Science and Religion in Dialogue

Volume One

[handwritten signature]

2014

SCIENCE AND RELIGION IN DIALOGUE

Volume One

Edited by

Melville Y. Stewart

A John Wiley & Sons, Ltd., Publication

This edition first published 2010
© 2010 Blackwell Publishing Ltd, except chapter 22 © 2009 Yale University

Blackwell Publishing was acquired by John Wiley & Sons in February 2007. Blackwell's publishing program has been merged with Wiley's global Scientific, Technical, and Medical business to form Wiley-Blackwell.

Registered Office
John Wiley & Sons Ltd, The Atrium, Southern Gate, Chichester, West Sussex, PO19 8SQ, United Kingdom

Editorial Offices
350 Main Street, Malden, MA 02148-5020, USA
9600 Garsington Road, Oxford, OX4 2DQ, UK
The Atrium, Southern Gate, Chichester, West Sussex, PO19 8SQ, UK

For details of our global editorial offices, for customer services, and for information about how to apply for permission to reuse the copyright material in this book please see our website at www.wiley.com/wiley-blackwell.

The right of Melville Y. Stewart to be identified as the author of the editorial material in this work has been asserted in accordance with the Copyright, Designs and Patents Act 1988.

Wiley also publishes its books in a variety of electronic formats. Some content that appears in print may not be available in electronic books.

Designations used by companies to distinguish their products are often claimed as trademarks. All brand names and product names used in this book are trade names, service marks, trademarks or registered trademarks of their respective owners. The publisher is not associated with any product or vendor mentioned in this book. This publication is designed to provide accurate and authoritative information in regard to the subject matter covered. It is sold on the understanding that the publisher is not engaged in rendering professional services. If professional advice or other expert assistance is required, the services of a competent professional should be sought.

Library of Congress Cataloging-in-Publication Data

Science and religion in dialogue / edited by Melville Y. Stewart.
    p. cm.
  Includes bibliographical references and index.
  ISBN 978-1-4051-8921-7 (hardcover : alk. paper)   1. Religion and science. I. Stewart, Melville Y.
  BL241.S3815 2010
  201'.65–dc22

                            2009032180

A catalogue record for this book is available from the British Library.

Set in 10/12.5pt Minion by SPi Publisher Services, Pondicherry, India
Printed and bound in Singapore by Fabulous Printers Pte Ltd

01 2010

To my loving wife, Donna Mae Stewart

Contents

VOLUME ONE

Lists of Figures and Tables   xii
Biographical Sketches   xiv
Preface   xx
Acknowledgements   xxvi

Introduction to Volume One   1
Melville Y. Stewart

Part 1   Has Science Really Destroyed Its Own Religious Roots?   39
1   The Nature of Science   41
Del Ratzsch
2   The Religious Roots of Science   54
Del Ratzsch
3   The Alleged Demise of Religion   69
Del Ratzsch

Part 2   God and Physical Reality: Relativity, Time, and Quantum Mechanics   85
4   Relativity, God, and Time   87
Thomas Greenlee
5   General Relativity, The Cosmic Microwave Background, and Moral Relativism   93
Thomas Greenlee
6   Quantum Mechanics and the Nature of Reality   97
Thomas Greenlee

Part 3   Interaction Between Science and Christianity   105
7   Science and Religion in Harmony   107
Deborah B. Haarsma
8   How Christians Reconcile Ancient Texts with Modern Science   120
Deborah B. Haarsma

9   Christian and Atheist Responses to Big Bang Cosmology   131
     Deborah B. Haarsma

Part 4   Interplay of Scientific and Religious Knowledge Regarding Evolution   151
10   Scientific Knowledge Does Not Replace Religious Knowledge   153
     Loren Haarsma
11   God, Evolution, and Design   168
     Loren Haarsma
12   Human Evolution and Objective Morality   181
     Loren Haarsma

Part 5   The Universe Makes It Probable That There Is A God   203
13   What Makes a Scientific Theory Probably True   205
     Richard Swinburne
14   The Argument to God from the Laws of Nature   213
     Richard Swinburne
15   The Argument to God from Fine-Tuning   223
     Richard Swinburne

Part 6   A Paleontologist Considers Science and Religion   235
16   Is Intelligent Design Really Intelligent?   237
     Peter Dodson
17   God and the Dinosaurs Revisited   243
     Peter Dodson
18   Science and Religion in the Public Square   251
     Peter Dodson

Part 7   Christian Faith and Biological Explanation   265
19   Evolutionary Creation: Common Descent and Christian Views of Origins   267
     Stephen Matheson
20   A Scientific and Religious Critique of Intelligent Design   278
     Stephen Matheson
21   Biology, the Incarnation, and Christian Materialism   290
     Stephen Matheson

Part 8   Religion, Naturalism, and Science   299
22   Science and Religion: Why Does the Debate Continue?   301
     Alvin Plantinga
23   Divine Action in the World   317
     Alvin Plantinga
24   The Evolutionary Argument Against Naturalism   324
     Alvin Plantinga

Part 9   Science and Theology as Faithful Human Activities   333
25   Two For the Ages: Origen and Newton   335
     Gary Patterson

26   The Holy Trinity of Nineteenth-Century British Science: Faraday,
      Maxwell, and Rayleigh   345
      Gary Patterson
27   A Professor in Dialogue with His Faith   359
      Gary Patterson

Part 10   Cosmology and Theology   **369**
28   Our Place in the Vast Universe   371
      Don N. Page
29   Does God So Love the Multiverse?   380
      Don N. Page
30   Scientific and Philosophical Challenges to Theism   396
      Don N. Page

Part 11   Science Under Stress in the Twentieth Century:
             Lessons from the Case of Early Nuclear Physics   **411**
31   The Copenhagen Spirit of Science and Birth of the Nuclear Atom   413
      Richard Peterson
32   When Scientists Go to War   420
      Richard Peterson
33   Scientific Responsibility: A Quest for Good Science and Good Applications 429
      Richard Peterson

Part 12   The Science of Religion   **437**
34   The Evolution of Religion: Adaptationist Accounts   439
      Michael J. Murray
35   The Evolution of Religion: Non-Adaptationist Accounts   458
      Michael J. Murray
36   Evolutionary Accounts of Religion: Explaining or Explaining Away   472
      Michael J. Murray

Part 13   Belief in God   **479**
37   How Real People Believe: Reason and Belief in God   481
      Kelly James Clark
38   Reformed Epistemology and the Cognitive Science of Religion   500
      Kelly James Clark
39   Explaining God Away?   514
      Kelly James Clark

VOLUME TWO

      Introduction to Volume Two   527
      Melville Y. Stewart

Part 14   Background Topics for the Science and Religion Dialogue   **603**
40   Reflections on the Scientific Revolution (1543–1687)   605
      Owen Gingerich

41 Designing a Universe Congenial for Life   618
    Owen Gingerich

**Part 15 Stewardship and Economic Harmony: Living Sustainability
          on Earth   629**
42 Earth's Biospheric Economy   631
    Calvin DeWitt
43 The Steward and the Economist   645
    Calvin DeWitt
44 Sustainable Living in the Biosphere   658
    Calvin DeWitt

Part 16 Cosmology and Theism   671
45 God, Time, and Infinity   673
    William Lane Craig
46 Time and Eternity   683
    William Lane Craig
47 The End of the World   703
    William Lane Craig

Part 17 Theology and Science in a Postmodern Context   721
48 Theology and Science in a Postmodern Context   723
    Nancey Murphy
49 Science and Divine Action   732
    Nancey Murphy
50 Theology, Science and Human Nature   740
    Nancey Murphy

Part 18 Darwin and Intelligent Design   749
51 Darwin and Intelligent Design   751
    Francisco J. Ayala

Part 19 The Laws of Physics and Bio-Friendliness   767
52 The Nature of the Laws of Physics and Their Mysterious Bio-Friendliness   769
    Paul Davies

Part 20 Time and Open Theism   789
53 The A-Theory of Time, Presentism, and Open Theism   791
    Dean Zimmerman

Part 21 Science and Scripture   811
54 A Kind of Darwinism   813
    Peter van Inwagen
55 Darwinism and Design   825
    Peter van Inwagen
56 Science and Scripture   835
    Peter van Inwagen

Part 22   The Mutuality of Science and Theology   847

57   Science and Religion in Western History: Models and Relationships   849
     Alan Padgett
58   Overcoming the Problem of Induction: Science and Religion
     as Ways of Knowing   862
     Alan Padgett
59   God and Time: Relative Timelessness Reconsidered   884
     Alan Padgett

Part 23   Physics and Scientific Materialism   893

60   The Laws of Physics and the Design of the Universe   895
     Stephen M. Barr
61   The Multiverse and the State of Fundamental Physics Today   911
     Stephen M. Barr
62   Philosophical Materialism and the Many-Worlds Interpretation
     of Quantum Mechanics   928
     Stephen M. Barr

Part 24   Biotechnology and Human Dignity   943

63   Embodied Being: Evolution and the Emergence of the Human Person   945
     William Hurlbut
64   Embryos, Ethics, and Human Dignity   960
     William Hurlbut
65   Biotechnology and the Human Future   974
     William Hurlbut

Part 25   Science, Emergence, and Religion   985

66   Freedom, Consciousness, and Science: An Emergentist Response
     to the Challenge   987
     Philip Clayton
67   Mediating Between Physicalism and Dualism: "Broad Naturalism"
     and the Study of Consciousness   999
     Philip Clayton

**Part 26   Theories and Unobservables: The Realist/Nonrealist
             Debate in Science and Religion**   1011

68   Scientific Realism   1013
     Bruce Reichenbach
69   Religious Realism   1034
     Bruce Reichenbach
70   Experience and the Unobservable   1053
     Bruce Reichenbach

Glossary   1078
Index   1087

Lists of Figures and Tables

VOLUME ONE

Figures

4.1	Graph of Galilean transformation equation	88
6.1	Illustration of quantum mechanics	98
6.2	Graph of a beam of photons entering a Michelson interferometer	98
7.1	The relation between nature and Scripture, science and Biblical scholarship	113
8.1	Egyptian representation of the world	127
17.1	*Triceratops* head	248
17.2	*Triceratops* in full	248
25.1	Isaac Newton	339
26.1	Michael Faraday	347
26.2	James Clerk Maxwell	349
26.3	John William Strutt	355
26.4	Lord Kelvin and Lord Rayleigh	357

Tables

8.1	Timeline of Natural History	121
8.2	Literary Structure of Genesis 1	126
8.3	Differences between Genesis 1 and *Enuma Elish*	128
34.1	The Prisoners' Dilemma	445

VOLUME TWO

Figures

40.1	The Copernican Transformation 1	609
40.2	The Copernican Transformation 2	610
40.3	The Copernican Transformation 3	610
40.4	Drawing by Copernicus, Sun-centered system in Copernicus' *De Revolutionibus* of 1543	611
42.1	Aerial photograph showing Lake Waubesa on the upper right and Waubesa Wetlands on the left with its central stream flowing into Lake Waubesa	632
42.2	Ecosystem services as identified and classified by the Millennium Ecosystem Assessment	634
42.3	Earth's ecosystem	636
43.1	The "sifting and winnowing" bronze plaque, University of Wisconsin-Madison	656
44.1	Variations of the Earth's surface temperature for the past 140 years	663
44.2	An ultra-light airplane leading a group of cranes	665
44.3	Illustration of Beijing Olympics 2008 motto	669
47.1	Oscillating Model	708
47.2	Oscillating Model with Entropy Increase	708
47.3	False vacuum state of the universe	709
47.4	Baby universes	709
47.5	Bubbles of true vacuum in a sea of false vacuum	711
47.6	Constraints on the Big Bang	713
64.1	Altered Nuclear Transfer (ANT)	969

Table

41.1	Number of compounds atoms of different elements can make with hydrogen	619

Biographical Sketches

Francisco J. Ayala is University Professor and Donald Bren Professor of Biological Sciences and Professor of Philosophy at the University of California, Irvine. He is a member of the National Academy of Sciences (NAS), a recipient of the 2001 National Medal of Science, and served as Chair of the Authoring Committee of *Science, Evolution, and Creationism*, jointly published in 2008 by the NAS and the Institute of Medicine. He has been President and Chairman of the Board of the American Association for the Advancement of Science (1993–6) and President of Sigma Xi, the Scientific Research Society of the United States (2004–5). Dr Ayala has written numerous books and articles about the intersection of science and religion, including *Darwin's Gift to Science and Religion* (2007).

Stephen M. Barr is Professor in the Department of Physics and Astronomy and the Bartol Research Institute of the University of Delaware. His research is in theoretical particle physics, with an emphasis on grand unified theories, the origin of particle masses, spacetime symmetries, and the cosmology of the early universe. He has published over 130 research articles in refereed physics journals, and is the author of the article on Grand Unified Theories in the *Encyclopedia of Physics*. He has written on the relation of science and religion for many publications, especially *First Things*, on whose editorial advisory board he serves. He is the author of two books, *Modern Physics and Ancient Faith* (2003) and *A Student's Guide to Natural Science* (2006).

Justin Barrett is Professor of Evolutionary Anthropology at the University of Oxford. He served on the psychology faculties of Calvin College, Grand Rapids, Michigan, and the University of Michigan (Ann Arbor), and as a research fellow of the Institute for Social Research. He is a founding editor of the *Journal of Cognition & Culture* and is author of numerous articles and chapters concerning the cognitive science of religion. His book *Why Would Anyone Believe in God?* (2004) presents a scientific account for the prevalence of religious beliefs. It represents the field's first relatively comprehensive introduction intended for a general audience.

Kelly James Clark has taught at the University of St. Andrews, Scotland, and is Professor of Philosophy at Calvin College, with specialties in Philosophy of Religion and Chinese Philosophy. He is Chair of the China Committee for the Society of Christian Philosophers, and Chair of the Executive Committee. He is a John Templeton Foundation recipient for initiatives in China, and he was awarded a grant for research at Oxford in 2010. His areas of specialty include philosophy of religion, death and the meaning of life, ethics, and Chinese philosophy. His main works include, *The Story of Ethics*, *Return To Reason* (also in Chinese), and *When Faith Is Not Enough*.

Philip Clayton is currently Professor of Religion and Philosophy at Claremont Graduate University and Ingraham Professor at Claremont School of Theology. Clayton's books and articles address the cultural battle currently raging between science and religion. Clayton has drawn on the resources of the sciences, philosophy, theology, and comparative religious thought to develop constructive partnerships between these two great cultural powers. As a public intellectual he seeks to address the burning ethical and political issues at the intersection of science, ethics, religion, and spirituality such as the stem cell debate, euthanasia, the environmental crisis, interreligious warfare. As a philosopher he works to show the compatibility of science with religious belief across the fields where the two may be integrated (emergence theory, evolution and religion, evolutionary psychology, neuroscience and consciousness).

William Lane Craig is Research Professor of Philosophy at Talbot School of Theology, La Mirada, California. He has authored or edited over 30 books, including *Assessing the New Testament Evidence for the Historicity of the Resurrection of Jesus* (1989); *Divine Foreknowledge and Human Freedom* (1991); *Theism, Atheism and Big Bang Cosmology* (with Quentin Smith, 1995); *The Kalam Cosmological Argument* (2000); and *God, Time and Eternity: The Coherence of Theism II: Eternity* (2001), as well as over a hundred articles in professional journals of philosophy and theology, including *The Journal of Philosophy*, *New Testament Studies*, *Journal for the Study of the New Testament*, *American Philosophical Quarterly*, *Philosophical Studies*, *Philosophy*, and *British Journal for Philosophy of Science*.

Paul Charles William Davies is currently a professor at Arizona State University and Director of BEYOND: Center for Fundamental Concepts in Science. His research interests are in the fields of cosmology, quantum field theory, and astrobiology. In 2005, he took up the chair of the SETI: Post-Detection Science and Technology Taskgroup of the International Academy of Astronautics. His numerous publications include: *The Last Three Minutes* (1994); *Are We Alone?* (1995); *The Fifth Miracle* (1999, 2001); *How to Build a Time Machine* (2001); *The Goldilocks Enigma* (2007), also published under the title *Cosmic Jackpot*: *Quantum Aspects of Life* (eds. Derek Abbott, Paul C. W. Davies, and Arun K. Pati, with foreword by Sir Roger Penrose, 2008).

Calvin B. DeWitt is Professor of Environmental Studies, Nelson Institute for Environmental Studies, University of Wisconsin-Madison. His many specialties include integrative framing of science, ethics, and praxis in the development and application of solutions to environmental issues and problems; intentional institution-building for ecological and economic sustainability/wetland ecosystem development and role in sequestering carbon and atmospheric solutes and particulates in maintaining a habitable earth, and agricultural ecology, ethical motivations for landscape preservation in the lives of John Muir and Theodore Roosevelt; and application of ecosystem services and systems analysis to ecological and societal sustainability. His many works include *Unsustainable Agriculture and Land Use: Restoring Stewardship for Biospheric Sustainability* (2009) and numerous journal articles and chapters in books.

Peter Dodson is Professor of Anatomy at the University of Pennsylvania School of Veterinary Medicine, and Professor of Paleontology in the Department of Earth and Environmental Science. He is a research associate at the Academy of Natural Sciences of Philadelphia. He is co-editor of *The Dinosauria* (1990, 2nd edn. 2004); author of *The Horned Dinosaurs* (1996); and of several children's books, including *An Alphabet of Dinosaurs* (1995). He is co-founder and first president of the Metanexus Institute for Religion and Science (1998–2001) and winner of a Templeton Science and Religion Course Award (1999). He is currently working on a book on the dinosaurs of China.

Owen Gingerich is Professor Emeritus of Astronomy and of the History of Science at the Harvard-Smithsonian Center for Astrophysics. He is a leading authority on the seventeenth-century German astronomer Johannes Kepler and on the sixteenth-century cosmologist Nicholas Copernicus, who proposed the heliocentric system. An account of his Copernican adventures, *The Book Nobody Read* (2004) has now been issued in 13 foreign editions. He is particularly interested in the science and religion dialogue, the context of his most recent book, *God's Universe* (2006). Professor Gingerich has been Vice-President of the American Philosophical Society, and has served as chairman of the US National Committee of the International Astronomical Union.

Thomas Greenlee is Associate Director of NASA's Minnesota Space Grant Consortium and served three years on the Editorial Board of Physics Resource Letters of the *American Journal of Physics* and six years as secretary of the Minnesota Area Association of Physics Teachers. He has had grants from 3 M for laser interferometry to measure roughness of surfaces and temperatures of gases. In 1993 and 1994, Dr. Greenlee was awarded a summer research fellowship in temperature measurement by infrared pyrometry at NASA – Lewis Research Center in Cleveland, Ohio. His other professional interests are connections between science and Christianity and chaos theory.

Deborah Haarsma is Associate Professor of Physics and Astronomy at Calvin College. Her specialties include extragalactic astronomy and cosmology. Her recent work is on galaxy clusters and evolution. Her main works include: "The Central Component of Gravitational Lens Q0957+561" (with J. N Winn, I. Shapiro, and J. Lehar, 2008); "The FIRST-Optical-VLA Survey for Lensed Radio Lobes" (with J. N Winn, E. E. Falco, et al., 2005); and "Origins: A Reformed Look at Creation, Design, and Evolution," *Faith Alive Resources* (with Loren D. Haarsma, 2007).

Loren Haarsma is an Associate Professor in the Physics and Astronomy Department of Calvin College. His scientific research is in electrophysiology, studying the activity of ion channels in developing nerve cells and other cell types. He is co-author of *Origins: A Reformed Look at Creation, Design, and Evolution* (2007), and he has written numerous other book chapters, articles, and lectures on topics at the intersection of science, philosophy, and religion.

William B. Hurlbut is Consulting Professor, Department of Neurology and Neurological Sciences, Stanford University Medical Center. His specialties include: ethical issues of advancing biomedical technology; biological basis of moral awareness; integration of theology and philosophy of biology. He has been a member of the President's Council on Bioethics, since 2002. He is author of Altered Nuclear Transfer, a proposed technological solution to the moral controversy over embryonic stem cell research. His works include, "Seeking Consensus: A Clarification and Defense of Altered Nuclear Transfer," *Hastings*

Center Report (2006) and "Science, Religion and the Human Spirit" in *The Oxford Handbook of Religion and Science* (2006).

Peter van Inwagen is the John Cardinal O'Hara Professor of Philosophy at the University of Notre Dame. He has delivered the Maurice Lectures at King's College, London, the Wilde Lectures at Oxford, the Stewart Lectures at Princeton, and the Gifford Lectures at St Andrews. His Gifford Lectures were published under the title *The Problem of Evil* (2006). His numerous books include *An Essay on Free Will* (1986), *Material Beings* (1995), *God, Knowledge, and Mystery: Essays in Philosophical Theology* (1995), *Ontology, Identity, and Modality: Essays in Metaphysics* (2001), and *Metaphysics* (2008), He was elected to the American Academy of Arts and Sciences in 2005, and is currently President of the Central Division of the American Philosophical Association.

Stephen Matheson is Associate Professor of Biology at Calvin College. Professor Matheson is a developmental biologist with a particular interest in neurobiology. His research is focused on the signaling systems in nerve cells that direct their structural and electrical development and has been published in journals such as *Development* and *Nature Cell Biology*. His weblog, "Quintessence of Dust," explores topics at the interface between Christian belief and modern biology and was featured in *The Open Laboratory*, an anthology of the best science writing online, in 2007 and 2008.

Nancey Murphy is Professor of Christian Philosophy at Fuller Theological Seminary. Professor Murphy serves on the board of the Center for Theology and the Natural Sciences, Berkeley, and is a member of the planning committee for conferences on science and theology sponsored by the Vatican Observatory. Her most recent publications are *Bodies and Souls, or Spirited Bodies?* (2006), *Evolution and Emergence: Systems, Organisms, Persons* (with William Stoeger, SJ, 2007), and *Did My Neurons Make Me Do It? Philosophical and Neurobiological Perspectives on Moral Responsibility and Free Will* (with Warren Brown, forthcoming). Professor Murphy serves as an editorial advisor for *Theology and Science* and *Theology Today*. Areas of expertise, research, writing, and teaching are: Anglo-American postmodern philosophy, theology and science, philosophy of mind.

Michael Murray is the Arthur and Katherine Shadek Professor in the Humanities and Philosophy at Franklin and Marshall College, Lancaster, PA. He has recently published *An Introduction to the Philosophy of Religion* (with Michael Rea, 2008) and *Nature Red in Tooth and Claw: Theism and the Problem of Animal Suffering* (2008), *The Believing Primate: Scientific, Philosophical, and Theological Reflections on the Origin of Religion* (with Jeffrey Schloss, 2009). He has two books forthcoming: *Predestination and Election* and *Divine Evil?* (with Michael Rea and Michael Bergmann). He is currently affiliated with the John Templeton Foundation.

Alan G. Padgett is Chair of the History – Theology division and Professor of Systematic Theology at Luther Seminary in Saint Paul, MN. He is well known for his many writings integrating theology, philosophy, and the sciences. He is the author of over 90 scholarly articles and book chapters, including the article "Religion and the Physical Sciences," *The Encyclopedia of Philosophy*, 2nd ed., 8 volumes (2006) and "Science and Christianity," *The Encyclopedia of Christianity*, 5 volumes (1999–2008). He is author or editor of nine books, including *God, Eternity and the Nature of Time* (1992), *Science and the Study of God* (2003), and co-author of *Christianity and Western Thought* (also in Chinese), vols. 2 and 3 (2000, 2009).

Don Page is Professor of Physics at the University of Alberta. He held a NATO Postdoctoral Fellowship in Science at the University of Cambridge, England, and worked as a research assistant under Stephen Hawking. He has taught at the University of Texas at Austin, the California Institute of Technology, and the University of California at Santa Barbara. His specialty is theoretical gravitational physics (black holes and cosmology), and his main works include 190 professional articles in science journals, including "Lectures on quantum cosmology" (1991), "Information in black hole radiation" (1993), "Black hole information" (1994), and "Aspects of quantum cosmology" (1995).

Gary D. Patterson is Professor of Chemistry at Carnegie Mellon University in Pittsburgh, PA. In his laboratory he studies the structure and dynamics of amorphous liquids and solutions using light-scattering spectroscopy. He received the National Academy of Sciences Award for Initiatives in Research in 1981 in recognition of his work on light scattering from polymers. He is currently active in History of Chemistry and has published on the history of the atomic doctrine and the development of polymer science. He has published many papers in polymer science in addition to his recent book, *Physical Chemistry of Macromolecules* (2007). He has also published on the interaction of Christianity and Science and teaches a humanities course on this topic.

Richard W. Peterson is currently Professor of Physics at Bethel University, MN. He was elected a Fellow of the American Physical Society (APS) and received the APS prize for research with undergraduates. Research areas have included optics, metrology, and acoustics, and he has been very active in physics teaching – recently serving as President of the American Association of Physics Teachers. He has authored over 100 papers in his areas of research, including "Still a 'Band of Myopic Brothers?'" (2005), "Primal Inquiry: Making Stuff Work," (2005), and "The Ping-Pong Cannon: A Closer Look," (2005, with B. N. Pulford and K. R. Stein). He enjoys working with a physics lecture demonstration apparatus for diverse audiences. He has also taught courses on the twentieth-century development of nuclear physics, leading physicists of that period, and ethical issues stimulated by the process of science and its interaction with society.

Alvin Plantinga is Professor of Philosophy at the University of Notre Dame. His areas of special interest include epistemology, metaphysics, and philosophy of religion. He has authored numerous journal articles and books including: *God and Other Minds* (1967), *The Nature of Necessity* (1974), *God, Freedom & Evil* (1974), which appears in a Russian translation, *Does God Have a Nature?* (1980), *Warrant: the Current Debate* (1993), and.*Warrant and Proper Function* (1993). His most recent book, *Warranted Christian Belief* (2000) has been translated into Chinese and appears in the *Weiming Translation Library* of Peking University Press. He has served as President of the Society of Christian Philosophers, and is Past-President of the Central Division of the American Philosophical Association.

Del Ratzsch is Chair of the Philosophy Department at Calvin College in Grand Rapids, Michigan. He is the author of various articles on science/religion issues as well as a number of books, including *The Battle of Beginnings: Why Neither Side Is Winning the Creation-Evolution Debate* (with Delvin Lee Ratzsch, 1996), *Science and Its Limits: The Natural Sciences in Christian Perspective* (2000) and *Nature, Design and Science: The Status of Design in Natural Science* (with Delvin Lee Ratzsch, 2001). The first two have been translated into Chinese and published in China.

Bruce R. Reichenbach is Professor of Philosophy, with a specialty in Philosophy of Religion at Augsburg College, Minneapolis. His main works include: *The Cosmological Argument: A Reassessment* (1972), *Is Man the Phoenix?: A Study of Immortality* (1982), *Evil and a Good God* (1982), *The Law of Karma: A Philosophical Study* (1991), *On Behalf of God: A Christian Ethic for Biology* (with Elving Anderson, 2002), *Introduction to Critical Thinking* (2002), *Religion and Religious Belief* (with Michael Peterson, William Hasker, and David Basinger, 2008) and *Philosophy of Religion: Selected Readings* (with Michael Peterson, William Hasker, and David Basinger, 2006).

Richard Swinburne is a Fellow of the British Academy and was Nolloth Professor of the Philosophy of the Christian Religion at Oriel College, University of Oxford (1985–2002), and is now Emeritus Nolloth Professor. He is best known for his trilogy on the philosophy of theism: *The Coherence of Theism* (1993), *The Existence of God* (2004), and *Faith and Reason* (2005). He gave the Gifford lectures at the University of Aberdeen from 1982 to 1984, resulting in the book, *The Evolution of the Soul*. His philosophical method reflects the influence of Thomas Aquinas. Besides the above, he has authored ten other major works in the areas of philosophy of science, philosophy of religion and epistemology. He has lectured widely in Europe, Russia, and Southeast Asia.

Dean Zimmerman is Professor of Philosophy at Rutgers University. His main areas of research are in metaphysics and the philosophy of religion. Current writing includes a book on the persistence of material objects and persons, and papers on temporal passage and the idea that God is "outside of time." He is the director of a (currently biennial) summer workshop, Metaphysical Mayhem, which he started at the University of Notre Dame in 1996. He is author/editor of: *Metaphysics: The Big Questions* (with Peter van Inwagen, 1998; 2nd edn., 2008), *The Oxford Handbook of Metaphysics* (with Michael Loux, 2003), *Persons: Human and Divine* (with Peter van Inwagen, 2007) and *Contemporary Debates in Metaphysics* (with Ted Sider and John Hawthorne, 2008).

Preface

The Science and Religion Series that took place every fall term from 2005 to 2009 at five of China's top universities comprises an interesting narrative context for the collection of papers included in this two-volume set. All I can hope to do here is share a few glimpses of those moments that are now history.

My teaching assignments in China began with my appointment as a Pew Scholar at Peking University, fall term of 1996. That came about as a result of a visit I had made from Russia in late spring and early summer of 1993. At that time I was teaching at St Petersburg State University while on a sabbatical from Bethel College (now Bethel University). My friend who was teaching at Moscow State University, Daniel Clendenin, was invited to give a short-term lecture series at Peking University in the early spring of 1993. Before he left for Beijing he asked me whether I would be interested in giving a lecture series at Peking University. I had always wanted to visit China so my response was an enthusiastic affirmative. My first book, *The Greater-Good Defense, An Essay on the Rationality of Faith* had just been published, so I sent it along with my *vita* in support of my proposal for a short-term lecture series in China. Clendenin returned from China with good news: I was invited to visit Peking the last few days of May and the first few days of June. Late afternoon May 26 I met with the leaders of the Department of Philosophy, and proposed a symposium idea that would bring 10 leading Western philosophers to Peking University to meet with a matching Chinese team. Ye Lang, the Chair, and Zhao Dunhua, the Vice Chair, and Zhang Zhigang another vice chair, voted for the symposium idea. At my urging, the idea was eventually picked up by the Society of Christian Philosophers (SCP) during Professor Eleonore Stump's presidency. Under her leadership it became a yearly conference sponsored by the SCP. The first five years the symposia were held at Peking University, but following 1999, the meetings moved to other campuses beginning with Xiamen University on Xiamen Island. The Xiamen conference was especially significant because I had proposed a Science and Religion theme which Templeton saw as a good idea, and so sponsored it. A book issued from this conference in Chinese with the title,《科学与宗教的对话》(*A Dialogue Between Science and Religion*).[1]

Another opportunity opened up that visit. Later that same day my wife and I stood on the shores of Nameless Lake (Weiming Hú) with Zhou Weichi our university guide, and I remarked, "I would love to come here some day to teach." Later I shared the idea with the faculty at Beida. Before I left Beijing that spring I had an invitation to teach the fall term of 1996. I was able to arrange a third sabbatical allowing me to honor the invitation. Zhu Donghua was one of my students. In fall 2008 I arranged to meet with Professor Wang Xiaochao at Tsinghau to talk about the possibility of teaching and conducting the last Science and Religion Series at Tsinghua. Imagine my surprise when I opened the door to our apartment at Peking's Shao Yuan Hotel to see my former student, Zhu Donghua, standing next to Wang. He was chosen to be my assistant at Tsinghua.

The year 2005 was a critical turning point for China initiatives. I was invited to teach at Wuhan University in Wuhan, but at the time I was unsure as to what would be the theme of my visit. The success of the science and religion symposium at Xiamen University on Xiamen Island gave reinforcement to the idea of a Science and Religion Series. Another SCP Science and Religion conference for Russian and American scholars had taken place at Notre Dame in 2003. I had taken part, and Michael Murray had been the planner. Early in 2005, thinking that a science and religion idea might work, I crafted a proposal for a Science and Religion Symposium at Wuhan for the fall of 2005 and submitted it to the John Templeton Foundation. The proposal, late as it was, met with a speedy approval. That fall my possible world became a spectacular actual world. Professor Changchi Hao and his students made public lectures and the Science and Religion venues rock. The response was so strong and enthusiastic, I dreamed of a larger proposal featuring the Science and Religion theme with a many-university expansion. The Proposal was an enlargement of the Wuhan model that focused on four main projects: (1) a teaching task at the host university involving at least one course in Science and Religion designed to set the stage for the visiting lecturers who were to give papers on the topic; (2) a Science and Religion Series, which included inviting a team of scholars, some representing the sciences and some philosophy; (3) co-edit with a resident Chinese scholar a book that would include the papers presented – the invited team members were to prepare three papers; (4) finally, there was the task of book distribution at the Series, and to libraries and leading scholars. Initially, teams numbered four presenters, but as time and circumstance would have it, the number of members expanded. The Series' list of host universities was soon firmed up to include: Wuhan University, fall term, 2005, co-editor, Changchi Hao; Fudan University, Shanghai, fall term, 2006, co-editor, Yingjin Xu; Shandong University, Jinan, fall term, 2007, co-editor, Fu Youde; Peking University, Beijing, fall term, 2008, co-editors, Xing Taotao, Xiangdong Xu; Tsinghua University, fall term, 2009, co-editor, Zhu Donghua. This five-year Series was funded largely by the John Templeton Foundation, with other supporting institutions including the Paul & Dawn Sjolund Foundation, and the Wooddale and Salem Foundations.

The Series allowed me to rekindle and build old friendships started at SCP symposia as well as establish new ones. New ideas brought about various faculty collaboratives, one of which led to the co-authoring of a *Dictionary of Western Philosophy, English, Pinyin, Chinese* by Professor Yingjin Xu and myself.[2]

Negotiations led to the appointment of key Chinese faculty as co-editors of the Chinese edition of the papers that are included in this two-volume set. Every co-editor also served as a co-director of the programs attending the Series.

The kick-off of the Series took Wuhan University's Department of Philosophy by storm. Changchi Hao's outgoing personality and abounding enthusiasm was contagious. He helped draw faculty and students from other departments. A PhD from Fordham University meant students had easy access to an instructor familiar with Western analytic and continental traditions.[3] So when students enrolled in my classes and attended the Series they were ready to take off with new ideas and arguments.

After we finished our assignment at Wuhan, there were many exciting ventures to follow in the lives of those impacted. Following our stay, Changchi Hao went on to become a Harvard-Yenshing Scholar[4] at Harvard University, and the year after he did further research on science and religion at Baylor University. In addition to serving as co-editor of the first volume in the Chinese *Series*, he arranged a review interview of our book that appeared in the *Science Times*,[5] a publication that enjoys a circulation of 100,000 in all 23 of China's provinces.

The first team of Templeton Scholars was right for the occasion: Del Ratzsch, who had been to China with Kelly James Clark and Michael Murray on short-term lecture series visits, was ready to connect meaningfully with students and faculty. He helped set the stage for the entire five-year *Series* giving account of the nature and origins of science. Tom Greenlee with Deborah and Loren Haarsma were forerunners for science installments which were to follow.

This first round inspired a new Four-Year Proposal application to Templeton that took these venues to new heights at four of China's highest-ranking universities, Fudan, Shandong, Peking, and Tsinghua.

The second round, held at Fudan University in Shanghai, helped bring about some other valuable collaboratives we had not anticipated. Were it not for Liu Ping (who had been a central figure in an SCP symposium in 2005), my invitation to Fudan might not have happened. When it was finalized, the enthusiastic response of the Department brought about a stay in the spectacular skyline city of Shanghai. Here, key scholars included Yingjin Xu, keen on contemporary Western analytic philosophy, and William (Willy) Wilson, a scholar from the West in New Testament studies. His popularity helped him establish a close-knit community of scholar friends ready for the Science and Religion focus.

Upon our arrival we were met by Professor Liu Ping and Vincent (Tang Jie). The latter was to become a creative and enthusiastic teaching assistant. The same model of paper distribution initiated by Li Yong at Wuhan became Vincent's. He initiated creative ways of promoting the Series. Upon arriving at Guanghua Towers, the place of the lectures and Series, I saw floor-to-ceiling posters strategically placed at the entrances to the elevators, and on the philosophy floors – 24–26. On the authority of Al Plantinga's "other-university repertoire," it is the most lofty Department of Philosophy in the world. The meeting place for this Series, West Wing, Room 2501, had a maximum seating capacity of 100. The gathering for Alvin Plantinga's lecture on "The Evolutionary Argument Against Naturalism," December 18, 2006, 6:30 p.m., pressed possible-room capacity to the max. Students and faculty filled every seat, table top and floor space all the way out of both doorways into both hallways. Others who served on the team for that Series, Richard Swinburne, Stephen Matheson, and Peter Dodson, drew capacity crowds. Science and Religion caught on in a big way in Shanghai. Yingjin Xu agreed to co-author a *Dictionary of Western Philosophy, English/Pinyin/Chinese* to help bridge the language gap for future Western teachers. Understanding Western categories and ideas became the name of the game spearheaded by Yingjin Xu and Tang Jie. Our final celebrative banquet held a few days before our departure was evidence of the impact and the enthusiasm the Series had generated.

The following year we went to Shandong University. Professor Fu Youde, Chair of the Department of Comparative Religion and Hebrew Studies had become a close friend when I taught there in 2004. We had served as co-editors of a book that followed a Society of

Christian Philosophers symposium held in 2001.[6] From the moment of our arrival, I knew he was enthusiastically committed to the Series.

Two key scientists from the West, Pam Holt with a PhD in biology, and Robbi Greenwood with a PhD in environmental science, had become good friends when I taught at Shandong in 2004. They were ready to run with the Series idea as soon as we arrived. Another key faculty, Professor Ed Mignot, teamed up with Holt and Greenwood urging students in their classes to attend the lectures. Scientists and philosophers packed the auditorium across from the University Hotel.

Stateside I had worked out the details of the Program for the Series, and had designed a cover for the pre-published booklet to be distributed to those who attended, but I couldn't find a Kinko shop to do the printing task in Jinan. Professor Fu Youde's teaching assistant, Ms Dottie Summer helped me find a printer, Gao Guoqing, owner of Jinan Huitong Scientific and Technological Printing Center. He ran off 300 copies of the booklet that contained the papers of Gary Patterson, Don Page, Kelly James Clark, Michael Murray and Richard Peterson. It was the start of a new process that helped spread the Science and Religion Series idea beyond the host campus to other universities in the greater metropolitan area. The engagement of the students was exciting. Refreshments and book distribution helped attract students majoring in philosophy and the sciences campus-wide. Professor Huang Fuwu (physics), was appointed by Fu Youde to do the translation task.

We will long remember eating at the Pizza Hut not too far from the old Shandong University campus (*laoxiao*) that features the magnificent landmark Hong Lou Roman Catholic cathedral. At night, floodlights are reflected on its beautiful twin spires lighting up the sky over the older part of the city.

Peking (affectionately called "Beida," a contraction of *Beijing Daxue, Beijing University*) was next on the calendar for 2008. I had taught there three times. I wasn't sure what to expect. I only knew that it was China's model for the academy, and some of China's best students eventually find their way to Beida, many from distant mountain villages. For any given year about 2000 scholars from the West serve as visiting faculty, and students are attracted from all over the world to study Chinese. This marvelous international mixture brought an exciting cultural dimension to my classes.

Key faculty were long-time friends: Zhao Dunhua, Chair of the Department of Philosophy and Religious Studies Department was a long-time acquaintance from my first visit to China in late spring of 1993. In 2004, during my United Board appointment at Beida, I team-taught a course on Plantinga's epistemology with Xing Taotao.[7] Xing Taotao and Xiangdong Xu were appointed as co-editors and co-planners of the Series at Beida.

The Series had a spectacular and quite unexpected turn. The week following my Templeton Series, Templeton had planned one of its own, a NewVision 400 Series, with scientists and philosophers gathering from all over the world at a kickoff event held at the Great Hall of the People. Consequently, some scholars I had hoped to get in earlier rounds were in Beijing for the 400 Series venue, and open to giving single papers at my Series, including Francisco J. Ayala, and Dean Zimmerman. Paul Davies was open to giving a paper, but his schedule was too full to attend. Fortunately, he was still willing to submit a paper for the Series (hence the inclusion of several single papers by leading scholars that appear in Volume II of the English, and Volume IV of the Chinese). The original team, Owen Gingerich, Calvin DeWitt, William Lane Craig, and Nancey Murphy were delighted with the fuller complement of scholars from the West.

The final round, according to the original plan, was to be actualized at Tsinghua University, rival to Peking for China's best. It is China's finest science and engineering university just across the street (Haidian Road) from Beida. An outstanding team was arranged for Tsinghua: William Hurlbut, Stephen M. Barr, Alan Padgett, Peter van Inwagen, and Bruce Reichenbach. The last three were members of the initial SCP symposium team to China during the fall of 1994.

The anticipated appearance of books from previous rounds reaching back to Wuhan including the Chinese and English editions meant an accumulation of seven volumes, I, II, III, IV and V of the Chinese Edition and One and Two of the English edition published by Blackwell Publishing of Oxford. Adding Yingjin Xu's and my *Dictionary* meant eight books would mark the culmination of the *Series*, and the beginning of new programs, collaboratives, and study programs abroad. Since my first trip to China from St Petersburg, Russia[8] in 1993, I have had the honor of teaching hundreds of students in a country we have come to regard as our second home.

Two key persons who had arranged my stay at Tsinghua, Wang Xiaochao and Zhu Donghua were actors center stage in the final chapter of the Series narrative. As noted above, I had met Professor Wang Xiaochao back in 1996, when I had visited Hangzhou University (now Zhejiang University) for a short-term lecture series during my sabbatical assignment funded by the Pew Foundation. Over time we became good friends. Eventually, his sphere of influence was expanded to include teaching positions at both Zhejiang and Tsinghua universities. But because his full-time position is at Zhejiang, he transferred the responsibility of negotiating my appointment to his former student and mine, Dr Zhu Donghua.

The foregoing narrative is not a simple A to Z, but a tale that brings heart-warming X t' Zs! That is, the narrative closure brought a sense of deep gratitude expressed in simple Chinese, *Xie Xie* (谢谢, *thank you*), to two persons who have become good, close friends, Zhao Dunhua, who played a central role in the opening of the Series narrative, and Zhu Donghua, who helped bring it to a wonderful closure; hence my heart-felt X t' Zs, *Xie Xie* (谢谢) to Zhao, and Xie Xie (谢谢) to Zhu.

For a person familiar with Chinese, I take pleasure in listing the five-volume set that includes the polished versions of the 70 papers presented at the host universities in China. A sixth entry, a book on Science and Religion that followed the Xiamen Symposium in 2000 is entered as an endnote.[9]

1) *Science and Religion in Dialogue*,《科学与宗教的对话》, ed. Melville Y. Stewart and Changchi Hao. Beijing: Peking University Press, 2007.
2) *Science and Religion: Twenty-first Century Dialogue*,《科学与宗教：二十一 世纪时对话》, ed. Melville Y. Stewart and Xu Yingjin. Shanghai: Fudan University Press, 2008.
3) *Science and Religion: Current Dialogue*,《科学与宗教：当前对话》, ed. Melville Y. Stewart and Fu Youde. Beijing, Peking University Press, May, 2009.
4) *Science and Religion: Twenty-first Century Issues*,《科学与宗教：二十一 世纪问题》, ed. Melville Y. Stewart and Xing Taotao. Beijing: Peking University Press, 2009.
5) *Science and Religion: Current Debate*,《科学与宗教：当前争论》, ed. Melville Y. Stewart and Zhu Donghua. Beijing, Peking University Press, 2009.

I am very pleased to see these 70 papers now appear in an English edition so beautifully bound with covers like their Chinese counterpart, featuring Hubble Telescope pictures, graphically portraying the seemingly infinite, resplendent glory of the heavens. It is hoped that the readers will respond to these papers in kind with those in who were the first readers and hearers.

Melville Y. Stewart

Notes

1   A person familiar with the Chinese will immediately see that the title of the book containing the proceedings from the Xiamen conference is identical to with the title of the volume that followed the Series at Wuhan University in 2005, only the English is reversed, *A Dialogue Between Science and Religion* (2000) *vis-à-vis Science and Religion in Diaogue* (2005).

2   Forthcoming, 2009, Peking University Press.

3   His doctoral dissertation focused on the writings of Merold Westphal, who was to become a guest lecturer at Wuhan.

4   Peking University was originally named Yenching University, and was a union venture blending Methodist, Presbyterian, and Congregational denominations both American and British, headed up by the American Board of Commissioners for Foreign Missions in Tungchow. The Christian university had its beginnings in 1916, and later moved to a new campus in the fall of 1926. The buildings were built featuring a modified "palace design," and were refurbished for the 100th anniversary of the university. When it was re-established by the Chinese government it was renamed, Peking University. See *Hallowed Halls, Protestant Colleges in Old China*, text by Martha Smalley, edited by Deke Erh and Tess Johston, Hong Kong: Old China Hand Press, 1998.

5   March 20, 2008. Interviewer is Yun Li, and interviewee, Changchi Hao.

6   《跨宗教对话：中国与西方》(*Interfaith Dialogue: East and West*). Editors, Fu Youde (Shandong University), Kelly James Clark (Calvin College), Melville Y. Stewart, (Capella Univerity), editors, Beijing: Social Science Publishers, 2004.

7   This led to his taking up the task of translating Alvin Platinga's *Warranted Christian Belief* into Chinese during a sabbatical spent at the University of Notre Dame.

8   I was a visiting philosopher the fall and spring terms (1992–93) at St. Petersburg State University, and the spring term at St. Petersburg Christian College, St. Petersburg, Russia.

9   《科学与宗教的对话》(*A Dialogue Between Science and Religion*; note that the English title has a different word order from entry 1, but the Chinese is identical). Proceedings of Xiamen I Symposium, Xiamen, People's Republic of China, October 16–20, 2000. Xiamen: Xiamen University Press, 2003. Chinese edition funded by the John Templeton Foundation. Chinese edition editors: Zhou Jianzhang (Xiamen University), Kelly James Clark (Calvin College), Melville Y. Stewart (University of St Thomas).

Acknowledgements

For a work of this magnitude I owe thanks to many.

First, I would like to thank the five host universities – Wuhan University, 2005, Fudan University, 2006, Shandong University, 2007, Peking University, 2008, and Tsinghua University, 2009 – for their gracious hospitality for our stays, the accommodations provided for the visiting Templeton scholars, and lecture hall arrangements.

My thanks also to the scholars appointed to serve as co-planners of the Series and co-editors of the Chinese version of the 70 papers, Changchi Hao (Wuhan), Yingjin Xu (Fudan), Fu Youde (Shandong), Xing Taotao and Xiangdon Xu (Peking), and Zhu Donghua (Tsinghua).

I want to add a note of thanks to my Teaching Assistants (TAs) at each of the host universities: they were indispensable for both the teaching assignments, and preparation for the *Series*. The list includes Li Yong at Wuhan University, Vincent (Tang Jie) at Fudan University, Martin (Dong Jianchao) at Shandong University, Ben (Yu Benxi) and Ivy (Yuan Yuan) at {Peking University}, and the TA to be assigned at Tsinghua University.

My special gratitude to Mr Drew Rick-Miller, Program Officer at the John Templeton Foundation for helping me to refine the two proposals that were finally approved. His patient review of my many revisions, ultimately led to two that worked, the one-year grant for the Wuhan Series, and the four-year grant that funded the Fudan, Shandong, Peking and Tsinghua Series. I also appreciate the assistance of Michael Murray at the Templeton Foundation for offering helpful information relating to funding for the various projects connected with the Series.

I am deeply indebted to the John Templeton Foundation for two grants covering my teaching assignments and five Science and Religion Series held at Wuhan (2005), Fudan (2006), Shandong (2007), Peking (2008) and Tsinghua (2009) universities. Their support helped actualize a dream now also realized in printed form.

There were other funding sources that helped make the teaching assignments and Science and Religion Series an outstanding success. I wish to express my gratitude to the Salem Foundation, under the direction of Pat Krohn, the Wooddale Foundation led by Tom Correll, and the Paul and Dawn Sjolund Foundation.

My thanks also to Robert Ess, Director of the Copy Center at Bethel University. He prepared preliminary copies of the volumes that were eventually to be translated and published in Chinese by Peking (volumes I, III, IV, and V) and Fudan (volume II) university presses. He also prepared pre-published bound copies for the copyediting process.

I wish to express my deep gratitude to my wife, Donna Mae, for proofreading parts of the manuscript, and for her many encouragements and her presence with me while on location at the host universities in China. Her company and love have been an inspiration in all of my teaching and writing efforts. Her love and faithfulness has been a stabilizing force in more ways than I can ever say.

I also wish to express my deep gratitude to the 26 Templeton scholars who served on the five teams over a five-year span (in the order of their papers): Del Ratzsch, Thomas Greenlee, Deborah Haarsma, Loren Haarsma, Richard Swinburne, Peter Dodson, Stephen Matheson, Alvin Plantinga, Gary Patterson, Don Page, Richard Peterson, Michael Murray, Kelly James Clark, Owen Gingerich, Calvin DeWitt, William Lane Craig, Nancey Murphy, Francisco J. Ayala, Paul Davies, Dean Zimmerman, Peter van Inwagen, Alan Padgett, Stephen M. Barr, William Hurlbut, Philip Clayton, and Bruce Reichenbach. I am indebted to their creative and scholarly commitment to the Series, to the original audiences, and the readers of the published papers. It has been my pleasure to read the manuscripts many times over while preparing the five-volume Chinese edition, and the English two-volume set. The coming together of 12 philosophers and 14 scientists, each with their own approaches to their respective practices of inquiry, was a joy. There was always a concern as to how they might interact with each other, with their primary audience, and with the keen anticipation that their initial presentations would appear in final polished form for readers worldwide. There is a marvelous variety of subtopics relating to the science-and-religion-in-dialogue theme enhanced by a rich variety of insights. I also want to thank each of the lecturers for friendly suggestions and corrections of summaries of their respective papers that form the main substance of the Introductions to each of the volumes. My special thanks to Alan Padgett and Bruce Reichenbach for reviewing early sections of both Introductions and for their recommended improvements. I also want to thank my longtime friend Roger Ames of the Center for Chinese Studies at the University of Hawaii for reviewing the Chinese entries in both Introductions. Chinese entries elsewhere were edited by my Teaching Assistants. Special thanks also to Deborah and Loren Haarsma for preparing most of the definitions of key terms that appear in the Glossary.

No manuscript ever enters the scene with every turn and term original with each passing page and diagram or cover picture. Hence the need for thanks to publishers who granted permission to include pieces, pictures, and passages of poetry, for enhancement and precision.

First, there are diagrams, pictures, and charts that appear in Volume One beginning with the three figures drawn by Thomas Greenlee, and the triangular graph and three charts crafted by Deborah Haarsma. Special thanks to Eisenbraun's publisher, Winnona Lake, Indiana, for permission to include the Egyptian engraving originally published in *The Symbolism of the Biblical World* authored by Oshmer Keel. Two pictures of "Horned Dinosaurs" for Peter Dodson's papers were submitted by Dodson's artist friend, Robert Walters. Three pictures appearing in Gary Patterson's papers were supplied by Wellcome Trust, London, UK, and the other two are in the public domain.

Figures and pictures in Volume Two include: Owen Gingerich's original drawings of the Copernicon Transformation, and the original drawing by Copernicus of the "Sun-Centered System," in Copernicus *De revolutionibus* of 1543 (public domain); Calvin DeWitt includes images of (1) The Wetlands, (2) the *S-E-P* Triad, (3) the Millenium Ecosystem Assessment Chart, University of Wisconsin Class Plaque, the University of Wisconsin, (4) variations of the Earth's surface temperature for the past 40 years, (5) the Cranes, and (6) "One World, One Dream" (*yige shijie, yige meng* (一个世界，一个梦). William Lane Craig supplied his original drawings of two Oscillating Models, false vacuum, baby universes, the bubbles of a true vacuum and the stalagmites and stalactites of the Big Bang theory, following Penrose's ideas. And finally, William Hurlbut provided his "Altered Nuclear Transfer" drawing.

The Hubble Telescope jacket pictures were incorporated by the design department of Wiley-Blackwell. My thanks to NASA for issuing contract NAS5-26555, which offers these beautiful pictures to the public. My special thanks to the Wiley-Blackwell cover artists for working with me in the selection of pictures so nicely representing the manifold beauty of the starry heavens, framing them in aesthetically pleasing color and design.

My special thanks to Dr Jeff Dean, Senior Acquisitions Editor, and his Assistant, Tiffany Mok at the Boston Wiley-Blackwell office for helpful advice, and for the many suggestions that led to refinements upgrading the quality of the publication. I am also very grateful to the freelance copyeditor appointed by the Oxford office, Janey Fisher, for her careful attention to detail and syntactical sensibility, all of which led to many significant improvements in the text; and to Wiley-Blackwell of Oxford both for having chosen to publish these papers in a two-volume library-bound edition for distribution in the West, and for allowing a Chinese edition to be published by Peking and Fudan university presses for distribution in Asia.

I want to close with a celebrative note, thanking and congratulating the students who comprised the first audiences for these papers in China. An exciting narrative unfolded as team after team visited one university after another. Every round was met with an enthusiastic welcome by students and faculty who packed lecture halls to hear the Templeton scholars. Those were wonderfully inspiring moments now etched in our memories. It was a coming together of minds in critical, constructive, and friendly dialogue. Many thanks to friends in the Chinese academy for helping to set this sort of affirmative stage in preparation for another audience, the readers of these volumes. It is hoped that readers East and West will find these pages as engaging, enjoyable and inspiring as did the first readers and hearers.

Melville Y. Stewart

Introduction

MELVILLE Y. STEWART

We live in a time of unprecedented scientific exploration, discovery, and achievement. This is as evident in China as it is in the United States. During the fourth round of the Science and Religion Series, my wife Donna and I lived at the Shao Yuan Hotel, room 109, Peking University. That year (2008), Chinese astronauts were sent into space, and a week later they landed safely in the desert to the north in Inner Mongolia. It was the lead story in all the Chinese media.

Nearly six years ago, *Time* magazine featured an article, "How the Universe Will End," which provided a flow-chart account of how the cosmos started and how scientists see it as ending in a Dark Era, comprised "… mostly of photons, neutrinos, electrons and positrons wandering through a universe bigger than the mind can conceive … [the author went on to say] From here into an infinite future, the universe remains cold, dark and dismal."[1] Science prognosticators paint a rather dismal picture for the human race and planet Earth. Many think that the sun will eventually fade into a ball scarcely bigger than our "home planet" and if the human species is going to survive at all, it will only be a vestigial remainder aboard a "galactic ark," transporting one generation after another of its human occupants on an endless search for some distant planet suited for human habitation beyond our nearest star (next to the sun), Proxima Centauri, some 4.3 light years away.

It is interesting that scientific prognosticators predict an end to the cosmos that bears a similarity to religious-end-type narrative. Paul in prophetic verse in New Testament passages predicts the dissolution of the heavens and the earth in a unity of the eschatological complex of events. However, as interesting as this intersection of comparative end-time accounts might be, there are other more significant points of intersection between the two areas of inquiry that are of special interest, namely those that relate to the foci of the papers included in these two volumes.

The task taken up in this collection of 70 papers involves exploring the disciplines of science and religion in dialogue, not in an unfriendly, disconnected, perhaps even warlike confrontational mode, but in constructive, congruent, perhaps even complementary affirmation. The assumption underlying the Science and Religion Series is: "the God of Christian theism provides a starting point, in terms of which the Book of Nature, as it is displayed in the starry heavens above and the manifest beauty of the Earth below," and "the Hebrew-Christian Scriptures, believed by Christians to be inspired by the Spirit of God, are viewed as two modes whereby God reveals two core attributes, his eternal faithfulness/consistency and ultimate rationality." If one affirms such a God exists, and further that this divine agent created the heavens and the earth, *and* inspired the Hebrew – Christian Scriptures, then *inter alia*, this may serve as a ground for the claim that there is a consistency and complementarity between the two Books, just in case the two modes of revelation are carefully and properly understood. Regarding the Book of Nature, in a recent article in *National Geographic*, featuring a cover story titled, "What Darwin Didn't Know: His First Clues, Evolution Now," Matt Ridley reports Darwin's comment, "All the organic beings which have ever lived on this earth have descended from some one primordial form," to which Ridley adds, "He was frankly guessing. To understand the story of evolution – both its narrative and its mechanism – modern Darwins don't have to guess. They consult *genetic scripture*."[2] Yes, there are *two scriptures*, one the physical cosmic Book of Nature, which includes as part of its "text," the *genetic scripture*, the other, the Hebrew, Greek, and Aramaic texts containing moral codes and religious teachings, each mode requiring disparate methods of *exegesis*, the former a natural-scientific "exegesis," and the latter, carefully crafted principles of a proven-trustworthy hermeneutic.

As the reader begins to take up topic after topic, discussed by team members invited for each round of the Series beginning at Wuhan University, it is important to note that world-class scientists, philosophers, and theologians enthusiastically committed themselves to science and religion dialogue. And while the two areas of inquiry doubtlessly generate differences, sometimes substantial, as to method, subject matter and objectives, some of which are noted passim by the authors, it is argued that there are also analogues, in some instances close parallels, points of intersection, significant complementarity, and yes, perhaps even elements of mutual support. Thus the two areas may be viewed as involving practices of inquiry[3] evidencing points of similarity, overall consistency, and complementarity. More specifically, one may see elements of analogy in their respective uses of (1) paradigm, (2) models of explanation, and, (3) their respective methods and criteria of rationality.[4]

The reader faces a huge enticing menu to choose from on topics covered. This is intentional. The rigor of the logic and persuasive rhetoric prima facie evident may make choices and the formulation of one's own belief system difficult, as authors "strut and fret their hour upon the stage" to present their case say, for the consistency and complementarity of the two disciplines. Notwithstanding divergences, there is an abiding and pervading general consensus on the part of the team members who seriously pursue Christian apologetic practices of inquiry, affirming that God has produced two books – two modes of revelation whereby God's consistency and truthfulness so central to his nature are reflected in the Book of Nature and the Eternal Word, both of which are readily accessible to human agents who are *prepared to receive* and interpret these revelations with *properly-functioning belief-forming mechanisms*.

This brings us to a consideration of another matter of introductory importance, the title of the two-volume set, which originates from the title of the first volume of the Chinese Series, *Science and Religion in Dialogue* (《科学与宗教的对话》).[5] The English meaning of the terms appearing in the title have a rather straightforward sense. *Science* is understood in contemporary idiom as including the *natural* and *social* sciences, and *religion* is understood denotatively as including belief-systems such as Christianity, the Hebrew faith, Islam, Hinduism, etc.[6] The English expression "in dialogue" means "the interchange and discussion of ideas." Some think that *dialogue* conveys the added idea (such as in the case of science and religion) that the two areas of inquiry have things in common, and enough in the way of a common universe of discourse, that there is no problem with exchange, since they are not only logically compatible when both are properly understood and described, they may also bear a relation of complementarity. This added meaning takes us beyond the simple understanding of dialogue as *meaningful exchange*.

The Chinese title is somewhat more complex both in terms of the words used, and what they might be viewed as conveying in terms of current usage and understanding. The Chinese term for science, *kexue* (科学), doesn't have the rich etymology associated with its English counterpart, which is traceable back to the Latin root terms, *scio, sciere* (I know, to know).[7] And while the Chinese term for religion, *zongjiao*, (宗教), has been understood as referring to a cultural phenomenon resting on myth and superstition, many in contemporary Chinese culture view the term as a denotative equivalent of the English term.

The phrase in Chinese that merits closer attention is, *de duihua* (的对话). "in dialogue." Roger Ames in, "Dialogue Between Chinese and Western Philosophy,"[8] says that in the early days of Western philosophical narrative, *dialogue* had the meaning of *talking through an issue*, with the end of securing truth on an issue by means of a dialogical exchange involving carefully crafted arguments. For Plato, in his *Republic*, on the highest level of his epistemology (in his Analogy of the Line),[9] the term involved a *backword movement* to unhypothesized Forms (*eide*, εἴδε) which he hoped would yield certainties. This is where he left things in the so-called Middle Period of his writings because he couldn't find the epistemological certainties he wanted. In the third period of his writings, in the *Parmenides*, he appears to have shifted to the view that *beliefs* (δόχα), can be *known*. Ames adds that Aristotle's use of the term *dialogue* had the meaning of *a pursuit of the ontes* (ὄντες, the being or essence) *of things*. Thus we see an essentialism traces of which can be found in the early Wittgenstein. Ames says, on this account, the philosopher can speak, but not listen, since his pursuit leads him to the truth, alone, without the helpful exchange of others.

By contrast, according to Ames, the Chinese term for *dialogue*, *duihua* (对话) suggests a "conversation, a *fitting responsiveness* between two persons." *Dui* (对) has the meaning, "to be a counterpart, to answer," that is, in the sense of "having what deserves to be heard."[10] This sense of *dialogue*, namely, *having what deserves to be heard*, is a factor that helps preserve and promote a central end contemplated in the Science and Religion Series. Recognized scholars with various takes on the main theme have ideas and arguments that *deserve to be heard*. If there are significant competing opinions and arguments on a topic covered, then *ceterus paribus*, they deserve to be heard as well. As with all topics aired in the public square of the academy, scholars engaging in science and religion dialogue need to follow this and other participant guidelines and expectations so as to safeguard and promote civility in the public square. *Listening to what needs to be heard* is linked to another principle, that of *mutual respect* for the participants engaged, and for the views, beliefs, and values presented. And since we are in a day when the idea of *pure objectivity* is passé for the academy, this means that each side to a dispute has to make its case carefully, with a respect for the opposition, and with a readiness to listen to counter-arguments and proposals. So the idea of, "having (and listening to) what deserves to be heard" is pivotal to helpful and constructive dialogue. It has been refreshing and encouraging from the start to observe that each of the Series held in China has evidenced this sort of response – faculty and students listening to each presenter with the attitude that the presentation deserves to be heard.

I hasten to add, that the principle, "listening to what deserves to be heard" is in need of preserving principles. Without such principles the public arena of the academy (and other places of exchange such as the media) opens itself to potential abuse on the part of those who might wish to take advantage of this openness in the public square for their own ends in inappropriate ways. So reasonable and appropriate boundaries need to be established that will protect and preserve the purpose(s) contemplated for pubic gatherings for exchange in the academy.

Initially, the Science and Religion Series, funded by the John Templeton Foundation, was put together for university audiences in China, with a special concern to engage members of the science and philosophy departments at various host universities in friendly discourse on topics relating to the main theme. The original audiences for these 70 papers issuing from the Series running from 2005–2009 at five of China's top universities, Wuhan, Fudan, Shandong, Peking and Tsinghua, is now expanded to the academy worldwide via the medium of the printed page in two editions, the Chinese, published by Fudan and Peking university presses, and the English, published by Wiley-Blackwell of Oxford.

Part 1   Has Science Really Destroyed Its Own Religious Roots?

The beginning three papers by Professor Del Ratzsch (philosophy, Calvin College) were chosen as the lead chapters for Volume One because they help set the stage for the essays that follow by introducing the reader to the nature of science, and the religious roots of science. In chapter 1, THE NATURE OF SCIENCE, Ratzsch draws upon past and present views of the nature of science. Part of his task is to show that over and above the wide variety of scientific theories historically, there has also been a difference of opinion as to the precise *nature* of science and the scientific method. He examines in detail the way elements which are beyond "observational data," "theories," and "principles of reason," still have a pivotal and legitimate role at the very "heart of science." This he believes opens the door to considering science and religion issues that figure historically in the development of science and the scientific method. Moreover, he contends that the criticisms of religious belief which relied upon outdated accounts of the nature of science are for this reason potentially ineffectual. He concludes that science cannot be reduced to some sort of logical connection between sets of data and theory. He adds that there are many influences which unavoidably play a part in the construction of scientific pictures of the world.

In chapter 2, THE RELIGIOUS ROOTS OF SCIENCE, he contends that it is a myth that science has been at war with religion from its inception. Not only is this a mistake, the truth of the matter lies in an entirely different direction. As he argues in the previous chapter, science rests on principles that are not entirely empirical. He goes on to argue that many of the principles operative in the sciences are rooted in the religious belief in creation. In a review of the history of Western philosophy, he sees the rise of science taking place against the backdrop of the creation story. He then asks why this happened, and more particularly, why it happened when it did. He contends that the rise took place at a period when various scientists worked with religious assumptions, such as, God created a good and orderly creation. This affirmation that creation was good and orderly provided grounds for science to proceed on the assumption that science was a worthwhile task and a fulfillment of divine mandates announced early in the creation account.

Chapter 3, THE ALLEGED DEMISE OF RELIGION, is a response to the charge that science has undercut the rationality of religious faith. Variant accounts of this charge are examined. Four challenges come under scrutiny including, (1) claims issuing from the basic assumptions of science and its method, (2) the putative overall picture science presents (assuming a realist versus a nonrealist approach to scientific models and paradigms), (3) selected elements of scientific theory and finally, (4) claims issuing from alleged conflicts between science and religion. His overall strategy is to show that none of these charges hold up under scrutiny, hence he concludes that any fundamental rift between the two is a fiction.

Part 2 God and Physical Reality: Relativity, Time, and Quantum Mechanics

Professor Thomas Greenlee (physics, Bethel University) begins with a focus on RELATIVITY, GOD, AND TIME (chapter 4). By way of introduction, he offers an account of classical mechanics, specifically Isaac Newton's laws of motion, contrasting Newton's model with Albert Einstein's Special Theory of Relativity. After drawing several consequences of Einstein's theory, he then brings various elements of this new scientific model to bear on issues relating to God and time, offering two cautionary notes. First, since traditional Christian theism contends that God made the laws of physics, he isn't subject to them. Second, Greenlee believes that at those points where the laws of physics reflect the way things are, if the inquirer wants to "think God's thoughts after Him," then following this procedure of viewing the laws of physics as reflective of reality might be a way of seeing things the way God sees them. He concludes that the account of God's relation to time most in harmony with special relativity is the view that God is outside of time, the view held by Boethius and many great thinkers in the history of all three of the main traditions of Christianity, and more recently defended by Eleonore Stump, Norman Kretzmann, and Brian Leftow. He then anticipates a few problems facing this view.

In chapter 5, GENERAL RELATIVITY, THE COSMIC MICROWAVE BACKGROUND, AND MORAL RELATIVISM, he discusses the relationship of space and time in the context of the general theory of relativity, and then reviews the cosmic microwave background radiation discovery which in principle opens up the possibility that one might be able to compare times of events and velocities of reference frames throughout the universe working with a single rest frame, thereby providing a universe-wide standard of sequence of events. He concludes that this strategy will not provide helpful information regarding a time function, and hence doesn't enable one to choose coordinates for a cosmology.

The concluding focus is upon scientific relativity theory and the possible bearing it might have, if any, on moral relativism. He argues that those who might be tempted to think that the conclusion of relativity theory, that one reference frame is not any more correct than another, is analogous to and supportive of the idea that there is no one moral point of view, is mistaken for two reasons. First, the language games are not only different, but more particularly on the scientific side, he observes that there are frame-independent absolutes in scientific relativity theory. Therefore the analogy fails on two counts.

Chapter 6, QUANTUM MECHANICS AND THE NATURE OF REALITY, brings two readings of quantum mechanics center stage: the *Copenhagen interpretation* and the *many-worlds formulation*. The former reading, by far the most popular, involves the contention that unobserved electrons do not have dynamic properties. This is called the "collapse of the wave function" because there is a collapse from many possibilities to one actuality. Contrariwise, the many-worlds theory formulation holds that the full range of possibilities occur but in disparate worlds.

His concluding focus is upon *hidden variable theory*, and possible Christian responses to quantum mechanics. He draws the conclusion that though there are philosophical problems with quantum mechanics, the theory is at least prima facie compatible with Christian belief. His final conclusion: there is no conflict between Christian belief and some of the most recent "experimentally-tested" areas of contemporary physics.

Part 3   Interactions Between Science and Christianity

The final round of papers presented at Wuhan University are by professors Deborah Haarsma (astronomy, physics, Calvin College), and her husband, Loren Haarsma. In the original delivery they took turns. They are reordered in this volume, starting with Deborah Haarsma's three papers (Part 3) followed by Loren Haarsma's three papers (Part 4).

Professor Deborah Haarsma's first chapter (chapter 7), SCIENCE AND RELIGION IN HARMONY, takes on the charge that some of the discoveries in modern science such as Big Bang Theory, the great age of the Earth, and the common descent of the species and human evolution clearly support the thesis that science and religion are fundamentally at war. She explores possible alternative models such as the relationship of *independence*, the view that science and religion are two separate non-intersecting spheres, *interaction*, which holds that both disciplines might address the same questions, hence implications may be drawn for each, and finally, a *foundational model*, according to which religious beliefs can provide philosophical grounds for science to flourish. Her examination of each in turn includes historical examples. She concludes that the foundational model allows persons of various religious traditions to work in a constructive and complementary way without compromising either science or religious beliefs.

In chapter 8, HOW CHRISTIANS RECONCILE ANCIENT TEXTS WITH MODERN SCIENCE, Deborah Haarsma focuses on the pivotal Christian belief that the Christian Scriptures are inspired. Operating on the assumption that this belief is correct, she explores different accounts of the inspired Genesis story against the scientific data relating to origins. She first observes that the creation account of Genesis which says that creation took six days to complete appears to contradict the account of geology and astrophysics which on most accounts strongly indicate that beginnings go back billions of years. She adds that Christian responses to this have been multifarious evidencing thereby the influence of elements of culture, religion, and conviction regarding the authority and specificity of the Scriptures, and scientific beliefs. The responses include (1) the *day-age* theory (which takes the Hebrew term *yom* as signifying an epoch rather than a 24-hour day), and (2) the *Young Earth hypothesis* which seeks to counter the influence and credibility of scientific evidence for evolution. The Young Earth hypothesis takes the days of Genesis as literally lasting 24 hours. She observes that some Christian theists think that the Young Earth hypothesis is significantly out of line with the scientific data, and so they have taken refuge in what is called (3) the *appearance theory*, which is the view that the Earth *looks like* it is billions of years old because God made it to appear that way, but in actuality, God created it less than 10,000 years ago. She subsumes day-age, appearance-of-age, gap, and various Young Earth views under *concordism*. Each of the views are taken as interpretations that attempt to match scientific evidence to the sequence of events in Genesis 1. She contends that a hermeneutic of Genesis 1 which takes into account its literary features and its historical and cultural context favors a non-concordist interpretation. This approach holds that the main point of Genesis 1 is theological, not historical or scientific. In its historical context, Genesis 1 clearly communicates a theological message – a message in sharp contrast to the surrounding polytheistic beliefs of that time. That theological content includes the idea that there is one God who created the heavens and the earth, and that the sun, moon, earth, sky, and seas are created things and not gods. She concludes that such a non-concordist interpretation is not only more in line with the Biblical intent; it is also more compatible with scientific data.

In her final chapter (9), CHRISTIAN AND ATHEIST RESPONSES TO BIG BANG COSMOLOGY, Deborah Haarsma contrasts the infinitely old universe notion – a universe with no beginning in time, a view that prevailed in the early twentieth century – with the more recent Big Bang proposal that the universe began with a colossal explosion about 14 billion years ago. According to a popular attending hypothesis, several properties of the universe – its matter density, the values of physical constants and nuclear reaction rates – are all so finely tuned as to create an environment well-suited for life, and more particularly human life. She examines *in seriatim* the following observable data relating to the fine-tuning hypothesis: (1) the expansion rate of the universe and gravity are both suited for long-lived stars; (2) the masses of elementary particles and fundamental physical forces are both suited for fusion; (3) the nuclear reaction rates are right for producing carbon in stars; (4) the water molecule is suited for life around stars. All of these factors are observable data, and on her account, they all fall in line with the claim that God created and designed the universe for life and human existence.

Deborah Haarsma takes up the issue of the immense size of the universe and observes that this might incline one to think that humans are by sheer size contrast clearly marginalized. How could creatures count as having meaning in such a vast universe? (See Don Page's paper, DOES GOD LOVE THE MULTIVERSE?, chapter 29.) Many have thought this factor raises questions with regard to the meaning of life and of human life in particular. How could a seemingly insignificant species really have an important place in the scheme of things? Several points are drawn by way of conclusion; most important among them is the claim that special revelation instructs us not to view the vastness of creation as an indicator of our unimportance before God. Rather we are to see our place in the universe by the standard and revelation of his infinite love expressed in the Living Word. Christ is lifted as the standard and measure of divine love, and God's Incarnation is viewed as a reaffirmation of an original plan in process of being restored, in which humans presently share a rulership of the universe as his vice gerents, and in the final eschatological denouement of the Kingdom they become co-inheritors and co-rulers forever into the future.

Part 4 Interplay of Scientific and Religious Knowledge Regarding Evolution

In his first chapter (10), SCIENTIFIC KNOWLEDGE DOES NOT REPLACE RELIGIOUS KNOWLEDGE, Professor Loren Haarsma (physics, Calvin College) points out that science usually tries to explain natural events such as the orbit of planets or the growth of vegetation in terms of mechanistic, impersonal processes. In contrast, attempts to explain natural phenomena using religious language show a different pattern. Often, the approach is one that invokes the divine spelled out in terms of "action and intention." And while one might think the two approaches are antagonistic or in polarity, Loren Haarsma contends contrariwise, that the two can be viewed as fitting together, that is, the religious offers foundational principles that provide a conceptual framework for viewing the universe as orderly and predictable. Viewing the universe as a divine creation gives an account of (1) beginnings and (2) a consistent continuance and preservation of natural laws according to the doctrine of divine Providence. On those occasions when science encounters a phenomenon which defies explanation in terms of known natural laws, whether those phenomena are taken as (1) a divine miracle, or (2) a random event, or (3) as an unknown natural process may not depend upon one's science, but upon one's predilection to certain religious beliefs. On his account, science neither proves nor disproves miracles. Accordingly, he says that science is one source of dependable knowledge, but it isn't the only source. A list of other sources include history, personal experience, and culture.

A distinction is drawn between *beliefs* and *faith commitments*; the former is more general and operative in all epistemological inquiries, and the latter involves a belief or set of beliefs which significantly impact our whole life and manner of living. Moreover, neither science nor faith need to be viewed as in polarity with reason, though there have been times in history when they have been thought to be in polarity. He concludes that polarity/conflict between scientific and religious knowledge is not an inevitable outcome, but instead, the two may be in significant ways complementary, and may in fact share important characteristics. He adds that there might be times when science may offer correctives to some religious beliefs, and religious beliefs may offer correctives to mistaken scientific beliefs or to mistaken philosophical interpretations of correct scientific beliefs. Thus on the reason/faith variant, reason and faith are not opposites. The opposite of reason is irrationality. The opposite of faith is unbelief – both are commitments. Faith and unbelief commitments can be rational or irrational, depending on the circumstances. A reasonable faith commitment is based upon, and may be open to correction from, multiple sources of knowledge, including science, history, personal experience, and the experience of others.

In chapter 11, GOD, EVOLUTION, AND DESIGN, Loren Haarsma acknowledges that the evidence for the evolutionary hypothesis abounds. While he discusses some of the issues raised in the previous paper, his focus is more particularly on evolution and design. A distinction is drawn between (1) Young Earth creationists, discussed and described in the previous chapter, and (2) progressive creationists. The latter allow that there is strong evidence for an earth that is billions of years old, a long history of life, and some evolution during that history, but adds that God has intervened miraculously in the evolutionary process so as to bring about new life forms. Evidence for such intervention is sought after to support the claim that life was "intelligently designed." There are still others, called "theistic evolutionists" or "evolutionary creationists," who hold the conjunction that evolution (without the need for miraculous intervention) *and* the system of Christian beliefs are true. The two are logically and factually compatible.

Loren Haarsma tends to favor the evolutionary creationist line of reasoning, arguing that God uses evolution to create new life forms in a way analogous to his maintaining gravity to preserve the pattern of the earth's orbit around the sun. He concludes that evolutionary mechanisms are a result of God's creativity, and the mechanisms themselves are designed to bring about richness in diversity of life forms in ways that are progressively adaptive to the changing demands of the environment. So he agrees with theist philosopher of science Robin Collins that the laws of nature in the cosmos appear fine-tuned for the existence and evolutionary development of life.

In his final chapter (12), HUMAN EVOLUTION AND OBJECTIVE MORALITY, Loren Haarsma challenges the idea often associated with the evolutionary hypothesis, that evolution tends to favor selfish interest. Since it is the fittest and strongest that survive, selfish interest would seem an easy corollary to the evolutionary hypothesis, and hence a natural and appropriate motive for the stronger member of any given species. He turns to the fields of sociobiology and evolutionary psychology to trace explanations the sciences might have for the genesis of altruistic behavior, the more general forms of moral consciousness, and the appearance of the religious consciousness. The general conclusion of these fields is that the origins of moral and religious consciousness can be explained scientifically by understanding their utility in promoting survival and reproduction in early human communal living. According to some philosophical interpretations, such scientific explanations undercut morality and altruism's integrity in particular, as well as the integrity of religious consciousness in any authentic form. As a counter, Loren Haarsma challenges the naturalistic philosophical underpinnings of the claims, contending that they are not essential to the scientific theories under scrutiny. And while moral and religious sentiments could have evolved biologically, which he avers is compatible with the idea of God creating the characteristics of all life forms via governance of natural processes, he wants to add to this story the traditional theological idea of supernatural personal revelation in human history. So in Aquinian fashion, he sees the supernatural as a transcending dimension beyond what may be found in the complex of natural law. Divine personal revelation adds a vertical dimension to the horizontal biological and social dimensions, bringing with it a fuller and richer account of the human condition. Moral and religious sentiments developed through evolutionary processes are supernaturally expanded according to divinely given moral disclosures providing warrant/justification, scope, and content for religious beliefs.

Part 5 The Universe Makes It Probable That There Is A God

Richard Swinburne (philosophy of religion, philosophy of science, University of Oxford), in his first chapter (13), WHAT MAKES A SCIENTIFIC THEORY PROBABLY TRUE, focuses upon explanations as to why things happen the way they do, and why the world is the way that it is. Two patterns of causal explanation of events are distinguished: the inanimate or scientific, which explains natural phenomena in terms of the so-called laws of nature and earlier conditions which might be thought to *cause* the phenomena in question. The second kind of explanation is personal: various factors relating to persons as causes are enumerated, such as the way a person's body is moved by the agent in question, and ways in which the agent's beliefs and intentions produce certain effects. We use explanations of different kinds in explaining different phenomena. Swinburne expands upon the former scientific explanation model, breaking it down into two categories according to whether the laws are universal or statistical. He contends that such explanations are "rigorous" and "scientific" when "the description C and the statement of L entail … the occurrence of E" or make it probable. The former he calls a "full explanation" and the latter a "partial" one.

After distinguishing the two models his attention is directed to what makes a postulated explanation probably true. He begins with the scientific sort of explanation. Here the question is, what sort of criteria are there that allow one to say a given explanation is probably true? His response is that the probability of L being a law of nature hinges on two factors, (1) its being a scientific hypothesis with great explanatory power and (2) its possessing a high prior probability. If the former occurs, the hypothesis in question has predictive power;

it makes probable the occurrence of the observed phenomena when it is not probable that the phenomena would occur if the hypothesis is false. The second, the prior probability of an hypothesis, is described as the probability it has independent of the phenomena whose occurrence it makes probable. The intrinsic probability hinges on its simplicity and scope. The calculation of the principles of probability is rendered in terms of the calculus of conditional probabilities formalized in Bayes' theorem. Thus the probability of a causal explanation, an explanatory hypothesis, can be formalized in terms of Bayes' theorem.

Swinburne distinguishes three basic kinds of probability: physical, statistical, and inductive. The first is a measure of the extent to which nature is prone to bringing forth certain events. Statistical probability is a proportional measure of events of one kind in some class of events; and inductive probability is the measure to which one proposition makes another probably true. In assessing probability he is concerned mainly with how far propositions which describe the evidence render them inductively probable.

After rendering his account of the criteria for a scientific or personal explanatory hypothesis being probable on the evidence, he acknowledges that while many philosophers of science might agree with some of his ideas, perhaps some might not agree with his claims regarding the criterion of simplicity and the suggested formulation in terms of Bayes' theorem. His claim that Bayes' theorem is true is succinctly expressed thus: "all statements about one probability being greater than, or equal to, or less than another probability, which can be deduced from the theorem are true."

In what follows, he hopes to assess whether arguments from various phenomena leading to a personal omnipotent, omniscient, and omnibenevolent God are correct *C*-inductive arguments – arguments in which the premises add to the probability of the conclusion, and perhaps correct *P*-inductive arguments – arguments which make the conclusion more probable than not.

In his second chapter (14), THE ARGUMENT TO GOD FROM THE LAWS OF NATURE, Swinburne argues that the "hypothesis of theism" that God exists, is not only a simple hypothesis (which satisfies a criterion discussed in his first chapter), but it is also quite probable that the God described would bring about free creatures with powers to change their lives and the lives of others in the ways that humans seem to be able to do. This focus is upon the personal type, since God is the explanatory hypothesis.

He starts off with a brief account of God conceived as essentially eternal, omnipotent, omniscient, and perfectly free. This is God's essence as it has been historically described by the three main traditions of the Christian faith, Roman Catholicism, historic Protestantism, and Orthodoxy. The first says in effect that God always was, is, and forever will be. The second says that he is able to bring about any logically possible set of states of affairs compatible with his nature. The third claims that he knows all logically consistent propositions that are logically possible for him to know. And finally, regarding his perfect freedom, he is not subject to irrational inclinations, and so can choose only those options which he believes to be good. Hence because he is omniscient, God knows which options are good, and because he is also perfectly free, he will be perfectly good.

The hypothesis of this God, he goes on to argue, makes probable a universe governed by the laws of nature, because such a universe is necessary for the existence of humans. That is, whether the observational evidence *e*, makes the hypothesis that God exists probable, hinges on whether *the existence of God* hypothesis explains all that is subsumed under *e*.

The simplicity of the hypothesis translates into its having a "high intrinsic and prior probability." He concludes that the data makes the hypothesis "quite probable."

He passes in review two central arguments for God's existence, the cosmological argument from the existence of the universe of many substances, and the argument from their uniform behavior (as governed by laws of nature), and he takes both as good C-inductive arguments, arguments of a scientific sort that satisfy the criteria given in his first chapter (simplicity and prior probability), and so he contends that the premises add considerably to the conclusion's probability, hence it is probable that God exists.

In his third chapter (15), THE ARGUMENT TO GOD FROM FINE-TUNING, Swinburne goes beyond the data that the universe is governed by the laws of nature, to consider the claim that the laws are fine-tuned for the existence and evolution of human life as we know it. He contends that the exact values of the constraints of the laws of nature and of the boundary conditions of the universe required for the development of human life are more likely, given the existence of the God described above, than if one were to deny this hypothesis. Hence fine-tuning increases the probability of the existence of God.

The final conclusion is that there is a powerful C-inductive argument, a scientific sort of explanation, which explains both the existence of the laws of nature, and the fine-tuning of the universe, and because the hypothesis offered explains both, he concludes that there is a greater range of phenomena explained.

Part 6 A Paleontologist Considers Science and Religion

In his three chapters Professor Peter Dodson (anatomy, geology, University of Pennsylvania) introduces the reader to the interesting and engaging practices of inquiry of the paleontologist. The first (chapter 16), Is INTELLIGENT DESIGN REALLY INTELLIGENT? is based on an earlier paper bearing the same title in the *American Paleontologist* (Spring, 2006).[11] He has updated and revised the study for inclusion in this collection.

He begins with an observation, as a scientist, that he sees "intelligent design in the dissection lab every single day." He then continues to enumerate examples that are his favorite, such as the musculoskeletal structure of the hand, and the elegant pattern of redundant vascularization of the gut, both of which are viewed as evidencing optimal design.

But then he adds in stark contrast what he considers to be counter-examples to design cases, such as the uprightness of the human species, and the specific phenomenon of the recurrent laryngeal nerve. It is the latter that Stephen Jay Gould categorizes as "evolutionary baggage." Regarding both examples, he observes that what may be viewed as prima facie imperfections of organic design may also provide insight into evolution. The process that brought about the recurrent laryngeal nerve is explained by an appeal to the evolutionary developmental path of fish.

He opines that Intelligent Design (ID) is made to carry too heavy a load. He explains, if the Designer is going to be praised for the good things he allegedly designs, then he must also be blamed for what appear to be dysteleological elements in nature. Thus he finds fault with scholars like biochemist Michael Behe (author of *Darwin's Black Box*), who formulates an account of ID to explain what Behe calls *irreducible complexities* (see chapter 20, Stephen Matheson's "A Scientific and Religious Critique of Intelligent Design"), contending that an evolutionary process could not have produced such complex structures, adding that only an "unspecified designer" could have done it.

While Dodson is critical of this account of ID, the view that God has to be introduced into the picture when giving account of the genesis of the universe, its particular forms of

life, and such things as irreducible complexities, he admits to being sympathetic to creationist ideas. He holds God to be the Supreme Creator and his modus operandi to be evolution. He makes clear his stand on this issue, with a reference to Haught and Ayala, who
believe that Darwin's evolutionary hypothesis is a "gift to theology."

While many if not most scientists dismiss the notion of purpose in their methodology,
Dodson judges that to draw the conclusion philosophically that there is no purpose of any
sort takes the scientist beyond the boundaries of science *qua* science. Or as Haught has put
it, it is to pretend that scientific description exhausts explanatory possibilities.

He concludes that there should be no fear of the scientific, if it is genuinely scientific.
Evolution should not be taken as a threat to the viability of God's existence or his creative
activity. Rather, this can serve as a helpful picture of how God might have brought about the
richness and diversity of the species, and of the stars and planets that fill the heavens. So
Haught's and Ayala's contention that evolution is "Darwin's gift to theology" is enthusiastically endorsed.

His second chapter (17), GOD AND THE DINOSAURS REVISITED, is based on an earlier
paper that appears in the *American Paleontologist* (May, 1997).[12] In this chapter, his focus is
upon two matters, his faith as a scientist, and how his science fits with his faith commitment. He begins by informing the reader of the range of his academic career that qualifies
him as a biologist, a dinosaur paleontologist, a veterinary anatomist, and an evolutionary
biologist. In addition to research in the United States, his commitment to these areas of science has taken him literally around the world, including Canada, India, Madagascar, Egypt,
Argentina, and China. He was doing research with Chinese scholars when this Introduction
was written.

His first focus is upon his personal perspective as a professional scientist firmly committed to a Christian life and worldview. He acknowledges that as important as science is to
human endeavors in the contemporary world, he sees the discipline as vastly incomplete
when it comes to issues such as living one's life, and human values. He sees the religious
perspective as "deeply imbedded" in human nature, in ways resembling Paul's descriptive
accounts in the Book of Romans (1:19, 21; and 2:14, 15).

He admits that for a good portion of his professional life, he had kept his faith a personal
matter, rarely, if ever, sharing it with others in his profession. But he admits now to a change
of mind. He doesn't hesitate to make his faith a public matter, as an added dimension, an
essential ingredient of one's humanity, worthy of examination and critical responses from
peers in the academy and its scientific counterpart. He refers to Bertrand Russell's outspo-
ken manner when he published his *Why I Am Not a Christian*. It was an announcement to
the academy that, until recent times, nearly stood alone in the philosophical literature.
Russell has since been joined by others who are center stage in contemporary science, such
as Carl Sagan, Jacques Monod, Steven Weinberg, Daniel Dennett, and Richard Dawkins.

Dodson laments the fact that, in the current literature, there are so many articulate models for the atheistic scientist, but not many who are supportive of theism. He sees John
Polkinghorne as a refreshing bearer of a "broader view of reality," one that takes into account
the fullness of human nature, and of the realities that form humanity's context in this universe. Here he is quick to add that he sees no reason or argument standing in the way of a
Christian embracing evolutionary theory.

For Dodson, religious belief that is carefully crafted in the light of Scripture need not
be the enemy of science when it is also carefully formulated in the light of the Book of
this world. On his account, without the God hypothesis, science would have ended a

stillbirth. But if the Book of Revelation and the Book of Nature are taken as two ways of knowing God, science flourishes and grows, as history has amply shown with its stellar cast of scientists such as Galileo, Kepler, Copernicus, Newton, Linnaeus, and William Buckland.

He then reviews four possible positions regarding the relation of science and religion, conflict, contrast, contact, or confirmation. The conflictive model is illustrated by the image of two snakes eating each other's tails. According to the contrast position, neither discipline intersects with the other since there is no overlap whatsoever. The two spheres are totally independent. The third, the contact or dialogical model, tries to find a fundamental harmony, notwithstanding a sense of struggle that underlies the endeavor. Dodson prefers the dialogue model according to which he sees science affirming his faith, and science and religion offering moments of reciprocal illumination.

The fourth model takes the two as integrated and harmonious because God is viewed as the creator of the natural world.

He concludes with a brief appreciatory note on dinosaurs. Dinosaurs have made his life as a scientist complete. His study of dinosaurs has not challenged his belief in God, only helped affirm it. He sees them as part of God's wonderful creation, as hundreds of species issuing from divine creative action reveal both his love and creativity for the benefit of humanity and the overall enhancement of creation.

His final focus on the demise of dinosaurs raises interesting questions that he briefly reviews in connection with the Genesis account of the creation of humans and the rest of Creation. Extinction is not viewed as something foreign to Creation, but as in integral part of it, making way for the coming into existence and flourishing of humans. Without dinosaur extinction, he avers, human existence would not likely have occurred. Their existence, not just a million years ago (Ma), but probably at least 6 Ma, gives us an expansive account of Creation that takes us way beyond the young-earth hypothesis that some literalists want to "impose" on the Genesis account. His research and scholarship challenges all who take this theistic hypothesis seriously, to reconsider literal renditions of terms like *yom* and various statements in early Genesis accounts of beginnings.

In his final chapter (18), Science and Religion in the Public Square, Professor Dodson acknowledges that science "touches" everyone on our planet. The incredibly rapid growth of science and our reliance upon it for so many good things has brought with it negative consequences as well. He observes that some have been inclined to go beyond giving it center stage. He adds that many in effect have deified nature and the sciences that study it. This turn has led some, no doubt many, to the conclusion that the religious dimension to life is no longer needed. For this sector, the religious is otiose, except for the masses that are emotionally attached to the putative myth of the religious. He adds, as Freud and Marx have contended, each working with different explanations of such phenomena, such inclinations and practices are seen as resulting from faulty belief-forming mechanisms. But Dodson contends to the contrary, that those who see nature as self-sufficient, as giving a full account of our humanity, are really infected by a disease especially contagious in this age of science. They are infected with a faulty vision, if they have one at all, of the deeper needs and longings of the human heart. For Dodson, the longing of the heart is not fully met by science. On such matters, *science doesn't have a lot to offer*. Dodson further points out that a substantial sector of the scientific community, as high as 40 percent, and perhaps even higher, believe in God. Those included in this number hold that "religious beliefs are intrinsic to what it means to be human."

He draws attention to Christian scholars/scientists who have emblazoned the pages of the history of science, marking off the seventeenth century onward as replete with persons of science who have assumed nature is God's creation. Moreover, the idea that science and religion are conflictive was at "best a crude caricature" if not a fraud.

On the religious side, he observes that "enlightened" religious thinking can be taken as a bridging, if not a process of eliminating the alleged "gap" between the two disciplines.

In his review of the Public Square and atheism's place in it, he opines that it once held a minority position. On the contemporary scene, he observes that while Richard Dawkins is obsessed with the idea of God, Dawkins charges it as a detestable hypothesis unworthy of serious consideration by anyone rationally inclined. Stephen Jay Gould's remark, that either "half of his colleagues are enormously stupid, or the science of Darwinism is fully compatible with conventional religious beliefs – and equally compatible with atheism" is set in the context of faith being a prerequisite of the understanding on such matters, as St. Anselm had contended in his famous *credo ut intelligam* dictum.

Dodson takes science as providing "provisional explanations," not absolute certainties. Moreover, provability for him is a "weaker notion" than truth. Hence he says, we are left with "staring through a glass darkly," as Paul claimed in 1 Corinthians 13:2.

In conclusion, he draws contrasting pictures of two understandings of the world, the atheistic worldview and the worldview of the theist. The former leaves us with a "blinding flash of light," with the attending vision of the world as an "unintended accident of the uncaring cosmos." This he contrasts with the Christian account, in which God said, "let there be light" and there was light. And however great this cosmos issuing from the "hand" of God may be, we can come to see that humans play a central role in it all. In place of an uncaring universe, we see that humans are "a little lower than the angels," and further, that "they are crowned with glory and honor" (Psalm 8:4, 5). Thus we find ourselves in a hospitable universe precisely because of the God hypothesis that underlies these positive elements supportive of humanity's flourishing in the world.

Part 7 Christian Faith and Biological Explanation

Professor Stephen Matheson (biology, Calvin College) examines three topics from a biologist's perspective, working with a Christian understanding of the Universe and human descent. His first chapter (19), EVOLUTIONARY CREATION: COMMON DESCENT AND CHRISTIAN VIEWS OF ORIGINS, is an attempt to examine evolutionary theory as a way of explaining fundamental aspects of the world of the living by drawing attention to the common ancestry of living things. The notion of common descent is understood as a biological theory, appealed to as an explanation of the many and varied phenomena of the world of biology, ranging from the geological distribution of such phenomena (biogeography), to the distribution of organisms on this earth, known as patterns of organizations of genomes. He fleshes out the theory, attempting to show its success as an hypothesis. His basic contention is that the explanation of common descent as evidenced in evolution is in no way conflictive with Christian belief, providing that the scientific beliefs are well-formed and well-founded representations of evolutionary theory, and that the religious beliefs are genuinely reflective of the Scriptural teachings. He adds that if there is a conflict for the theist, it probably arises from the existence of certain aspects of religious belief that some find difficult to place in evolutionary history and theory.

He advances the idea that common descent is an "excellent and successful scientific explanation." But some object that it includes no supernatural elements, and hence does not fit with the Christian worldview. Second, the account of common descent is quite different from the Biblical picture of human life. Matheson concludes that there is no necessary conflict of any kind between a sound view of common ancestry and Christian belief. The account of the biological sciences, properly rendered, is not in conflict with God's own work. The latter, he contends, is just left unspecified as to mode. And while some Christians might counter that evolution isn't God's way, careful study of the Scriptural data arguably does not supply a careful reader with specifics as to the mode of God's fiat. If anything, the Scriptures leave the mode open-ended.

He allows that there may be one area of possible conflict, that having to do with the Biblical account of the fall of humanity, if taken historically, in contrast to claims of evolutionary biology. But even here, Matheson thinks that the issues are resolvable, and that common descent is still unthreatened, as are those religious beliefs which take human origins into account.

Professor Matheson's second chapter (20), A Scientific and Religious Critique of Intelligent Design, is a careful study of the intelligent design (ID) movement, which claims that the world has properties that could not come about as a result of purely natural (evolutionary) processes, and that these phenomena show forth the properties of intelligent design. Matheson examines this basic contention, and comes to conclude that the ID movement fails to offer a viable challenge to evolutionary theory.

Matheson formulates his account of ID by viewing it on two levels, first in terms of its social and political engagement with naturalism, and secondly in its attempt to define "design" in the natural world. The author notes that many in the ID movement reject common descent and natural selection. The key motivating factor energizing the ID movement is the rejection of the underlying naturalism that motivates many scientists who want to work without a God hypothesis.

According to Matheson, the major goal of the ID movement is to identify "design" in the natural world. He acknowledges that design, specifically intelligent design, is "the very basis of many scientific theories." Here, design is viewed as the creation of humans or aliens.

Two concepts of ID theory are reviewed for the reader, "specified complexity," and "irreducible complexity." The former is defined denotatively (by example), as when we have a page of English letters showing a measurable complexity. The latter is defined by Michael Behe as one "which is composed of several interacting parts that contribute to the basic function, and where the removal of any one of the parts causes the system to effectively cease functioning." An example of both is the flagellum, a molecular machine, used by some bacteria for movement. As such, it is a specified complexity. It is also an irreducible complexity. If so, then as the ID theorists argue, it is an example of something that evolution by itself could not produce; hence the door opens to the idea of deliberate design by a Creator.

Matheson counters by invoking a conclusion drawn from the first chapter in his series. He rejects the idea that natural explanations rule out "the existence of supernatural influences." He takes the ID theorist as contending that if something can be explained by natural phenomena, it is an enemy to theism. Matheson rejects this as a mistaken inference. If there is a valuable contribution of ID, it is its challenge to naturalism and its "inappropriate claims of philosophical naturalism especially in science." But he sees an unfortunate turn in ID, when it conflates philosophical naturalism, the view that matter is all that matters, with "methodological naturalism," the method that confines itself to nature's empirical data.

Matheson finds Dembski's and Behe's claim regarding specified complexity and irreducible complexity unconvincing. The claim is that natural processes cannot produce irreducible complexities. According to Matheson, this remains to be shown. And while Behe allows that the bacterial flagellum does not deny common ancestry, his challenge to evolutionary biology is clear. Behe contends that the flagellum could not have arisen through selection acting on variation, and he further notes that Darwinian mechanisms have not shown how such mechanisms could have produced them. Matheson concludes that while there are elements of ID which are fascinating, even intriguing, he finds the proposals "unconvincing as challenges to natural selection."

His general conclusion is that there is no real serious conflict between evolutionary science and Christian belief. There is no push coming from the ID movement that should incline Christian theists to side with these sorts of explanation. Rather, Christians should listen to science when it is authentic, and embrace "natural explanations as far as they take us."

Matheson begins his final chapter (21), BIOLOGY, THE INCARNATION, AND CHRISTIAN MATERIALISM, with the note that all three of his contributions have a common theme: biological explanation can be meaningful in the context of the Christian faith. While the previous chapters record interaction between faith and evolutionary theory, the third involves interactions between the Christian faith and neurobiology, with a special focus on the soul as it may be thought to relate to scientific explanation. His focus is not so much upon philosophical discourse that arises in connection with metaphysical dualism of mind and body, but rather on keeping dualism's principal ideas in the forefront as he discourses on biological explanation.

He immediately draws a distinction between materialism as a view of persons, which allows supernatural beings such as God, and materialism, which is the view that all of reality is material. The former is a dualism, even though the view of persons is not, while the latter rules out the dualism that allows that there might be non-material beings such as God.

His first main focus is upon body and soul and the sort of dualism often found in the literature of the Christian traditions. Such accounts usually begin with the Genesis story about God taking the "dust" of the ground, the material side, and breathing into it the breath of life, thereby making man a living soul. Reference is also made to the first chapter of Genesis, where humans are spoken of as being created in God's image. Since God is spoken of as being spirit (in John 4:24), the image passage (Genesis 1:26, 27) has been interpreted to mean that humans share a non-material nature with God, that is, they have an immaterial soul or spirit. To this he adds the observation that some passages suggest that humans experience a disembodied state, resembling in some ways Plato's hope with regard to the soul at death. Under dualism and scientific explanation, he observes that most of the problems thought to face dualism arise in the context of philosophical accounts of the relationship between the two substances, mind and body.

His attention is directed to the idea that the soul (or spirit or mind) is the source of various functions such as freedom-of-choice willing, reason, moral behavior, love, and spirituality. But neuroscience is viewed by many as providing explanations for all of these functions; consequently the soul is losing its explanatory power and role. Matheson takes a closer look at these functions/attributes,[13] and carefully reviews evidence for the claim that neuroscience is capable of explaining these functions in the purely material mode.

His first focus is upon moral agency. He draws upon the case of Phineas Gage (1848), who was unfortunately injured by a metal bar penetrating his skull. Amazingly, Gage wasn't killed, and he had an extraordinary recovery. Studies of his skull led to sophisticated theories regarding the interaction of emotion and rational moral-reasoning processes. It is a case where moral agency appears to be explainable via the tools of neuroscience without any reference to the soulish substance of philosophers and theologians.

And what of the capacity to *love*? Surely this is beyond any sort of neuroscientific explanation. Matheson affirms that life devoted to unconditional love is a fundamental Christian virtue. But he observes that such love can be altered by brain damage, as we find in cases of Capgras delusion. And while those affected by such circumstances may recognize loved ones, they often see them as imposters. If an immaterial soulish part leads persons to love others, it is important to take note that physical damage to certain areas of the brain might diminish the explanatory value of souls.

Similar sorts of appraisals are offered with regard to accounts of religious experience, very much in the limelight just now. Many scientists boldly claim that they have found the physical roots/biological explanations of religious experience.[14]

And what of the "sense of the self"? A sense of the self, according to V. S. Ramachandran[15] is the "last remaining great mystery in science." This sense viewed as comprising the elements of, (1) continuity (through time), (2) unity or coherence of the self, (3) sense of ownership, (4) sense of agency, and (5) sense of self-awareness, are all elements known to be affected by various brain dysfunctions.

Finally, Matheson takes a look at free will. But here too, notwithstanding philosophical argumentation offered in support of free will, brain studies show that simple motor tasks are connected to anterior brain activities.

The above leads Matheson to conclude that neuroscience has "significantly eroded the explanatory value of immaterial souls." Malcolm Jeeves and Warren Brown have declared neuroscience "strongly questions a separate, non-material agency for the soul by which certain domains of human experience can remain unaffected by changes in the brain function." In response, Matheson says that Christians need not abandon the soul concept, but may have to reconsider the value of the idea weighed solely on the basis of its explanatory value.

He reviews two remaining arguments, (1) one which sees the Scriptures as teaching that there are souls, and (2) the line based on Christian understandings of human nature which asserts that humans are more than biological machines. He sees the first as unpersuasive; that is, he contends that the Biblical passages do not require dualism. He argues contrariwise that Biblical history involves embodiment. He sees the second as also resolvable, if one takes a holistic line.

He finally examines the non-reductive physicalism option. He asserts that while there is no need to assert dualism regarding human persons, it is important to add that all of human behavior may not be wholly explainable in biological terms.

Now the question is, how can a human be both a soul and a body, while asserting that a human being is purely physical? He holds that Kevin Corcoran's Constitution View (CV) works. On this account, persons are constituted by their body, but they are not identical with it. Perhaps he would be sympathetic to Bruce Reichenbach's account of a materialistic view of person that sees the human spirit or soul as a descriptive way of talking about the vertical dimension between humans and God. Or he might be open to William Hasker's notion that the soul emerges from the body, thereby comprising an emergent dualism.

His final focus is upon incarnation, resurrection, and ascension, which on his account are concepts clearly relating to bodies. The Incarnation as defined by the Nicene Creed is understood as emphasizing that Christ's humanity involved a body. Via the Incarnation, God became flesh.[16]

Another central belief of Christianity is the hope of the resurrection, which involves a bodily resurrection. He observes that even the ascension of Christ is described in terms of a return to heaven with a body.

In Matheson's summary of the three chapters, his intention has been to focus on the interactions between scientific explanations and the Christian faith. His purpose is to give a careful account of the effectiveness of biological explanations so that Christians may give them serious consideration. He believes that paying attention to the effective methods of science might help them avoid numerous errors, and secondly, a unified view of God's creative activity, which doesn't draw an artificial boundary between the natural and supernatural, gives a healthy place to biology as a way of understanding the natural world that God created. Finally, the embodied nature of Christ offers a framework for understanding biological human nature that is compatible with Christian theism.

Part 8 Religion, Naturalism, and Science

Alvin Plantinga (philosophy of religion, epistemology, philosophy of mind, formerly University of Notre Dame) observes, at the beginning of his first chapter (22), SCIENCE AND RELIGION: WHY DOES THE DEBATE CONTINUE?, that there is a debate that is still running, and it centers on the contention that there is opposition between "serious religious belief" and science, resulting in religion being in danger when confronted with science claims. Some have even observed the dwindling of religious belief because of advances in science.

Regarding the debate between science and religion, he wishes to make a contribution to an answer as to why the debate continues as it addresses two of six loci. These two are: the association of science with secularism, the scientific worldview, and second, the alleged conflict between evolutionary theory and Christian beliefs.

In his discussion of the first, for a starter he observes that some think that science requires or implies secularism. That to be a scientist one must not be involved with the religious. He expands the range to include any activity x. And then he asks, what is it to be secular with regard to all of life, *tout court*? He answers: this universalizes the reaches of the secular such that all of life, every dimension, is lived without any reference or appeal to the religious.

When his attention is on the academy, he says that there are two very different accounts in the West. One is examined (and rejected) by Bas van Fraassen in his *The Empirical Stance*, which says roughly, that scientific "objectifying inquiry" is enough, enough as a guide to life, and "enough for rightly fixing opinion." It is not only all that we need to know, it is all that we can know. While attention is directed at the first variety, he observes there is another.

The second kind, offered by Richard Rorty in a review of van Fraassen's book, sees science in utilitarian terms, and further holds that science has failed, and that humans and thus scientists are not therefore reaching out for and achieving any truth about the world, but rather are constructing truth about the world. Or as he has put it in another context, "there is truth as 'what our peers will let us get away with saying.'" This slant leads to the conclusion that we don't need anything transcendent, that we are autonomous agents.

Plantinga's main concern is with the former, scientific secularism. Here, the buzz phrase is, "getting ourselves out of the picture," with the result that one's likes and dislikes, fears and loves do not enter into the inquiry. Thus there is a kind of objectivity which leaves out both personal moral judgments and other moral sentiments more generally conceived. This bracketing move is expanded to exclude one's tendency to think teleologically because of a practical bent, as when one thinks such-and-such, asking the question, "is it useful?" These sentiments, he adds, have been seen as the source of methodological naturalism (MN). He continues, MN is not to be confused with philosophical naturalism, which eliminates God out of the picture altogether. Furthermore, MN is a "proposed condition on natural science," that is, there is no need to introduce the supernatural in the doing of science, but it is not a statement about the nature of the universe as is scientific secularism, which is secularism *tout court*.

Under the heading, "Evolution," he asks the question, where does conflict or alleged conflict arise? He reviews various accounts of evolutionary theory that work with one or more of the following ideas: (1) the Ancient Earth hypothesis; (2) the progression of life from simple forms to more complex forms; (3) the idea of descent with modification; (4) the common ancestry hypothesis; (5) the idea that certain mechanisms drive the process of descent with modification; (6) the idea that life developed from non-living matter without any creative act of God.

Some conflicts arise for theists who take a Young Earth hypothesis, that God created the heavens and the earth in five literal days. More significant conflict might arise for those who maintain that God created humans in his own image. While there may be problems, he judges that the Creation hypothesis is not incompatible with the ancient earth hypothesis or evolution (see Peter Dodson's papers and Steve Matheson papers in Volume One).

According to Plantinga, what is incompatible with the Christian God hypothesis is the idea that the process of evolution is unguided, that neither God nor any other agent was involved in its guidance, shaping or orchestration. Plantinga considers the example of Richard Dawkins who, in the *Blind Watchmaker*, claims that the world is without design. Plantinga counters that Dawkins' argument for this claim is wildly invalid.

And what of Daniel Dennett's contention in *Darwin's Dangerous Idea*, that evolution is a dangerous idea? Plantinga's rejoinder is, roughly, that while Dennett's contention conflicts with the Christian account of the world, it isn't necessarily dangerous to Christian belief, unless there is reason to believe Dennett's contention.

In response to Dennett's challenge, Plantinga questions the evidence for Dennett's claim, contending that it certainly doesn't issue from anything that has to do with natural science. He contends that there is a "confusion of natural science and unguided natural selection." On Plantinga's account, there is no conflict. There is no reason why God couldn't shape, direct, and supervise the natural process. This confusion between guided and unguided Darwinism, says Plantinga, lies at the root of some of the furor surrounding the ID movement. ID essentially claims that many phenomena cannot be explained by unguided evolution. Therefore, contrary to what many think, ID doesn't oppose Darwinism as such, but only unguided Darwinism.

He concludes with two possible objections. The first involves the view that Darwinism and theism are compatible, because "it could be that God causes the random genetic mutations involved." But the question then is how could there be random mutations with God in control? The answer might be that according to evolutionary theory, these mutations are random in a biological sense: they don't arise "out of the design plan of the creature" and are not correlated with the needs of the organism. But then it is perfectly possible both that God brought about these mutations and that they are random in the sense suggested.

The second is an objection tendered by Alex Pruss, who claims that modern neo-Darwinism claims two things: (1) there is a full ancestral history of each population of organisms (going back to the first ancestor); (2) an explanation of the diversity of life is given in terms of natural selection via random genetic mutation.

Plantinga observes that the explanation, call it *E*, Darwinism offers is statistical, "the explanation works by showing how the *explanans* is not unlikely. Pruss claims that if one accepts *E*, he cannot accept the hypothesis that God intended to create human beings." But Plantinga counters that *E* as it stands is incomplete, and for this reason is not in itself incompatible with theism, thus Pruss's contention is unfounded.

The second chapter (23), DIVINE ACTION IN THE WORLD, takes up the alleged conflict between science and the idea that God acts specially in the world, for example in the performing of miracles, in operations of divine providence, and in ways in which he works in the hearts of believers.

Regarding miracles, the problem may be seen to arise if God's bringing them about involves a violation of natural physical law as David Hume thought. Plantinga observes that those who see this as a problem are thinking in terms of classical science, such as Newtonian mechanics. God on this account creates the universe with fixed natural laws. But this need not lead to a "hands-off theology," advanced by Rudolph Bultmann and Philip Clayton. Plantinga notes that the principles espoused by Newton apply to "closed and isolated systems." But if God were to act specially in the world, the world at that time would not be falsifying any natural law. God could change the velocity or direction of a particle or create *ex nihilo* a full-grown horse without going against any natural law.

So while some theologians have problems when they take miracles as contrary to science, this need not be the case. God's performing miracles is in no way incompatible with classical Newtonian science. With quantum mechanics there is even less reason to claim conflict between science and miracles. That is because quantum mechanics is probabilistic, rather than deterministic; miracles will be improbable on a quantum mechanics model, but it won't be precluded by it.

Then Plantinga asks: what is the problem with intervention? Indeed, given quantum mechanics, what *is* intervention? Several readings are possible: (1) God acts such that had he not, a state of affairs *A* would not have happened; (2) that act which God performs which is neither conservation nor creation, but that causes *A* such that had he not acted *A* would not have occurred; (3) an act that God performs that is very improbable, given the previous state of the world; (4) *intervention* as defined in terms of *low-level generalizations, not entailed by quantum mechanics*. Plantinga sees none of these accounts as working; hence, he concludes that it still isn't clear what intervention "is supposed to be," and why writers think God would never intervene in the world.

Plantinga's final chapter (24), THE EVOLUTIONARY ARGUMENT AGAINST NATURALISM, is a focus on naturalism as such. He begins with the observation that naturalism as it stands is not a religion. But since it provides adherents with a worldview, it performs one of the cognitive or doxastic functions of religion. So he accords it the status of an honorary religion.

Now the problem arises if operating with a naturalist hypothesis we consider what the naturalist conceives the ultimate purpose of our cognitive faculties to be? The naturalist answer is, it is not to produce true beliefs, but to promote reproductive fitness. Here, Plantinga draws attention to what he calls a doubt expressed by Darwin in the question: are the "convictions of man's mind ... of any value or [are they] at all trustworthy?" What if, our cognitive faculties promote our reproductive fitness, but do not furnish us with true beliefs? Darwin is viewed as worrying about this and, Plantinga adds, well he should have.

Natural selection rewards adaptive behavior, but it doesn't care at all what one believes; and doesn't care whether what one believes is true.

Plantinga pursues this problem, and his first step is to assimilate materialism to naturalism: in which case, humans are mere physical beings. As such, a belief held by a physical being will be something like a neuronal structure attended by another property; it will have content. Two possible routes are considered, one in which the content of belief does not enter the causal chain leading to behavior, the other where it does. He argues that on the materialist line, it is hard to see how belief can enter that causal chain; but if it doesn't, the probability that our cognitive faculties are reliable is low. And even if belief does enter the causal chain leading to behavior, false belief doesn't guarantee maladaptive action.

After examining in detail a series of possible ways to rescue the naturalist line of Darwin, Plantinga comes to conclude that there *is* a religion/science conflict not between Christian belief authentically conceived and science *simpliciter*, but between philosophical naturalism and science.

Part 9 Science and Theology as Faithful Human Activities

Gary Patterson (chemical physics, polymer science, Carnegie Mellon University) opened the first week of the Series at Shandong with two papers offering an historical perspective featuring five luminaries, one from theology and four from science. Chapter 25, Two FOR THE AGES: ORIGEN AND NEWTON, gives center stage to two classic authors who in their own special way saw science, or what was then called "natural philosophy," and theology as "natural" complements: Origen, the Patristic theologian, and Isaac Newton, the world-renowned scientist who invented calculus, classical mechanics, modern optics, and also introduced what is now known as Biblical critical studies. Both scholars have been acclaimed as intellectually brilliant and innovative in their respective disciplines.

Origen's place of birth, Alexandria, Egypt, in the second half of the second century AD was outwardly hostile to the Christian faith. Conversion was a crime, and Origen's father, who had become a Christian, was martyred. Origen bravely accepted the headship of the catechetical school of Alexandria, and eventually began his own Didascalion. Books were produced including Bible commentaries. His approach to education involved reading famous books, followed by discussion sessions led by the instructors. Origen's philosophy of education involved a strong commitment to the unity of knowledge and faith. The historical record pictures him as having a strong mastery of argumentation, and this led to his being invited to various institutions in Arabia, Cappadocia, and Jerusalem to settle disputes.

During the reign of Decius in 247, Origen was arrested and, following his father, was martyred for his faith. He lived and died in an age transparently unfriendly to the Christian faith. Origen was persuaded that truth is found in many areas of inquiry. He earned a reputation for his devotion to a scholarly study of the Scriptures in their original languages. For him, it was important to synthesize faith with the insights and findings of his day. His masterpiece, *On First Principles*, is a model of scholarship embracing Scriptural truth claims and learning in the world.

The second actor center stage, Isaac Newton, grew up in the manor house of Woolsthorpe, England in the seventeenth century. He was abandoned by his stepfather, an Anglican clergyman, but in spite of this continued in the journey of faith begun in his youth. Eventually, his maternal grandmother and the Ayscough family that had raised him were influential in getting him into Cambridge University, as a subsizar (a poor student) at Trinity College in 1661.

During this period, the plague interrupted his stay at Cambridge, and he returned to Woolsthorpe. Though he was away from formal education, his initial exposure to Descartes' geometry helped incline him in the direction of developing the calculus. When he returned to Cambridge, he had so advanced in mathematics and mechanics that he was elected a Fellow of Trinity College, and worked toward a Master's degree. His interests included math, natural philosophy (natural science), chemistry, and theology; and though he is celebrated today for his math and natural philosophy, his personal interests were centered more on chemistry and theology.

Patterson notes further that the central underlying principle in Newton's approach to physics, as with science in general, was the basic premise that God was the foundational principle in terms of which science made sense. His approach saw two spheres, the natural world and specially revealed theology as contained in the Scriptures, as valid areas of inquiry ultimately relating to the Author of all truth, God. He saw himself as set aside by God to make clear the truths of nature, and the truths of the spirit, hence the self-descriptive phrase, "priest-scientist." In the sense that he saw all truth coming together in God, he was similar in stance to Origin, who saw himself as one seeking after all truth.

Origen worked with the analogy of two books, the Book of Nature, and the Book which he revered as the Word of God. It was an analogy which enjoyed a wide currency in the seventeenth century. Origen's special turn on the analogy was the idea that underlying all of nature and the Scriptures is the principle of simplicity.

Patterson's final focus brings to light Newton's strong interest in history. For him, God as Trinity is the epicenter of history, with simplicity and coherence as central principles bringing everything together in a meaningful whole. Newton looked for a common ground that he hoped would bring the various strands of Christians together.

Patterson observes that for both Origen and Newton, the pursuit of truth included giving a central place to the Scriptures, with an interdisciplinary expansion that allowed insights to be unified around the idea that God is the source of all truth.

In his second historical chapter (26), THE HOLY TRINITY OF NINETEENTH-CENTURY BRITISH SCIENCE: FARADAY, MAXWELL, AND RAYLEIGH, Patterson's focus is upon British physicists of the nineteenth century, in particular three of the most notable scientists, Michael Faraday, James Clerk Maxwell, and Lord Rayleigh. These celebrated scientists are portrayed as fully committed to the truth of the Christian faith. Faith and science were viewed by all three as patently complementary.

The first figure, Michael Faraday, better known today for his work in electricity and magnetism, viewed pure science "as a place of peace and order," after the manner in which God had originally created the world. Again, Patterson zooms in on the fact that Faraday was both famous for his scientific work and discovery, and also a devout Christian who served as an elder, took seriously the tasks of visiting the sick and needy, and faithfully ministered the Word. As he approached the end of his life, he was confident in the hope of life after death. His contemplation of death brought with it no sense of fear.

The second study is about James Clerk Maxwell, who was of Scottish descent, a scientist of the first magnitude, and who had such a command of the Biblical text that he could hold his own with the best Biblical scholars of his day.

Maxwell's training in the sciences began at the age of 12 when his father took him to the Edinburgh Royal Society. He wrote a paper on the construction of generalized ovals in geometry that was read before the Society by Professor James D. Forbes of Edinburgh University.

Maxwell took a serious interest in philosophy, communicating with the philosophers of the day. He left Edinburgh and continued his education at Cambridge, centering attention on math and theology. Maxwell had a keen interest in philosophy, theology, and science, and he saw all of these disciplines as fitting together with God as the fundamental unifying assumption.

In addition to being the poet laureate of the scientific world, he earned his place as a Fellow of Trinity College, Cambridge. His classic paper, "A Dynamical Theory of the Electromagnetic Field" and the book *Treatise on Electricity and Magnetism* were produced while he was at King's College, London. From here, he moved back to Cambridge, taking up the supervision of the Cavendish Laboratories for Experimental Physics. Thus his faith and his place as a world-renowned scientist, along with his poetic talent etched for him a place of distinction in the world of scholarly discourse and education.

While at Cambridge, he was urged to become a member of the Victoria Institute which promoted the interaction of theology and science. Maxwell, knowing that the sciences move from theory to theory, recommended that theologians approach the sciences carefully, and that instead of endorsing particular theories, they should rather reach for the truth found in God's world.

The third actor on the scientific stage, John William Strutt, 3rd Baron Rayleigh, was offered Maxwell's position at Cambridge at Maxwell's death. Rayleigh, along with J. J. Thomson, received the Nobel Prize in physics in 1906. His religious life involved regular attendance at church at both morning and evening services. With Lord Kelvin, he shared a deep love of science and an even deeper love for Christ.

In a new book, Gary Patterson has a chapter entitled, "Two Themes from an Evangelical Stance: A Professor in Dialog with His Faith." In this book, and so in the chapter included in this volume (27), A PROFESSOR IN DIALOGUE WITH HIS FAITH, Patterson presents the two themes from the original chapter, (1) An Evangelical Natural Philosophy, and (2) An Evangelical Anthropology. Regarding the former, the author urges that the "proper response" to contemporary science sees it as "knowledgeable about the past, engaged in the present, and open to the future."

Patterson points out that theist John Polkinghorne tends to see the world as faithful and flexible, without which attributes life as we know it would not be possible. But atheists tend to see it as rigid and chaotic. Patterson registers surprise at the number of theists who gravitate toward the latter view. He points out that there are two basic concepts used to describe the physical world, structure and dynamics. Regarding the former, the ancients tended to see the divine as spherical, holding that God like a sphere is a perfect entity. Regarding the latter, there are various understandings of physical reality proffered by some of the leading authors in science and religion. Patterson judges that while there are disparate ways of taking the world God has created, such as, for example, one that emphasizes his simplicity, another which appears to evidence his complexity, perhaps the better way is to affirm both as somehow reflective of the God who has brought the universe into existence.

In an "Evangelical Anthropology," he takes seriously the idea that humans are created in God's image, claiming that we are "fearfully and wonderfully made." Contemporary findings in physiology, psychology, and sociology are reviewed with an underlying commitment to an

Evangelical theoretical framework regarding human personhood. Various topics are examined, including the issue of the human mind and consciousness. While some writers are inclined to reduce consciousness to the categories of physics or chemistry, where attention is given to quantum indeterminacy or messenger molecules (see Stephen Matheson's chapters 19–21, Don Page's chapters 28–30, both in Volume One of this book, and Stephen M. Barr's chapters 60 – 62 in Volume Two), Patterson refuses to go in the direction of the "lowest-level processes … required for human thought," spelled out in terms of neurons. Patterson suggests that there is more promise in higher-level regions of the brain and sensors outside the brain. Here, where computers are able to perform many tasks thought to be unique to human thought processes, there are still functions that mechanical devices, no matter how complex, cannot perform, "activities that are worthy of beings created in His image." For Patterson, while there might be molecular "counterparts," the emotions are as "real" as the molecules. So he wants the Evangelical mindset to beware of a basic metaphysical distinction he thinks is necessary to a proper account of mind or soul versus machines and organisms.

At the same time, he wants to affirm an organic wholeness of person, and the essential goodness of both the soul and the body in terms of which person is instantiated. That is, there is not a separable soul plus a body, but rather as Nancey Murphy argues (see her chapters in Part 17, THEOLOGY, SCIENCE, AND HUMAN NATURE, in Volume Two) there is a body with a soul internally instantiated in it.

For Patterson, the term spirit is understood as "a direct gift from God," that allows humans to have a direct relationship with God. Other concepts reviewed in chapter 27 include original sin, the Kingdom of God, and the notions of individuals and families. The final concluding idea is an essential unity of humankind.

Part 10 Cosmology and Theology

The main focus of Don Page (physics, the University of Alberta) in his first chapter (28), OUR PLACE IN THE VAST UNIVERSE, is upon the incredible vastness of the universe viewed in terms of inflationary theory, quantum theory, disparate sorts or dimensions of space, carrying the notion of expansions to the level of "googolplexes" of spaces comprising many possible universes. The end result is that the immensity of the universe is expansively fleshed out in terms of these various ways of measuring its size thereby overwhelming the overall weight and measure of the average human. It is a scientist's take on, "What is a human, that you take him/her into account?"

Mapping his account in greater detail, he commences with the familiar measurement of the ancient Greeks, beginning with Aristarchus, who assumed a heliocentric picture of everything with earth as the center because humans made it their home. As for the Middle Ages, Page sees this period as involving something of a paradigm shift from the early ancient positive appraisal of the heliocentric picture, to the view that sees this centrality position as non-significant if not completely negative. Galileo, for example, saw it as the "dump heap of the filth and dregs of the universe."

Page's attention then shifts from a study of the size of the solar system, to the issue of how far the stars and galaxies reach out beyond the earth. Various measurements are pursued employing "cosmic distance scales." In the context of this method of measurement, planets are grouped as solar systems, and stars are grouped in galaxies (examples of which the reader finds depicted on the covers of the Chinese volumes in the Science and Religion

Series). He notes that the distances of far-off galaxies are roughly proportional to their velocities as they move away from planet earth.

This leads him to draw a pivotal quantifiable distance variable, the distance light has traveled since the beginning of the universe, roughly, a distance of 14 billion light years. Beyond this, he observes, we cannot see further. So he concludes that the observable universe is all that is within 13.7 billion light years in all directions, or what amounts to roughly a million billion times the distance between the earth and sun. This unimaginable number is contrasted starkly with the volume of the average human.

Then he turns to consider the many-universe/multiverse hypothesis as another way of expanding on the idea of the immensity of what lies beyond this planet. The idea of different "laws of physics" is viewed as another device for marking off possibly disparate universes. That is, perhaps there are other laws of physics operating in other universes.[17]

With all of the above measurement-devices in view, he asks what sort of analogy would work as a way of comparing a human with the vastness of the entirety of reality beyond and including our planet. His response? Calculations relating to the vastness of the universe, expanded so as to include the googolplexes of particular universes (what are called Everett worlds), are analogically compared to the listing of the sequence of about 3 billion DNA base pairs, which he says requires a specification involving about 2 billion digits. This figure, many judge, far exceeds the number of expansions imagined in connection with the immensity of the multiverse. His conclusion on this matter is, "the google of digits that specifies which of the Everett many-worlds describes our universe could be taken as analogous to a specification of which person one is out of all those with the same genes."

One inductive move on the vastness of the multiverse makes it probable that almost all possible human experiences would occur somewhere. This leads him to conclude, that if inflation theory is true, then this makes it probable that there are multiple copies of individuals throughout the universe.

Now, all of the above makes the question of the Psalmist, "What is a human, that You are mindful of him/her?" far more complex than many may have initially imagined.

Page concludes that though one might have some concern for the uniqueness of the human species, or even the uniqueness of a particular human, uniqueness on either level is not essential to the value either of a single human, or of the human species. The sense of the term *value* he draws upon here, is the value of the human species viewed as in a different spectrum from those which are purely quantifiable. The point of the Psalmist is an emphasis on the vertical dimension – humans are created "a little lower than the angels." Hence the Psalmist's metaphysical/anthropological question, why? In response, Page asks, can't humans be important merely because of who they are, not because of any measure of uniqueness in a possibly immeasurably vast universe?

Having drawn the picture of the immensity of the universe as a background consideration, he next asks the question, in Chapter 29, how far does God's love extend? Does God love all that he has made, viz., DOES GOD SO LOVE THE MULTIVERSE? He begins with the thesis that God loves all humans. His account runs the entire historical gamut from Genesis 1, where he creates humans in his image, to the book of Ruth, where God gives account of his love as extending beyond the boundaries of Israel, to Ruth who was from Moab. The stretch includes Jonah, which symbolically suggests that divine love embraced people in the city of Nineveh. God loves Israel, and those outside Israel. Does it reach yet further? In the New Testament, the Gospels and Book of Acts evidence God's love for all people, and according to Acts 10, that love extends to the Gentiles.

Page then draws parallels between evolution and the multiverse notion as a way of expanding on the notion of *divine love*. Attention is directed to the distinctness of the human race as evidence of God's "separate and individual design." He sees a similar move now with regard to those who see fine-tuning as evidence of divine design. He judges that this move could be "equally mistaken." How so? If the multiverse hypothesis is correct, then it is possible that there are many universes out there that are finely tuned for human-like instantiations. Thus, he comments, perhaps the universe is much larger than we imagine it to be, and such restrictive pictures are reflective of a narrower-than-appropriate view of what God might actually be like, and what he might actually have brought into existence.

He moves on to consider the fine-tuning argument, and possible explanations of fine tuning. David Lewis' view that all logically possible worlds exist is straightforwardly rejected. He then critically reflects on the proposal that, "it is sufficient to explain what we see by a multiverse theory in which there are enough different conditions that ours necessarily occurs somewhere." This he rejects because there is the further requirement that the conditions observed are not too rare "over the entire universe."

In the next section he goes beyond explanations of fine tuning, to a consideration of the application of Bayes' theorem in three areas, drawing the *a posteriori* probabilities of each. *Inter alia*, attention is given to a single universe with a single set of physical constants. His conclusion is that it is better to conclude (for various reasons) that God created a variety of sets of constants in physics, and so a multiverse, which proposal is not incompatible with a Christian view of reality.

Under the heading, "Toy Multiverse Model from Arithmetic," he offers an analogue drawn from an example in mathematics. Here, he draws the conclusion that from this simple analogue, one's observations in a single universe might be a reliable sample of the whole, and if the sample is sufficiently rich, this sampling might give us a fuller picture of the whole.

In the section, "The Growth of our Knowledge of the Universe," he urges that if our universe is large enough, then corresponding to the multiverse hypothesis, we will allow the inclusion of conscious extraterrestrials, and so conscious beings in other hypothetically conceived universes on condition they are instantiated.

Various philosophical objections to multiverse ideas are considered, and he concludes that the multiverse idea does undercut the fine-tuning argument at the level of there being a single set of constants in physics. Here he observes that the loss of one argument (the standard fine-tuning argument) does not mean the conclusion is false.

In response to various theological objections to the multiverse hypothesis, he urges that it might just be that if there are multiverses, then the death of Christ on the cross might be viewed as applying beyond this universe to others in a multiverse reality. His general conclusion is, there is no really good reason to deny the possible reality of a multiverse expansion beyond our world.

His final chapter (30), SCIENTIFIC AND PHILOSOPHICAL CHALLENGES TO THEISM, examines various issues that are potentially worrisome to the author. He begins with the after-life awareness problem. The challenge examined issues from the Carter – Leslie – Nielsen – Gott's doomsday argument when applied to the after-life. The argument rests on the observation "that we are among the first hundred billion or so humans" and this "reduces the prior probability that we find ourselves in a species whose total lifetime number of individuals is much higher." If the growth in population continues another hundred or so years, it is unlikely that we would find ourselves as members of the small number alive now. But if the human race were to end sooner, then we would not be unusual. The argument implies that unless the *a priori* probability is very high for far more individuals in the future than in the past, "then our observations of how many humans there have been in the past makes the *a posteriori* probability low for far more humans in the future."

He judges that similar consequences would apply to the after-life hypothesis concerned with after-death experiences. That is, if one were not absolutely certain that an afterlife would last enormously longer than the pre-death life, then "the observation that we are experiencing pre-death life rather than after-death life significantly reduces the *a posteriori* epistemic probability for a very long afterlife."

Page considers an analogous application of this strategy to an area in physics, namely, the formation of brains by vacuum fluctuations. A problem arises if the universe lasts too long. Brains thus formed resemble Boltzman brains which also arise from thermal fluctuations. He reviews various solutions to the Boltzmann brain problem, and concludes that none have a wide acceptance. For a tentative solution, he suggests that, instead of working with the idea that the universe exists indefinitely into the future, suppose that it is decaying "quantum mechanically at a rate comparable to its exponential expansion rate," bringing about a rate of decay "fast enough to make the expectation value of the four-volume of the co-moving region finite and at the same time not so big that Boltzmann brains would dominate over ordinary observers." If this strategy were applied to the after-life awareness problem, he believes it might resolve this difficulty as well.

His final strategy for the after-life awareness problem is to attempt to somehow connect consciousness to physics. So he reformulates the problem in terms of the *measures* of conscious experiences. All of the problems considered arise from comparing the probability of an experience to be "one of those which do not fit our observations" to that of being an *ordinary observer*. In his analysis, he claims to have "formulated a framework for connecting consciousness to physics by means of a measurement of each conscious perception being measured by the expectation value of a corresponding quantum operator." One possibility is, the "after-life is not an infinite set of after-life awarenesses, but a single eternal experience."

He next considers the problem of free will. After review, he rejects the idea that human free will could help choose the laws and the quantum state of the universe. An even stronger argument against free will is the claim that "God creates everything logically contingent other than Himself."[18] He is inclined to think that this is the case, and so comes to conclude that humans are not free but rather determined by the laws of physics established by God. He expands on related ideas under the heading Divine Free Will and Information Content.

He begins his discourse on Divine Free Will and Information Content with the admission that he has assumed that God has "libertarian free will." This assumption is then viewed in the light of the claim some make that the laws of the universe are fixed, that not even God could change them. This is reinforced by an earlier idea in Anselm, that God is necessary, and that he created the world the way he did because his creative activity is also necessary.[19] Here he interjects that God does not need to be completely necessary, that is, his necessity doesn't need to extend to what he creates or brings about.

The information content idea for Page is God's choice between conceptual possibilities. In this context he observes that if God is entirely necessary, then he would have no information content, because there would be no possibles, only necessary sets of states of affairs. This he rejects because he holds that God enjoys libertarian free will.

Under the heading, "The Complexity and Probability of God," he draws distinctions between a simple and complex world, and observes that the former is more probable than the latter. His conclusion to this section is that the God of the Bible and the Koran "seems complex," but the entirety of God might be simple.

His final focus is upon the problem of evil, which he sees as really a problem of elegance. That is, when considering the level of beauty of the laws of nature, the universe seems quantifiably more elegant than ugly. He expresses this turn via the following question: Why does the beauty found in math appear to far outweigh the moral good in the universe? This construal is more worrisome to him, since he's not sure it would be more worrisome to others than traditional constructions of the problem.

Part 11 Science Under Stress in the Twentieth Century: Lessons from the Case of Early Nuclear Physics

In Chapter 31, THE COPENHAGEN SPIRIT OF SCIENCE AND BIRTH OF THE NUCLEAR ATOM, Richard Peterson (physics, Bethel University) paints a picture of Niels Bohr as one nurtured in the shadows of Søren Kierkegaard and Harold Hoffding, and as leading his fellow workers toward a sub-nuclear, atomic, and molecular foundation for modern science that is based on complementarity – yet still anchored solidly in the real empirical world. He begins with the experimental mentoring of Ernest Rutherford, tracing the Copenhagen impact on quantum mechanics, neutron physics, and fission, and Nils Bohr's engaging approach for doing science while inspiring experimental and theoretical teamwork on an international scale. Bohr's transition from Copenhagen to Cambridge, and then to Rutherford's laboratory at the University of Manchester, was a geographic transition that helped give birth to the "Bohr atom," a revolutionary construct, a crucial stepping-stone paradigm shift to the "full-blown" quantum mechanics of the late 1920s and nuclear physics of the 1930s.

During the period between 1926 and 1928, Bohr's fiercely intense thinking often depended upon brilliant younger colleagues serving as a "sounding board." His reflection on the ethics of work on the atomic bomb evidenced the complementary relationships within scientific and the ethical perspectives. He convinced colleagues that they should take into account the complementary perspectives of the tragically *negative* destructive power of this weapon versus the need to consider its *positive* ethical imperatives. And he along with Oppenheimer would struggle the rest of their lives to help nations see that such a weapon would make any just war on a strategic scale impossible, and that lasting peace would be possible only through international control.

The closing focus of Chapter 31 is upon the aftermath of the Lise Meitner and Otto Frisch deliberations on the mechanism of nuclear fission in the woods near the Swedish town of Kungälv.

In his second chapter (32), WHEN SCIENTISTS GO TO WAR, Peterson remarks that "beset by the ethical imperatives and dilemmas of racism, fanatical dictatorships, weapons for mass civilian destruction, human egotism, and pride, the physicists still persevere to build a 'gadget' that can shake the earth and usher in a new perspective of warfare on a new and frightening scale." He reviews the pacifism of Albert Einstein, the Quaker heritage of Robert R. Wilson, and the Christian Mennonite background of Arthur H. Compton, as these internationally famous physicists faced the pressures of national survival and moral outrage. He asks, can we say real "science" is being done when wartime censorship of work becomes the norm, and open publication among peers stops? Is there a legitimate case for scientific work on weapons designed for the mass destruction of hundreds of thousands of civilians? He concludes the chapter with personal reflections on the responses of Los Alamos scientists in the aftermath of the test of the first atomic bomb.

In his final chapter (33), SCIENTIFIC RESPONSIBILITY: A QUEST FOR GOOD SCIENCE AND GOOD APPLICATIONS, Peterson observes that prior to and after Hiroshima and Nagasaki, nuclear scientists and engineers have debated the issue of their proper and influential role in trying to guide the use of their work. Some scientists like Leo Szilard, Niels Bohr, Edward Teller, Robert Oppenheimer, Joseph Rotblat, and Andrei Sakharov have spoken out strongly in the political arena and in public affairs. Robert Oppenheimer, who led the development of the atomic bomb, stated after World War II that "physicists have known sin" in the war years, and Peterson considers the implications of such a statement and what might properly comprise "sin" within the process and pursuit of science. H-bomb development (by the US, Soviet Union, England, France, and China) in the decades that followed World War II presented technical, strategic, and ethical problems that are still with us today. Peterson concludes his chapter with a few examples and challenges posed by exemplary human motivations for active participation and teaching within the global scientific community.

Part 12 The Science of Religion

In chapter 34, THE EVOLUTION OF RELIGION: ADAPTATIONIST ACCOUNTS, Michael Murray (philosophy of science, philosophy of religion, Franklin and Marshall College) observes that anthropologists, psychologists, and evolutionary theorists have put together a number of scientific accounts of the origin and persistence of religious beliefs.

Early in this chapter, he takes up the task of defining religion, noting Paul Griffith's comment on the task as similar to writing a diet book, "it never stops, and none of it does much good." He turns to psychologist Scott Atran for his definition as sufficient for the tasks at hand in this chapter, "Religion is a community's costly commitments to a world of strange and unusual supernatural agents which serve to master people's existential anxieties, such as death and deception." He further notes that religion is universal and is transmitted vertically and horizontally, or via both. The horizontal sort of transmission is from person to person, or social group to social group. The vertical sort includes what some think amounts to a hard-wiring of the religious – we have dispositions to believe. Those which are vertical are ultimately explained in terms of evolutionary adaptation.

The above leads him to say that if he is correct that religion is a human universal, and that all human universals are transmitted vertically, is he also correct that all vertically transmitted traits have a biological basis along with the religious? He observes that while religion is universal it seems maladaptive. Having made this point, he draws attention to the fact that scientists have been cataloging cases of what appear to be maladaptive characteristics while looking for explanations as to why they arise. He considers religious behavior. which, because it is maladaptive, is a Darwinian anomaly. Two sorts of evolutionary explanation are offered as to why this happens, those which see the religious as adaptive, and those which explain it as a byproduct or spandrel.

In this chapter, Murray offers a descriptive account of the three most widely known adaptationist evolutionary models for religion: punishment theories, commitment signaling theories, and group selection theories. Drawing from Robert Hinde, four types of questions are listed as contributing to an adequate explanation: (1) the causal question, what factors figure in the causal picture?; (2) the developmental question, how did the causal factors that produced the behavior bring the organism about?; (3) the functional question, what are the immediate benefits of the behavior to the organism?; (4) the evolutionary question: what are the evolutionary stages involved?

Punishment theories may be traceable to the religious notion of fear of retribution. But on initial inspection this seems highly implausible because though the threat of divine punishment might work for a while, if a person cheats and gets away with it, they might think that they can fool the gods. Though there are these sorts of counters, it has been found that humans tend to cooperate when they are given evidence that human behavior is being watched.

The second sort of explanation is *commitment signaling*. Here, the idea is that the more I interact with others, the more opportunities there are for watching relationships, predicting the behavior of others, and maintaining positive social dispositions. But again, there are ways of sneaking around the establishment of alliances on the basis of putative reliable commitment signaling. As a counter, hard-to-fake signals are proffered. But the question is, are there reliable cues of this sort that enable people to distinguish between those who cooperate and those who cheat?

Murray then examines ways in which religion could be tied to commitment signaling. He concludes that commitment signaling is not fully satisfactory as a scientific account of the origin and persistence of religion. Two reasons are given: first, hard-to-fake signaling fails to explain why religion is pan-cultural, and second, it does not explain why religion has such broad similarities in respect to belief and ritual structure.

Finally, *group selection theories* give a different account of the origin and persistence of religion in culture. The other two sorts, punishment and signaling theories, offer special explanations as to how altruists can avoid being exploited into extinction. By contrast, group selection altruists may contribute to group fitness without ever benefiting personally. Nevertheless, group selection is a minority position for various reasons, one of which is that it plays no role in evolutionary development. Second, group selection accounts are "mind-blind" in the sense that the behaviors are not really religious as such, but religious people following religious norms. The final reason is that group selection theories of religion rest on an argument that looks at the contribution that altruists make to the fitness of the group, contending that if they didn't thus contribute, the group would be less well off. But the arguments are judged invalid. Murray concludes that adaptationist theories of the origin and persistence of religion give us an old theory in new attire, but that religion as such can account for these alleged benefits.

In chapter 35, THE EVOLUTION OF RELIGION: NON-ADAPTATIONIST ACCOUNTS, Murray critically reviews the non-adaptive or maladaptive consequences of other traits which are adaptations, traits which are often referred to as spandrels. He examines the two most widely held theories of religion, the cognitive theories and the meme theories, and then evaluates their effectiveness as scientific accounts of religion.

Under cognitive theories of religion, he identifies the common features of this view: (1) they are counter-intuitive which makes them suited for recall and transmission; (2) they spring from cognitive mechanisms that produce beliefs about agents (see chapter 38 by Kelly James Clark, in this volume); (3) They are "inference rich"which allows one to draw narratives that are enhancing and aid in our remembering them; (4) they represent the religious entities as *minded agents*.

Murray, like Kelly Clark in his study of cognitive science and religion, gives account of certain devices called "hyper-active agency detection devices," or HADD. Such devices are a help to our fitness since they make us wary of circumstances where predators might present a danger. He notes that the best-known theorists advocating this model are strongly inclined to affirm that religion confers no fitness benefits at all. Rather, religion is to be understood as a mere by-product brought about by "a chance confluence of cognitive circumstances." We happen to engage in HADD, and the result is religion.

Finally, Murray appraises the cognitive accounts. The main problem with this approach is that the view is incapable of offering an explanation of the pervasiveness of religion across times and cultures.

His second focus is upon *memetic accounts*. These units of culture are the "potentially spreadable forms of behavior which are "conceptually mediated." More recent theorists in this camp argue that memes are not just units of cultural information, but informational units which are (1) codes for a behavior that are (2) learned by imitation. And while no one has yet worked out a complete memetic theory of religion, many have asserted that religion is a meme.

Murray thinks that this approach is not very helpful. At best it may serve as an epidemiology of religion, because it can help to show that religious claims as with other memes are good at "infecting minds, and spreading from mind to mind." But notwithstanding this virtue, it still fails to explain any of the most important aspects of religion.

He concludes that non-adaptationist explanations of religion emerge because they piggyback on other traits that are adaptive, or they are a mere spandrel or by-product. And finally, meme theory is not much in the way of a scientific theory or account of religion.

In the final chapter of his set (36), EVOLUTIONARY ACCOUNTS OF RELIGION: EXPLAINING OR EXPLAINING AWAY, Murray asks whether accounts of the sort discussed explain religion, or explain it away. He offers a critical review of the scientific accounts of religion designed to show that religious beliefs cannot be taken with the seriousness religious believers attach to them, looking closely at the arguments drawn in support of this main conclusion. His task is to examine five reasons that have been offered in support of the claim that the various psychological mechanisms "honed" by natural selection are epistemically unjustified.

Reason 1:   the explanations don't explain religion away; all that they do is explain the origins of religious beliefs. As for whether such genetic accounts undermine justification of religious beliefs, while he admits that they sometimes do, he asks, do they always? He puts off an answer because it would involve too much detail in this chapter. But he does begin to develop an answer in response to Reason 2.

Reason 2:   the most widely endorsed psychological account of the origins of religious belief are those nurtured by a mental tool called a "hypersensitive agency detection device" (HADD). One problem he says it encounters is that it generates too many false positives, and so is unreliable. However, Murray argues that HADD is also reliable under some conditions. Until we can identify the conditions that lead to false positives, we cannot plausibly argue that HADD- generated beliefs are unjustified.

Reason 3:   here, the tool in question is judged to yield "contrary beliefs about the same domain of objects in roughly equivalent epistemic conditions." Murray agrees that religious beliefs are largely mutually inconsistent across cultures. For this argument to succeed one would have to show that the incompatible aspects of beliefs arise from the functions of the cognitive faculties, and not through cultural accretions and influences.

Reason 4:   some think that there is still something about these accounts that undermine religious belief. It is the idea that such accounts can account for religious belief in a way that makes no reference or requires no causal connection with a supernatural reality. This raises the whole question of the right relation regarding the causal explanation in one of two senses: one involves some sort of reliability of the account, and the other is the strong one that there be some sort of causal connection between the external world and the belief that is produced. Here a distinction is drawn between an internalism, where justification hinges on facts "inside the head," and externalism, which holds that justification depends upon whether the belief has the right relation to the facts out there in the world. Murray concludes that psychological theorists who offer such explanations cannot by these alone undermine the justification of religious belief. Other facts/assumptions have to be at work to generate this result.

Reason 5:   here it is argued that belief-forming mechanisms are reliable just in case they involve the right sort of "winnowing" of natural selection. Murray sees two mistakes, (1) the mistaken claim that natural selection can winnow "reliable from unreliable belief-forming mechanisms"; (2) there is no reason to think that evolutionary pressures would lead us to false beliefs in the domain of religion. In conclusion, evolutionary explanations of religion may be true as far as they go. But he adds, "Nothing about such explanations undermines, or trumps, explanations in theistic or alethic terms." Explanation is not equivalent, he says, to explaining away. Justification may still have a place.

Part 13 Belief in God

In his first chapter (37), How Real People Believe: Reason and Belief in God, Kelly James Clark (philosophy, Calvin College) draws a contrast between Reformed epistemology and Enlightenment evidentialism. The former rejects the evidentialist assumption that one has to have evidence for belief in God in order to be rational. Clark says that evidence in this context is to be understood as propositional argument, or theistic proof for the existence of God. In order for belief in God to be rational, it does not have to have this sort of evidence/argument. His basic contention is that this sort of demand for evidence cannot be "met" with the equipment that God has given the creature.

In his discussion of "The demand for evidence," he gives account of W. K. Clifford's claim in "The Ethics of Belief," that it is wrong, "always and everywhere, for anyone to believe anything on insufficient evidence." Clark agrees that some beliefs do require evidence, but he denies that beliefs in every circumstance do. As a way of establishing his claim, he considers the regress argument: if one always has to have evidence for a belief, the process of tracing evidence would generate an infinite regress.

He then takes up the idea that belief begins with *trust*. Many of the beliefs one holds are embraced because someone one trusts has passed on the information/beliefs in question.

He next turns to Reid's view of the human cognitive faculties, and draws the conclusion that we are equipped with cognitive faculties that produce beliefs that we can reason from. This is Reid's counter-proposal to the Enlightenment project that he took as unable to offer adequate information for reasoning from sense experience to the material world. Reid claimed that relying upon reason would not give sufficient information with which reason could work. Reid's view is that the belief-producing faculties of sense and memory are as much a part of who we are epistemologically speaking, as is reason which Descartes and his followers enshrined. Hence reason should not be put above sense and memory. Reid also argued that we must accept that we have minds and that there is a past (which is assumed in every historical belief), and the external world. He concluded the vast majority of beliefs held are not ones reasoned to, but rather are produced "immediately, non-reflectively by our various cognitive faculties."

Clark then turns to consider if we have a Reid-like disposition to believe in God immediately and non-inferentially. He first considers Calvin's claim that all humans have been given an innate sense of God, a *sensus divinitatis*. Clark argues that if there is a God who cares for human beings, then it is reasonable to assume that he gave us cognitive faculties that generally produce beliefs without the need for evidence. Those of the Reformed epistemology camp trace their historical roots to John Calvin (1509–64), and find good company with thinkers such as Alvin Plantinga, Nicholas Wolterstorff, and William Alston. They share the belief that one may properly believe and even know that God exists without the support of proof or inferential evidence. Plantinga, unlike Calvin, holds that the range of beliefs produced by the *sensus divinitatis* includes the idea that God is an omnipotent, omniscient, and perfectly good Creator.

Clark notes that cognitive science has uncovered a wide range of various functions of the human mind, and has come to conclude that there is a set of cognitive faculties that dispose us to religious beliefs. This instinctive religious sense produces a family-resemblance repertoire of beliefs that might fall under a range of concepts such as, "religion," "spiritual," "supernatural," "ritual," and "worldview."

Some cognitive scientists have claimed more extravagantly that there is a "God" part of the brain, a "genetically inherited instinct." Another has suggested that there is a "God gene," associated with brain receptors that are activated when a person has feelings of self-transcendence and interconnectedness with the universe. Clark contends that there is no evidence for these claims.

In his section on "Reason and Belief in God," Clark lists four reasons for believing that it is "proper or rational for a person to accept belief in God without the need for argument."

(1)   He has argued that belief begins with a trust in our cognitive faculties unless we have reason to think that they are unreliable. To this he adds that we should extend this to the god-faculty unless we find reason or evidence to the contrary.

(2)   Though philosophers may require arguments in favor of their positions, surely ordinary persons are not required to hold proofs in order to believe rationally in the external world or other persons/minds or even God.

(3)   If God exists, it is reasonable to assume that he has given us a sense of himself that doesn't require arguments for religious beliefs to be rational or proper.

(4)   Belief in God is more like a belief in a person than in a scientific theory. Clark's strategy has been to offer a descriptive account of the ordinary acquisition of beliefs via the cognitive faculties, including the god-faculty. Persons may rationally belief in God's existence without evidence or argument.

In his second chapter (38), REFORMED EPISTEMOLOGY AND THE COGNITIVE SCIENCE OF RELIGION, Clark claims that there has been a convergence of Reformed epistemology and cognitive science on the issue of belief in God. Reformed epistemologists claim that belief in God is properly basic or natural; that is, immediately produced by our cognitive faculties. Interestingly, contemporary cognitive scientists contend that religious beliefs, or belief in some kind of god, can be non-reflectively and instinctively produced by the human cognitive faculties. Clark aims to show points of convergence and points of dissimilarity between the two projects.

Regarding the cognitive science of religion, Clark gives special attention to the cognitive scientist's account of belief in God. He points out that a general picture has emerged as to how our cognitive faculties incline us to beliefs in God. The faculties in question are thought to have evolved in response to various environmental pressures. He says that religious beliefs have arisen partly because humans are equipped with "an agency-detecting device" that generates beliefs about agency, sometimes with minutial stimulation. With these stimulations, the devices produce beliefs about agents without argument or inference. This "hypersensitive agency detection device" (HADD) has obvious value for the possessor in respect to adaptive advantages.

Justin Barrett contends that we are equipped with pattern detectors "fine-tuned to detect agency." And when this happens, the mind begins to function and ascribe beliefs, desires, and purposes to the agent(s) in question.

The cognitive science of religion is often associated with evolutionary explanations of the origins of our cognitive faculties, and many in this field hold that belief in God is a spandrel which is an "adaptive trait that is a by-product," not a "direct consequence of natural selection." But some spandrels may prove adaptive over time.

In the section entitled "The internal witness: the *sensus divinitatis*," attention is directed to ideas espoused by John Calvin. Calvin distinguished between two sources of knowledge of God, the internal and the external. The former is an immediate or innate knowledge of God produced by a divinely given belief-forming faculty. Calvin believed that all persons have an internal sense of God written upon their hearts. This knowledge includes all that is involved in the idea of a God as creator but little if anything in the way of information regarding human redemption. He goes on to add that most persons lack "pure and clear knowledge of God."

In "Reformed epistemology and cognitive science," Clark draws a distinction between Calvin's view and Plantinga's. Calvin held that the *sensus divinitatis* is not a faculty of the soul that is initiated or triggered by some circumstance, but rather an *innate* bit of information about God. Plantinga, however, holds that the *sensus divinitatis* is a disposition, which is more in line with the cognitive science literature's description of HADD. But Plantinga does not handle belief in God as an "evolutionary spandrel." Clark also notes that an atheistic cognitive scientist might hold that the god-faculty cannot produce justified religious beliefs precisely because it is unreliable, whereas Plantinga holds that the cognitive faculty can produce justified religious beliefs.

Regarding "Obstinacy in belief," Clark notes that there is an agreement between Calvin and contemporary cognitive scientists on the issue that belief in God is the "natural state of belief for humans," and it can't be abandoned.

Finally, attention is given to the external witness: the order of the cosmos. Calvin held that there is an external witness to God's existence, in the "fashioning of the universe and its governance." And while Calvin gave a place to arguments for God's existence, he held that it was completely unnecessary because of the "elegance of the universe." Clark holds that Plantinga himself appears to hold to something similar to Calvin's idea here, but he calls beliefs that are produced by the order and symmetry of the universe "grounded" rather than "inferential."

In a concluding remark, Clark allows that if there is a God who wants humans to be in a divine – human relationship, might he not so superintend the evolutionary process so that "favorable traits naturally develop in human beings?"

Kelly Clark's main task in chapter 39, EXPLAINING GOD AWAY?, is to examine the claim that evolutionary explanations of religion undermine the rationality of belief in God. His approach to the rationality of belief here follows the Plantingian model, which holds that belief in God is rational even if it is not inferred from other beliefs but rather is immediately produced by one's cognitive capacities, perhaps in response to a religious experience.

He examines the claim that evolutionary explanations of religious belief undermine the rationality of belief in God by considering the findings of cognitive psychology of religion which claims that humans have a tendecy to believe in gods, which he calls, for short, "the god-faculty". He then examines evolutionary explanations of the origin of this faculty, and finally presents the reader with responses to arguments that claim that evolutionary psychology undermines the rationality of belief in God.

Contemporary research in cognitive science suggests that a shared biological heritage and relatively similar environmental backgrounds lead to similar minds and similar beliefs. Instead of Locke's notion of the *tabula rasa*, contemporary cognitive psychologists hold that our minds are equipped with cognitive capacities that influence our perceptions and conceptions of the world. Regarding the religious, the claim is that our cognitive capacities have a natural tendency to produce belief in god.

The capacities that produce this sort of beliefs include an agency-detecting device which generates beliefs about agency. This tendency helps us avoid dangers from a predators or an enemies. The survival value of this agency-detecting device is obvious. Barrett has called the disposition to form such beliefs in flight-or-fight situations a "hypersensitive agency detection device," or HADD. Observe here that while the device might lead to good ends, hypersensitivity permits of false positives.

HADD not only brings about many good results in response to animals and enemies, it also issues forth in beliefs about gods. Really big events are accounted for by HADD in terms of really big agents. Thus humans have pattern detectors fine-tuned to detect agency. When another faculty, the Theory of Mind, is activated, it ascribes beliefs, desires, and purposes to the agent. Finally, cognitive psychology claims to have found a cognitive faculty or set of faculties that "detect the kind of design that is often alleged to support God's existence." Cognitive scientists claim that humans are equipped with pattern detectors, and these capacities organize experiences into orderly meaningful patterns. Belief in God is thus a natural state of beliefs held by humans, which beliefs arise non-reflectively or non-inferentially through these dispositions to believe.

Where did this god-faculty come from? How or why did it evolve? Why are human beings naturally inclined to believe in God or gods? The answer is traced back to our ancestors who were faced with survival pressures. If religious beliefs do not help us fight, flee, feed or reproduce, they must be by-products of capacities that do have survival value. Evolutionary by-products are called spandrels. This term, from Gould and Lewontin, means a by-product trait, not a direct consequence of natural selection.

So a belief spandrel is a belief that is a by-product of cognitive faculties or capacities brought about for the production of other kinds of beliefs which do have survival value. Beliefs about gods are widely treated as spandrels – by-products of HADD.

If religious beliefs arise as by-products, many claim that such beliefs are perforce irrational. Also, if there is a natural explanation of the putatively supernatural, the reality of the supernatural is undercut. But Clark counters that a naturalistic cause of certain phenomena counts neither against the existence of God nor against the rationality of belief in God.

Clark contends that rejecting spandrel or by-product beliefs as irrational is too sweeping, since, for example, the whole of contemporary science is effectively a belief spandrel.

But perhaps the god-faculty cannot produce justified religious beliefs because the faculty is not reliable – it has too many false positives. Clark argues that HADD and ToM[20] are generally reliable in agency detection. But, given the plethora of religious beliefs, perhaps HADD and ToM are spiritually unreliable; that is, they are unreliable when it comes to religious beliefs themselves. Clark argues to the contrary that the god-faculty, instead of being unreliable, may be simply "imprecise and coarse-grained." Maybe it produces roughly true religious/moral beliefs.

Clark suggests that perhaps rational reflection may lead to deeper, and truer moral and religious beliefs. But because of their course-grained nature, there may be divergent formulations.

While Kelly does not claim to have proved that there is a God, he does claim to have succeeded in showing that evolutionary psychology of religion has not undermined the rationality of religious belief. If the line is taken that the religious is thereby undermined, then the argument used to bring about this conclusion leads to the further conclusion that modern/contemporary science is also undermined.

These 39 insightful and carefully crafted chapters found keenly attentive and predominantly young audiences when they were presented. And now it is the pleasure and delight of the editor that these papers have come to this final form, so as to make them available to the wider audience in the West as well as the East. The narrative accompanying the Series will never fade or lose its place in our hearts. We are bound to a people, culture, and language that have become part of who we are. We only hope that readers will find insight and engagement as these two practices of inquiry are brought together with a passion and commitment that merits a response in kind. May this contribution bring about other collaboratives, and ultimately greater clarity and understanding of issues so pivotal to questions relating to the meaning, value, and purpose of human existence for the good of all.

Melville Y. Stewart

Editor

Notes

1   *Time*, June 25, 2001, cover story.

2   Matt Ridley, Part Two: "Modern Darwins," *National Geographic*, February 2009, (italics added) which follows an article by David Quammen, "The Darwin Bicentennial," Part One. The special issue is in celebration of the 200th birthday of Charles Darwin, February 10, 1809. To the "genetic scripture," one might also add, the "astronomical scripture," referencing the Psalmist's exclamation, "The heavens declare the glory of God," Psalm 19. No doubt there might be others.

3   I am indebted to Professor Nicholas Wolterstorff for his account of practices of inquiry in the context of education and ethical theory in a paper delivered at a Society of Christian Philosophers symposium held at Fudan University, October 15–19, 2005 (the year of the first Series). See his paper, "Religion in the Academy and in the Political Order."

4   See my article, "The Complementarity of Science and Religion," *Dialogue of Philosophies, Religions and Civilizations in the Era of Globalization*, ed. Zhao Dunhua. Department of Philosophy, Peking University, The Council for Research in Values and Philosophy, 2007, and regarding items (1), (2), (3) and (4) see my article, 《科学与宗教中的范式》 ("Paradigm in Science and Religion"), in 《科学与宗教的对话》 (*A Dialogue Between Science and Religion*), co-eds. Zhou

Zianzhang (Xiamen University), Kang Phee Sang (Hong Kong Baptist University), Kelly James Clark (Calvin College), and Melville Y. Stewart (University of St. Thomas). Xiamen: Xiamen University Press, 2001.

5   The titles of the four succeeding volumes in the study have variant endings added to Science and Religion so as to distinguish the volumes.

6   *Religion* is not as easy to define as suggested here. While some work at stipulative definitions, John Hick, in *Philosophy of Religion*, 3rd ed., offers a Wittgensteinian "family resemblance" approach, which singles out one point of family resemblance, the *salvific structure*, which he variously terms, "salvation," or "liberation," p. 3.

7   *Scientia* is synonymous with *cognitio* and *notitia*, and conveys knowledge generally, and specifically, knowledge acquired by demonstration. See, Richard A. Muller, *Dictionary of Latin and Greek Theological Terms*, Grand Rapids, Baker Book House, 1985, p. 274.

8   Roger Ames, "Dialogue Between Chinese and Western Philosophy," in *Dialogue of Philosophies, Religions and Civilizations in the Era of Globalization*, Chinese Philosophical Studies, XXV, ed. Zhao Dunhua, 2007. I want to thank Professor Roger Ames for reviewing the Chinese entries.

9   See Book VI of the *Republic*, 509 D-511 E, Oxford: Oxford University Press, 1941.

10   Book of Songs, 257, in "Dialogue Between Chinese and Western Philosophy," *Dialogue of Philosophies, Religions and Civilizations in the Era of Globalization*, Chinese Philosohical Studies XXV, ed. Zhao Dunhua, Peking University.

11   The editor wishes to thank Professor Dodson for his inclusion of this very important revised and updated version of an earlier paper that appeared in the *American Paleontologist* (Spring, 2006).

12   The editor wishes to thank the publisher of the *American Paleontologist*, and Peter Dodson, for allowing the inclusion of this revision in this Collection.

13   Philosopically speaking, these two terms can have rather distinct meanings, *function* is what something *does*, whereas *attribute* is what that something *is*.

14   See Kelly James Clark's second chapter, and the paper he team-presented with Justin Barrett, both in Volume One (chapters 38 and 39).

15   *The Empirical Stance* (New Haven, CT: Yale University Press, 2002).

16   Or as some might contend more precisely, *He took on flesh*.

17   Interestingly, when the NewVision 400 Science Series sponsored by the Templeton Foundation took place a week after the Peking Science and Religion Series, this was one of the topics for heated discussion.

18   Here of course, if God is not logically contingent (as most Christian theists hold), there would be no need to add the phrase, "other than himself."

19   I suggest a similar idea in, "Trinitarian Willing and Salvifc Initiatives," *The Trinity: East/West Dialogue*, Vol. 24 (Dordrecht: Kluwer Academic Publishers, 2003), p. 66, "God is essentially a creator as well as lover." In the Russian edition, *Пресвятая Троица*, ed. Alexander Kyrlezhev (Moscow: Moscow Patriarchate), 2002, p. 86. Also see, "Свобода, Необходимость Искупление," ("Freedom, Necessity and the Atonement") in *Искуплениа* (*The Atonement*) (St Petersburg School of Religion and Philosophy Press, 1999), pp. 256–80.

20   ToM stands for Theory of Mind.

Part 1

Has Science Really Destroyed Its Own Religious Roots?

1

The Nature of Science

DEL RATZSCH

Although it is widely recognized that different scientific theories have been accepted in different historical periods, it is less widely known that the very concepts of science and scientific method have also varied substantially over time. This chapter begins with a brief survey of some of those changes, revealing a trend toward ever-growing recognition of the extent to which things beyond just (a) observational data, (b) theories, and (c) principles of reason play absolutely essential and rationally legitimate roles in the heart of science itself. That opens interesting possibilities for science/religion issues, and also means that many traditional criticisms of religious belief – which often incorporate outdated views of what science is – are no longer effective.

Few things have changed human history more profoundly than have the rise, growth, and products – both conceptual, practical and technological – of the natural sciences. Yet despite science's profound shaping role in modern history and culture, despite the near reverence in which its capabilities are sometimes held, contemporary culture does not really understand science's theories, its capacities, its limitations, or its basic character.

I Conceptions of Science

The first question to ask is: what *is* science? In its broadest sense, science is an epistemological project – an attempt to understand, to generate knowledge. A tradition going back to various Greek thinkers claimed that genuine knowledge required certainty. For some matters, certainty was not in principle problematic. Under the right conditions, we could have certainty concerning various truths which were objective and necessary – mathematical or logical propositions, for instance. We could also in principle often have absolute certainty concerning some truths which were both subjective and contingent – concerning our own internal mental states, for instance. However, natural science typically operates in areas falling between those two regions – dealing with objective contingencies.

Generating genuine knowledge – including the required certainty – in this domain posed a variety of potential difficulties. What gradually emerged historically was the belief that acquiring genuine knowledge of the objective contingencies of nature required a strictly structured method (which would screen out fallible human subjectivity) guided by the appropriate logic (which would secure the required certainty). Of course, since science operated in the realm of contingency, the logic would have to be appropriate to that realm.

Inductivism

The earliest influential modern conception of science came from Francis Bacon in the early seventeenth century. Bacon's proposal, which dominated conceptions of science nearly to the present, was in effect to let nature dictate the principles, concepts and theories constituting science, while holding subjective human conceptual intrusions at bay.

According to Bacon's picture, science rested ultimately on nothing but pure objective, dispassionately collected observational data. Scientists carefully followed set, stringent procedures (the "scientific method") in their observations and reasoning, and scientific results, scientific theories, and scientific knowledge were the rigorous outcomes of applying pure reason (mathematics or logic) to the observational data in accord with the dictates of the specific scientific method. Since the logic which defined the backbone of this method was an inductive logic, Bacon's views are generally referred to as "inductivism."

The contention was that if one (a) began exclusively from what nature said (empirical, experimental data), (b) built upon that foundation only what rigorous reason permitted, and (c) accepted only facts, laws, and principles which this stringent scientific method dictated, then (d) all pronouncements of science would ultimately represent the authoritative voice of nature itself, and no human subjective taint could force its way into science. Purity, objectivity, and certainty were thus to be rationally guaranteed. Scientific method was, then, a set of rigid rules – the alleged "rules of science" – both for human epistemological empowerment (allowing us to reach truths otherwise beyond unaided human capabilities), and for overcoming other human weaknesses (protecting science from subjectivities which would otherwise cripple it).

This picture of science was dominant historically, was made into something like the official cultural conception by the Positivist movement of the early twentieth century, and still underlies many popular ideas about science. The view was quite attractive in that it seemed to offer a comforting certainty to human beings.

Indeed, on some systems of thought, science very nearly became a religion. A variety of groups have attempted (and some continue to attempt) either to construct broad philosophical systems purely on the basis of modern science, or to acquire support for pre-existing philosophical systems from science, or, on the basis of science, to generate challenges to broad philosophical systems or religious worldviews. For instance, Positivists were widely known for thinking that science was the only legitimate source of knowledge and truth, that science represented our only hope of answering whatever questions humans had, and that to the extent there could be such, science – not metaphysics, not philosophy, not religion – constituted the only reliable guide to human life. Thus, the noted biologist C. H. Waddington:

> Science by itself is able to provide mankind with a way of life which is, firstly self-consistent and harmonious, and secondly, free for the exercise of that objective reason on which our material

progress depends. So far as I can see, the scientific attitude of mind is the *only* one which is, at the present day, adequate in both these respects.[1]

Speaking of the position science has in fact come to occupy in contemporary society, the Marxist biologist Richard Lewontin says that for an institution or practice to become a source of intellectual and societal authority it must meet three conditions:

(1)   It must be something beyond just a *human* institution that gives it its authority.
(2)   Its ideas and principles must go far beyond human fallibility – representing absolute truth.
(3)   Its deep truths must go beyond what ordinary people can understand, its deep details clear only to specialists.

Lewontin then says:

> The Christian Church or indeed any revealed religion fits these requirements perfectly … But this description also fits science and has made it possible for science to replace religion as the chief legitimating force in modern society.[2]

But while a Baconian picture might attractively promise secure certainties, it has been known for half a century to be irreparably defective, disintegrating at nearly every point, thus destroying any hope of building philosophical or other *certainties* upon it. One of the most serious difficulties was that there simply is *no* form of logic by which theories, laws and the like can be *inferred* from empirical data alone. There is no procedure of logic which can begin with only data and rigorously produce a theory of that data. The implication was that science could not be *just* rigorous reason applied to objective data – that sort of conceptual purity was impossible. I'll say more about that shortly.[3]

Hypothetico-deductivism

If theories cannot be logically generated from data, how do they originate? The answer is: a leap of human creativity. Of course, since such leaps do not seem to follow any logical rules, giving human creativity a key role in science seemed to re-open the door to subjectivity. The immediate problem was that not only was there no logic of invention, but that invention essentially involved all sorts of unruly, untamed subjective processes. A creative leap could be triggered by some bizarre idea, hunch, twinge, dream, fantasy, or virtually *anything* else, including philosophical speculation, religious presuppositions, political doctrines, or metaphysical bias. That seemed to open the doors wide for human subjectivity to flood back into science. Evidently, then, one had to choose between barring scientific theories from science altogether, or finding some way of containing the threat of subjectivity. The most popular such approach was the idea that a scientific theory could be thought up or *proposed* for any reason (or no reason) whatever, but that any theory had to pass stringent empirical and logical tests before being actually *admitted* into science. Thus, the subjectivity of theory invention could not penetrate science itself, because again, nature itself via objective empirical, experimental results, had the final say in the theory's fate – in whether a theory did or did not actually gain access into the body of accepted science.

The structure of such tests, however, had significant implications for the character of science. The only way to test proposed hypotheses and theories against nature was apparently to deduce experimental or other observational predictions from the hypothesis or theory then see whether or not prediction matched reality – either confirming or contradicting what the theory said. (Since it involved *deduction* of predictions from *hypotheses*, it became known as the "hypothetico-deductive method".) However, correct predictions do not *conclusively prove* theoretical truth, because no matter how many tests a theory successfully passed, it was still possible that some new result – tomorrow or in three centuries – would contradict what the theory said. To think otherwise was to commit the logical fallacy of Affirming the Consequent.

In fact, it is in principle *possible* for a false theory to make infinitely many correct predictions. Worse yet, it is in principle possible for multiple *competing* theories to *all* be consistent with any collection of empirical data. No matter how large one's collection of data, there are always *in principle* infinitely many theoretical interpretations consistent with that data (just as there are always infinitely many lines that can be drawn through any given finite collection of points on a graph). This is generally referred to as the *underdetermination* of theory by empirical data.

Every scientific theory is underdetermined in this sense. Any collection of data – no matter how large – can *in principle* be explained by multiple alternative theories, each of which is logically consistent with, and offers a potential explanation for, all the data. Even if we had the complete collection of empirical data from the entire cosmos we could not rigorously *infer* any substantive scientific theory.

Further, where two alternative theories are "empirically equivalent" (where they make all the same empirical predictions), science cannot choose one theory over the other on *purely empirical* grounds. The data, being consistent with both, simply cannot discriminate between the two. Of course, we typically do take specific scientific theories to be *true*. But given that empirical data alone cannot discriminate among empirically equivalent theories, it follows immediately that when we select one theory from among the competing theories as being true, our selection must inescapably be based on something beyond merely empirical evidence.

So science *has* to involve things beyond just logic and data, and among those additional things are such deeply human matters as *creativity* – because there simply is no *logic* which could produce theories from data. Humans have to construct them. Furthermore, certainty and proof of theories could no longer be hoped for, so theories have to be held with at least some degree of *tentativity*.

But it was still believed that experimental results could provide some degree of positive *confirmation* to theories, and that our best theories could still be shown to be highly *probable* by scientific inductive logics.

Falsificationism

But things were about to get worse. A number of people – most notably Karl Popper[4] – concluded that theories could not even be confirmed in the usually understood sense (much less proven). Popper believed that it was not possible even to establish the *probable* truth of a theory by means of confirming its implications. Genuine scientific theories had to be *general* (applying to all space and time) and thus had infinitely many possible empirical implications. It was obviously impossible to check *all* of them, and given that the number of possible implications was infinite, checking and confirming any finite subset of them, no matter how large, conferred exactly zero probability upon the theory in question. There thus was, according to Popper, no such thing as proper scientific induction. Confirmation in *any* degree was simply out of the question, as was, apparently, even *tentative* acceptance of theories as even *probably* true. The only thing even in principle within science's capabilities was to show a theory to be *false* by uncovering empirical data contrary to the theory's predictions. Most "Popperians" thus claim that scientific truth can never be proven or even confirmed – the only thing science can do is to disprove scientific error.

Unfortunately, even that modest claim turns out to be too strong. Theories make no predictions at all just by themselves, but only in conjunction with a significant cluster of other claims – boundary conditions, auxiliary hypotheses, instrumentation theories, and others. For instance, if one tests a theory's predictions by using a particle accelerator, one is automatically assuming some theories about how particle accelerators work, as well as assuming some theories about the sorts of particles being used in the accelerator, and quite a few other things. Thus, failure of a prediction can be blamed on either the theory being tested, *or* it can be blamed on any number of those other factors, some of which (auxiliary hypotheses, instrumentation theories) are themselves unavoidably lacking absolute certainty. (They lack certainty because they too are scientific theories, and thus like any theory cannot be conclusively proven by empirical data.)

The inescapable implication is that observational or experimental failure of a prediction confronts science with a human *choice* concerning what to abandon and what to keep – a choice never *quite* empirically closed. So subjective human processes were part of theory discovery and construction, theories could never be *proven* to be true, and Popper now argued that theories could not even be shown to be *probably* true. And in even trying to *show* that mistaken theories were false, one had to employ *human* choices. Science thus did not look like a rigorously certain foundation for human *life*, as Waddington and others had claimed. But worse (for the usual view of science) was yet to come.

Post-empiricism

Remember that on the usual view of science, science rested on the absolute solid bedrock of empirical, observational data. Historically it was almost universally believed that perception was (at least under ideal conditions) completely neutral in the sense that beliefs, presupposition, philosophical preferences, and other such factors did not affect what an honest, careful observer *saw*. That neutrality guaranteed the objectivity and utter trustworthiness of the empirical data which constituted the secure foundation of science. But in the 1960s, that neutrality came under attack. It was argued (perhaps most influentially by Thomas Kuhn[5]) that perception itself was an active – not passive – process, deeply affected by the broad conceptual frameworks – or *paradigms* – to which one had prior allegiances.

Thus, not only was the allegedly rigid logic structure of science gone, but the pure objectivity of its foundations was threatened. Furthermore paradigms influenced not only perception, but theory evaluation, theory acceptance, conceptual resources, normative judgments within science, and a host of other extremely consequential matters. According to Kuhn, a paradigm is a blended complex of four primary constituents – what he called "symbolic generalizations" (equations), metaphysical commitments, values, and exemplars. Such paradigms constitute normative (or governing) conceptual frameworks which are accepted by a scientific community and which define proper procedures for investigation, dictate criteria for theory evaluation, determine what conceptual resources may and may not be employed in theories, and in general stipulate the character and boundaries of scientific legitimacy within and in terms of which scientific work is normally conducted and evaluated. Since paradigms were partially *defined* by, among other things, *metaphysical* commitments and *values*, nonempirical, human-rooted factors seeped into scientific method at all levels.

And the human factors could not be completely removed from science. Recall one consequence of underdetermination was that if humans chose some specific scientific theory to claim as *true*, the choice of that theory *had* to involve (at least implicitly) factors *beyond* just the empirical.

Postmodernism

Some people – often lumped together under the term "postmodernist" – have argued for the nearly *complete* subjectivism of science. From that perspective, science can no longer be seen as an objective, epistemological project at all, but must be seen as a human social construction, an invention, wielded as a repressive weapon in a social power game, typically employed by dominant classes or groups as a means of perpetuating and legitimating their own perspective, power, privilege and position. However, that extreme view has not fared well outside certain circles. Indeed, it apparently cannot even account for so basic a fact as that science and scientific results *work,* and it also appears to be self-contradicting as well. In short, it is generally seen, at least in extreme form, as a failure. One lesson of the history of philosophy of science in this century is that any proper conception of science must accommodate the fact that nonempirical factors play a fundamental and essential role in science. But a lesson of the failure of postmodernism's runaway subjectivism is that there are limits on those factors. Kuhn's own less extreme conception of science has come in for a variety of serious criticisms also. His interpretation of the history of science, his specific theory of human perception, his failure to construct any precise definition of his most fundamental concept – *paradigm* – and others of his claims have all come under serious and persuasive criticisms.[6] But despite the apparent difficulties in Kuhn's positions, many contemporary philosophers of science believe that his views contain important lessons and raise important questions which cannot be ignored. And the developing answers to such questions have deeply affected contemporary conceptions of science.

Current views

According to the old ideal, the results and theories of science were rigorous outcomes of rigid scientific reason operating on pure empirical data in ways dictated by scientific method. But historical investigation showed that science had never in fact matched that ideal historically. Political, philosophical, psychological, social, and other human factors often influenced science. And even what scientists themselves took proper scientific method to be had changed several times historically. There simply were no such things as universal "rules of science."

Furthermore, the ideal was an *impossible* one anyway. As we have seen, theories are not logically dictated by data, and there is no logic for the invention of theories at all. Beyond that, theories cannot be conclusively *proven* by empirical data, and according to Popper could not even be shown to be probable. Refuting a theory turned out to involve human choices. Indeed, even in principle almost no part of science could operate without human choices, human concepts, and human presuppositions.

Does that mean that science can claim no epistemological authority at all? Does it mean that in science just anything goes? Not at all. But saying exactly where various boundaries are, or exactly what can or cannot factor legitimately into science is extremely difficult. Although disagreeing on numerous specifics, most mainline commentators argue that despite the irremovable dependence of science upon resources beyond just empirical data and reason, scientific results can still claim significant rational justification and epistemic legitimacy. Rigor, objectivity, and warrant may be less than absolute, but science *can* still at least approach theoretical truth. In modest form, realism (the view that science can – and sometimes does – get at truth) still seems defensible.

Of course, such realist claims are plausible only if we have grounds for confidence in the human perceptual and cognitive structures which inescapably function within science. Beyond that, the principle of underdetermination of theory by data entails that science requires a conceptual environment richer than the merely empirical. Historically, that indispensable conceptual richness was drawn from religious principles. I will be talking specifically on that topic in the next chapter.

II Beyond the Empirical

But a number of related important questions must be addressed. Remember that empirical data and logic alone can never tell us that any *one* specific theory is the right one. But we do pick particular theories as being the right theory, or the true theory, or the best theory all the time. Such selections thus *have* to be made on partially nonempirical grounds. What are our nonempirical selection criteria? Some of the factors are obvious and familiar – for instance, the presupposition that nature is uniform, that natural laws operate everywhere in the cosmos, that theories should be consistent with empirical observation, that human minds, human reason, and human senses are the right sort for understanding nature, and so on.

But where do these nonempirical principles come from? Why do – or should – we accept them? How can we *rationally* justify our use of them? Science *itself* cannot provide the rational justification for them. Why not? Very briefly, doing science requires use of presuppositions involving criteria for theory construction, theory evaluation, and boundaries of concept legitimacy, plausibility structures, and a host of other matters. Such presuppositions are not direct *results* of science – they are among the conceptual materials which science itself depends upon and without which there simply would be no science. So if we are rationally justified in accepting the legitimacy of science then we must be rationally justified in accepting those foundational presuppositions. But if they are not *results* of science, then their rational justification cannot rest upon science, but must lie somewhere *beyond* the borders of science. Thus, if we take science itself to be rationally justified, we are thereby committed to the position that science is *not* the only source and basis for rational justification. So if science does provide rational justification for anything, science cannot itself be the only foundation for rational justification. There must be some *deeper* source of rational justification.

This result is important enough to make it worthwhile to see the reasoning in detail:

(1) Science itself rests upon a foundation of a number of presuppositions.

Thus:

(2)   Science itself is not rationally legitimate *unless* those foundational presuppositions are themselves rationally legitimate.

But

(3)   Science cannot operate unless those foundational presuppositions are *already* in place.

So:

(4)   Science cannot be the original source of rational justification for its own foundational presuppositions.

Therefore:

(5)   If science is rationally legitimate, then science cannot be the *only* source of rational justification.

Thus:

(6)   If science itself is rationally legitimate, then there must be some other *deeper* source of rational justification.

What will be that deeper source? In the next chapter, I will specifically discuss the role that Christian concepts, doctrines and beliefs played in the origin of modern science.

III Points of Contact

As it turns out, a lot of philosophical, political, social, and religious factors have come to bear upon science historically. How do various nonempirical factors function in science? It is obvious that such factors can bear upon the uses to which science is put, upon the directions of technological development, upon what questions are funded for investigation, and so forth. But important as those matters are, I want to leave them aside and probe a bit more deeply into the inner workings of science itself. Let us begin with three simple examples.

(1)   Europeans once accepted the very simple theory that all swans were white. But given one confirmed observation of one genuine black swan, that theory was *immediately* abandoned as no longer strictly true.

(2)   Virtually every scientists in the early eighteenth century accepted Newtonian theory as the correct description and explanation of planetary movement. Oddly enough, the Newtonian predictions were known to be wrong concerning one parameter of the moon's motion, and (later) concerning certain motions of Mercury. But no one seemed overly concerned – in particular, Newtonian theory was not abandoned until *over 200* years after it was first published.

(3)   All scientific activity operates on the presupposition that physical reality at some deep level is consistent, that nature functions uniformly. That presupposition underlies extrapolation from present knowledge to distant times (the past in e.g., geology and the past and future in cosmology) and to distant parts of the cosmos (in e.g., astronomy and cosmology). This postulated uniformity is absolutely indispensable to science. Inductive inferences depend upon it, and ultimately even what is or is not taken to need scientific explanation often depends upon it. The upshot is that no matter what we observed, we would not abandon the idea of nature's fundamental uniformity on some level. We might conclude that what we had previously *thought* represented uniformity really did not, but the foundational principle that there *was* some ultimate uniformity would only be abandoned with the abandonment of science itself.

Such examples suggest that within the conceptual structure of science, and within the larger conceptual context in which science is embedded, there are different levels. The above cases illustrate the fact that different components operate at different levels within the conceptual structure of science, and that evaluative procedures and other processes vary from level to level. The simple swan theory was abandoned easily on the basis of a single bit of data. Newtonian theory was much more tenacious and stubborn – it took two centuries, a lot of data, and some special conditions to bring about even its partial rejection. And the principle of the uniformity of nature seems to be in no possible danger from any possible empirical data ever.

In what follows, I will present a brief picture of that structure – an interrelated hierarchy of levels on which different components of science operate. Along the way, I will briefly discuss where and how at the different levels of that hierarchy, several of the nonempirical factors which shape scientific thought and explanations may come to bear upon the general scientific project.

IV The Hierarchy

The principal components of the hierarchy, with brief descriptions and some illustrative examples, are as follows.

Worldview

Principles, beliefs, intentions, and stances tied to the deepest level of human commitment and dedication constitute *worldviews*. The constituents at this level represent the most foundational, most all-encompassing components of one's conceptual framework, and include one's answers to the broadest human questions. For instance, what lies at the ultimate foundation of reality – is it Mind, or a Being, or purely mindless matter, or abstract and immaterial principles of reason, or eternal chaos, or nothing? Ultimate religious issues fit here – is there a supernatural being who brought the cosmos into existence? Here also are one's governing presuppositions concerning the ultimate nature of human beings and of human life.

Such considerations have sometimes played very specific roles in science. For instance, what is now considered to be the correct principle of conservation of momentum was first stated by the French mathematician/philosopher Descartes on grounds which were strongly theological. Newton accepted a particular theory concerning both the quality and quantity of matter in the cosmos in large part because he thought that that theory more appropriately reflected God's glory and power than did alternative theories.

Metaphysics

This category involves issues which are indeed deep, but not quite as ultimately fundamental as are those in the previous category. With respect to the reality around us – is it purely material? mechanical? corpuscular? continuous? intelligible? living? chaotic? determined? static? orderly? in process? uniform? governed by law? fundamentally mathematical? partly constituted by us? independent of us? Is reality a designed and created artifact, or itself eternal, or itself sentient, or a random entity thrown into existence out of some abyss of negation, or something else? What are the appropriate categories for conceptualizing and describing reality?

Here are two examples. Einstein had a deep philosophical commitment to reality being ultimately deterministic, and thus was hostile toward the Copenhagen interpretation of quantum mechanics. And Copernicus' decision to try to restructure astronomical theory and the particular type of restructuring he pursued both grew out of his philosophical commitment to a neo-Platonic metaphysics.

Epistemology

Science is a human knowledge-seeking enterprise. Thus, the nature of knowledge and of rationality, and the nature and capabilities of human knowers have consequences for the nature, scope, and competence of science, and for its proper aims and methods. Questions concerning the nature of knowledge, the character of truth, the means for producing knowledge, criteria for recognizing when genuine knowledge has or has not been reached – all will have to be addressed, or answers to them will have to be assumed.

Axiology

How science is actually pursued depends in part on what one takes the *aims* of science to be, what one thinks science is *for*. Historically, a variety of aims can be seen – e.g., the discovery of truth, identification of rational belief, understanding, empirical adequacy, control of nature, empowerment of human beings, ennoblement of human beings, and so on. Clearly, what one thinks that science should be *for* will affect how and where one pursues science, and will also determine when one *quits* – when one takes the pursuit to have been successfully or unsuccessfully *completed*.

Epistemic values

Given that the empirical alone does not single out specific theories (underdetermination), theory choice and evaluation have often been in terms of characteristics which were thought to be relatively reliable *indicators* of empirical and/or theoretical truth. Standard lists of such epistemic values include consistency, simplicity, breadth, intelligibility, fruitfulness, beauty, explanatory power, problem-solving power, progressiveness, and the like. Since theories which exhibited such characteristics were held to be more likely true than those lacking such properties, they were regarded as *epistemic* indicators or *epistemic values* as they are usually called. Obviously, what theory characteristics one takes to be reliable indicators of truth will depend in part on one's deeper views concerning reality, the nature of truth, the extent of human capacities, and so forth.

Methodology

Method is often identified as the very core of science. Scientific method is widely seen as what defines science, as what gives science its distinctive character, as what underlies the epistemological legitimacy, reliability, and power of science, and as what distinguishes science from non-science and pseudo-science. In broadest terms, method encompasses the procedures by which nature is to be asked questions, and the procedures by which her answers are to be heard and incorporated into the larger scientific picture. A number of factors can affect one's conception of method. For instance, Aristotle and Bacon had very different views of how one should investigate nature, those differences stemming in part from their differing views of human capabilities and faculties. (More on that in the next chapter.) If one takes *scientific truth* to be what scientific method produces, then different conceptions of method will often result in different conceptions of scientific truth.

Pragmatics

Pragmatics broadly includes constraints and strategies imposed by various limits under which science finds itself having to operate. Some pragmatic matters which are "external" to science include economics, government policies, technological capabilities, military needs, and so forth. But there are also "internal" pragmatic matters – considerations which shape science, not because there is any particularly good reason to think they reflect deep reality, but because they are inescapable in practice. For instance, in doing realist theoretical science, there seems no way to avoid assuming that in some way the observed and the observable are keys to the unobserved and the unobservable, that artificial and humanly constructed experiments really do reveal natural truths, that basic laws governing our area of time and space are representative of nature in general, and so on. Pretty clearly, the actual direction science has gone has been affected by such matters.

Theory

Theories are in some ways the centerpieces of science. But saying exactly what a theory *is* is difficult. Candidate analyses in this century have included everything from merely compact descriptive summations of past data, to formal axiom systems, to descriptions (perhaps metaphorical) of some causal substratum, to sets of universally quantified subjunctives, to sets of interpreted models, to trajectories in *n*-dimensional state spaces. But despite difficulties in rigorously *defining* theories, most of us are nonetheless able to identify them.

It is evident that theory characteristics, evaluative criteria, selection criteria, and other related matters are anchored in other levels of the hierarchy. Further, as some see it there is a texture of humanness built even more deeply into the very heart of theories themselves.

(This issue will be discussed in detail later.) And again, since theories cannot be directly *inferred* from data, theories themselves are results of human *creativity* – with possibly far-reaching implications. And the concepts and other resources constituting theories seem, obviously, to be *human* concepts growing out of *human* interpretations of *human* experiences.

Data

It is, again, increasingly widely believed in the West that human sensory observation is not merely a passive process of the mind registering what nature unambiguously presents to us. Perception is an active process, and data are subtly shaped by the observer's mindset, prior beliefs, and broader conceptual framework. This is often summed up by the phrase that "all data are *theory-laden*." If that is correct – and it seems to be to some degree – then influences from the larger conceptual context can have some effects even upon the empirical data which are popularly taken to be the bedrock upon which science is built.

V Interconnections

The above hierarchy components are not free-standing and independent. As indicated in a number of the examples given above, they interact, intermesh, mutually interpenetrate, and affect each other. Here is just one example. Over the past two or three decades, quite a number of scientists have become increasingly impressed with the fact that the cosmos *appears* to be exquisitely adjusted and constructed to allow the emergence, development, and continued existence of life. There is an extensive and growing catalogue of principles of nature, natural constants, and other physical matters which fall within *incredibly* narrow limits necessary for the very possibility of basic conditions for life – the existence of planets, of heavy elements, and so on. For instance, if some of the specific natural constants upon which life depends were different by as little as 1 part in 10^{60} there apparently would have been no possibility of life in this universe.

Now, this apparent *fine-tuning* (as it is called) is a very striking fact. How might we explain it? One theory which has received a lot of attention is that there are actually infinitely many distinct, separate, mutually isolated universes, each with its own unique set of laws, constants, and conditions, and that given infinitely many such chances, at least a few of them – such as ours – are likely to be finely tuned, to fall within the right zone for producing suns, planets, and other conditions necessary for the development of life.

But a theory which postulates infinitely many universes seems a bit extravagant. The fact that they are distinct *universes* seems to imply that each such universe is utterly inaccessible to every other such universe – meaning that we can not even in principle have *empirical* evidence even of their existence. Why might someone adopt such an extravagant cosmological theory for which there could never even in principle be any direct empirical evidence?

The reason has a direct worldview basis. The fact that this universe operates *within* such staggeringly tight constraints has struck many as being empirical evidence that the cosmos was deliberately *designed* for life. The improbability of the cosmos fitting all the constraints for life so exactly seemed to some to be vastly too huge to be explained just in terms of coincidence, lucky accident, or random chance. However, the possible explanation that there is a cosmic Designer seemed to some scientists to be much too religious-sounding for their taste. But then without a Designer how could one explain the fine-tuning, the huge improbability, and the exquisite fit? Their answer: by postulating infinitely many undetectable, mutually isolated universes to try to overpower the huge improbability. Thus, one frequent impulse behind this cosmological theory is a world-view-driven desire to avoid what appears to be a religiously significant implication of the existence of cosmic fine-tuning. (Similarly, some scientists initially resisted Big Bang theory, because it looked too much like a creation.)

VI Conclusion

What does all this mean? It means among other things that science is not just a simple matter of data and theory with logic connecting the two. It means further that a wide array of influences beyond the purely empirical play unavoidable, significant, substantive, and legitimate roles in the structure and content of our scientific picture of the world. It means that science has an irremovable human flavor. And it raises at least the possibility of an integrated conception of science – a science in which all the main currents of human concern have (perhaps highly indirect) points of contact with nature.

In the next chapter, I will examine the roots of science and look at the religious conceptual context from which the necessary additional principles and values came. Then in the chapter following that I will talk about whether science damages the rationality of religious belief.

Notes

1   C. H. Waddington, *The Scientific Attitude*, p. 170 (my emphasis).
2   Richard Lewontin, *Biology as Ideology*, pp. 7–8.
3   For a general introduction to philosophy of science, see Del Ratzsch, *Science and its Limits*.
4   Karl Popper's best known works in this area are *The Logic of Scientific Discovery* and *Conjectures and Refutations*.
5   Thomas Kuhn's best known work is *The Structure of Scientific Revolutions*.
6   These issues are discussed in detail in my *Science and Its Limits*.

Bibliography

Kuhn, Thomas *The Structure of Scientific Revolutions* (Chicago: University of Chicago Press, 1962; 2nd edn. 1970).
Lewontin, Richard *Biology as Ideology* (New York: Harper Collins, 1991).
Popper, Karl *Conjectures and Refutations* (New York: Harper, 1963, 2nd edn. 1965).
Popper, Karl *The Logic of Scientific Discovery* (New York: Harper, 1959, 2nd edn. 1968).
Ratzsch, Del *Science and its Limits* (Downers Grove, IL: InterVarsity Press, 2000).
Waddington, C. H. *The Scientific Attitude* (West Drayton, UK: Penguin, 1941, 2nd edn. 1948).

2

The Religious Roots of Science

DEL RATZSCH

There is a widespread but historically inaccurate myth that science, since its very birth, has been bitterly opposed by religion. That myth is not merely inaccurate, but with respect to the birth of science, the truth is in a different direction entirely. As indicated in the previous chapter, science's very existence crucially depends upon a variety of principles that are not merely empirical. In this chapter, it will be argued that the rational justification for – and in some cases the source of – many of those essential principles was rooted in the theological doctrine of creation. To some degree, then, the foundations of science itself may ultimately depend upon a theologically-shaped picture.

The beginnings and rise of modern science are usually traced to the sixteenth and seventeenth centuries, and to a number of key thinkers in Western Europe – Francis Bacon, Nicholas Copernicus, Robert Boyle, Johann Kepler, Galileo, Isaac Newton, and others. We might ask several questions. The type of investigation which developed involved a special combination of properties we identify as being characteristically scientific – a dependence upon empirical observation, an emphasis on experimentation, a materialistic conception of causation, a structure patterned upon principles of rationality, reason, and logic. What underlay those particular characteristics? Why did it develop in Europe? And why just at that particular period of history? Other cultures flourished earlier – e.g., ancient Greece, Rome – and some had much longer histories than Western European culture – e.g., China, India, and Egypt. Why did the type of investigation we identify as being characteristically *scientific* emerge and flourish precisely when and precisely where it did? As it turns out, the answers to those questions are connected. To see how, we first look deeper into Western history.

I A Brief History

Most Western intellectual histories begin with ancient Greece, starting roughly 25 centuries ago. There were widely divergent currents of thought in ancient Greece, but two or three are of particular relevance.

Italian Greek

The first, sometimes identified as the Italian Greek tradition, which included such figures as Parmenides, Pythagoras, and Plato, held that ultimate reality was not the reality we see around us, but that the foundational constituents of reality consisted of *immaterial* things – numbers, mathematical objects, forms, essences – existing in an immaterial, transcendent realm. This immaterial, ultimate reality had a very specific type of structure – its existence, character, and constitution were dictated by, exemplified, and indeed constituted, ultimate principles of reason, the essence of rationality.

This ultimate reality and the essence of rationality it defined were eternal and unchanging, and rigidly governed everything else that truly existed. Since true reality had at its core that framework of rationality, its structure corresponded in important ways to the structure of the thought of any rational mind – including human minds. There was a special fittingness between the immaterial, rational principles of ultimate reality, and *mind*. That meant not only that this eternal, unchanging immaterial realm was the proper focus and object of thought, but that processes of the mind could parallel the structure of reality – in short, that a rational mind had the potential to *understand* reality.

Furthermore, seeing reality as ultimately structured according to principles of reason and as conforming to the dictates and demands of *mind*, made it both easy and natural to see reality in mind-related terms – purposes, goals, and aims, for instance. In fact, some Greeks saw rational order and 'The Good' as deeply connected. Reality on this view was suffused with *value*.

Finally, since ultimate reality was unchanging, and since the things in the physical realm were contingent, changing, and temporary, physical things were not part of what was ultimately real. The senses, however, grasp only things in the physical realm, and thus did not make contact with the fully real. It was inferred that the senses did not provide a path to genuine truth. The pure activity of the mind, then, was the only means to understanding and to truth that we humans had.

Ionian Greek

The second Greek tradition, sometimes called the Ionian tradition, took a very different view. Thales, Anaximander, Anaximenes, and others within this tradition sought for explanations of reality in terms of physical principles and processes, rather than appealing to abstractions, immaterial factors, or anything of that sort. Basically, the Ionian thinkers attempted to explain experienced physical events and regularities in nature in terms of physical, experiential categories – familiar *observed* substances (earth, air, fire, water), familiar *observed* processes (flotation, falling), familiar *observed* properties (hot, cold, wet, dry).

In this Ionian Greek tradition, ordinary physical phenomena were important parts of genuine reality – Ionians rejected the idea that only the immaterial realm had *real* existence and status. And since the senses provided our access to the physical realm, sensory experience and observation provided genuine information and pieces of truth about reality, given the reality of the physical realm.

Indeed, some Greek thinkers – for example, Atomists such as Democritus and Leucippus – went further, declaring that atoms of various sorts constituted the only reality there was. Atomists were later interpreted as holding that *everything* consisted only of bits of matter in motion. Although that was not quite accurate, the Atomists did believe that the fundamental principles that ultimately *govern* reality were not reflections of mind, reason, or intellect.

In very broad terms, what we see among the ancient Greek thinkers are the beginnings of two strands which in fact persisted in identifiable form down to the modern era – one focusing upon highly abstract reason as the key to understanding an immaterial, ideal reality, and the other focusing upon sensory experience and experiential concepts as the key to understanding a material, observable reality. So Italian Greeks elevated reason to the point of denying empirical observation any real role in the process of investigating reality, and even denied the full reality of the physical realm itself. The Ionian tradition, in extreme form, admitted the existence *only* of the material realm, and denied that there even was any deep rational structure in the cosmos for the mind to understand.

Aristotle

One can see Aristotle as attempting to blend these two strands into a unified harmony. Although Aristotle accepted the Italian Greek conception of reality as ultimately rationally structured, that rational structure was intimately, inseparably bound up within the physical realm itself, and the physical realm, rather than being less than fully real and less than fully rational, now itself was part of the rational order of reality. Aristotle in effect kept the rational structures of the Italian Greeks, but shifted the location of that order and the focus of attention to the physical world of the Ionians. With the focus on the physical realm, the physical senses and observation again provided foundations of knowledge, but reason and the intellect (as well as such related concepts as *purpose* and *goal*) still played crucial roles in the acquisition and content of knowledge.

While Aristotle believed that investigation had to rest on observation he believed that such observation need not be extensive and need not involve elaborate experimentation. According to Aristotle, we had an *inductive* mental faculty which from just a few bits of observational data could extract the general rational patterns embedded in the observed reality in question. Thus, extensive observation was not necessary. And Aristotle saw experimentation as potentially *distorting* nature. But if nature in experimental circumstances were distorted or coerced into doing things it *otherwise would not* do, then the results of any such experimentation obviously would not reveal any basic truths about real nature itself. In effect, experimental results would in part be human artifacts.

The physical realm itself was often taken to be (or to be governed by) active, even living agencies. Some Greeks had seen *nature* itself as a separate 'overseer' of the physical realm, or postulated something like a 'world soul' which had a type of autonomous, vital existence above the purely physical components of nature. The proper conceptual organizing metaphor for thinking about the cosmos was that of a living *organism*. That provided another reason for refraining from experimental poking at nature – it could be dangerous or even sacrilegious.

Despite important differences between the two original traditions, and despite a number of unique aspects of Aristotle's thought, nearly all the Greek philosophers believed that on its most fundamental level, ultimate reality – whether that was matter or atoms or immaterial principles or Forms – was eternal, fixed, unchanging, and governed by structures and principles of reason.

Given this rigid, logical structuring of the ultimate, governing level of reality, most Greeks thought that any 'nature' or 'world soul' – and even the gods themselves – were subject to, and had to work within or around, the boundaries imposed by this eternal, rigid, ultimate order of reality.

This general Greek view was in various ways philosophically fruitful, but it did not directly result in any enduring tradition that was identifiably scientific, in the sense of the later Scientific Revolution. In fact, several of the aspects of Greek thought outlined above may have *hindered* development of anything like modern science. And that general effect long outlived Greek culture itself. As the Christian religion rose to Western cultural dominance within the medieval era, Greek views – basically the only body of worked-out intellectual thought known to medieval scholars – were appropriated by Christian culture and integrated into Christian intellectual structures. Greek philosophy – either that of Plato (via e.g., Augustine) or that of Aristotle (via e.g., Aquinas) subsequently dominated Western thought for centuries.

II The Rise of Science and the Doctrine of Creation

But modern science did emerge – explosively – in the Scientific Revolution of the sixteenth and seventeenth centuries. Something evidently changed, breaking the barriers which Greek-shaped thought had constituted. Exactly what changed? The story is complicated, and the exact role of all the factors is not completely settled. But major historians now believe that one key factor (among others) was a focus on a basic doctrine of Christian theology – the doctrine of creation.

Very briefly, the strongest version of the doctrine of creation says that the cosmos and everything that exists in it was *created* by a transcendent, rational God. That implies that the cosmos had a *beginning* – it has not existed always and is not eternal. The only thing eternal, according to this doctrine, is God. Everything else is created. This doctrine also says that the things which God created were created *out of nothing* – that God brought the cosmos itself into existence by His decree and command, and did not merely fashion the cosmos out of some pre-existing materials or matter. Further, according to this doctrine, since only God is eternal, there were no pre-existing rules or principles or boundaries that He had to work within. He was not subject to any constraints in choosing what to create, so everything else – is made by Him – was utterly subject to His will and free decisions.[1]

But how could that theological doctrine have any relevance to the character and shape of modern science? What exactly are the connections which historians see here? And even if there really are such connections, is there any reason whatever to think that the people who actually got modern science up and running – Newton, Galileo, Bacon, Boyle, Descartes – were aware of the connections? Even more to the point, is there any evidence that they had them consciously in mind or explicitly employed them?

Many historians of science believe that the answer to all those questions is "yes." In support of that answer, the following are a number of key implications of the doctrine of creation as it was understood in the early modern period, and a number of revealing statements by major early modern scientists themselves. The quotations in the following are merely illustrative of vastly many more which could be cited.

Contingency and empirical investigation

Since God had created the cosmos out of nothing, and since in creating it He had not been bound by prior principles or inherent properties of pre-existing matter, the structure and character of the cosmos had not been dictated by any preexisting necessities. That meant that the principles and structure of the cosmos were contingent. There was no one way that they *had* to be, and thus they could not be deduced just from *a priori* principles of reason, logic, or mathematics. In creating, God had been *free*, and consequently in order to discover what God had done, we had to actually *look*. It followed that science must have part of its foundation in *observation*.

Various early scientists specifically endorsed the idea of God being *free* to *choose* what and how to create. (This was known as the doctrine of *divine voluntarism*.) For instance, in his *Reason and Religion*, Robert Boyle, often considered to be the founder of modern chemistry, says: "God [is] the author of the universe, and the free establisher of the laws of motion.... [These laws] depend perfectly upon his will..."[2] and in his *The Christian Virtuoso* again notes: "The laws of nature ... were at first arbitrarily instituted by God."[3]

But did early scientists make the explicit inference from the fact that God freely chose what and how to create, to the conclusion that we had to proceed in our investigations of nature by empirical observation? Indeed they did, as exhibited in the following by Roger Cotes in the Preface of Isaac Newton's major work, *Principia Mathematica*:

> Without all doubt this world, so diversified with that variety of forms and motions we find in it, could arise from nothing but the perfect free will of God directing and presiding over all.
>
> From this fountain it is that those laws, which we call the laws of Nature, have flowed, in which there appear many traces of the most wise contrivance but not the least shadow of necessity. These therefore we must not seek from uncertain conjectures, but *learn them from observations and experiments*.[4]

All of that raises an immediate question. For the Greeks, it was exactly the necessities built into reality which made it intelligible. But if the Creator was completely free in choosing what and how to create, if there were no constraints at all, no binding necessities, then could we humans have any hope whatever of *understanding* that creation? The answer, given Christian doctrine, was "yes." That answer emerged as follows.

Coherence/intelligibility of creation

God is a rational being. Since the things which a rational being does reflects the being's nature, the cosmos God constructed would be constructed according to principles and laws He chose in his wisdom There would thus be reason to nature's structures. So in a basic sense, nature would be *coherent* and *intelligible* – a principle which is a precondition to any rational understanding of nature. The cosmos actually being a creation, it could be expected to embody patterns that reflected and resonated with a *mind* – things like simplicity, elegance, and other such properties.

But even if the cosmos embodied deep principles of wisdom and rationality built into its structure and governance, since those principles were principles freely chosen by a *supernatural*, omniscient being, would there be any realistic hope that *we* – finite, limited beings – could ever actually understand it? Here again, Christian doctrine implied that the answer was "yes."

Understandability of creation

Since God had also created human beings and human intellect, and since according to Christian doctrine God had created humans *in his own image*, we at least had a head start toward understanding nature and its governing principles, since the intellect with which we tried to understand the cosmos reflected in some degree the intellect which had planned and created the cosmos, and whose thought principles were structured into the cosmos itself. That connection is explicitly stated by a number of the early founders of modern science. For instance, Kepler in a 1597 letter to Maestlin said:

> [In publishing the *Mysterium Cosmographicum*] the effect which I strove to obtain [was] that the belief in the creation of the world be fortified through this external support, that thought of the creator be recognized in its nature ... Then man will at least measure the power of his mind on the true scale, and will realize that God, who founded everything in the world according to the norm of quantity, also has endowed man with a mind which can comprehend these norms.[5]

Even more specifically, in a 1599 letter to Johannes Georg Herwart von Hohenburg, Kepler says:

> Those [laws] are within the grasp of the human mind. God wanted us to recognize them by creating us after his own image so that we could share in his own thoughts ... and, if piety allows us to say so, our understanding is in this respect of the same kind as the divine, at least as far as we are able to grasp something of it in our mortal life.[6]

Galileo, in the *Dialogues Concerning the Two Chief World Systems* makes a similar connection:

> I say that as to the truth of the knowledge which is given by mathematical proofs, this is the same that Divine wisdom recognizes, [although] our understanding ... is infinitely surpassed by the Divine. [Yet] when I consider what marvelous things and how many of them men have understood, inquired into, and contrived, I recognize and understand only too clearly that the human mind is a work of God's, and one of the most excellent.[7]

On the general idea of linking the image of God in humans to an ability to understand, Aquinas in his *Summa Theologica* says:

> Only in rational creatures is there found a likeness of God which counts as an image ... As far as a likeness of the divine nature is concerned, rational creatures seem somehow to attain a representation of [that] type in virtue of imitating God not only in this, that he is and lives, but especially in this, that he understands.[8]

But that raised a further question. If our intellects partially reflected that of God, then was empirical investigation really essential? Perhaps we needed a few empirical hints since God had created freely, but if our minds really did partially reflect God's, wouldn't just a few such hints be sufficient (as Aristotle had thought)? The answer was "no." First of all, many early scientists were extremely insistent concerning the degree of and implications of our human finitude. As noted above, Galileo said that our understanding was *infinitely* surpassed by God's. And Roger Cotes again:

> He who is presumptuous enough to think that he can find the true principles of physics and the laws of natural things by the force alone of his own mind, and the internal light of his reason, must either suppose that the world exists by necessity, and by the same necessity follows the laws proposed; or if the order of nature was established by the will of God, that himself, a miserable reptile, can tell what was fittest to be done.[9]

We *could* understand nature, but our limitations as compared to God meant that we needed all the empirical help we could get. So Francis Bacon in *The Great Instauration of Learning* says:

> All depends on keeping the eye steadily fixed upon the facts of nature and so receiving their images simply as they are. [Only by so doing can we hope to discover] a true vision of the footsteps of the Creator imprinted on his creation.[10]

All depends on keeping our eyes *steadily* on the facts of nature – that is our *only* hope of getting at nature's truths.

A Preliminary results (1)

To this point, we can see that the doctrine of creation was consciously taken by major early scientists as implying that while the cosmos was contingent it was still intelligible, but that the only way we could arrive at a real understanding of it was through intense, extended empirical investigation.[11] That represented a crucial difference from earlier thought, and a difference which was essential for the birth of modern science.[12] But that change alone was not yet enough. Older systems often pictured the cosmos in terms appropriate to *organisms* – growth, development, reproduction, love, hate (and even justice and injustice). Again, many earlier thinkers had even construed *nature itself* as being very like an active, living being – perhaps even a god. That general metaphor for thinking about the world was not ultimately fruitful, and Christian theology provided part of the foundation for the needed change.

Nature's dependence

According to the Christian doctrine of creation, nature was completely dependent upon and subject to God's actions and commands. The cosmos was consequently seen as not only *distinct* from God, but as being of a fundamentally different kind than God. Thus, Bacon in *The Advancement of Learning*: "[Non-Christians] suppose the world to be the image of God … But the Scriptures never vouchsafe to attribute to the world that honor, as to be the image of God, but only the work of his hands".[13]

Nature was seen not as a *being* but as a *thing*, a work of God's hands, an *artifact*, governed by God according to rules appropriate to an artifact. Thus Boyle in his *Notion of Nature*:

> [N]ature is not to be looked on, as a distinct or separate *agent*, but as a rule, or rather a system of rules, according to which these agents and the bodies they work on, are, by the great Author of things, determined to act and suffer.[14]

The earlier organism metaphor and the picture of nature as itself nearly alive (with a soul) and acting on its own was replaced by a picture more suited to a dependent object, an artifact, obeying laws decreed for it. That picture was the *machine* metaphor – nature as purely physical and operating according to mechanical principles.

That switch proved to be enormously fruitful – indeed, modern science probably could not have begun without it. But what *justified* that switch? Surprisingly enough, early scientists appealed to theology here. Thus, Boyle (again in *Notion of Nature*) says that nature is

> like a rare clock ... where all things are so skilfully contrived, that the engine being once set a-moving, all things proceed, according to the artificer's first design ... by whose laws the grand agents in the universe were empowered and determined to act, according to the respective natures he had given them ... [T]his, I say, I think to be a notion more respectful of divine providence than to imagine ... that God has appointed an intelligent and powerful being, called nature, to be ... his vice regent ...[15]

That change and the theological justification for abandoning the older picture are explicitly expressed also by Cotton Mather:

> ... there is no such thing as an universal Soul, animating the vast system of the World, [as] according to Plato; nor any substantial Forms [as] according to Aristotle. ... These unintelligent Beings are derogatory from the Wisdom and Power of the great God, who can easily govern the Machine He could create, by more direct Methods than employing such subservient divinities ... It is now plain from the most evident principles, that the great God ... has the springs of this immense machine, and all the several parts of it, in his own Hand ...[16]

Notice that the change of metaphor is defended by reference to the new metaphor involving a more *respectful* concept of God and the old one involving a more *derogatory* concept of God.

The doctrine of God's creation and direct control of the cosmos, on the one hand, and the mechanistic conception of nature on the other, is explicit in Boyle's *The Excellency and Grounds of the Mechanical Hypothesis*:

> Thus the universe being once framed by God and the laws of motion settled and all upheld by his perpetual concourse and general providence; the same philosophy teaches, that the phenomena of the world are physically produced by the mechanical properties of the parts of matter, and that they operate upon one another according to mechanical laws.[17]

This idea of the world as an *artifact* also had a further crucial consequence, involving the status of experiments.

Experiment legitimacy

Since the cosmos was created, it was itself an artifact. But if nature is an artifact, and if we as image bearers of God are similar in activities, concepts, and so on, then our art, our products (artificially manipulating nature) are on the same continuum as nature. That idea is explicit in this passage from Descartes' *Principles of Philosophy*:

"I know of no distinction between those things [human artifacts] and natural bodies except that the operations of things made by skill are, for the most part, performed by apparatus large enough to be easily perceived by the senses."[18] That idea – that artificial, human-produced things and processes were except for their scale essentially the same as those in nature – was crucial for the development of modern science, because it suggested that the artificial experimentation done by human scientists was not distortion of nature as many Greeks (including Aristotle) had held. That meant that experimentation could be an important source of the reliable information about nature itself which we, because of our finitude, *had* to have in order to make progress in understanding the cosmos.

There was one other important implication of the doctrine of creation as it related to experimentation.

Experiment permissibility

Since the cosmos was a creation, it was not a *deity* of any sort, as many earlier belief systems and religions had held. The cosmos being a creation, an artifact, a thing, and especially not a deity, it did not have to be approached with fear or worship – it was neither inappropriate nor sacrilegious to try to understand it, to manipulate it, to pry into it experimentally. The only deity that there was – God – was transcendent over nature, not a part of or constitutive of it. Indeed, according to Christian theology, humans had been given *dominion* over the world, and had been given the task of *subduing* it. That idea of *subduing* nature included, for many thinkers, the task of investigating and understanding it – of subduing nature intellectually.

B Preliminary results (2)

Contemporary historians of science generally believe that there were a number of essential developments which either triggered, or were at least key necessary conditions for, the rise of science. Most agree that the emphasis on empirical observation, the importance of deliberate experimentation, and thinking of nature as mechanical were indispensable for the birth of modern science. That meant that the earlier view of the cosmos as ruled by *necessities* had to be replaced by a view of the cosmos and its structure as contingent; that the earlier view that deliberate manipulation of nature generated distortion had to be replaced by the view that deliberate experimentation revealed genuine facts of nature; and that the earlier view of nature as a being or a deity had to be replaced by a view of nature as an object. As we now see, various aspects of and implications of the Christian doctrine of creation provided the resources and the motivation for rejecting each of those earlier views, and also provided materials or suggestions for constructing the needed alternative views. The transitions in question were all explicitly drawn by various key early scientists, who explicitly made the connections between their Christian doctrine, rejection of the earlier views, and acceptance of the new views.

III "Why there?"

That at least *suggests* that the answer to our original question – "why did modern science begin *there*? why Western Europe?" was that this the only location where there were available conceptual conditions necessary to allow the required intellectual and methodological developments. That is obviously not to say that science could only be pursued in a context shaped by a Christian doctrine of creation, or that even in principle modern science could only have arisen in such a context. Nor is it to say that there were not a multitude of other necessary conditions. But as a historical fact it was only in Western Europe that the conditions necessary for its beginnings were in place, and as a historical fact some of those conditions grew out of a Christian theological context. It is worth noting that Paul Davies, an important figure in contemporary physics, and not, as far as I know, a Christian himself, recently remarked: "Science began as an outgrowth of theology, and all scientists, whether atheists or theists ... accept an essentially theological worldview."[19]

If Davies is correct, it may be that even if science had somehow begun completely independently of any religious influence, the structure it would have to have taken would nonetheless be parallel to that which Christian theology would have given it.

IV "Why then?"

What of the related question – why did modern science begin just *then*? – why the sixteenth and seventeenth centuries? Why not earlier? After all, the Christian tradition had been dominant in Western Europe for centuries prior to the actual rise of modern science. This second question is a bit more difficult, but in broad outline I think that we can answer it as well. Although some other key factors also came together at that time, the sixteenth and seventeenth centuries represented the period in history where the key transitions mentioned above were firmly enough in place for modern science to emerge. The three Greek outlooks mentioned above had to be replaced, and that turned out not to be as easy as might have been expected. The reason was that – as already noted – the general Greek conceptual structure was incorporated deeply into Western Christian theology, by such extremely influential Christian thinkers as Augustine and Aquinas. Various strands of Greek thought were so firmly entrenched that in some Western universities in the thirteenth century one could actually be fined for simply disagreeing with Aristotle, and it was possible to get into legal trouble for attacking Aristotle as late as 1543 – the year, oddly enough, when Copernicus' book was published. For the necessary changes to occur, that tight grip had to be broken, and new ways of thinking had to be worked out and accepted. That process was complicated by the fact that the secular, religious, and academic authorities were in general firmly committed to the reigning blend of Greek thought and Christian theology, and thus change had to come in part from less influential, less powerful sources outside various official authority hierarchies.

The process took some time, but a number of historians of science believe that the real *beginning* of the breaking of the grip of Greek thought can be precisely dated to 1277, and precisely located in Paris. According to the historian of science Pierre Duhem:

> If we had to assign a date for the birth of modern science, we should undoubtedly choose the year 1277, when the bishop of Paris solemnly proclaimed that there could exist many worlds, and that the ensemble of celestial spheres could, without contradiction, be moved in a straight line.[20]

Exactly why would Duhem say that?

Although Aquinas's blend of Christian theology and Aristotelian thought was powerfully influential, the fit between the two was in some areas not very smooth. The tensions became problematic enough that in 1277 the Bishop of Paris issued an official Church Condemnation of 219 principles – most of them related to Aristotle or to Aquinas' combined system of Aristotle and Christian theology. Although the 219 principles ranged rather widely, the primary focus was on the idea that since fundamental principles of rationality were logically necessary, and since God was fully rational, then God *had* to create and govern the cosmos in ways strictly dictated by those principles of rationality. The Bishop rejected that as infringing on God's sovereign *freedom* to create and to govern what and how He freely chose. If that insistence on God's freedom in creating was indeed the beginning of the events and changes that ultimately led to modern natural science, then the ultimate triggering event in the rise of modern science was a religious document issued by a Christian bishop on a specific dispute over one aspect of the Christian doctrine of creation.

V Other Implications and Parallels

The Christian doctrine of creation also provided justification for a variety of other essential – but perhaps less unique – principles and components of science and scientific method. I will very briefly discuss a few of those.

Laws of nature

The change from the metaphor of organism to that of machine was not merely a small change in the mental picture of nature, but had deeper consequences. Organisms act from their own *inner* principles, whereas machines simply *obey* the laws that govern them or are *imposed* on them. The shift in metaphor from organism to machine was thus associated with the idea of things in nature being wholly subject to laws. The concept of nature as strictly law-governed is essential to science. Where did such laws originate? Since the cosmos had come into existence and continued in existence by God's decree and command, some scientists saw God's decrees as the source of natural law. (Voluntarism, remember, suggested that there were no laws *prior* to God's creational decrees.) For example Boyle in his *Notion of Nature* says: "The nature of this or that body is but the law of God prescribed to it [and] to speak properly, a law [is] but a notional rule of acting according to the declared will of a superior."[21] Others argued that what we take to be "natural laws" were actually just descriptions of God's own ongoing direct activities in governing the world. For example, Charles Kingsley: "there are no laws of Nature, but merely customs of God."[22]

In any case, the character of natural laws as in some sense normative for nature (*nomologically* necessary) and the foundation of natural laws were also located in their arising from God's sovereign decrees.[23]

Uniformity of natural law

The creations of a person typically reflect some of the character of that person. Given the Christian doctrine of God's faithfulness and unchanging reliability, one would expect that in a cosmos created by God there would be pattern, consistency, and *uniformity*. The principle of the uniformity of nature is, of course, absolutely essential to science, to inductive inference, and so forth. Newton's spokesman, Samuel Clarke, linked that uniformity to God: "… what men commonly call the course of nature … is nothing else but the will of God producing certain effects in a continued, constant, and uniform manner."[24]

But what exactly underpins that reliable uniformity? Here again we find justifications in terms of theological doctrines – the following one from the late fifteenth century: "[God rules nature with] an unfailing [conditional] necessity … appropriate to God … because of his promise, that is, his covenant, or established law."[25] God's promise – his covenant of faithfulness – is here applied to nature itself as a foundation for the uniformity of the principles of God's governance – the laws of nature. This instance is particularly interesting, since it is less plausible to claim that this is merely an after-the-fact co-opting of theology as a rationalization for something already scientifically entrenched. And, of course, the Condemnation of 1277 can not be viewed as theology conforming itself to match modern science, because (a) it occurred long before modern science, and (b) it was in flat defiance of the reigning Aristotelian science of the time.

The same connection was made in William Ames's 1623 work, *The Marrow of Theology,* where he speaks of

> the establishment of law and order, which is to be observed perpetually in the thing to which ordaining power applies. The constancy of God shines forth in that he would have all creatures observe their order, not for days or years but to the end of the world.[26]

Ames was not a scientist, but his book *Marrow* was extremely influential. It went through about 17 editions in several languages, and was for a time required reading for divinity students at such schools as Leiden, Harvard, and Yale.

Universality of natural law

Science requires the principle that the laws of nature hold universally, and Newton believed that principle was justified in theistic terms:

> If there be an universal life and all space be the sensorium of a thinking being [God] who by immediate presence perceives all things in it [then] the laws of motion arising from life or will may be of universal extent.[27]

There were a variety of other more indirect scientifically positive inputs from Christian doctrine, three of which briefly follow.

The creation as good

Since in the Bible God had declared the creation to be good, examining and exploring the physical realm would not degrade one, as some Greeks and even some medieval thinkers had believed. The creation was fully real, and fully legitimate, and according to many Christians, part of the very *reason* humans had been created was to work with physical things – specifically, to tend the earth and to be caretakers of the earth. And Christ was raised in the family of a carpenter, and a number of his leading disciples were fishermen. The doctrine of the goodness of the creation removed one previous barrier to doing science.

The creation as worth studying

Since the cosmos was a creation of God, and represented God's own work, it was *worth* studying. In fact, some Christians saw investigation of the creation as itself having *religious* significance – learning to appreciate what God had done – and they saw scientific work itself as a type of religious obedience to God. That was all the more true if the Biblical command to subdue the earth included (or at least depended upon) bringing nature under human comprehension and understanding, as some Christians believed.

Furthermore, many believed that since God had created and designed the cosmos, study of it could even teach us about God himself. That intuition underlay the whole 'natural theology' movement of the early 19th century and had provided important motivation for some earlier scientific efforts as well. For instance, in a 1692 letter to Richard Bentley, Newton said:

> When I wrote my Treatise about our system [the *Principia*] I had an eye upon such principles as might work with considering men, for the belief of a deity, and nothing can rejoice me more than to find it useful for that purpose.[28]

Science as "good work"

Religious belief provided not only a legitimation (a sanction) but a further motivation for some scientific efforts, construing them as good works and as obedience to various divine mandates – and perhaps even as evidences of salvation.

VI Conclusion

During the past century or so in the West it has been frequently claimed that religious institutions and religious belief have hindered science, or have even been completely opposed to and inconsistent with a scientific outlook. While it is certainly true that there have been various – sometimes serious – tensions in relations between science and religion, it is worth keeping firmly in mind that given the path which human history has actually taken, had there been no Christian intellectual context, there might well have been no modern science, or its rise might at least have been much later and more difficult than it was.

In the next chapter I will look more directly at the familiar claim that science has destroyed the rational legitimacy of religious belief.

Notes

1   There have been disputes historically within the Christian community over whether or not the basic laws of logic constituted boundaries within which God had to work. We need not settle that question for present purposes, but one can read "constraints" as "substantive constraints" if so desired.

2   Robert Boyle, "Some considerations about the Reasonableness of Reason and Religion", Vol. 8, p. 251–2. In Michael Hunter and Edward Davis (eds.), *The Works of Robert Boyle* (London: Pickering and Chato, 1999–2000).

3   Robert Boyle, "The Christian Virtuoso," Appendix I, in Hunter and Davis, *Works of Robert Boyle*, vol. 12, p. 423. This basic idea can be found earlier, of course – e.g., Occam, Nehemiah Grew (discoverer of the fact that plants reproduced sexually), and others.

4   Roger Cotes, Preface to the second edition of Newton's *Principia*, reprinted in H. S. Thayer (ed.), *Newton's Philosophy of Nature* (New York: Hafner, 1953, pp. 116–134), pp. 132–3 (my emphasis). There are at least suggestions in early literature that our empirical faculties might have been intended precisely for that purpose. For instance, Bacon in *Refutation of Philosophies*:

> [God] did not give you reliable and trustworthy senses in order that you might study the writings of a few men. Study the Heaven and the Earth, the works of God Himself, and do so while

celebrating His praises and singing hymns to your Creator. (*The Philosophy of Francis Bacon*, trans. Benjamin Farrington. Liverpool University Press, 1964, p. 107)

The idea as well that empirical investigation could be a reliable route to truth was held by earlier pioneers – e.g., Buridan in the fourteenth century.

5   Quoted in Gerald Holton, *Thematic Origins of Scientific Thought: Kepler to Einstein* (Cambridge, MA: Harvard University Press, 1988), p. 84 (p. 68 revised edition).

6   Quoted in Christopher Kaiser, *Toward a Theology of Scientific Endeavor* (Aldershot: Ashgate, 2007), p. 144.

7   Galileo, *Dialogue Concerning the Two Chief World Systems*, trans. Stillman Drake (Berkeley: University of California Press, 1967), p. 104.

8   Thomas Aquinas, *Summa Theologica*, Ia Q93 A6 (Allen, Texas: Christian Classics, 1948), vol. I, p. 473.

9   Roger Cotes, Preface, p. 133.

10   Francis Bacon, Preface to *Magna Instauratio*, in Robert Foster Jones (ed.), *Essays, Advancement of Learning, New Atlantis, and other pieces* (New York: Odyssey, 1937), p. 264.

11   The doctrine of voluntarism was taken as implying that empirical investigation was *essential*, but the doctrine of creation *ex nihilo* was also apparently taken by some as implying that empirical investigation could be *adequate*. A being (e.g., a demiurge) trying to impose intelligibility on preexisting, independently existing, and recalcitrant matter could not do so wholly successfully. The governing principles would thus not be truly reflected in physical things and getting to the truth would require somehow going to a level *beyond* the empirical. However, in creating out of nothing, an omnipotent God could obviously create matter precisely appropriate for the purpose, and thus the relevant governing principles would be perfectly exemplified in the things created, and it would not be necessary to go beyond the empirical to discover them. That was, perhaps, seen by some as a good thing, because according to, for example, Descartes, we could not understand God's deeper purposes in the creation, since God's purposes were much too far beyond us. See Foster, *Essays*, on these general points.

12   This combination of characteristics has been linked by some to the Galilean and Keplerian insistence both that nature does admit of systematic mathematical description (rationality), but that which mathematical description (or later, which mathematics) is actually correct must be determined and checked empirically (voluntarism). See Michael Foster, *Mind* 1936.

13   Francis Bacon, *The Advancement of Learning*, ed. William Aldis Wright (Oxford: Clarendon Press, 1900), p. 109.

14   Robert Boyle, *A Free Inquiry into the Vulgarly Receiv'd Notion of Nature*. in Hunter and Davis, *Works of Robert Boyle*, vol. 10, p. 523 (my emphasis).

15   Ibid., p. 448.

16   Cotton Mather, *The Christian Philosopher*, ed. Winton Solberg (Urbana: University of Illinois Press, 1994), p. 94.

17   Robert Boyle, *The Excellency and Grounds of the Mechanical Hypothesis*, in Hunter and Davis, *Works of Robert Boyle*, vol. 8, p. 104.

18   René Descartes, *Principles of Philosophy*, trans. V. R. Miller and R. P. Miller (Dordrecht: Reidel, 1983), Part IV, Article 203, p. 285.

19   Paul Davies, *Are We Alone?* (New York: Basic Books, 1996), p. 138.

20   Pierre Duhem, *Etudes sur Leonard de Vinci* (Paris: A. Hermann, 1906–13), vol. ii, p. 412.

21   Robert Boyle, *A Free Enquiry into the Vulgarly Received Notion of Nature*, ed. Edward Davis, and Michael Hunter (Cambridge: Cambridge University Press, 1996), p. 24.

22   *Charles Kingsley: His Letters and Life*, ed. Francis Kingsley (London: King and Co., 1877), Vol. II, p. 67.

23   This sort of "legal" terminology was already being used by late medieval times, in for example, Buridan and Occam.

24   Samuel Clarke, *A Demonstration of the Being and Attributes of God, and other Writings*, ed. E. Vailati (Cambridge: Cambridge University Press, 1998), p. 149.

25   Robert Holcot, *Super Libros Sapientiae.* Quoted in Heiko Oberman, *Forerunners of the Reformation* (Cambridge: James Clarke Company, 2002), p. 149.

26   William Ames, *The Marrow of Theology*, ed. John Eusden (Grand Rapids, MI: Baker, 1997). p. 104.

27   This statement is contained in an unpublished draft of Query 31 of the *Opticks*. Quoted in John Hedley Brooke, *Science and Religion: Some Historical Perspectives* (Cambridge: Cambridge University Press, 1991), p. 139.

28   *Isaac Newton's Papers and Letters on Natural Philosophy*, ed. I. B. Cohen (Cambridge, MA: Harvard University Press, 1958), p. 280. And Kepler, in *Mysterium Cosmographicum* says:

   There were three things in particular about which I persistently sought the reasons why they were such and not otherwise: the number, the size and the motion of the circles. That I dared so much was due to the splendid harmony of those things which are at rest, the sun, the fixed stars and the intermediate space, with God the Father, and the Son, and the Holy Spirit. (*Johannes Kepler: Mysterium Cosmographicum*, trans. A. M. Duncan. New York: Abaris Books, 1981, p. 63).

Appendix

Some implications of the doctrine of creation and the doctrine of divine voluntarism:

Nature is created with God's wisdom
   so Nature is intelligible in itself
Nature is contingent
   so science must depend upon observation
   and science must be empirical
Humans are created in God's image
   so human minds are capable of understanding truths about nature
   i.e., Nature is intelligible to humans
   and human senses are capable of reporting truths about nature
   i.e., Nature is accessible to humans
Nature is uniform
Nature is coherent
Nature is subject to law
Natural laws are universal
Nature is an artifact (not a deity)
   so experimentation on Nature is permissible
   and experimentation can give is clues to hidden levels of Nature
Nature/the creation is good
Nature/the creation is worth studying
Nature can reveal to us truths about God

3

The Alleged Demise of Religion: Greatly Exaggerated Reports from the Science/ Religion "Wars"

DEL RATZSCH

It is frequently claimed that science has damaged, if not destroyed, the rational legitimacy of religious belief. Various authors cite a number of different grounds for that claim. Popular grounds include appeals to (a) some alleged basic presuppositions of science and scientific method, (b) the overall character of the picture of reality alleged produced by science, (c) selected particular scientific theories, (d) alleged historical trends in the interactions between science and religious belief, and others. In this chapter, I examine those and similar cases in detail, and argue that none of the popular attempts of this sort withstand critical scrutiny.

There is a widespread intuition that the continuing triumphal march of science has shown religious belief to be irrational.[1] In what follows, I shall examine some of the alleged justification for that view, and will argue that none of the anti-religiouis arguments based on science really work.

I Refutation: some preliminaries[2]

The worst difficulty science could pose for religious belief would be direct scientific refutation of essential religious principles. But refutation can emerge only out of genuine conflict, and that fact imposes some boundaries. For instance, many believe that science and religion operate in different domains or levels.[3] If such positions are correct, there can be no genuine conflict. Furthermore, serious conflict between science and religious belief is possible only if *both* purport to be true. It follows that science taken anti-realistically (instrumentalism, social constructivism, etc.) poses minimal challenge.

Suppose, however, that science can conflict with religion. Where would conflicts occur? We can separate religious claims into two rough categories – core beliefs shared by nearly every religion, and the more varied beliefs constituting the specialized, characteristic beliefs of particular religious groups. The core usually includes the following:

(1)   A supernatural person – God – created the cosmos.

(2)   God cares about humans.

(3)   God ultimately controls cosmic and human history.

(4)   God can intervene in earthly events.

(5)   There is objective meaning/significance to human life both now and after death.

There are only limited possibilities of science contradicting that core. Plate tectonics, stellar and biological evolution, the periodic table, relativity, quantum mechanics, or other such results of science do not even come close to contradicting any of the above. Evolution, for example, could be the means God used to achieve certain desired results, or the world could be quantum mechanical because that is the way God wanted the cosmos to operate. If those claims are *coherent* (whether scientific or true), then the theories in question do not contradict (1)–(5).[4]

The typically cited "conflicts" nearly always involve specialized beliefs outside the core, such beliefs often being ascribed to special sources of information (e.g., revelation). For instance, many believers historically took the earth to be stationary at the center of the cosmos. Some contemporary religious groups see the earth as quite young. Others take the basic kinds of organisms to be unchanged since the creation. These and other specialized religion-inspired claims are widely perceived as having been discredited by science. But would that be problematic for deeper religious belief? How would an antireligious argument proceed from there? One line of thought is that such refutations undermine the claims to "revealed truth" and that since even the deeper-core religious principles rest on that same source, they are thus rationally unsupported. A different line is that multiple consistent failures even of peripheral religious beliefs support an inductive case for the falsehood of religious principles in general, including the more fundamental core beliefs. Both will be discussed later.

Even if genuine conflicts were in principle possible, proposed refutations of religious belief would still have to meet legitimate rational standards. Antireligious cases resting on naive and/or inadequate traditional philosophies of science (for instance, broadly positivistic conceptions of science) will be of little beyond political, social, or psychological interest. And of course, science does not rigorously establish the truth or falsehood of theoretical matters even on its own turn. So even in the case of such conflict, it could not legitimately be claimed that science *conclusively proved* that religious belief was mistaken.

Antireligious cases based upon outdated scientific pictures (e.g., strict Newtonian determinisms) will be of little significance. The history of science is from one perspective a long history of enthusiastically endorsed scientific positions being subsequently discovered to be simply mistaken. For instance, when science abandoned strict determinism early in twentieth century, antireligious arguments resting upon that determinism were no longer viable.

Dismissals of religion relying on implicit co-opting of current climate of opinion are also of little philosophical interest. Just as there are music fads, clothing fads, and decorating fads, there are intellectual fads as well. Regardless of how effective in the contemporary academy, neither bald assertions concerning "what the truly educated person" or the "truly modern mind" can or cannot believe; neither allegations of what is or is not intellectually old-fashioned, nor the sneers of various intellectual idols are of particular importance. Thus, when Richard Dawkins in "Universal Darwinism" says (speaking of built-in capacities for or drives toward increasing perfection): "To the modern mind this is not really a theory at all, and I shall not bother to discuss it. It is obviously mystical, and does not explain anything that it does not assume to start with."[5]

We need not be impressed by that haughty dismissal until it is backed by genuinely substantive *arguments*.

II Foundations – Deep Conflict?

Science would challenge religious belief if there were principles essential to scientific method, scientific explanations, and so on, which were thus presupposed in the very existence of science, and which conflicted with essential core components of religion. For instance, Norman and Lucia Hall claim that: "Science and religion are diametrically opposed at their deepest philosophical level.... [There is a] fundamental incompatibility between the supernaturalism of traditional religion and the experimental method of science."[6] Is that correct?

The larger web

First, some cautions. Since most scientists historically were religious believers, we have to attribute intellectual blindness, self-deception, or hypocrisy to those scientists, who missed this "fundamental incompatibility." But classifying Copernicus, Galileo, Newton, Kepler, Boyle, Maxwell, Faraday, and their ilk, as imperceptive or as religious hypocrites violates substantial historical evidence.[7] And since a significant percentage of current scientists classify themselves as believers (about 40 percent in the US), and since even many unbelievers see no fundamental *conflict* here, the present charge would indict the majority of scientists who ever lived as not fully grasping what they were doing. That seems implausible.

Furthermore, any science-based case against the rationality of religion must presume the rational justification of science itself, including its foundational presuppositions – the uniformity of nature, the basic reliability of human observation, the appropriateness of human conceptual and cognitive resources, and so on. But science cannot straightforwardly establish the legitimacy of the foundations upon which it itself rests. If science is the only source of rational justification, then the foundational principles upon which science itself rests must be simply accepted on brute faith – effectively undermining a key purported distinction between science and religion. Otherwise, science's foundational presuppositions must obtain rational legitimation elsewhere. So science could not be the *only* source of rational justification.

Here once again is the argument in explicit form:

(1)   Science itself rests upon a foundation of a number of presuppositions

Thus:

(2)   Science itself is not rationally legitimate *unless* those foundational presuppositions are themselves rationally legitimate.

But

(3)   Science cannot operate unless those foundational presuppositions are *already* in place.

So:

(4)   Science cannot be the original source of rational justification for its own foundational presuppositions.

Therefore:

(5)   If science is rationally legitimate, then science cannot be the *only* source of rational justification.

Thus:

(6)   If science itself is rationally legitimate, then there must be some other *deeper* source of rational justification.

But what other source of rational justification – a justification on which science itself depends – might there be? As we saw in the previous chapter, Christian scientists in the past proposed religiously based solutions to justification problems. Historians of science no longer question the foundational role which religion played in the birth of modern science itself.[8]

Those foundations may be of more than merely historical interest. Despite centuries of development science may implicitly depend upon those roots even now. As noted in the previous chapter, physicist Paul Davies remarks: "Science began as an outgrowth of theology, and all scientists, whether atheists or theists … accept an essentially theological worldview."[9] If Davies is right, prospects for antireligious cases of the present sort are not promising, since science *still depends* upon foundational structures appropriated from its religious world-view heritage, and thus seems unlikely to constitute a refutation of them.

Cases

Let us nonetheless look at two examples.

1 Naturalism: philosophical and methodological

Again, the Halls: "Science … assumes that there are no transcendent, immaterial forces and that all forces which do exist within the universe behave in an ultimately objective or random fashion. … [N]aturalism is the unifying theory for all of science."[10]

But does science require philosophical naturalism – the assumption that the natural realm is all that exists? Many scientists – believers and non-believers – argue that science requires only *methodological* naturalism. Advocates of this position argue that whether or not reality includes more than only just the natural realm, science by its very nature can deal only with the purely natural and must rigidly restrict itself to that realm. For instance, Eugenie Scott:

> Science has made a little deal with itself; because you can't put God in a test tube (or keep it [sic] out of one) science acts as if the supernatural did not exist. This methodological materialism is the cornerstone of modern science.[11]

It is interesting that the deal science purportedly makes is with *itself*. Shouldn't science be making deals with *nature*?

A particularly forceful statement of methodological (at least) naturalism as a faith claim comes from Harvard biologist Richard Lewontin:

> Our willingness to accept scientific claims that are against common sense is the key to an understanding of the real struggle between science and the supernatural. We take the side of science ... because we have a prior commitment, a commitment to materialism. It is not that the methods and institutions of science somehow compel us to accept a material explanation of the phenomenal world, but, on the contrary, that we are forced by our a priori adherence to material causes to create an apparatus of investigation and a set of concepts that produce material explanations, no matter how counter-intuitive, no matter how mystifying to the uninitiated. Moreover, that materialism is absolute, for we cannot allow a Divine Foot in the door.[12]

On this version of methodological naturalism, science must pretend that what it cannot control either does not exist or has no relevant bearing on science, and so science must operate *as if* there is no supernatural realm.[13]

It is evident that whether or not there is a nonnatural realm, the methods science would employ and the results science would obtain presupposing philosophical naturalism would be *identical* to those it would obtain employing methodological naturalism of this sort.[14] There is thus no *scientific* reason for insisting on philosophical as opposed to this methodological naturalism – whatever the *philosophical* rewards might be.

The critic might take a different tack here, claiming that science does require the assumption of methodological naturalism, but that the continued success which science has achieved using that assumption constitutes indirect confirmation that the natural realm is after all the only reality – that is, that philosophical naturalism is true.

That move is sensible but not completely simple. First, science may not *require* even *methodological* naturalism. Science historically sometimes employed a nonnaturalistic conception of *law* as regularities in God's immediate governance of the cosmos.[15] A second reason involves what *success* means in this context. Most scientists do take methodological naturalism as a practical working principle. That means that methodological naturalism defines the terms in which acceptability of scientific theories is assessed. Thus if a theory is inadequate, it will *as a matter of scientific policy* be replaced only by some alternative theory which also meets methodological naturalistic criteria. Nonnaturalistic theories – regardless of how explanatorily powerful – will simply be ruled out of consideration at the start. Given this procedure, only "naturalistic" theories – whatever their problems – can ever be candidates for "success." The claim, then, that naturalism has a monopoly on scientific success is thus not surprising and doesn't really tell us much.[16]

In any case, conflicts between science and religion do not automatically mean that religion is in trouble unless we *assume* that science and its presuppositions takes precedence over religion and its presuppositions. That is a philosophical – not a scientific – assertion, and will be discussed later.[17]

2 The larger conceptual matrix

Richard Dawkins believes that religion's foundational outlook is profoundly misdirected. On his view, religion does have empirical content.[18] But unfortunately for religion, he says, the empirical expectations it generates are precisely wrong – science shows us a completely *meaningless* universe.[19] The problem is not just that some specific scientific theory associated with religion is mistaken, but that science shows us that this universe is nothing like the one religion would lead us to expect.

It is not obvious that Dawkins is right. (Even many scientists disagree with him.) Some would deny that *empirical scientific* results bear upon issues of *meaning* at all. And could we even in principle distinguish a purposeless universe from a designed, purposeful universe in which something has gone badly wrong (a familiar religious claim)? While Dawkins' intuitions here may be understandable, they are not rationally required.

In any case, if we do form religious expectations about the world, and if we observe aspects of the world which clash with those expectations, the problems *may* lie in our expectations. It is worth noting that nearly every *scientific* revolution has involved reality itself violating our previous best *scientific* expectations concerning the natural world. But that does not mean that there is some deep problem with science. (Indeed, it indicates that we are actually learning something from nature.) Our human expectations concerning the *super*natural world may also be far off the mark. And it must be kept in mind that the world also exhibits characteristics we would not expect *unless* it were supernaturally created – beauty, joy, complex detail, marvelous structures.

Science itself may have something to say on this side of the issue. Although controversial, cosmological fine-tuning is at least suggestive.[20]

III Epistemic Undertows: Dissolving Rationality

A number of "scientific" critiques of religious belief consist of

(1)   citing purported causes of such belief

then

(2)   claiming that those causes are not rationally legitimate.

While such considerations would not show the *falsehood* of religious belief, wouldn't they undercut its *rationality*?[21] Let us look briefly at popular versions of this critique.

According to Freudian theory, for example, religious belief represents wish fulfillment. We have deep, hidden psychological needs and terrors, and we construct emotionally comforting religious beliefs in response to them. But nonconscious, need-driven processes of forming beliefs are not rational ways to generate beliefs of any sort. That way of acquiring beliefs represents profound immaturity (indeed, neurosis), and would not produce beliefs accurately reflecting the actualities of the world and ourselves. Other critics of religion argue that religion is an empty promise of future compensation for present suffering whose true (societal) causes it deliberately conceals. In both cases, the belief-producing process is aimed toward something other than *truth*. The governing aim is psychological protection or psychological compensation. Both processes involve belief directed at something other than uncovering truth, and consequently do not deliver rational justification.

Success for this type of critique requires two things. First, there must be a plausible case that the proposed source of belief is in fact its actual source – which religious belief really *does* arise from fear of death, immaturity, or something like that. Such cases are not easy to construct. Freud produced speculative stories involving a hypothetical domineering prehistoric father and his conscience-ridden cannibal sons.[22] It is not clear that such unverifiable speculations constitute a genuinely scientific threat to religious rationality.

Second, such criticisms require a case for thinking that the proposed religion-producing tendencies are indeed unreliable – that they were not, for instance, placed in us by God exactly for the purpose of alerting us to spiritual matters. Showing that is not easy.

Several additional points are worth noting. This kind of criticism cuts in both directions. Some people may, as Freud said, embrace religion because of fear of death. But it is equally possible that some people embrace antireligion because they fear being held accountable in an after-life, or because they have difficulty dealing with the idea of some Being immeasurably superior to them, or because they cannot cope with being mere dependent creatures, and so on.

Furthermore, if Darwin is right – as most critics of religion believe – then natural selection produced the faculties and mental structures with which we form beliefs and pursue science. The governing aim of natural selection is reproductive success – *not* theoretical truth.[23] In fact, Darwin *himself* worried about his own theory undercutting the mind's reliability:

> [W]ith me the horrid doubt always arises whether the convictions of man's mind, which has been developed from the mind of the lower animals, are of any value or at all trustworthy. Would anyone trust in the convictions of a monkey's mind, if there are any convictions in such a mind?[24]

But if the governing aim of a belief-production mechanism being other than truth undercuts the rational legitimacy of the beliefs so produced – as Freudian and other criticisms presuppose – then *exactly* the same principle poses potential problems for scientific beliefs *and for antireligious arguments produced by* cognitive faculties developed by Darwinian processes which are ultimately pointed toward enhancing reproductive fitness.

Finally, the present criticism categorizes religion as an explanatory hypothesis competing with other hypotheses and thus having to answer to scientific criteria appropriate to such hypotheses. Later I will discuss one ground for questioning that.[25]

IV Conflicting Mindsets

Some cases involve psychological contrasts. For instance, Darwin's cousin, Francis Galton, remarked that: "The pursuit of science is uncongenial to the priestly character."[26]

The usual claim is that science requires an open, tentative, inquiring – even skeptical – mindset, whereas religious belief requires a closed, dogmatic, authority-accepting mindset. One mind, it is claimed, cannot easily be of both sorts. Nobel physicist Richard Feynman describes as "a kind of conflict between science and religion" the "human difficulty that happens when you are educated two ways."[27]

The claim is not obviously true – at least there are important exceptions (Copernicus, Mendel, and LeMaitre,[28] for instance, were priests). But even if different mindsets operated in different areas, there would not necessarily have to be conflict. Rational people have different traits in different areas. The first collection of traits – tentativity, skepticism – might be inappropriate and even irrational in the interpersonal relationships even of a scientist. The second set – tenacity of belief, even dogmatism – might be inappropriate and even irrational in anyone's practical pursuits.

Furthermore, the mindsets are not as distinct as critics would have it. Kuhn and others have taught us that certain degrees of dogmatism, tenacity, and similar traits are absolutely essential to the effective operation of *science itself*. Many scientists accept what they believe to be scientifically essential presuppositions as virtually non-negotiable faith commitments. Some hold specific theories pretty dogmatically – for example, the opponent of religion Richard Dawkins:

> The theory of evolution by cumulative natural selection is the only theory we know that is in principle *capable* of explaining the existence of organized complexity. Even if the evidence did not favor it, it would *still* be the best theory available.[29]

Obviously, Dawkins does not hold evolution just tentatively.

On the other hand, numerous religious traditions have valued – and devoted enormous effort to – reasoned justifications for their beliefs. In fact, basic theistic belief seems to be perfectly consistent with a 'scientific' mindset. There were those in the nineteenth-century natural theology movement who refused to accept religious authority and revelation as legitimate and who wanted to accept beliefs about the supernatural *only* to the extent that such beliefs could be empirically supported. Many of them were convinced that God's existence and some of His properties could be scientifically, rationally discovered.

V Historical Erosion

The problem science purportedly presents for religion is often seen not in terms of decisive confrontation episodes between the two, but as gradual historical erosion. Religion, the story goes, supplied pre-scientific explanations for otherwise puzzling aspects of human experiences. These explanations might in their time have been rationally defensible but, the story continues, science has progressively undermined all of those areas – religious conceptual foundations, explanatory resources, proposed explanations, and in some cases even the alleged phenomena "explained." Science has irreversibly eroded the conceptual foundations by making it progressively clearer that the cosmos simply does not match what religion leads us to believe. Thus, Alfred North Whitehead:

> [F]or over two centuries religion has been on the defensive, and on a weak defensive. The period has been one of unprecedented intellectual progress. In this way a series of novel situations have been produced for thought. Each such occasion has found the religious thinkers unprepared. Something which has been proclaimed to be [theologically] vital, has finally, after struggle, distress, and anathema, been modified and otherwise interpreted. ... The result of the continuous repetition of this undignified retreat, during many generations, has at last almost entirely destroyed the intellectual authority of religious thinkers.[30]

Dissolution by induction

One continuation of this story goes as follows. The various bits and pieces which have crumbled away from the religious conceptual scheme might not, *individually*, have been essential to religious belief, but added together over the longer haul they constitute a track record of continuing failure of religious beliefs.

Such objections are quite popular. Stephen Hawking suggests that explanatory appeal to God may no longer be appropriate even for the bare existence of the cosmos:

> [T]he quantum theory of gravity has opened up a new possibility, in which there would be no boundary to space-time … The universe would be completely self-contained … But if the universe is really completely self-contained, having no boundary or edge, it would have neither beginning nor end; it would simply be. What place, then, for a creator?[31]

1 Imploding the gaps

One common way of packaging this "what place?" challenge is the "God-of-the-gaps" picture. According to this picture, religious explanations flourished before science began to conquer the vast plains of human ignorance. But as that conquest got under way, religious "explanations" simply could not compete with the confirmable explanations produced by science, and were increasingly displaced by them. The available field of operations for religious explanations inevitably shrunk, reducing religion to fighting for its life in doomed rearguard actions from within whatever gaps in the broader scientific picture happened to be (as yet) unclosed. But even those temporary shelters are, if not exhausted, well within the current gunsights of scientific inevitability.

Such objections are not without surface plausibility, but they may be less powerful than their advocates believe. First, there still are gaps in our scientific pictures. Although there are recurrent claims that we finally have in hand all the necessary materials for completing the scientific picture (and such claims have a long and to this point unsuccessful history[32]), such promises rest upon optimistic induction at best and prior philosophical commitments at worst, and share the hazards such processes embody. Second, Kuhn argued that revolutions and advances sometimes reopen scientific issues previously thought to be settled. Since there is no guarantee that closed gaps will stay closed, closed gaps may be an unstable launching platform for critiques.

Third, it is not clear that religion exhibits an unbroken record of being driven into gaps in scientific explanations. For nearly two centuries, some scientists have argued that the fundamental empirically discovered structure of nature (natural constants, governing laws, etc.) can best – maybe *only* – be sensibly explained in terms of deliberate design and adjustment. Indeed, theistic sympathies raised by "fine-tuning" considerations get progressively more pronounced the *more* we know about nomic structures, incredibly tightly constrained natural constants, and so forth. Such positions have become noticeably stronger recently, and have attracted even some scientists who are not traditional religious believers.[33] There are, of course, proposed cosmologies which militate in the opposite direction – Hawking's view above, many-worlds theories, and so on. But such cosmologies are currently largely speculative, and speculative cosmologies have been quite unstable historically.[34] And keep in mind that some cosmologies – including some many-world theories – have been embraced by some precisely *for* the purpose of escaping what otherwise look like broadly religious implications of apparent cosmic fine tuning.

2 Creeping marginalization

I am all in favor of a dialogue between science and religion, but not a destructive dialogue. One of the great achievements of science has been, if not to make it impossible for intelligent people to be religious, then at least to make it possible for them not to be religious. We should not retreat from this accomplishment[35].

The perception expressed here by Nobel physicist Steven Weinberg represents a variant erosion theme. Perhaps science has not rendered religious belief completely irrational, but it does make explanatory appeal to any supernatural agency unnecessary – even pointless. Religion is superfluous because (a) its primary purported function is explanatory, and (b) any domain of actual reality it might claim to explain will ultimately be covered by science. That is guaranteed by science's potential explanatory completeness – a potential inductively supported by its continually expanding history to this point. So, Weinberg thinks, perhaps one can still accept religion if one wants, but one should not be fooled into thinking that religious belief does any essential explanatory work or is otherwise rationally indispensable.

Contention (a) will be addressed shortly. Concerning (b), we may need to be a bit careful. We must appreciate the power science has and the incredible things it has achieved. But we must not overlook the fact that perceptions of science's potential completeness are at this point projections involving surprising leaps, and some of the remaining gaps are worth reflection. For instance, few things are more familiar than the fall of a raindrop. Yet no scientist anywhere has ever accurately predicted – let alone observed, measured, and confirmed – the path of a single descending raindrop. There are, of course, readily proposed, perhaps perfectly correct, explanations for that. But the *fact* is that assertions of global scientific capabilities constitute an unfulfilled future prediction even for vast stretches of the most familiar, directly observable physical events.

One other point for reflection here. Those who advance an "erosion" picture assume that science drove the process. But that is an historical claim, and may not be totally accurate. On a closely related issue, historian John Henry says: "Far from being the predominant driving force in secularization, the practice of science itself was secularized as a result of influence from the wider culture."[36] The "credit" for the erosion may not be science's to claim – other perhaps not completely rational factors may have been driving the evolution of science itself.

Revelation

The claimed erosion of religion over time by science also factors into another popular critique. Suppose that some person claims to have a special source of supernaturally revealed truth, but that the alleged revelation is frequently mistaken in easily testable areas. Suspicion of the claim to special revelation would certainly be understandable – maybe even proper. (There is, of course, the possibility that the mistakes result from human misinterpretation of genuine revelation – not to mention the possibility that the alleged refuting scientific results are where the mistake lies.) But suppose that the revelation – even all revelation – were shown to be not genuine. Would religion have to abandon all claims of rational justification?

That follows only if the core religious beliefs rest solely on alleged revelation – now discredited – and is lacking all other possible rational justification. By "rational justification," critics typically mean argumentation, evidence, experiences, observations, explanatory hypotheses, and the like. Of course, some believers (e.g., mystics) have cited special sorts of direct experience. Others, during nearly every historical period, have constructed formal arguments. Such attempts are generally rejected by critics. The usual assumption is that any legitimate rational justification must conform to something like a scientific model of rationality.[37] But is that assumption correct? That question will be addressed shortly.

VII Conflict and Rational Justification

Conflict: limited significance

As noted earlier, some argue that science and religion operate in different arenas and cannot even in principle conflict, meaning that science *cannot* undercut religion. Perhaps that is true. But suppose that there is genuine conflict. What would the significance of that be? As noted, conflict would inevitably destroy religious belief only given the epistemic priority of science – and establishing that may not be straightforward for several reasons.

(1)   Although we often speak of "scientific proof," the logical structure of scientific investigation and confirmation precludes rigorous proof of scientific theories and results. That well-known fact is one reason why science is typically described as provisional and always willing to give up specific positions when necessary. The possibility that specific scientific beliefs involved in science/religion conflict are mistaken should not be over-looked.

(2)   Science is done by humans, and reflects human limitations. For instance, scientific theories and results are of necessity limited to reasoning, concepts, observations, measurements, and other resources which human faculties can, either directly or indirectly, connect to. Regardless of how far instruments, computers, and other aids can extend humanity's scientific reach, that reach must have traceable ties ultimately to a fundamentally human basis. The anchors of human science must catch there, because our human faculties and capabilities are the only ones we have, and without such connections we could neither grasp nor pursue our own science. Although we try – via the "scientific method" – rigorously to govern, correct, and test our faculties, reasoning, concepts, and theories, we have no alternative but to employ and ultimately to trust fundamental human capacities and insights. Claiming that we subject them to *nature's* verdicts does not circumvent the loop. After all, we must ultimately rely on *our* convictions concerning what constitutes a *scientific test*, on *our* convictions concerning what constitutes *passing* such tests, on *our* convictions concerning what the *evidence* of such passing does or does not include, on *our* convictions concerning what proper *evaluation* of such attempts involves – and none of these matters are just dictated to us by nature. Careful, methodical, and responsible as we might try to be, those matters *inevitably* have human fingerprints all over them.

(3)   Ultimately, then, we have no choice but to accept some deliverances of some basic human faculties as cognitive foundation for any human enterprise. But the cognitive faculties and intuitions underlying science are not the only ones we humans have – or if they are, they also underlie other characteristic human projects which may thus have ultimate foundations exactly as legitimate as science's. If, then, there *is* any deep conflict between science and religion, each side may rest upon fundamental aspects of human nature and each may have equally legitimate claims on us. In that case, science would have no more inherent claim to deeper allegiance than does religious belief. It may be that other dimensions of broader human existence (faith, loyalty, perseverance, love, religious commitment) *should*

sometimes outweigh commitment to the abstract, provisional, inductive, theoretical, highly indirect, only partially confirmed theories and hypotheses of the scientific dimension of human existence – and on precisely the same ultimate grounds that science ought some-times to overrule specific religious beliefs. That seems at least *possible*, and if so, then the mere fact of even genuine and irresolvable conflict would not automatically imply that religious belief should always give way to science.

(4)   The history of science itself provides a caution here. Historically, most scientific theories ever proposed or accepted by scientists have turned out to be incorrect, at least in detail. Anyone who had risked everything for nearly any scientific theory in the past would have lost everything. Future generations may well say exactly the same about present sci-ence. If so, then those who advocate the absolute primacy of science must either argue that at last *we* now happen to be the lucky generation that finally got things right (which seems both unlikely and overly self-congratulatory), or else they must base that claim of the abso-lute primacy of science on the prediction that although science has not yet gotten things quite right, it someday will. That latter means that theory-based scientific cases against religious belief rest partially upon *faith* in a promise for the future.

(5)   The implications of inconsistency and conflict are not always straightforward even within science itself.

a)   *Theory/data conflict.* Nearly every successful scientific theory is proposed, developed and accepted in the context of *known* contradicting data. That has been so prevalent historically that one historian of science remarked that *every* theory is *born* refuted. *Were* problematic data an automatic reason to reject scientific theories, we'd have to reject them all – and that would kill science.

b)   *Theory/theory conflict.* General relativity and quantum mechanics – two of the best theories contemporary science owns – are mathematically inconsistent with each other. But science has so far – *perfectly properly* – refused to part with either. Logical ambiguity is where we flesh and blood humans – scientists included – must sometimes live.

Rational justification: sources

The conception of religious belief as constituting an explanatory hypothesis competing with science, and whose rational credentials depend upon successfully meeting the criteria for such hypotheses, has arisen repeatedly in the foregoing. Is that conception correct? Very recently, some scholars have been struck by the fact that virtually none of our truly funda-mental, common sense, life-governing beliefs are generated by argumentation, nor are they mere provisional explanatory hypotheses or anything of the sort. Nor do we acquire or justify beliefs that those around us have minds, that there has been a past, that our reason-ing applies to reality, or that there is an external world, on some "scientific" model of argu-mentation, hypothesis, testing, and confirmation. *We could not do so were we to try* – as the long history of failed philosophical attempts (such as Descartes) shows. And belief that one's spouse loves one is neither a hypothesis to explain otherwise puzzling behaviors, some sort of induction, nor an empty irrelevancy. Furthermore, centuries of serious *skeptical* arguments from various philosophical movements have failed to make the slightest dent in our commitment to such pervasive and persistent beliefs as that we know that there is a real external world. Yet despite not having the support of formal arguments such fundamental beliefs are surely rational if any of our beliefs are. Rational justification here must thus have some different and deeper source, and artificially limiting acceptable grounds to explanatory hypotheses, argumentation, and the like, does serious violence to human rationality. That has led some "Reformed epistemologists"[38] to suggest similarly that those artificially limiting possible grounds of rational justification of religious beliefs to a set of "scientific" procedures which is demonstrably inadequate even for the world of ordinary experience may be equally mistaken. We may, they argue, have deep inbuilt faculties which generate religious belief, just as we apparently have deep inbuilt faculties which generate the bulk of our common-sense beliefs. (Indeed, the indispensable presuppositions of science itself may ultimately rest upon an exactly similar foundation.) Relevant assessments of rationality may in each case require an approach very different from more formal "scientific" ones.

If that proves correct, then some common demands – for example, that religious believers produce science-like arguments, or identify empirical areas in which religion withstands all empirical challenges – may simply be inappropriate. Any inability of religious believers to meet such demands may be as unimportant as the inability of any human to produce arguments for the existence of the external world, the minds of their friends, the reality of the past – or for the legitimacy of fundamental presuppositions of science itself. In none of these areas would any such inability alone establish the absence of rational justification.

VII Conclusion

I have not tried to show that a theistic worldview is correct, or that science supports such a worldview, or that there have not been historical tensions between science and religion, or that there are no present tensions. In fact, tension seems to be the natural condition of most truly open human projects – intellectual or otherwise. But making the case that science undercuts core religious beliefs is not as easy as some claims would make it seem. And if science really *is* to be our intellectual model here, as some critics suggest, then given standard claims that science differs from blind religious dogma in being tentative, provisional, and always prepared to revise in the face of new information and insight, perhaps some critics of religious belief should be a bit more tentative in their criticisms.

Acknowledgments

This paper is a modified version of my earlier "The Demise of Religion," in Michael Peterson and Raymond Van Arragon (eds.), *Contemporary Debates in Philosophy of Religion* (Malden, MA: Blackwell, 2004), pp. 72–87. Materials used by permission.

I wish to thank my colleagues in the Calvin College Philosophy Department, especially Steve Wykstra, Kelly Clark, and David Van Baak.

Notes

1   For instance, Julian Huxley:

The supernatural is being swept out of the universe in the flood of new knowledge of what is natural. It will soon be as impossible for an intelligent, educated man or woman to believe in god as it is now to believe that the earth is flat, that flies can be spontaneously generated ... or that death is always due to witchcraft. (*Religion without Revelation* (New York: Mentor, 1957, p. 62)

2   Additional discussion of several points can be found in my *Science and its Limits* (Downers Grove, IL: InterVarsity Press, 2000), and in "Space exploration and challenges to religion," *Monist*, vol. 70(4), Oct. 1987, pp. 101–13.

3   For instance, see Stephen Jay Gould's Non-Overlapping Magisteria – "NOMA" – principle.

4   It might be countered that this sort of reference to God is empirically empty and adds no *content* to the scientific claims in question. That may or may not be true, but if it is true then the proposition that *God made the world to be quantum mechanical* is logically consistent if the claim that *the world is quantum mechanical* is consistent. Religious claims cannot be simultaneously empirically empty *and* empirically refuted.

5   Richard Dawkins, "Universal Darwinism", pp. 15–38 in David Hull and Michael Ruse (eds.), *The Philosophy of Biology* (Oxford: Oxford University Press, 1998), p. 18.

6   Norman F. Hall, and K. B. Lucia, p. 27 of "Is the war between science and religion over?", *The Humanist*, May/June 1986, pp. 26–8.

7   We cannot just let these scientists off the hook by claiming that the specific scientific facts and theories which generated problems were not yet known in their day, if the conflict flowed out of the very structure and necessary presuppositions of the scientific project itself in which they were intensely engaged.

8   In fact, some historians of science believe that scientific method was developed *as* empirical and experimental precisely *because* as early scientists saw it, given the doctrines that God had created *freely*, unhampered by substantive constraints, science had to actually *look* to see how the cosmos was structured and governed.

9   Paul Davies, *Are We Alone?* (New York: Basic Books, 1995), p. 138.

10   Ibid. pp. 26, 27 (lengthy elipsis).

11   Eugenie Scott, "Darwin Prosecuted", *Creation/Evolution* Vol. 13, no. 2, Winter 1993, p. 43.

12   "Billions and billions of demons," *New York Review of Books*, Jan. 9, 1997, 44 (1).

13   As Steven Wykstra has pointed out to me, the range of what is considered "natural" could be different in theistic and non-theistic universes. That would imply that a principle that science can involve only what is *natural* is *not* equivalent to the principle that science must proceed as if the natural is all that exists, as Scott and others seem to believe. Wykstra is developing this point in a MS currently in progress.

14   Of course, if philosophical naturalism is not true, then assuming either philosophical or methodological naturalism in science may well lead science irretrievably off track, but that is a different issue.

15   Such views may even offer the *only* available explanation of unique logical characteristics of "natural laws." See Del Ratzsch, "Nomo(theo)logical Necessity," (*Faith and Philosophy*, vol. 4 (1987), 383–402). Those unique characteristics include their being located between material generalizations and necessities, their support of counterfactuals, and so on.

16   It is worth keeping in mind that the evidence in question (the claimed success of naturalism in science) is not only contingent, historical, and problematic, but that the conclusion it is supposed to support – philosophical naturalism – is *philosophical*. Such cross-categorial moves are not straightforward even under the best of circumstances.

17   It is often argued that methodological naturalism acts as an important safeguard against scientific investigation being shortcircuited by scientists being too ready to take the easy way out by citing supernatural explanations for phenomena for which genuine scientific explanations could be found were investigations to continue. That might be true, but even if it is that justifies methodological naturalism only as a *pragmatic* strategy, which has no substantive implications in the present context.

18   Dawkins says:

[Y]ou can't escape the scientific implications of religion. A universe with a God would look quite different from a universe without one. A physics, a biology where there is a God is bound to look different. So the most basic claims of religion *are* scientific. Religion *is* a scientific theory. (*The Nullifidian* [an e-journal], vol. 1(8), Dec. 1994)

And Julian Huxley again:

The supernatural hypothesis, taken as involving both the god hypothesis and the spirit hypothesis and the various consequences drawn from them, appears to have reached the limits of its usefulness as an interpretation of the universe and of human destiny, and as a satisfactory basis for religion. It is no longer adequate to deal with phenomena, as disclosed by the advance of knowledge and discovery. (*Religion without Revelation*, p. 185)

19   In *River out of Eden* (London: Weidenfeld & Nicolson, 1995), p. 132–3, Dawkins says:

[I]f the universe were just electrons and selfish genes, meaningless tragedies ... are exactly what we should expect, along with equally meaningless *good* fortune.... In a universe of blind physical forces and genetic replication, some people are going to get hurt, other people are going to get lucky, and you won't find any rhyme or reason in it, nor any justice. The universe we observe has precisely the properties we should expect if there is, at bottom, no design, no purpose, no evil and no good, nothing but blind, pitiless indifference.

See also Peter Atkins, *The Creation* (San Francisco: W. H. Freeman, 1981), pp. 17, 23.

20   None of this is to say that there is not a problem here for religious believers. In any case, religious believers, far from ducking this and related problems historically, have been among those most insistent on coming to grips with them.

21   There are a number of technical qualifications that would be required even for that more modest project, but I shall bypass most of them.

22   Sigmund Freud, *Moses and Monotheism* (New York: Vintage, 1958), p. 102 ff.

23   Thus, Patricia Churchland:

There is a fatal tendency to think of the brain ... as a device whose primary function is to acquire propositional knowledge. ... From a biological perspective, however, this does not make much sense.

   Looked at from an evolutionary point of view ... [t]he principle chore of nervous systems is to get the body parts where they should be in order that the organism may survive. ... Improvements in sensorimotor control confer an evolutionary advantage: a fancier style of representing is advantageous *so long as it is geared to the organism's way of life and enhances the organism's chances of survival.* Truth, whatever that is, definitely takes the hindmost. ("Epistemology in the age of Neuroscience," pp. 548–9 in *Journal of Philosophy*, vol. LXXXIV, no.10, Oct. 1987, pp. 544–53 [her emphasis])

24   See his July 3, 1881 letter to William Graham, in Francis Darwin (ed.), *The Life and Letters of Charles Darwin* (New York, 1889) n.p.

25   Indeed, the implications apply even to the faculties Darwin employed in forming his own beliefs that evolution explained the existence of those same faculties. One might claim that the successful track record of the Darwinian-produced faculties has established their reliability, but that is not completely unproblematic, given that the judgment of "successfulness" essentially employs and depends upon *precisely* the cognitive faculties in question. Also, the recent dismal fates of both Freudianism and Marxist systems might be worth pondering here as well. Other similar deconstructive critiques – e.g., postmodernism – also seem well on their way to dismal fates.

26   Francis Galton, *English Men of Science: Their Nature and Nurture*. (London: Macmillan, 1874), p. 24.

27   Richard Feynman, *The Meaning of it All* (Reading, MA: Perseus, 1998), p. 38. Even John Wesley noted this sort of difficulty (at least for some, including himself): "I am convinced, from many experiments, I could not study, to any degree of perfection, either mathematics, arithmetic, or algebra, without being a Deist, if not an Atheist." (From Wesley's sermon "The use of money", *The Works of John Wesley*, vol. VI, Peabody, MA: Hendrickson Publishing, 1984, p. 128)

28   It was LeMaitre who first proposed the Big Bang theory. Other examples are, of course, numerous.

29   *The Blind Watchmaker* (New York: Norton, 1987), p. 317 (his emphasis).

30   A. N. Whitehead, "Religion and science," in *Science and the Modern World* (New York: Free Press, 1997).

31   Stephen Hawking, *A Brief History of Time*, pp. 136, 141. See also Atkins, *The Creation*, p. 17.

32   For instance, Peter Atkins, *The Creation*, p. 127, says: "Complete knowledge is just within our grasp."

33   Furthermore, the initial emergence of this focus not on objects in nature but on design-friendly law structures underlying nature was not part of a retreat from Darwin (as it is frequently characterized), but predated Darwin by a number of decades.

34   The physicist John Archibald Wheeler reports one of his colleagues as advising people not to chase after a bus, a member of the opposite sex, or a cosmological theory – since, after all, in each case there will be another one along in about three minutes.

35   Steven Weinberg, "A Designer Universe?" *New York Review of Books*, Oct. 21, 1999, p. 48.

36   "Atheism," pp. 182–8 in Gary B. Ferngren (ed.), *The History of Science and Religion in the Western Tradition* (New York: Garland, 2000), p. 186.

37   Some – e.g., Nancey Murphy and Michael Banner – have argued that there are significant formal parallels between science and religious belief.

38   That group includes, Alvin Plantinga, Nicholas Wolterstorff, Kelly Clark, and others.

Part 2

God and Physical Reality: Relativity, Time, and Quantum Mechanics

4

Relativity, God, and Time

THOMAS GREENLEE

In this chapter I give a brief introduction to the contrasts between classical mechanics and the special theory of relativity. Then I discuss some consequences of special relativity. This discussion leads to some thoughts on God's relation to time.

Classical Mechanics

To many people the theory of relativity seems strange, mysterious, and hard to understand because many of the results violate our common sense, which has been built up over years and decades by observing objects moving slowly compared to the speed of light. A good starting point, then, for examining relativity is to review what our common sense tells us about objects and events viewed by observers moving with respect to each other. As you read the next few paragraphs, imagine an observer standing on the ground and another going by in a truck that is moving in a straight line at a constant speed. Both observers, we will assume, are in inertial frames of reference, frames in which an object stays at rest or in straight-line motion at constant speed unless the object is acted on by a force external to the object.

First, if the two observers have identically constructed watches, the "stationary" watch and the "moving" watch will tick at the same rate. If both watches were synchronized at a certain time, then they will continue to read the same time, no matter what the speed of one watch is with respect to the other. From this simple observation comes a far-reaching conclusion: there is one universal rate of progression of time throughout the universe. For all observers time is progressing at the same rate.

Secondly, lengths will be the same for the moving and stationary observers. The two observers will agree on the dimensions of objects both along and perpendicular to the direction of motion of the truck. Both observers will see a meter stick as 1 meter long no matter what the orientation of the stick is.

Two events, for example two firecracker explosions, which are simultaneous to one observer, are simultaneous to the other. That is, the light and sound from the two explosions may not reach an observer at the same time, but the observer can, knowing the location of the two events and the speeds of light and sound, calculate the time of each explosion

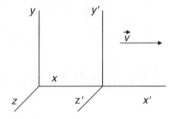

Figure 4.1   Graph of Galilean transformation equation.

and determine that the two events, to within experimental uncertainties, were simultaneous. If one observer so determines that the events were simultaneous, then all observers will, regardless of their locations and motions with respect to each other.

If the observer in the truck sees a ball flying in the direction of motion of the truck with speed u', and if the truck is moving at speed v with respect to the observer on the ground, then the observer on the ground will see the ball move with speed $v + u'$.

These are some things that seem self-evident to us, and based on these ideas a set of simple equations was developed to relate the observations of one observer to those of the other. These equations, called the Galilean Transformation,[1] relate the coordinates and time of an event in one reference frame to those in another reference frame. In Figure 4.1 above, $t = t' = 0$ when the origins of the two coordinate systems coincide. The $x'y'z'$ frame is moving in the positive x direction at speed v with respect to the xyz frame. Then the Galilean transformation is:

$$x' = x - vt \quad y' = y \quad z' = z \quad t' = t$$

Notice that the time of an event in the moving frame is independent of the position of the event in either frame; time is not coupled to space but evolves independently of space.

One of the great beauties of classical physics is that Isaac Newton's laws of motion have the same mathematical form for any two frames of reference related by the Galilean transformation.[2] The practical conclusion of this is that any set of experiments that can be developed that use Newton's laws will give the same results in the stationary frame as in the moving frame; if you are in a windowless room you cannot tell by such a set of experiments whether you are "stationary" or "moving." So there is no one definable rest frame; all inertial frames, no matter what their speeds and directions of motion, are equivalent with respect to Newton's laws.

In the late nineteenth century, however, it was discovered that not all inertial frames of reference were equivalent with respect to the laws of electromagnetism, in particular, with respect to the propagation of light. Maxwell's equations for electromagnetism can be combined to produce equations for electromagnetic waves. The speed of the waves, according to the equations, should be different in different reference frames if the Galilean transformation were valid.

To the nineteenth-century physicists, this made sense. Their view was that light, as any wave, needed a medium through which to propagate. The proposed medium, which was believed to fill all of space, was called the ether. Observers moving at different speeds with respect to the ether should see light moving at different speeds.

From these considerations came the idea for a profound experiment: measuring the speed of the earth with respect to the ether rest frame! In the late 1880s Albert Michelson and Edward Morley carried out an experiment to determine that speed.[3] Their result surprised their contemporaries: there was no detectable speed of the Earth with respect to the ether. After some attempts to retain the idea of the ether, physicists were forced to conclude that the ether did not exist.

Special Relativity

In 1905 Albert Einstein, working from theoretical considerations and not from the Michelson – Morley experiment, published what is now called the special theory of relativity. This theory does explain the Michelson – Morley experiment. Einstein based his theory on two postulates: (1) the mathematical form of the laws of physics is the same in all inertial reference frames; (2) The speed of light in a vacuum ($c = 300,000$ km/s) is the same in all inertial frames, regardless of the speeds and directions of those frames.

Many people have heard the second postulate before; in fact, they may have heard it so often that it seems easy to accept. But if we think about what it means physically, it is strange. For instance, consider the situation of a rocket that is speeding towards a person standing still. If a light beam shines out of the rocket's nose towards the observer, the second postulate says that an observer in the rocket, moving with the source of the light, will measure the same speed of light as the stationary observer does, no matter how fast the rocket is moving. Conversely, if the stationary observer shines a flashlight or a laser at the rocket, both an observer in the rocket and the stationary observer would measure the speed of that light to be c, again no matter how fast the rocket is going.

From the postulates of special relativity physicists can derive many surprising consequences. The first I will discuss is time dilation. In general, the time between two events is different in reference frames moving with respect to each other. For example, consider an observer in a spaceship setting off two firecrackers in the same place a time T_0 apart. The time measured between the two explosions in the "stationary" frame is $T = T_0/\sqrt{(1 - v^2/c^2)}$. If v is almost equal to c, T will be much greater than T_0. Therefore, to an observer on the ground, a clock in the spaceship will tick slower than an identically made clock on the ground. Many experiments have proven this behavior.[4] Unstable radioactive particles have a longer average life when they move at high speed than when they are still. Atomic clocks carried around the world on planes have shown the expected time differences with clocks on the ground.

This leads to a startling conclusion: there is no universal rate of progression of time! The times for different events are different for observers in motion with respect to each other.

A second consequence of special relativity is length contraction. A stick of length L_0 held in the direction of motion of another observer will have, in that observer's frame, length $L_0 \sqrt{(1 - v^2/c^2)}$, a contracted length. If the stick is held perpendicular to the other observer's direction of motion, both observers will measure length L_0.

A third consequence is the breakdown of simultaneity. If one observer sees two events as simultaneous, those events will not be simultaneous to an observer moving with respect to the first. For example, referring to Figure 1 above, an observer moving with the $x'y'z'$ frame will see an event at $x = 5$ light years happening before a simultaneous (in the xyz frame) event at $x = 0$.

The relationships between the "moving" and "stationary" frames that incorporate the special theory of relativity are called the Lorentz transformation.[5] They are:

$$x' = \gamma(x - vt),\ y' = y,\ z' = z,\quad \text{and } t' = \gamma(t - vx/c^2),\quad \text{where } \gamma = 1/\sqrt{(1 - v^2/c^2)}.$$

Let's look at two events that are simultaneous in the stationary frame. They happen at $t=0$ and $x = 0$ and $x = X$. If we apply the Lorentz transformation to these events, we see that the event at $t = 0$ and $x = 0$ occurs at $t' = 0$ and $x' = 0$. However, the event at $t = 0$ and $x = X$ happens, in the moving frame, at $t' = (1/\sqrt{(1 - v^2/c^2)}) (-vX/c^2)$. The farther right the event is, the earlier it happens in the moving frame.

Notice the drastic change between this view and the classical physics view. In classical physics, all observers in inertial frames will see the two events as simultaneous. Time evolves independently of space. In special relativity, space and time are intertwined. The time that an event appears in one frame depends on its location in another reference frame.

This time-space connection led Albert Einstein[6] to comment that in special relativity, "It appears therefore more natural to think of physical reality as a four-dimensional existence, instead of, as hitherto, the evolution of a three-dimensional existence." Our everyday experience is of the evolution in time of the three-dimensional reality we see around us, but that is not the most natural perspective for special relativity.

For completeness, I should include two other famous results of special relativity, even though for our purposes they are not as profound as the relationships between space and time. The first is the variation of momentum with speed. Classically, momentum is the mass times the velocity: $p = mv$. In special relativity, $p = \gamma mv$, where again $\gamma = 1/\sqrt{(1 - v^2/c^2)}$. As a consequence, as $v \rightarrow c$, $p \rightarrow \infty$, so it would take an infinite force to propel a mass to the speed of light or beyond. Therefore, c is the upper bound of possible speed that any object can have. This expression for momentum also leaves open the possibility of a particle's traveling at speed c, with $m = 0$ and yet having a nonzero momentum.

Perhaps the most famous result of special relativity is the equation $E = mc^2$. A plausibility argument (not a proof) is this.[7] A calculation, using the new expression for momentum, of the kinetic energy of an object that starts from rest and is accelerated to speed v gives the result $mc^2/\sqrt{(1 - v^2/c^2)} - mc^2$. The first term varies with v, and the second term is constant. This suggests (but does not prove) that the first term is the total energy and that the second term is a kind of energy inherent in the objects mass. We call this the rest energy of the object, the energy that would be created if the mass were somehow converted to energy. Because c^2 is so large, a tiny amount of mass, if converted, yields a huge amount of energy. For example: 1 gram of mass, completely converted to energy, would exceed the energy of a 20-kiloton nuclear weapon.

Relativity, God, and Time

It could be very misleading, I think, to look to the laws of physics to deduce something about God's mode of existence. According to the Christian theist, God made the laws of physics; He is not subject to them. However, the laws of physics can tell us about the nature of physical reality. If our investigation of nature is an attempt to "think God's thoughts after Him," then perhaps our knowledge of the laws of physics can give us a God's-eye view of material reality.

The picture given to us by relativity is of a four-dimensional reality, *spacetime*, in which the spatial and time parts are intertwined. In special relativity, the time interval between events in one reference frame is not, in general, the same as the interval in another reference frame, and the relationship between those times depends on the locations of the events.

Therefore, it seems to me that the picture of God's relationship to time most in harmony with special relativity is that God sees all events at all times and places, that He does not experience time sequentially, as we do. To illustrate this, I would like to start with a belief that all Christians, I think, agree with: at any particular time, God is present throughout space. Therefore, if in my reference frame there are two simultaneous events, even events spaced millions of light years apart, God is present at those two events. However, as we saw before, in the reference frame of someone moving with respect to me (let's call him Professor Stewart), those events are widely separated in time as well as space. Indeed, since God is present everywhere in my reference frame at a particular time, that must mean He is present at all times in Professor Stewart's frame. But if He is omnipresent at any particular time in Professor Stewart's frame and if He is present at all times in Professor Stewart's frame, then God must experience all times and places.

Many people are uncomfortable with this picture of God because it raises problems of human free will versus predestination. I will not attempt to resolve this apparent paradox, but perhaps I can address some of the cause of the discomfort. Just as our picture of reality is built up by our daily experience, our picture of God's interaction with the physical world owes something to our experiences. We are fairly comfortable with the idea of God's omnipresence at any moment of time, I believe, at least partly because most of us have had the experience of viewing large areas of space "all at once." We look down from mountaintops or airplanes, or we look up into the night sky, and we see vast reaches of space. However, we do not have the experience of viewing many times "all at once"; in fact, that expression is inconsistent because "all at once" is a relationship within time, and to view many times we would have to be outside of time. We can speak in analogies, for example, the analogy of being in a helicopter viewing a parade, seeing the whole length of the parade while people at a particular spot on the ground view the parade one small segment at a time.

The question of God's relationship to time is not just an academic or theoretical question. Our view of that relationship can have practical, even daily consequences. For example, the Christian theist's view of God and time can influence what the believer may pray about. Suppose that a friend of mine had an operation, and I do not already know the outcome. Does it make any sense for me now to pray about the result of that operation? If I believe that God experiences time sequentially and that that operation is in His past, then the answer to that question is "no.". However, if, in the language of Eleonore Stump and Norman Kretzmann,[8] my prayer is ET-simultaneous with the operation, then God, before or at the time of the operation, can certainly respond to my present prayer by acting at the time of the operation. However, the limitation is that I not know the result of the operation. If I know the result, then I know God's will, and it would not be useful to ask God to change His will.

My view of God's relationship with time will also affect my prayer about future events. Some would say that if God "already" sees those future events, why should I pray about those since they are determined? C. S. Lewis[9] answered that: If I pray, God takes my prayers into account in His whole creative act, which includes those future events.

Conclusion

The picture of physical reality presented by special relativity is of a four-dimensional reality (three spatial dimensions and time), with no particular inertial reference frame's having claim to being more fundamental than any other inertial frame. In my opinion, as a theist, the relation of God to time most in harmony with this picture is that of God's being independent of time, having created time and space, and viewing all events.

Notes

1   Arthur Beiser, *Concepts of Modern Physics*, 6th edn. (New York: McGraw-Hill, 2003), pp. 37–8.
2   P. A. Tipler and R. A. Llewellyn, *Modern Physics*, 3rd edn. (New York: W. H. Freeman, 1999),
3   Ibid., pp. 10–14.
4   H. O. Hooper and P. Gwynne, *Physics and the Physical Perspective*, 2nd edn. (San Francisco: Harper & Row, 1980), p. 648. See Beiser, *Concepts*, pp. 15–16. See also Jacob Bronowski, *The Ascent of Man* (Boston: Little & Brown, 1973), 255.
5   Beiser, *Concepts*, pp. 38–41.
6   Albert Einstein, *Relativity, the Special and the General Theory* (New York: Crown, 1961), p. 150.
7   Beiser, *Concepts*, pp. 26–8.
8   Eleonore Stump and Norman Kretzmann, "Eternity," in Edward Craig (ed.), *Routledge Encyclopedia of Philosophy*, vol. 3 (London, New York: Routledge, 1998), p. 423.
9   C. S. Lewis, *The Screwtape Letters* (New York: Macmillan, 1970), pp. 127–8.

5

General Relativity, The Cosmic Microwave Background, and Moral Relativism

THOMAS GREENLEE

In this chapter I discus the relationship of space and time in general relativity, the possibility of the cosmic microwave background's giving a universe-wide standard of the sequence of events, and the misuse of the language of relativity by those believing in moral relativism.

General Relativity

If space and time are intertwined in special relativity, their identities merge even more in general relativity. General relativity was created to deal with gravity and accelerating reference frames. These are the two main postulates of general relativity:

(1)   The laws of physics can be written in such a way that they are valid no matter what the observer's state of motion.[1]

(2)   No experiment performed inside a closed laboratory can determine whether the laboratory is in a uniform gravitational field or is accelerating. That is, if you are in a closed laboratory and drop a ball, you cannot tell whether it accelerates downward because you are in a gravitational field or because your frame is accelerating upwards compared with an inertial frame.[2]

A consequence of the second postulate is that, although light has no rest mass, its path is bent in the presence of a massive object. The path of light in an inertial frame would be a straight line. In an accelerated frame, the path would appear bent. Therefore, the path must be bent in a gravitational field. The bending of starlight, seen in the solar eclipse of 1919, was one of the first experimental tests of general relativity.

General relativity explains gravity as the consequence of warped spacetime around a massive object. The massive object causes the spacetime around it to curve. The curvature of spacetime causes objects near the massive object to accelerate.[3]

In special relativity, space and time are intertwined. In some instances in general relativity spatial dimensions can actually take on timelike properties. The most extreme example of this is in a black hole.

A black hole can, we believe, be formed when a massive star collapses. If the mass is around 3 or more solar masses, nothing that we know that can stop the collapse can provide the pressure needed to keep the mass from being drawn into a smaller and smaller volume by its own gravity. What results is a point of infinite density, called the singularity, which warps the spacetime around it to an unimaginable degree.

Around the singularity is a boundary called the event horizon. This is the boundary of no return. Objects coming closer than this are inexorably drawn into the singularity with no possibility of escape. Objects close to the horizon but outside of it have, at least in theory, the possibility of escape. Why is there no possibility of escape? One might think that the gravitational force is just too strong or that space is warped into curves that always go back toward the singularity, but those are not quite accurate answers. The reason why there is no possibility of escape within the horizon is stranger than science fiction, and it takes some mathematics to gain a clearer picture of that reason.

In the familiar Euclidean space of classical physics, small displacements of dx, dy, and dz in the x, y, and z directions lead to a total squared displacement of $ds^2 = dx^2 + dy^2 + dz^2$. In special relativity, the displacement squared between two events in spacetime, called the spacetime interval, is $ds^2 = c^2\, dt^2 - dx^2 - dy^2 - dz^2$, where c is the speed of light and dt is a small change in time. Notice that the time variation has a positive sign in the spacetime interval while the spatial variations have negative signs.

Near a black hole, general relativity tells us that the spacetime interval is[4]

$$dt^2 = (1 - 2M/r)\, dt^2 - dr^2 / (1 - 2M/r) - r^2\, d\varphi^2$$

where r is the distance from the center of the black hole and φ is an angle from a specified direction. Here time and mass have been multiplied by physical constants to give them the same units as length. The horizon is at $r = 2M$. Notice what happens to the spacetime interval at $r < 2M$. The time part becomes negative, and the spatial part becomes positive. That means that the spatial coordinate, r, which still indicates a distance from the singularity, has become timelike!

What does that mean from the standpoint of someone falling into the black hole? In our three spatial dimensions we can, with some mechanical assistance, control our direction and speed; we can move back and forth, left and right, up and down. However, none of us can control our motion through time; we are inexorably drawn through time. That inexorable quality has, within a black hole, been acquired by the spatial coordinate r. As explained in one classic text on general relativity,[5]

What does it mean for r to "change in character from a spacelike coordinate to a timelike one"? The explorer in his jet-powered spaceship prior to arrival at $r = 2M$ always has the option to turn on his jets and change his motion from decreasing r (infall) to increasing r (escape). Quite the contrary is the situation when he has once allowed himself to fall inside $r = 2M$. Then the further decrease of r represents the passage of time. No command that the traveler can give to his jet engine will turn back time. That unseen power of the world which drags everyone forward willy-nilly from age twenty to forty and from forty to eighty also drags the rocket in from time coordinate $r = 2M$ to the later value of the time coordinate $r = 0$. No human act of will, no engine, no rocket, no force ... can make time stand still. As surely as cells die, as surely as the traveler's watch ticks away "the unforgiving minutes," with equal certainty, and with never one halt along the way, r drops from $2M$ to 0.

In general relativity, observations of events and their times vary drastically depending on the frame of reference, and space can even acquire time-like characteristics within a black hole.

The Cosmic Microwave Background

Physicists, from their earliest education in relativity, learn that there is no "preferred" rest frame, that all inertial frames are equally valid. However, in the 1960s a discovery was made which presents the possibility, in principle, of comparing times of events and velocities of reference frames throughout the universe with one rest frame. That discovery was the cosmic microwave background radiation.[6]

This radiation comes to us from all directions in space. The spectrum and intensity differ very little with direction, and the greatest part of that variation, due to the Earth's motion, shows up as a shifting of the spectrum to shorter wavelengths in radiation coming from one direction and a shifting to longer wavelengths in radiation coming from the opposite direction. This is called the Doppler Effect. Therefore, it is easy to tell our direction and speed with respect to a frame in which the radiation would be uniform in every direction, which I will call the "rest frame" of the radiation.

Most astrophysicists believe that this radiation originated when the universe had cooled to the point that electrons and protons combined to form neutral hydrogen atoms. Since hydrogen is transparent, that allowed the thermal radiation that was present in the universe to travel without the interference from matter. That radiation was characteristic of the temperature of the universe at that time. As the universe has expanded and cooled, the temperature of the radiation has dropped, which means that the wavelengths have become longer and longer.

Now, imagine that two events happen at widely separated points in the universe. In principle, an observer at each event can measure the temperature of the blackbody radiation. The event with the cooler radiation therefore took place later in the development of the universe than the event with the hotter radiation. There would be uncertainties in the measurements of the temperatures due to the *Heisenberg uncertainty principle*, and it would be difficult to assign a definite difference in times to the events because of uncertainty about the history of the rate of expansion of the universe, but the sequence of the events could be determined.

Also, any observer in the universe can, in principle, measure his or her speed and direction with respect to the rest frame of the radiation. That would be true for any other rest frame, so that does not make the rest frame of the background radiation unique, but it is intriguing that the measurements with respect to the cosmic microwave background could be done so easily for any observer anywhere in the universe. However, there are difficulties in using this reference frame. According to relativity expert Don Page[7] of the University of Alberta, a system that uses the cosmic microwave background as a definition of rest does not lead to the choice of a time function and so is not useful as a choice of coordinates for cosmology.

Relativity and Moral Relativism

In relativity we say that observers in different reference frames see things differently. They see different lengths for the same objects, see different times for the same events, and if one observer sees two events as simultaneous, the other will not see them as simultaneous. There is no reference frame that is more correct than any other.

When we use language like this, it is not surprising that some people will apply the language to the moral realm. They will say: "See, the theory of relativity proves that there is no one valid moral point of view. Everything depends on your own reference frame, your own way of looking at things. So there is no absolute morality."

Not only does this argument err in applying a theory in physics to the moral realm; such statements show a misunderstanding of the basis of relativity theory. There are frame-independent absolutes in relativity theory. In special relativity, the laws of physics, correctly expressed, are the same in all inertial frames. The speed of light is the same in all inertial frames. In general relativity, the laws of physics, correctly expressed, are the same in all reference frames, whether accelerated or in gravitational fields or inertial frames. Therefore, there are absolutes in relativity theory, and attempts to justify moral relativism by appealing to relativity theory are mistaken.

Acknowledgment

I owe many thanks to my friend, Professor Don Page of the University of Alberta for his answers to many questions that came up as I worked on this chapter and the next one.

Notes

1   Albert Einstein, *Relativity, the Special and General Theory* (New York: Crown, 1961), pp. 97–9.
2   Arthur Beiser, *Concepts of Modern Physics*, 6th edn. (New York: McGraw-Hill, 2003), p. 33.
3   Michael Seeds, *Foundations of Astronomy*, 4th edn. (Belmont, CA: Wadsworth, 1997), p. 93.
4   E. F. Taylor and J. A. Wheeler, *Exploring Black Holes: Introduction to General Relativity* (San Francisco: Addison Wesley Longman, 2000), pp. 2–19.
5   C. W. Mismer, K. S. Thorne, and J. A. Wheeler, *Gravitation* (San Francisco, CA: W. H. Freeman, 1973), p. 823.
6   Michael Seeds, *Horizons: Exploring the Universe*, 9th edn. (Belmont, CA: Thomson Brooks/Cole, 2006), pp. 331–3.
7   Don Page, University of Alberta, private communication, Nov. 2005.

6

Quantum Mechanics and the Nature of Reality

THOMAS GREENLEE

In this paper I discuss two interpretations of quantum mechanics: the Copenhagen interpretation and the many-worlds interpretation. The possibility of a hidden-variable theory is discussed, and some Christian responses to quantum mechanics are presented.

Introduction

To illustrate quantum mechanics, following Feynman[1] I will use a system of two tiny slits separated by a small amount, an electron "gun" emitting a stream of electrons toward the slits, and a screen after the slits which will detect the electrons as they hit. According to classical mechanics, we would expect the pattern of electrons on the screen to be two thin lines where the particles would hit if they traveled in straight lines through the slits. What we find experimentally in similar situations, as quantum mechanics predicts, is a series of high and low probability areas we call "interference fringes." If only one slit is open, the pattern becomes a broader pattern called a "single slit diffraction pattern." These patterns are characteristic of waves in classical physics, so we say that the electrons display some wave qualities; there is a "wave-particle duality" in the behavior of electrons and all other particles.

One of the central mysteries of quantum mechanics is shown if we reduce the intensity of the beam until only one electron at a time is between the slits and the screen (see Figure 6.1). We still get the same pattern. Why? Does one electron interfere with itself? How does the electron "know" whether one or both slits are open; how does it know where it is or is not allowed to land?

One possible answer would be that the slits are so close together that the electron, which has a wavelength, is spread out enough in space to be affected by the opening or closing of a slit even though it does not go through that slit. However, another system governed by quantum mechanics shows that that is not the answer. That system is a beam of photons entering a Michelson interferometer, as shown in figure 6.2.

In this system, the pattern on the screen depends on the positions of the mirrors and the tilt of $M2$ with respect to the beam. Again, the pattern is predictable from classical wave theory. But if the beam is reduced so that only one photon at a time is between the beamsplitter and

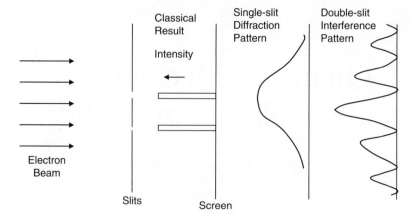

Figure 6.1   Illustration of quantum mechanics.

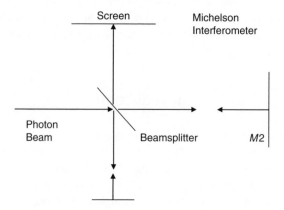

Figure 6.2   Graph of a beam of photons entering a Michelson interferometer.

the screen, how does a photon that reflects from *M*1 know the position and tilt of *M*2 and therefore where it should or should not land on the screen? Here the distance between mirrors can be several centimeters, much greater than the wavelength of a photon. If we were to put a detector in the path to each mirror, we would find that each photon would go down only one path, so the photon does not split and interfere with itself.

The Wave Function

The quantum mechanical explanation for this behavior is that there is a wave function associated with each particle. The wave function is a mathematical function of position and time that determines the probability that the particle will land in a certain area of the screen. The wave function depends on the placement of slits, whether one or both are open, and the locations and tilt of the mirrors in the interferometer. For electrons of the same momentum, direction, and spin orientation, the wave function for each particle is the same as for the other particles, so the same probability distribution on the screen governs the placement of all of the particles.

The mystery can now be rephrased: What physical interaction governs the establishment of the wave function? We say that the wave function exists, but we do not really know how it is formed. However, I will discuss two proposed explanations of how the wave function produces results in a physical system.

The Copenhagen interpretation

The Copenhagen interpretation of quantum mechanics is the "orthodox" position,[2] the philosophical position that has been the most popular over time. Let's return to the slits–screen–electron beam system described above, with only one electron between the slits and screen at any time. The Copenhagen interpretation says that between the slits and the screen the electron has no dynamical properties: position, momentum, angular momentum. The wave function contains all of the possibilities for those properties of the electron. However, when the electron is observed, out of all of those possibilities, only one is "actualized"; only one becomes a reality. This is called "the collapse of the wave function."

The more one thinks about this idea of the collapse of the wave function, the stranger it seems. The wave function is a complex-valued number, physically immeasurable, a mathematical construct. And the act of observation is said to give a particle a definite location and maybe other properties. Some people argue that the electron does not have an existence of its own but is just a correlation between two observable events, the production and the detection. And since a correlation is the product of the human mind, electrons (and other particles) do not exist apart from the human mind. Gary Zukav writes:

> "Correlation" is a concept. Subatomic particles are correlations. If we weren't here to make them, there would not be any concepts, including the concept of "correlation". In short, if we weren't here to make them, there wouldn't be any particles![3]

Some people extend this idea to the idea of the wave function of the universe, a function describing all possible physical events. But these probabilities are constantly being turned into actualities by our observations. According to Zukav,[4]

> Without perception, the universe continues, via the Schrodinger equation, to generate an endless profusion of possibilities. The effect of perception, however, is immediate and dramatic. All of the wave function representing the observed system collapses, except one part, which actualizes into reality."

Therefore, his argument goes, we are creating the universe by the act of observation.

> Who is looking at the universe? Put another way, "How is the universe being actualized?" The answer comes full circle. *We* are actualizing the universe. Since we are part of the universe, that makes the universe (and us) self-actualizing.[5]

Some people, then, conclude from the collapse of the wave function that we (the observers) are creating the universe and that there is no reality apart from what we create. A corollary of this is that there is no objective physical reality independent of human thought.

Most physicists still go about their work as if there were an independent external reality which it is their job to investigate. I know few physicists who deny such a reality. But, as Zukav illustrates, those who reject such a reality sometimes use quantum mechanics to support their rejection.

The many-worlds theory

In contrast to the Copenhagen interpretation, the many-worlds theory maintains that rather than a collapse from many possibilities to one actuality, what happens is that all of the possibilities actually happen![6] They just happen in different worlds. That is, at the moment of observation, the universe actually divides into many parallel universes, and in each of those universes one of the possibilities occurs. Imagine the uncountable physical systems in the universe. Each second there are many collisions of atoms or electrons, many photons going through holes or scattering around obstacles, with diffraction happening each time a wave goes through a hole or around an obstacle. And for each diffracted photon, the universe splits into multiple universes, in each of which the photon hits one of the locations allowed by the wave function.

Local and nonlocal theories

In the decades since quantum mechanics was first developed, many people have been uncomfortable with the Copenhagen interpretation and the many-worlds interpretation. The creation of infinite numbers of universes each second or the notion of a particle's only having definite properties with the collapse of the wave function are bizarre ideas, but the discomfort has often been at a more basic level than that. The need to use probabilities for systems that, in classical physics, were completely predictable has been repulsive to many people, including Albert Einstein, whose response to quantum mechanics included the famous quote, "God does not play dice with the universe."

One of the responses has been to propose that there are laws deeper than quantum mechanics by which we could predict completely the behavior of systems. These laws are called "hidden-variable theories" because the variables that would allow us to predict behavior precisely are unknown to us, and are therefore "hidden."[7] Quantum mechanics, according to this argument, is a partial description of reality, hence it isn't complete.

We can put hidden-variable theories into two classes: local and nonlocal. In local theories, information travels at the speed of light or more slowly. In my chapter on special relativity (chapter 4) I assumed that information was traveling at the speed of light or more slowly when I discussed the spacetime interval. This type of theory is called "local" because, for a time interval t, only events within a distance ct can influence an event at the point of interest. For instance, if I make a measurement of a physical system at a certain location, and a time t later someone else makes a measurement of another system farther than ct away from me, my measurement cannot affect that observer's measurement. In nonlocal theories there is some means by which information can travel faster than the speed of light, and therefore, for some theories, recent events far away can influence events here: my measurement could affect the outcome of the other observer's measurement.

Quantum mechanics is a nonlocal theory. In 1935 Einstein, Podolsky, and Rosen[8] presented a thought experiment involving measurements of spins of particles in a specially prepared system. Their conclusion, called the EPR paradox, was that some types of information in quantum mechanics could travel faster than the speed of light, that one observer's measurement of a particle's spin, even though at a great distance, could instantaneously affect the measurement of the other particle's spin. Therefore, they maintained that quantum mechanics had to be incomplete.

The Bell inequality and the resulting alternatives

Until 1964 we knew of no way to test whether quantum mechanics was a basic description of nature or the incomplete expression of a hidden-variable theory. In that year J.S. Bell[9] proved that quantum mechanics is incompatible with any local hidden-variable theory. He did this by proposing a generalization of the EPR experiment that involved rotating the two detectors independently and looking at the correlations of spin measurements. The results would be different for "orthodox" quantum mechanics, in which the particle does not have a definite spin component until a measurement is made, and local hidden-variable theories, which assume that each particle has a definite spin from the moment it is created, but that we do not know that spin until it is measured.

Since 1964, several experiments of this type have been carried out. The results are unambiguous: local hidden-variable theories fail; they cannot be true descriptions of reality.

In the words of David Griffiths,[10]

> It is a curious twist of fate that the EPR paradox, which *assumed* locality in order to *prove* realism, led finally to the demise of locality and left the issue of realism undecided – the outcome (as Mermin[11] put it) Einstein would have liked *least*."

It appears that the two options left are quantum mechanics (either the Copenhagen interpretation or the many-worlds interpretation), which is nonlocal, or nonlocal hidden variable theories, which are not tested by the Bell inequality. It appears that reality is nonlocal, that events far away can instantaneously influence events near us.

However, that influence is very limited. In a Bell's inequality experiment, both observers measure what seem to them random orientations of particle spins and make lists of their results. In a particular rest frame, Observer A, who makes an observation first, cannot control the outcome of his own experiment; he or she just measures the particle's spin. Therefore, Observer A cannot send a message to Observer B by determining the outcome of Observer B's measurement. Only after the measurements are made and the two observers compare their lists can they observe the correlation of the spins. To show how strange an influence this is, realize that in a different reference frame Observer B would make the measurements first, but this would not violate causality because A and B could not observe the correlation until they compare the two lists. So Observer A's measurements, in a particular reference frame, can be said to influence Observer B's measurements, not determine the results of individual measurements.

Possible Christian Responses to Quantum Mechanics

Accept quantum mechanics

First, I do not believe that Christians should refuse to accept quantum mechanics. There are philosophical difficulties with quantum mechanics apart from those I have mentioned, but we must admit that quantum mechanics has explained and predicted many things. There is no known physical phenomenon that seems to contradict quantum mechanics. If refutation of a Creator were intrinsic to quantum mechanics and an inescapable conclusion derived from it, then the theist would have to take a stand by faith that quantum mechanics is incorrect. I hope to show below that such a refutation is not inevitable if one accepts quantum mechanics. Therefore, it is more fruitful, I believe, to examine the assumption behind the claim that the universe is self-actualizing than it is to try to refute such an experimentally well-tested principle.

The use of probabilities

There are elements of quantum mechanics that are very compatible with Christianity. Under classical physics, in principle, once the initial conditions of the universe were established, once the forces were set up and the original particles given their positions and velocities, the rest of the history of the universe was predetermined. (Modern chaos theory has modified that conclusion, as far as our ability to predict the behavior of systems, but if the initial conditions are precisely known, the outcome is still determined.) A conclusion some people came to was that, if God created the universe, after that creation He was unnecessary.

On the other hand, quantum mechanics introduces unpredictability into the basic nature of matter. People now have to admit their limited knowledge and inability to control what will happen. When the uncertainties required by the Heisenberg uncertainty principle are combined with the predictions of chaos theory, we see that even for systems governed by classical physics our ability to predict is very limited.

The idea of an objective reality, independent of our minds

If we are to accept quantum mechanics at all, we have to be careful in the use of the words, "objective," "independent," and "external to the human mind." The interaction of the observed system and the observer, the dependence of the observations on what we choose to observe, are verified experimentally. Our decision to observe certain properties of the system will determine what other properties we could observe simultaneously. Once we make an observation, the wave function describing alternative ways the system could develop will not be the same as it would be had we not made the observation. So reality will not be "independent" of us in the sense that it will simply go its way unaffected by us.

However, saying that we influence a system is much different from saying we create it or control it. We can observe which slit the electron goes through, but we do not control which slit that is. Our observation of the electron's position on the screen "actualizes" one possibility but does not determine which possibility is actualized. We still have to accept the occurrences that nature gives us. We still cannot mold the reality to our will or desire or preference; we still must be in submission to it. That is, we still must bring our thoughts and actions into accord with the reality or live in unreality, in a dream world. It is an interesting piece of logic to claim that particles viewed as correlations are concepts that we create by our own reasoning. But my reasoning cannot determine what happens if I grab both terminals of a high-voltage power supply; the electrons will flow through me without regard for my desires.

The claim that the universe is created by us

There is a crucial assumption behind the claim that the universe is created by us, by our observations. "Who is looking at the universe? … We are actualizing the universe." The assumption is that we (and possibly other intelligent beings on other planets) are the only ones doing the observing. Therefore, the assumption is that there is no God observing the universe. If there is a God who is observing the universe and sees everything that has happened and will happen, then quantum mechanics gives our observations the same role they had under classical physics: we see things God has "already" observed.

There is another assumption in Zukav's argument that many physicists would disagree with: the assumption that human perception or consciousness is required for an "observation" or "measurement." What many physicists define as a "measurement" is an interaction of the microscopic system (governed by quantum mechanics) with a macroscopic system (governed by classical physics) in a way that leaves a permanent record.[12]

It would be fun to try to develop a detailed picture of how God works through quantum mechanics to actualize the universe by his observations. However, I do not think it would be best to base too much on such a picture because someday quantum mechanics may be scrapped. In talking about Christianity I believe it is best to base our claims and arguments on what cannot be shaken while at the same time refuting erroneous claims that are based on current intellectual fashions. In the case of quantum mechanics, the claim that we are the creators of the universe turns out to be based on the assumption that there is no God and on a very disputable concept of measurement, not on anything intrinsic to quantum mechanics.

The nonlocal nature of reality

At present, it appears that reality is described either by quantum mechanics or by nonlocal hidden variable theories. Both types of theories are nonlocal; they admit the possibility that information, at least in some special circumstances, can travel faster than light. This is unsettling to many physicists, but it should not be to Christians. We believe in a universe that is connected by the presence of God, filled with the presence of God. Therefore, whatever God observes in one part of the universe could influence what He does in another part of the universe billions of light years away. In theory, my prayers tonight could instantly influence an event in the Andromeda Galaxy, 2 million light years away. Of course, prayer about present or future events on earth does not depend on the nonlocal nature of reality, because light travels so quickly that information can reach anywhere on earth is less than a tenth of a second. But the basic idea of a nonlocal reality is one Christians can readily accept.

The things that cannot be shaken

A little earlier I mentioned that I thought it was best to base our claims for Christianity on what cannot be shaken, what is not just current intellectual fashion. I have to admit that there is nothing that I know of that is beyond any possible disproof, but there are things that have stood through centuries, even millennia. Some of those things are the historical evidence for the resurrection of Christ, the words and lives of the apostles, and the fulfillment of Bible prophecies. Some things that also encourage me are the times that I have seen God work in my life and His work in the lives of others. In day-to-day living, those things strengthen me more than the compatibility of Christianity with quantum mechanics. But it is reassuring that there is no conflict, I think, between Christian beliefs and one of the most experimentally tested areas of modern physics.

Notes

1 R. Feynman, R. Leighton, and M. Sanda, *The Feynman Lectures on Physics* (Reading, MA: Addison-Wesley, 1965), pp. 1–4.
2 David J. Griffiths, *Introduction to Quantum Mechanics*, 2nd edn. (Upper Saddle River, NJ: Pearson Prentice-Hall, 2005), p. 305.
3 Gary Zukav, *The Dancing Wu Li Masters* (New York: Bantam, 1980), p. 71.
4 Ibid, p. 79.
5 Ibid., p. 79.
6 D. Styer, M. Balkin, K. Becker, M. Burns, C. Dudley, S. Forth, et al., "Nine formulations of quantum mechanics," *American Journal of Physics* 42 (2002), 295.
7 Griffiths, *Introduction*, p. 3.
8 A. Einstein, B. Podolsky, and N. Rosen, *Physical Review* 47 (1935), 777.
9 J. Bell, *Physics* 1 (1964), 195.
10 Griffiths, *Introduction*, p. 427.
11 N. David Mermin, "Is the moon there when nobody looks?" *Physics Today*, April, 1985, 39.
12 Griffiths, *Introduction*, p. 431.

Part 3

Interaction Between Science and Christianity

7

Science and Religion in Harmony

DEBORAH B. HAARSMA

Some religious beliefs appear to conflict with some discoveries of modern science, including the Big Bang, the great age of the Earth, common descent of species, and human evolution. Some people claim that science and religion are fundamentally at war, but this is only one way to model the relationship between science and religion. Other models for this relationship include independence (science and religion each deal with separate questions), interaction (science and religion can speak to the same questions and influence each other positively), and foundational (religious beliefs can provide a philosophical foundation and context for doing science). Each type of relationship will be described using examples from Christianity, including the conflict between Galileo and the Catholic Church in the early seventeenth century. The foundational model demonstrates that adherents of different religions can collaborate on science successfully without denying their own religious beliefs.

Introduction

In 1633, Galileo stood trial in Rome for his view that the Earth moved in orbit around the Sun. The Vatican charged him with heresy, banned his book, and confined him to house arrest. Galileo's experience is used today as a prime example of the conflict between science[1] and religion, particularly science and Christianity. Yet when we look at this historical incident more closely, we will find that many cultural and interpersonal factors led to Galileo's condemnation in addition to the Church's objection to his scientific conclusion.

Nearly four centuries later, scientists around the globe are studying the natural world. These scientists hold to a variety of beliefs: Christianity, Judaism, Islam, Hinduism, Buddhism, agnosticism, atheism, and so on (I will refer to these collectively as "worldviews"[2]). Some scientists simply view science and religion as pertaining to different parts of their lives, and don't attempt to reconcile apparent conflicts between their scientific work and their beliefs. Others find that their scientific work has a major impact on their belief system (and vice versa), and strive to reconcile their beliefs with science. Scientists who are committed Christians tend to fall in the second group. Christianity requires that all of life (work, family, recreation, etc.) be governed by our belief in the God of the Bible, not just religious activities like attending church or praying. Thus, Christians find it very important to determine how science is related to their faith. While Christians do not agree on how the two are related, many believe it is possible to harmonize science and religion, in large part because we believe that God created the natural world that we study in the laboratory.

In this paper, I will discuss four models[3] for how science and religion may be related:

1) *Warfare*: Science and religion are in conflict, in historical and contemporary situations, due to their fundamental differences.
2) *Unrelated*: Science and religion are entirely independent and explore separate realms.
3) *Interacting*: Science and religion have some similarities of method, and can correct and enhance each other.
4) *Foundational:* Religion provides a philosophical framework needed to do science.

For each model, I will give examples from Christianity, since that is my own religion, but these models are also applicable to other worldviews. All four models are useful in some respects, but models 3 and 4 are more accurate and useful depictions of the relationship between religion and science.

1 Warfare (Conflict) Model

In the warfare model, science and religion have been in conflict throughout the history of science up to the present day, due to the fundamental differences between them. Two influential histories of science cast the interaction as warfare: *History of the Conflict between Religion and Science*, written by J. W. Draper in 1874,[4] and *A History of the Warfare of Science with Theology in Christendom* written by Andrew White in 1896.[5] White wrote: "Hardly a generation since [Galileo] has not seen some ecclesiastic suppressing evidence, or torturing expressions, or inventing theories to blacken the memory of Galileo." Both histories use the Galileo incident as the prime example that religion and science are at war.

While conflicts between science and religion have occurred in the past, warfare is not the primary interaction between religion and science. In most scientific fields (e.g., geochemistry, atomic physics, cell biology), conflicts between religion and science are barely mentioned. Many scientists are personally religious, and see no inconsistency between their religious beliefs and their scientific activities. When clashes due occur, they often are due in part (and sometimes in large part) to extraneous factors, such as cultural and personality conflicts or bad logic, rather than a direct struggle between religion and science.

Cultural and personal conflicts

Let us take the Galileo incident as a case study. The story is used frequently in discussions of science and faith and in introductory astronomy textbooks, so much so that the actual events are often forgotten. People argue that Galileo had incontrovertible scientific proof that the earth orbits the sun, but the Church was ignorant of science. The Church attacked Galileo's ideas because they could not be reconciled with the Bible,[6] and they didn't admit he was right until 1992.[7] But the actual events were much more complicated. Here I offer an overview of some of the circumstances which show this conflict was not primarily between science and religion.[8]

Galileo's observations were convincing proof against the geocentric model of the solar system developed by Ptolemy around AD 200, in which the Sun and all planets orbit the Earth. But his observations did not disprove *all* geocentric models. Tycho Brahe had recently proposed another geocentric model where only the Sun orbited the Earth, and all the other planets orbited the Sun. Galileo's data were technically consistent with the stationary Earth of Brahe's model, but he argued strongly that he had proved the Earth moved.

Galileo was himself a Christian. He was devout and pious in his beliefs and religious practice. He wrote not only about his scientific discoveries, but about how those discoveries were not in contradiction with the Bible.[9] He famously said, quoting Cardinal Baronius, that: "The Bible teaches how to go to heaven, not how the heavens go."

The tide of Church opinion was actually supportive of Galileo early in his career. The Jesuit scholars in the Church were very interested in his work, and once they had confirmed his observations themselves, they publicly supported Galileo. Galileo also had a positive relationship with various Church leaders, including the cardinal who later became Pope Urban VIII (the pope who condemned him). In 1614, a Dominican friar preached a sermon against Galileo, but the leader of the Dominicans issued a formal apology.

The conflict that later developed between the Church and Galileo was "a complex power struggle of personal and professional pride, envy and ambition, affected by pressures of bureaucratic politics."[10] Galileo's personality didn't help. By all accounts he was arrogant and short-tempered, and didn't hesitate to use foul language when talking about his opponents. This kind of personality would have made enemies regardless of his views! It had already made him enemies at his university, where his views on buoyancy and friction were counter to the accepted Aristotelian physics (this was well before his first telescopic observations and astronomical research). On the other side, the Church was on the defensive following the Protestant Reformation, particularly on the issue of Church authority. The Church was not so much anti-science as pro-tradition, opposing the Reformation idea that each person could interpret the Bible for themselves.

In 1642, Galileo died under house arrest, with growing interest in his discoveries from around Europe. That same year saw the birth of Isaac Newton, who went on to publish the universal law of gravity in 1687. It was this new understanding of gravity that turned most opinion in favor of the heliocentric view (clearly the Sun is the most massive object in the solar system, so gravity would cause all planets to orbit the Sun). The Church officially withdrew its condemnation of Galileo in 1992, but they demonstrated a changed view much earlier: in 1824, the Church dropped Galileo's publications from their list of banned books, and in 1891 founded the Vatican Observatory. The Observatory is still in operation today – Church funds support current astronomical research, a testimony to the harmony of science and religion.

Logic problems

Some apparent conflicts between science and religion are based on arguments that fall apart under scrutiny. For example, one modern conflict can be framed as follows:

Premiss 1: Christianity requires that the Earth is less than 10,000 years old.
Premiss 2: Science proves the Earth is billions of years old.
Conclusion: Christianity is false or irrelevant.

Christians obviously disagree with the Conclusion. The Conclusion doesn't follow from the premisses, since only one aspect of Christian belief is mentioned in Premiss 1. But many Christians have argued against the Conclusion by attempting to invalidate Premiss 2. Similarly, atheists will make their case by arguing for the strength of the scientific evidence for Premiss 2. Impressively, people on both extremes of the argument implicitly agree with Premiss 1. But, as I will argue in my second lecture, the problem is actually in Premiss 1: the Bible does not necessarily require the Earth to be younger than science has found. Similarly, other modern conflicts between religion and science often are bogged down in a false understanding of religious beliefs, or in unstated assumptions. In many conflicts, both sides assume that *either* science *or* religion must be wrong and do not admit the possibility that the two could be reconciled.

Another poor argument is the "God of the gaps" argument. The argument is framed as follows: Consider an event or phenomenon for which science has not found a natural mechanism, in other words, a gap in scientific knowledge. Many people conclude that the cause of the event must be supernatural, that is, God. But at some later date, scientists may find a natural mechanism that explains the phenomena, and there is no longer a need for God as the immediate cause of that event. As science continues to advance, the gaps in scientific knowledge get ever smaller, and the "god" of the gaps shrinks away, pushed out by science. For example, before the time of Newton, most Westerners assumed that God caused the regular motions of the planets. Then Newton discovered the law of gravity, and could scientifically explain and predict planetary orbits. Many people felt that God was no longer needed and had been replaced by science. The answer to this argument is to understand properly how Christians view God's interaction with the world: God sustains the physical universe, and it is only by his action that matter continues to exist and natural laws continue to function.[11] God is the ultimate cause of both the events that science can explain (for which we understand the natural mechanism), *and* of events that science cannot (yet) explain. The Christian God is not a god of the gaps.

Worldview conflicts

If a dispute between science and religion is stripped of side issues such as personality conflicts and bad arguments, is there still a fundamental disagreement? Proponents of the warfare model would say yes. P. W. Atkins, a lecturer in physical chemistry at Oxford University, writes:

> A scientist's explanation is in terms of a purposeless, knowable, and understandable fully reduced simplicity. Religion, on the other hand, seeks to explain in terms of a purposeful, unknowable, and incomprehensible irreducible complexity. Science and religion cannot be reconciled.[12]

J. W. Draper wrote

> The antagonism we thus witness between Religion and Science is the continuation of a struggle that commenced when Christianity began to attain political power. A divine revelation must necessarily be intolerant of contradiction; it must repudiate all improvement in itself, and view with disdain that arising from the progressive intellectual development of man.[13]

Atkins and Draper argue that religion and science have fundamentally different methods, purposes, and ways of determining knowledge, and conclude that this fundamental difference means the two must be in direct conflict. (By the way, very few scientists in my experience in the United States have such a strong view of materialism; Atkins is rare, not typical.)

I agree that there is a fundamental conflict here, but it is not between religion and science. It is between religion and the worldview of reductive materialism. This worldview claims that the physical world is all there is, God and supernatural phenomena do not exist, the only truth is that which can be proved logically or experimentally, and religion is merely foolish superstition and self-deception. Clearly materialism is a worldview in conflict with religion, but *science* is not in conflict with religion. Materialism claims that science has disproved religion, but science itself is not able to offer such philosophical proofs. Science is the study of the *physical* world, and finds models and theories which describe how the physical world works. Furthermore, it is circular logic to first assume that only the physical world is relevant (all knowledge is scientific), and then cite science as proof that there is nothing beyond the physical world.

Materialist arguments often take the form of "nothing but" arguments. For example, "Human beings are *nothing but* chemical machines, governed by their genetics and hormonal reactions", that is, the only relevant way to understand humans is at the physical level. But there are many valid levels of explanation besides the purely scientific.[14] In our daily experience, we routinely gain and use knowledge from other sources. For instance, we use non-scientific knowledge and methods to judge the trustworthiness of another person, to build a legal case in court, to appreciate a piece of artwork, or to understand the character of God. These other types of knowledge do not involve controlled scientific experiments and equations, but they are valid, rational ways for gaining knowledge that is somewhat reliable and consistent. Without them we would be sorely limited in our encounters with the world around us. For instance, a strictly scientific analysis of a Shakespearean poem would only yield a chemical analysis of the paper and ink. But using our understanding of language, literature, and human experience, we know that a poem is not only ink on paper, but letters and words, rhyme and meter, allusion and metaphor, and expressions of love or pathos. Thus, we would never say "A poem is *nothing but* ink on paper." To remind ourselves that there are other levels of knowledge, simply replace "nothing but" with "not only." Human beings are not only chemical machines, but complex biological systems, which relate to one another in social groups, groups which form cultural institutions and religious practices.

2 Unrelated/Compartmentalized/Independent Model

In this model, science and religion are entirely independent and explore separate realms, with each discipline answering different kinds of questions. Stephen Jay Gould writes:

> No such conflict [between science and religion] should exist because each subject has a legitimate magisterium, or domain of teaching authority … The net of science covers the empirical universe: what is it made of (fact) and why does it work this way (theory). The net of religion extends over questions of moral meaning and value.[15]

Gould is an atheist like Atkins, but their views of science and religion are very different. While Atkins argues that science and religion are in conflict (and science has won), Gould argues for coexistence. While Atkins claims that science is of unlimited utility, Gould says science cannot answer religious questions. Gould argues that religious knowledge is a valid but separate type of knowledge from science. In his view, all apparent conflicts between science and religion are due to misunderstandings about the kinds of questions each can answer. If the boundary line is drawn carefully enough, every issue can be separated into religious questions and scientific questions, and then each discipline can be used to answer its own type of question. This compartmentalized view of religion and science is probably the most common view among Western scientists (of all worldviews). It fits nicely with moral relativism – these scientists will agree to disagree about religious questions, and agree that religion has no impact on their scientific work.

This model of science and religion has some important strength. Science is indeed limited – it addresses questions about the regular functioning of the material world (what, how, when). Science cannot directly answer questions of purpose, personhood, God, or why the universe exists. Similarly, religion is limited – it cannot answer questions like "what is the mass of an electron." By separating religious and scientific questions, many apparent conflicts can be easily resolved.

But this model is incomplete. First, a thoughtful person of any worldview will want to have a consistent philosophy of life that applies to scientific as well as moral questions, rather than compartmentalizing them into separate areas of life. Moreover, Christianity and other religions consist of more than moral values and personal opinion; many religions make universal truth claims, claims related to the material world as well as the spiritual. Some key questions, such as human origins, require both scientific and spiritual approaches to construct a complete and meaningful answer; while one's worldview will provide the primary answer, science can provide important evidence that will affect the answer. Finally, a better view of science and religion would go beyond avoiding warfare to exploring what positive interactions the two might have.

3 Interacting/Complementary/Dialogue Model

In this view, science and religion have some similarities of approach, and can interact with each other in both positive and negative ways. Pope John Paul II wrote, "Science can purify religion from error and superstition; religion can purify science from idolatry and false absolutes. Each can draw the other into a wider world, a world in which both can flourish."[16]

One positive interaction is the sense of the spiritual that many people experience in their interaction with the physical world. This may come through visits to mountains or seashores, or when encountering the world through the microscope, telescope, or theoretical calculations. Many people have a sense that they are viewing more than mountains, cells, or stars, but encountering something beautiful that goes beyond the purely physical or something that affects how they view their place and purpose in the world. Although such encounters do not provide logical proof of God and can certainly be explained without God, many who experience it find that it is evidence in support of a belief in God.

Christian theology has long included beliefs which are similar to the interacting model, as a way to understand the religious alongside the material world. Christians believe that God made the entire physical universe (nature), and that this same God inspired the Bible (Scripture). In Christian thought, an analogy is used for this idea, in which nature

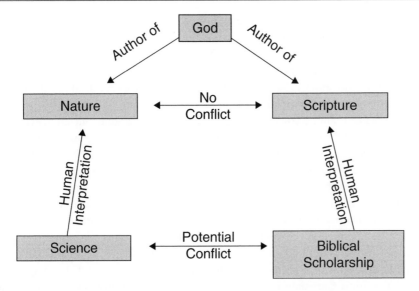

Figure 7.1   The relation between nature and Scripture, science and Biblical scholarship.

and Scripture are referred to as two "books" that God has "authored." For example, the Belgic Confession states:

> We know [God] by two means:
>
> First, by the creation, preservation, and government of the universe, since that universe is before our eyes like a beautiful book in which all creatures, great and small, are as letters to make us ponder the invisible things of God: his eternal power and his divinity, as the apostle Paul says in Romans 1:20. All these things are enough to convict men and to leave them without excuse.
>
> Second, he makes himself known to us more openly by his holy and divine Word [the Bible], as much as we need in this life, for his glory and for the salvation of his own.[17]

In other terms, the physical world is called God's "general revelation," which is visible to all, and the Bible is called God's "special revelation," in which he reveals himself more specifically to Christians. Christians view the Bible as *inspired* by God, meaning that God taught the message to (the many) human authors, then the human authors composed the words within their own cultural context.[18] Because of this divine origin, Christians view the Bible as authoritative, but Christians still disagree about what some parts of the Bible mean.

The analogy of two "books" emphasizes that nature and Scripture are not at war, but are fundamentally related: both have their origin in God. Moreover, it is impossible for them to conflict with each other, because God cannot conflict with himself. This is illustrated in the top part of the diagram, figure 7.1.[19]

The conflicts we experience are represented in the lower part of the diagram, which is the human level. Conflicts arise because the human understanding of one or both "books" may be in error. Both sides of the diagram follow the pattern of critical realism. At the top is something real and true (the physical world, the text of Scripture). At the bottom is the human understanding of each – science is the human understanding of nature, and Christian theology is the human understanding of Scripture. In both cases, the human understanding can be in error, due to our limited intelligence, sinfulness, and whatever biases and assumptions we bring to the process. But in both cases, a closer examination of the original "book," along with discussion with other people who interpret it differently, leads to a better understanding of the underlying truth.

This view of science and Christianity gives a useful framework for dealing with apparent conflicts. It points out the divine authority on both sides. When a conflict arises, we should not assume science is always correct and ignore the Bible, or assume our interpretation of the Bible is correct and ignore the physical universe God made. Our response should instead be to examine *both* the science *and* the Biblical scholarship more carefully, to find and correct the error in our human understanding. We should not ignore one side or the other, but hang on to both with the good hope that ultimately we will grasp the underlying unity of God as author of both revelations. Thus, my Christian worldview causes me to examine certain scientific claims more skeptically than my non-Christian colleagues, and to study certain Scripture passages more carefully than my fellow Christians.

This is not to say that all conflicts are easily dealt with. There are serious issues, and Christians have serious disagreements about how to resolve them. But this diagram is a framework that most Christians agree on – that nature and Scripture are both important, and that the problem is at a human level – while still disagreeing about where exactly the problem is (in science or in Biblical scholarship). The other chapters in this volume by Loren Haarsma and myself illustrate how this can work out for several particular issues, such as the age of the universe, evolution, the Big Bang, and human morality.

Despite the strength and utility of this model, it does not capture all of the aspects of the relationship between science and religion. For another view, we turn to the final model.

4 Foundational Model

In the Foundational model, a religion or worldview provides the philosophical foundation and framework needed to do science. All scientists (of whatever worldview or religion) hold certain beliefs (presuppositions) which are necessary in order to do science, yet cannot be proved from science. Science is based on beliefs not found in science itself. These beliefs can originate in culture or religion, or may simply be personal convictions on the part of the scientist.

In order to do modern science, a scientist must believe that:[20]

1) Humans have the ability to study nature and understand (at least in part) how it functions.
2) Events in the natural world typically have (immediate) causes in the natural world. (For example, a tree falls because the wind exerts a force on it, not because it "wants" to fall, not because the "forest god" made it fall, not because it was simply fated to fall.)
3) Natural phenomena are regular across space and time. Scientists will find the same experimental result in laboratories all over the earth, and will find the same result today as they found last week. This consistency allows the phenomena to be studied using logic and (at times) mathematical precision.
4) Observations and experiments are necessary to build and test scientific models which correctly describe natural phenomena; logic and deduction are not sufficient to build an accurate understanding of the natural world.
5) Scientific study of the natural world is a worthwhile use of human time and resources.

Today, these beliefs may seem to be obviously true, but for most of human history, most people did not hold all of these beliefs. Animists, who believe in gods inhabiting many aspects of the physical world, would have very different views of cause and effect and of the regularity of nature. Plato and Aristotle developed logical and beautiful theories about the workings of the natural world, but did not place enough priority on experimental tests and got the wrong answers. Even today, some worldviews are inconsistent with these beliefs – an antirealist or relativist would have trouble believing that all scientists could obtain the same scientific model, independent of the opinions of the scientists.

Scientists hold a wide range of views on other topics, such as the existence of God and the meaning of human life, but they still share the beliefs listed above. This commonality is what allows scientists of all worldviews to work together, using the same methods and obtaining the same results.

There are other worldview beliefs that are part of the scientific process, but (unlike the ones I list above), scientists do not all have to agree on them in order to do science. For instance, a scientist *could* do their work with an antirealist or instrumentalist view of science, not believing that their models say anything about the truth of physical reality (but I have never met a scientist with this view.) Most scientists believe some form of critical realism: the universe is real, and our models are approaching an accurate understanding of what that reality is. Another way worldviews impact the sciences is through cultural influences on what phenomena are interesting to study. For example, Chinese astronomers around AD 1000 made careful scientific observations of astronomical phenomena, with a focus on transient, occasional events (such as sunspots, comets, and star variability) rather than on regular patterns (such as the motions of planets relative to the stars).[21] This cultural tradition (and the flourishing of Chinese culture during the European dark ages) meant that the Chinese made detailed records of a supernova explosion in AD 1054 in which a "star" appeared bright enough to be seen in the day time – modern astronomers used these records to find and photograph the remnants of this explosion. Finally, worldview and culture influence how a scientist chooses between competing models. When individual scientists are deciding which model is best, they value accuracy (good match to past and predicted observations), scope (the model explains many phenomena), fruitfulness (leads to new, feasible studies), and simplicity (the model has beauty, symmetry, and/or a lack of ad hoc additions). These are subjective judgments, and beliefs from outside of science can affect how a scientist views a particular model.

Let us return to the list of beliefs necessary for science. While scientists today share these philosophical beliefs, they do not necessarily hold them for the same reasons. Some scientists simply believe them because they work. Paul Davies wrote:

> The success of the scientific method at unlocking the secrets of nature is so dazzling [that] it can blind us to the greatest scientific miracle of all: science works. Scientists themselves normally take it for granted that we live in a rational, ordered cosmos subject to precise laws that can be uncovered by human reasoning. Yet why this is so remains a tantalizing mystery.[22]

But other scientists have worldviews which can explain why this is so. For example, an atheist might justify the beliefs in the following way:

- We can understand nature because intelligence, and the ability to make predictions, are adaptive features granted to us by evolution (our ancestors who had those abilities in greater measure than their competitors produced more offspring).

- Nature typically operates with regular, repeatable, universal patterns because matter simply has the properties of self-existence and regularity, and since the material world is all there is, there are no supernatural entities to disturb these patterns.
- Experiments are needed because our intelligence and rationality have only evolved so far; perhaps a being with greater intelligence could figure out the laws of nature without experiments, but we cannot.
- Science is worth doing because science is interesting and the knowledge gained gives us power to help ourselves and help other people.

A Christian might justify those same philosophical beliefs in an entirely different way.

- We can understand nature because we are made in God's image (*e.g.*, Genesis 1:27) and God has given humans the abilities to do science.
- Nature typically operates with regular, repeatable, universal patterns because nature is not filled with capricious gods, but ruled by one God in a faithful consistent manner (e.g., Psalm 119:89–90).
- Experiments are necessary because God was free to create in many ways, while we humans are sinful and limited, and are not able to understand God's ways perfectly (e.g., Job 38); our scientific models must be tested by careful comparison to what God actually made.
- Science is worth doing because we are studying God's handiwork, because God wants us to learn about nature, and because the knowledge we gain helps us benefit others (e.g., Genesis 1:28, 2:19–20, Proverbs 25:2, Psalm 19:1).

For a Christian, the Bbiblical teachings about God and the natural world provide support and motivation for doing science, and a basis for understanding why science is so successful.[23] A theist doing science is not acting "as if God doesn't exist." Rather, he or she is acting like there is a God – not a capricious God, but the God of the Bible, who made an orderly world and who still governs it in an orderly fashion. As Donald MacKay wrote,

> We have … [taken the] mandate for the scientific enterprise from the biblical view of our world and its dependence on God. Contrary to widely propagated belief, we have found nothing but encouragement to build up experimentally based knowledge into a theoretically integrated explanatory framework [i.e. to do science] …. Of irreconcilable contradiction" we have found no trace.[24]

Thus, religion is not at war with science, nor a separate realm from science, but rather can serve as a fundamental foundation for how and why to do science.

A Christian and a Scientist

Let me close with some personal reflections on the ways in which Christian faith does, and does not affect, the work of a scientist like myself. The scientific process can be described in broad terms as follows:

1) *The basis for science:* Can we discover new truths about nature? If so, how and why are we able to do so?

2) *The processes of science:* What are effective scientific methods for learning about nature?

3) *The discoveries of science:* What do we learn about nature when we apply these methods?

4) *The inferences of science:* Do scientific discoveries have implications for society, philosophy, religion?

5) *The human aspect of science:* What are our motives, ethics, and goals for doing science?[25]

When conflicts occur between science and religion, they typically arise in the inferences of science (4), as people of different worldviews disagree about the implications of particular scientific discoveries, and use (or misuse) scientific results to argue their world-view agenda. As a Christian, the Warfare and Interacting models remind me to inspect such claims carefully, since they are based not purely on science but on other beliefs. Science and religion mostly deal with different questions, so when inferences are made from science (4), the Independent model reminds me that science is limited and cannot answer all questions. But the Foundational model shows that the fundamental interaction of Christian faith with science is through the basis for science (1), the processes of science (2), and the motives and goals of science (5).

Note that the discoveries of science (3) are not much affected by Christian beliefs. Christians can and should come to the same conclusions in a particular experiment as other scientists do. Christian beliefs may have some effect on what scientific questions a scientist finds interesting to pursue,[26] or cause me to inspect some scientific results more skeptically (Interacting Model), but it does not bar me from studying certain questions, nor bind me to some predetermined conclusion in conflict with the scientific evidence. Rather, Christianity declares that "All Truth is God's Truth": whether I study the tiniest elementary particles or the largest galaxy cluster, I will never come across an object or physical process that did not originate in God. All areas of scientific inquiry are open; studying the universe will only deepen my understanding of God and His revelation in nature.

Finally, my Christian beliefs help me notice the attributes of God displayed in the physical universe he has made. The Bible says:

> The heavens declare the glory of God;
> the skies proclaim the work of his hands.
> Day to day they pour forth speech;
> Night after night they reveal knowledge.
> There is no speech or language where their voice is not heard.
> The voice goes out into all the earth, their words to the ends of the world.[27]

In my studies of the heavens, I hear them declaring not only God's glory, but also his other attributes, such as beauty, creativity, faithfulness, immensity, and intricacy. The author Annie Dillard writes: "The creator churns out the intricate texture of ... the world with a spendthrift genius and an extravagance of care."[28] John Calvin lists more attributes: "The whole world is a theater for the display of the Divine goodness, wisdom, justice, and power."[29] The heavens "speak" of these things without words or language, but in a way that can be understood by people of all places and cultures.

For a Christian, Scripture is the primary guide to understanding God and his character. But God's work in nature enhances this knowledge by *illustrating* God's character in ways that words on a printed page could never do. The view of the clear night sky from a dark location, with the Milky Way sparkling overhead, displays God's glory in a way accessible to people of all cultures. Recently astronomers have discovered stars which explode in "hyper-novae," shining (for a moment) brighter than thousands of galaxies; these display God's power in a way we couldn't detect until gamma-ray telescopes were built in the last few decades. The Bible teaches Christians that God is glorious and powerful, but it is nature which *demonstrates* this on a scale that touches my spirit and emotions more than the written text.

From Galileo to the present day, many Christians have made extraordinary contributions to our scientific knowledge. While some still argue that science has triumphed over religion, many scientists show by their example that science and religion are in harmony. More than coexisting, science and Christianity have a positive relationship, which enhances each without weakening the integrity of scientific practice or compromising Christian beliefs.

Notes

1   By "science," I mean the natural sciences (e.g., astronomy, chemistry, biology). In places my comments could apply more broadly to the social sciences or academic knowledge in general, but my primary meaning is the natural sciences.

2   A "worldview" or "world and life view" is the belief system a person uses to answer the big questions of life, such as the origin of the universe and of humanity, the purpose of human existence, the existence of God and how one should relate to God, etc. In this context, atheism is not the mere absence of religion, but a competing belief system which answers these questions differently.

3   I am indebted to Ian Barbour for this framework, although I define the last two categories somewhat differently than he. Ian Barbour, *Religion and Science* (San Francisco: Harper, 1997), ch. 4.

4   John W. Draper, *History of the Conflict between Religion and Science* (New York: D. Appleton, 1874).

5   Andrew Dickson White, *A History of the Warfare of Science with Theology in Christendom* (New York, D. Appleton, 1896).

6   Roger A. Freedman and William J. Kaufmann II, *Universe: Stars & Galaxies* (New York: W. H. Freeman, 2002), p. 71.

7   Andrew Fraknoi, David Morrison, and Sidney C. Wolff, *Voyages to the Stars and Galaxies*, 2nd edn. (Philadelphia: Saunders College Publishing, 2003), p. 33.

8   More extended histories of the life of Galileo can be found in many books, including Charles E. Hummel, *The Galileo Connection* (Downer's Grove, IL: InterVarsity Press, 1986), and Stillman Drake, *The Discoveries and Opinions of Galileo* (Anchor, 1957) (includes translations of some of Galileo's writings).

9   Galileo, *Letter to the Grand Duchess Christina*, 1615.

10   Hummel, *The Galileo Connection*, p. 116.

11   For more on Christian beliefs about God's interaction with the physical world, see chapter 10, SCIENTIFIC KNOWLEDGE DOES NOT REPLACE RELIGIOUS KNOWLEDGE, in this volume.

12   P. W. Atkins, *Nature's Imagination: The Frontiers of Scientific Vision*, ed. J. Cornwell (Oxford: Oxford University Press, 1995).

13   Draper, *History of the Conflict between Religion and Science*.

14   For more on other types of knowledge, see chapter 10, SCIENTIFIC KNOWLEDGE DOES NOT REPLACE RELIGIOUS KNOWLEDGE, in this volume.

15   Stephen Jay Gould, "Nonoverlapping magisteria," *Natural History*, vol. 106, March 1997.

16   Pope John Paul II, *John Paul II on Science and Religion* (Vatican Observatory Publications, distributed by University of Notre Dame Press, Notre Dame, Indiana, 1990).

17   Article 2 of the Belgic Confession, written by Guido de Brás in 1561, and revised and adopted by the Reformed churches of the Netherlands in the late 1500s. This document is still at the heart of Reformed Christian doctrine today, and all ministers and officials are required to subscribe to it. The full text is available at http://www.reformed.org/documents/BelgicConfession.html.

18   For more on the doctrine of inspiration, see How CHRISTIANS RECONCILE ANCIENT TEXTS WITH MODERN SCIENCE, chapter 8 in this volume.

19   A similar diagram appears in Hummel, *The Galileo Connection,* p. 263.

20   Loren Haarsma, "Does science exclude God? Natural law, chance, miracles, and scientific practice," in Keith B. Miller (ed.), *Perspectives on an Evolving Creation* (Grand Rapids, MI: Eerdmans, 2005).

21   Fang Li Zhi, "Note on the Interface between science and religion" in the anthology *John Paul II on Science and Religion* (Vatican Observatory Publications, distributed by University of Notre Dame Press, Notre Dame, Indiana 1990).

22   Paul Davies, *The Mind of God: The Scientific Basis for a Rational World* (New York: Simon & Schuster, 1992), p. 20.

23   In fact, the beginnings of modern science in Western Europe were influenced by these Christian beliefs, see Del Ratzsch, THE RELIGIOUS ROOTS OF SCIENCE – WHAT SCIENCE OWES TO THEOLOGY, chapter 2 in this volume.

24   Donald MacKay, *Science, Chance, and Providence* (Oxford: Oxford University Press, 1978).

25   Loren Haarsma, "Is Intelligent Design scientific?" invited talk at the annual conference of the American Scientific Affiliation, Aug. 5–8, 2005: http://www.asa3.org/ASA/meetings/Messiah2005/papers/IsIDScientific_ASA2005.htm.

26   For an example, see CHRISTIAN AND ATHEIST RESPONSES TO BIG BANG COSMOLOGY, chapter 9 in this volume.

27   Psalm 19:1–4, *The Bible: New International Version.* Grand Rapids, IL: Zondervan Publishing.

28   Annie Dillard, *Pilgrim at Tinker Creek.* Harper's Magazine Press (New York: Bantam Books) 1975.

29   John Calvin, *Commentary of the Psalms,* 135:13. Calvin's theater metaphor is discussed more fully in "The World as a Theatre of God's Glory" by Belden Lane, *Perspectives,* Nov. 2001, 7.

8

How Christians Reconcile Ancient Texts with Modern Science

DEBORAH B. HAARSMA

For Christians, the entire text of the Bible is inspired by God and no part is to be dismissed as merely human writing. Yet the Bible's description of creation in six days appears to conflict with the billions of years of natural history found by modern geology and astronomy. Christians have responded to this apparent conflict with a multitude of interpretative approaches, reflecting their culture, their views of science, and their understanding of Biblical inspiration. One approach is to compare the Biblical accounts to other creation texts from ancient Babylon and Egypt written at about the same time. By understanding this cultural context into which God first inspired the text, we can see more clearly God's original intent; the result is an interpretation of the Biblical creation account which upholds the authority of God's word but is consistent with the great age of the earth and the universe.

1 The Problem

In the last century, our scientific understanding of natural history has grown dramatically. We can now write down, with some confidence, the sequence and timing of major events in the development of the universe, the solar system, and life on our planet (see figure 8.1). More information about this timeline can be found in standard textbooks[1] of astronomy, geology, paleontology, and archeology.

The first chapter of the Bible, Genesis 1, also lays out a sequence of events in the development of the physical world, life, and human culture. (The origin of the physical world and God's work as creator is actually described in several places in the Bible – Genesis 2, Psalm 104, John 1:1–5, Colossians 1:15–20 – but these other texts have a less chronological character and thus are in less direct conflict with the chronology of natural history.) Genesis 1 describes God creating the world in six days (see the text of Genesis 1, and Table 8.2 below). Genesis 2 describes the origin of the first humans, Adam and Eve. A few pages later, Genesis chapters 6–9 describe a worldwide flood lasting several months, which destroyed all life except for Noah, his family, and the animals aboard his boat. The early chapters of Genesis also list a genealogy of Adam's descendents. The Bible goes on to record the lives of Abraham

Table 8.1   Timeline of Natural History

Time	Event	Dating Techniques
13.7 billion years ago	Big Bang	cosmic microwave background and galaxy recession
(+3 minutes)	first nuclei	ratio of elements
(+300,000 years)	first atoms	cosmic microwave background
(+100 million years)	first stars	Simulations and high-redshift observations
(+ 1 billion years)	first galaxies	high-redshift observations
~10 billion years ago	our galaxy forms	stellar evolution
5–12 billion years ago	stars in our galaxy make heavy elements	stellar evolution
4.6 billion years ago	sun and earth formed	radioactive dating (RD)
4.2 billion years ago	first life (prokaryotic)	fossils (F), RD, geologic strata (GS)
2 billion years ago	eukaryotic life	F, RD, GS
1–1.8 billion years ago	multicellular life	F, RD, GS
530 million years ago	"Cambrian explosion"	DNA dating, F, RD, GS
70 million years ago	dinosaurs wiped out	meteor impact
40 million years ago	early primates	DNA, F, RD, GS
5 million years ago	Mediterranean Sea forms	RD, GS
2.5 million years ago	stone tools	F, RD, GS
120,000 years ago	modern humans	F, RD, GS
10,000+ years ago	agriculture	carbon dating, F, RD, archeology
7,500 years ago	Black Sea fills	F, RD, GS
5,000 years ago	continuous written history	

and his family, and the formation and history of the nation of Israel (the Jews), and ultimately the life of Jesus Christ and the growth of the early Church. This historical and genealogical information, if taken literally, can be used to calculate backwards to determine the year in which God made the universe. Archbishop James Ussher of Ireland (1581–1656) did this calculation with impressive precision, and declared the exact date of creation to be Sunday, October 23, 4004 BC.[2]

The differences between the Biblical chronology and the scientific chronology could be easily brushed aside by deciding that some (or all) of the Bible is only folk tales and fiction, rather than a serious historical record of actual events. This, however, is not an option for Christians. Christians view all parts of the Bible as *inspired* by God. This means that the text is more than the ideas of the human authors; rather, God taught the message to the human authors, then the human authors composed the words within their own cultural context.[3] The Biblical text was written over thousands of years in several cultures and multiple languages, yet the thematic consistency through the Bible is evidence for its common origin in God. A verse in the Bible says: "All Scripture is inspired by God and useful for teaching, rebuking, correcting, and training in righteousness, so that the people of God may be thoroughly equipped for every good work."[4] This means that all Scripture is equally sacred and authoritative, and Christians cannot arbitrarily choose which passages they will ignore and which passages they will believe and obey.

On the other hand, the differences between the Bible and natural history could be brushed aside by completely ignoring the modern scientific evidence. This is not an option for a serious scientist, who understands the wealth of evidence for a universe that is billions of years old. Moreover, it is a poor response from a purely theological perspective. Recall (chapter 7 in this volume) the Christian idea of two "books," nature and Scripture, both authored by God. If the physical world itself is from God, it is wrong to completely ignore its testimony about its origin (i.e., natural history).

The task of this chapter is to discuss the various ways Christians have reconciled the significant differences between the Biblical timeline and the natural history timeline (beyond simply ignoring one or the other).[5] This reconciliation is done through various interpretations of the Genesis 1 text, and there are *many* such interpretations (I will discuss half-a-dozen of them). The question for Christians is: "If I believe in the Bible, is it possible to also accept the scientific understanding of nature?" The question for scientists is: "If I take the physical evidence seriously, is it possible to also believe in the Bible?"

2 Responses, Past and Present

In the seventeenth and eighteenth centuries, the field of geology began to develop an understanding of long-term processes and the historical record fixed in rock. Many geologists at that time (particularly in Britain) started from the assumption (based on the Bible) that a global flood had happened in the earth's past, and that the earth was only a few thousand years old.[6] But as they studied the fossil record, volcanic processes, erosion, and so on, they found that these processes must have been ongoing for millions of years, if not longer. To resolve this tension with the Biblical timeline, two new interpretations of Genesis 1 were proposed: the Gap interpretation, and the Day-Age interpretation.

The Gap Interpretation focuses on the meaning of the first two verses of Genesis 1. The first verse ("In the beginning, God created the heavens and the earth") is viewed not as an introduction to what follows, but as a complete statement that God made the whole universe millions or billions of years ago. The second verse ("The earth was formless and empty") refers to some more recent catastrophe that destroyed life on the surface of the earth. The remaining verses of Genesis 1 then are viewed as the restoration (not creation) of the earth, occurring just a few thousand years ago. Thus, there is a long gap of time between the creation of the geological earth billions of years ago, time for the long historical record of geology to take place. Then the rest of Biblical history starts less than 10,000 years ago and proceeds onward with the development of plants, animals, and humans. Although this interpretation solved the discrepancies between Genesis 1 and the geological evidence, it did not account for the long history of biological life that had become apparent in the fossil record.

The Day-Age Interpretation focuses on the word "day" in the Genesis account. The original Hebrew word used is *yom*, which can be translated as a 24-hour day, or as a long indefinite time period (epoch). If the second meaning is intended, then each "day" in Genesis 1 could be millions or billions of years long, allowing enough time for both geological and biological processes to happen. This resolves issues of the *length* of time needed, but it does not resolve issues about the *sequence* of events. For example, in Genesis 1, birds arrive before land creatures, rather than arriving after land animals as we learn from the fossil record. A second problem with this interpretation is the clear statement "there was evening and there was morning, the *X*th day" at the end of each day in Genesis 1, clearly indicating that *yom* is meant to refer to 24-hour days rather than long epochs.

In 1859, Charles Darwin published *On the Origin of Species,* and his theory of biological evolution has been debated by Christians ever since.[7] Despite some strong resistance to Darwinian evolution, Christian views of the age of the earth did not change much. Ronald Numbers writes:

> By the late 1800s, even the most conservative Christians readily conceded that the Bible allowed for an ancient earth and pre-Edenic life. With few exceptions, they accommodated the findings of historical geology and paleontology using day-age theory, or gap theory.[8]

The early twentieth century in North America brought continued debate between Christians on several issues, including the authority of the Bible and whether Jesus rose from the dead. This led to a split between conservative "fundamentalist" Christians and liberal Christians. Although evolution was a key issues in these debates (e.g., the famous Scopes trial in 1925), both sides still accepted the findings of great age from geology, paleontology, and astronomy.

Things changed in 1960, when theologian John Whitcomb and engineer Henry Morris published *The Genesis Flood.*[9] This book started the modern Young Earth Creationism movement. In this interpretation, Genesis is taken mostly literally,[10] with the universe, Earth, and all life formed in a six-day period less than 10,000 years ago, followed shortly by a global flood. The goal of this movement was to develop a modern scientific model which shows that the scientific evidence actually supports a young Earth and global flood.[11] For instance, all geological layers and fossils were formed in the flood, rather than over millions of years. In contrast to earlier Christian positions, this movement asked to be judged on scientific grounds, not just on its theological position. Unfortunately, its scientific claims have been shown (in several recent books)[12] to be unjustified or inconsistent with well-established scientific principles. The motivation for the Young Earth Creation movement was to counter evolution and the increasingly prominent worldview of atheism that is often attached to it. These Christians viewed the issue with a warfare mentality,[13] For example, Morris wrote:

> If the system of flood geology can be established on a sound scientific basis, and be effectively promoted and publicized, then the entire evolutionary cosmology, at least in its present neo-Darwinian form, will collapse. This, in turn, would mean that every anti-Christian system and movement (communism, racism, humanism, libertinism, behaviorism, and all the rest) would be deprived of their pseudo-intellectual foundation.[14]

The movement rapidly spread throughout fundamentalist and evangelical Christians in North America.

The large scientific problems with the Young Earth position have led some conservative Christians to adopt the Appearance of Age Interpretation. In this view, God created the Earth less than 10,000 years ago, but made it such that it appears billions of years old. This interpretation is a way to maintain a literal reading of the Biblical text while also believing all of the scientific evidence, thus neatly avoiding all conflict with the science. It has, however, a significant theological problem. In this view, God made sedimentary rocks with layers which appear millions of years old, fossils that represent extinct life forms which never actually existed, and photons traveling to us from distant galaxies showing supernova explosions which never happened. Of course, God is omnipotent and could have created this way if he chose, but the problem is that this is inconsistent with the character of God taught in the rest of the Bible. Would God have created the universe with a long, rich embedded history, but ask us to believe *in spite of the physical evidence*[15] that he created it much more recently? This is inconsistent with God's truthfulness and the faith commitment he asks of us.

The views I've mentioned so far (gap interpretation, day-age interpretation, young earth creationism, and appearance of age) all fit under the umbrella of *concordism*. Concordist interpretations are those in which God made the Earth using the same sequence of events as describe in Genesis 1. Some concordist views allow God to use a longer time period than six 24-hour days (i.e., the day-age interpretation), but in all cases the sequence is the same (i.e., God made light first, then sky and ocean, then dry land, etc.).

3 The Hermeneutical Principle

Other Christians hold to *non-concordist* interpretations of Genesis 1. In these views, the text is considered divinely inspired and authoritative for the message originally intended, but the intended message is seen as primarily theological. In other words, the passage did not intend to convey scientific or historical information of the sort we think of in the modern world today; it wasn't intended to be a science textbook or an eye-witness account. The sequence and timing of events described in the text may have some cultural or literary significance, but are not meant to be taken as literal scientific truth.

Non-concordist views are *not* a concession made to reconcile the text with modern science. There is a good theological reason for a Christian to read Genesis 1 this way. To explain this further, let me discuss briefly a principle of good Biblical hermeneutics (interpretation),[16] which I will call "the hermeneutical principle." This is a principle which should be used when attempting to understand any Biblical passage, not just Genesis 1.

To best comprehend what the text means, we should seek to understand how the original author and intended audience viewed the text. What meaning did they think it to have? In what ways was it significant, or trivial? There are several ways to gain this understanding. First, we need a good translation, which captures well the meaning and nuance of the text in the original language. Second, we can look at the internal content and literary genre of the text – is it written as history? parable? poetry? prophesy? Finally, we can consider the cultural-historical context of the passage, such as what did surrounding cultures think? what historical events preceded and followed this writing? Using all of these techniques, we gain a better understanding of what the original human author intended and what the original audience heard.

Does this make it too difficult for the average person to understand the Bible? A key Protestant belief is the doctrine of perspicacity (clarity), which says that the primary message of a Biblical text is clear to any Christian, and does not need to be interpreted for them by church leaders. Similarly, the meaning should be clear to any Christian without having to consult experts on the original language and culture. Note, however, that this doctrine applies to the *primary* message of the passage. In the case of Genesis 1, the obvious message is clear: God created the whole world and it is good. This basic message can be understood by any reader, but the details and implications of each word in the passage might not be correctly understood unless the reader makes an effort to understand the literary genre and the cultural and historical context. Thus, if we want to understand the *details* of how Genesis 1 relates to the modern scientific chronology, we need to do our homework first.

The hermeneutical principle of interpretation has several important advantages. It discourages the modern reader from assuming that all ideas in the text have the same meaning and implications that they would if written today for our culture. Also, since this same principle can (and should) be used for all Scripture passages, it gives us a consistent approach to understanding the Bible, rather than simply deciding that any passage which doesn't agree with modern science must be figurative. The following examples show that the hermeneutical principle can lead to both figurative and literal interpretations.

Consider the account of Jesus' life in the Gospel of Luke. The human author, Luke, begins the book with these words:

> Many have undertaken to draw up an account of the things that have been fulfilled among us, just as they were handed down to us by those who from the first were eyewitnesses. ... Therefore, since I myself have carefully investigated everything from the beginning, it seemed good also to me to write an orderly account for you, most excellent Theophilus.[17]

This passage has all the earmarks of a nearly modern style of historical writing, including an explanation of sources and methods. The internal content shows that the Gospel of Luke was clearly intended by Luke (and understood by his first readers) to be a literal account of what happened. Applying the hermeneutical principle, we find that we, too, should understand the events recorded in the book as actual historical events. This includes the death and resurrection of Jesus Christ, even though science has no way to explain the miracle of someone rising from the dead.[18]

Consider next this poem from the book of Psalms:

> The Lord reigns, he is robed in majesty;
> the Lord is robed in majesty and is armed with strength.
> The world is firmly established;
> it cannot be moved.
> Your throne was established long ago;
> you are from all eternity.[19]

The middle stanza of this passage was used in the time of Galileo to argue that the Earth is not in motion around the Sun, but rather must be fixed in space, with the Sun, planets, and stars orbiting the Earth. Galileo responded to such arguments by quoting Cardinal Baronius saying "The Bible teaches how to go to heaven, not how the heavens go." Similarly, modern Christians have no difficulty with reading this stanza as figurative, given its context. The parallel statements of the world and God's throne clearly suggest that the world *is* God's throne and is thus stably maintained by him – no human action could move the earth or dislodge God from his throne. The intended message was spiritual, not scientific.

4 Other texts from the Ancient Near East

With the hermeneutical principle in hand, let us return to the text of Genesis 1. Its internal content reveals it to be a carefully structured narrative.[20] Although it does not follow the typical patterns of other Hebrew poetry, it does show important rhythms and repetition.

Table 8.2 Literary Structure of Genesis 1

Initially, Earth is ...	Days of forming	Days of filling
Dark	Day 1: light	Day 4: sun, moon, and stars
watery abyss	Day 2: separate the waters into sky and ocean	Day 5: birds and fish
formless earth	Day 3: separate the dry land from ocean, plants	Day 6: animals and humans

Most striking is the structure of the six days. The initial state of the Earth is described in Genesis 1:2: "The earth was formless and empty, and darkness was over the surface of the deep waters." This initial condition is overcome throughout the six days of creating, as shown in the table above.[21] During the first three days, the Earth goes from formless darkness to light and clearly defined structures of dry land, ocean, and sky. During the second three days, the empty world is filled with motion and life.

The careful structure of this passage shows that the original author had poetic factors in mind when selecting the sequence of events. The original intent was to convey the completeness of God's creation (all aspects of existence, both structures and moving creatures), its orderliness in contrast to its initial dark chaos, and its goodness. The author may also have designed the text to be easy to remember and pass down through oral history.

Our best understanding of Genesis 1 comes when we consider not only the internal content, but the original cultural context. The ancient Hebrews were neighbors to (and sometimes exiles in) the ancient near east nations of Egypt and Babylon.[22] The Hebrews certainly would be aware of how those peoples viewed the origin of the world. First, consider the Egyptian engraving shown in figure 8.1.

In this highly symbolic Egyptian representation of the world, the starry sky (the lady of heaven – the goddess Nut) arches over the reclining earth (the god Geb). Above her is the upper ocean in which the solar barque [boat] sails to carry the Sun (the falcon-headed god Re) from the eastern horizon up to the zenith and then down to the western horizon. (Re is accompanied by the goddess Maat with her identifying feather; she is the daughter of Re, who is the source of world order.) Kneeling above the Earth (reclining Geb) and holding up the sky (Nut) is the atmosphere god Shu; he holds in both hands the symbol of the breath of life. At the lower right is Osiris, the great god of the world of the dead. Not represented here is the subterranean ocean which the solar barque traverses at night to return the sun at dawn to the eastern horizon. That ocean is clearly shown in other symbolic representations.[23]

This view of the world has important structural similarities to the picture in Genesis 1 and other Biblical passages.[24] A solid sky dome (or firmament) covers the earth, holding up primeval waters above the sky. Although this firmament seems bizarre to us now, it was a way for a pre-scientific culture to make sense of the world around them. Without any understanding of evaporation and precipitation, they simply concluded that there must be an ocean of water above the sky; a solid dome holds the waters up, and occasional "floodgates" open and allow rain to fall. The primeval waters were also thought to exist under the Earth, as evidenced by springs where water rises up out of the land. Without any understanding of the Earth rotating on its axis, they assumed the Sun literally traveled from east to west each day,[25] and under the Earth each night to return to the east. The place of the dead is under the Earth.

Figure 8.1   Egyptian representation of the world. From *The Symbolism of the Biblical World: Ancient Near Eastern Iconography and the Book of Psalms* by Othmar Keel (New York: Crossroad, 1985). Reproduced by permission of Eisenbraun publishers.

Next, consider the Babylonian epoch *Enuma Elish*.[26] This is another story of the creation of the world, with many similarities to Genesis 1. It begins with primeval chaos, and describes the origin of light, a sky-dome, dry land, and a means of marking time. It ends with the gods resting and celebrating in a banquet.

Both the Egyptian and the Babylonian cosmologies have similarities to the physical structures in Genesis 1. But they also have sharp differences. In both the Egyptian engraving and the Enuma Elish text, a pantheon of gods is present, with gods inhabiting various parts of the physical world. In *Enuma Elish*, matter is co-eternal with the gods. Six generations of gods spring from the first pair of gods, Apsu and Tiamat; ultimately Tiamat is defeated by the god Marduk, who splits Tiamat's body like a shellfish, using half to form the sky dome. Marduk also sets the lesser gods in "stations" to mark days, months, and seasons. At the end of the story, humans are made from the flesh of a defeated god, in order to be slaves to the gods and servants at the banquet.

To the Hebrew original audience, the physical structures and events in Genesis 1 would have been familiar from their knowledge of other cultures. But the role and character of God in Genesis 1 would have stood out as strikingly different compared to the gods in the Egyptian and Babylonian pictures. The following table shows the theological differences between Genesis 1 and the *Enuma Elish*.

Given these pronounced differences, the new and striking message for the original audience in Genesis 1 would have been the theological content, not the sequence of physical events. God inspired the human author of Genesis 1 to tell the story in a way that conveyed these theological truths. Imagine if the text attempted to also correct scientific misconceptions, by explaining that the Earth is round (not flat) and the sky is gaseous (not a solid

Table 8.3   Differences between Genesis 1 and *Enuma Elish*

Genesis 1	Enuma Elish
One God	pantheon of gods
God creates an ordered world by the authority of his word	the world is formed by a battle among the gods
God declares all parts of the world good	matter is partially good and partially bad
God created men and women in His image, as the culmination of the story, and declared them very good. He gave them responsibility to be stewards of creation.	humans are made from the flesh of a defeated god in order to be slaves to the gods,
No part of the physical world is divine. For example, the sun and moon are referred to as greater and lesser lights, to avoid mention of proper names related to deities	the sun and moon and other physical objects are gods

dome) – it would have baffled them completely! Moreover, it would have completely distracted them from the theological message. As John Calvin wrote,

> The Holy Spirit had no intention to teach astronomy; and in proposing instruction meant to be common to the simplest and most uneducated person, He made use by Moses and other prophets of the popular language that none might shelter himself under the pretext of obscurity.[27]

God graciously accommodated himself to the needs of the people by communicating the spiritual message in the clearest means possible, rather than obscuring it in scientific information.

Now we return to the hermeneutical principle. Based on the message heard by the first audience, we see that we too should understand Genesis as teaching spiritual truths, not scientific information. Although the original audience may have understood the events and structures as literally true, they wouldn't have considered them the main point of the text. God's purposes in Genesis 1 did not include teaching scientific truths, so we should not look to this passage for scientific information about the age or development of the world. For us, as for the original audience, the message is theological.

In conclusion, we have taken the best method of Biblical interpretation (the hermeneutical principle), which is applicable to the whole Bible, and applied it to Genesis 1. By considering the internal content, the literary genre, and the cultural context, we find that the text was never intended to teach scientific information about the structure, age, or natural history of the world. Thus, it is not, and can never be, in conflict with the sequence of events found by scientific methods. Instead, the text teaches us of one sovereign God, who makes light from darkness, an ordered world from chaos, and fills an empty world with good creatures. Humans need not fear the capricious whims of a pantheon of gods, but can instead trust in the one true God, and work as his stewards to care for the physical world around us.

Notes

1   In addition to textbooks, see "Radiometric dating: A Christian perspective", R. C. Wiens, at http://www.asa3.org/ASA/resources/wiens.html and "An Ancient Universe," and http://www.astrosociety.org/education/publications/tnl/56/index.html.

2   A diagram showing this sort of timeline is available at http://www.geobkt.com/biblestudy/genesis09.htm.

3   Note that Christians do not believe that God *dictated* the actual words of the text, except for a few prophetic passages.

4   2 Timothy 3:16. *The Bible: New International Version* (Grand Rapids, IL: Zondervan, 1973; hereafter NIV).

5   Much more on the history of Christian views of the age of the universe can be found in: Ronald Numbers, *The Creationists* (Berkeley: University of California Press, 1993); Howard J. Van Till, Robert E. Snow, John H. Stek and Davis A. Young, *Portraits of Creation: Biblical and Scientific Perspectives on the World's Formation* (Grand Rapids, IL: Eerdmans, 1990); and papers by Edward B. Davis, Mark A. Noll, and David Livingstone in Keith Miller (ed.), *Perspectives on an Evolving Creation* (Grand Rapids, IL: Eerdmans, 2003).

6   Davis Young, "The discovery of terrestrial history," in Van Till et al., *Portraits of Creation*.

7   Christian responses to evolution are discussed in Loren Haarsma, GOD, EVOLUTION, AND DESIGN, chapter 11 in this volume.

8   Ronald Numbers, *The Creationists*.

9   John Whitcomb and Henry Morris, *The Genesis Flood*. (Phillipsburg, NJ: P & R Publishing, 1960).

10   Note that Young Earth Creationism is not a completely literal interpretation. A completely literal interpretation would view the earth as flat (rather than a globe), with a solid sky dome (rather than an atmosphere). See section 4 of this chapter.

11   The Young Earth creation model claims

     that life cannot evolve from non-life, that geological strata show evidence of recent formation and a global flood, that the fossil record should lack transitions between species, that evolution is limited to microevolution, that mutations cannot produce increased biological complexity, and that there are no ape-human transition fossils. ("Why believe in a creator? Perspectives on evolution," L. Haarsma, *The World & I*, v.11 n.1, 1996, pp. 323–7)

12   Some examples by both Christian and non-Christian authors: Howard J. Van Till, Davis A. Young, and Clarence Menninga, *Science Held Hostage* (Downers Grove: InterVarsity Press, 1988); Alan Hayward, *Creation and Evolution: The Facts and Fallacies* (London: Triangle, 1985); Van Till et. al., *Portraits of Creation*; Niles Eldredge, *The Monkey Business* (New York: Washington Square, 1982); Norman Newell, *Creation and Evolution* (New York: Columbia University Press, 1982); Phillip Kitcher, *Abusing Science* (Cambridge: MIT Press, 1982); Michael Ruse, *Darwinism Defended* (Reading: Addison-Wesley, 1982).

13   See chapter 7 in this volume, SCIENCE AND RELIGION IN HARMONY, section 1 on the warfare interaction.

14   Henry Morris, ed., *Scientific Creationism* (San Diego: Creation-Life Publishers, 1974), p. 252.

15   See SCIENTIFIC KNOWLEDGE DOES NOT REPLACE RELIGIOUS KNOWLEDGE, chapter 10 in this volume, on reasonable faith commitments.

16   For more on Biblical hermeneutics, see Gordon D. Fee and Douglas Stuart, *How to Read the Bible for All It's Worth* (Grand Rapids, MI: Zondervan, 1982) and Hummel, *The Galileo Connection* (Downers Grove, IL: InterVarsity Press, 1986), chapter 8.

17   Luke 1:1–3 (NIV).

18   See SCIENTIFIC KNOWLEDGE DOES NOT REPLACE RELIGIOUS KNOWLEDGE, chapter 10 in this volume, for more on miracles and science.

19   Psalm 93:1–2 (NIV).

20   For a more detailed analysis of Genesis 1, see Hummel, *The Galileo Connection,* ch. 10; John Stek, "What says the scripture?" in *Portraits of Creation;* Conrad Hyers "Comparing Biblical and scientific maps of origins," in Keith Miller (ed.), *Perspectives on an Evolving Creation.*

21   Hyers, in *Perspectives on an Evolving Creation,* p. 30.

22   For a longer discussion of Ancient Near East cosmologies, see John Stek, "What says the scripture?"

23   Caption from John Stek, "What says the scripture?" p. 227.

24   For a detailed list of passages besides Genesis 1 that refer to this physical picture of the world, see Loren Haarsma, http://www.asa3.org/archive/asa/200205/0743.html.

25   Psalm 19:4–6 (NIV).

26   The complete text can be found in James Pritchard, *Ancient Near East Text Relating to the Old Testament,* 3rd edn. (Princeton, NJ: Princeton University Press, 1969). An English translation is also available at http://www.cresourcei.org/enumaelish.html.

27   John Calvin, *Commentary on Psalms* (Grand Rapids, MI: Eerdmans, 1981) vol. 5, pp. 184–5.

9

Christian and Atheist Responses to Big Bang Cosmology

DEBORAH B. HAARSMA

In the early twentieth century, most astronomers believed that the universe was infinitely old and had no beginning in time. Modern astronomy and cosmology has shown that our universe formed abruptly about 14 billion years ago in a great explosion of matter, energy, and space-time (the Big Bang). Moreover, the properties of the universe (e.g., its matter density, the values of physical constants, nuclear reaction rates) appear to be "fine-tuned" to produce a universe that is particularly well-suited for life as we know it. These astronomical discoveries support the Christian view that God created the universe from nothing and designed it to support intelligent life, but atheists (as well as agnostics and some Christians) have proposed alternate ways to view this scientific evidence. The discovery that the universe is vastly larger than the Earth, or even the solar system, raises questions about the meaning and significance of human existence in such an immense cosmos, questions which are answered very differently by atheists and by Christians.

A century ago, the prevailing view among astronomers was that the universe was infinitely old and that its overall properties did not change over time. The tremendous astronomical discoveries since then have shown this view to be completely wrong. The current standard scientific model for cosmology is the Big Bang. In this model, the universe began about 14 billion years ago in an extremely hot, dense state. Then space itself expanded, carrying the material with it and spreading it out. The gasses cooled, and 300,000 years later the universe consisted of nearly uniform hydrogen and helium gas at a temperature of 3,000 degrees Celsius. The regions that were slightly denser began to collapse under gravity, forming the first generation of stars. Gradually, billions of galaxies formed throughout the observable universe, each containing billions of stars. About 4.6 billion years ago, the Sun formed within the Milky Way galaxy, and eventually life appeared on Earth. The history of the cosmos as we now understand it is much richer and more dynamic than a uniform infinite past.

The discoveries of modern cosmology have some compelling implications for religious and philosophical views of the natural world. One discovery is that the universe is billions of years old. This appears to conflict with Christianity, since the Bible records only a few thousand years of history since the creation of the universe. In chapter 8 of this volume, How Christians Reconcile Ancient Texts with Modern Science, I have discussed this issue in detail, and shown that the best interpretation of the Genesis text is completely consistent with the scientific evidence for billions of years of history. In this chapter I turn to four other aspects of modern cosmology with implications for philosophy and religion: (1) the universe had a beginning (rather than an infinite past); (2) the universe is extremely well-suited for life; (3) the universe will end someday; and (4) the universe is much larger than the Earth and humanity.

1   Our Universe Had a Beginning in Time

1.1   Scientific evidence

In the standard Big Bang model, our universe is not infinitely old. This model is supported by several strong lines of evidence. First, we observe that all galaxies are moving away from us; in a pattern which indicates that space itself is still expanding (this was discovered by Edwin Hubble in 1929). By mentally "rewinding" this expansion, we can calculate the time at which the expansion began, and thus the beginning of the universe. Second, we can observe the heat left over from the Big Bang, in the form of weak thermal radiation reaching us uniformly from all over the sky (discovered by Arno Penzias and Robert Wilson in 1965). This is called the Cosmic Microwave Background Radiation, and dates back to 300,000 years after the Big Bang. Third, we detect evidence of the processes which occurred in the first few minutes of the Big Bang, namely fusion of hydrogen into helium. We can calculate the fraction of hydrogen that would have fused into helium, then compare it to observations; when we measure gasses which have been unaltered since the Big Bang, they exactly match the predicted value. Thus, the scientific community has a strong consensus about what happened in the minutes and years following the Big Bang.

We do not, however, have a good understanding of the first instant of the Big Bang. How did the expansion get started? What was the source of matter and energy? In the standard Big Bang model, these questions cannot (yet) be answered scientifically. When physicists calculate back to the first instant (the first 10^{-43} seconds after the Big Bang), we find such extremely high densities and energies that the conditions cannot be replicated in current experiments. Moreover, the modern theories of quantum mechanics and general relativity (each of which are an excellent match to data in most situations), give contradictory answers for the initial moment. According to general relativity (but not quantum mechanics), the universe was initially a singularity, in which matter was infinitely compressed, and space and time had their beginning. (The phrases "at a time before the Big Bang" or "the Big Bang expanded into space" do not have meaning in the standard model, since there is no time or space apart from the spacetime of our universe, which originated in the Big Bang.) On the other hand, quantum mechanics says that no such singularity can exist, because it would violate the *uncertainty principle*. The uncertainty principle is a fundamental result of quantum mechanics, and states that the position of an object cannot be known with infinite precision, therefore matter cannot be confined to an infinitely small singularity. These contradictory answers tell us that our physical theories are simply not yet capable of answering questions about the beginning of the Big Bang; we know that we don't know the answers.[1]

Even before scientists reached a consensus about the Big Bang, they had become aware that the universe could not be infinitely old. Arthur Eddington wrote in 1931 about the implications of modern thermodynamics. The second law of thermodynamics states that entropy, a quantity that measures disorder, must always increase in a closed system. Since the universe is a closed system (in the sense that energy does not enter it from "outside"), its entropy must have been smaller in the past. At some point the entropy must have been zero, a condition when "the matter and energy of the world had the maximum possible organization. To go back further is impossible. We have come to an abrupt end of space-time – only we generally call it the 'beginning.'"[2] Another implication of an infinitely old universe was explained by Fred Hoyle in 1950:[3] all the hydrogen in the universe would have long ago been converted into helium through fusion in stars. An infinitely old universe does not explain the fact that the majority of protons in the universe are still in the form of hydrogen rather than heavier elements.

1.2 Christian responses

A beginning to the universe is consistent with the Bible and the traditional Christian doctrine of creation. This doctrine includes several ideas, only a few of which will be discussed here.[4] One aspect is *creation originans*, the idea that everything (time, space, matter, and energy) was miraculously made by God[5] at some point in the finite past. This is closely related to *creation ex nihilo* ("creation from nothing"), the idea that God made all that is. The opening lines of the Gospel of John speak of Jesus Christ (the Word) and his role in creation:

> In the beginning was the Word and the Word was with God, and the Word was God. He was with God in the beginning. Through him all things were made; without him nothing was made that has been made.[6]

Everything in the universe owes its existence to God. Matter is not self-existing, nor co-eternal with God, rather it was made by God. Thus, Christian doctrine is consistent with God starting the Big Bang.

But the Christian doctrine of creation does not consist solely of God's action at the beginning. It also includes *creation continuans:* the idea that everything (time, space, matter, energy) is preserved and sustained by God. Paul wrote "By him [Christ] all things were created: things in heaven and on earth, visible and invisible ... He is before all things, and in him all things hold together."[7] Christians believe that God directly upholds the ongoing function of the physical laws and the continuing existence of matter.

The beginning of the universe can also be used to argue for the existence of God on philosophical grounds.[8] One example of this is the *kalam* argument for the existence of God, which has its roots in Islamic thought. It can be summarized as follows,[9]

(1)   Everything that begins to exist has a cause of its existence.

(2)   The universe began to exist.

(3)   Therefore, the universe has a cause of its existence.

(4)   Scientists do not have a scientific explanation for a causal origin of the universe.

(5)   Therefore, the cause of the universe must be a personal agent.

The evidence I presented in section 1.1 supports premisses (2) and (4). If you grant premiss (1), then an eternal personal being (God) is required to cause the Big Bang.

1.3 Atheistic responses

Many atheists agree with something like the *kalam* argument, and many also agree that such arguments are more consistent with Christianity than with atheism. Arthur Eddington, after explaining the entropy argument for a beginning (see section 1.1) wrote "I have no 'philosophical axe to grind' in this discussion. Philosophically, the notion of a beginning of the present order of nature is repugnant to me."[10] He personally disliked the idea of the beginning, but was convinced by the scientific evidence that the universe could not be infinitely old. Similarly, Fred Hoyle closes his explanation of the hydrogen argument for a beginning (section 1.1) with "So we see that the universe being what it is, the creation issue simply cannot be dodged."[11] Hoyle goes on to explain his Steady-State model of the universe (section 1.4), an alternative model in which the universe is infinitely old.

Comments like those of Eddington and Hoyle (and Hawking, below) suggest that there was (and is) an atheistic motivation among some scientists to develop alternative scientific models[12] to the Big Bang. They want a model that would explain the data in terms of a universe infinite in time, or at least recast the Big Bang in a way that avoids a beginning of time. This would challenge premisses (2) and (4) of the *kalam* argument, and thus avoid its conclusion. In contrast, Christians have been more open to investigating the Big Bang model. One of the earliest of these was Georges Lemaître, a Belgian cleric who developed some of the first mathematical models for the expansion of the universe.[13]

1.4 Alternative scientific models

Steady State universe

In the 1940s, Hoyle developed his model for the Steady State universe (and in 1999[14] he was still arguing for a version of it). Note that this model was developed at a time when there was much less evidence for the Big Bang model (recall the three major pieces of evidence outlined in 1.1). By the 1940s, there was strong evidence for the expansion of the universe, but the evidence of the early heat and the fusion reactions was not yet known, nor was the evidence that galaxies had different properties in the past than today. Hoyle's hypothesis was more reasonable then than it is now.

In the Steady State model, the universe is expanding (matter is moving apart), but the average density of the universe stays constant (constant amount of matter per square meter). These two ideas are contradictory, so the model requires the ongoing creation of matter to maintain the same spatial density. The matter arrives in the form of hydrogen atoms which spontaneously appear in space. Consider a certain nearby galaxy, which we observe to be moving away from us due to the expansion of the universe. In the distant future that galaxy will be much further away, but in the meantime hydrogen atoms will appear and form another nearby galaxy in its place, maintaining the average density of galaxies. Although the ongoing creation of new hydrogen atoms violates the conservation of matter-energy, Hoyle argued that it was not an unreasonable theory.

The whole idea of creation is queer. In the older theories all the matter in the universe is supposed to have appeared at one instant of time, the whole creation process taking the form of one big bang. For myself I find this idea very much queerer than continuous creation.[15]

In the decades since Hoyle first developed the Steady State model, a tremendous amount of scientific evidence has appeared which contradicts it. The Steady State model has been revised in attempts to fit the new evidence,[16] and the small number of astronomers who still pursue it[17] argue that the Big Bang model also has several arbitrary physical processes, unconfirmed claims, and contradictory evidence.[18] But virtually all astronomers feel the evidence is a much better fit to the Big Bang model than to the Steady State model.

Oscillating universe

Another model for an infinitely old universe involves an eternal cycle. The universe would expand for a time, then collapse back down to a condition of extreme heat and density (similar to the Big Bang), then bounce back into another expansion. Analysis of this model shows, however, that it is not possible to make an infinite universe this way (entropy would increase at each bounce and should be infinite by now)[19]. An oscillating universe would still require a beginning in time.

Hawking's "no boundary condition" universe

Stephen Hawking has developed a different mathematical picture of the Big Bang based on ideas of quantum gravity.[20] As mentioned above, the standard Big Bang model is based on general relativity; the universe started with a singularity, where space was infinitely small at time zero. This is a "boundary condition": certain parameters of the universe are set at time zero, and then the universe proceeds into the future. Hawking has incorporated ideas from quantum mechanics into general relativity, and developed a model in which the Big Bang is *not* a singularity. Instead, the spacetime of the universe is redefined in new coordinates ("imaginary time") and shaped in such a way that there is no edge. The result is a model in which time never equals zero. The conclusion is that there are no boundary conditions and no beginning.

Hawking reflects on the implications of his theory:

The idea that space and time may form a closed surface without boundary also has profound implications for the role of God in the affairs of the universe. With the success of scientific theories in describing events, most people have come to believe that God allows the universe to evolve according to a set of laws and does not intervene in the universe to break these laws. However, the laws do not tell us what the universe should have looked like when it started – it would still be up to God to wind up the clockwork and choose how to start it off. So long as the universe had a beginning, we could suppose it had a creator. But if the universe is really completely self-contained, having no boundary or edge, it would have neither beginning nor end: it would simply be. What place, then for a creator?[21]

Carl Sagan, in the introduction to Hawking's book, takes this a step further.

Hawking is attempting, as he explicitly states, to understand the mind of God. And this makes all the more unexpected the conclusion of the effort, at least so far: a universe with no edge in space, no beginning or end in time, and nothing for a Creator to do.[22]

If Hawking's model is correct, it would be philosophically similar to an eternal universe (no beginning, so no need for God); yet still consistent with dynamic changes occurring in the universe in the minutes and years following the Big Bang.

There are several weaknesses in this argument, when viewed from the perspectives of science, philosophy, and religion.[23] Scientifically, the model is suggestive and mathematically correct, but it has not been experimentally confirmed. Moreover, it makes no physical predictions that *could* be used to test it. Philosophically, Hawking is inconsistent when describing how the model relates to reality. He writes "we may regard our use of imaginary time and Euclidean spacetime as merely a mathematical device (or trick) to calculate answers about real space-time",[24] but goes on to argue that the results for imaginary time are a true description of the beginning, true enough to draw philosophical and religious implications.

Another weakness is in the way Hawking describes God and his role in the universe. Hawking and Sagan are using a "straw man" argument: they define God in a simplistic way (as a deistic god who only starts things off and is not otherwise involved), and then they argue that such a god is no longer required. As discussed above, actual Christian doctrine (*creation continuans*) teaches that God does much more than start the universe – God continually upholds the existence of matter-energy and the functioning of physical laws. Hawking and Sagan also imply that God exists in the timeline of this universe, by implying that he would need to be around "before" time zero to start things off. But God is transcendent (beyond) the spacetime of this universe, and creates it apart from himself. God is completely capable of creating spacetime without a boundary. Hawking and Sagan have not succeeded in disproving the existence of the God of the Bible. God's interaction with the universe is much richer and ongoing then simply "winding the watch" at the beginning.

Mother universe

Other scientific alternatives to the Big Bang model take a different approach. Rather than arguing for an infinite universe, they seek some natural process (some scientific explanation) for how the universe started. Typically this takes the form of a "mother" universe, an eternal preexisting reality, which brought about the Big Bang of our universe (and presumably many other universes) via some mechanism. That mechanism could be a quantum fluctuation of some energy field, a black hole singularity, or colliding membranes in a higher spatial dimension. Some scientists have even suggested that an alien life form may have obtained the intelligence and technology to produce new universes.[25]

Although some of these proposed mechanisms have some mathematical basis, none has yet made physical predictions which could be used to test and verify the mechanism. There are also philosophical problems with the argument. If the mother universe is eternal and God does not exist, then the matter of an eternal mother universe would have nearly divine properties, such as eternal self-existence, and the ability to produce new time and spatial dimensions. The problem of divinity hasn't been eliminated. Finally, a mother-universe model does not necessarily eliminate God's role in starting creation – God could have created the mother universe in the finite past, and then used it (and natural mechanism) to bring about the universe we live in. Note that it is impossible to measure the age of the mother universe, since our measurements are confined to the spacetime of this universe. Thus, the mother universe could be finite in age or infinite, but we would have no way to determine that scientifically. Thus, the mother universe model will never be able to disprove the finite age of the universe, nor disprove the existence of the Christian God.

1.5 Comments

These alternative scientific models for the history of the universe have a notable lack of any supporting experimental evidence, and most do not even make physical predictions which could be tested (the Steady State model makes predictions, but the test results have been negative). This places most of these models in the realm of mathematical speculation rather than in the realm of science. They are interesting to consider, but they cannot support the weight of serious philosophical argument.

Thus, we are left without any convincing scientific explanation for the first moment of the Big Bang, either via standard or alternative models. As a Christian and a cosmologist, I am torn between two views,[26] both of which are consistent with the current scientific evidence and with Christian doctrine. Either

(1)   God started the Big Bang in a supernatural miracle, in which he created matter, energy, space, time, and established the physical laws governing them.

or

(2)   God used some natural mechanism to produce the Big Bang from some preexisting material that we could learn about through scientific study. To be consistent with *creation ex nihilo*, the preexisting material would have been created by God in a supernatural act at some earlier point (this option pushes *creation ex nihilo* back to some earlier time).

The first option has the risk of becoming a "god of the gaps" argument[27] - an attempt to prove the existence of God based on our lack of scientific understanding, if we forget God's role in events we do understand. But the second option seems needlessly convoluted given the current evidence – the Big Bang is the obvious beginning to the space and time of the universe we experience, and thus is an obvious place to put the moment of *creation ex nihilo*. In either case, as a Christian I believe God created the universe by his word at some time in the finite past, and that the universe is not co-eternal with God.

2 The Universe Appears Fine-Tuned For "Life As We Know It"

2.1 Scientific evidence

When we consider the universe around us, we can imagine all sorts of ways it could be different, and most of those ways are completely incompatible with life as we know it. Instead, observations show that the universe is amazingly well suited for our existence. We are life-forms which have a complex chemistry (including long-chain molecules and a variety of atoms) and rely on the radiant energy of a nearby star. The preceding sentence is a fairly conservative definition of "life as we know it." It is hard for us to imagine a life-form that could develop and exist without energy from a star or without a variety of atoms to support complex information. Life stranger than this may exist, but this definition is compelling enough to raise some interesting questions about the universe. Note that stars are important for life for two major reasons: as an energy source, and as a factory to produce all the elements in the periodic table. Hydrogen and helium were produced in the Big Bang, and after the Big Bang the universe was a simple gas of (mostly) these two elements. Virtually all other elements formed later in stars. When the stars die, the elements are distributed into space and made available to be formed into new stars, planets, and lifeforms.

As I will describe below,[28] the properties of the universe appear to be "fine-tuned." The analogy here is to a radio dial, which has to be turned to the correct setting ("tuned")to pick up a radio station. The universe appears to have parameters, particles, and forces all tuned to the correct values in order to allow life. Another phrase that is used is "just right," where the value is not too far one direction or the other, but at the precise value that is required.[29]

The expansion rate of the universe is just right for long-lived stars

We can imagine a universe where stars would never have formed. For instance, the universe could have expanded much more rapidly after the Big Bang, pulling the gas clouds apart before they could collapse into stars. Or, the universe could have expanded more slowly, such that it could not overcome its own gravity, and would have quickly collapsed back down into a singularity before stars had a chance to form. Instead, we observe the universe expanding at just the right rate to allow stars to form. The expansion rate is affected by some properties of the universe as a whole (its matter density, dark energy, and spatial curvature). We observe a spatially flat universe, and when we calculate back in time we find that it must have been precisely spatially flat at the beginning. So, to explain why the expansion rate is just the right value, we also would need to explain why the spatial curvature is exactly at this special value.

The force of gravity is just right for long-lived stars

We can imagine a universe where the force of gravity was weaker or stronger. If the gravitational force was too weak, it wouldn't be able to hold a star together (the gas pressure in a star would blow it apart if gravity was not present). If the gravitational force was too strong, it would easily hold stars together, but the stars would be denser and burn faster and thus would burn out very quickly. The force of gravity we observe is set just right to allow stable, long-lived stars.

The masses of elementary particles are just right for fusion

We can imagine a universe where protons and neutrons had very different masses. This would prevent them from fusing together into heavier elements. What we observe is that the mass of a neutron is very nearly the sum of the proton mass and the electron mass. This allows protons and neutrons to transform from one to another and to fuse together to form the elements in the periodic table. If the protons had much more mass than the neutrons (or vice versa), fusion reactions would not work in the same way. The masses of the proton and neutron are finely tuned to just the right values.

The fundamental physical forces are balanced just right for fusion

We can imagine a universe where the physical forces had different strengths. Three physical forces are involved in fusion reactions: the strong nuclear force, the weak nuclear force, and the electromagnetic force. We observe that the strengths of these forces are balanced so that protons and neutrons can successfully fuse together, and so that atoms can exist stably without falling apart. If the strengths were different, fusion reactions would not occur properly, and the only stable element in the universe would be hydrogen.

Nuclear reaction rates are just right to produce carbon in stars

We can imagine a universe without carbon. Why care about carbon? It is one of the few elements that can form long-chain molecules with hydrogen (hydrocarbons), and long-chain molecules are very well suited for complex chemical life such as ourselves. Carbon is made in the cores of stars, as part of a sequence of fusion reactions involving other elements. Even with the masses and forces balanced just right so that fusion works in general, the rates of each particular reaction must also be set correctly to produce carbon. In a star, the first reaction is when beryllium and helium fuse together to form carbon (destroying the beryllium). Then, carbon fuses with more helium to form oxygen (destroying carbon). Ultimately the star comes to the end of its life and the elements are dispersed into the universe to form planets and other smaller bodies. If the two reactions proceeded at the same speed, all the carbon would be used up and there would be no carbon left in the star at the end of its life. What we observe instead is that carbon has a nuclear-excited state which allows the first reaction to proceed quickly. Oxygen does not have a similar nuclear-excited state, so the second reaction proceeds slowly. Thus, the nuclear properties of these atoms are finely tuned so that a substantial amount of carbon is produced in stars.

The water molecule is just right for life around stars

We can imagine a universe where water would not be as useful for life as it is. Water is useful on Earth because of its molecular properties. It can exist on Earth as a solid, liquid, or gas, and it is a solvent for many other molecules and ions. Another property is its transparency. Water is opaque at most wavelengths (infrared, ultraviolet, x-ray), but it is transparent to light in a narrow window around 400–700 nm (the wavelengths our eyes can see). This happens to be the part of the spectrum where light from the Sun (and other long-lived stars) is the brightest. There is no physical reason that the light emitted by stars should have any correlation with the transparency of a useful molecule, and yet these are related in a way that is particularly beneficial to life. One or the other is fine-tuned for life as we know it.

Even more parameters may be fine-tuned.[30] In fact some writers have developed very long lists of them. Unfortunately they sometimes overcount the number of fine-tuned parameters by double counting those that are not independent of each other. I have tried to avoid this in my description above, for instance by referring to the *balance* of force strengths (their ratio) rather than the strength of each force individually (two or three separate parameters). Many writers also attempt to calculate the numerical probability that the universe is fine-tuned, and come up with extraordinarily small probabilities.[31] The problem with those calculations is that we have only one universe to study, so it is nearly impossible to know the range of possible universes, and that range is a key component of the probability calculation.[32] The evidence for fine-tuning is strong and compelling, but *quantitative* measures of it are not completely reliable.

2.2 Christian responses

William Paley[33] famously argued that the careful design of the universe is evidence that it is the work of an intelligent designer. He used the analogy of walking along and finding a watch lying on the ground. One could compare the watch to a rock lying nearby, and it would be immediately obvious that the watch is more complicated than the rock. Moreover, it is apparent that the watch has a purpose and function, and that it was carefully designed for that function. We can extend this analogy by imagining that one discovers not merely a functioning watch, but a bunch of parts which (when shaken) would self-assemble into a watch. The design of the self-assembling watch pieces would be even more impressive than the design of a standard watch, since the pieces have to fit and lock together as they are shaken and form into a functioning whole in the end. Similarly, the careful construction of the universe, with so many parameters set to be just right for life, is evidence that it was designed by an intelligent agent, such as God.[34] The design is impressive in its economy and productivity. The system has a small number of physical forces, particles, and universal properties, but as it changes over time it produces the incredible variety and complexity that we see in the universe and on earth. This points to an intelligent person who constructed the system. God designed this system to bring about not only the universe and the earth, but intelligent life forms (us) that can relate to him.

2.3 Atheist and other responses

Of course, theism is not the only response to the scientific evidence for fine tuning. Here are some other responses.

Blind coincidence

Some people view the fine-tuned parameters as simply coincidence, or blind chance. They see no significance to this evidence for fine-tuning, nothing that requires further explanation on our part. Most people (of all worldviews) find this unsatisfying. The scientific information seems full of implications that we should try to understand.

The Anthropic principle

Another set of responses come from John Barrow and Frank Tipler, authors of *The Anthropic Cosmological Principle*.[35] The Weak Anthropic principle states that we should not be surprised that the universe appears fine-tuned to support life. Consider the alternative: if the universe did not have the necessary properties to support intelligent life, then we wouldn't be here to ask the question! Even if it was unlikely for the universe to be just right for life, the simple fact that we exist means that we will necessarily observe a universe that can support life, however probable or improbable.[36] This view is useful, at a minimum, in countering overzealous application of the "Copernican principle" (see section 4.2).

   The problem with the Weak Anthropic principle is that it doesn't have any explanatory power. It would be the same whether we determined that universes like ours are typical or extremely rare. John Leslie[37] uses a "firing-square" analogy: a prisoner is taken out to be executed, and 50 sharpshooters aim at him from short range. They all fire, and yet he is not hit. Would the prisoner say afterwards, "Oh, that's not significant – if they hadn't all missed, I wouldn't be alive here to consider it"? No, he would look for a *reason* why all the shooters missed. The fact that we're here doesn't explain *why* the universe is the way it is.

Barrow and Tipler propose other versions of the principle which go farther. The Strong Anthropic principle states that the universe *must* be such that intelligent life would arise at some point, that is, the purpose of the universe is to produce *us*. At their most extreme, Barrow and Tipler suggest the Final Anthropic principle, which states intelligent life must arise, *and* that it will go on to fill the whole universe to the point that the universe consists only of our biological and machine descendents and the information they produce (this is called the "omega point"). Thus, the universe *becomes* us. I don't know of any scientist who holds these views, or who would even give serious consideration to the Final Anthropic principle.

Only one logically possible universe

Another unusual response to fine-tuning is the suggestion that this universe is *not* rare and unlikely, but rather is the only logical possibility. Paul Davies writes:

> Christians claim that this particular universe can be explained as God's choice, taken from an infinite range of alternatives, for reasons what are unknown to us. But even an omnipotent God cannot break the rules of logic. God cannot make 2 = 3 or make a square a circle. The hasty assumption that God can create any universe must be qualified by the restriction that it be logically consistent. Now if there exists only one logically consistent universe then God would effectively have had no choice at all.[38]

The idea here is that if God could only make one universe, then of course that is the one we live in and there is nothing remarkable about it. But the argument rests on an unlikely premise, that "there exists only one logically consistent universe". Scientists (of all world-views) can imagine a vast variety of possible universes! Our scientific models have many free parameters and we can easily construct logically consistent mathematical models which do not match the reality of our universe.

2.4 Alternative scientific models: Multiple universes

Some scientists respond to fine-tuning by looking for a natural explanation. This is typically done by arguing for multiple universes.[39] The idea is that our universe is one of many universes in existence. These universes originate through some natural mechanism, such as those described above. The universes do not all have the same values for the physical constants (force strengths, particle masses, cosmological explanation rate, etc.), but have a variety of values for those constants. Of the many universes, a few will happen to have physical parameters with values appropriate for life. Then, by the Weak Anthropic Principle, we can conclude that we must be living in a universe appropriate for life. Thus, if there are many universes, our universe no longer looks fine tuned, it just looks like home. Analogously, if you go to the clothing store and there is only one shirt in the whole store, it would be very surprising to find that it fits you exactly, but if the store caries many shirts with a wide range of size it is not surprising at all.[40]

A major problem with this view, as mentioned above, is that the mechanisms for producing multiple universes have no experimental evidence to support them, and don't even make predictions that could be tested. Even if multiple universes exist, fine-tuning would not be eliminated. The "mother universe" which produces the multiple universes would also have to be somewhat fine-tuned. Its parameters would have to be set correctly to produce many universes, and to produce them with a range of physical constants that include the values appropriate for life. Such a model would reduce the number of fine-tuned parameters, but not eliminate fine-tuning.

2.5 Comments

Further scientific study may eventually explain some parameters previously thought to be fine-tuned. In fact, this has already happened, in the inflation model for the early universe. This model is an addition to standard Big Bang cosmology, in which a new natural mechanism causes the universe to expand (inflate) *extremely* rapidly at 10^{-35} seconds after the Big Bang. This rapid expansion *causes* the universe to be precisely spatially flat, which is one of the fine-tuned properties I discussed in section 2A. Thus, the flatness property need no longer be caused by an initial supernatural (miraculous) action, but instead could have been set using this natural process. Moreover, this new natural mechanism provides answers to two other puzzles in the standard Big Bang model: the uniformity of temperature over the whole sky, and the absence of magnetic monopoles.[41] It does not merely introduce one new mechanism to explain one new fine-tuned property, but introduces one mechanism which explains at least three properties of the universe. So, will the other fine-tuned parameters ultimately be explained through new scientific explanations within our universe? Both atheists and Christians seem to feel this is unlikely. If atheists thought this was a possibility, they would propose that sort of research rather than the multiple universe models. And many Christians are comfortable viewing the fine-tuned parameters as God's supernatural action and do not feel a desire to seek natural explanations.

Speaking as an astronomer, the scientific evidence for fine-tuning is strong. Speaking as a Christian, I see God at work both in processes (like inflation) that we can describe scientifically, and in the "coincidences" and fine-tuned parameters that do not have natural explanations. The evidence for fine-tuning is consistent with Christian beliefs about God's purposes in creation. It is evidence which supports my belief in God, and it is compelling evidence that should cause a non-theist to consider whether there is a God. I find the philosophical and scientific alternatives to be weak and unconvincing. Thus, I believe God used a small number of physical forces and particles, and crafted them in such as way as to produce everything from a symmetric spiral galaxy to the sweet scent of a rose, from the crystalline structure of a snowflake to intelligent persons which could in turn relate to God. If we find natural explanations for values we currently think are fine-tuned, it would speak even more highly of God's craftsmanship in making a self-assembling universe with even fewer knobs to tune.

3 The Universe Will End

3.1 Scientific evidence

Astronomers have abundant evidence that our universe is a dynamic, evolving place, and that it will not continue into the future with the same properties it has now. Assuming the laws and constants of physics stay the same, we can sketch out a scientific prediction for the future. About 5 billion years from now, our galaxy will collide with our neighbor the Andromeda galaxy. This will have only a mild effect on the solar system, but will be an impressive lightshow in the sky as millions of new stars form during the collision. Our concerns will be closer to home, because around that time the Sun will reach the end of its life and become a red giant star. It will be thousands of times brighter than it is now, which will destroy our atmosphere and burn up the surface of the Earth. In the more distant future (trillions of years), all gasses in the universe will be converted into stars, and then all the remaining stars will die (becoming white dwarfs, neutron stars, or black holes). At that point the universe will be a cold, dark place with no starlight to provide energy. In the far future, the entropy of the universe will reach a maximum value, bringing about the "heat death" of the universe. But before that time, the universe might experience the "Big Rip," when the accelerating expansion of the universe pulls all matter apart from itself. An alternative distant future is the "Big Crunch," in which the universe collapses back on itself and heats up (the Big Bang in reverse). Regardless of the details, it is a virtual certainty that the Earth will not survive into the infinite future. (Remember, all of these predictions assume the physical laws continue to operate as they have so far.)

3.2 Atheistic responses

Bertrand Russell wrote in 1903:

> The world which science presents for our belief is even more purposeless, more void of meaning, [than a world in which God is malevolent]. Amid such a world, if anywhere, our ideals henceforward must find a home. That man is the product of causes which had no prevision of the end they were achieving; that his origin, his growth, his hopes and fears, his loves and his beliefs, are but the outcome of accidental collocations of atoms; that no fire, no heroism, no intensity of thought and feeling, can preserve an individual life beyond the grave; that all the labors of the ages, all the devotion, all the inspiration, all the noonday brightness of human genius, are destined to extinction in the vast death of the solar system, and the whole temple of Man's achievement must inevitably be buried beneath the debris of a universe in ruins – all these things, if not quite beyond dispute, are yet so nearly certain that no philosophy which rejects them can hope to stand. Only within the scaffolding of these truths, only on the firm foundation of unyielding despair, can the soul's habitation henceforth be safely built.[42]

Steven Weinberg wrote in 1988:

> It is almost irresistible for humans to believe that we have some special relation to the universe, that human life is not just a more-or-less farcical outcome of a chain of accidents reaching back to the first three minutes, but that we were somehow built in from the beginning.... It is very hard to realize that [the Earth] is just a tiny part of an overwhelmingly hostile universe. It is even harder to realize that this present universe has evolved from an unspeakably unfamiliar early condition, and faces a future extinction of endless cold or intolerable heat. The more the universe seems comprehensible, the more it also seems pointless.... The effort to understand the universe is one of the very few things that lifts human life a little above the level of farce, and gives it some of the grace of tragedy.[43]

These writers look at the scientific prediction for the future and see only ruins and hopelessness. I wonder what they expected from the future *before* this scientific picture developed. Certainly they were smart enough not to hope for their own immortality, but perhaps they hoped in the immortality of the human race, or that humanity's achievements would have some eternal impact on the universe. Whatever their hope was, it has been dashed by the news that the universe will end someday. Other atheists have a less pessimistic view of the future, but the scientific picture has removed the option for atheists to place their hope in the ultimate future of humanity, to rest their sense of meaning and purpose in our long-term impact on the universe.

3.3 Christian response

Christians are not surprised to learn that the universe will end some day. The Bible includes many prophesies that God will ultimately destroy the heavens and the earth, and then remake them. Long before modern science, Christians were aware of not only their personal mortality, but the mortality of the human race and of the whole world. In the face of this, the Bible teaches us to put our hope in Jesus Christ. All who commit their lives to him will be saved from the coming destruction and preserved in the new world. The Bible says:

> I am making everything new.... A new heaven and a new earth.... The first earth will pass away.... Now the dwelling of God is with men. They will be his people, and God himself will be with them and be their God. He will wipe every tear from their eyes. There will be no more death or mourning or crying or pain, for the old order of things has passed away.[44]

God will destroy the heavens and the earth as a way to ultimately destroy all evil and suffering, but will preserve his people to live in a new world of peace. Thus, Christians look forward to the end of the world with hope.

The Bible specifically teaches that we cannot know when the end will come, and Christian theology has taught that it could be anytime – today, next year, or in a thousand years. Trillions of years seem long, simply because God's interaction with humanity has so far occurred on time scales of hundreds and thousands of years, not billions or trillions. In any case, the Biblical description strongly suggests a *supernatural* end to the current universe, rather than the natural ends discussed in section 3A. At any time, God could choose to discontinue his regular governance of the world, and bring about destruction and a new creation.

4 The Universe is Much Larger than Humanity

4.1 Scientific evidence

The discoveries of astronomy have shown that humanity is a small part of a very large universe, not only in terms of size,[45] but in terms of time and of substance. In terms of time, the universe has existed for about 13.7 billion years (or more, if you believe the mother universe models), while humanity as a race has been around about 100,000 years and an individual human lives in the order of 100 years. In terms of size, the part of the universe we can observe is on the order of 100,000,000,000,000,000,000,000,000 meters across, while the Earth is only about 10,000 meters across and a human is only 2 meters tall. And just in the last decade it has become clear that humanity is in the minority in terms of substance. Our bodies are made of protons and neutrons, which make up only

4 percent of the material in the universe. Another 23 percent of the universe is made of "dark matter," a substance which has mass but does not emit light (perhaps exotic particles left over from the Big Bang). The majority of the universe (73 percent) is made of "dark energy" which is so new and exotic that we have very little idea of what it is. The universe is vastly beyond the size and time scale of our human existence, and is mostly made of material we don't understand.

4.2 Atheistic responses

One way to understand our place in the universe is the "Copernican principle." This is the idea that our location in the universe is not special or unique, but typical of the universe around us. It dates back to the discoveries of Nicolas Copernicus. He was the first modern scientist to argue that the Sun is at the center of the universe. This was counter to the prevailing view that the Earth was at the center of the universe. Copernicus showed that the Earth is not unique, but one of many planets. In the centuries that followed, it became clear that our Sun is not unique, but one of many stars. And later, we found that the Sun is not at the center of the universe. In fact, the Sun is an ordinary star in orbit around our galaxy. By this time the pattern was becoming obvious, so it wasn't a shock (at a philosophical level) to find that our galaxy is not unique, nor at the center of the universe, but is one of many galaxies. Currently, some scientists speculate that this pattern continues further, that our universe is one of many universes. Thus, the pattern called the Copernican principle gives a context for the evidence that we are very small compared to the universe – it is yet another way in which we are not unique compared to the universe.

This Copernican principle is easy to apply when merely considering our physical location in the universe, but it is harder to apply to questions like the materials we are made of, or the epoch of the universe that we live in. The fact that we are part of the 4 percent of the universe made of protons and neutrons looks like we are "special" rather than typical of the universe at large. To avoid nonsense conclusions, the Copernican principle must be coupled with the Weak Anthropic principle. The Copernican principle could be revised to say that our location in the universe is not unique *when compared to the set of locations that could support life*. Thus, it is not a violation of the Copernican principle to find that Earth is in a galaxy (even though most of the universe is empty space), because it is the stars in a galaxy that can support the complex chemistry needed for life.

The preceding description of the Copernican principle is not particularly atheistic. But the principle is often cast in stronger terms relating to the *significance* of humanity in the universe. Proponents say that the medieval Church viewed the Earth as central and thus the most important place in the universe, and opposed Copernicus' model because it would "de-throne" the Earth and make humanity less significant in the universe. The continuation of the pattern to stars and galaxies is then cast as a continuing triumph of science over Christianity, and a continuing demotion of humanity. Carl Sagan is reported to have said "Who are we? We find that we live on an insignificant planet of a humdrum star lost in a galaxy tucked away in some forgotten corner of the universe." Sagan wrote "Our planet is a lonely speck in the great enveloping cosmic dark. In our obscurity, in all this vastness, there is no hint that help will come from elsewhere to save us from ourselves."[46] From the scientific evidence that humanity is trillions of times smaller than the universe, they conclude that humanity must be completely insignificant.

4.3 Christian responses

As a Christian who believes in the teachings of the Bible, I find that the scientific vastness of the universe does not challenge or disprove those beliefs, and in fact can strengthen them.

The origin of the Copernican principle and its philosophical overtones has been studied by Dennis Danielson,[47] a historian of science. He finds that at the time of Copernicus and Galileo, the Church and Western society did *not* view the center of the universe as the best or most significant location. Rather, the center was the place of imperfection and sin (recall Dante's *Inferno,* which places hell at the center of the Earth). The heavens were the place of perfection, and when Copernicus showed that Earth moved, he promoted Earth to one of the heavenly bodies. In that culture it was not a demotion, nor did it lower the cosmological significance of humanity. It was later authors who combined scientific history with the modern view that the center is the most significant location. The Copernican principle may have some use in describing a pattern in the history of science, but its philosophical significance is viewed very differently by people of different cultures. The principle alone cannot prove that humanity is insignificant.

Implicit in the response of atheists like Sagan is the view that "God" is merely an idea invented by humanity. If this is so, then the smallness of humanity in the universe would indeed make "God" small, and Sagan could rightly conclude that "no help will come from elsewhere to save us from ourselves." But Christian doctrine has always stated that God came before humans, and that God rules the whole cosmos, not just the Earth. The scientific discovery of the vastness of the universe does not contradict this belief, but rather strengthens it by demonstrating the vastness of God's reign and creative power.

Still, some Christians wonder why this powerful God would care about us if he is governing such a large universe. Is it audacious to believe that God loves us when we are such a small component of what he has made? This is not a new question. Over 3,000 years ago, the poet David looked up at the night sky and wrote:

> O Lord, our Lord,
> how majestic is your name in all the earth!
> When I look at your heavens,
> the work of your fingers,
> the moon and the stars
> that you have established,
> What are human beings that you are mindful of them,
> mortals that you care for them?[48]

David goes on to answer the question in the following verses, by reminding us that God gave humanity responsibility to care for the Earth:

> Yet you have made them a little lower than God,
> and crowned them with glory and honor.
> You have made them rulers over the works of your hands;
> You put everything under their feet.[49]

Thus, God gave us a significant role to play in the cosmos, in caring for this planet.

Another Biblical answer comes with these lines:

> God does not treat us as our sins deserve
> or repay us according to our iniquities.
> For as high as the heavens are above the earth,
> so great is his love for those who fear him;
> as far as the east is from the west,
> so far has he removed our transgressions from us.[50]

In Ancient Near Eastern cultures,[51] the full extent of the cosmos was from the flat earth up to the hard dome of heaven, and from the eastern horizon to the western horizon. Thus, these verses refer to the entire created universe, not just some part of the Earth. This is the object lesson used to illustrate the love of God for humanity. This revelation from God in the Bible clearly states that we are not to view the vastness of the cosmos as a sign of our smallness in God's eyes, but rather as a sign of the greatness of God's love and forgiveness.

That love has been demonstrated by God in many ways, but centrally in the person of his Son, Jesus Christ. Christ reigned with God, governing the universe, and then set this aside to become incarnate as a human being. He was born as a human baby – how much more approachable could a powerful God become? He lived on earth as one of us – how can he not understand our human needs and troubles? He died a cruel death to pay the punishment for our sins – how can he not attentively listen to our prayers for forgiveness of sin? He rose from the dead and reigns in heaven, preparing a place for us to dwell in his presence – why should we fear the future of the universe? For a Christian, our significance in the universe is based on our significance in God's eyes, not in our physical size and composition.

Notes

1 This is an example of what Loren Haarsma calls a "scientifically unexplainable event" or "unknown natural mechanism" in chapter 10 of this volume, SCIENTIFIC KNOWLEDGE DOES NOT REPLACE RELIGIOUS KNOWLEDGE. He discusses five ways scientists respond to such situations, and in the remainder of this chapter I'll point out examples of each.

2 Arthur S. Eddington "The End of the World: From the Standpoint of Mathematical Physics," *Nature* (Supplement), 127.3203 (March 21, 1931), as reprinted in the anthology Dennis Danielson (ed.), *The Book of the Cosmos* (hereafter *BoC*) (Cambridge: Perseus, 2001), p. 403.

3 Fred Hoyle *The Nature of the Universe* (Oxford: Basil Blackwell, 1950), reprinted in *BoC*, p. 413.

4 For a bit more discussion, see William Lane Craig, "'What place, then for a creator?' Hawking on God and Creation," *British Journal of Philosophical Science* 41 (1990), 473–91, reprinted in the anthology Melville Y. Stewart and Xing Taotao (eds.), *Philosophy of Religion* (hereafter *PoR*) (Beijing: Peking University Press), 2005, p. 481.

5 An example of Loren Haarsma's "reponses to unknown natural mechanisms", type (b) a supernatural event.

6 John 1:1–3. *The Bible: New International Version* (Grand Rapids, MI: Zondervan) (hereafter *NIV*).

7 Colossians 1:16–17 (*NIV*).

8 For a detailed summary of philosophical arguments from cosmology, see Bruce Reichenbach, "The Cosmological Argument," *Stanford Encyclopedia of Philosophy*, reprinted in *PoR*, pp. 119–35.

9 Ibid., p. 125.

10 Eddington, in *BoC*, p. 403.

11 Hoyle, in *BoC*, p. 413.

12 An example of Loren Haarsma's "reponses to unknown natural mechanisms", type (a) an unknown natural law.

13   For example, Georges Édouard Lemaître, "The Evolution of the Universe," *Nature* (Supplement) 128.3234 (October 24, 1931), reprinted in *BoC*, pp. 407–10.

14   Geoffrey Burbidge, Fred Hoyle, and Jayant V. Narlikar, "A Different Approach to Cosmology," *Physics Today* (April 1999), pp. 38–46.

15   Hoyle, in Danielson, *BoC*, p. 413. It is here that Hoyle coined the term "Big Bang".

16   Burbidge, Hoyle, and Narlikar.

17   Erik Lerner (and 33 co-signers), "An Open Letter to the Scientific Community" published in *New Scientist*, 2448 (May 22, 2004), also available at http://www.cosmologystatement.org.

18   The assumptions used in each include the following. The Big Bang model assumes the creation of matter in the first instant, the existence of (poorly understood) dark matter and (very poorly understood) dark energy, and the inflation process. The Steady State model assumes the ongoing creation of matter, the location and type of the newly created matter, that deuterium can some-how be made in stars (rather than in the Big Bang), a 100-billion-year oscillation period that is turned around by a poorly understood energy field, and odd dust grains to convert star light into the uniform microwave background radiation.

19   Steven Weinberg explains that the ratio of photons to nuclear particles (the entropy per nuclear particle) would increase at each cycle. If the cycle has gone on into the infinite past, that ratio would now be infinite, but we observe it be merely large. *The First Three Minutes* (New York: Basic Books 1988), p. 154.

20   Stephen Hawking, *A Brief History of Time* (New York: Bantam Books, 1988).

21   Hawking, *Brief History*, p. 141.

22   Sagan, Introduction to *A Brief History of Time*.

23   For a complete discussion, see Craig, in *PoR*, pp. 479–93.

24   Hawking, *Brief History*, p. 135.

25   An example of Loren Haarsma's "reponses to unknown natural mechanisms," type (c) natural but super-human intellect or technology.

26   These correspond to Loren Haarsma's "reponses to unknown natural mechanisms", type (b) supernatural event, and type (a) a new natural law. I find the other three responses dissatisfying for the beginning of the universe.

27   See my SCIENCE AND RELIGION IN HARMONY, chapter 7 in this volume, section 1.

28   Most of the scientific arguments in this section are discussed in more detail by Lee Smolin in *The Life of the Cosmos* (New York: Oxford University Press, 1997); excerpts reprinted in *BoC*, pp. 467–81.

29   This idea of "just right" is captured in the well-known Western children's story "Goldilocks and the Three Bears." The text is available at http://www.dltk-kids.com/rhymes/goldilocks_story.htm (typically the story is accompanied by many pictures and is read to small children at bedtime).

30   For examples, see Smolin in *BoC*, pp. 467–81; Robin Collins, "God, Design, and Fine-Tuning," in *PoR*, pp. 161–80; and books by Hugh Ross, such as *The Creator and the Cosmos* (Colorado Springs: NavPress, 1995).

31   Smolin (*BoC*, p. 473) calculates a probability of 1 in 10^{226}; and Eddington (*BoC* p. 403) calculates a probability of roughly 1 in $10^{10000000000}$.

32   For example, consider rolling a die and getting the number 3. How surprised should you be to get 3? We know that the probability is 1 in 6, because there are six options on the die, all with equal probability. Now consider some parameter in our universe that has the value 3. We might calcu-late that only values between 2 and 4 could support life as we know it. How likely is it that our universe has the value 3? We have no way of knowing, because we don't know the range this parameter can have. We only see the number 3, and there are not multiple universes to study to see what other options are available. The parameter might have a range from 1 to 6, or from 0.1 to 600, or from 1 to 10^{60}; we just don't know. Therefore we can't determine if the probability is 1 in 6 or 1 in 10^{60}.

33   William Paley *Natural Theology* (London, 1802), excerpts reprinted in *BoC*, pp. 291–3.

34 For a detailed discussion of the design argument for God, see Collins, in *PoR* pp. 161–80. Note that this argument is somewhat different than the argument made by the current "Intelligent Design" movement in the United States (see Loren Haarsma, GOD, EVOLUTION, AND DESIGN, chapter 11 in this volume).

35 John D. Barrow and Frank J. Tipler, *The Anthropic Cosmological Principle* (Oxford: Oxford University Press, 1986); excerpts reprinted in *BoC*, p. 442.

36 An example of Loren Haarsma's "reponses to unknown natural mechanisms", type (d) an improbable event simply occurred.

37 John Leslie "How to Draw Conclusions From a Fine-Tuned Cosmos" in Robert Russell et al. (eds.) *Physics, Philosophy, and Theology: A Common Quest for Understanding* (Vatican City: Vatican Observatory Press, 1988), p. 304, quoted in Collins in *PoR*, p. 169.

38 Paul Davies, *God and The New Physics* (New York: Simon & Schuster, 1983), p. 222.

39 Smolin, in *BoC*, pp. 478–9; Martin Rees, *Before the Beginning: Our Universe and Others* (Reading, MA: Helix/Perseus Books, 1997), excerpts reprinted in *BoC*, pp. 464–6. This is an example of Loren Haarsma's "reponses to unknown natural mechanisms", type (e) improbable event in one of many universes.

40 This example is borrowed from Martin Rees, as told by Danielson, *BoC*, p. 464.

41 Inflation explains the flatness of space in this way: if space initially were curved (like a small balloon), the extreme expansion (like inflating the balloon) would have stretched it out, so that the portion of the universe we see is spatially flat (like an ant living on the balloon would find a square inch to be flatter after the inflation than before). In section 1A, I mentioned the cosmic microwave background radiation, the heat radiation leftover from the Big Bang. When we calculate what the radiation should look like, we find that regions in different parts of the sky could easily have had different temperatures. But we observe that this radiation is virtually the same in all directions. There is no known way (in the standard Big Bang model) for the universe to have the same temperature in every direction, because the regions now on opposite sides of the sky would never have been in thermal contact with each other. But in the inflation model, regions that are now on opposite sides of our sky would have been close enough together before inflation to be in thermal equilibrium, and thus would have the same temperature. The third puzzle is related to magnetic monopoles, which are predicted to be copiously produced in the Big Bang, yet we haven't observed even one. Inflation explains this, since it stretches out space so much that the monopoles are extremely far apart. See Alan Guth, *The Inflationary Universe: The Quest for a New Theory of Cosmic Origins* (Reading, MA: Addison-Wesley/Hexlis Books, 1997); excerpts reprinted in *BoC* pp. 484–7.

42 Bertrand Russell quoted by Barrow and Tipler, *BoC*, pp. 443–4.

43 Weinberg, *The First Three Minutes*, pp.154–5.

44 Excerpts from Revelation 21:1–5 (*NIV*).

45 This is dramatically described by Werner Gitt, *Stars and Their Purpose: Signposts in Space,* trans. Jaap Kies (Bielefeld: CLV, 1996), reprinted in *BoC*, pp. 418–22.

46 Carl Sagan in *The Pale Blue Dot* (New York: Random House, 1994).

47 Dennis Danielson, "Copernicus and Tale of the Pale Blue Dot", available at http://faculty.arts.ubc.ca/ddaniels/.

48 Psalm 8:1, 3–4. *The Bible: New Revised Standard Version* (Grand Rapids: Zondervan Publishing).

49 Psalm 8:5–6. *The Bible: New Revised Standard Version* (Grand Rapids: Zondervan Publishing).

50 Psalm 103:11–12 (*NIV*).

51 See HOW CHRISTIANS RECONCILE ANCIENT TEXTS WITH MODERN SCIENCE, chapter 8 in this volume, section 4.

Part 4

Interplay of Scientific and Religious Knowledge Regarding Evolution

10

Scientific Knowledge Does Not Replace Religious Knowledge

LOREN HAARSMA

Science usually explains natural events – such as the orbit of planets or the growth of trees – in terms of mechanistic, impersonal natural processes. Religions usually explain these same events in terms of divine action and intention. These two levels of explanation might seem at first to conflict. However, these two explanations can be harmonized through the religious idea of a God who created and designed the laws of nature, and who typically governs creation through those natural laws. Occasionally, events happen which cannot be explained through known natural laws. Whether someone thinks an unexplained event is a divine miracle, a random event, or an unknown natural process often depends not on the science, but on their religious beliefs. Religious beliefs and scientific reason do not need to conflict. In fact, making reasoned decisions as a scientist and making reasonable faith commitments in a religion, while not exactly the same thing, share many of the same characteristics.

For centuries, humans have watched the motions of planets and stars. Throughout history, most cultures developed religious explanations, saying that the motions of planets and stars were caused by God or the gods.

About 320 years ago, Sir Isaac Newton developed a scientific explanation for the motion of planets and stars. Newton proposed some basic principles which he believed to be universally true for all motion: that two objects always exert equal and opposite forces on each other, that objects change their momentum at a rate proportional to the force acting on them, and that any two objects attract each other with a gravitational force which is proportional to their masses and inversely proportional to the square of the distance between them. He then showed mathematically that if we combine these principles, or "laws of nature," we can explain and predict not only the motion of objects here on Earth, but also the motion of the moon and the planets.

Newton was religious. He believed that God created the universe and continues to govern it. Newton did not think that his scientific explanation replaced his religious beliefs. In fact, he saw his scientific discovery as supporting his religious belief in God. He wrote, "This most beautiful system of the Sun, planets, and comets could only proceed from the counsel and dominion of an intelligent and powerful Being."[1]

About a century after Newton, another brilliant mathematician and scientist named Pierre Laplace built on the work of Newton and other scientists and wrote several books which scientifically explained and predicted the motion of the moons and planets in great mathematical detail.[2] There is an often-repeated story that when Laplace formally presented a copy of his work to the Emperor Napoleon Bonaparte, Napoleon observed that Laplace had written a huge book on astronomy without once mentioning the Creator of the universe. Laplace is said to have replied, "Sir, I have no need for that hypothesis."

People have interpreted Laplace's statement in a variety of ways over the centuries. The most common interpretation of Laplace's statement is something like this: "Now that we have a scientific explanation for how the planets move, we no longer need to use God as an explanation." It seems that for Laplace, the scientific explanation for planetary motion did replace a religious explanation.

Atheist and Theist Views of Natural Laws

Newton and Laplace represent two of the most common views held by scientists today about the relationship between religion and scientific explanations of the natural world. Laplace represents a view in which matter and energy simply exist and interact impersonally and mechanistically in regular patterns which we call "natural laws." This mechanistic picture of matter and energy is most commonly held by atheists. Atheism, as a philosophical view, asserts that the material universe is all that exists and that there is no such thing as God or the supernatural. While there might be some atheists who do not have a mechanistic view of matter and energy, in my experience, atheists who are scientists almost invariably have a mechanistic view of the natural world.[3]

Isaac Newton represents a theistic view of nature which is consistent with the traditional teachings of Judaism, Christianity, and Islam. Theism is a general term which refers to belief in the existence of a God. In this chapter, I will use the term *theism* specifically to refer to the beliefs shared by Judaism, Christianity, and Islam, that there is one God who not only created the universe, but also continues to sustain it, govern it, and interact with it. In theism, God governs the universe, and because God governs consistently, matter and energy behave in regular patterns, and we call those patterns "natural laws."[4]

Donald MacKay, a physicist and neuroscientist who was also a Christian, described his view of nature this way: "…The continuing existence of our world is not something to be taken for granted. Rather it hangs moment by moment on the continuance of the upholding word of power of its Creator."[5] MacKay called this view "dynamic stability," and he illustrated it with the following modern analogy. Suppose you are playing a simple computer game in which electronic balls and racquets appear to move around the computer screen. The balls and racquets on the computer screen appear to be stable, and they appear to move and interact in regular, repeatable, mathematically predictable patterns. However, we know that the balls and racquets on the computer screen are not really solid or stable. They only appear stable because a stream of electrons from a cathode ray tube continually strikes the fluorescent pixels on the screen. The rules which determine the motion of the balls and racquets are not intrinsic to the balls and racquets themselves. Rather, the rules come from the computer which controls the cathode ray tube. In the same way, MacKay argues, the matter, energy, and laws of nature of this universe are not themselves intrinsically self-existing and stable, but rather owe their continued existence and apparent stability to the fact that God continually sustains them.

Isaac Newton did not invent the idea that God not only created the universe, but also continually governs it. This idea goes back in Christian and Jewish tradition for thousands of years.[6] Many passages of the Bible proclaim that the universe continues to exist, and behaves in an orderly fashion, only because of God's continual sustaining action. One example comes from Psalm 104, where a poet writes in praise to God:

> The moon marks off the seasons,
> and the Sun knows when to go down.
> You bring darkness, it becomes night,
> and all the beasts of the forest prowl.
> The lions roar for their prey
> and seek their food from God.
> The Sun rises, and they steal away;
> they return and lie down in their dens.[7]

Note the parallel levels of description in that passage. The Sun goes down (a natural event), and God brings night (divine action). The lions hunt prey (a natural event), and they seek their food from God (divine governance). The Biblical perspective is clear. If something happens "naturally," God is still in charge. This psalm was written more than 2,000 years before modern science existed, so the poet probably wasn't thinking in terms of "natural laws." However, the poet certainly knew the difference between ordinary natural events and extraordinary events. The psalms are filled with praise to God for the times in Israel's history when God did something unusual, something miraculous. So the poet undoubtedly understood that there is a difference between a supernatural miracle and an ordinary event like the Sun going down or lion hunting. Yet the poet insisted that God was in charge of natural events every bit as much as God was in charge of supernatural events. In fact, God is to be praised and worshipped for those natural events.

Scientists sometimes talk about natural laws "governing" the universe. In a theistic perspective, however, natural laws themselves do not govern the universe; rather, natural laws are the means by which God governs the universe. God can supersede the ordinary functioning of natural laws when he chooses, but most of the time God chooses to work in consistent ways through those natural laws. As we study the universe scientifically, we build mathematical models and descriptions of those natural laws which God created and uses. Theists believe that rationality and regularity of these laws of nature should be seen as a gift from God without which we would not be able to understand our world.

Atheist and Theist Views of Chance

One of the surprising discoveries of physics within the last century is that the laws of nature do not appear to be completely deterministic. Classical mechanics, as developed by Isaac Newton and scientists who followed him, is deterministic. In classical mechanics, it is in principle possible to know with absolute precision every physical variable (position, velocity, energy, etc.) of any particle. But in the last century, physicists discovered that they need a new theory, quantum mechanics, to describe the behavior of tiny particles. From quantum mechanics we have learned that, in fact, it is impossible to measure every physical variable of a particle with complete accuracy. In quantum mechanics, even when we know as much as there is to know about initial conditions of a particle or a system of particles, it is impossible to predict the exact outcome of some measurements. Some quantum mechanical events have results which – not just in practice, but in principle – are randomly determined. Randomness or "chance" is built into the very mathematical formalism of quantum mechanics.[8]

Scientists also use the term "chance" outside of quantum mechanics, but in a different way. In classical mechanics, if a system is sufficiently complicated (a "chaotic" system) it is practically impossible to have sufficiently complete knowledge of its initial conditions. The final state of the system depends so sensitively upon the initial conditions that, in practice, it is impossible to predict exactly what will happen. Some common examples of "chaotic" systems include throwing dice, flipping a coin, and predicting the weather. In these systems, based upon experience and certain general considerations, various outcomes can be assigned probabilities of occurring, but the particular outcome of any single event cannot be predicted. Biologists use the word "chance" this way. In evolutionary biology, a "chance" event is simply an event which affects an organism's survival (for example, a natural disaster) or genetic information (a mutation) but one which was not caused by the organism itself and could not have been predicted. "Chance" in evolutionary biology or any other branch of science is a statement about scientists' inability to precisely predict final outcomes.

Some people interpret the existence of random events in nature atheistically. They use the word "chance" as an alternative explanation to God. When they say that something happened "by chance," they believe that it had no purpose, no significance of any kind, nothing guiding it, no purpose which cares about the final results. This is not the scientific meaning of the word *chance*, although some scientists do use the word this way in their popular writings. Noting the role played by random events in evolutionary theory, George G. Simpson has written, "Man is the result of a purposeless and natural process that did not have him in mind."[9] Similarly, Douglas Futuyma has written, "Some shrink from the conclusion that the human species was not designed, has no purpose, and is the product of mere mechanical mechanisms – but this seems to be the message of evolution."[10] When scientists use the concept of chance in this way, they are taking the scientific meaning of the word "chance" and adding some philosophical, atheistic interpretations to it.

When scientists use the concept of chance in a strictly scientific sense, they mean simply this: they could not completely predict the final state of a system based on their knowledge of earlier states. In a scientific theory, the term "chance" is not a statement about causation (or lack of causation); rather, it is a statement about predictability.

Theists believe that this scientific use of the term *chance* is also entirely compatible with the theistic view of God's governance of nature. Many passages in the Bible describe God working through apparently random events. For example, thousands of years ago, priests would sometimes throw dice or "cast lots" to determine God's will for a particular decision. The book of Proverbs in the Bible describes their belief this way: "The lot is cast into the lap, but its every decision is from the Lord."[11] Centuries before modern science existed, people understood that some events are unpredictable. Biblical writers proclaimed that God was sovereign over apparently random events like casting lots. Biblical writers also proclaimed God's sovereignty over events which we now describe scientifically using probabilities (for example: the weather). Scientific randomness poses no fundamental problem to a Biblical understanding of God's governance. Just because we human beings cannot scientifically predict the outcome of an event doesn't mean that God cannot be involved in the event, giving it purpose and meaning. Quite the opposite. In a theistic view of nature, chance events are another means by which God can govern.

An analogy or two might be helpful to explain this concept. A scientist at the Massachusetts Institute of Technology once described writing a computer simulation of leaves randomly falling off a tree. To anyone observing the computer simulation, the timing of the falling leaves appears random. However, this scientist can control her computer program to cause any one particular leaf to fall at a particular time and a particular place. An observer would be unable to predict this event and could not tell the difference between a truly randomly falling leaf and a leaf whose fall was controlled by the scientist. In an analogous fashion, God could select the outcome of scientifically unpredictable events in order to achieve particular outcomes.[12] God could do this subtly, interacting with creation in ways which are significant but which we could not detect scientifically.

John Polkinghorne, a particle physicist and an Anglican priest, has argued that another way God might use random processes is to give the created world a bit of freedom.[13] In this view, through laws of nature which include both some determinism and some randomness, God has given the matter and energy of the universe a range of possibilities to explore and the freedom to explore that range. For an analogy, consider how some computer programmers are using "genetic algorithms" in their work. They design a computer program with a goal (for example: to control a complex manufacturing process). Rather than specify all of the variables in that computer program, the programmers specify for each variable a range of values. The computer randomly selects the variables from the allowed ranges, and then measures its own performance on how well it performs its given task. It then randomly alters one or more of the variables, performs the task again, and sees whether it did better or worse. In this way, after enough trials, the computer converges on a set of variables which are ideally suited to performing a particular task. Genetic algorithms in computer programs can also be used for artistic purposes. Some multi-variable mathematical functions, when creatively displayed, make very beautiful pictures. An artist can allow the computer program to change one variable randomly, and then another, and another, allowing the computer to explore a wide range of possibilities, generating a whole series of beautiful and unique pictures.[14] Some theists argue that God created the laws of nature with some randomness built in, through the laws of quantum mechanics, so that nature could explore the wide range of beautiful possibilities which God gave it the potential to become.

Atheist and Theist Views of Why Science Works

I have described two views about the universe which are fairly common amongst scientists today: The first is an atheist view in which God doesn't exist, natural laws and random events happen mechanistically, and scientific explanations for events in nature should replace all religious explanations. The second is a theist view in which God continually governs the universe in consistent patterns which we interpret as natural laws, God can interact with nature through apparently random events, and scientific explanations for events in nature add to our understanding of how God governs the universe but do not replace our religious knowledge. There are, of course, more than just these two views amongst scientists, but the atheist and theist views which I just described are probably the two most common religious views amongst scientists today.

This leads to the question of why scientists with such different philosophical and religious views about the universe can work together and reach consensus about their scientific theories and equations. Atheist and theist scientists agree with each other that Newton's laws of classical mechanics, improved upon by Albert Einstein's theories of relativity, accurately describe how large objects move and gravitationally attract each other. Atheist and theist scientists agree with each other that quantum field theory does a superb job of describing the motion of small particles and the electromagnetic and nuclear forces. Some people wonder how scientists can hold very different religious beliefs about the universe and still agree about the science.

One answer that has been proposed is that science is "methodologically atheistic."[15] The scientific equations and theories of Newton and Einstein and Charles Darwin do not refer to God or the supernatural. Therefore, according to this view, scientific equations and theories are methodologically atheistic. They act "as if God doesn't exist." A scientist does not have to be an atheist to do science. A scientist may still believe that God exists; however, according to this view, a scientist must act as if God does not exist when he or she does science.

It is true that scientific theories and equations do not directly refer to God's existence or action. However, describing science as "methodologically atheistic" is misleading in some important respects because it implies that the scientific method is more compatible with atheism than it is with theism or other belief systems. Theists argue that the scientific method is at least as compatible with theism as it is with atheism.

Although scientists can have very different religious beliefs in general, nearly all scientists share a certain core set of philosophical beliefs about nature. Nearly all scientists believe that there are regular, repeatable, universal patterns of cause and effect in nature which we can understand through a process of observation, hypothesis formation, and experimentation. These beliefs are not, strictly speaking, scientific beliefs. Science cannot prove that they are true. These beliefs come from philosophy and religion. This core of philosophical beliefs about nature is compatible with atheism. As we have seen, this core set of philosophical beliefs about nature is also compatible with theism. For example, the Bible teaches that God created the universe and continually governs it in a faithful, consistent fashion. A theist believes that this is why science works. A theist who does science, looking for regular patterns of cause and effect in the natural world, is not "pretending as if God doesn't exist." Rather, he/she looks for regular patterns of cause and effect in the natural world precisely because he/she believes in the God described in the Bible.

Scientific knowledge, and the use of scientific methods to learn about nature, is compatible with more than one religious belief system. Science is compatible with atheism, theism, and other religious beliefs. This allows scientists of many different religious beliefs to work side by side, studying nature together, sharing the results of their research with each other, and reaching consensus on the properties, functioning, and history of the natural world.

Miracles

The fact that science is so successful in helping us understand the natural world does not prove either theism or atheism. Nevertheless, some people try to use science to support their religious beliefs by trying to show either that science can prove that a miracle has occurred, or by trying to show that science disproves the possibility of any miracle ever happening.

The word "miracle" has a number of meanings.[16] In Biblical writings, it does not automatically imply a violation of natural cause and effect. Many miracles in the Bible are given cause-and-effect explanations, or such explanations are at least consistent with the written account. However, when the idea of "miracle" is discussed in the context of science and religion, usually people are thinking of an event which includes a supernatural break in ordinary natural chains of cause and effect.

Science can describe how natural events typically happen today and how they have happened in the past. However, science by itself cannot prove that those events will always happen the same way in the future. In a theistic view, there is no reason to expect that the success of science in general disproves the possibility of miracles in particular cases. If natural laws are the way God normally oversees his creation, then God can supersede that ordinary governance in special instances for a good reason. Human beings sometimes behave in unexpected ways for good reasons. You might know a friend very well, know how he typically behaves, and know his habits to the point where you can accurately predict how he will act in most situations. Then one day, he does something totally unexpected. But if you investigate why he did something different that day, you'll find out that there were special circumstances – circumstances which you originally didn't understand. Given those special circumstances, you now understand that he actually had good reasons for doing that surprising thing on that particular day – reasons which are completely consistent with his character. In the Bible, that is often how miracles are depicted.

As an example of this, consider the dramatic Biblical story of the prophet Elijah on Mount Carmel.[17] Elijah was a prophet of God, but during Elijah's lifetime, the king and queen of the nation of Israel were killing the prophets of God and encouraging everyone to worship an idol named Baal. Elijah arranged a contest. Two altars were set up on Mount Carmel – one to God, and one to Baal. Animal sacrifices were placed on both altars, but no fire. The prophets of Baal chanted and shouted for hours for Baal to send fire from heaven and light the altar, but of course nothing happened. Then Elijah drenched his alter with water to make sure that all the witnesses would know that he hadn't hidden any fire under the wood, and then he prayed a simple prayer to God. God immediately answered by sending fire from heaven to Elijah's altar. This is a very unusual event – a miracle. God did not routinely send down fire from heaven onto sacrificial altars. But from the context of this story, it is clear that this was an unusual time, a critical time, in the history of the nation of Israel. The king and queen had nearly turned the entire nation away from the worship of God. And so God answered the prayer of this prophet for a dramatic demonstration. God did something dramatically different, something unexpected based upon how God ordinarily governs creation, but entirely appropriate considering the special circumstances, and the event was accompanied by a verbal explanation of what God was doing and why he was doing it.

Science neither proves nor disproves the possibility of supernatural miracles

Science is an excellent tool for discovering the ordinary patterns of the behavior of nature. On the other hand, science is a poor tool for understanding the philosophical or religious significance of an unexpected event. For this reason, science cannot be used to prove that a miracle has ever happened. When an unexpected event happens or is reported to have happened, the most that science can say is that the unexpected event was highly improbable or impossible given our current understanding of natural laws.[18]

When scientists study a natural event (for example a supernova, or biological development from a single-celled zygote to an adult organism), they try to build empirical models of the process based on known natural laws plus information about the conditions before, during, and after the process. Attempts to build empirical models meet with varying degrees of success. As scientists study these puzzling events, they could reach three general types of conclusions about the event:

(1)   It is an "explainable event." Good empirical models predict that known natural laws can explain the event. (There might still be some puzzling features, but most of the event is well understood.)

(2)   It is a "partially explainable event." Our empirical models are not sufficiently thorough to explain the event entirely. However, based upon what we have done so far, we believe that known natural mechanisms are sufficient to account for the event. We believe that future improvements in knowledge, more elegant models, and more computing power will eventually allow us to prove that the event is "explainable."

(3)   It is an "unexplainable event." No known natural laws can explain this event. In fact, there are good, empirical reasons for ruling out any model which relies on known natural laws.

Scientists don't always agree with each other. For any particular event, there may be some debates in the scientific community as to whether it is explainable, partially explainable, or unexplainable. Yet even when there are debates, the great majority of scientists usually do have consensus. For example, most scientists would agree that planetary orbits, the formation of mountains, and supernovas are "explainable" events. Most scientists would agree that the development of animals from single-celled zygotes into mature adults falls into the category of "partially explainable." A small number of scientists argue that the origin of first life on Earth is unexplainable in terms of known natural laws, but most scientists argue that the formation of first life on Earth should be considered "partially explainable."

The vast majority of puzzles which scientists study fall into the categories of "explainable" or "partially explainable." There are, however, some rare occasions when the scientific community is forced to admit that the event is simply unexplainable in terms of known natural law; and, in fact, strong empirical arguments can be made ruling out models employing only known natural laws.

The energy source of the Sun was once scientifically "unexplainable." By the late 1800s, geologists had established that the Earth was hundreds of millions or billions of years old, with life existing on Earth for most of that time. Presumably, the Sun must have been shining all that time. However, scientists calculated that two mechanisms proposed to be the Sun's energy source – chemical reactions and gravitational compression – could not have powered the Sun for more than a few hundred thousand years. For several decades, scientists had to admit that no known natural mechanism could account for the Sun shining for billions of years.

Two closely related modern examples of scientifically "unexplainable" events are the source of the Big Bang and the apparent fine-tuning of the laws of nature for life to exist. Cosmologists can model the history of the universe backwards in time to a tiny fraction of a second after the Big Bang, but no known natural laws can account for why the Big Bang actually happened. Moreover, the laws of nature in our universe appear to be finely tuned to allow life to exist.[17] If the masses of some fundamental particles or the strengths of the fundamental forces were increased or decreased by small amounts, our universe would not have the properties necessary for life to exist. Scientists currently do not have any scientific explanation for why the fundamental constants of nature are these particular values. As far as we know at present, these fundamental constants could have taken any of a wide variety of values. No known law of nature explains why they fall into an extremely narrow range which makes life possible.

What do scientists do when confronted with scientifically "unexplainable" events? Usually there is no consensus. Individual scientists could reach (at least) five different meta-scientific conclusions about the cause of a scientifically unexplainable event:

(A) An unknown natural law is responsible.

(B) A supernatural event occurred.

(C) Natural but super-human intellect or technology is responsible.

(D) An improbable event simply occurred.

(E) There are many universes. The event was improbable for our observable universe, but the entire universe is vastly larger than our observable universe and/or there are a very large number (perhaps an infinite number) of parallel universes, so it is not surprising that this event happened somewhere, and we are living in the universe where it happened.

The first of these five was the correct conclusion for the energy source of the Sun. In the early twentieth century, scientists discovered a new natural process – nuclear fusion – and conclusively showed this to be the energy source of the Sun.

Today, there are cosmologists who advocate each of these five possibilities for the source of the Big Bang and the fine-tuning of the laws of nature for life. Some propose that an unknown natural law is responsible. They believe that when physicists finally discover the most fundamental law of nature – the "Theory of Everything" – it will explain why the masses of particles and strength of forces have the exact values that they do. Others scientists propose that God caused the Big Bang to occur out of nothing and designed the laws of nature so that they are finely tuned for life. Others propose that our universe is a result of super-human technology. Just as we might someday be able to create technology that allows us to construct new black holes, so they speculate that perhaps scientists in a parallel universe somewhere have created technology which allows them to create entire new universes and set the fundamental laws of nature in those universes; they choose to create universes where life could evolve. Others propose that we simply got lucky that the universe exists and that the laws of nature of our universe allow for life. One of the most popular proposals these days is the "many universes" hypothesis. In this proposal, there are a vast number, perhaps an infinite number, of causally disconnected universes. A mother universe creates lots of daughter universes, each with its own fundamental laws of nature, and some tiny fraction of these daughter universes have conditions suitable for life to evolve.[19]

Another modern example of a potentially "unexplainable" event is the origin of first life on Earth. Most scientists today believe that, although we do not yet have a good scientific explanation for the origin of first life, it is not in principle unexplainable. Most scientists, including myself, believe that we will eventually be able to construct a scientific explanation for first life in terms of known natural laws and the conditions of the early Earth. However, there is a minority of scientists who believe that life-forms, even the simplest ones are too complex to have self-organized on the early Earth via known natural laws. Amongst this group of scientists, there are advocates of each of the five meta-scientific hypotheses listed above. Some propose that as-yet-unknown natural laws were responsible. Some propose that God did a miracle to form first life. Some propose that life on Earth was seeded from outer space. Some propose that we simply got lucky. Some propose that the universe is vastly larger than our observable universe, thereby increasing the odds that life should happen on some planet somewhere.

The five meta-scientific hypotheses listed above are very different from each other philosophically and, in some cases, religiously. However, they play virtually identical roles in *scientific* models. In scientific models, they simply allow scientists to get from before an event to after an event when the event itself is currently scientifically unexplainable. Regardless of their philosophical and religious disagreements, scientists can, at least in principle, reach consensus on whether certain events are explainable, partially explainable, or unexplainable in terms of known natural laws.

For those rare events which are scientifically unexplainable, a person's religious beliefs sometimes play an important role in choosing which of these meta-scientific hypothesis he/she finds acceptable. A particular unexplainable event might lead someone to conclude that a certain religious belief is probably true. For example, some scientists believe that the Big Bang and the fine-tuning of natural laws provide support for belief in the existence of God. Or for example, in the story of the prophet Elijah on Mount Carmel, any witnesses at the event would very likely believe that the event was a supernatural miracle rather than simply an improbable event. These conclusions, however, rely on other sources of information than the merely scientific.

The mere fact that an event is scientifically unexplainable neither proves nor disproves any particular religious belief, because scientifically "unexplainable" events allow for multiple meta-scientific explanations. Science alone cannot settle the issue. Other sources of knowledge beyond science are necessary to determine the meta-scientific implications of unusual events.

Scientific Knowledge Is Not the Only Kind of Reliable Knowledge

Wherever possible, scientific investigations use empirical and objective measurements. Scientists double-check each other's work. As a result, we usually find scientific knowledge trustworthy. When we take an antibiotic for a disease or fly in an airplane, we literally trust our lives to the scientific methods behind those discoveries. Because science has been so successful, science is sometimes portrayed as the one and only way of obtaining reliable knowledge.

There are, however, other ways of obtaining reliable knowledge besides the scientific method. For example: if you want to know what George Washington, the first president of the United States, did while he was president, you wouldn't use the scientific method. You would use historical methods of obtaining knowledge, by studying historical records. Another example: if someone accuses your friend of being a rude, selfish, egotistical person, you probably won't do a scientific experiment on your friend to test that hypothesis. Instead, you would rely on your personal experiences with that friend to determine to what extent that accusation is true. Your personal experiences with your friend may be subjective experiences which you cannot share with any other person, yet if you have spent a lot of time with your friend, those personal experiences could provide you with sufficient information to form a reliable conclusion about your friend's character. Another example: if you want to know whether a certain charity is worthy of your time and money, you might rely on social knowledge, that is, you might ask people whose opinion you trust what experiences they have had with the charity. One more example: if there is a God who interacts with human beings, this allows for another source of reliable knowledge, divinely revealed knowledge.

Every day, we make decisions based on non-scientific sources of knowledge. We can take significant risks based on sources of knowledge which are non-scientific but which nevertheless we have good reason to consider reliable. An historian might risk her career to publish an unpopular hypothesis if she believes she has reliable historical evidence. Someone might give a lot of time and money to a charity based on its good reputation. Based on their personal experiences with a friend, someone might be willing to risk their money or even their life to help that friend.

Science is one valid way of gaining reliable knowledge, but it is not the only valid way. Knowledge gained from science augments, but does not replace, important truths we might have gained from studying history, from our personal experiences, and from our culture through the experiences of the people around us.

To illustrate this, imagine a boy who grows up in a village on the edge of the forest. The boy takes great joy playing in the forest – learning all the best trees for climbing, the best hiding places, fields for playing games, bushes near a small stream which grow tasty berries. The boy also learns from his parents the cultural importance of the forest to the village, and he learns from the village elders the history of how the village was first settled near the forest. Now when this boy is older, he goes to the university and studies science. In biology class, he learns about the ecology of the plants and animals of the forest. In geology class, he learns the natural history of the forest stretching back centuries in time. This scientific knowledge should augment, not replace, everything he learned about the forest before he came to the university. When the boy was growing up in the village, he learned some folk legends about the ancient history of the forest which conflict with what he learns studying geology. Perhaps some people in his village told him stories about some legendary animals thought to live in the forest, and this turns out not to be true, based on what he learns in biology class. It's true that the boy's new scientific knowledge might correct a few mistaken things he thought he knew about the forest before he studied science. However, most of what the boy learned about the forest – about the history of how the village grew up near the forest, about the cultural importance of the forest for his village, and most of all about his personal experiences of playing in and exploring the forest, and the great joy he took in that – that knowledge is not replaced by the boy's new scientific knowledge. If anything, his knowledge about the cultural importance of the forest, and his personal knowledge he gained by exploring the forest as a boy, should be enhanced by his new scientific knowledge.

Reasonable Scientific Decisions and Reasonable Faith Commitments

My personal story, as a scientist, is somewhat analogous to the boy in the story I just told – not about a forest, but about my Christian faith. My parents and grandparents are Christians. My uncles and aunts and cousins and most of the people I grew up with are Christians. So I learned the beliefs of the Christian religion ever since I was very young. As I grew older, I learned about other philosophies and religions, and from time to time questioned some of the things I had been taught, but I continue to believe that the fundamental teachings of Christianity are true. I continue to believe those fundamental teachings of Christianity based partly on what I have learned from science, based partly on historical evidence, but based primarily on my own personal experiences of God when I read the Bible, pray, and worship, and when I hear from my friends and family about their own experiences of God.

In college, I majored in physics. After college, I went to Harvard University to earn a PhD in physics, and after that I worked for five years doing full-time research in neuroscience. Since 1999, I have taught physics at Calvin College. I have been studying, researching, and teaching science for about twenty years of my life. The science I have learned has not replaced, but rather enhanced, what I learned from my religion.

There have been a few corrections along the way. For example, the first chapter in the book of Genesis in the Bible has a poetic account, written about 3,000 years ago, of God creating the Earth. When I was growing up, my parents and my pastors – who are not trained scientists – taught me to interpret that particular passage to mean that God miracu-lously created the Earth about 10,000 years ago. Now, they didn't insist that this was the only correct interpretation of that creation poem. It was simply the interpretation that they had learned from their parents.

As I studied science, I learned that the Earth and the universe have a history stretching back billions of years. This conflicts with one thing I had been taught as a boy. But while I was learning science, I also learned that the 3,000-year-old creation poem in the book of Genesis has other interpretations besides the one I had been taught as a boy. In fact, Christian theologians who had studied that poem in great detail had far better understandings of it – understandings which still respected it as a divinely inspired poem, but which were also compatible with what modern science was teaching us about the history of the Earth.[20]

So scientific knowledge corrected one particular belief I had from my childhood about the history of the Earth. And for that, I am very grateful. But that was a rare event. On the whole, the science that I have learned has not contradicted or replaced my religious beliefs. Fundamental Christian beliefs which I learned as a boy about God, God's governance of universe, and how God chooses to relate to us human beings – in my experience, those fundamental beliefs were supported, enhanced, and enriched by the science that I have learned over the years.

During my scientific career, I have encountered a few scientists who have told me – in person or through their writings – that science is fundamentally incompatible with religious belief. Usually, their objections to religion were along the following lines: "Science is all about Reason. In science, you only believe things based on evidence. Religion is about Faith. Faith means believing in something despite lack of evidence, or in spite of contradictory evidence. Reason and Faith are incompatible."

This sort of argument against religion, I believe, depends upon a misunderstanding of what is meant by the word "faith." In Christianity, the word "faith" includes the idea of believing in God's existence, even when one has not personally seen God. However, that is not primarily what the word *faith* is about. A more complete definition of the word would include the following ideas. First, a Christian has faith in God analogous to the way one might have faith in a friend. We trust that God will be good to us. We trust God's good character and we trust God's ability to do what God has promised to do. Second, as we live our lives and make daily decisions about how we use our time and our money and how we treat other people, we act "in good faith" towards God and towards other people. If you trust a friend to keep his promises, you can gladly act on the basis of those promises. You trust that your friend will treat you well, so you, in turn, treat your friend well. That is what it means to act "in good faith." Third, religious faith means being faithful to your commitments even when it is difficult. We believe in God and God's promises, and therefore we try to live the way God wants us to live, even in the times when it seems very costly to do so.[21]

A faith commitment, the way I am using the term in this chapter, is a belief or a set of beliefs which deeply affect the way a person lives his or her life. In this sense, faith commitments could be non-religious. Marriage could be seen as a sort of faith commitment to another person. Some people make faith commitments to ethical philosophies such as Confucianism as the basis for their moral choices. A person could also make a faith commitment to a political philosophy. For example, a person might be deeply committed to the idea that communism is the best way to organize society to deliver the most good for most people, while another person might be deeply committed to the idea that capitalism is the best way to organize society to deliver the most good for most people.

Not all beliefs are faith commitments. In fact, most beliefs do not rise to the level of faith commitments. A person might believe that a particular charity is worthy of receiving their time and money, or that Confucianism is a good moral philosophy, or that communism or capitalism is the best way to organize society, without having those beliefs make any significant impact on the way that they make their daily decisions or live their lives. A person might even say that they believe that the basic tenets of the Christian religion are true, without actually living their life according to those tenets. Such a person's belief has not become a faith commitment. A faith commitment, the way Christians typically mean the term, is a commitment to a set of beliefs which profoundly affects the way that person lives his or her life.

Faith is not the opposite of Reason. The opposite of Reason is irrationality. Scientific beliefs can be either rational or irrational. For example, 120 years ago, it would have been very rational for a scientist to believe that mass is always conserved. The best scientific theories and the best experimental work at that time all pointed to the idea that mass is always conserved. But in the year 1905, Albert Einstein published his famous work on the theory of relativity showing that mass can be converted into energy, and energy can be converted into mass.[22] Since that time, there has been abundant experimental confirmation of Einstein's theories. Today, it would be irrational for a scientist to disbelieve Einstein's theory and still insist that mass is always conserved.

Faith commitments also can be irrational or rational. Having faith in the promises of another person can be either rational or irrational, depending on whether or not that person has shown himself in the past to be either honest or dishonest. Having faith in a social organization can be either rational or irrational, depending on whether that organization has shown itself to work for the public good, or only to work for its own selfish interests. Faith commitments to a political philosophy could be rational or irrational, depending on a person's experience with how that philosophy impacts the lives of other people. Religious faith can be irrational, if there is strong evidence against its fundamental teachings. Religious faith can also be rational, if its core beliefs are compatible with the findings of modern science, and if one has evidence from history and from personal experience which support those beliefs.[23]

Conclusion

I have argued that the findings of modern science about the natural world can be compatible with an atheist's belief that matter, energy, and the laws of nature are fundamentally impersonal, mechanistic things. Science also can be compatible with a theist's belief that matter, energy, and the laws of nature were created by God and continue to be governed by God in a regular, consistent fashion. Although science is not consistent with every conceivable religious system, science is almost certainly compatible with other religious belief systems besides the two I just mentioned.

Because science is compatible with multiple religious belief systems, scientists of different religions can work together and reach consensus on scientific issues. If a scientist – or any individual – wants to choose between competing religions, science can only provide partial guidance. An individual in pursuit of religious truth will have to seek other sources of knowledge such as historical sources, personal experience, and the experiences of other trusted teachers and friends.

Because I am a Christian, I have paid particular attention to how scientific knowledge interacts with the religious beliefs of myself and my fellow Christians. I have found that science can occasionally correct a mistaken belief about the natural world. But primarily, science has added new layers of knowledge about the world without contradicting knowledge that I had gained from other sources. In my own experience as a scientist and as a Christian, scientific knowledge has not replaced, but rather enhanced, knowledge I have gained from my religion, history, culture, and personal experience.

Notes

1   Isaac Newton, *Principia Mathematica* (1687).
2   Pierre Laplace, *Treatise on Celestial Mechanics* (1799–1825).
3   For example: P. W. Atkins, "The limitless power of science" in John Cornwell (ed.) *Nature's Imagination – The Frontiers of Scientific Vision,* (Oxford University Press, 1995). There is another philosophical view called "deism" which asserts that God initially created the material universe and the laws of nature, but now simply lets it go on its way without interacting with it. For example, cosmologist Stephen Hawking in his popular book *A Brief History of Time* (New York: Bantam Books, 1988), after describing the laws of nature which help us understand scientifically the behavior of the universe in the first moments after the Big Bang, writes the following: "These laws may have originally been decreed by God, but it appears that he has since left the universe to evolve according to them and does not now intervene in it," (p. 122). Atheism and deism share the view that matter, energy, and the fundamental laws of nature operate mechanistically and impersonally.
4   There are at least two different ways for understanding the status of natural laws, both of which are within the tradition of Christian orthodoxy. One view: God proscriptively determines the activity of all material objects from moment to moment. Natural laws are formulas which merely describe the regularity with which God normally acts. Breaks in "natural laws" are instances where God acts, for particular reasons, in ways which are contrary to, or at least extremely improbable from the standpoint of, the regular patterns of God's governance. Breaks in natural laws are not a fundamentally different type of God's activity, but rather instances where God, because of special circumstances, proscribes activity which is (from our perspective). A second view: God has gifted his creation and everything in it with certain creaturely capacities. These capacities are designed to interact with each other in regular fashions which we call natural laws. They do not operate independently of God, but are dependent upon God for their creation, design, and continued existence. God can interact with his creation through these creaturely capacities within the uncertainty and flexibility of the system (e.g., flexibility evident in quantum and/or "chaotic" systems). God can also interact with his creation through acts of radical reorganization. Some miracles are breaks in natural laws (or very improbable workings through natural laws) which have special personal and/or spiritual significance. Both of these views have proponents amongst Christian scientists.

It is worth being aware of both of these views; however, for the purposes of this chapter, it is not worth debating their differences and relative merits.

5   Donald MacKay, *The Open Mind and Other Essays* (Leicester, UK: InterVarsity Press, 1988), p. 23.

6   Portions of the next few paragraphs are adapted, with small changes, from: Loren Haarsma. "Does science exclude God? Natural law, chance, miracles, and scientific practice" in Keith B. Miller (ed.), *Perspectives on an Evolving Creation* (Grand Rapids, MI: Eerdmans, 2003).

7   Psalm 104:19–24. *The Bible: New International Version* (Grand Rapids, MI: Zondervan; hereafter *NIV*).

8   Portions of the next few paragraphs are adapted, with small changes, from: Loren Haarsma, "Does science exclude God?"

9   George G. Simpson, *The Meaning of Evolution* (New Haven, CT: Yale University Press, 1967).

10 Douglas Futuyma, *Science on Trial: The Case for Evolution* (New York: Pantheon, 1983), pp. 12–13.

11 Proverbs 16:33, (*NIV*).

12 A recent collection of essays on this topic is found in: Nancey Murphy, et. al., *Quantum Cosmology and the Laws of Nature: Scientific Perspectives on Divine Action* (Notre Dame: University of Notre Dame Press, 1997).

13 John Polkinghorne, *Science and Providence* (Boston, MA: Shambhala, 1989).

14 Other Christian authors writing on the subject of natural laws, chance, and God's governance: Donald MacKay, *Science, Chance and Providence* (Oxford: Oxford University Press, 1978); John Polkinghorne, *Science and Providence*; Howard Van Till, Davis Young, and Clarence Menninga, *Science Held Hostage* (Downers Grove, IL: InterVarsity Press, 1988); Charles E. Hummel, *The Galileo Connection* (Downers Grove, IL: InterVarsity Press, 1986); George L. Murphy, *Toward a Christian View of a Scientific World* (Lima, OH: CSS, 2001).

15 For example: Nancey Murphy, "Phillip Johnson on trial," *Perspectives on Science and Christian Faith* 45, no. 1, pp. 33–4; Richard E. Dickerson, "The Game of Science," *Perspectives on Science and Christian Faith* 44, no. 2, p. 137.

16 In the Bible, miracles are performed in contexts where the spiritual message should have been clear to the observers. Miracles can be ordinary events with extraordinary timing. (e.g., the famine which began and ended with the prophet Elijah's proclamations: 1 Kings 18–19.) Such miracles are not scientifically impossible or even improbable, but the timing was specially arranged by God and accompanied by a spoken revelation explaining the spiritual significance of the event. Other miracles described in the Bible are events which defy any explanation on the basis of natural laws (e.g., Jesus' resurrection and post-resurrection appearances: Luke 24, John 20–1, Acts 1).

17 1 Kings 18:16–56 (*NIV*).

18 Portions of the next few paragraphs are adapted, with small changes, from: Loren Haarsma, "Does science exclude God?"

19 These are discussed in greater depth by Deborah B. Haarsma in CHRISTIAN AND ATHEIST RESPONSES TO BIG BANG COSMOLOGY, chapter 9 in this volume.

20 A book which was particularly helpful to me is: Howard van Till, Robert E. Snow, John H. Stek, and Davis A. Young, *Portraits of Creation*. (Grand Rapids, MI: Eerdmans,1990).

21 This understanding of the Christian concept of "faith" is further explained in C. S. Lewis, *Mere Christianity* (San Francisco: Harper, 2001. [New York: Macmillan, 1943]).

22 Albert Einstein, *Annals D. Phys* 18 (1905), 639.

23 Some current Christian philosophers who have written about rationality and religious faith include: Alvin Plantinga. *Warranted Christian Belief*. (Oxford: Oxford University Press); A. Plantinga and N. Wolterstorff, *Faith and Rationality: Reason and Belief in God* (Notre Dame: University of Notre Dame Press, 1984).

11

God, Evolution, and Design

LOREN HAARSMA

There is a great deal of scientific evidence supporting Darwin's theory of biological evolution. Some philosophers and scientists have claimed that if evolution is true, then religious beliefs such as Christianity must be false. Christians in North America have responded to this claim in a variety of ways. Some Christians, often called "Young Earth creationists," reject evolution in order to maintain a semi-literal interpretation of certain biblical passages. Other Christians, called "progressive creationists," accept the scientific evidence for some evolution over a long history of the earth, but also insist that God must have performed some miracles during that history to create new life-forms. The theory of Intelligent Design, as it is promoted in North America is a form of progressive creation. Still other Christians, called "theistic evolutionists" or "evolutionary creationists," assert that the scientific theory of evolution and the religious beliefs of Christianity can both be true. In this last view, God used evolution to create life-forms, similar to the way that God uses gravity to keep the earth in orbit around the sun. Evolutionary mechanisms are designed by God to produce abundance and a wide variety of complex, well-adapted, and continually adapting life-forms.

After Charles Darwin published his book, *On the Origin of Species,* in 1859, his theories quickly became a battleground for competing scientific, philosophical, and religious claims. In the decades that followed, scientists discovered more and more evidence supporting Darwin's theories. Today, Darwin's theory of evolution is one of the fundamental theories of biology. Scientists still study and debate the application of Darwin's theories to particular biological systems. Scientists sometimes disagree with each other about just how particular features of particular species evolved. However, scientists today generally agree that the theory of evolution is essentially correct in its broad picture of the history of life on earth.

In the realm of philosophy and religion, however, Darwin's theories are still a battleground for debate. Some people, most particularly some atheists, try to claim that Darwin's scientific theories support their particular philosophical or religious beliefs. Other people oppose Darwin's scientific theories not primarily because of any scientific data, but rather because they believe that Darwin's scientific theories inevitably lead to some unacceptable philosophical or religious conclusions.

The Term "Evolution" Has a Variety of Meanings

The word "evolution" has taken on more than one meaning. Confusion over these meanings often fuels the controversy. For this chapter, I am first going to distinguish four different meanings: (1) *microevolution,* (2) *pattern of evolution,* (3) *theory of evolution,* and (4) *evolutionism.*

   (1)   By *microevolution,* I mean the following: "biological species change over time due to random mutations and differential reproductive success." Examples of microevolution would include disease organisms developing a resistance to antibiotics, or insects developing a resistance to a pesticide, or any plant or animal which adapts over the course of several generations to new environmental conditions. Microevolution can be studied experimentally in laboratories, and it can be observed in nature over the course of several decades. Within human history, many species have shown small but noticeable changes, and several species have split into two or more separate species. I am restricting the term "microevolution" to small-scale changes in species which can happen in a few decades or a few centuries at most. Microevolution is not a source of controversy. I am not aware of anyone who disputes the idea that microevolution happens.

   (2)   By *pattern of evolution,* I mean the following: the fossil record reveals that there has been a long history of biological life on Earth going back billions of years. Species have changed throughout that time. Modern species look somewhat like species in the recent past, less like species in the more distant past, and only a little bit like species in the very distant past. Species in the distant past are generally simpler than modern species. When a species first appears in the fossil record, it looks a lot like other species which exist at the same time, and then progressively changes over time. This pattern of evolution, as I have defined it, acknowledges that species have changed over time in the history of the earth, but it makes no conclusion about the reason or the mechanism for that pattern of change.

   (3)   By *theory of evolution,* I mean essentially Darwin's theory that all plants and animals share a common ancestry, and that all living and extinct species – with their complex and diverse biologies – were produced by mutations and differential reproductive success operating over billions of years. Darwin's theory of evolution seeks to explain the mechanism behind the pattern of evolution seen in the fossil record. That mechanism is mutation and differential reproductive success. Before Darwin, it was widely believed that each lifeform must have been specially created, since after all, apple seeds only grow into apple trees (and not any other kind of plant), and cats give birth only to kittens (and not some other kind of animal). Before Darwin, the amazing intricacy of biological organs such as wings, eyes, and ears was seen as clear evidence that these things must have been specially created by an intelligent designer. Darwin's theory of evolution challenges the idea that each individual species was specially created.

   (4)   By *evolutionism* I mean the following: Some people try to use Darwin's scientific theory of evolution to support some atheistic, materialistic philosophical claims. The claims

of evolutionism include the following: there is no absolute morality because human ethics is merely the result of heredity and environmental influences; humans were not designed but arose merely by chance; there is no higher purpose to human existence; there is no Creator who cares for the world.

Evolutionism in the Public Debate over Evolution

A number of scientists and philosophers have written books and articles which support evolutionism. Here are just a few recent examples:

> It is already evident that all the objective phenomena of the history of life can be explained by purely naturalistic, or in the proper meaning of a much abused word, materialistic factors.... Man is the result of a purposeless and natural process that did not have him in mind.[1]
>
> It is almost irresistible for humans to believe that we have some special relation to the universe, that human life is not just a more-or-less farcical outcome of a chain of accidents reaching back to the first three minutes... It is very hard to realize that [the earth] is just a tiny part of an overwhelmingly hostile universe. It is even harder to realize that this present universe has evolved from an unspeakably unfamiliar early condition, and faces a future extinction of endless cold or intolerable heat. The more the universe seems comprehensible, the more it also seems pointless.[2]
>
> Some shrink from the conclusion that the human species was not designed, has no purpose, and is the product of mere mechanical mechanisms – but this seems to be the message of evolution.[3]

I should point out that not all atheists agree with these claims of evolutionism. Some scientists who are atheists have said quite clearly that they believe that Darwin's scientific theory of evolution is compatible with a belief in God.[4]

However, because there are some scientists who publicly advocate evolutionism in books and articles written for non-scientists, it should be no surprise that there is a philosophical and religious debate over evolution. People who may not understand the subtleties of the scientific theory of evolution – but who are certain that they disagree with these antireligious assertions of evolutionism – ask: "Have scientists really proven these claims? Does science really teach that there is no God? Are they teaching that to our children in school in science classes?"

Belief in a Creator

To understand why some people react so strongly against evolutionism, it is important to understand some of the reasons why people believe that there is a God who created this universe.

Nearly 3,000 years ago, a Jewish poet contemplated the world around him and wrote: "The heavens declare the glory of God; the skies proclaim the work of his hands. Day after day they pour forth speech; night after night they display knowledge."[5] Since that poem was written, over a hundred generations of worshipers have shared this profoundly religious experience. Belief that there is a Creator who loves and cares for creation is, for some people, strongly motivated by their experience of nature. These feelings are an intuitive response to the order and intricacy of the natural world. Many scientists today share this experience. They believe there is a God who created the universe, and this belief is increased, not diminished, by their scientific knowledge.[6]

The sense that human existence has ultimate purpose, and that there really is a universal standard for moral behavior, motivates many people to believe in a Creator. Humans have an innate sense of right and wrong which seems, to many people, to go deeper than mere moral instinct or social convention. Something in our psyche makes most of us believe that there is an ultimate standard of right and wrong, and that this standard came from our Creator.[7]

While these feelings may predispose some people to believe in a God who created the universe, the real power of belief, the real certainty for most people, comes from what they believe to be the experience of God's presence in daily life. A few believers have experienced dramatic answers to prayers which they consider to be miraculous. For most other believers, God's presence is felt in acts of worship, prayer, and studying the Bible, in acts of love from friends and family, in the community of fellow believers, in the voice of conscience open to guidance, and in the honest desire to put God's will ahead of their own selfish inclinations. These experiences do not prove that God exists, but for those who experience divine love as real and as personal as the love of family and friends; they believe it would be intellectually dishonest and deliberately self-deceptive not to believe in a Creator.

For Christians, the Bible plays a central role in their beliefs.[8] The Bible records the words and historical events which claim to be direct revelations from God. Most Christians believe that God not only inspired the scriptures, but also insured that they are fully reliable. In an important sense the Bible is a source of true knowledge about the God and the world.[9]

Some fundamental beliefs of Christianity include the idea that the universe was created by a God who governs it; that human beings were made by God for a purpose; that God cares for us; and God has objective moral standards for human behavior. These beliefs conflict with the philosophical claims of evolutionism listed earlier.

All Christians reject the philosophical claims of evolutionism. However, Christians do not all agree with each other about the scientific claims of the theory of evolution. Because the science of the theory of evolution is so often linked with the philosophy of evolutionism, Christians have responded to scientific claims of evolution in a variety of ways.

Some Christians are "Young Earth creationists." They dispute both the theory of evolution and the scientific claim that there is a pattern of evolution in the history of life. They believe that God specially created the Earth and modern life-forms a few thousand years ago. Other Christians are "progressive creationists" who accept the pattern of evolutionary change in the history of life over billions of years; however, they reject the idea that the mechanisms proposed by Darwin in his theory of evolution can account for the pattern. They believe that God must have miraculously guided or intervened at various points in the history of life to produce modern life-forms. A third category of Christians is "evolutionary creationists." They accept the pattern of evolution and agree that Darwin's theory of evolution is a good scientific description of the history of life. They believe that God used the natural processes of evolution to bring about modern life-forms, in an analogous way to how God uses the natural mechanism of gravity to keep the Earth in a stable orbit around the Sun.[10]

Young Earth creationism

Young Earth creationists believe that the Earth and all modern life-forms were created, mature and fully functioning, during six days approximately ten thousand years ago. This belief comes from a particular interpretation of the creation poem in the first chapter of the book of Genesis in the Bible. Young Earth creationists believe that this poem must be literally true and historically accurate in some (though not quite all) of its details.[11] They believe that interpreting this poem non-literally and non-historically calls into question the historical accuracy of other Biblical events fundamental to Christianity, such as the crucifixion, resurrection, and post-resurrection appearances of Jesus. They believe that interpreting this poem non-literally and non-historically would undermine the very idea that the Bible is a true revelation from God, and would undermine other fundamental Christian doctrines about how human beings relate to God.[12]

During the past 30 years, Young Earth creationists have tried to prove scientifically that their view is correct. They have tried to make numerous scientific arguments that the Earth is only thousands of years old, and they have disputed the scientific evidence from astronomy and geology that the universe and the earth are billions of years old. They reject the idea that the pattern of fossils shows an evolutionary history, and instead have tried to explain the pattern of fossils in terms of a catastrophic global flood. Their arguments were not published in the mainstream scientific literature because the vast majority of scientists saw their arguments as having serious scientific flaws. Young Earth creationists instead published their arguments in books and magazines aimed at non-scientists.[13] Today, several Young Earth creationist organizations have web sites where they publish their arguments.[14]

In response to these publications, several scientists have written books pointing out flaws in the scientific arguments made by Young Earth creationists.[15] And today, there are websites dedicated to this same task.[16]

Young Earth creationism is a fairly common belief amongst protestant Christians in North America who do not have a university education in science. But because there is abundant scientific evidence that the earth is billions of years old and abundant scientific evidence for the pattern of evolution in the history of life,[17] there are very few Young Earth creationists who have advanced degrees in science. Nevertheless, because they have strong religious motivations for believing that the Earth must be young, they continue to try to build scientific arguments in favor of their view.

Progressive creationism

Progressive creationists accept the astronomical and geological evidence that the Earth is several billion years old, and they accept that the fossil and genetic data shows a pattern of evolutionary change in life-forms during the history of life on Earth. Many progressive creationists accept that there is good evidence that all modern life-forms share a common ancestry in earlier life-forms. However, they dispute whether the mechanism proposed by Darwin – random mutation plus differential reproductive success – can fully account for this pattern.

Progressive creationists accept microevolution. They agree that random mutation plus differential reproductive success can produce small-scale changes and adaptations in species. However, progressive creationists are skeptical that life on Earth could have arisen purely by natural processes without divine intervention, and they are skeptical that Darwin's theory can account for the large-scale increases in biological complexity which we see during the history of life. They believe that God acted miraculously several times throughout biological history, first of all in order to create the very first life-forms, and then at various times throughout history to introduce new biological features and increased biological complexity into the history of life.

When scientists write books for non-scientists trying to explain the theory of evolution, they often argue that highly complex organs, such as the eye, the ear, or the wing, could have evolved from simpler organs through a sequence of minor, adaptive mutations. (For example, in the case of the eye: a few light-sensitive cells form an eyespot, the eyespot becomes recessed to increase the light-gathering area and to allow directional sense, the opening narrows to create a "pin-hole camera" eye, fluid fills the space for protection, the fluid becomes a lens.)[18] Progressive creationists point out that these stories are very speculative and unempirical. The actual sequence of genetic mutations is not even hypothesized. Additional factors, such as the complex signal-processing circuitry required to make an eye useful, are typically ignored in these stories. Possible maladaptive factors in the sequence of mutations are not considered.[19]

Progressive creationists also point out that many biological structures are not just complex, they are "irreducibly complex." That is, several independently coded proteins must function together in order for the system to work properly. If any one of the proteins is removed or significantly altered, the structure does not function at all. The bacteria flagellum is one example. The flagellum is a tiny whip-like structure found on the membrane walls of some single-celled organisms. It is constructed out of more than a dozen different proteins, fit together in just the right way, which allows the organism to move. Progressive creationists argue that it is very unlikely for a sequence of random mutations to produce such an irreducibly complex system.[20]

The scientific arguments of progressive creationists seem to be valid in the following limited sense. The evolution of complex biological features such as eyes, or bacteria flagella, is a very hard problem to solve scientifically. Even if research in evolutionary biology proceeds quickly, it will probably take decades before scientists will be able to figure out a specific sequence of genetic mutations which could reasonably produce such complex features. It is still an open scientific question as to whether or not Darwin's proposed mechanisms of random mutation and differential reproductive success are sufficient to explain the increases in biological complexity seen in the history of life.

Progressive creationists believe that future scientific research ultimately will show that Darwin's theory cannot do the job, and that the scientific evidence ultimately will point towards non-natural or supernatural mechanisms as being necessary to explain biological complexity.[21]

Evolutionary creationism

Consider the following claim: "If Darwin's scientific theory of evolution is true, then the philosophical claims of evolutionism must also be true." If you disagree with the philosophical claims of evolutionism, then you seem to have two choices.

You could attack the scientific underpinnings of Darwin's scientific theory of evolution. This is what Young Earth creationists and progressive creationists do. Evolutionary creationists, on the other hand, believe that Darwin's theory of evolution is an accurate scientific picture of the history of life on Earth. Evolutionary creationists strongly disagree with the claim that if the theory of evolution is true, then the philosophical claims of evolutionism must also be true. Evolutionary creationists believe that Darwin's theory of evolution can be fully compatible with their religious beliefs that the universe was created by a God who governs it, that human beings were made by God for a purpose, that God cares for humans, and that God has objective moral standards for human behavior.

The philosophical claims of evolutionism seem to rely on the assumptions that if something happens via scientifically explainable natural mechanisms then God wasn't involved in that process, and that if something seemed to happen "by chance" (such as an apparently random mutation), then God had nothing to do with the event. I have already argued in chapter 10 that these assumptions are not true. Scientific explanations in terms of natural laws and apparently random events are fully compatible with the Christian belief in a God who created the universe, designed the laws of nature, and can continue to interact with that creation in subtle but effective ways through events which seem scientifically random to us.

Evolutionary creationists believe that if it is reasonable to believe that God might choose to use the scientifically understandable mechanism of gravitational attraction to keep the earth in a stable orbit around the sun, then it is also reasonable to believe that God might choose to use the mechanisms of genetic mutation and differential reproductive success gradually to create a wide variety of life-forms, each life-form well-adapted to its environment.[22]

An Analysis of Intelligent Design Theory

Within the last ten years, some progressive creationists have rephrased some of their arguments in ways which they are calling "Intelligent Design theory." Two arguments are at the core of Intelligent Design (ID) theory. The first argument is that it is very, very improbable that complex biological features such as the eye, or the bacteria flagellum, could have evolved purely by the Darwinian mechanisms of random mutation and differential reproductive success. The second argument is that if the evolution of biological complexity is very improbable, then biological complexity also has some additional features which indicate that this complexity was assembled by the action of an intelligent agent.

The second argument requires some explanation. Many events are improbable, but not all improbable events are "designed." For example, suppose there is a computer keyboard sitting on the far side of the room from where I am standing. Suppose I throw 15 small rocks at the keyboard, hitting 15 keys. When I was done throwing rocks, you would expect to see a string of 15 apparently random symbols on the computer. There are about 80 keys on a typical English computer keyboard, and if I am truly hitting the keys randomly, then the odds that I will happen to hit any particular string of 15 symbols is 80 to the power of 15, or about 1 in 3×10^{28}. So each particular string of 15 symbols is highly improbable. However, if the 15 symbols which I hit look random and don't spell anything in particular, you would not conclude that the event was "designed." You would conclude that it was a random event. If an event does not seem to serve any conceivable purpose, even if that event is very improbable, we generally conclude that the event is simply random. Suppose, however, that after I threw the 15 rocks, the symbols on the computer spelled out the sentence, "I love my wife." Now you would be suspicious. It seems very unlikely that 15 randomly thrown rocks would spell out anything intelligible. You would probably conclude that either I am very good at throwing rocks, or maybe someone rigged the computer ahead of time. Either way, you would conclude that this particular event was not truly random, but was caused by some intelligent agent guiding the process.

In the same way, Intelligent Design theory argues that if the evolution of the eye or the bacteria flagellum is very improbable via random processes, the fact that these organs are so useful for living organisms should lead us to the conclusion that some intelligent agent – and they would say that this intelligent agent was probably God – was guiding the process.[23]

Most of the debate over Intelligent Design theory has been over whether or not it should be considered "scientific." Advocates of Intelligent Design say that their arguments are scientific, and can be evaluated purely on their scientific merits apart from any religious considerations. Most opponents of Intelligent Design say that these arguments are unscientific, that they are completely religious arguments and therefore should stay out of science.

In my opinion, the debates over whether Intelligent Design is wholly "scientific" or wholly "religious" have been useless debates. This is because Intelligent Design, as a whole package, is partly scientific, partly philosophical, and, yes, partly religious. The scientific, philosophical, and religious parts of ID should each be evaluated on their own merits.

The first core argument of ID is that it is very, very improbable that complex biological features such as the eye, or the bacteria flagellum, could have evolved by a Darwinian process. This is clearly a scientific argument and can be evaluated on its scientific merits. This is, however, an exceedingly difficult question to answer scientifically.

On the one hand, scientists do not yet have enough information to attempt to explain how complexity in a particular organism could have evolved. Scientists would have to sequence the entire genome of the organism and of closely related organisms, and then figure out the function of every gene in the organism, and then figure out how the genes are regulated during the development of the organism, and then deduce the genetic ancestry of the organism, and learn something about the environment of the ancestral organisms. Only then could a truly convincing, detailed, step-by-step model be constructed for the evolution of a particular biological feature. Scientists are still many decades away from being able to accomplish this.

On the other hand, advocates of ID have an even harder task. They are trying to argue that some complex biological features could not have evolved via any known natural evolutionary mechanisms. They face the special challenge of being as thorough as possible in accounting for all known natural mechanisms. Advocates of ID frequently do make flawed scientific arguments because they are not sufficiently careful in accounting for all known natural mechanisms. I will give two examples.

We could imagine a warm pond of water with various simple molecules dissolved in it in various concentrations, and then calculate the probability that the right molecules will just randomly collide together, all at once, to spontaneously form a living cell. The probability of that happening is extremely low. If we were to conclude on the basis of this calculation that first life on Earth probably didn't form via that mechanism that would be a solid scientific conclusion. But if one were to conclude on the basis of this model that first life on Earth probably didn't form via any natural mechanisms that would be a flawed scientific conclusion. Scientists who are researching the origin of life long ago rejected the idea that the first cell was formed via a single, random collision of millions of molecules. Scientists today have other natural mechanisms in mind for the origin of first life, and if you are going to attempt a meaningful probability calculation, those other mechanisms need to be studied and taken into account.[24]

Another example: The simplest version of biological evolution – and this is how evolution is often presented in the popular literature – looks something like this: each gene only produces a single protein; each protein only has a single function in the cell; the only kinds of mutations are point mutations; and the only way in which a mutation can be fixed in a population is through natural selection. We can build a mathematical model of evolution using just that limited set of natural mechanisms, and we can calculate that, under those conditions, the evolution of certain kinds of biological complexity is extremely improbable. On the basis of this model, a solid scientific conclusion would be that biological complexity probably didn't evolve via that limited set of mechanisms. A flawed scientific conclusion would be to claim, on the basis of the model I just described, that this model proves that biological complexity cannot evolve at all. Scientists have determined that biological evolution is a lot more complicated than the simplified model which I just presented. A more thorough model of evolution would include an accounting of at least all of the following natural mechanisms: reproductive isolation, founder effects, neutral drift, sexual selection, environment-dependent gene expression, gene duplication, horizontal gene transfer, allo-polyploidy, endosymbiont capture, differential RNA editing, ambiguous tRNA sequences, multiple proteins encoded by the same gene, and single proteins having multiple functions for a single protein. This is just a partial list of natural evolutionary mechanisms which go beyond the simplest version of biological evolution outlined earlier. Many of these mechanisms make the evolution of complexity far more probable.[25]

The evolution of complexity is a relatively new and growing field of scientific study. It can be simulated on a computer,[26] and progress is being made in the study of biological complexity. There are many natural mechanisms to consider, and we don't fully understand many of them. Given how much we have yet to learn about the mechanisms of evolution, it seems to me that two limited types of scientific conclusions are reasonable for advocates of ID to draw. The first type would be:

On the basis of specific models with well-defined assumptions, we can rule out certain limited sets of natural mechanisms as being adequate, by themselves, to account for first life or to account for specific examples of biological complexity. Any evolutionary account will need to make use of additional natural mechanisms that aren't included in our initial models.[27]

There is a second type of scientific conclusion which I think is defensible. An advocate of ID could say:

It seems to me (that is, it is my scientific intuition) that once *all* natural mechanisms are accounted for in detail, we will be able to show that first life and certain types of biological complexity (*e.g.*, bacteria flagella) truly are unexplainable in terms of all known natural mechanisms. We can't prove it for sure right now, but I believe that is where the data is pointing.

These are conservative claims, but given our current state of knowledge, it seems unwise for advocates of ID to claim that current scientific evidence warrants anything stronger.

To summarize: the great majority of scientists believe that all of the biological complexity which we see today could have evolved via natural Darwinian mechanisms. However, it is currently well beyond our scientific abilities to prove conclusively that this has happened. A small minority of scientists, such as those in the Intelligent Design movement, believes that biological complexity could not have evolved; however, they are also unable to prove their claims. Presumably, further scientific research eventually will resolve this question.

A Philosophical and Religious Consideration:
Both Evolution and "Design" Could Be True

Advocates of evolutionism believe that Darwin's theory of evolution is scientifically true and that biological life was not designed by any God. Most of the debate about evolution during the past ten years has been arguments between these two groups. However, evolutionary creationists offer a third option. Evolutionary creationists believe that Darwin's theory of evolution is scientifically true and that biological life was designed by God. Both "evolution" and "design" could be true.

To illustrate this, consider two hypothetical plastic bags each of which contain a collection of tiny mechanical parts (springs, hooks, levers, gears, etc.). The first bag contains all the parts of a mechanical music box which has been disassembled. If you seal this bag, you could shake it up and down continuously, 24 hours a day for years and years, and the music box would never reassemble. It would remain a bag full of separate pieces. Now consider a second bag similar to the first, except that all the pieces are designed to latch onto each other in specific ways. Spring, hooks, levers, and gears are designed so that when any two parts which belong together happen to collide in the right way, they latch together and stay latched together. The more you shake this bag, the more the pieces come together in the right way. So if this bag is shaken for a few hours, eventually, an entire functional music box will self-assemble out of all the component pieces. (I don't know if anyone has ever built such a self-assembly music box, but I believe that it could be done with enough time, determination, and cleverness.)

Advocates of Intelligent Design theory think of "design" in biology like the first music box. In order to become a functional music box, someone must put together all the pieces together by hand. Once that is done, the finished product is clearly a designed object. So also, advocates of Intelligent Design believe that complex biological features like eyes and ears could not have evolved, but must have been assembled specially by God, and therefore are designed.

Evolutionary creationists think of "design" in biology like the second music box – the one that self-assembles. If anyone could make all of the parts of a self-assembling music box, it clearly would be a cleverly designed object. So also, evolutionary creationists believe that the fundamental laws of nature were designed in order that life and biological complexity could self-assemble out of the component pieces by evolutionary processes. For evolutionary creationists, the focus of the term "design" is less on the final products such as eyes and ears, and more on the entire process which makes the evolution of complexity possible. The evolutionary mechanisms were designed by God to produce a wide variety of complex plants and animals, each species well-adapted to its environment, and the whole system continually adapting to environmental changes.

There is evidence for self-assembly in astronomy and physics. The laws of nature appear to be very finely tuned so that the fundamental particles produced in the Big Bang could self-assemble into atoms.[28] And these atoms could self-assemble into stars and galaxies. And inside stars through the process of nuclear fusion, heavier atoms can self-assemble out of simpler atoms. And these heavier atoms can self-assemble into simple molecules and planets with land and atmospheres and oceans. All of these steps are already fairly well understood scientifically. Evolutionary creationists believe that the same pattern will probably hold in evolutionary biology as well. They believe that the laws of nature probably are also very finely tuned to allow simple life to self-assemble out of chemicals on the early earth, and that the laws of nature are finely tuned to allow biological complexity to evolve out of simpler life-forms.

I have participated in discussions and debates between Christians who are progressive creationists (and therefore favor Intelligent Design theory) and Christians who are evolutionary creationists. The scientific arguments are inconclusive, because scientists cannot yet prove whether or not biological complexity can evolve by natural mechanisms. Therefore, not surprisingly, the discussion sometimes turns to religious arguments. Christians who are progressive creationists look for evidence of God's activity in the history of life on Earth by looking for places where, perhaps, the ordinary operation of natural laws was broken by a supernatural miracle. This can be very attractive to Christians, because if scientists really could prove that natural evolutionary mechanisms are incapable of producing biological complexity, while this would not prove the existence of God, it would be counted by many people as evidence in favor of God's existence.

Evolutionary creationists, on the other hand, believe that the ordinary operation of natural laws was God's chosen method for governing the history of life on Earth and for producing the world we live in today. This makes God's activity far less obvious. However, evolutionary creationists find religious support for this idea in the Christian theological concept of *kenosis*. *Kenosis* is a Greek term meaning "to empty," and it is used in the Bible to describe God, in the person of Jesus Christ, emptying Himself of His divine power. Christian theology considers that the ultimate expression of God's good character is shown not in His great power or His great knowledge, but in His self-emptying and self-sacrifice. In the person of Jesus Christ, God emptied Himself of divine power and lived as a human being. And as a human being, he suffered rejection, betrayal, torture, and murder – all the worst evils that humans inflict on each other. And then, instead of striking out in retribution, he forgave the evils that were done to him. In Christian theology, God permitted himself to suffer human evils, and then offered forgiveness for those evils. That is considered to be the ultimate expression of God's good character, the ultimate example for us human beings to follow in our relationships with each other, and the ultimate plan of God to bring about a renewed relationship between Him and humanity. In Christian theology, God does not supernaturally force human beings to give up their evil ways and become good people, although He could do so. God instead chooses to respect the ability of free choice which He gave to human beings, and instead seeks – through the seemingly weak acts of self-emptying and self-sacrifice – to persuade human beings to choose good over evil and to follow Him.

Several evolutionary creationists have written books and articles arguing that this theological concept of *kenosis* can also help us understand the history of life on Earth. God has the power, at any time, to break the ordinary laws of nature and supernaturally force the world into whatever form he chooses. But God chooses to respect the creation that He made, and to work through the ordinary laws of nature by which it operates. According to evolutionary creationists, God accomplishes His design in the natural world, as He does in the human world, not primarily through supernatural miracles, but by respecting and by working through the ordinary capabilities of His creatures.[29]

Notes

1   George G. Simpson, *The Meaning of Evolution* (New Haven: Yale University Press, 1967).
2   Steven Weinberg, *The First Three Minutes: A Modern View of the Origin of the Universe* (New York: Bantam, 1979).

3 Douglas Futuyma, *Science on Trial: The Case for Evolution* (New York: Pantheon, 1983), pp. 12–13.

4 For example: Stephen J. Gould, "Nonoverlapping magisteria," *Natural History* 106 (2) (1997), 16–22.

5 Psalm 19:1–2, *New International Version Study Bible* (Grand Rapids, MI: Zondervan, 1985).

6 Some organizations of scientists who share these beliefs include: the American Scientific Affiliation, Ipswich, MA; the Association of Christian Engineers and Scientists, Vernonia, OR; the Association of Christians in Mathematical Sciences; Wheaton, IL; the Christian Association for Psychological Studies, Temecula, CA; the Christian Medical and Dental Society, Richardson, TX.

7 C. S. Lewis makes this argument more carefully in *Mere Christianity* (New York: Macmillian, 1943).

8 I am writing this chapter from a Christian point of view because I am a Christian myself and am most familiar with the Christian tradition. Believers in Judaism and Islam also believe in God and oppose evolutionism. Judaism, Christianity, and Islam share many of the Scriptures which teach about God's creation of the universe.

9 While all Christians agree that the Bible is a revelation from God, Christians do not all agree on the best ways to interpret some passages in the Bible. Deborah Haarsma writes, in How Christians Reconcile Ancient Texts with Modern Science, chapter 8 of this volume, about the variety of ways in which Christians have interpreted the creation poem in the first chapter of the book of Genesis.

10 Loren Haarsma, "Why believe in a creator? Perspectives on evolution," *The World & I* 11 no.1 (1996) pp. 323–37; J. P. Moreland and John Mark Reynolds (eds.), *Three Views on Creation and Evolution* (Grand Rapids, MI: Zondervan, 1999).

11 I will not discuss the details of this interpretation in this paper because Deborah B. Haarsma discusses it in chapter 8 of this volume, How Christians Reconcile Ancient Texts with Modern Science.

12 One of the foundational books on Young Earth creationism which makes these arguments is: Henry Morris, *Scientific Creationism* (San Diego: Creation-Life Publishers, 1974).

13 For example: H. Morris and G. Parker. *What is Scientific Creationism?* (San Diego: Creation-Life Publishers, 1982); J. C. Whitcomb and H. Morris, *The Genesis Flood: The Biblical Record and Its Scientific Implications* (Grand Rapids, MI: Baker, 1961, 2nd edn. 1993). G. T. Gish, *Evolution: The Challenge of the Fossil Record* (San Diego: Creation-Life Publishers, 1985).

14 For example: www.icr.org; www.creationresearch.org.

15 Some examples by both Christian and non-Christian authors: Howard J. Van Till, Davis A. Young, and Clarence Menninga, *Science Held Hostage* (Downers Grove, IL: InterVarsity Press, 1988); Alan Hayward, *Creation and Evolution: The Facts and Fallacies* (London: Triangle, 1985); Howard J. Van Till, Robert E. Snow, John H. Stek, and Davis A. Young, *Portraits of Creation* (Grand Rapids, MI: Eerdmans, 1990); Niles Eldredge, *The Monkey Business* (New York: Washington Square, 1982); Norman Newell, *Creation and Evolution* (New York: Columbia University Press, 1982); Phillip Kitcher, *Abusing Science* (Cambridge, MA: MIT Press, 1982); Michael Ruse, *Darwinism Defended* (Reading, MA: Addison-Wesley, 1982).

16 For example: www.talkorigins.org.

17 There isn't space in this chapter to list the many evidences from astronomy and geology that the Earth is billions of years old, and the many evidences for the pattern of evolution from the fossil record, from the geographic distribution of species, from developmental biology and from genetics. Good textbooks provide some of the best summaries of these evidences.

18 For example: Richard Dawkins. *River Out of Eden* ([London: Basic Books, 1995). Kenneth Miller, "Life's grand design," *Technology Review* 97, no. 2 (Feb./Mar. 1994), 24–32.

19 Phillip Johnson. *Darwin on Trial* (Downers Grove, IL: InterVarsity Press, 1993).

20 Michael Behe. *Darwin's Black Box* (New York: Touchstone Press, 1996).

21 For example: William Dembski, *The Design Inference* (Cambridge: Cambridge University Press, 1998).

22   Some books by evolutionary creationists which make these arguments include: Howard J. Van Till, Davis A. Young and Clarence Menninga, *Science Held Hostage*, (Downers Grove, IL: InterVarsity Press, 1988); Kenneth Miller, *Finding Darwin's God* (New York: HarperCollins, 1999); Darrel Falk, *Coming to Peace with Science* (Downers Grove, IL: InterVarsity Press, 2004); Keith Miller (ed.), *Perspectives on an Evolving Creation* (Grand Rapids, MI: Eerdmans, 2003).

23   See earlier footnote on *The Design Inference* by William Dembski. In addition, a website where Intelligent Design advocates publish these sorts of arguments is: www.discovery.org.

24   For two reviews of research on the origins of life see: L. E. Orgel, "The origin of life – a review of facts and speculations," *Trends Biochemical Sciences* 23 (1998), 491–5; Andri Brack (ed.), *The Molecular Origins of Life: Assembling Pieces of the Puzzle* (Cambridge: Cambridge University Press, 2004).

25   Loren Haarsma, "Self-organized Complexity and Design" in Keith B. Miller (ed.), *Perspectives on an Evolving Creation* (Grand Rapids, MI: Eerdmans, 2003).

26   Some examples: Barbara Drossel, "Simple Model for the Formation of a Complex Organism," *Physical Review Letters* 82 (21 June 1999), 5144–7; Steven Levy, *Artificial Life* (New York: Pantheon Books, 1992); Stuart Kauffman, *The Origins of Order: Self Organization and Selection in Evolution* (New York: Oxford University Press, 1993). And the websites: www.alcyone.com/max/links/alife. html; www.santafe.edu/~smfr/tierra/intro.html; http://dlife.annexia.org. See also previous footnote on "Self-organized Complexity and Design."

27   A recently published paper by an ID advocate which makes such a limited claim: M. Behe and D. W. Snoke, "Simulating evolution by gene duplication. ..." *Protein Science* 13 (2004), p. 2651.

28   These apparent "fine-tunings" of the laws of nature are discussed in greater depth by Deborah B. Haarsma in chapter 7 of this volume.

29   Two examples: Denis Edwards, *The God of Evolution: A Trinitarian Theology* (Mahwah, NJ: Paulist Press, 1999); John Polkinghorne, *The Work of Love: Creation as Kenosis* (Grand Rapids, MI: Eerdmans, 2001).

12

Human Evolution and Objective Morality

LOREN HAARSMA

Evolution is usually thought to reward selfish behavior. There is good scientific evidence that humans evolved, so the question of why humans often behave morally and altruistically is a scientific puzzle. The scientific fields of sociobiology and evolutionary psychology have offered several hypotheses for how altruism, a sense of morality, and religious dispositions could have evolved in human beings. However, when these scientific hypotheses are presented, they are often used to support philosophical claims that morality and religion are nothing more than genetic and social constructs which make us behave in ways which increase our chances of reproducing, that human morality cannot be objective, and that religious beliefs cannot be true. These philosophical claims are unnecessary additions; they can be separated from the scientific hypotheses without any scientific loss. Human moral and religious sentiments are intrinsic parts of our biological nature, and therefore could have evolved. But many religions also include the concept of divine revelation in human history. The concept of divine revelation enriches the horizontal, human dimension of morality and adds a vertical, divine – human dimension to morality. Combining human evolution of moral and religious sentiments with the idea of divine revelation allows a full picture of objective morality and religious beliefs.[1]

Feelings of Guilt as Adaptive

Are feelings of guilt adaptive?

Cartoonist Sidney Harris has drawn a cartoon which pictures two identical atoms. One is captioned, "atom in a bird's brain"; the other is captioned, "atom in a human's brain."[2] This cartoon makes some people laugh precisely because it makes them uncomfortable. If the captions in Harris's cartoon had read "atom in a bird's liver" and "atom in a human's liver," it wouldn't bother people so much. Most people have made peace with the idea that human bodies and animal bodies are composed of exactly the same atoms obeying exactly the same physical laws. When someone talks about the human brain, however, they are implicitly talking about human intelligence and human behavior. It does bother many people to suggest that human behavior – including our moral sentiments – were shaped by exactly the same natural forces of evolutionary selection which shaped animal behavior. This disturbing claim is at the heart of the scientific fields of sociobiology and evolutionary psychology.

Animal behavior can be studied without reference to evolution, but behavioral studies which ignore evolution are increasingly considered incomplete and unsatisfying. Consider the following questions: Why is it that, when hungry rats or mice are placed in a new environment with food available, some species will usually first eat and then explore, while other species will usually first explore and then eat? Or: Why are some species of birds mostly monogamous while other bird species are not?[3] In its simplest form, evolution predicts that a species' most common behavioral dispositions ought to be "adaptive." This means that individual animals which display the most common behavioral dispositions of a species ought, on average, to produce more offspring than individuals with different behavioral dispositions.[4] Over the past several decades, evolutionary studies of animal behaviors have produced some interesting insights into adaptive behaviors which seemed, at first glance, to have been maladaptive.

Sociobiology and evolutionary psychology extend the evolutionary study of animal behavior into the study of human behavior. Some scientific hypotheses are fairly uncontroversial. For example, the observation that humans enjoy eating sweet foods seems well-suited to an evolutionary explanation. Natural foods with high sugar content, such as fruit, typically are also highly nutritious, so it makes sense that animals and humans would evolve brain circuitry which would take pleasure in eating sweet foods. Similar hypotheses could be made about the human predisposition to eat in groups rather than eating alone, for example. Evolutionary hypotheses about such predispositions, while still sketchy and incomplete, do not generate much controversy and seem useful for stimulating further scientific research.

Sociobiology and evolutionary psychology rapidly become controversial when they make hypotheses about morality and religion. Religion typically asks whether behaviors are morally right or wrong, and whether religious beliefs are true or false. Traditional Christian theology, for example, would say that morality has an absolute, objective basis in God's will. God has a standard for human behavior, even if we humans do not all agree with that standard.

Biologists, by contrast, do not ask whether behaviors are right or wrong. Biologists typically ask whether behaviors are adaptive. Consider, for example, feelings of guilt. Lions, we presume, feel no guilt when they kill in order to eat. An evolutionary argument could be made that feelings of guilt are maladaptive in lions. Lions who felt guilt at killing gazelles would not hunt as well, and therefore would leave fewer offspring than lions who felt no guilt. Humans, however, do feel guilt, at least when it comes to harming other human beings. The feeling of guilt when harming another human being is so common amongst human beings that we say that humans who do not feel guilt at harming other humans are abnormal – that they are pathological.

First we should ask a scientific question: Can we construct an evolutionary explanation for why human ancestors who felt guilt tended to produce more offspring than those who did not feel guilt? Second we should ask a philosophical question: Suppose scientists can successfully construct such an evolutionary explanation for human guilt. Would that mean that guilt is nothing but an evolutionary construct imposed by our genes and that there is no objective reason for one human to feel guilt when harming another human being?

If guilt is adaptive, so what?

According to some writers, the answer to both of those questions is, "Yes." This claim is the source of much controversy. Sociobiology and evolutionary psychology are not the first scientific theories to become a battleground for competing philosophical ideologies. Centuries ago, Isaac Newton's laws of mechanics were used to support a metaphysical belief that the universe followed a sort of clockwork determinism. Darwin's theories of biological evolution have been co-opted to serve a variety of philosophical ideologies: social Darwinism, eugenics, a metaphysics of Chance, and claims that there is no longer any reason to believe in a Creator. Today, the scientific field of evolutionary psychology is being used, by some scholars to support philosophical positions such as moral relativism,[5] or to support the claim that religion is nothing more than a delusion which, at best, might help one individual or group successfully compete against another individual or group.[6]

Analyzing these claims requires that they be broken into at least two steps. First there is the scientific claim that we can construct accurate evolutionary explanations for the existence of human moral and religious sentiments. Second there is the philosophical claim that if these evolutionary explanations are scientifically accurate, then human moral and religious beliefs have no objective status or truth content.

Many people, including myself, dispute the idea that human moral and religious beliefs have no objective status or truth content. Some people have chosen to attack the scientific claim – that human moral and religious sentiments allow for an evolutionary explanation – in hopes of undercutting the philosophical claim of moral and religious relativism.[7] I am convinced, however, that this is an unproductive strategy. I believe that the flaw lies in the second claim. I believe that it is possible that we can construct evolutionary explanations for the existence of human moral and religious sentiments, and yet still have it be true that morality and religion have objective status and objective truth content.

Altruism and Evolutionary Theory

Well-established scientific theories: Kin selection and reciprocal altruism

Evolutionary accounts of human morality usually start with altruism. In everyday use, the word *altruism* often refers to having feelings of goodwill towards others, without expecting anything in return. In the science of sociobiology, the word *altruism* has a more technical definition. An altruistic act is one which reduces an organism's own reproductive chances while benefiting the reproductive chances of others. Examples of altruistic acts could include sharing a scarce resource with another member of the species, or giving a warning call when a predator is noticed. While these two definitions of altruism are linked, it's important to distinguish between altruistic feelings and altruistic acts.

At first glance, the existence of altruistic acts would seem to be a problem for evolutionary theory. The caricature of evolution is that it rewards selfishness. If a population includes both selfish and altruistic individuals, so the theory goes, the selfish individuals will produce more offspring than the altruists. Assuming these traits are inherited, after enough generations selfishness would completely take over the population. That line of reasoning, however, is too simple. It turns out that there are some intriguing ways in which evolution can "reward" altruism.

The most obvious case of altruism is parental care of their young. From the strict sociobiological definition, parental care typically is not an altruistic act because animals that care for their young often are, in fact, increasing the number of their offspring who survive. I mention it for two reasons. First, parental care is probably an evolutionary precursor to the other kinds of altruism we will discuss. Second, parental care ties into the emotional and motivational use of the word "altruism." It seems a fair, although unproven, assumption that some animals – particularly the more intelligent primates – experience emotions analogous to human emotions when they care for their young. It is evolutionarily beneficial for these animals to have altruistic feelings towards their children. It seems likely that the genes which promote parental altruistic feelings and behaviors are involved in altruistic feelings and behavior towards non-offspring. Parental care of offspring, which is evolutionarily rewarded, sets the stage for other forms of altruism.

One way in which evolution can "reward" altruism is through kin selection.[8] Suppose you have genes which make you behave altruistically towards your relatives – perhaps by giving warning calls when you spot predators. Chances are that your relatives share the same genes. Your altruistic behavior may reduce your own chance of reproducing, but increase the chances of all of your relatives surviving and reproducing. Thus, the number of individuals with altruistic genes in the next generation increases. Mathematical models of kin selection have been constructed, and it has been observationally studied in a variety of animal species.

Another way in which evolution can "reward" altruism is reciprocal altruism.[9] I do something good for you today, an act which has a small cost to me but a large benefit to you. And I expect that in the future you will help me out in the same way. In order for reciprocal altruism to work, there has to be a way for cheaters – individuals who accept help but never give help – to be punished or excluded from receiving help in the future. Again, mathematical models of reciprocal altruism have been constructed, and it has been studied observationally in a variety of animal species.

Human beings display altruistic emotions and behaviors which go beyond kin selection and reciprocal altruism. I will very briefly sketch some competing evolutionary hypotheses for how human beings could come to possess altruistic tendencies beyond kin and beyond reciprocation.

Non-adaptive evolutionary theories of altruism: Side-effects, cultural evolution, and memes

The first group of scientific hypotheses supposes that altruistic behavior (beyond kin selection and beyond reciprocal altruism) really is non-adaptive. Like hypothetical lions who feel guilty for killing a gazelle, strictly from a genetic and reproductive point of view, humans should not have altruistic tendencies. So why do we? One hypothesis is that our altruism – and more broadly, our sense of morality – is a side-effect of other mental characteristics which are adaptive.[10] (As an example of an evolutionary "side effect", the fact that our blood is red is not an adaptive characteristic. There is no evolutionary selection for redness in blood color. Our blood is red because the chemical hemoglobin happens to be red when oxygenated. There is evolutionary selection for blood which contains hemoglobin. Our blood is red as a side-effect.) What mental characteristics of humans are thought to be adaptive? We are intelligent. We have the ability to predict probable outcomes of our actions. We have the ability to make value judgments, that is, to select some outcomes as being more desirable than others. We are self-aware, and we perceive other humans as being self-aware individuals with their own knowledge and goals. We have empathy for the mental state of others. All of these mental abilities might be adaptive. Individuals who have these mental abilities in greater degrees are more likely to produce offspring. And, when you put all of them together, you get altruism and morality as an inevitable side-effect.

Another hypothesis which supposes that altruism and morality are non-adaptive is the hypothesis that altruism and morality are cultural (not genetic) phenomena.[11] According to this theory, our genes do not particularly predispose us to morality, but our culture teaches us to be moral and altruistic. Groups of humans who have a culture that promotes altruism and morality will tend to do better than groups of humans who have a very selfish culture. Cultures which promote morality will therefore tend to replace or convert cultures which do not. This effect could feed back to the genetic level. Individuals who are predisposed to moral behavior will tend to do well in cultures which promote morality, so that eventually the genes might "catch up" with culture and co-evolve with culture to promote moral sentiments.

Another hypothesis is that altruism and morality are like a kind of mental virus, sometimes called a "meme."[12] The idea of morality spreads from individual to individual and group to group, infecting brains in ways analogous to the way that viruses infect bodies. Although the altruism meme tends to kill off its hosts, or at least make them less likely to reproduce, the meme keeps infecting new hosts.

Adaptive theories for the evolution of altruism: Individual selection

Another set of hypotheses propose that altruism and morality are, in fact, adaptive. Humans who behave morally really do tend, on average, to produce more offspring than humans who do not behave morally. The most cynical version proposes that, when someone behaves altruistically in front of you, what they are really doing is manipulating you into being nice to them in the future.[13] A slightly less cynical version is that being altruistic and behaving morally enhances your reputation, increases your social status, and thereby brings you benefits in the long run.[14] A variation on this hypothesis is that behaving morally is a sort of "price of admission" to be part of a group. A human being's chances of survival and reproduction are greatly enhanced when he or she is part of successful group. Groups don't tolerate members who are constantly selfish.

Another version of this hypothesis is that altruism is adaptive because of sexual selection. When humans look for potential mates, part of the criteria is selecting for moral behavior as an indicator of ability and willingness to care for offspring over a long period of time.[15]

All of these "individual selection" hypotheses share a common feature. Altruistic acts (such as behaving according to a moral code) might cost you in the short term, but, on average, tend to give you even greater benefits in the long term. Therefore, individuals whose genes predispose them to behaving altruistically and morally will tend to have more offspring than individuals whose genes predispose them constantly towards selfish behavior.

Adaptive theories for the evolution of altruism: Group selection

A third class of hypotheses for the evolution of altruism is group-selection.[16] In this hypothesis, altruistic individuals really do produce fewer offspring than selfish individuals within the same group. However, the benefits of being in a group composed mostly of altruistic individuals outweigh the costs imposed by the small number of selfish individuals within the group. This hypothesis works to make altruism genetically successful if there is a large amount of group – group competition and if there is occasional mixing of group membership – especially if there is a certain amount of self-selection into groups so that altruists can find each other and form groups together.

Avoiding scientific oversimplification

In examining these scientific hypotheses, it should be noted that when scientists hypothesize that there are genes "for" altruism and morality, they understand that this is a simplification. It is almost certainly not the case that there are just a few genes whose purpose, and whose only purpose, is to make humans more altruistic or moral. Genes regulate proteins. Proteins influence cell growth and signaling. Cell growth and signaling affects how the brain is wired. Certain brain structures and circuits need to exist in order for humans to behave altruistically and morally, but those brain circuits do many more tasks than simply promote altruistic behavior. So if altruism and morality do have a genetic basis, it is undoubtedly the result of many genes working in combination to produce the sorts of brain structures and circuits which permit many kinds of actions, not just altruistic acts.

Gene expression is affected by environmental context. Genes "for" altruism and morality would only work properly in the context of extensive social training and reinforcement. Chimpanzees that are raised in isolation, for example, have great difficulty adapting to life in a social group. Similarly, human children who are raised without normal social and moral training often develop moral pathologies as they grow up. This is a clear example of genetic evolution and cultural evolution being intertwined.

In addition, even if there is a genetic basis for human altruism and morality, as several of the preceding hypotheses suggest, this should not lead to the expectation that humans should be perfectly altruistic or moral. Selfish behavior also has a genetic basis. Certain forms of selfish behavior are also, presumably, adaptive. Evolutionary hypotheses about human altruism endeavor to explain, not that humans are perfectly altruistic, but rather why humans have the capacity to choose between selfish and altruistic acts and why they feel inclinations to sometimes choose altruism.

Common features of evolutionary theories about altruism

Clearly, there is a wide variety of competing evolutionary hypotheses for why human beings display altruistic behaviors and emotions beyond mere kin selection and reciprocal altruism. All of these scientific hypotheses are in a preliminary stage. There is a great deal of theoretical speculation, and only a small amount of hard data to help scientists determine which of them are correct. It will take decades of research before scientists know which one, or which combination of hypotheses, withstand scientific scrutiny.

All of these hypotheses presuppose a critical role for human intelligence, memory, rationality, and long-term interpersonal interaction in complex social groups. Under those conditions, all of these hypotheses agree that the natural evolutionary development of moral sentiments and moral systems is not only possible, but perhaps even inevitable.

Both as a scientist and as a Christian, I find all of these scientific hypotheses intriguing. I cannot think of any compelling scientific or religious reason why one of them must be true. Nor can I think of any compelling scientific or theological reason why one of them must be wholly false.

Moral and Religious Relativism Are Philosophical Ideas Sometimes Added to the Science

Within the fields of sociobiology and evolutionary psychology, a great deal of the popular literature aimed at non-scientists – and even some of the professional literature aimed at scientists – has philosophical arguments added to the scientific hypotheses. Often the philosophical arguments are mixed with the science to the point where it takes some serious scholarly effort to see where science ends and philosophy begins.

Leaping from "how morality evolved" to "why morality exists"

Science is very good at answering the question of how something works or how something changed over time. Once we have a successful scientific hypothesis for how something exists, it is very tempting to make the philosophical move and say that this is also why is exists. A beautiful example of this line of reasoning can be found in a Calvin and Hobbes cartoon written by Bill Watterson.[17] The young boy Calvin asks his tiger friend Hobbes, as a representative of nature, "What is our purpose in life?" Hobbes immediately answers, "We are here to devour each other alive." Hobbes knows how tigers live. Tigers live by devouring other animals. Therefore, Hobbes concludes that this must be why things exist. To Hobbes, the purpose of living organisms is to eat each other.

The same philosophical step – going from how something exists to concluding that this must be why it exists – is often made regarding the evolution of human morality. For example, Michael Ruse and Edward O. Wilson propose a scientific hypothesis regarding how morality evolved. They believe that morality is adaptive. Once human beings started living in large groups with complex social hierarchies, individuals whose genes made them constantly selfish were punished by the group, and therefore produced fewer offspring than individuals whose genes made them believe in an objective moral code. Ruse and Wilson then very quickly move from the "how" to the "why" and write, "Morality, or more strictly our belief in morality, is merely an adaptation put in place to further our reproductive end."[18] Why does morality exist? According to Ruse and Wilson, morality exists so that we can pass on more of our genes.

Richard Dawkins advances a similar argument in his book *The Selfish Gene,*[19] and in other writings. Most people who know something about genetics probably would say that the reason genes exist is so that organisms can reproduce. Dawkins flips that upside down. Organisms don't reproduce copies of themselves (at least not exactly); it is genes which reproduce exact copies of themselves. According to Dawkins, therefore, organisms are merely robots whose purpose it is to make more copies of the genes. Genes are selfish in the sense that their only concern is to make copies of themselves. Complex, intelligent organisms are just a way to accomplish that. The selfish-gene analogy is actually an interesting and sometimes useful tool for thinking about certain kinds of scientific problems. But Dawkins does not intend for us to think of the selfish-gene hypothesis only as a scientific tool. He advances it to a sort of ontological claim. The purpose of human beings, and in particular the purpose of human morality, is to make more copies of those genes.

I believe this line of reasoning is an example of what neuroscientist Donald MacKay called "the fallacy of nothing but-tery."[20] This is the assertion that a description of something at one level renders other levels of description meaningless. "Nothing but-tery," however, is a self-defeating strategy. If a biologist asserts that organisms are nothing but robots to make copies of genes, what shall we make of a chemist's claim that genes are nothing but arrangements of atoms obeying chemical laws? What shall we make of a physicist's claim that atoms are nothing but arrangements of quarks and electrons obeying deeper mechanistic laws? Which level of description trumps the others?

From our everyday experience, we know that a successful description on one level does not invalidate other levels of description. For example, one might assert that a Shakespeare sonnet is "nothing but" ink blots on a page. It is true that one way you can describe a Shakespeare sonnet is to specify precisely the coordinates of every ink blot on a piece of paper. Such a description would be valid and complete on its own level. However, one can also analyze the sonnet linguistically, emotionally, socially, historically, and on many other levels. If you are programming an inkjet printer, of course, the most important description of the sonnet is in terms of ink-blot coordinates. For almost every other purpose in life, however, that is perhaps the least important description of the sonnet.[21]

I am not disputing Ruse and Wilson's scientific hypothesis about how morality evolved; rather, I am disputing their philosophical extrapolation as to why morality exists. If we allow the hypothesis that there is a God who used evolutionary mechanisms to create human beings, then the philosophical extrapolation from "how" to "why" is defeated. Consider the following analogy. Suppose I built a robot which could do a variety of useful things: mow the lawn, walk the dog, clean the house, grade homework, write scholarly lectures, and so forth. Suppose one of the things this robot can do is, given a complete set of spare parts, to build an exact replica of itself. Whenever I find the need for another robot, I give one of my robots a set of spare parts and have it build a replica of itself. So, amongst all the software subroutines within this robot, there is a set of subroutines which govern the robot's self-replication, including the replication of those self-replication subroutines. Now, would it be valid to say that the purpose of the robot's existence is merely to reproduce those self-replication subroutines? Would it be valid to say that all of the other software and hardware of the robot – which allow it to mow the lawn, walk the dog, and so on – merely further the reproductive ends of those self-replication subroutines. Well, not from where I'm standing. It is true that, at one level, the robot hardware and software serves to reproduce those self-replication software routines. At another level, those self-replication software routines serve the robot to produce more copies of itself. At another level still, those self-replication software routines serve the robot's creator to make it unnecessary for him to construct each new robot himself. The creator of the robot certainly gets the last word as to which of those levels of description is most important.

So in human beings, does morality exist in order to further the reproduction of certain genes? Or do genes exist in order to allow for the production of new human beings who can behave morally? Humanity's Creator is the one who ultimately gets to answer that question.

"Selfishness" Language

Some of the popular literature in sociobiology and evolutionary psychology employs a sort of linguistic trick in which every action which improves the reproductive chances of someone's genes is labeled "selfish."[22] No matter how purely altruistic one's motives might have been psychologically, if the action has the slightest long-term benefit to one's genetic reproduction, then the action is labeled "selfish." Whenever someone eats or sleeps or takes medicine to stay healthy, even if those acts don't harm anyone else, even when those actions improve one's ability to provide help to other individuals, those acts are labeled "selfish." Parental care of offspring is called "genetic selfishness." Altruistic acts which cost the individual who does the act but which benefit the group which shares those genes are called "reproductively selfish" acts. Lee Cronk takes this to an interesting extreme. When one individual gives a gift to another, this is called "manipulation."[23] When one individual openly and honestly communicates with another individual in hopes of altering his or her behavior, the open and honest communication is called "non-deceptive manipulation."

In this line of reasoning, the word "selfish" becomes attached to all possible acts which a human being could commit. It matters not what an individual's psychological motives might be. All acts are openly selfish, secretly selfish, or (in the case of acts which genuinely harm one's reproductive chances), unsuccessfully selfish. (It is not the case that all writers in sociobiology employ this linguistic trick. Several of them have, however, so it is worth spending some time analyzing it.)

We can accept the scientific hypothesis that some human actions which are motivationally altruistic are also evolutionarily adaptive. If we're nice to other people, we tend on average to have more children. One philosophical interpretation to put on this scientific hypothesis is to describe such altruistic acts as reproductively selfish. But another equally supportable philosophical interpretation would be to say that being nice to others causes individuals and groups to flourish. The natural laws of evolution are such that, when intelligent individuals live in complex social hierarchies where individuals interact with each other over long periods of time and where cooperation is frequently rewarded both directly and indirectly, nice people really do succeed, on average.

Is there any scientific utility in labeling all actions, even those with altruistic motives, as "selfish"? I would argue that it is scientifically counter-productive. Human beings display a spectrum of behaviors. Some behaviors have almost purely selfish motives, some have almost purely altruistic motives, and most behaviors are somewhere in-between. Some behaviors clearly enhance the reproductive probability of an individual's genes, some behaviors clearly reduce the probability, and many behaviors are difficult to judge. Some behaviors benefit the person who acts while also benefiting others. Some behaviors benefit the person who acts while harming others. Many behaviors which benefit the person who acts neither harm nor help anyone else directly, but do improve that person's ability to care for him and others in the future. Sociobiologists point out that we humans invest a lot of our mental resources into "cheater detection," that is, into figuring out who amongst us obeys the moral codes all the time – even when no one is watching – and who amongst us disobeys the moral codes whenever they think they can get away with it.[24] Human brains are genetically wired to recognize and sort out a variety of motivations in other human beings. If the goal of scientists is to understand, better and better, the rich spectrums of human behaviors and motivations, then the linguistic trick of giving every action on that spectrum a single label – selfish – is scientifically unhelpful.

Free Will

Another common philosophical concern is that evolutionary explanations of morality will destroy our concept of human free will. This concern is an understandable. Most of the popular literature – and even the professional literature – is written as if there is just one gene for each type of behavior: a gene for altruism and a competing gene for selfishness; a gene for monogamy and a competing gene for polygamy; and so forth. Scientists know that this is just convenient shorthand, an over-simplification. Sociobiologists and evolutionary psychologists know that whole suites of genes act in very complex ways to influence behavior. Rather than saying that there are genes "for" certain behaviors, it is far more accurate to say that certain genes, under certain circumstances, will increase or decrease one's predisposition towards certain behaviors. Some scholars in sociobiology, such as Janet Radcliffe Richards[25] and Langdon Gilkey,[26] make these distinctions very clearly for their readers.

Some people do argue that the theory of evolution undercuts our idea of human free will. I believe, however, that the scientific fields of sociobiology and evolutionary psychology are not the source of their denial of free will. The source of the belief that free will is an illusion is a philosophical commitment to certain kinds of materialism – that is, that everything that exists is ultimately reducible to mechanistic, material interactions between fundamental physical particles. It is these versions of philosophical materialism, not evolutionary theories *per se*, which lead to a denial of free will.

If anything, evolutionary studies of human behavior undercut the notion that all human behaviors are strictly determined. Anthony O'Hear[27] and others point out that the various scientific hypotheses within evolutionary psychology do seem to agree that, for human beings, behavioral plasticity is adaptive. Because humans are intelligent and live in complex social groups, individuals who have a great range of possible behaviors tend to be more reproductively successful than individuals who have a limited range of possible behaviors. Individuals who have a greater ability to predict outcomes of behaviors and select behaviors accordingly tend to be more reproductively successful than other individuals. Behavioral plasticity is adaptive. Free will, assuming it is possible at all, would therefore seem to be adaptive. An evolutionary picture of human behavior should, it seems to me, actually strengthen belief that some form of free will is possible.

Moral Responsibility

Another philosophical concern is that scientific study into "genetic predispositions" towards certain behaviors will undercut our understanding of human responsibility for our actions. It is tempting to conclude that if I have genetic predisposition towards a certain behavior, then I am less responsible for that behavior. I argue, however, that the opposite is true. Knowledge about genetic factors which influences my behavior actually increases my responsibility for my behavior.

It is tempting to compartmentalize behavior as either being due to free choice or being due to some biological factor such as genetics or neurotransmitter levels. If we classify behavior that way – free choice or biologically determined – then every new fact we learn about the biological basis for behavior would seem to reduce free choice. The problem stems from the simplistic compartmentalization of behavior. Both our everyday experience and the results of modern neuroscience seem to indicate is that we cannot separate our biological and psychological aspects. As neuroscientist Malcolm Jeeves[28] and others point out, the direction of causation in our brains seems to go both bottom – up and top – down. Levels of neurotransmitters in my brain can affect my conscious state of mind. It is also true that conscious decisions I make can, over time, affect levels of neurotransmitters in my brain. For example, addiction to alcohol or various drugs can have a genetic component which predisposes someone to addiction. Once the addiction takes hold, there are physical and chemical changes in the brain which strengthen the addiction. However, for many recovering addicts, the road to recovery requires daily, difficult, conscious choices to do the right thing. A pattern of such choices, over time, can have a top – down effect and change the physical and chemical state of the brain.

The more we know about genetic factors which affect our behavior, the more we can take responsibility for our actions. Note the peculiar phrase, "taking" responsibility. It acknowledges that biological factors beyond our control were, to a greater or lesser extent, responsible for our current unpleasant situation – whether that is drug addiction, or depression, or a quick temper, or a hateful or prideful attitude. However, now that we are aware of those biological factors, we can do something about them, which makes us responsible for doing something about them. We take responsibility. Armed with our knowledge about those biological factors, we are better able to design an effective strategy, possibly using a combination of biochemical, medical, behavioral, social and spiritual strategies, to improve our behavior. And since this knowledge makes us better able to improve our behavior, we are therefore more responsible for doing so.

The "Science or God" Fallacy

Implicit in a great deal of popular writings on human evolution is the "science or God" fallacy. This is the idea that if we can come up with a scientific explanation for human behavior in terms of natural evolutionary processes, then we have proven that God is uninvolved, unnecessary, or perhaps even nonexistent. I have already devoted an entire chapter (10) to examining this fallacy. So for now, I will simply summarize the conclusion of that chapter. In Christian theology, a scientific explanation for how something happened does not at all diminish God's involvement in the event. God is in control of every natural event, and scientific explanations for events tell us something about *how* God accomplished the event, rather than excluding God from the event.

Religious Explanations *versus* Mechanistic Explanations

Another source of philosophical confusion comes from an apparent conflict between religious explanations and evolutionary explanations about why things happen. Religious explanations are typically teleological (that is, they refer to something having a design and purpose):

Why are human beings moral and religious? Because our Creator made us to be moral and religious.

Evolutionary explanations are typically mechanistic and functional.

Why are human beings moral and religious? Because moral and religious sentiments evolved through the mechanisms of mutation and natural selection, and they serve the function of increasing the reproductive chances of certain genes.

At first glance, these two types of answers to the same question seem incompatible because both seem to provide different "because" answers to the same "why" question. This apparent conflict is worthy of further analysis.

Instead of starting with morality or religion, let's start with a more ordinary "why/because" question for which an evolutionary explanation might seem to conflict with a theological explanation.

Question: Why do polar bears have thick fur?
Theological answer: Polar bears have thick fur because God created them to live in cold climates.
Evolutionary answer-A: Polar bears have thick fur because they evolved through natural processes to live in cold climates, where thick fur provided a selective advantage.

I don't think that these two explanations conflict. To see why they don't conflict, I will restate the evolutionary answer in a different way. In particular, I will eliminate the word "because" from the evolutionary explanation.

Evolutionary answer-B: Some millions of years ago, the ancestors of polar bears had thinner fur. Some individuals in that population had random genetic mutations which gave them thicker fur. In their environment (where, presumably, there were readily available food sources to the north in colder climates), individuals with thick-fur mutations tended on average to produce more offspring. The mutations were adaptive and spread through the population. This process continued through several fur-thickening mutations, until we reach the current species of polar bear with thick fur.

Now it's easier to see why a mechanistic evolutionary explanation should not conflict with the theological explanation. There is no conflict between the two explanations if you are willing to accept the idea that God might choose to create thick-furred polar bears over time through a process of mutation and natural selection. If there is any lingering sense of conflict between the theological and the evolutionary explanations, that sense of conflict probably focuses on that word "random." What do we mean by a "random" genetic mutation? As I argued earlier in this chapter, science does not require that a random event must be metaphysically uncaused. Scientifically, all that is required by the word "random" is that the particular mutation was scientifically unpredictable and not in some way caused by the organism itself. Theologically, scripture teaches that God can work providentially through events which appear random to us. So theologically, there should be no problem believing that God could choose to use random genetic mutations when creating a species.

Now let us consider the question of human religious sentiments. (I am choosing to focus for now on religious sentiments, rather than moral sentiments, because there would seem to be greater potential for conflict between theological and evolutionary answers.)

Question: Why do humans generally have religious sentiments and spiritual beliefs?
Theological answer: Humans have religious sentiments and spiritual beliefs because we were created to live in a relationship with God.
Evolutionary answer A: Religious sentiments and spiritual beliefs evolved in humans because, millions of years ago, individuals and groups who had religious sentiments and beliefs were better able to compete, and therefore left more offspring, than individuals and groups who lacked religious sentiments and beliefs.

Following the polar-bear example, let's re-state the evolutionary explanation without using the word "because."

Evolutionary answer B: Thousands or millions of years ago, hominids were living in social groups. Some individuals had random genetic mutations which predisposed them to have religious sentiments and beliefs. Groups who had these individuals developed cultures which included religious elements. Groups which had religious cultures, and individuals whose genes predisposed them to having religious beliefs, were better able to compete and therefore left more offspring than individuals or groups who lacked religious beliefs. Genes for religious sentiments and beliefs are adaptive.

Does *evolutionary answer B* conflict with the theological explanation? I don't believe that it does. If we are willing to accept the idea that God might choose to create certain behavioral dispositions in humans over time by using the natural evolutionary mechanisms which God designed, then there is no conflict.

Now we arrive at a critical point: Evolutionary explanations do not tell us *why* a particular individual random mutation happened. Evolutionary explanations only postulate that such random mutations do occur, and then consider under what conditions those mutations are adaptive. Evolutionary explanations are statements about changes in groups and populations, but they do not, by themselves, say anything about why a particular genetic mutation might have happened. To illustrate how evolutionary explanations function at the group level, rather than the individual level, it is worth looking at a particular recently published work on the evolution of religious sentiments.

David Sloan Wilson believes that religious sentiments are adaptive, and he is particularly interested in the group-selection hypothesis. To look for evidence in favor of that hypothesis, he studies modern religions to find examples of groups whose religious beliefs caused them to be very successful, relative to neighboring groups who did not share those religious beliefs. In a recent publication,[29] Wilson studied the city of Geneva at the time of John Calvin. Wilson gathered historical evidence that John Calvin's teachings did much to turn the troublesome, quarrelsome city of Geneva into a smoothly functioning, successful city. The teachings of Calvinism did this by instituting an effective system of group control over individual selfish behavior and by motivating its citizens to subordinate their selfish goals to the common good. Wilson knows that this one example does not prove his hypothesis about the evolution of religion – a great deal more work needs to be done. Calvinism in Geneva does, however, provide an example of how religion might have operated in humanity's distant past, to help groups of individuals unite, work together for the common good, and thereby succeed where other groups failed. Calvinism in Geneva is taken to be an example which increases the plausibility of Wilson's evolutionary hypothesis.

Lurking within Wilson's analysis on Calvinism is an idea which could be very troublesome to Christian theology. It almost sounds like Wilson is proposing that Calvinism was successful in Geneva, and spread beyond Geneva, precisely because Calvinism was so good at instituting social controls.

If we leave aside the broader question of the evolution of religious sentiments, and focus specifically on Geneva and Calvinism, we can frame a question which might seem to have contradictory theological and evolutionary answers.

Question: Why did many people in Geneva and beyond Geneva come to believe and practice the Calvinist form of Christianity?

Theological answer: Calvinism spread in Geneva and beyond because, when people heard the gospel preached by Calvinists and saw the gospel lived by Calvinists, the Holy Spirit worked in their hearts and minds and gave many people a living faith.

Evolutionary answer A: Calvinism spread in Geneva and beyond because Calvinism was so good at implementing social controls. The successful practice of social controls resulted in great benefits both to individuals and to the entire city. Therefore, Calvinist Geneva competed very well with other social/religious systems around at the time. Therefore, more individuals and groups adopted Calvinism and it spread beyond Geneva.

Those two explanations seem to be incompatible; however, as we've done before, let's remove the "because" word from the evolutionary explanation.

Evolutionary answer B: In Geneva at the time of Calvin, some individuals happened to start believing and practicing Calvinism. Once enough powerful citizens of Geneva became Calvinists, Calvinism became the basis for Genevan society. Calvinism in Geneva was very good at implementing social controls. The successful implementation of social controls resulted in great benefits both to individuals and to the entire city. The city prospered. Individuals and groups outside Geneva saw this. Calvinism was adopted by individuals and groups outside of Geneva.

Does evolutionary answer B conflict with the theological answer? Not necessarily. The focal point of contention seems to be this question: Why did some individuals (and not others) come to believe and practice Calvinism? Why did some individuals (and not others), when hearing and seeing the gospel preached by Calvinists, come to believe that the gospel they heard was true? Christian theology, while accepting the importance of social factors in the preaching of the gospel, stresses the work of the Holy Spirit in prompting such belief. Does this conflict with Wilson's evolutionary analysis of Calvinism?

I can think of at least two ways of interpreting Wilson's analysis of Geneva and Calvinism. The first interpretation is an evolutionary explanation which functions purely at the level of groups and populations. When Calvinism (or any religion) functions well at coordinating group action, then we would expect, in general, more individuals to come to believe that this religion is true. In other words, there is simply a correlation between the success of a religion at promoting collective action and numbers of individual people who come to believe that religion is true. This interpretation, it seems to me, is easily compatible with Christian theology. Indeed, the Bible states that when Christians love each other, this is a powerful witness which the Holy Spirit can use to convince people of the truth of the gospel.[30] Christian theology reinforces the idea that we should not be surprised to see a correlation between the success of a religion at promoting collective action and numbers of individual people coming to believe that religion is true.

A second way of interpreting Wilson's analysis of Geneva and Calvinism is to augment the evolutionary explanation, which only functions at the group level, with an auxiliary hypothesis at the individual level. This auxiliary hypothesis might be that Calvinism's success as coordinating collective action in Geneva is what caused many of its citizens to come to believe that Calvinism was true. In other words, the success of Calvinism at promoting social order is sufficient, at a neuropsychological level, to cause many individuals to believe that God exists and Calvinism is true – irrespective of whether or not God actually exists. Does this auxiliary hypothesis conflict with Christian theological beliefs that the work of the Holy Spirit is necessary if an individual is to become a believing and faithful Christian. Perhaps, although perhaps not if we remember that, in Christian theology, the Holy Spirit can work through natural mechanisms as well as through miraculous mechanisms. In order to sort out this difficult issue, Christians would need to do a lot of careful thinking about what we mean, theologically, when we say that the Holy Spirit's work is necessary if someone is to become a believing and faithful Christian, and we would need to think about the various ways in which the Holy Spirit could accomplish this. I will not address that issue in this chapter.

What we should particularly notice is that this second interpretation requires an auxiliary hypothesis which goes beyond evolutionary explanations into the realm of neuropsychological explanations. If we restrict ourselves to purely evolutionary hypotheses, all that is required for Wilson to be correct is a correlation between the success of a religion at promoting collective action and numbers of individual people coming to believe that Calvinism is true. If, however, the claim is made that promoting social order is sufficient, at a neuropsychological level, to cause many individuals to believe in Calvinism, then an entirely different sort of data will have to be collected at the neuropsychological level. The evolutionary story, by itself, does not require the neuropsychological auxiliary hypothesis. And the evolutionary story by itself, without the neuropsychological hypothesis, is easily compatible with Christian theology.

Functional Arguments

If we can construct a successful evolutionary hypothesis for the existence of religious sentiments in humans, does this undercut the idea that religious beliefs could have any truth content? Some authors imply this.[31] The human ability to hear is adaptive because sound exists. If human religious sentiments are adaptive, this could be taken as evidence that God exists. However, these authors point out, perhaps correctly, that human religious sentiments may have an adaptive function regardless of whether or not God actually exists. If their scientific hypothesis is correct, that religious beliefs can be adaptive regardless of whether or not the supernatural exists, does this undercut belief in God? There are at least two reasons why this argument fails.

First, an evolutionary explanation for the existence of religious sentiments should no more undercut belief in God than evolutionary explanations for the existence of stars and planets. Let us suppose that one of God's important goals in creating the universe (not the only goal, but one important goal) was the production of intelligent persons with moral and religious sentiments. In order for them to exist in this universe, first of all stars and planets must exist. I have already argued that naturalistic explanations for the existence of things like stars and planets should not undercut belief in God – at least not the God of the Bible – because the Biblical picture is that God can work through natural processes just as much as through miracles. If our picture of God is informed by the Bible, then evolutionary explanations for the existence of anything – stars, planets, or religious sentiments – do not imply a lack of God's activity. Successful evolutionary explanations give us information about how God created those particular things. Theologically, there seems little difficulty with the idea that God used evolutionary, adaptive mechanisms to bring about religious sentiments in human beings, and later, through divine special revelation, informed human beings about how to properly exercise those sentiments.

Second, it may be self-defeating to claim that the discovery of an adaptive function for beliefs undercuts the truth content of those beliefs. If such a claim is made about moral and religious beliefs, it can also be made about scientific beliefs. The human ability to do science relies on several human characteristics which are almost certainly adaptive: intelligence, memory, rationality, ability to notice correlations, ability to reason causal connections, and the like. The scientific method itself rests upon certain basic metaphysical beliefs which might be adaptive: belief in the regularity of causes and effects over time and space, belief that repeated trial-and-error testing can lead to valuable knowledge, and so on. If these abilities and beliefs which allow us to do science are also adaptive, does this undercut any claims regarding their truth? Should we suspect all of our scientific knowledge simply because some of the abilities and beliefs necessary to do science are adaptive? If, on the one hand, we say that adaptive beliefs are intrinsically suspect, then the scientific reasoning which we used to determine that religious beliefs are adaptive is itself automatically suspect. Since adaptive beliefs are unreliable truth guides, we cannot use scientific arguments to say anything about the truth of religious beliefs. If, on the other hand, we say that adaptive beliefs are not intrinsically suspect, and moreover claim that the adaptive beliefs which undergird science could very well be true regardless of their adaptive status, then it also follows that the adaptive status of religious beliefs is irrelevant in determining whether or not religious beliefs are true.

Philosophical Materialism, Moral Relativism, and Objective Morality

If human beings developed moral sentiments through evolutionary processes, does that mean that humans are doomed to moral relativism? Moral relativism is probably the most frequently debated philosophical topic surrounding sociobiology and evolutionary psychology. It seems quite commonplace for some scholars to assume that if evolutionary accounts of morality are true, then moral relativism is the inevitable result. A fair number of philosophers and scientists have published articles arguing for that very point.[32] However, several non-Christian philosophers and scientists have published articles arguing against that very point.[33] The more I have read the debates over moral relativism, the more I have come to the conclusion that the central issue in these debates is not evolutionary theory itself. The absolutely central issue in these debates is philosophical materialism. Does the worldview of philosophical materialism allow for normative, objective moral systems, or does the worldview of philosophical materialism necessarily imply moral relativism? Some philosophical materialists reject moral relativism. They argue that it is possible, within philosophical materialism, to construct moral systems which are, in some sense, normative and objective. They offer a number of possible non-supernatural sources for objective moral authority, such as reason, community, and nature.[34]

The majority of Christians who have entered this debate have argued that philosophical materialism, does, indeed, necessarily imply moral relativism. Unless God exists, so the argument goes, there is no objective reason to choose one moral code over another. In Christian theology, the ultimate source of objective moral authority is God. Philosophical materialism rejects the existence of God, so it is not surprising that many Christians would believe that materialism implies moral relativism.

However, there are various versions of philosophical materialism. One version is reductive materialism. Reductive materialism says that matter is, and always will be, nothing but mindless stuff mindlessly going through mechanical processes. Anything constructed only of matter, no matter how it is combined and organized, must fundamentally be nothing but mindless stuff mindlessly going through mechanical processes. Reductive materialism does seem to imply moral relativism. However, reductive materialism is only one version of philosophical materialism. a great many probably a majority – of philosophical materialists hold some form of emergent materialism. they believe that mind, awareness and self-consciousness are emergent properties of matter when it has the right sort of organized complexity. it's not clear to me whether or not emergent materialism necessarily implies moral relativism. this is an area of ongoing scholarly debate.

Philosophical materialism, in all of its forms, says that there is no such thing as God or the supernatural. It might or might not be the case that philosophical materialism necessarily leads to the conclusion that all human moral codes are subjective and relative.

God's Special Revelation

Christians, however, believe not only that God exists, but also that God has given some special revelations to human beings, throughout human history. These are special occasions in which God has communicated to humans on a personal level, through words and images and actions. According to Christian theology, special revelation has sometimes taken the form of God speaking directly to people, or through the words of a human prophet who was inspired by God and commissioned to speak on God's behalf. Special revelation could include words of wisdom from a teacher or a priest, answers to prayers, or the promptings of a person's conscience to do the right thing. Christians consider the Bible to be a special revelation from God because, although it was written by humans, it contains an historical record of many events in which God revealed himself in the ways just described. And Christians believe that the ultimate personal revelation from God is to be found in the life, death, and resurrection of Jesus.

For Christians, then, an evolutionary account of human moral and religious sentiments could be true, but it would be incomplete. The evolutionary account could explain, scientifically, how humans came to possess a sense of morality and an inclination to be religious. But this would only be part of the story. If God has personally revealed truth to human beings throughout human history, then human morality and religion certainly could have objective truth content.

In Christian theology, divine special revelation in human history could add the following elements to our human understanding or morality and religion:

1) *Content.* Our biology – through our emotions and our reason and our conscience – gives us a basic sense of right and wrong behavior. However, our biology alone cannot completely determine the entire content of our moral and religious beliefs. Our culture, which we as humans create, determines much of the detailed content of our moral and religious belief systems. Divine revelation can add information at the cultural level about the proper content of moral and religious beliefs.

2) *Clarification.* When we use only our human abilities – our reason, our conscience and our collective wisdom – we cannot all agree on the correct moral code. On some moral

questions nearly all humans agree, but on other moral questions, wise and well-intentioned humans sometimes disagree with each other. Divine revelation could, whenever God so chose, clarify moral ambiguities.

3) *Objectivity*. Divine special revelation can give humans objective, normative standards for morality. God knows, and can communicate, the moral standards by which I ought to live, even if I refuse to assent to those standards.

4) *Scope*. Without divine revelation, it is very tempting for humans to think that morality consists of loving those who love us and hating those who hate us. Divine revelation tells us to increase the scope of our love. Divine revelation tells us to love strangers and even our enemies.

5) *Divine context*. Through divine revelation, we learn that our relationship with God depends very much on how we treat our fellow human beings. We cannot love God while at the same time hating our fellow human beings.

6) *Accountability*. Through divine revelation, we learn that we are morally accountable for our actions not only to our family and our tribe, but also to God. God can and does hold us accountable for our actions more perfectly than our family or tribe ever could.

7) *Significance*. According to the Bible, the consequences of our moral choices are not limited to this world and this lifetime. God has plans for human beings beyond this lifetime. What we do in this life to help or harm our fellow human beings has consequences, on them and on ourselves, beyond our earthly lives.

8) *Ordering*. Of all our moral obligations, which are the most important? Christians believe that God has revealed to humans, through scripture, that the two most important moral obligations are, first: "Love the Lord your God with all your heart and with all your soul and with all your mind," and second: 'Love your neighbor as you love yourself."[35]

9) *Grace*. One of the first things that humans learn, when they start to encounter God personally, is that none of us can live up to God's moral standards. No human being is able to live a perfect life. God's answer to our human failure is to give us divine grace – forgiveness that we do not deserve. In response to divine grace, we as human beings are instructed by God to give grace to other humans.[36]

10) *Example*. In Christian theology, God gave us a supreme example of proper moral and religious behavior in the person of Jesus Christ. God himself, in the person of Jesus, personally suffered all the worst evils that humans inflict on each other. Then, instead of eradicating human evil by an act of divine power which overwhelms our free will, God chose to work through our human free will, offering to forgive the evils which each of us have committed, and inviting us freely to choose to follow Jesus' example of living a life of love and forgiveness.

Conclusion

In summary, sociobiology and evolutionary psychology offer some scientific hypotheses for how humans came to posses feelings of altruism, a sense of morality, and inclinations to be religious. Several scholars have tried to liken these scientific hypotheses to philosophical claims that morality must be purely subjective and relative, and that religious beliefs in the supernatural must necessarily be false. These philosophical claims, however, are not required by science. The scientific hypotheses could be true, and it could still be the case that human morality and religious beliefs could have objective status. Christian theology offers one way in which this could happen – through divine personal revelation from God in human history.

Notes

1   An edited version of this paper was published in: Loren Haarsma, "Evolution and divine revelation: Synergy, not conflict, in understanding morality," in Philip Clayton and Jeff Schloss (eds.), *Evolution and Ethics: Human Morality in Biological and Religious Perspective* (Grand Rapids, MI: Eerdmans, 2004).

2   S. Harris, *Freudian Slips: Cartoons on Psychology* (New Brunswick, NJ: Rutgers University Press, 1997).

3   J. Cartwright, *Evolution and Human Behavior* (Cambridge, MA: MIT Press, 2000); N. B. Davis, *Dunnock Behavior and Social Evolution* (Oxford: Oxford University Press, 1992); J. R. Krebs and N. B. Davies (eds.), *Behavioral Ecology* (Oxford: Blackwell, 1991).

4   Adaptive explanations should take into account complicating factors such as the possibility that a species' current environment may be different from its environments in the past, or that some behaviors may be maladaptive but necessary by-products of other adaptive behaviors, or that some behavioral dispositions may be neither adaptive nor maladaptive.

5   Richard D. Alexander, "Biological considerations in the analysis of morality," pp. 163–96 in Matthew H. Nitecki and Doris V. Nitecki (eds.), *Evolutionary Ethics* (New York: State University of New York Press, 1993); Susan Blackmore, "The memes' eye view," pp. 25–42 in Robert Aunger (ed.), *Darwinizing Culture: The Status of Memetics As a Science* (Oxford University Press, 2000); Lee Cronk, "Evolutionary theories of morality and the manipulative use of signals," *Zygon: Journal of Religion & Science* 29(1) (1994), 81–101; Helena Cronin, *The Ant and the Peacock: Altruism and Sexual Selection from Darwin to Today*: ch. 11, "Altruism now," pp. 253–265 (Cambridge University Press, 1991); Richard Dawkins, *The Selfish Gene*: Ch. 1, "Why are people?" pp. 1–11 (Oxford University Press, 1976); Michael Ruse, "Evolutionary theory and christian ethics: Are they in harmony?" *Zygon: Journal of Religion & Science*, vol. 29(1) (1994), 5–24; Michael Ruse and Edward O. Wilson, "The approach of sociobiology: The evolution of ethics," in James E. Huchingson (ed.), *Religion and the Natural Sciences* (Fort Worth: Harcourt Brace Javonovich College, 1993); Robert Trivers, "Deceit and self-deception: The relationship between communication and consciousness," p. 175–191 in Michael Robinson and Lionel Tiger (eds.) *Man and Beast Revised* (Smithsonian Institution Press, 1991); Bart Voorzanger, "No norms and no nature – the moral relevance of evolutionary biology" *Biology & Philosophy* 2 (1987), 253–70; Edward O. Wilson, *On Human Nature*: ch. 7, "Altruism," pp. 149–67 (Cambridge, MA: Harvard University Press, 1978).

6   Richard D. Alexander, "Group-living, conflicts of interest, and the concept of God," 2001, unpublished paper; Geoffrey Miller, "Sexual selection for cultural displays." Ch. 5, pp. 71–91 in Robin Dunbar, Chris Knight, and Camilla Power (eds.), *The Evolution of Culture: An Interdisciplinary View*. (1999); Steven Mithen, "Symbolism and the supernatural." Ch. 8, pp. 147–72, in Dunbar et al., *The Evolution of Culture*; David Sloan Wilson, *Darwin's Cathedral: Evolution, Religion, and the Nature of Society* (University of Chicago Press, 2002.)

7   Just two examples: Philip Yancey, "The unmoral prophets," *Christianity Today* 42 no. 11 (Oct. 5 1998), 76–9; Charles Colson, "The Devil in the DNA," *Christianity Today* 42 no. 9 (Aug. 10 1998), 80.

8   W. D. Hamilton, "The genetical evolution of social behavior," *Journal of Theoretical Biology* 7 (1964), 1–16.

9   R. L. Trivers, "The evolution of reciprocal altruism," *Quarterly Review of Biology* 46 (1971), 35–9.

10 Francisco J. Ayala, "The difference of being human: Ethical behavior as an evolutionary byproduct." Ch. 5, pp. 113–135, in Rolston Holmes III (ed.), *Biology, Ethics, and the Origins of*

Life (Jones & Bartlett, 1995); S. J. Gould and R. C. Lewontin, "The spandrels of San Marco and the Panglossian Paradigm: A critique of the adaptationist programme," *Proceedings of the Royal Society of London. Series B, Biological Sciences* The Evolution of Adaptation by Natural Selection, vol. 205 (1161), 581–98, (1979); Susan Oyama, *Evolution's Eye: A Systems View of the Biology-Culture Divide*: Ch. 9, "Bodies and minds: Dualism in evolutionary theory," pp. 153–66 (Durham, NC: Duke University Press, 2000); Barry Schwartz, *The Battle for Human Nature: Science, Morality, and Modern Life*: ch. 7, "The limits of evolutionary biology," pp.182–215 (New York: W. W. Norton, 1986); Ian Vine, "Altruism and human nature: Resolving the evolutionary paradox." Ch. 4, p. 73–103, in Pearl M. Oliner, Samuel P. Oliner, Lawrence Baron, Lawrence A. Blum, Dennis L. Krebs and M. Zuzanna Smolenska (eds.), *Embracing the Other: Philosophical, Psychological, and Historical Perspectives on Altruism* (New York: SUNY Press, 1992).

11   Eric Smith, "Three styles in the evolutionary analysis of human behavior." Ch. 2, pp. 37–46, in Lee Cronk, Napoleon Chagnon, and William Irons (eds.), *Adaptation and Human Behavior: An Anthropological Perspective* (Hawthorne, NY: Aldine de Gruyter, 2000); Barry Schwartz, *The Battle for Human Nature: Science, Morality, and Modern Life*: ch. 7, "The limits of evolutionary biology," pp. 182–215. (New York: W.W. Norton & Company, 1986); George C. Williams, "Huxley's evolution and ethics in sociobiological perspective." *Zygon: Journal of Religion & Science,* vol. 23(4) (1988), 383–407.

12   Susan Blackmore, "The memes' eye view," pp. 25–42 in Robert Aunger, (ed.), *Darwinizing Culture: The Status of Memetics As a Science* (Oxford University Press, 2000).

13   Lee Cronk, "Evolutionary theories."

14   Richard D. Alexander, "Evolutionary selection and the nature of humanity"; Richard D. Alexander, "Biological considerations in the analysis of morality," pp. 163–196 in Matthew H. Nitecki and Doris V. Nitecki, (eds.), *Evolutionary Ethics,* (New York: SUNY Press, 1993); Michael Ruse and Edward O. Wilson, "The approach of sociobiology: the evolution of ethics," in James E. Huchingson (ed.), *Religion and the Natural Sciences* (Fort Worth: Harcourt Brace Javonovich College, 1993).

15   Helena Cronin, *The Ant and The Peacock: Altruism and Sexual Selection from Darwin to Today.* Ch. 11, "Altruism now," pp. 253–65 (Cambridge University Press, 1991); Geoffrey Miller, "Sexual selection for cultural displays," pp. 71–91 in Robin Dunbar, Chris Knight, and Camilla Power, (eds.), *The Evolution of Culture: An Interdisciplinary View.* (New Brunswick, NJ: Rutgers University Press, 1999).

16   David Sloan Wilson, *Darwin's Cathedral: Evolution, Religion, and the Nature of Society* (Chicago: University of Chicago Press, 2002).

17   B. Watterson, *The Days are Just Packed* (Kansas City: Andrews and McMeel, 1993).

18   Michael Ruse and Edward O. Wilson, "The approach of sociobiology: The evolution of ethics." in James E. Huchingson (ed.), *Religion and the Natural Sciences* (Fort Worth: Harcourt Brace Javonovich College, 1993).

19   Richard Dawkins, *The Selfish Gene*: ch. 1, "Why are people?" pp. 1–11. (Oxford: Oxford University Press, 1976).

20   D. MacKay, *Christianity in a Mechanistic Universe* (Chicago, Illinois: InterVarsity Press, 1965).

21   This analogy is explored in more depth by Deborah Haarsma in chapter 9 in this volume.

22   Richard Dawkins, *The Selfish Gene,* ch. 1; Ruse and Wilson, "The approach of sociobiology"; Richard D. Alexander, "Evolutionary selection and the nature of humanity."

23   Lee Cronk, "Evolutionary theories."

24   Richard D. Alexander, "Group-living."

25   J. R. Richards, *Human Nature After Darwin: a Philosophical Introduction* (New York: Routledge, 2000).

26   Langdon Gilkey, "Evolution, culture, and sin: Responding to Philip Hefner's proposal." *Zygon: Journal of Religion & Science,* vol. 30(2) (1995), 293–308.

27   A. O'Hear, *Beyond Evolution: Human Nature and the Limits of Evolutionary Explanation* (Oxford: Oxford University Press, 1997).

28 M. Jeeves, *Mind Fields: Reflections on the Science of Mind and Brain* (Grand Rapids, MI: Baker Books, 1993).

29 David Sloan Wilson, *Darwin's Cathedral: Evolution, Religion, and the Nature of Society*. (Chicago: University of Chicago Press, 2002).

30 Cf. John 13:35.

31 Richard Dawkins, "Darwin triumphant: Darwinism as a universal truth," pp. 23–39, in Michael Robinson and Lionel Tiger, (eds.), *Man and Beast Revised* (Smithsonian Institution Press, 1991); Susan Blackmore, "The memes' eye view"; Richard D. Alexander, "Group-living"; Geoffrey Miller, "Sexual selection for cultural displays"; Steven Mithen, "Symbolism and the supernatural" pp. 147–72, in Dunbar et al., *The Evolution of Culture: An Interdisciplinary View*.

32 Richard D. Alexander, "Biological Considerations in the Analysis of Morality," pp. 163–196 in Nitecki and Nitecki, *Evolutionary Ethics*. (; Susan Blackmore, "The memes' eye view"; Lee Cronk, "Evolutionary theories"; Helena Cronin, "Altruism now." Richard Dawkins, *The Selfish Gene*. Ch. 1; Michael Ruse, "Evolutionary theory"; Robert Trivers, "Deceit and self-deception: The relationship between communication and consciousness," pp. 175–91 in Michael Robinson and Lionel Tiger (eds.), *Man and Beast Revised* (Smithsonian Institution Press, 1991); Bart Voorzanger, "No norms and no nature"; Edward O. Wilson, *On Human Nature*: ch. 7, "Altruism."

33 J. R. Richards, *Human Nature After Darwin: A Philosophical Introduction* (New York: Routledge 2000); A. O'Hear, *Beyond Evolution: Human Nature and the Limits of Evolutionary Explanation* (Oxford: Oxford University Press 1997).

34 Larry Arnhart, *Darwinian Natural Right: The Biological Ethics of Human Nature* (Albany, NY: SUNY Press, 1998); as well as the books by J. R. Richards and A. O'Hear in the previous footnote.

35 Matthew 22:37–9, *New International Version* (Grand Rapids, MI: Zondervan, 1985).

36 Denis Edwards, *The God of Evolution: A Trinitarian Theology* (Mahwah, NJ: Paulist Press 1999); Jeffrey P. Schloss " 'Love creation's final law?': Emerging accounts of altruism's evolution." Ch. 8. in Stephen Pope, Lynne Underwood, Jeffrey Schloss, and William Hurlbut (eds.), *Altruism and Altruistic Love: Science, Philosophy, and Religion in Dialogue* (Oxford: Oxford University Press, 2001).

Part 5

The Universe Makes
It Probable That There
Is A God

13

What Makes a Scientific Theory Probably True

RICHARD SWINBURNE

There are two different ways of explaining the occurrence of an event. Inanimate (or scientific) explanation explains an event in terms of laws of nature and initial conditions which together cause it. Personal explanation explains an event in terms of a person, his powers (e.g., to move his body in certain ways) his purposes (to produce some effect) and his beliefs (e.g., about which bodily movement will produce that effect). An explanation H is probably true in so far as it has great explanatory power (that is, in so far as it predicts many data which it is not probable would otherwise occur) and has great prior probability (that is, "fits with" hypotheses rendered probable by the "background evidence" about how things behave in other fields of inquiry and is intrinsically probable. Its intrinsic probability depends on its simplicity and scope). These principles of probability are spelled out in terms of Bayes's theorem.

We try to explain why things have happened, why the world is the way it is. There are two different patterns of causal explanation which we use all the time. The first is what I shall call inanimate (or "scientific") explanation – we explain an event E by a previous state of affairs C (its initial conditions or cause) and a regularity L roughly of the form "Events like C bring about events like E." When the regularity is sufficiently general, we call it a law of nature. A law may be either universal ("All events like C bring about events like E") or statistical (for example "96 percent events like C bring about events like E"). The explanation becomes rigorous and scientific, when the description of C and the statement of L entail (in the case of a universal L) the occurrence of E, or (in the case of a statistical L) make probable the occurrence of E. The former is a full explanation; the latter is only a partial explanation of the occurrence of E.

We explain a particular explosion by the ignition of a particular volume of gunpowder in certain conditions of temperature, pressure, and humidity, and the generalization that under such circumstances ignited gunpowder explodes. We explain a particular piece of litmus paper's turning red by its having been immersed in acid and the generalization that litmus paper being immersed in acid always turns red. Sophisticated scientific explanations invoke many laws of generalizations and a complex description of previous events, of which it is a somewhat remote deductive consequence that the event of state to be explained occurs. It is a consequence of Newton's laws and arrangements of the Sun and planets thousands of years ago that they are in the positions in which they are today, and the former explain their being in those positions.

Science does not explain only particular events, but it may also explain laws. It explains less fundamental laws by more fundamental laws. If it is a consequence of L_1 that under particular conditions C) L_2 operates, then L_1 (together with C) explains the operation of L_2. Newton's laws of motion explain the operation of Kepler's laws, under conditions of a certain arrangement and initial velocity of sun and planets. This account of scientific or, as I prefer to say, inanimate, explanation is that classically expounded and developed by C. G. Hempel.[1]

But we use a different pattern of explanation when we explain some event as brought about by a rational agent, such as a human, intentionally (that is, meaning to bring it about.) He may bring it about either as a basic action or as a mediated action. By a basic action I mean an action which someone does, "just like that," not by doing any other action. Moving our limbs or uttering sentences are for most of us, basic actions. I move my finger or say "I'll tell the police" not by intentionally doing some other action but directly (even though of course certain events have to happen in my body, if I am to perform the basic action). Often by my basic actions I intentionally bring about further states of affairs. By squeezing my finger when it is pressing against the trigger of a gun pointing at you, I may intentionally kill you; or by pressing certain keys on my computer I may send you an e-mail. Or by saying "I'll tell the police," I frighten you. Killing or sending an e-mail or frightening you are then mediated (that is, non-basic) actions. When we explain some event E (e.g., the motion of my finger) as brought about by a basic action, we explain it in terms of some rational agent P (myself), his purpose J to bring it about, and his powers (to move his limbs in various ways). P having J and X explain the occurrence of E. When we explain some event E (e.g., your death) as brought about by a mediated action, we explain it in terms of a rational agent P having a purpose J (to bring about E), a belief that bringing about some other event F (squeezing my finger) will cause E, his powers X to bring about F, and the causal fact that F will cause E. The latter causal fact is no doubt explicable by an inanimate explanation. So inanimate explanation involves laws and initial conditions; personal explanation involves rational agents, their beliefs, powers, and purposes. Just as one scientific law may be able to explain the operation of a less fundamental law, so a scientific law may be able to explain the existence and operation of the factors involved in personal explanation.

So much for the patterns of explanations. But what are our criteria for saying that some postulated explanation is probably true?[2] I began with inanimate explanation. A postulated explanation of E by L and C (when L and C entail E or make E probable) is probably true in so far as it is probable that L is a law of nature, and it is probable that C occurred. It is probable that L is a law of nature insofar as it belongs to a scientific theory which has great explanatory power and high prior probability.

A theory has great predictive power insofar as it makes probable the occurrence of all of many diverse observed phenomena. Newton's theory of motion, as put forward in his *Principia* in 1687, consisted of his three laws of motion and his law of gravitational attraction. The theory had enormous predictive power in that it rendered very probable the observed behavior of bodies of very different kinds in very different circumstances – the motions of planets, the rise and fall of tides, the interactions of colliding bodies, the movements of pendula, and so on. A theory has great explanatory power, insofar as it has great predictive power and also the phenomena that is predicts are not to be expected, whether or not the theory is true. I shall come back shortly to considering how we can assess the latter when I"ve discussed the notion of prior probability.

The prior probability of a theory is its probability independently of the phenomena whose occurrence it makes probable, that is its predictions. The prior probability depends both on the extent to which the theory "fits with" our other theories about how the world works which are rendered probable by our "background evidence," and on features intrinsic to the theory (its simplicity and scope). A theory "fits with" other theories in so far as the entities and laws which it postulates are of the same kind as those postulated by those other theories. Thus a theory about the behavior of argon at low temperatures would fit well with background evidence, in so far as that background evidence renders probable a theory with laws of a similar kind for another inert gas, for example neon, at low temperatures. The "background evidence" is the evidence which makes probable those other theories. However theories of very large scope may purport to explain so much that there are no neighboring fields about which we have background evidence; and in those cases the prior probability of a theory will depend only on features intrinsic to the theory. For example Newton's theory in purporting to explain the mechanical interactions of all bodies everywhere (not for example only mechanical interactions on Earth, or only the behavior of pendula), did not leave much of the relevant scientific knowledge known in 1689 outside its scope with which it could fit; there were then no established laws of electromagnetism or of light or of chemical combination. Its degree of simplicity and its scope determine the intrinsic probability of a theory, its probability independent of its relation to any evidence. The simpler a theory, the more probable it is. A theory is simple in so far as it has few short mathematically simple laws governing few entities and properties, few kinds of entities and properties, and the entities and properties are simple in the sense being readily observable or definable in terms of things readily observable.

A theory of fundamental particles, for example, would be simple to the extent to which it postulates only a few kinds of particle with properties (for example, mass and electric charge) of which we can observe other instances on the larger scale, and whose behavior is governed by simple mathematical formulae. Newton's theory was simple because there were only four very general laws of very great mathematical simplicity stating the mechanical relations that hold between all material bodies (that is, bodies having mass, a property that we feel on the human scale). Thus the law of gravitation stated that all material bodies attract each other in pairs with forces proportional to the product of the masses of each, m and m^1, and inversely proportional to the square of their distances apart (r), $F = mm^1/r^2$. The relations are mathematically simple because the distance is not raised to a complicated power (for example, we do not have $r^{2.0003}$ or $r^{\log 2}$), there is only one term (for example, we do not have $mm^1/r^2 + mm^1/r^4 + mm^1/r^6$), and so on.

Yet, a theory's intrinsic probability is diminished in so far as its scope is great. What I mean by this is that, in so far as it purports to apply to more and more objects and to tell you more and more about them, it is less probable. Clearly the more you assert, the more likely you are to make a mistake. The force of this criterion is to render theories less probable in so far as they are about all material bodies rather than (for example) just all bodies near the Earth, or about all metals rather than just about copper. But typically, if a theory loses scope, it loses simplicity too, because any restriction of scope is often arbitrary and complicating. Why arbitrary restrictions to all bodies near the Earth? A claim about the behavior of all material bodies is simpler. (It mentions fewer entities.) For this reason I do not think that the criterion of small scope is of great importance in determining prior probability. Newton's theory had large scope, but it satisfied the other criteria so well that this did not, I suggest, greatly diminish its probability. Hence I shall concentrate on simplicity as the main criterion of intrinsic probability.

I said earlier that a theory has great explanatory power in so far as it has great predictive power, and in so far as what it predicts is not otherwise to be expected, that is whether or not the theory is true. We can now see that what this latter amounts to is that no other theory with significant prior probability predicts the relevant phenomena nearly as well as does the theory in question. If another equally simple theory had predicted all that Newton's theory predicted in all its detail, the evidence would not have supported Newton's theory nearly as strongly. But no other simple theory could predict that.

These criteria have to be weighed against each other in order to yield a verdict about how probable a theory is overall on the available evidence. For example, although a theory has greater prior probability in so far as it is simple, it is often the case that only a theory that is less than perfectly simple can satisfy the other criteria (for example, explanatory power) for probable truth. The best theory may be less than perfectly simple; but, other things being equal, the simpler, the more probably true. And the different facets of simplicity which I have mentioned (number of laws, numbers of kinds of property, properties being observable, etc.) need to be weighed against each other to determine which theory is the simplest overall. It may be, for example that only a theory which postulates properties related only very remotely to observable properties (e.g., having some faint analogy with some observable property, is very simple in other respects (numbers of kinds of property, mathematical simplicity etc.)

An explanation of a phenomena E by L and C is probably true in so far as it is probable that L is a true law and that C, the postulated initial conditions actually occurred. Our grounds for believing the initial conditions C occurred are either that they were observed to occur, or, less directly, that the supposition that C occurred has itself great prior probability and explanatory power. It is for a reason of the latter kind that we suppose unobservable entities such as distant planets to exist. We observe a distant star moving in a certain way, and we can explain this if we suppose that there is close to it a massive planet that, in accordance with Newton's laws, is exerting on it an attraction so as to make it move in that way. If we suppose that Newton's laws operate (for which there is the vast amount of evidence that I have just outlined), we can account simply for the behavior of the star by postulating at least one unobserved body that is exerting a gravitational force on the star. Such behavior would otherwise be very improbable. If we were, for example, to postulate that some force of attraction other than the gravitational force were at work, we should be postulating the operation of a force de termining star motion other than the forces that determined all other star motion, and this would lead to a more complicated world picture than the postulation of an unobserved planet. It is clearly simpler to suppose that there is only one such body rather than many such bodies producing the observed phenomenon, and so this is the supposition with maximum prior probability and explanatory power.

It is also for a reason of this kind that we suppose unobservable entities such as atoms, molecules, photons, and protons to exist, to interact, and to have effects. An explanation of the occurrence of certain clicks of Geiger counters and spots on photographic plates by the supposition that certain such particles have produced them is probably true because it has high explanatory power and is simple (in postulating a few kinds of particles with a few kinds of properties causing the various patterns of tracks on photographic plates).

So then, to summarize, our grounds for judging a proposed scientific explanation h of a phenomenon E to be probably true, are the prior probability of h and its explanatory power with respect to the observed phenomena (that is, data or evidence). The same criteria are at work in judging the probability of a personal explanation. Suppose that a safe has been burgled. A detective finds these clues (his observed evidence): John's fingerprints on a burgled safe, John having a lot of money hidden in his house, and someone looking like John being seen near the scene of the burglary at the time when it was committed. The detective may also have background evidence best explained by supposing that John has robbed safes previously; and he will have also very general background evidence of an obvious kind, about the powers humans have over their bodies. The detective then suggests an explanation of the three new clues: the explanation that John robbed the safe. The explanation has good predictive power: if John robbed the safe, you would expect to find (that is, it would not be very improbable that you would find) his fingerprints on the safe, someone looking like John being seen near the scene of the crime, and John having a lot of money in his house or some place owned by him. We have no other reason to expect these phenomena. For although we could postulate other hypotheses equally able to predict the phenomena, these hypotheses would be complicated and so have low prior probability. We could suggest for example that Brown planted John's fingerprints on the safe, Smith dressed up to look like John at the scene of the crime, and without any collusion with the others Robinson hid the money in John's house. But this hypothesis postulates three persons acting independently, whereas the original hypothesis postulates one person – John, doing one deed – robbing the safe, which leads us to expect the several phenomena which we find. The detective postulates that John robs the safe in virtue of his powers (to move his body) similar to those of other humans, a purpose to rob the safe (of a kind which he had had a previous occasions), and true beliefs about how to do so using his bodily powers (the same as those which he had previously). The detective's hypothesis, that John robbed the safe is therefore probable. It has good explanatory power because it predicts phenomena which there are otherwise no reason to expect. And it has high prior probability; it fits in well with background knowledge, in the purposes, powers, and beliefs it ascribes to John, and it is simple in postulating only one person causing the phenomena.

I stress the enormous importance of the criterion of simplicity, an importance that is not always appreciated. Sometimes people ignore it and say that what makes a theory probable is just its explanatory power, or, worse still, just the fact that we can deduce from it statements reporting the phenomena that have been observed (that is, our data or evidence.) The trouble with this claim is that, for any finite collection of phenomena, there will always be an infinite number of different theories of equal scope such that from each (together with the same statements of initial conditions) can be deduced statements reporting the phenomena observed with perfect accuracy (and such that unless one of these theories is true, these phenomena are not to be expected). The theories agree in leading us to expect what has been observed so far, but disagree in their subsequent predictions. We may wait for new observations of phenomena to enable us to choose between theories. But, however many theories we eliminate by finding them incompatible with new observations, we will always be left with an infinite number of theories between which to choose, on grounds other than their explanatory power. If there are no theories of neighboring fields rendered probable by background evidence with which some theories fit better than others, the crucial criterion is that of simplicity. And when our theories are very large scale, there will be no theories of neighboring fields. And anyway "fitting with" such theories just having the simplest overall theory of the new observational evidence which leads us to expect both the new evidence and the background evidence.

This point about the indispensability of the criterion of simplicity may be illustrated by what is known as the "curve-fitting" problem. Consider Kepler studying the motion of Mars. Suppose that he has as data a large finite number of past positions of Mars. He wishes to know the path along which Mars is moving, knowledge that will enable him to predict its future positions. He can mark on a map of the sky the past positions; but through those positions he can draw an infinite number of different curves, which diverge from each other in the future. One theory is, of course, that Mars moves in an ellipse. Another is that Mars moves in a spiral that diverges hardly at all from an ellipse during the period studied so far, but will diverge significantly hereafter. Another is that Mars moves along a path that describes increasingly large ellipses and eventually becomes parabolic. And so on. Of course very few of these theories would have been set out and seriously considered by Kepler or anyone else investigating the field. But my point is that, if the sole criterion for judging between theories was their explanatory power, all these theories would be equally likely to be true, for all of them would have been so far equally successful in predicting, and unless one of them was true the phenomena would have been unlikely to occur. The fact that many of the theories were not seriously considered is grounds for supposing that some other criterion was at work, and clearly it was the criterion of simplicity. Most theories that predict the data are theories that describe Mars as moving in a very contorted curve that can only be described by a very complicated equation. The theory that Mars moved in an ellipse was very simple one.

My points about how to assess the probability of an explanatory hypothesis can be put in formal terms with the aid of the probability calculus. But before I do so, I need to make clear the kind of probability which I am discussing. There are, in my view, three basic kinds of probability – physical, statistical, and inductive. Physical probability is a measure of the extent to which nature has a propensity towards bringing forth events. The propensity may vary with time. A possible event has a probability of 1 if and when it is predetermined to happen and a probability of 0 if and when it is predetermined not to happen; values intermediate between 1 and 0 of the probability of an event measure the extent of the bias in nature towards the occurrence of that event. Statistical probability is a measure of the proportion of events of one kind in some class of events. The probability of an American voting for George Bush in the 2004 election just is the proportion of Americans who did so vote. The class may be an actual class (as in this example) or a hypothetical class – for example, the proportion of heads in a series of tosses of this coin if we were to toss it indefinitely often (and to have a clear notion, we need to specify the conditions under which the toss would be made and to make the notion of "indefinitely often" more precise). Finally there is inductive probability, which is a measure of the extent to which one proposition makes another proposition likely to be true. I distinguish two species of inductive probability – logical probability as the probability of one proposition on another by correct criteria of inductive probability, and subjective probability as the measure of this by a certain person (or group) using their own criteria of inductive probability. This latter measure is person-relative. My main concern in this lecture is with inductive probability: and – given that there are ways of assessing whether a scientific or other theory is probable or not – with logical probability.

To formalize my argument, I represent by lower-case letters such as e, h, p, and q propositions. $P(p|q)$ represents the logical probability of p given q. Thus p might represent the proposition: "the next toss of this coin will land heads," and q might represent the proposition: "505 of the last 1,000 tosses of this coin have landed heads," that is "the statistical probability of a toss in the last 1,000 tosses of this coin being heads is 505/1000." Then $P\,(p|q)$ represents the probability that the next toss of the coin will land heads, given that 505 of the last 1,000 tosses have landed heads. (The value of $P\,(p|q)$ would then generally be supposed to be 0.505). However, the relation between p and q may be of a much more complex kind; and clearly we normally assess the probability of claims on evidence other than or additional to that of relative frequencies. p may be some scientific hypothesis – for example Einstein's general theory of relativity; and q may be the conjunction of all the reports of the evidence of observation and experiment that scientists have collected relevant to the theory. Then $P\,(p|q)$ represents the logical probability of Einstein's general theory given all the reports of relevant observations and experiments.

I can now put my points in formal terms. Our interest is in $P\,(h|e\&k)$, the "posterior probability" of an hypothesis h, that is the probability of the hypothesis, given our background evidence k and our relevant immediate observational evidence e. We have seen that this probability is a function of the prior probability of h, $P\,(h|k)$; and of its explanatory power with respect to e. This latter is a factor that increases with the predictive power of h, $P\,(e|h\&k)$; and decreases with $P\,(e|k)$ the prior probability of e, that is its probability whether or not h.

So the more h makes e probable, to be expected, the greater is $\dfrac{P(e|h\&k)}{P(e|k)}$. It is easy to show that that value increases or decreases with

$$\frac{P(e\,|\,h\,\&\,k)}{P(e\,|\,{-}h\,\&\,k)}$$

as one would expect. For, given some particular value of $P(e|h\&k)$, e is more likely to occur whether or not h is true if and only if it is more likely to occur if h is false.

These points are made explicit by a basic theorem of probability theory, Bayes's theorem, as follows:

$$P(h\,|\,e\,\&\,k)=\frac{P(e\,|\,h\,\&\,k)\,P(h\,|\,k)}{P(e\,|\,k)}$$

This theorem follows directly from the axioms of the mathematical calculus of probability expressed in terms of relations between propositions. It holds for any propositions at all, but for present purposes I understand h, e and k as I have stated. $P\,(h|k)$, the prior probability of h, depends as we have seen, in the normal case both on the intrinsic simplicity of h (and its narrowness of scope) and also on how well h fits in with our general background evidence about the world contained in k. However, the division between observational and background evidence is often rather arbitrary, and the theorem holds however we make that division. Normally it is convenient to call the latest piece of observational evidence e and the rest k; but sometimes it is convenient to let e be all observational evidence and let k be mere "tautological evidence"(in effect, no evidence at all). In the latter case the prior probability $P\,(h|k)$ is the intrinsic probability of h, and will depend mainly on the simplicity of h (as well as to a lesser extent on its narrowness of scope). But, if k contains logically contingent evidence of what there is in the world and how it works, $P\,(h|k)$ will depend also on how well h fits in with that evidence. Where k is mere "tautological evidence," $P\,(e|k)$ will be what I term the intrinsic probability of e.

I believe that the axioms of the calculus capture our intuitive judgments about what is evidence for what; and so the derivability of Bayes's theorem from them is further grounds for believing my account of what makes explanatory hypotheses probable. But we cannot normally ascribe exact numerical values to the probabilities involved. It would be very odd to say that there is a 0.965 probability that quantum theory is true on such-and-such evidence. So what does it mean for Bayes's theorem to be true? It means that, in so far as for various e, h, and k, the probabilities occurring in the theorem can be given a numerical value, it correctly states the numerical relationships that hold between them. In so far as they cannot be given precise numerical values, my claim that Bayes's theorem is true is simply the claim that all statements about one probability being greater than, or equal to, or less than another probability, which can be deduced from the theorem are true. For example it follows from Bayes's theorem that, if there are two hypotheses h_1 and h_2 such that $P(e|h_1\&k) = P(e|h_2\&k)$, then $P(h_1|e\&k) > P(h_2|e\&k)$ if and only if $P(h_1|k) > P(h_2|k)$. This says that, if h_1 and h_2 both make it equally probable that we will find evidence e, given background knowledge k, then one of them h_1 will be more probable than the other on the total evidence (e and k), if and only if h_1 was more probable than h_2 on the background evidence alone. Put more technically: if h_1 and h_2 have equal predictive power, h_1 will have greater posterior probability than h_2, if and only if it has greater prior probability. It follows immediately from Bayes's theorem that $P(h|e\&k) > P(h|k)$ if and only if $P(e|h\&k) > P(e|k)$. This important principle is called the "relevance criterion." It follows from it by a fairly short step of logic that $P(h|e\&k) > P(h|k)$ if and only if $P(e|h\&k) > P(e|\sim h\&k)$. This says that a hypothesis h is confirmed by evidence e if and only if that evidence is more likely to occur if the hypothesis is true than if it is false. I call an inductive argument from e (and k) to h a correct C-inductive argument if (and only if) a (given k) e is more likely to be found if h is true than if h is false; and a correct P-inductive argument if (and only if) $P(h|e\&k) > 1/2$.

I have now given you my account of the criteria for a scientific or any other explanatory theory being rendered probable by evidence. Many of these claims would be agreed by many philosophers of science; some, especially my claims about simplicity and the formalizability of the criteria in terms of Bayes's theorem, would not. I leave you to assess the arguments which I have given. In my other two chapters (14 and 15 in this volume) I shall apply the results of this chapter to assessing the probability of the existence of God on the very obvious evidence that our world is governed by simple laws of nature and that these laws are such as (together with the initial conditions of the universe) to bring about the existence of human beings. In other words I shall be assessing whether the arguments from these phenomena constitute at least correct C-inductive and perhaps correct P-inductive arguments to the existence of God.

Notes

1   For a simple exposition, see C. G. Hempel, *Philosophy of Natural Science* (Upper Saddle River, NJ: Prentice Hall, 1966), chapter 5. The original article dealing only with deductive-nomological explanation is C. G. Hempel and P. Oppenheim, "Studies in the logic of explanation," *Philosophy of Science* 15 (1948), 135–75.

2   My account of the criteria for a suggested explanation either of the inanimate or of the personal kind, being probably true, are taken from a full account in my book *Epistemic Justification* (Oxford: Oxford University Press, 2001), chapters 3 and 4.

14

The Argument to God from the Laws of Nature

RICHARD SWINBURNE

The principles of chapter 13 are applied to the probability of theism, that is the theory that there is a God (a person who is omnipotent, omniscient, perfectly free, and everlasting – from which it follows that he is perfectly good). In this chapter I consider the data that there is a physical universe governed by simple laws of nature; and I argue that it is most improbable that this would occur if there is no God, but it is quite probable that it would occur if there is a God. Theism is a theory of such wide scope that there are no other theories with which it needs to fit, and – despite that large scope – it is so simple that it has high intrinsic and so prior probability. Hence the data make the theory quite probable.

I have campaigned for many years for the view that most of the traditional arguments for the existence of God can be construed as inductive arguments from phenomena to the hypothesis of theism (that there is a God) which best explains them.[1] Each of these phenomena gives some probability to the hypothesis, and together they make it more probable than not. The phenomena can be arranged in decreasing order of generality. The cosmological argument argues from the existence of the universe; the argument from temporal order argues from the universe being governed by simple laws of nature; the argument from fine-tuning argues from the initial conditions and the form and constants of the laws of nature being such as to lead (somewhere in the universe) to the evolution of human beings. Then we have arguments from those humans being conscious, from various particular characteristics of humans and their environment (their free will, capacity for causing limited good and harm to each other, and especially molding their own characters for good or ill), various historical events (including violations of natural laws), and finally the religious experiences of so many millions of humans. Arguments against the existence of God, for example from the existence of evil, must also be taken into account, and these may reduce the probability of the existence of God.

I begin by setting out my hypothesis and its consequences. The arguments are arguments to the hypothesis of the existence of "God" in the traditional sense of a personal being essentially eternal, omnipotent, omniscient, and perfectly free. I shall understand by his being eternal that he is everlasting; he existed at each moment of past time, exists now, and will exist at each moment of future time. I understand by his being omnipotent that he is able to do anything logically possible that is anything the doing of which does not involve a contradiction. He cannot make me exist and not exist at the same time – because that supposition makes no sense. But he can create or abolish universes immediately (as a basic action, to use the terminology I used in the previous chapter). He is omniscient in the sense that he knows at any time anything which it is logically possible to know at that time. He knows whether it rained in Shanghai exactly one million years ago today, and how many electrons there are in the universe. But if it is not logically possible to know (without the possibility of mistake) what I will do freely tomorrow, then he does not know that. He is perfectly free in the sense that nothing nonrational in any way influences him to do what he does. (Rational considerations alone influence him.) All God's other properties follow from these four properties which are supposed to be essential to him.

In particular it follows from these properties that God is perfectly good. To believe some action to be "good" involves having some motivation to do it. You couldn't really believe that it was good to repay a debt and yet have no inclination to do so. But we humans are subject to irrational considerations; we desire to keep the money. But being perfectly free, God will (unlike ourselves) be subject to no irrational inclinations deterring him from pursuing what he believes to be good; being omniscient, he will have true beliefs about which actions are good, and so he will be perfectly good, understood as being as good as it is logically possible to be. That means that he will do only what is good and will do the best action insofar as that is logically possible. So he will inevitably being about a unique best possible world (if there is one), or one of a disjunction of equal best possible worlds (if there are such). But if for every good possible world, there is a better, all that God's perfect goodness can amount to is that he will bring about a good possible world. So God will bring about any state of affairs which belongs to the best of all the equal best of all the good possible worlds. If there is some state of affairs which is such that any world is equally good for having it or not having it, then there is a probability of ½ that he will bring it about. God exercises this choice among worlds (and so states of affairs) which it is logically possible for him to bring about and which he has the moral right to bring about. There are some very good possible worlds and states thereof which God cannot for logical reasons intentionally bring about, such as worlds where agents with a choice between good and evil always freely choose the good.(One cannot make someone do something freely.)

I claimed in the previous chapter that (with background evidence *k*) evidence *e* makes a hypothesis *h* probable insofar as *h* has great explanatory power (that is, given *h*, it is probable that *e* will occur and it is not otherwise probable that *e* will occur), and *h* has great prior probability. When there is no contingent background evidence (that is, evidence from a wider field of inquiry), the prior probability of a hypothesis is a matter of its simplicity, and to a much smaller extent its scope. If we are comparing theism with rival theories such as naturalism, the view that the universe and its laws of nature are ultimate and have no further explanation, then for both there is no contingent evidence (because both purport to tell us about all there is) and both have similar scope. Hence their relative prior probability must depend on their relative simplicity. The hypothesis of theism I claim is a very simple theory, for in postulating a person of unlimited power, true belief, freedom, and length of life it is postulating the existence of a being with zero limits to the degree of those properties which make a person.

Scientists have always seen postulating infinite degrees of some quantity as simpler than postulating some very large finite degree of that quantity, and have always done the former when it predicted observations equally well. Newton's theory of gravity postulated that the gravitational force traveled with infinite velocity, rather than with some very large finite velocity (say 2,000,000,000.325 km/sec.) which would have predicted the observations equally well within the limit of accuracy to which measurements could be made. Only when Einstein's General Theory of Relativity, concerned with electromagnetism as well as with gravity, was adopted as the simplest theory covering a vast range of data did scientists accept as a consequence of that theory that the gravitational force traveled with a finite velocity. Likewise in the Middle Ages people believed that light traveled with an infinite velocity rather than with some large finite velocity equally compatible with observations. Only when observations were made by Römer in the seventeenth century incompatible with the infinite-velocity theory was it accepted that light had a finite velocity.

Persons, as I have noted, are beings with powers, purposes, and beliefs. If the action of a person is to explain the existence and operation of the universe, he will need to be a very powerful person. It is a simpler hypothesis to postulate that his power is infinite rather than just very large. If we said that he was powerful enough to make a universe of such and such mass but not powerful enough to make a more massive one, the question would arise as to why there was just that rather than any other limit to his power. It naturally fits the suggestion that God's power is infinite that there are no causal influences from outside God influencing how he exercises that power, and so it is simplest to hold that his freedom too is infinite. In order to exercise power effectively, you need to know what the consequences of your actions are. Hence it naturally fits the claim that God is infinitely powerful and free to claim that he is infinitely knowledgeable. It is simpler also to suppose that God exists eternally. If he came into existence only at a certain past moment of time, there would have been some earlier period of time at which what happened would have had nothing to do with God. Other forces would have been at work, and it would have depended on them whether God came into being at all. And so our hypothesis postulated to explain how the world is would inevitably become more complicated, in postulating other forces and to that extent limited divine power. And the same applies if we supposed that God could cease to exist in future. I conclude that the principles which we use in science and history and all other human enquiries into causes indicate that, if we are to explain the world in terms of personal explanation, we should postulate an eternal personal being of infinite power, knowledge, and freedom.

It seems to me that it is simpler to postulate not merely that God is eternally infinitely powerful, knowledgeable, and free, but that he is so essentially. If we say that it is only an accident that God is infinitely powerful, and so on, we allow that God could, if he so chose, abdicate. He could reduce Himself to a being of limited power. He could even commit suicide. And then it would be open to some rival to become infinitely powerful instead. But, in that case, it would have been an accident that our God was in charge of the universe; it could have been, and could yet happen, that another God took charge (maybe with less extensive powers.) All of that would make it much less foundational brute fact that our God is the source of all that is. It would need to be explained why God had not already limited his powers or committed suicide. And even if that could be explained, there would have to be other causal principles, besides God, which would determine what would happen if God abdicated. That complexity is no longer required if we suppose that God is essentially omnipotent, omniscient, perfectly free, and eternal.

So, I claim, the hypothesis of theism is a very simple hypothesis and so has quite high prior probability. I noted in the previous lecture that you can divide evidence between observational evidence (e) and background evidence (k) in any way you like. I shall put all our relevant contingent evidence (for or against h) into e. Then whether the evidence, the phenomena which I listed at the beginning of this lecture, makes that hypothesis overall probable will depend also on the explanatory power of the hypothesis of theism to explain all the contingent evidence. The arguments from the phenomena which I listed at the beginning of the lecture will be cogent arguments insofar as it is quite probable that the phenomena will occur if there is a God, and quite improbable that they will occur if there is no God. The arguments are, I claim cumulative. In each case the argument goes that the cited phenomena are unlikely to occur, given only the phenomena mentioned in the previous argument. That is, the existence of the universe is improbable *a priori* (i.e., if we assume no contingent background evidence); the universe being governed by laws of nature is improbable, given only the existence of the universe – and so on. Each argument then claims that if there is a God, its phenomena are much more to be expected (more probable) than if there is no God; and hence they each increase (from its prior probability) the probability that there is a God. In this chapter I shall discuss very briefly the first argument, the cosmological argument from the existence of the universe; and devote my main attention to the second argument, the argument from the universe being governed by simple laws of nature. In my final chapter (15) I shall discuss the argument from fine-tuning.

So let me set out the two pieces of evidence with which I shall be concerned in this chapter. First there is the existence of at least one physical universe, "the" universe or our universe. I understand by a physical universe an enormous number of physical objects each at some distance and direction from each other. The second piece of evidence is that in our universe all the physical objects are governed by relatively simple laws of nature – the four forces of gravity, electromagnetism, the Weak force, and the Strong force, subject to the overriding laws of quantum theory and relativity theory. Possibly all of this may be derivable from a slightly more unified system of laws – "Grand Unified Theory" or a "theory of everything." These laws are such that they enable humans to produce different effects, good and bad. But what is a law of nature? What are we saying, for example, when we say that it is a law of nature that all bodies attract each other with forces proportional to the product of their masses and inversely proportional to the square of their distance apart?

One view due to Hume[2] and developed in a more sophisticated way in recent years by David Lewis[3] is the view that they are just regularities in the behavior of objects. All bodies just do behave in the same way; for example they attract each other in the way that Newton's laws state. But if many things all have the same characteristics, and thereby we can infer what will happen in future if we interfere with the world in a certain way and what will happen if we do not, we should try if we can to explain all this. If all the coins found in a deposit have the same markings, we look for an explanation. And even if the fact that all bodies have behaved in the same way up till yesterday was the result of a vast coincidence, why were we able yesterday to predict so successfully how they would behave today: that the Sun would rise, and tables and chairs stay on the ground? There must be some feature of things which makes them behave in the same way as they have behaved up to now. So talk of "laws" must be understood as talk about a feature of the world additional to the mere succession of events, a feature of physical necessity which is part of the world. This feature of physical necessity may be thought of either as separate from the objects which are governed by it, or as a constitutive aspect of those objects. The former approach leads to a picture of the world as consisting of events (constituted perhaps by substances with their properties) on the one hand, and laws of nature on the other hand. Laws of nature are thus ontologically concrete entities. There is an event of the Sun being where it is, and the Earth being where it is and having a certain velocity; and a law of nature outside the event which forces the Earth to move on a certain elliptical path; so that the first event is followed by a succession of events of the Earth being now here, now there on the path. The version of this account which has been much discussed recently is the version due to David Armstrong,[4] Michael Tooley,[5] and Fred Dretske[6] which claims that laws of nature are logically contingent relations between universals. Universals are properties such as being green or square, each of which can be instantiated in different objects; many different ties can be green, many different houses can be square, and so on. The operation of laws of nature is a matter of universals being tied together in certain ways, so that if one is instantiated the other comes with it. On this view it being a fundamental law of nature that "all photons travel at 300,000 km/sec relative to every inertial reference frame" is a matter of the universal "photon" and the universal "travels at 300,000 km/sec relative to every inertial frame" being tied together. If you cause the existence of a photon and so instantiate the universal "photon," you instantiate with it the universal "travels at 300,000 km/sec relative to every inertial frame." On this view there are many bundles of connections between universals situated in some timeless heaven; and if you bring one down to earth you bring others with it. I shall call this account of understanding laws of nature as the relations-between-universals (RBU) account.

The alternative to thinking of the physical necessity involved in laws of nature as separate from the objects governed by it is to think of it as built into those objects. The way in which this is normally developed is what we may call the substances-powers-and-liabilities (SPL) account of laws of nature. The "objects" which cause are individual substances – this planet, those molecules of water. They cause effects in virtue of their powers to do so and their liabilities (deterministic or probabilistic) to exercise those powers under certain conditions, often when caused to do so by other substances. Powers and liabilities are thus among the properties of substances. Laws of nature are then just (logically) contingent regularities – not of mere spatio-temporal succession (as with Hume), but of causal succession, regularities in the causal powers (manifested and unmanifested) of substances of various kinds. That heated copper expands is a law is just a matter of every piece of copper having the causal power to expand, and the liability to exercise that power when heated. As a matter of contingent fact substances fall into kinds, such that all objects of the same kind have the same powers and liabilities. The powers and liabilities of large-scale things (lumps of copper) derive from the powers and liabilities of the small-scale things which compose them – atoms, and ultimately fundamental particles. These latter belong to a few kinds (electrons, protons, neutrons etc), differing from each other in the degrees of a few simple properties which they possess (mass, charge, spin, etc.) Every fundamental particle of the same kind (e.g., every electron) has exactly the same powers and liabilities as every other particle of that kind. And these powers and liabilities are specific forms of more general powers and liabilities possessed by all particles of all kinds (e.g., the power to cause an effect proportional in a certain way to their mass, charge, spin, etc., and the liability to exercise that under conditions varying with the mass, charge, spin, etc., of other objects). Because the powers and liabilities of a thing belong to its essence, that explains why (under the same conditions) it will do the same thing again. The copper retains its power to expand and its liability to do so when heated – so if you heat it a second time, it will behave in the same way, And all bits of copper behave in the same way as each other because being copper consists (at least in part) in having certain specific powers and liabilities. This way of explaining things was the way familiar to the ancient and medieval world, before they ever used the expression "laws of nature" (as they came to do in the sixteenth century). It was revived by Rom Harré and E. H. Madden in *Causal Powers*[7] and developed most recently by Brian Ellis in his *Scientific Essentialism*.[8] I find this a far more plausible account of why things happen than the RBU account, for the reason that it provides an explanation of a similar kind to a way of explaining that we have to use anyway. We ourselves have powers to do basic actions (e.g., to move our limbs), as I have pointed out in both these chapters. The difference between ourselves and inanimate objects is just that we choose when and how to exercise these powers; the inanimate objects have liabilities (inevitably or with great probability) to exercise them under certain specific conditions. But how can universals act on the world? This is a very mysterious causal relation between the non-spatio-temporal world and our world for which we have no analogue. For this reason I shall in future assume the correctness of the SPL account (although I believe that my argument can be expressed equally well on the RBU account.)

So that is the evidence. There is a universe of physical objects governed by simple laws of nature. The latter fact consists in each physical object belonging to one of a few simple kinds; each object of a kind behaves in the same simple observable way as each other object of that kind, and all objects behave in certain respects in exactly the same way as each other. If there is an omnipotent God, he could bring it about that there is a physical universe and that there are such laws. How probable is it that he would do so? Among the good worlds which a perfectly good God has reason to make are ones in which there are creatures with a limited free choice between good and evil and limited powers to make deeply significant differences to themselves, each other, and their world by those choices (including the power to increase their powers and freedom of choice). In order to have a choice between good and evil such creatures must, as I noted earlier, be subject to irrational inclinations deterring them from pursuing the good, and then they will have a choice between yielding to such inclinations and pursuing the good despite them. The goodness of significant free choice is, I hope, evident. We think it is a good gift to give to our children that they choose their own path in life for good or ill, and influence the kinds of persons (with what kinds of character and powers) they and others are to be. But good though this is, there is the risk that those who have such free will make bad choices, form bad characters for themselves, hurt others, and make their characters evil. For this reason I suggest that it would not be a good action to create beings with freedom of choice between good and evil and unlimited power to put such choices into effect. If God creates beings with the freedom to choose between good and evil, they must be finite, limited creatures. Even so, the risks are – as we know very well – considerable; and so, I suggest that God would not inevitably bring about such a world. So my own moral intuition is that any world which God could make containing such creatures would be no worse for not containing such creatures, and that any world which God could make to which you add such creatures would be none the worse for such an addition. In that case there is a probability of ½ that he will make such a world. You may weigh the goodness of creating such creatures differently from me; and my arguments do not depend on giving such a precise or such a high probability to God (if there is a God) making such a world. But I do suggest to you that it is such a good thing that there be beings with a free choice between good and evil, that there is some significant probability that a God would make them; and that is all that is required for my argument to have force.

Let us call beings with limited powers of the above kinds free rational beings. If humans have (libertarian) free will (as is not implausible), evidently our world is a world containing such beings. We humans make deeply significant choices, affecting ourselves, each other, and our world; and our choices include choices to take steps to increase our powers and freedom, and form our characters for good or ill. If humans are to able to make choices which affect each other, they must be able to get hold of each other and do things to each other, and that means that they must have a public location; and if they are to have only limited powers, they must have limited public locations – that is bodies. My body is a public object on which the functioning of my mental life depends, and the means by which I can learn about the world (by light waves etc. stimulating my sense organs) and make a difference to it (by my basic actions). If I did not have a body to which I was tied down, you could not communicate with me or improve or harm my powers. You could not tell me things, cause warm feelings in me by embracing me, give me food to keep me alive, cause pain to me by kicking me, or maim or kill me and so forth. Nor could doctors improve my sensory capacities or my abilities to perform basic actions. It is through our bodies that we belong to a mutually dependent community.

Our world is thus a world of a kind which God can (with significant probability) be expected to make. Free rational beings will have to begin life with a limited range of control, and the power to choose to extend that range or – alternatively – not to bother to do so. That limited range is their bodies. In order for them to be able to extend their range of control, there must be some procedure which they can utilize – this bodily movement will have this predictable extra-bodily effect, and that bodily movement will have that effect. That is, the world must be subject to regularities, simple natural laws (either deterministic or probabilistic), which such creatures can choose to try to discover and then choose to utilize to make differences to things distant in space and time. You can learn that if you plant seeds and water them, they will grow into edible plants which will enable you to keep yourself and others alive; or that if you pull the trigger of a gun loaded in a certain way and pointing in a certain direction, it will kill some distant person. And so on. We can choose whether to seek out such knowledge (of how to keep alive or kill) or not to bother; and we can choose whether to utilize this knowledge for good or ill. In a chaotic world, that would not be possible – for there would be no recipes for producing effects.

So, given that – as I argued – there is a significant probability that a God would create free rational beings (as defined earlier), there is a significant probability that he will create this necessary condition for the existence of such beings – a physical universe regular in its conformity to simple natural laws by which a variety of different sorts of effects are produced. It is not sufficient that there be natural laws; they must be sufficiently simple to be discoverable by rational beings. This involves their being instantiated frequently, and that the simplest extrapolation from their past instantiations will often yield correct predictions. There could be a world with a trillion unconnected laws of nature, each determining that an event of a certain kind would be followed by an event of a certain other kind, but where there were only one or two events of each former kind in the history of the universe. No rational being could discover such laws. Or there could be laws governing events of a type frequently instantiated, but of such enormous mathematical complexity that the simplest extrapolation from past occurrences would never yield correct predictions. The laws must be sufficiently simple and frequently instantiated to be discoverable from a study of past history at least by a logically omniscient rational being (one who could entertain all possible scientific theories, recognize the simplest, and draw the logical consequences thereof). And all this spelled out in terms of the SPL account of laws means that there must be substances of a few simple kinds whose combinations will produce many different effects. I summarize this as the uniformity of the powers and liabilities of substances.

How probable is it that if there is no God, there would be a law-governed universe of this kind? If gods are at work, monotheism of the traditional kind is far more probable than polytheism, that is, many independent gods of finite powers. For polytheism is a far less simple hypothesis than theism. And if polytheism were true, one would expect the universe to show signs of different craftsmanship in different parts or different aspects. But we do not find this. To what extent can there be an explanation of the inanimate (or scientific) kind for the existence of the law-governed universe? This is impossible. For while science could and does explain the existence of the universe today in terms of its existence yesterday and the law of the conversation of matter-energy, it could not by its very nature explain why there are any physical objects at all on which its laws could operate. And while we can explain less fundamental laws by more fundamental ones, there cannot be an explanation (of the inanimate kind) of the conformity of nature to the most fundamental laws. For it is with them that explanation stops. Nevertheless it is possible for there to be an inanimate explanation of the magnitude of our universe and the extent of its regular behavior in terms of a somewhat simpler universe.

Today's universe consists of enormous numbers of things of different kinds (with uniform powers and liabilities) distributed in clumps of various sizes throughout possibly infinite space. On the SPL account it is possible for there to be an inanimate explanation of why there are so many particles exhibiting this uniformity, in terms of the ancestry of the particles. On this account a substance can have the powers and liabilities it does because it was produced by another substance exercising (in virtue of some liability to do so) its power to produce a substance with just those powers and liabilities. If a proton is produced (together with an electron and an antineutron) by the decay of a neutron, then the proton's powers and liabilities are caused by the neutron, in virtue of its powers and liabilities. There are then different ways in which it could have come about that there are many substances falling into a small number of kinds in the way described, according to whether this process had a beginning and of what kind that beginning was.

Suppose, first, that the universe did have a beginning, a "Big Bang" of some sort. There are two different kinds of theories of a beginning. The first state might have been a spatially extended state, or a spatially point-like state. In the first case, we would still have a lot of substances, but perhaps crammed into a very small space. In terms of the Big Bang model, there would not have been literally a singularity; it would just have been that as you approach the first instant in the temporally backward direction, you would find denser and denser states; but it really all started in a very but not infinitely dense state. If that state was to give rise to our present universe of very few kinds of substance, it must itself have consisted of a very large number of substances of very few kinds. The alternative first state would be a literally point-like one. In the first instant on this theory, there was an unextended point, endowed with the power to decay into innumerable substances of very few kinds, and liability to exercise that power at some time or other. Suppose now that the universe has an infinite age. The properties (of powers and liabilities) of every substance are then caused by those of a preceding substance. So there can only be many substances with exactly the same such properties (including the power to produce substances of the existing kinds) if there always have been.

Study of the present data of physics and cosmology will allow us to say roughly how probable on those data are the three different theories – on the basis of how probable it is that we would find these data given each of the theories, and of how simple are the different theories. My assessment of the present state of cosmology is that a beginning is more probable than an infinite age; and that evolution from a very dense state is more probable than evolution from an infinitely dense state. (All matter-energy occupying an unextended point is, I suspect, not a possibility allowed by the current theory of matter-energy, which would require considerable complication in order to allow for this while continuing making the present data probable). But of course new data could change the probabilities.

The issue for us, however, is not what are posterior probabilities on the physical data that the different theories are true, but how probable it is *a priori* if there is no God that the true theory will be such as to lead to many substances of a very few kinds. This will depend solely on the simplicity of the three theories, and the probability on each of these theories that many substances of very few kinds would result. Simplicity is the sole relevant *a priori* criterion. There is no doubt that the theory that the universe began at a point is simpler than any particular theory that it began with many substances or that it always consisted of many substances.

But how probable is it, even if it did begin from a point, that it would begin with a power to produce the total regularity combined with variety in the behavior of observed substances such as we find? There are many alternative powers and liabilities with which an initial singularity might be endowed. It might have no powers, or powers with no liability to exercise them unless interfered with, or merely the power and liability to keep itself in being, or the power and liability to produce other substances which themselves had no power to sustain themselves in being for long, or the power and liability to produce other substances which themselves would have all kinds of different and unconnected powers and liabilities, or the power and liability to produce only identical substances so that there was no scope for creatures to bring about a variety of sorts of effect. And so on. Simplicity alone can determine which is the most probable *a priori*. And many variants of the initial singularity theory, although themselves relatively simple will not lead to a continuing universe with simple laws. And the simplest form of the variant which does – the point having the power and liability to produce many identical substances which themselves produce many identical substances – will not yield a sufficiently varied universe. And for each way of producing substances with similar powers and liabilities yielding simple laws, there are innumerable ways of producing substances with chaotic and erratic powers. All told, the prior probability of the point being such as to produce the right sort of laws is going to be very small.

Yet, plausibly, the very low probability of the singularity having the character just described is not as low as the *a priori* probability for all of very many substances of few kinds beginnning their existence uncaused in a Godless universe with the same powers and liabilities, or always having had the same powers and liabilities in a Godless universe. For each of these suppositions involves many substances exhibiting enormous coincidences in their behavior.

All told, the prior probability that the physical universe would either everlastingly or beginning from the right kind of beginning come to consist of innumerable particles with uniform powers and liabilities is very small; much smaller than the simplicity of what we have seen to be a very simple supposition – theism, just one substance of a very simple kind. Theism leads us to expect that by one of these routes a universe will be produced in which many substances of few kinds have all the same powers and liabilities, and will be conserved by God in this state. Either he will bring about an initial point of the right kind or a right arrangement of substances with the right powers and liabilities and conserve substances in subsequent existence with their resulting powers and liabilities; or he will always have kept in existence substances with the right powers and liabilities.

I have been assuming so far that there is only one universe. But there may be many universes. If there actually exist all possible universes, some of them would exhibit uniformity of the right kind. However it would be the height of irrationality to postulate innumerable universes just to explain the particular features of our universe, when we can do so by postulating just one additional entity – God. Science requires us to postulate the simplest explanation of the data, and one simple entity is simpler than a trillion complex ones. The only possible grounds we could have for believing that there are other universes would be if extrapolating back from the present state of our universe in accord with the mathematically simplest supposition about what are its laws leads us to a state at which there was a universe split, a state in which those laws will have dictated that another universe would "bud off" from our universe. But in that case the other universe would be governed by the same fundamental laws as govern our universe, and so we can consider the two universes (or however many universes we learn about) as one multiverse, and the whole preceding structure of argument gives the same results as before. So it does not affect the issue of why things are law-governed if we suppose (on good evidence) that there is more than one universe. I conclude that it is *a priori* very improbable that a Godless universe would consist of many substances governed by simple laws, but there is quite a significant probability that a God-created universe would consist of many substances governed by simple laws; and the hypothesis that there is a God is a very simple hypothesis, much simpler than any other possible origin of things. Explanation has to stop somewhere; the most probable stopping place (the cause of everything) is the simplest stopping place.

So I have condensed into one two arguments for the existence of God – the cosmological argument from the existence of the universe of many substances, and the argument from their uniform behavior, that is their being governed by simple laws of nature. These are good *C*-inductive arguments by the criteria which I stated in my first chapter; in each case the premises add considerably to the probability of the conclusion.

Notes

1   See especially my *The Existence of God*, rev. edn. (Oxford: Clarendon Press, 1990). For the detailed argument from laws of nature, see chapter 8 of that work. See also the shorter version of this: *Is There a God?* (Oxford: Oxford University Press, 1996; Chinese translation, Beijing: Peking University Press, 2005). See chapter 4 of that book for the argument from laws of nature.

2   See David Hume, *A Treatise on Human Nature*, 1. 3. 14. where what we call "laws of nature" are analysed simply as regularities in the behaviour of objects. For Hume, there is no "necessity" in the world which brings about these regularities.

3   For his programme see David Lewis, *Philosophical Papers*, vol. 2 (Oxford: Oxford University Press (1986), Introduction. Some subsequent chapters in the volume contain some of the ideas of his "Humean" programme.

4   D. M. Armstrong, *What is a Law of Nature?* (Cambridge: Cambridge University Press, 1983).

5   Michael Tooley, "The Nature of Laws," *Canadian Journal of Philosophy* 7 (1977), 667–98.

6   F. I. Dretske, "Laws of Nature", *Philosophy of Science* 44 (1977), 248–68.

7   Oxford: Blackwell, 1975.

8   Cambridge: Cambridge University Press, 2001.

15

The Argument to God
from Fine-Tuning

RICHARD SWINBURNE

In this chapter[1] I consider the data that not merely is the universe governed by laws of nature, but that these laws are fine-tuned for the evolution of human-type bodies. Human bodies are public objects which enable conscious human beings to learn about the world and to make a difference to it. Hence they need sense organs, an information processor, a memory bank, brain states causing good and bad desires influencing but not fully causing purposes which then cause brain states, and a processor to turn these latter states into limb movements. I argue that even if the universe is governed by simple laws of nature, it is most improbable that the laws and the boundary conditions of the universe would have the characteristics needed to produce such human bodies; but that if there is a God it is quite probable that they would have these characteristics. Hence "fine-tuning" increases the probability of the existence of God beyond that reached in the previous chapter.

I argued in chapter 13 that an explanatory hypothesis h was rendered probable by evidence e in so far as h has great explanatory power (that is, it makes the occurrence of e probable, when it would not otherwise be probable), and h has great prior probability. When we are dealing with a very large-scale hypothesis such as theism, prior probability is primarily a matter of its intrinsic probability which is primarily a matter of how simple it is.

I argued in chapter 14 that the hypothesis of theism, the hypothesis that there is a God, is a very simple hypothesis; and that it is quite probable that God would bring about the existence of free rational beings, embodied beings with powers to make great differences to themselves, each other, and the world, and freedom to choose which differences to make – such as we believe humans to be.[2] If he is to bring about human beings with these powers, he must bring about the necessary conditions for their existence. These include a physical universe governed by simple laws of nature. I argued in chapter 14 that it was very improbable that there would be a physical universe governed by simple laws of nature unless there is a God; and that this phenomenon provides very considerable evidence for the existence of God. But it is not enough that there be simple laws of nature. God must bring about human bodies, which – being physical objects – must be governed by those same laws of nature. God could have brought about human bodies (so governed) by an instantaneous act; alternatively, he could have made the universe at an early stage in such a state as to lead to the evolution of human bodes. In view of the fact that the inanimate universe itself evolving into galaxies and stars and planets is a beautiful thing, and so too are the plants and animals which it produced, I cannot see any particular reason why God should have created humans intact rather than brought them about through the evolutionary process. But clearly he did not do the former – there is massive evidence from geology of the gradual evolution of humans from lower animals through monkeys and the great apes. And there seems to me pretty good evidence that the lower animals evolved from primitive organisms, these evolved from the lifeless matter of the early Earth, and this matter evolved from the primeval soup of energy which existed at the time of the Big Bang, the moment some 14 billion years ago when our universe (or at least its present stage) began. Since God has reason to bring about human bodies, he has reason to bring about an initial state of the universe and laws of nature of such a kind (rather than of any other kind), so as to lead eventually (at some place in the universe at some later time) to the existence of human bodies.

My argument, I stress, is an argument from the existence of human bodies. It is a further phenomenon that these are bodies of conscious beings. For the existence of organic matter arranged and operative in the way it is in human bodies does not entail that there is a mental life associated with them. The process of evolution which produced human bodies might have produced unconscious robots, which react to stimuli (spoken and written sentences, for example) by way of output (including spoken and written sentences) without any conscious awareness lying between the input and output. Consciousness is a further phenomenon which in my view leads to a further argument to the existence of God. But given the desirability for the reason which I gave in my previous chapter that humans should be embodied. God would need to bring about human bodies through which human conscious life could be expressed.

So what kind of bodies do free rational beings need in order for them to have the features discussed in the previous chapter? To be the body of a rational being of this kind, a body needs to be suited for the acquisition of true beliefs about the environment, the formation of purposes in the light of desires, and the expression of them via chosen basic actions designed to affect the agent, others, and the world for good or ill. To do this job a body needs: (1) sense organs with an enormous variety of possible states varying with an enormous variety of different inputs caused by different distant world states; (2) an information processor that can turn the states of sense organs into brain states that give rise to beliefs of moral or prudential importance; (3) a memory bank, to file states correlated with past experiences (we could not consciously reason about anything unless we could recall our past experiences and what others have told us); (4) brain states that give rise to desires, good and evil (desires to eat and drink, to care for others or to hurt them, and to discover whether or not there is a God); (5) brain states caused by many different purposes that we have; (6) a processor to turn these states into limb and other voluntary movements (to turn, for example, my purpose of telling you that today is Friday into those twists of tongue and lip that will produce an English sentence with that meaning ; and (7) brain states that are not fully determined by other physical states. (As far as physical laws are concerned, there needs to be a certain amount of indeterminism in the brain if free human choices are to determine what happens in the brain.)

Clearly human bodies have characteristics (1) to (6). Fairly clearly too there is a small amount of indeterminism in the brain, for, if the laws of quantum theory that govern matter on the smaller scale have no deeper deterministic explanation (as most physicists claim), then the behavior of objects on the small scale is not fully determined. The brain is an extremely complicated system in which small differences cause large differences.

Human bodies have evolved by natural processes from inorganic matter. But clearly the evolution can have taken place only given certain special physical laws. These are, first, the chemical laws stating how under certain circumstances inorganic molecules combine to make organic ones, and organic ones combine to make organisms. And, secondly, there are the biological laws of evolution stating how complex organisms evolve from simpler organisms. But then why were there these laws of chemistry and biology that led to the inorganic matter being formed into human bodies? Presumably because these laws follow from the fundamental laws of physics. And why was there the original inorganic matter? Physics tells us that there was a Big Bang some 14 billion years ago, which produced matter-energy that condensed into the fundamental particles that came together to form the chemical elements that eventually condensed to form the inorganic matter at the beginning of the history of planet Earth. But why were there the laws of physics that brought this about, and the laws of chemistry and biology which follow from them?; and why was there the right sort of initial matter-energy, such that – together with those laws of physics – would lead to the evolution of human bodies? Why was there just the right sort of laws of nature, and the right kind of initial matter-energy for human bodies to evolve? I shall argue that the laws and initial conditions being such as to lead to the evolution of human bodies is very improbable *a priori*, but fairly probable if there is a God who brought it about, and so we have a further substantial *C*-inductive argument for the existence of God (that is, an argument which raises substantially the probability of the existence of God, beyond that provided by the argument from the mere existence of laws of nature).

Fine-Tuning

Not all initial conditions or laws of nature would lead to, or even permit, the existence of human bodies at some place or other at some time or other in the universe. So we may say that the universe is "tuned" for the evolution of human bodies if the laws and initial conditions make this significantly probable. And, fairly evidently, it is tuned. Indeed there is a considerable, but not unanimous, scientific view that the laws and initial conditions of our universe make it very probable that human life will evolve in more than one place in the universe. If only a very narrow range of laws and initial conditions allow such evolution, then we may say that the universe is "fine-tuned" for this evolution. If the fundamental laws and initial conditions are, as we suppose, the laws of quantum theory and relativity theory with the four forces (strong force, weak force, electromagnetic force, and gravity) governing the basic array of fundamental particles (photons; leptons, including electrons; mesons; and baryons, including protons and neutrons) – what I shall call the standard theory – and the initial conditions are such conditions as the velocity, density, and degree of isotropy of the matter-energy of the universe immediately after the time of the Big Bang; and these are measured in normal ways, then – recent work has shown – the universe is fine-tuned. On this there is no scientific dispute. The constants of its laws and the variables of its initial conditions needed to lie within very narrow ranges if human bodies were ever to exist. One such set of narrow ranges are those centered on the actual values (as we believe them to be) of the constants of laws and variables of initial conditions. It is worthwhile giving a sample of the kind of scientific evidence for this fine-tuning. Given the standard theory with constants and variables of initial conditions having their actual values, it is highly doubtful whether there could be any other kind of intelligent life, except carbon-based life (though arguments of a similar kind for the need for the universe to be fine-tuned if it is to produce carbon-based life could be given if we suppose that the universe is to produce a silicon-based life.) The build-up of the atoms required for carbon-based life requires the four forces to have certain strengths, relative to each other. If there are to be stable nuclei, the strong force that keeps the protons and neutrons together in the nucleus has to be strong enough to overcome the electromagnetic repulsion between the protons. A 50 per cent decrease in the strong force "would undercut the stability of all elements essential for carbon-based life, with a slightly larger decrease eliminating all elements except hydrogen."[3] A 30-fold decrease in the weak force would lead to stars being made almost entirely of helium and so having a short life (of about 300 million years) in no way conducive to the evolution of intelligent life.[4] An increase in the strength of the gravitational force by a factor of 3,000 would lead to stars with lives of no more than a billion years (compared to the 10 billion years of our Sun's lifetime), which would make the development of intelligent life much less probable.[5]

In general the kinds of increases or decreases in the strengths of the forces mentioned above (50 percent, 4 percent, etc.) compatible with the production of carbon-based life represent a very small range indeed of the values of the strengths of the forces involved within that range of actual values of any of the forces, and an infinitesimal range within the range of logically possible values of the forces. For example, G has to lie between 0 and $3,000 G$, which represents one part in 10^{36} of the range of values of the force constants. And so on for the other constants.[6] The expansion of the universe is governed by the strength of the initial Big Bang, and the restraining effect of gravity possibly diminished or increased by the value (positive or negative) of the cosmological constant ($\boxed{}$), which latter may be regarded as determining a fifth force. This needs to lie extremely close to zero if space is not to expand so rapidly that every object in the universe flies apart, or to collapse so rapidly that every object is the universe is crushed.[7]

Further, given the actual laws of nature or laws at all similar thereto, initial conditions would have to lie within a narrow range of the present conditions if intelligent life was to evolve (or else they would have to lie well outside that range; this point will be discussed later). The initial rate of expansion is critical. It has been calculated that (barring a possible qualification from "inflation theory" to which we shall come shortly) a reduction in the rate of expansion of one part in a million would lead to premature collapse, and an increase by one part in a million would have prevented the evolution of stars and heavier elements.[8] Some initial inhomogeneity in the distribution of matter-energy is needed if galaxies, and so stars, are to be produced; too much would lead to black holes being formed before stars could form.[9] In the beginning there was a slight excess of baryons over antibaryons; all but the excess baryons became matter-energy. If the excess number had been even slighter, there would not have been enough matter for galaxies or stars to form. If it had been much greater, there would have been too much radiation for planets to form.[10] And so on. The universe has to start with the right density and amount of inhomogeneity of radiation and velocity of expansion, and that means (within a very narrow range) the actual amount. Recent work, has suggested[11] that, if a number of the constants and variables were all significantly different, each having a value within a different small range, human bodies could still evolve. That is, there are several small islands within the space of possible values of constants and variables within which human life could evolve. But this does not alter significantly the point that such islands are the exceptions and the tuning needs to be fine-tuning for human life to evolve. If standard theory provides the ultimate explanation of the universe (and so God does not bring it about that standard theory operates), such fine-tuning is *a priori* very improbable. For the form in which any theory, including the standard theory, is stated by scientists in their books and articles is its simplest form. Scientists do not try to complicate things for themselves and their readers unnecessarily. This form involves variables and constants being measured in the normal way. It is the form in which we judge the simplicity of the theory that determines (for theories of equal scope) the intrinsic probability of its truth. Versions of standard theory expressed in its simplest form will differ only in respect of the values of constants of laws and of variables of boundary conditions therein. Given all that, a version that claims that a constant or variable lies within one range will not differ greatly[12] in simplicity from theories that claim that it lies within another range of equal size; and so each such version will be approximately equally probable *a priori*. But since only a few versions of standard theory in which constants vary over a very small range are tuned for the evolution of human bodies, such evolution is *a priori* very improbable. In slightly more technical terms, the claim is that the density of the prior probability for constants and variables measured in the normal way is roughly constant (that is, the prior probability that these will lie close to a given value is roughly constant for all values of the constants and variables of standard theory).[13]

It is worth noting the effect of not choosing the simplest formulation of a theory, on the probability density of different constants and variables. I take a very easy example, Newton's law of gravitational attraction $F = \dfrac{Gmm^1}{r^2}$ could be expressed as $F = \dfrac{mm^1}{d^3 r^2}$ where d is defined as $G^{-1/3}$. A constant probability density distribution for d (that is, the assumption that it is equally probable that d lies within any range of given size) will not yield a constant probability density distribution for G, and conversely. A constant probability distribution for d (that is, the assumption that it is equally probable that d lies within any range of given size) will not yield a constant probability density distribution for G, and conversely. A constant probability distribution for d will yield the result that d is equally likely to lie between 8 and infinity (i.e., to have any value whatsoever above 8). Expressing the laws of our standard theory in very complicated forms, logically equivalent to their simplest forms, and assuming a constant probability density for the constants and variables of these forms, could have the consequence that much greater variation of these (far less "fine-tuning") would be compatible with the universe being hospitable to human bodies. But laws are judged simpler and so to have greater prior probability in virtue of the features of their simplest forms. Since a constant is simpler than a constant to the power $(-1/3)$, the traditional form of Newton's law is the simplest and so most fundamental form. And, more generally, insistence on the simplest form of a law should yield a unique probability density distribution for the constants and variables of laws of that kind (or, at most, if there are a number of equally simple forms of a law, a few different probability density distributions that are not likely to make much difference to the need for fine-tuning.) So, given standard theory and no more fundamental explanation thereof (physical or theistic), tuning is *a priori* immensely improbable.

Physical cosmology is a very unstable branch of physics. New theories are produced each year. It might be discovered that the laws are other than previously supposed, again in such a way that they bring forth intelligent life out of a much wider range of boundary conditions than had hitherto been supposed. "Inflation theory" suggests just that. Inflation theory tells us that regions of the universe with certain features may have been subject soon after the Big Bang, to a vast faster-than-light expansion, leading to them very quickly becoming cool homogeneous and isotropic regions. So features such as homogeneity and isotropy for which a narrow range of initial conditions were thought vital are – according to inflation theory – to be expected, given certain laws, to arise from a wider range of initial conditions. Yet it may well be that inflation theory can be successful, in any of its many variants in removing the need for fine-tuning from the initial conditions only by putting more fine-tuning into the laws.[14] There remains however a consensus that, given an initial Big Bang, variables such as the initial velocity of recession have (even on inflation theory) to lie within a narrow range.

It is also just possible that physicists might come to adopt a theory that the universe is infinitely old. It would still be the case that the values of the constants in the laws of standard theory (as opposed to the variables of initial conditions) must lie within very narrow ranges if life is to evolve anywhere in the universe – ranges that include the actual values of the constants and probably a few other small ranges in which the values of several of the constants are different from their actual ones. There would of course be no "initial conditions," but there would still be boundary conditions, states possessed by the universe at each moment of time, required for the evolution of intelligent life (such as the kind, quantity and average density of matter-energy.) There may be a more fundamental physical theory that explains the standard theory, and a constant probability density for the constants and variables of the boundary conditions of the simplest form of that fundamental theory may have somewhat different consequences for the prior probability of tuning (for example, that the consequence that the more readily observable variables can take only certain values)[15] More generally, there are innumerable possible scientific theories differing in their form from each other, and innumerable different kinds of boundary conditions differing in the number of entities that they postulate (big and small universes), each allowing many different sets of constants and boundary condition variables. A constant probability density over the latter (when each theory is expressed in its simplest form) will yield for each theory a different probability that a universe conforming to it will be tuned. The theories (although of equal scope – telling us about everything) themselves will differ in their simplicity, and so in their prior probability. Hence, given a precise way of measuring simplicity, there will be a true value for the prior probability, the probability if there is no God, that any universe will be tuned. It will be (loosely) that proportion of logically possible universes that are conducive to the evolution of human bodies, each weighted by the simplicity of the laws that govern it and the fewness and simplicity of entities in its boundary conditions. And, given the rough way we have of measuring simplicity, we could still give a rough value to this. So it does not matter – for the purposes of an argument from fine – tuning – whether we have the correct theory of our universe, or whether there is a more ultimate physical explanation of the forces that govern it; and whether only a small proportion of versions of the correct theory lead to a tuned universe. For the prior probability (in a Godless universe), that a universe will be tuned is a function not of the true physical theory and actual kinds of boundary conditions that govern our universe, but of all the possible theories and boundary conditions there could be for any universe at all.

It is not, however, within my ability to calculate this value, nor do I suspect within the ability of any present-day mathematician.

What however, I suggest, is fairly obvious is that *no* relatively simple universe would be tuned. For consider the seven features required by a human body listed earlier in this lecture. Such body has parts. But the parts have to form one body distinct from other bodies and from the inanimate world. In our world this is secured by chemistry whereby only some bits of matter link to other bits of matter. If I put my hand into a sandpit, my hand will not absorb the sand; but, if I eat some bread, it will become part of my body. Sense organs require an enormous variety of stimuli impinging on a place, which vary with their distant source. In our universe the best of all such stimuli are light waves-an enormous variety of different light waves arrive every second at our eyes, which vary with the states of objects many meters away. The sense organs respond differently to each very small range of incoming stimuli. But we humans are interested only in certain aspects of the states of distant objects – whether they are the bodies of predators, or prey, or mates, and so on for a million possible differences. The stimuli have to cause brain states that give us information of moral or prudential importance. Our information processor will utilize states caused by past experiences to turn the states of sense organs into useful brain states. And, if we are not to be just automata but to reason consciously from past experiences, we need a memory bank to file those states in recoverable form. This requires a chemistry of stable states (so that memories remain the same as time passes) and metastable states so that certain kinds of input will alter a brain element from one state to another (as we learn that some previous belief was erroneous). And for output we need again an enormous variety of brain states corresponding to the different purposes we could form, a processor to turn these into the relevant limb movements (for example, if I want to tell you that today is Friday, to produce the twists of tongue and lip that will cause the appropriate sounds of the English language). And we need a stable inorganic world to which we can make a difference that remains; there is no point in trying to build a house if the bricks immediately liquidify.

All this involves extended bodies, each composed of many fundamental particles of a number of different kinds, each particle capable of existing in a few different discrete states; the differences between bodies being a matter of the number and arrangement of the units and the discrete states of each. Change has to be affected through a particle (or group of particles) changing their states, causing other particles to change their states. To secure stable bodies that are nevertheless capable of existing in many different states, you need more than one simple force. One simple force of attraction would lead to crushed lumps of matter incapable of sensitive reaction; and one simple force of repulsion would lead to there being no extended bodies at all. Minimally a combination of two different simple forces (possibly both derivable from one more complicated force) is required. A force of attraction between particles inversely proportional to the square of the distance apart of the particles would be required to be balanced, for example, by a force of repulsion inversely proportional to the cube of their distance apart. Forces of these kinds of the right strength would lead to particles coming together but not collapsing on top of each other. But to preserve states (of the brain correlates of belief for example) intact, we have to rule out small variations. We need metastability – systems that remain unchanged under forces of a certain strength but that change from one discrete state to another discrete state when the strength of the force exceeds a certain amount. This is ensured in our universe by the laws of quantum theory, which guarantee the stability of the atom. And, to have distinct bodies that do not merge with each other, and distinct brain states that are open to change only under certain kinds of input, we need something like a chemistry allowing substances to combine easily with some substances but not with other substances. This is secured in our universe by chemical substances different from each other by the charge on their nucleus and the arrangements of charge-balancing electrons in shells around the nucleus-in other words, protons, neutrons, and the Pauli principle.[16] And so on.

So we need large numbers of particles of a few different kinds and forces of some complexity acting between them. But universes are simpler, the fewer objects (for example, particles) they contain and the fewer kinds of mathematically simple forces that operate between them. No very simple universe could be tuned, whatever its boundary conditions. Clearly more complicated kinds of possible universes (for example, ours) can be tuned, and maybe normally the tuning needs to be fine-tuning. Maybe, too, some very complicated kinds of universe would produce human bodies for most values of constants and variables of boundary conditions. But the considerable *a priori* weight of simplicity suggests that in a Godless universe it is *a priori* very improbable that any one universe will be tuned so as to yield human bodies.

Of course, if there were an infinite number of universes, each with different laws and different boundary conditions, one might expect at least one to be tuned. In the previous chapter I made the point that it is the height of irrationality to postulate an infinite number of universes never causally connected with each other, merely to avoid the hypothesis of theism. Given that simplicity makes for prior probability, and a theory is simpler the fewer entities it postulates, it is far simpler to postulate one God than an infinite number of universes, each differing from each other in accord with a regular formula, uncaused by anything else. There might, however, be particular features of our universe (other than its tuning) that are most simply explained by supposing that it "budded off" from another universe in consequence of a law whereby universes produce daughter universes differing from them in boundary conditions and laws; and so our universe explained as one of a collection of an infinite number of universes (originally causally connected with each other) differing from each other in boundary conditions and laws. But that is tantamount to postulating a multiverse that has laws and boundary conditions such that it will contain at some time or other a tuned universe. But then there are an infinite number of logically possible multiverses that do not have this characteristic, and the shape of the problem has in no way changed. For the problem that concerns us is not really why there is one (in my sense) universe that is tuned for life, but why among all the universes there are (one or many) there is a universe tuned for life. One way in which this could come about is by there being only one such universe. But another way is by there being a universe-generating mechanism that produces universes of various kinds, including a universe tuned for life. But, although the existence of this possibility does not change the shape of the problem, it draws our attention to a way in which a universe tuned for life could have come into existence. And so, in order to assess the prior probability that there be a universe tuned for life, we need to assess the probability that that would come about by one or other route. And taking this into account may lead us to reassess the value of that probability.

It might seem that the value would turn out to be much higher than we originally supposed. Let us individuate universe-generating mechanisms by the multiverse (the collection of universes) that they generate (at some time or another). Then, if we consider all the possible multiverses each consisting of r universes, chosen from n logically possible kinds of universe,only one of which is tuned for life, it follows mathematically that a proportion

$\dfrac{r}{n+r-1}$ of these multiverses will contain a universe tuned for life. For any $r > 1$ ($r = 1$ being the case where there is only one universe), this will exceed $1/n$ (the proportion of possible universes tuned for life). And the more universes in a multiverse (the larger is r), the closer this value will be to 1. So it might seem that, as we consider more and more possible universe-generating mechanisms (generating more and more universes, that is r getting larger and larger), the total proportion of universe-generating mechanisms that will generate a universe tuned for life will approach 1. So if it were equally probable that there exist any possible universe-generating mechanism (most of them generating far more universes than the number of logically possible kinds of universe), it would seem to be very probable that there would occur at least one universe tuned for life.

However, we cannot calculate the prior probability (in a Godless world) of a universe-generating mechanism being such as to produce a universe tuned for life merely by counting the proportion of mechanisms that have this characteristic among the total number of possible such mechanisms. To start with, there will be an infinite number of possible mechanisms of which an infinite number will have the required feature. And infinity divided by infinity has no definite value. We have to divide up mechanisms into a finite number of kinds of mechanism, and then weight each kind by the prior probability of a mechanism being of that kind which will be a function of the simplicity of the laws involved in the mechanism. Now, clearly mechanisms that yield universes varying from each other only in the constants involved in their laws will be much simpler than mechanisms that yield universes differing in the kinds of laws they have. A mechanism that produced universes with laws of totally different kinds from each other would need itself to be governed by some very complicated laws. Yet, if we are confined to mechanisms that yield only laws of one kind, my earlier arguments suggest that very few such mechanisms yielding only laws of relatively simple kinds (that is laws no more complex than are those of our universe) will yield a universe tuned for life. Secondly, mechanisms that produce universes with simple laws are simpler and so intrinsically more probable than mechanisms that produce universes with more and more complex laws as well. And, thirdly, the existence of a multiverse with a universe-generating mechanism is a more complex supposition than the existence of one universe without such a mechanism.

So, even if there is a large range of possible multiverses tuned for life (in the sense of producing a universe tuned for life), and the proportion of the range of possible multiverses tuned for life is vastly greater than the proportion of the range of single universes to tuned, this holds only because the former range includes very complex multiverses that are intrinsically very improbable. So I stick by my point that it is intrinsically very improbable that there be a universe tuned for life (whether it is a sole universe or a universe produced by a universe-generating mechanism). Yet it may well be that this improbability is less than the improbability that a single universe would be tuned for life.

A God however, I argued earlier, has good reason for bringing about free rational free beings, such as human beings appear to be; and so, on the hypothesis of theism, it is moderately probable that the universe will be tuned – that is, such as to make significantly probable the existence of human bodies. In terms of the probability calculus – I represent this evidence of the nature of the laws and boundary conditions as e, with h as the hypothesis of theism, and k as the background knowledge that formed the evidence of the arguments considered in the previous lecture – that there is a universe governed by simple laws of nature. The probability then, if there is no God, that the laws and boundary conditions will be such as to have this further feature of bringing about human bodies is $P(e| \sim h \& k)$. The probability that this will happen if there is a God is $P(e|h \& k)$. I have argued that $P(e|h \& k) \gg P(e| \sim h \& k)$, and so – by Bayes's theorem – $P(h|e \& h) \gg P(h|k)$. We have here a powerful C-inductive argument for the existence of God.

Notes

1   This chapter is a summary of the argument of the later part of chapter 8 of my book *The Existence of God*, 2nd edn. (Oxford: Clarendon Press, 2004). The original classical physical analysis of the extent of fine-tuning in the universe is J. D. Barrow and F. J. Tipler, *The Anthropic Cosmological Principle* (Oxford: Clarendon Press, 1986). This has been carefully reanalyzed and updated in Robin Collins, "Evidence for Fine-Tuning," in N. A. Mansom (ed.), *God and Design* (London: Routledge, 2003). I am much indebted to both of these sources for their presentation of the latest results of the relevant physics.

2   I am assuming that humans have free will, that is, we often have a choice between alternative actions despite all the causes which influence us. It seems to us that we do often choose freely. For further argument in defence of the claim that humans have free will, see my *The Evolution of the Soul*, rev. edn. (Oxford: Clarendon Press, 1997), ch. 13. Given free will, it is evident that humans are a species of free rational beings. The argument of this chapter is really an argument to God from the existence of free rational beings. But since the only such beings of which we have knowledge are humans, I express it hereafter as an argument from the existence of humans.

3   Collins, "Evidence for fine-tuning," p. 183.

4   Ibid., pp. 188–9.

5   Ibid., pp. 189–90, 192–4.

6   Ibid., pp. 183 and 190. The strengths of the actual forces span a range between the strength of the strong force and the strength of the gravitational force. On one widely used dimensionless measure the strength of the strong force is 10^{40} times the strength of the gravitational force.

7   Ibid., pp. 180–2.

8   Papers by W. W. Hawking and by R. H. Dicke and P. J. E. Peebles cited in J. Leslie, *Universes* (London: Routledge, 1989), p. 29.

9   Barrow and Tipler, *Anthropic Cosmological Principle*, pp. 414–19.

10   Ibid., pp. 401–8.

11   For one example, see Collins, "Evidence for fine-tuning," p. 185.

12   It will differ a little if the simplest formulation of the theory yields a unique zero point for measurement of some variable or constant (a unique point at which some quantity has its lowest value), as, for example, does the Kelvin scale for temperature measurement (0°K being that temperature at which an ideal gas would exert no pressure, and no lower temperature is possible). For then it will be a non-arbitrary matter whether the value of the constant or variable lies within a lower range or a higher range of possible values. It will be a bit more probable that it lies within the former, for the reason that laws containing small integers are simpler than ones containing larger integers (see *The Existence of God*, p. 54) and, more fully, my *Epistemic Justification* (Oxford: Clarendon Press, 2001), p. 90.

13   The constants and variables of standard theory with which we are concerned do in general have unique zero points (see n. 11 above). In measuring the density of matter-energy, or the velocity of relative recession of the galaxies, for example, velocity and density have unique zero points on the simplest way of measuring them. Hence lower values of these are somewhat more probable than higher values. This has the consequence that, although there is an infinite range of possible values of these constants and variables, there can be an infinite probability that some such constant will have a value lying within any given range. But, if the constant or variable having a value

within a range of given size was the same throughout the infinite range (as would be the case for constants and variables without a unique zero point), the probability of it lying within any finite range would be infinitesimal. (For the need to use infinitesimals in assessing probabilities, see my *Epistemic Justification*, Additional Note G). So, either by ascribing higher intrinsic probabilities to lower values of the constants and variables, or by using infinitesimals, I avoid what is known as the "normalizability problem." (See, e.g., Timothy McGrew *et al.*, "Probabilities and the fine-tuning argument," in N. A. Manson, *God and Design,*.

14   See J. Earman and J. Mostevin, "A critical look at inflationary cosmology," *Philosophy of Science* 66 (1999), 1–49.

15   It is possible that the derivation of the fundamental laws of nature from string theory would greatly reduce the need for fine-tuning. This has been argued in G. L. Kane et al., "The beginning and end of the anthropic principle," astro-ph/0001197. They suggest that all string theories are equivalent; and that different possible "vacua" uniquely determine all the constants and initial values of variables of laws of nature. They acknowledge that much work needs to be done before (if ever) string theory is established and their result can be demonstrated. But, even granted all this tentative speculation, they acknowledge that "there will be a large number of possible vacua"; and that means that if humans are to evolve the universe has to be fine-tuned in the respect that it has to be characterized by one unique vacuum rather than any other of that large number.

16   This principle (applying to all fermions – for example, electrons and protons) says that in any one system (for example, one atom) only one particle of the same kind can be in a given quantum state. In consequence there are only a small number of possible energy states for the electrons of an atom, and only a small number of electrons can be in each energy state. While the basic laws of quantum theory ensure the stability of the atom – electrons do not collapse onto the nucleus – the Pauli principle leads to the electrons being arranged in "shells." Hence atoms of a finite number of different kinds can be formed by different numbers of electrons surrounding the nucleus, and molecules of different kinds can be formed by bonds of different kinds between the electrons in the outer shells of certain combinations of atoms but not of others.

Part 6

A Paleontologist Considers Science and Religion

16

Is Intelligent Design Really Intelligent?

PETER DODSON

The theory of Intelligent Design is a theory of guided evolution that addresses the supposed shortcomings of Darwinian evolution by adding an unspecified Designer to the evolutionary process. It is a thinly veiled secret that the Designer is the Judaeo-Christian God. Although many writers take a romantic view of nature, emphasizing the beauty, swiftness, and grace of living creatures, it was obvious to Darwin that nature is filled with inefficiency and cruelty. Drawing on anatomical design, I point out many suboptimal structures in humans and animals that are the result of poor design. If God designed all of nature, then God must be held accountable for the cruelty and efficiency of nature. But if God created the evolutionary process and granted freedom to his Creation, his love, omniscience, and benevolence are not compromised. This is Darwin's gift to theology.

I wear many hats. With three degrees in Earth science, I am a professor of animal biology in a School of Veterinary Medicine at the University of Pennsylvania, my academic home for 33 years. (I tell my graduate students to expect the unexpected – their careers may turn out in surprising ways – mine certainly did.) In the School of Arts and Sciences I have taught courses in three different departments: geology, history and sociology of science, and religious studies). I consider myself fortunate indeed. Few are the vertebrate paleontologists who are privileged to teach gross anatomy – most who do, teach the boring kind, human anatomy (we joke in the veterinary profession that doctors are veterinarians who know only one species). I teach veterinary anatomy, and we dissect dogs, cats, horses, and goats in detail, and have passing encounters with avian theropods (*aka* chickens) and fish. Veterinary gross anatomy is intrinsically comparative in nature (and thus implicitly evolutionary) from the very first day of laboratory. Veterinary anatomy would still be comparative even if we studied only the dog. One reason for this is that the names of anatomical structures in domestic animals are nearly the same as those in humans even though these names may not be appropriate for dogs or cats. Veterinary students quickly learn that, while the human biceps brachii has two heads and the human triceps has three heads, one head suffices in the biceps for good tetrapods, while four heads is a better number for the triceps (granted, rather few vet students know that some precursors of modern mammals have up to six heads in their triceps!). My students learn these facts, not because we insist that they know the human condition, but because the names proclaim the structure: biceps means "two heads" and triceps means "three heads."

I see intelligent design in the dissection lab every single day. So many anatomical structures are elegant in their design and function. I have my favorites. The musculoskeletal structure of the hand is extraordinary, and even more extraordinary is the fact that the same fundamental structure obtains, whether the species is dog, cat, horse, or human! Charles Darwin rightly understood that anatomy provides compelling evidence of evolution. Consider your own hand. Each finger but the thumb has three segments, which are called phalanges. What is truly elegant is the pattern by which the digital flexors and extensors originate from several bellies, form a single thick tendon in the carpal canal, and then break into separate tendons going to each finger. The flexor muscles bend each joint of the hand separately to form a firm grip. The interosseus muscles flex the metacarpal – phalangeal ("knuckle") joint of each finger; the superficial digital flexor tendon splits over each first phalanx, forms a sleeve around the deep digital flexor tendon, and inserts on the base of the second phalanx; and the deep digital flexor passes through the sleeve or manica and reaches the base of the third (last) phalanx. By contrast, the extensor tendons of the hand that loosen the grip attach only on the third phalanx. Lovely ring (annular) ligaments keep the tendons in alignment, just like the line guides on a fishing pole. The consequence of this arrangement is that we humans have exquisite control over flexion (closing) of our fingers, but extension (opening) is much cruder (imagine trying to play the piano with your fingers upside down!). Horses have this arrangement as well – granted that their tendons are 3 or 4 centimeters wide, and they (and they alone) have but a single digit and one tendon where we have five.

Another intelligent design is the elegant pattern of redundant vascularization of the gut. The gut starts out in early development as a simple tube in the abdomen with three principal arteries that arise directly from the aorta, the huge arterial trunk that arises directly from the heart. Whereas paired organs such as kidneys, adrenals, and gonads are supplied by paired arteries, the intestinal arteries are unpaired, but anastomose or connect with each other in such a way that any segment of gut can potentially receive blood from two different directions. The longest part of the small intestine, the jejunum, has an elegant radial blood supply that ensures that no segment of gut is more than two centimeters or so from the nearest radial artery. Smaller arteries radiate out from their central point of origin like spokes on a bicycle wheel, where the jejunum is the wheel itself. The most direct principal artery is the cranial mesenteric artery; but in the event of a blockage of this artery, whether by clot, parasite, or tumor, blood can reach the gut from either the celiac artery cranially or the caudal mesenteric artery caudally. This redundant blood supply (technically known as collateral circulation) is an example of highly technical design. Foolproof? No. Nothing made of mechanical parts subject to wear is foolproof. But it is pretty good.

When we examine anatomical structures such as these, we readily recognize their optimal design. When we gaze in wonderment at a running cheetah, a leaping gazelle, or a graceful thoroughbred gliding across the finish line in full extension, we may thrill with thoughts of the perfection of organic structures. Certainly, these were the features of nature that Rev. William Paley had in mind when he wrote his *Natural Theology; Or, Evidences of the Existence and Attributes of the Deity* in 1802. However, nature isn't always intelligently designed.

Charles Darwin was very troubled by the imperfections of nature, and the frank cruelties with which nature abounds. He had great difficulty reconciling the unsavory aspects of nature (ichneumon wasps laying their eggs inside of caterpillars, so the wasp larvae can eat their way out of their live hosts; preying mantis queens biting the heads off the males that are inseminating them) with the idea of a loving God.

Humans have a plethora of anatomical structures that are highly suspect. As a dinosaur paleontologist, I have always thought it strange for humans to stand on two legs without the security of a counterbalancing tail. The spinal curves necessitated by making a tetrapod stand upright on two legs wreak all sorts of havoc, especially in the lumbar region – where all sorts of surgeries are performed. Similarly, balancing a heavy globular head on top of a fairly flimsy neck leads to all sorts of injuries, both acute (whiplash) and chronic (arthritic); both problems provide paychecks for neurosurgeons. And there is the case of wisdom teeth! Do humans have two molars or three? Sometimes that pesky third molar erupts normally, and sometimes it impacts and causes nothing but trouble. Could the Designer not have made up his mind? Childbirth is a risky business in humans, both for infants and for their mothers due to the conflict between the large head size of our babies and small size of the birth canal in the mothers. Also, about 20 percent of human pregnancies suffer spontaneous abortion (Ayala, 2007).

One of my favorite examples of really bad design, something no Designer or even promising Design Apprentice, would have come up, with is the recurrent laryngeal nerve. The larynx itself is a really sophisticated and complex structure. Also known as the voice box, it allows us to produce articulated speech, but more generally it is designed to protect the airway from foreign objects, a job it does very well in animals, but less well in humans due to the conflicting design requirements of speaking, breathing, and swallowing. The muscles of the larynx are operated by the tenth cranial nerve, called the vagus nerve. Two branches of the vagus nerve go to the larynx. The cranial laryngeal nerve does just what you would expect: it follows the shortest, most direct course from the parent nerve to the target structure. The second branch does not. It follows an absurd course. The vagus ("wanderer") nerve is appropriately named, for this odd cranial nerve leaves the brain and wanders down the neck, through the thorax, and into the abdomen, where it innervates smooth muscle in the intestinal tract. In the thorax, it detaches a branch called the recurrent laryngeal nerve that loops around the aorta and runs back up the neck in the opposite direction from which it came (hence the name "recurrent"), before it reaches the larynx.

The recurrent laryngeal nerve is a prime example of what Stephen Jay Gould termed "evolutionary baggage." It is the imperfections of organic design that provide the deepest insight into evolution. What is inexplicable incompetence in design terms makes sense in the light of evolution. Fishes have hearts and vagus nerves but lack necks – the heart is situated between the gills underneath the back of the head. The vagus nerve and its branches once had a direct course, but in the development of land-living tetrapods, the neck developed and the heart was pushed back into the thorax, and the recurrent laryngeal nerve was literally stretched out into an absurd loop in the process.

Another example of a strange design is provided by the so-called splint bones of horses. Horses have remarkable feet. They walk (and run) on a single toe, equivalent to our middle finger. The weight of the body passes down the leg, through the cannon bone, or third metacarpal, (equivalent to the long knuckle bone of our middle finger), down to the tip of the toe. The cannon bone is robust and well constructed for its purpose. However, on either side of the cannon bone is a pair of slender, tapering "splint bones." They participate in the carpal (wrist) joint but they taper to slender blunt points well above the bottom of the cannon bone, and thus do not transmit weight to the ground. They are mechanically useless. Moreover, they sometimes become inflamed and painful, and require therapeutic intervention to fuse them and eliminate their troublesome movement. Once again we see an example of poor biomechanical design, but one that is readily explained in evolutionary terms. *Eocene Hyracotherium*, the most famous ancestral horse, had four toes in front and three in back. Three-toed horses flourished in the Oligocene and Miocene periods. As late as the Pliocene, footprints in volcanic mud of *Hipparion* – associated with hominids at Laetoli, Tanzania – reveal the pattern of three toes. It is just about as clear as any fact of paleontology can be that the splint bones of modern horses are vestiges of the second and fourth metatarsals, which were progressively reduced in equid evolution.

Those of us who count the decades of our lives on the fingers of two hands are acutely aware of the imperfections of human design. Geologist/humorist Don Wise has drawn on the imperfections of the human body to develop his own theory of imperfections of ID: Incomplete Design! Foremost among these is the need for aging males to "pee in Morse code" due to prostate enlargement.

The problem is that Intelligent Design carries too great a burden. If the Designer gets credit for all the good things, then the same Designer should be condemned for all the bad design and just plain malevolence in nature. Intelligent Design is dubious theologically as well as dubious scientifically. The great British theologian, John Henry Newman, rejected William Paley's theory of Intelligent Design on the former grounds in 1852, some 124 years before Richard Dawkins achieved the feat in *The Blind Watchmaker*. Dawkins, no theological adept, seems to have believed that he had thereby disproved the existence of God, but in fact had merely rediscovered and successfully rebutted a difficulty that grew out of Isaac Newton's mechanical view of the universe.

Today's ID movement is a religiously motivated attempt to sidestep the implications of evolution by adding some unspecified form of guidance to the process of evolution without directly appealing to the God of the Bible. Biochemist Michael Behe (1996), author of *Darwin's Black Box*, gave rise to the concept of Intelligent Design (ID) with his notion of irreducible complexity, the idea that some structures are too complex to have evolved, but must have had help form an unspecified "designer," a none-too-subtly disguised euphemism for God. Although Darwin directly addressed the steps by which the eye could have evolved at the gross level, Behe pointed out that at the level of biochemistry, molecular pathways of vision are orders of magnitude more complex. With the involvement of mathematician William Dembski, the Intelligent Design movement was born, and with it the infamous "wedge strategy" designed to separate science from its naturalistic assumptions. Scientists have nearly uniformly rejected ID, because it seems a counsel of despair – if the problem is too tough to solve, we will just fall back on the Designer. Whatever the merits of this strategy prior to 1859, it is a non-starter today.

In 2005 Judge John E. Jones III heard a celebrated case in a federal district court in Harrisburg, Pennsylvania, of the suit brought by Tammy Kitzmiller et al. against the Dover Area School District. The suit arose from the attempt by the school board to insert a cautionary statement about the validity of evolution coupled with the option for instruction in intelligent design theory into the school science curriculum. As in previous similar cases, the high-profile court case drew intense scrutiny from national and international media. In a 139-page opinion delivered on December 20, 2005, Judge Jones slammed the door on the teaching of ID in Dover, PA. Judge Jones could not be convinced that ID was anything but a sectarian religious doctrine, scientific creationism in new clothing, clearly not a scientific theory, and thus unconstitutional to include in school science curricula. Since the Dover decision was delivered, it has had a chilling effect on similar attempts elsewhere, most recently Ohio.

As a theistic evolutionist myself, I am not without sympathy for creationists. They work at their jobs, shovel their snow, cut their grass, shop at the grocery store, pay their taxes, and vote. Sometimes, they even vote the right way (the Dover school board that had passed the ID resolution was voted out in the following election). Creationists do not have two heads, cloven hooves, or pointed tails tucked inside their pants; they are just people who try to make sense of their daily lives like the rest of us. The problem is that they try to read the Bible as a comprehensive scientific account of nature, for which it was never intended, rather than as a spiritual guide for daily life. Scientists who use evolution as a bludgeon to defeat religious belief, equally gratuitously, illustrate the flip side of the coin. Judge Jones labeled as "utterly false" the presupposition "that evolutionary theory is antithetical to the existence of a supreme being and to religion in general." Indeed, in this and previous federal court cases against creationism in Arkansas and Louisiana, religious believers have testified for the plaintiffs against creationism, which is neither good for science nor good theology.

In fact, several authors have recently pointed out that evolution by natural selection is Darwin's gift to theology (Haught, 1998; Ayala, 2007). Victorian theologian Aubrey Moore wrote, "Darwinism appeared, and, under the guise of a foe, did the work of a friend" (Ayala, 2007). Darwin accomplished this by relieving God of the burden of explicitly creating death, disease, deformity, and every manifestation of biological imperfection. These natural evils from which every human suffers are not the result of the malevolence or impotence of God, but are intrinsic to the evolving world which God created. How could it be otherwise if we are to be truly free, not mere puppets of our Maker?

Richard Dawkins famously wrote that Darwin made it possible to be an intellectually satisfied atheist, and the barrage of evangelical writings of scientists and philosophers of science against religious believers continues, with recent books by Dawkins, Dennett, Harris, and Hitchens. Where does that leave the religious believer in the age of science? The profound intuition of the religious believer is that life has meaning and purpose, and this intuition provides the basis for cosmic hope – is it a coincidence that atheists seem to be typically pessimists? (Theologian John Haught quips, "I tried to be a philosopher, but happiness kept breaking out.") I use the term *intuition* advisedly, because that feeling does not derive from science. Likewise, atheistic assumptions are not intrinsic to science but arise outside of, or properly, before science. No amount of pontificating by Nobel prizewinners such as Jacques Monod or Steven Weinberg is likely to disabuse a religious person of the cherished notion of purpose in life. It is also a profound religious intuition that our existence on this planet is not a matter of chance or accident; we are not the unintended consequence of the uncaring cosmos, otherwise populated only by "billions and billions of stars," as Carl Sagan and S. J. Gould would have us believe.

How can we reconcile acceptance of evolution with its reliance on random mutations and apparent lack of direction with a sense of cosmic purpose? We might as well ask, how could science possibly detect purpose, even if it exists? Science intentionally excludes purpose from its discourse, and is successful because of that omission. Science can discuss the mechanism by which water boils, but cannot detect that the reason the water is boiling is because I want a cup of tea. Science can describe in exquisite detail the flight of an airplane in terms of chemical energy, kinetic energy, aerodynamics, altitude, airspeed, ground speed, position, direction, and so on, without any knowledge of the destination of the flight or of its internal control, that is to say, its purpose. Science will necessarily always be limited in what it can determine; scientific knowledge is intrinsically incomplete. Any scientist who declaims on purpose is speaking outside of science. We may also question what the word "random" actually means. Is random not an admission of ignorance on our part rather than an objective statement? We do not know the cause of an event or are unable to detect the pattern, so we label it "random." Can randomness coexist with purpose? We are familiar with statistical behavior of large populations of molecules in a gas. Similarly, traffic engineers can describe the flow of automobiles on a freeway at rush hour, including annoying the stop-and-start tie-ups with which we are all too familiar. They can do this despite the fact that each car is on the road with a strict purpose and intentionality.

There is no reason for religious believers to fear science. Evolution is fairly viewed as God's way of creating. A number of Biblical texts invite us to take creation (i.e., *nature*) seriously (e.g. Psalm 33:4; Romans, 1:20). An evolutionary outlook helps us to understand some of the puzzling aspects of creation, such as its obviously unfinished character. Creation is still evolving – the sixth day has not yet ended. Evolution is indeed "Darwin's gift to theology." We can and must embrace evolution but we need not turn our backs on religion in our rational quest for the fullness of life.

Acknowledgment

This chapter is based on an essay by Peter Dodson entitled "How Intelligent is Intelligent Design?" *American Paleontologist* (Spring, 2006).

References

Ayala, F. J. (2007) *Darwin's Gift to Science and Religion.* Washington, DC: John Henry Press.

Behe, M. (1996) *Darwin's Black Box – the Biochemical Challenge to Evolution.* New York: The Free Press.

Haught, J. F. (1998) Darwin's gift to theology. In R. J. Russell, W. R. Stoeger, and F. J. Ayala (eds.) *Evolutionary Biology and Molecular Biology: Scientific Perspective on Divine Action*, pp. 393–418 (Notre Dame, IN: University of Notre Dame Press).

17

God and the Dinosaurs Revisited

PETER DODSON

> In this chapter, I would like to talk about two central matters, my faith as a scientist, and how my science fits together with that faith, rather than challenges it.

I am a geologist, a dinosaur paleontologist, a veterinary anatomist, an evolutionary biologist, and a deeply committed Christian. I am also a husband and a proud father. Not unreasonably, I seek a healthy degree of integration of these facets of my life; schizophrenia is not a healthy human condition. To some, acceptance of Christian faith may seem contradictory to my scientific pursuits. It is not.

For forty years, it has been my privilege and my joy to study dinosaurs, first in Canada, then in the United States, more recently in India, Madagascar, Egypt, and Argentina, and especially in China, where I have returned for the eighth time in the summer of 2007. My students and I have named four new dinosaurs (*Avaceratops* from Montana; *Paralititan* from Egypt, *Suuwassea* from Montana, and most recently *Auroraceratops* from China). I have co-edited two editions of the definitive scholarly reference, *The Dinosauria* (Weishampel, Dodson and Osmolska, 1990, 2004). I have also written *The Horned Dinosaurs* (Dodson, 1996).

Dinosaurs were not particularly popular when I was a child, either in the public eye or scientifically. Nonetheless, I caught the "bug," encouraged by my father, E. O. Dodson, a religiously inclined evolutionary biologist himself. The 1950s and 1960s were a "quiet time" in dinosaur paleontology, but the field exploded in 1970s, the time in which I completed my PhD and entered academic life. The field is even more active today, fueled by spectacular dinosaur discoveries in China during the past decade (Wang and Dodson, 2006).

The Faith of a Scientist

I find my activities in science deeply satisfying, and I am profoundly grateful for the opportunities I have enjoyed over the years. But science is not enough for me. As the distinguished evolutionary biologist Francisco Ayala once remarked, science by itself is woefully inadequate for human affairs:

> Successful as it is, and universally encompassing as its subject is, a scientific view of the world is hopelessly incomplete. Matters of value and meaning are utside of science's scope. Even when we have a satisfying scientific understanding of a natural object or process, we are still missing matters that may well be thought by many to be of equal or greater import. (Ayala, 2007, p. 178)

Science is a tremendously valuable human endeavor, but it cannot tell me how to live my life. For that I turn to religion. I practice the Christian faith, which has provided me with the strength and guidance I need to be a fulfilled though imperfect human being. Given that religious belief is deeply embedded in human nature, one may at least raise the question as to whether persons who eschew religion are completely whole psychologically.

For years I was quiet about my faith in a professional context even though it was an essential part of my life as an adult. The quietness on my part was not matched by certain scientists on the other side of the religious divide. Every generation has had its public atheists. The brilliant British scientist Bertrand Russell once wrote a book, *Why I am Not a Christian*. Such public figures were then recognized as outside the norm. In recent years there has been a cacophony of scientific voices preaching a gospel of atheism, supposedly but not actually arising out of science. Prominent among them are the late Carl Sagan and Jacques Monod, Stephen Weinberg, Peter Atkins, William Provine, Richard Lewontin, Daniel Dennett, and above all, the highly visible, articulate and prolific Richard Dawkins, author of the egregious bestseller, *The God Delusion* (2006). Dawkins manages to convey a profound emotional revulsion for Christianity while simultaneously avoiding intellectual engagement with its content. I avoid including in this list the late Harvard paleontologist Stephen Jay Gould and also E. O. Wilson. Gould (1999), an agnostic, was respectful of religion, and recognized its importance in the fullness of human life. Harvard University evolutionary biologist Wilson lost the Christian faith he brought with him to university, but he has not lost respect for the importance of faith in the lives of people; indeed, he recently (Wilson, 2006) solicited the help of people of faith to save the biosphere.

There are many articulate models for the scientist as atheist, but rather fewer these days for the scientist as believer. For years it was lonely to be a religious believer among my scientific colleagues. Silence prevailed. Religion was never discussed. Ten years ago I decided to break my professional silence, and so I wrote a brief essay entitled "God and the Dinosaurs" in a paleontological newsletter, *American Paleontologist* (Dodson, 1997). The effect of coming out of the closet was remarkable. It encouraged religious believers to come out of the woodwork and to feel comfortable with their beliefs, encouraging them to break down painful mental barriers between the scientific side and the human side of their lives. In consequence, I have received a number of invitations to speak at scientific meetings, in museums, and on campuses, not only in the United States but at Fudan University in China. Moreover, despite the efforts of Weinberg and Dawkins to ridicule it, the science and religion dialogue is stronger than ever, with numerous conferences going on literally around the world every year, and with major organizations devoted to the exploration of the harmonious interaction of science and religion (e.g., ESSAT, the European Society for Science and Theology; IRAS, Institute for Religion in the Age of Science; the Metanexus Institute for Religion and Science). Moreover, a number of prominent scientists have recently published books expressing their Christian faith in relation to their science (e.g., Godfrey and Smith,

2005; Gingerich, 2006; Collins, 2006; Roughgarden, 2006). Distinguished philosopher and historian of science Michael Ruse (2000) enquired "Can a Christian be a Darwinian?" His answer was a resounding "yes," as the authors cited above all attest. Theologian John Haught (1998) has described evolution as "Darwin's gift to theology," a refrain taken up by Ayala (2007), whose masterful book is entitled *Darwin's Gift to Science and Religion*.

I will add my few words as a theistic evolutionist to advocate what physicist-theologian John Polkinghorne (1994) terms "a broader view of reality." That a scientist can accept evolution and believe in God is a much-misunderstood position, but one with a long tradition. Cornell University evolutionary biologist William Provine has labeled such a position "hypocrisy," although when I pressed him, he magnanimously allowed that I may not actually be a hypocrite, "merely blinded by powerful cultural traditions." The position that Peter Dodson is blind but that Will Provine sees clearly may lack some of the objectivity that science requires for its operation.

Religious belief is not the enemy of science, or vice versa. In fact, it has been observed more than once that the Judeo-Christian view of the cosmos that prevailed in Western Europe during past centuries was the correct view to permit science to develop and flourish. Greco-Roman pantheism that saw gods behind every rock and tree did not work; the view that God was apart from nature was fruitful. Aristotle's view of eternal unchanging essences, and worse yet, Plato's view of true reality as incorporeal essences barely flickering on the wall of a cave, were philosophies that did not permit natural science to prosper.

As Stanley Jaki (1978) phrased it so memorably, in these cultures, yes, science was born, but it was a stillbirth! Similarly, the Chinese view that respect of elders is a superior virtue to respect of truth could not allow science to flower. In the thirteenth century, Thomas Aquinas baptized Aristotle, eschewing Augustine's neo-Platonism that focused on treasures eternal to the neglect of the things of this Earth. Christians were invited to take God's creation seriously. Thus was added to the Book of Revelation the Book of Nature, two ways of knowing God. Many of the great scientists who pioneered the development of science, Kepler, Copernicus, Newton, Linnaeus, and William Buckland, to name but a few, regarded their activities as studying the Creator through his works. The notion that the world could be viewed independently of God is a product of the so-called Enlightenment.

Theologian Jack Haught (1995), in his masterful book *Science and Religion - From Conflict to Conversation*, characterizes the relationship between science and religion as taking one of four postures: conflict, contrast, contact, or confirmation.

(1)   *Conflict* is a primitive form of the relationship between science and religion, as in the model of two snakes eating each other's tails, neither granting the other the right to exist. Scientists have predicted the disappearance of religion since the Enlightenment. As E. O. Wilson (1978) admits in his book, *On Human Nature*, this isn't going to happen. Indeed, Larson and Witham (1997) recently published in *Nature* a survey revealing that about 40 percent of scientists believe in a personal God, a number essentially unchanged since early in this century! The extreme "scientific" position of *non-tolerance* is termed *materialism* or *scientific naturalism*. This is a philosophical position in no way intrinsic to science that entails the *a priori* belief that science is the *only* path to knowledge. William Provine, Daniel Dennett, and Richard Dawkins all espouse this view in their writings. For example, Dennett, in his compelling book, *Darwin's Dangerous Idea*, describes Darwinism as "universal acid" which destroys all non-materialistic belief systems. The religious counterpart of non-tolerance is scientific creationism, an outgrowth of the fundamentalist belief in biblical literalism, a view

discredited by liberal Christians since the fifth century, when Augustine observed that the purpose of the Bible is to teach us how to go to heaven, not how the heavens go.

(2)   A second level of relationship between science and religion is the *contrast position*, seemingly espoused by Gould. This is the position that science and religion operate in completely non-overlapping spheres. This permits each to hold sway in its own domain, but also denies the possibility of any dialogue between them. I for one find this position too restrictive. This way leads to an all-too-painful schizophrenia. I require more integration in my life. I refuse to leave my brain at the back of the church!

(3)   A *contact* or *dialogue* position seeks to recognize the fundamental harmony between science and religion. A religion that battles science is too thin for me. As Polkinghorne (1994) says, "A scientist expects a fundamental theory to be tough, surprising and exciting," no less in religion than in science. My science informs my view of God. The order and regularity I see and study in nature are reflections of the nature of God. My God is not a trickster or a magician. My God is also a God who grants freedom to His creation. Natural objects realize their natures, even when this means that the Earth quakes and volcanoes spew lava, winds turn violent and raging waters overwhelm unlucky humans. God grants the same freedom to people, who freely choose good or evil. Haught observes that natural selection may be no more problematic than gravitation with respect to the existence of God. And I would add that the existence of dinosaurs doesn't detract from God, or creation, but rather just the opposite, it enhances the history of this planet and expands the dimension of human fascination and pleasure.

The metaphor of the second law of thermodynamics, the law of entropy, has transferred to human culture to a remarkable degree. Jacques Monod and Steven Weinberg are among those who have preached cosmic pessimism. The universe is going to come to an end in 15 billion years, either in an agonizing ball of fire or in unending cold and dark, so human existence is pointless, a tragic farce. But 15 billion years is a timescale that is utterly irrelevant for human affairs. Moreover, our supposed understanding of the second law of thermodynamics accords poorly with our experience of the universe. Far from running downhill, the universe is an unimaginably creative, happening place! Only two elements, hydrogen and helium, were present at the Creation; today there are 111 elements and counting. Life did not create complex organic molecules; life is an (inevitable?) consequence of the upward spiral of ontological complexity of which organic evolution is but a manifestation. Matter experimenting with novelty is a trend that life did not invent but merely jumped astride, as Haught so aptly expressed it. Do these facts not suggest that the second law of thermodynamics is an inappropriate metaphor for culture? Haught instead asks, "Why is the Universe so intolerant of monotony?"

(4)   The highest stage of relationship between science and religion is a vision that *integrates both endeavors.* One such view is that a universe created by God must be an evolutionary one. God's providential love for us is infinite, and by definition this cannot be poured out in an instant but is necessarily ongoing and open-ended. Creation is not finished: stars are exploding, comets are impacting, new elements are being created, life is evolving, species are multiplying.

I have great respect for science. It is one of the most important and satisfying activities of my life, but it is only part of my life. I respect the limits of science. When at last physicists achieve their Holy Grail, their Theory of Everything (ToE), I fear that with their few equations they will have explained almost nothing because they will have touched little that is most human of all. How can a few numbers explain the richness of human experience; Shakespeare, the Bible, the Mona Lisa, Brahms' *Requiem*, or the resurrection of Christ? As powerful as science is in its proper domain, it is woefully incomplete as a prescription for human affairs. Science does not tell me how I should lead my life and what I should do for my neighbor.

Science Informs Faith

I am glad for the existence of dinosaurs. I am a connoisseur of these magnificent beasts; I have been as long as I can remember. It has been a great privilege to devote my professional life to the study of these creatures, and I have realized my goal of writing my own dinosaur book, *The Horned Dinosaurs*, on which I have worked off and on since I was a graduate student nearly forty years ago. They are among the most interesting of dinosaurs – surely grist for a good book. Their bones are the primary documents of my science. Indeed, paleontologists are scientists who love bones. We find them aesthetically appealing, complex, interesting, even sensuous objects. Certainly artist Georgia O'Keeffe found them so.

As a scientist, I take up many questions in my book relating to the genesis, life, and demise of dinosaurs. My study of issues relating to these questions in no way challenges my belief in God. Rather, pursuing the data and "tracks" they have left enhances my belief in God, as when I entertain the idea that His creative fiat brought them into existence as an enhancement to His Creation, and as a revelation of His expansive love.

One of those questions centers on what led to the extinction of dinosaurs? Near the end of my book, I take up the matter, "And then there were none." Now extinction was once a serious theological problem. It was once believed that extinction was theologically impossible, because it would seem to imply the imperfection of Creation, and thus the imperfection of the Creator. Several centuries of exploration of the Earth have made it clear that not only are dinosaurs extinct, so are 99 percent of the organisms that have ever lived on Earth. It is necessary for theology to take this fact into account. The Earth is round, the Earth revolves around the Sun, and extinction must be part of the divine plan. The fossil record demonstrates that evolution is the process by which God creates, and extinction is an intrinsic part of Creation. Had dinosaurs not become extinct, the Earth would not have become hospitable for human beings.

Ceratopsians (they were rhinoceros-like animals, see Figure 17.1) were among the last dinosaurs on Earth. If the reign of the dinosaurs eroded in a blazing catastrophe, Triceratops (see Figure 17.2), may have witnessed it. Let us examined this statement a little more closely. The span of the dinosaurs exceeded 163 million years. The oldest dinosaur currently known dates from rocks in Argentina dated at 228 Ma (million years ago). The last dinosaur skeletons come from Late Cretaceous rocks formed early in the age of mammals, most plausibly derived as sedimentary particles by erosion of soft sediments of Cretaceous age. The last geological division of Cretaceous time is called the Maastrichtian stage. As it lasted six million years or so, it represents too much time to document dinosaur extinction directly. The Edmontonian fauna of Alberta recorded in the Horseshoe Canyon, Wapiti, and St. Mary River formations are early Maastrichtian in age, roughly 70 Ma. The last dinosaurs on Earth are those of the late Maastrichtian, particularly well documented in the Hell Creek Formation of Montana and the Dakotas, but also seen in the Lance Formation of Wyoming, the Scollard of Alberta,

Figure 17.1 Head of *Triceratops*. From Peter Dodson (1996) p. 24. Illustration by Robert Walters.

Figure 17.2 *Triceratops* in full display. From Peter Dodson (1996), p. 270. Illustration by Robert Walters.

the Frenchman in Saskatchewan, and the Laramie of Colorado. The Lancian dinosaurs, dating from 68–65 Ma, are the dinosaurs that witnessed extinction. There were two common Lancian dinosaurs. *Triceratops* is far and away the most abundant, and *Edmontosaurus* is a distant second. *Leptoceratops* and *Torosaurus* are rather rare ceratopsian members of the fauna; *Ankylosaurus*, *Pachycephalosaurus*, and *Thescelosaurus* are also noteworthy.

The great question of dinosaur extinction is whether they disappeared with a whimper or with a bang. This question is much debated. The "bang" scenario is high profile and has been very popular ever since it was articulated by Nobel Prize-winning physicist Luis Alvarez, his geologist son Walter, and their colleagues Frank Asaro and Helen Michel in 1980. They observed the physical evidence of enrichment in the heavy metal element iridium of Cretaceous/Tertiary (K/T) boundary sediments at many locations around the world. In the same sediments they found grains of shocked quartz (in which the crystal structure is disrupted by fracture planes that only occur at extremely high pressures). From these observations they devised a scenario that involves the impact of a large asteroid, some 10 km or more in diameter, at the very end of the Cretaceous. The impact would have raised great clouds of dust that circled the globe, causing complete darkness for weeks or months, blocking out sunlight, and causing plants to die and animals to starve to death. Additionally there were freezing temperatures, storms, acid rain, global wildfires – the *horsemen of the apocalypse* were abroad, and dinosaurs could not withstand their wrath! Lest there be any doubt about all this, a 200-km-wide crater named Chicxulub is reported from Yucatan, where it is buried deep beneath the surface of the jungle (Dodson (1996), p. 280, n. 27). With such a gruesome scenario, who could doubt that dinosaurs became extinct like this? Well, I doubt it! The problem I have is that this grim scenario explains too much, not too little. Although many species on land, in the air, and in the seas became extinct during the Maastrichtian, it is less apparent to me that this distinction was all that sudden. Many extinctions in the seas (of ammonites, inoceramid and rudistid clams) demonstrably began at least 6 million years before the final extinction at the boundary, and on land there was a pattern of massive survival: of mammals, crocodiles, turtles, lizards, frogs, salamanders, fishes. Plant communities, especially those documented in North Dakota and Montana, suffered disturbances but seemingly not massive extinctions.

And what of the dinosaurs? There too I see a pattern of dwindling. Ten million years before the end, there were two subfamilies of ceratopsids, the centrosaurines and the chasmosaurines. At the end, only the chasmosaurines were left. Ten million years before the end, there were two subfamilies of hadrosaurs, the crested lambeosaurines and the flat-headed hadrosaurines. At the end, only the hadrosaurines were left. Ten million years before the end, there were two families of armored dinosaurs, the ankylosaurids and the nodosaurids. At the end, only the ankylosaurids were left. By comparison with the fauna of the Judith River Formation of Alberta, the dinosaur fauna of Hell Creek Formation is boring, completely dominated by a single kind of dinosaur: *Triceratops*.

I do not know the cause of dinosaur extinction. I suspect it was due to a symphony of causes, no one of which was unique or totally explanatory. Among them were changing sea levels, increasingly seasonal climate, volcanism, mountain building – the usual physical culprits. Indeed, dinosaurs may have witnessed an asteroid impact that gave them the final nudge into oblivion. But my position is very clear: they were already failing. The impact was at best only the last straw.

Ceratopsian dinosaurs were magnificent animals by any standard. The small ones are found in North America and Asia; the large ones are unique North American treasures. They were not paragons of intelligence, but little stood in the way of their success. No animals on Earth have ever had larger skulls, nor more interestingly appointed ones. They were colorful, noisy, gregarious, belligerent, feisty, lovable creatures. They were the last major group of dinosaurs to appear on Earth, and one of the last to witness the calamity that erased the last dinosaurs from the face of the Earth. How keenly I regret their passing. Why did it have to end this way?

Concluding Thoughts

All of the above is part of a serious examination of issues relating to both science and faith that I have engaged in for nearly forty years. During that time of study, I have found little if anything to support or necessitate the warlike antagonism between science and religion pictured by Dawkins and like-minded scientists, who are animated by motives other than pure, disinterested science. Rather, my lifetime of study has made me awed by the power and providence of the God who must have loved these creatures more than I ever dreamed possible. Moreover, it is the stretch of history, and an expanse of a group of organisms that fascinates the human mind and attracts us even more to the Agent who brought them about for our study, amazement, and enjoyment. Is there anything in Creation that attracts kids and adults to museums more than the magnificent dinosaurs?

As a religious scientist, I have a particular perspective on the evolutionary process. What then of dinosaurs? In a word, dinosaurs were the jewels of God's creation. By no means failures, they graced the planet for 160 million years. Like all of His Creation, they gave Him praise. God loved dinosaurs.

References

Ayala, F. J. (2007) *Darwin's Gift to Science and Religion*. Washington, DC: Joseph Henry Press.

Collins, F. S. (2006) *The Language of God: A Scientist Presents Evidence for Belief*. New York: Free Press.

Dawkins, Richard, *The God Delusion*. Boston, MA: Houghton Mifflin, 2006.

Dodson, P. (1996) *The Horned Dinosaurs - A Natural History*. Princeton, NJ: Princeton University Press.

Dodson, P. (1997) God and the dinosaurs. *American Paleontologist* 5 (2), 6–8.

Gingerich, O. (2006) *God's Universe*. Cambridge, MA: Belknap Press.

Godfrey, S. J. and Smith, C. R. (2005) *Paradigms on Pilgrimage – Creationism, Paleontology, and Biblical Interpretation*. Toronto: Clements.

Gould, S. J. (1999) *Rocks of Ages – Science and Religion in the Fullness of Life*. Library of Contemporary Thought, New York: Ballantine.

Haught, J. F. (1995) *Science and Religion – from Conflict to Conversation*. Mahwah, NJ: Paulist Press.

Haught, J. F. (1998) Darwin's gift to theology. In R. J. Russell, W. R. Stoeger, and F. J. Ayala (eds.) *Evolutionary Biology and Molecular Biology: Scientific Perspective on Divine Action*, pp. 393–418. Notre Dame, IN: University of Notre Dame Press.

Jaki, S. (1978) *The Road of Science and the Ways to God*. Chicago: University of Chicago Press.

Larson, E. J. (1997) and Witham, L. Scientists are still keeping the faith. *Nature* 386, 435–6.

Polkinghorne, J. (1994) *Faith of a Physicist*. Princeton, NJ: Princeton University Press.

Roughgarden, J. (2006) *Evolution and Christian Faith – Reflections of an Evolutionary Biologist*. Washington, DC: Island Press.

Ruse, M. (2000) *Can a Darwinian be a Christian? : The Relationship between Science and Religion*. Cambridge, MA: Harvard University Press.

Wang, S. C. and Dodson, P. Estimating the diversity of dinosaurs. *Proceedings of the National Academy of Sciences* 103 (2006), 13601–5.

Weishampel, P. Dodson and H. Osmólska (eds) (1990; 2nd edn., 2004) *The Dinosauria*. (Berkeley: University of California Press).

Wilson, E. O. (1978) *On Human Nature*. Cambridge, MA: Harvard University Press.

Wilson, E. O. (2007) *The Creation, An Appeal to Save Life on Earth*. New York: W. W. Norton.

18

Science and Religion
in the Public Square

PETER DODSON

In the following, I argue that religion (Judaism and Christianity) is not anti-science. In fact, throughout the history of science from the seventeenth century onward, scientists were motivated by the desire to understand God's creation. And enlightened religious thinking today goes a long way towards bridging the supposed gap between science and religion by accommodating evolutionary thought within a wider view of reality than that provided by reductionist science. Various Christian groups appear to have rejected the findings of modern science, which has resulted in many among the unbelieving worldviewing all Christians as anti-evolution. I contend that nothing could be further from the case. I want to suggest that each side pursue a clearer understanding of the contrasting approach to reality – the naturalistic scientific community needs to understand the religious, and the religious needs to appreciate the findings of science. While the public square must allow for contrasting worldviews, that of the atheist and the contrasting theist, I argue that the central claims of the Christian faith need not be viewed as in conflict with evolution, and many other hypotheses advanced in the sciences.

It is a truism that we live in a scientific culture. Modern science, medicine, and technology have brought about countless miracles (literally, "wonderful things") that we all too easily take for granted. The human genome has been decoded; the death rate from cancer is beginning to drop even though the population is rising; a diagnosis of AIDS is no longer regarded as a death sentence, at least in the West. Electronic communications allow nearly instant connectivity around the globe; the click of a few keys can result in an avalanche of information within mere microseconds. For example, entering the term "sex" in a well-known web-browser results in 29,400,000 hits in .06 seconds! "God" results in a staggering 402 million hits in 0.08 seconds. Computers deliver more and more speed, computational power and storage at smaller and smaller size and less cost. Although science has unquestionably contributed greatly to human well-being, it is by no means without its dark side – nuclear technology that cures disease has also immolated thousands of innocent civilians; medical technology that heals is also used to prolong lives in ghoulish, ventilator-dependent states; fossil fuel combustion that contributes to human prosperity and freedom of movement now threatens the very existence of civilization in the near future due to global warming.

Science touches the lives of nearly everyone on the planet today. So successful is the scientific enterprise that some scientists are inclined to overreach the legitimate boundaries of science and make philosophical claims for science that cannot possibly be justified. It is one thing to acknowledge that science is a powerful tool for unlocking the secrets of nature, for who can deny this? It is quite another to claim that science is the *only* valid source of knowledge. This view, which has been characterized as philosophical naturalism, has been espoused with vigor by such authors such as Oxford University evolutionary biologist Richard Dawkins (1986, 2006, and others), Tufts University philosopher Daniel C. Dennett (1995, 2006), the late Cornell University astronomer Carl Sagan (1996), and many others. Cornell University evolutionary biologist and historian of science Will Provine (1988) is blunt and to the point. According to him, modern evolutionary biology demonstrates that there is no God, no soul, no life after death, and even no free will. He charges that religiously oriented scientists are effectively atheists, or believe things that are demonstrably unscientific or assert the existence of entities or processes for which not a shred of evidence exists. Such scientists are alleged to be intellectually dishonest, subject to wishful thinking, and blinded by religious training or other powerful cultural traditions. A religious scientist must check his brains at the church house door.

The social climate of science has come a long way since Charles Darwin published *On the Origin of Species* in 1859. Darwin concluded that masterful work with these words:

> There is grandeur in this view of life, with its several powers, having been originally breathed by the Creator into a few forms or into one; and that, whilst this planet has gone cycling on according to the fixed law of gravity, from so simple a beginning endless forms most beautiful and most wonderful have been, and are being, evolved.

These are not the words of an atheist, and in his autobiography Darwin stated "In my most extreme fluctuations I have never been an Atheist in the sense of denying the existence of a God" (Francis Darwin, 1887, p. 304). In 1879, his secretary, writing for Darwin to a German student, wrote, "He considers that the theory of Evolution is quite compatible with the belief in a God; but that you must remember that different persons have different definitions of what they mean by God" (F. Darwin, 1887, p. 307). Cosans (2005) makes the remarkable case that Richard Owen, Darwin's contemporary antagonist, considered Darwin too much of a creationist, because he believed in only one or a very few episodes of origin of life, whereas Owen himself believed that life originated continually wherever physicochemical conditions permitted, and that single-celled life forms observable today were merely recently evolved stages in the ongoing transformation of life. Evolution does not disprove the existence of God and does not necessitate atheism. Georgetown University theologian John F. Haught (2000, 2003; see also Ayala, 2007) has actually made the case that evolution is Darwin's gift to theology, a view we shall consider below.

Modern science grew up and matured in Western Europe during the Renaissance, although contributions from Greek geometry and Arabic algebra and astronomy, among others, may be freely acknowledged. With few exceptions until the Enlightenment, scientists or, more properly, natural philosophers (the term "scientist" was coined by Whewell in 1833), were religiously motivated, and often were ordained men of God, a circumstance that prevailed well into the nineteenth century. Isaac Newton considered himself a theologian much more than a scientist and his writings in theology were far more extensive than his writings as a scientist. Well into the twentieth century, prominent evolutionary biologists remained explicitly and devoutly Christian, including two giants of the new evolutionary ("neo-Darwinian") synthesis, R. A. Fisher (1890–1962) and Theodosius Dobzhansky (1900–75. Contemporary evolutionary biologists and paleontologists who have explicitly referred to their Christian faith include Kenneth Miller (1999), Simon Conway-Morris (2003), Stephen Godfrey (2005), Daryl Domning (2006), Francis Collins (2006), and Joan Roughgarden (2006. Of course I number myself among this host (Dodson 1997, 1999, 2005, 2006).

Despite the plethora of scientists willing to come forth and expound on their atheist views, it turns out that religious views are actually common among scientists in the United States (Larson and Witham, 1997), with no evidence of a decline in numbers during the twentieth century. Even among scientists who are not religious believers, it is acknowledged that religious beliefs are intrinsic to what it means to be a human. E. O. Wilson (1978) describes religious belief as the most powerful and complex force in all of human nature, and believes it to be ineradicable. Religious belief may have some degree of evolutionary explanation in terms of survivorship benefits of belonging to cohesive social units (e.g., Wilson, 1998). The suggestion is even made that our brains are hard-wired for religious belief. For example, Andrew Newberg, MD, and associates have studied Tibetan monks and Franciscan nuns during meditation and have discovered areas of the brain that are active (frontal lobe) and areas that are physiologically quiet (parietal lobe) (Newberg et al., 2001). It should not be a great surprise that religious experiences are processed in the brain rather than in the elbow or the big toe! An evolutionary explanation for the origin of religion neither supports nor negates the question of the existence of God.

Judaism and Christianity are in no way anti-science. Because modern science originated in a particular time in a specific place, namely in Western Europe during the Renaissance, we are entitled to ask what it is about that culture as opposed to that of Ancient Greece, Rome, Egypt, India, or China that permitted science to flourish. A case can be made that the prevailing philosophies of those societies did not provide suitable substrates for science to develop. Plato believed that the senses provide unreliable information about reality, and that true reality belongs to higher realm; the world encountered by the senses represents mere shadows of eternal unchanging forms. Evolutionary thought was unlikely to develop in the world of Plato and Aristotle. Similarly, pantheism that sees gods in every rock, flower, tree, river, sea, star, sun and moon discourages de-constructive investigation for fear of angering the deity. The radical monotheism of Judaeo-Christianity sees Creation (the natural world) as separate from the Creator God. The Judaeo-Christian God is a God of lawful order, not of chaos. Science could not develop in a cosmos of chaos. History and historical science also benefit from the Judaeo-Christian concept of linear time (Adam's fall in the past, the coming of the Messiah in the future) unlike the cycles of time that characterize Hinduism and Buddhism (Gould, 1987; Rudwick, 2005). The rationality of the universe reflects the rationality of God; Christian theology has always emphasized rationality. Two of the giants of Christianity, Augustine of Hippo (AD 354–430) and Thomas Aquinas (AD 1225–74) are two of the most rational humans who have ever lived. Augustine is associated with philosophy of Plato, but most especially the neo-Platonism of the Roman Plotinus (Augustine did not read Greek). Aristotle's work did not survive in the West, but was preserved by Islam until finally translated into Latin in the thirteenth century. Augustine was notably liberal in his interpretation of Scripture, and taught that "the purpose of the Bible is to tell us how to go to heaven, not how the heavens go." He provided the following principles:

> First, because God is the author of the Bible and also the creator of the natural world, there can be no contradiction between the interpretation of the Bible and established scientific knowledge. From this it follows that if there appears to be some disagreement, it must be due to a misunderstanding or to inadequate knowledge. St. Augustine was quite clear that if a truth about the natural world was definitely established, then the Bible could not be interpreted in a way that contradicts that truth. (Hodgson, 2005)

Aquinas was heavily influenced by Aristotle, and in a sense "Christianized" him. Thomas saw God working through secondary causes, the laws of nature, to create a world with its own ordering and processes. Galileo (1564–1642) was heavily influenced by Augustine and Aquinas, and spoke of God's two books, the Book of Revelation (the Bible) and the Book of Nature; both books had God as their author, so they could not contradict one another.

Throughout the history of science from the seventeenth century onward, men of science had been motivated by the desire to understand God's creation. The idea of an inherent conflict between science and religion is at best a crude caricature ("little more than Victorian propaganda" according to Orr, 2004), and at worst an outright fraud promulgated by books with lurid titles such as *History of the Conflict Between Science and Religion* by John William Draper (1874) and *The Warfare of Science with Theology Within Christendom* (1896) by Andrew Dickson White, the first president of Cornell University. These benighted authors, for example, wrote that Christians believed that the Earth is flat long past all reason, which is not remotely true. No serious historian of science accepts the thesis that science and religion are irretrievably at odds with each other (e.g., Lindberg and Numbers, 1986; Brooke, 1991; Grant, 1996). Even Thomas Henry Huxley, Darwin's pugnacious defender who reputedly battled Bishop Wilberforce over Darwin's concept of evolution, showed signs of mellowing in his later years. In 1887 Huxley praised three sermons by important bishops as indicating "the possibility of bringing about an honorable *modus vivendi* between science and theology" (McGrath, 2005). Also, as a member of the Royal Commission on Public Education, he insisted on the teaching of the Bible as an integral part of British culture (Dyson, 2006). The social context of the struggle in Victorian England between science and religion in the latter half of the nineteenth century was the professionalization of science and the loosening of the grip of established religion on the public institutions in which a professional science was emerging (McGrath, 2005). In a sense scientists have always been opposed to authoritative power structures, whether they be religious as in previous eras or political as today (Dyson, 1995). The supposed conflict between science and religion is not intrinsic to a Judaeo-Christian understanding of either God or nature but may be merely a diverting bit of Victorian history (Orr, 2007) that makes little sense today except perhaps in limited locations where the methods and conclusions of modern science are not welcomed.

Enlightened religious thinking today goes a long way towards bridging the supposed gap between religion and science by accommodating evolutionary thought within a wider view of reality than that provided by reductionist science. As we have seen, Georgetown University theologian John F. Haught (1998) describes evolution as "Darwin's gift to theology," an insight also reflected in the title of a book by University of California-Irvine evolutionary biologist and National Academy of Science member Francisco Ayala (2007): *Darwin's Gift to Science and Religion.* In a series of books, Haught (1995, 2000, 2003, 2006) points to the unfinished nature of Creation. Genesis 1: 31 records the thought that God's work is "very good" but not perfect. God's infinite love continues to transform Creation, which evolves under the action of Divine love. He believes that God gives "inexhaustible depth to Creation" that cannot be plumbed comprehensively either by modern science or by literal reading of the Bible. Both scientific naturalism and Biblical literalism are the result of superficial readings of nature and Scripture, respectively.

If the human mind is only the result of evolution, how can it discover Truth? This is a problem that disturbed Darwin:

> The horrid doubt always arises whether the convictions of man's mind, which has been developed from the mind of the lower animals, are of any value or are at all trustworthy. Would anybody trust the convictions of a monkey's mind, if there are any convictions at all?" (Darwin, 1887, p. 316)

This is a problem that has by no means disappeared today. For example, David Sloan Wilson wrote: "Rationality is not the gold standard against which all other forms of thought are to be judged. Adaptation is the gold standard by which rationality is to be judged" (Wilson, 2002, p. 228). Philosopher Richard Rorty (1995) writes: "The idea that one species of organism is, unlike all others, oriented not only towards its own increased prosperity, but towards Truth, is as un-Darwinian as the idea that every human being has its own built-in moral compass." These quotes suggest a rather startling limit to the ability of science to deliver Truth, the desire for which, as Haught (2006) notes, is one of the defining characters of human nature. We can never be satisfied with mere illusion.

Science is an immensely valuable and productive enterprise, but it works precisely because it is limited, encompassing physical reality, which is the "easy" part of reality. Objects that can be weighed, measured, and timed are the proper domain of science. The objectivity of science and irrelevance of the observer make science relatively impervious to the biases of language, culture, and nationality, and this is both strength and a weakness. As Polkinghorne (1994) observed, we cannot live in the lunar landscape of reductionism. A science that leaves humans and human experience out of its purview cannot pretend to provide the only knowledge worth knowing. Like a bird soaring to the skies, the human mind reflexively soars beyond the limits of science.

Christianity in the Public Square

Most religious people in the United States, be they Christians, Jews, Muslims, Hindus, Buddhists, or of other faiths, go about their daily lives without ostentation, giving to Caesar what is Caesar's, paying their taxes, voting in elections, educating their children, working at their jobs, buying their daily bread, and so on. People generally do not wear their religions on their sleeves. Several events have recently brought religion into the public square. The terrorist attacks on the United States on September 11, 2001 have suddenly elevated Islam into high profile and have subjected it to intense public scrutiny. Although the overwhelming majority of Muslims around the globe are gentle, peace-loving people, it is also true that some of the most appalling violence around the world today is committed by Islamic fundamentalists, who seem particularly fond of slaughtering infidels and coreligionists alike by means of suicide bombs.

   In the United States Christian fundamentalists rarely if ever are moved to violence. We understand fundamentalists to be those Protestant Christians who believe in the literal truth of the Bible, and who tend to reject extra-Biblical sources of knowledge. Because fundamentalists accept a literal account of Creation, especially as expressed in Genesis chapters 1 and 2, they believe the Earth to be roughly six thousand years old, and accordingly reject evolution as well as the sciences in support of it. Moreover, evolution is thought to be a philosophy that has contributed to the moral decline of society (Ruse, 2005). Although evolution rightly occupies its place in school science curricula, for several decades fundamentalists have attempted either to outlaw the teaching of evolution in schools or substitute "creation science" courses. Generally these attempts have been unsuccessful, and have been rejected by decisions in federal court, including those challenging laws in Arkansas in 1981 and Louisiana in 1987, on the grounds that such courses favored the teachings of specific sectarian religions. The latest attempt is the so-called intelligent design (ID) movement that argues on the basis of "irreducible complexity" that because some structures are believed to be too complex to have evolved incrementally, such structures must therefore have been designed by an unspecified designer or Designer. The names most closely associated with the ID movement are Lehigh University biochemist Michael Behe (1996, 2007), mathematician and philosopher William Dembski (1998), and University of California lawyer and anti-Darwinian polemicist Phillip E. Johnson (1993, 1997, 2002). The recent attempt to insert ID into the science curriculum in Dover, PA was decisively defeated in federal court by Judge John Jones (Slack, 2007). The constant battles to keep sectarian creationist accounts out of the science classroom require constant vigilance by the scientific community, which are often spearheaded by the National Center for Science Education, and its tireless executive director, Eugenie Scott (2004).

   Because certain Christian groups have apparently rejected the findings of modern science, there is a tendency among non-believers in general and the press in particular to regard all Christians as anti-evolution. Nothing could be farther from the case, as the references above must indicate compellingly. No less an authority than Pope John Paul II (1996) described evolution as "more than a theory." Biblical literalism as opposed to Christian belief presents certain difficulties. Augustine complained about the scandal to the Christian faith caused by the faithful ignorant of the fundamental facts of the natural world when confronting knowledgeable infidels. The Bible cannot be regarded as scientifically authoritative, nor was that ever its intention (Hyers, 1984). For example, the Bible lists the names of about 130 kinds of plants and 200 kinds of animals according to the *Catholic Encyclopedia*. The 50 birds mentioned (Grigg, 1996) are only a tiny fraction of the 9600 species in the world today. The 130 species of plants mentioned in the Bible constitute barely 4 percent of the three thousand plants in the Holy Land today. The Bible barely mentions the rich invertebrate and vertebrate life of the seas, the crucially important realm of the microscopic, the biota of the unexplored New World, the unique diversity of the tropics or the depauperate biota of the boreal realms. The Bible is not a credible treatise of chemistry or of meteorology or of any other science for that matter. It is necessary to believe that God intended for humans to use the divine gift of intellect to explore and understand the world, thereby giving praise to its Creator. Why the study of evolution, unique among the sciences, should be exempt from the divine mandate to explore the world is far from obvious.

   Those who chose to live in a world whose age is measured at six thousand years have a narrowed chronological perspective to be sure. The newly opened Creation Museum in Petersburg, Kentucky, incorporates dinosaurs and all other prehistoric life into that compressed timeframe. Many opinion polls demonstrate widespread acceptance of Creationists beliefs in the United States. A USA Today/Gallup poll taken on June 1–3, 2007 listed 18 percent of the population as accepting evolution as "probably true" and 28 percent rejecting evolution as "probably false." This poll is perhaps unusual inasmuch as the sum of those accepting evolution as true or probably true is 53 percent, while those rejecting evolution as false or probably false is 44 percent. Inconsistently, the same poll reported that 56 percent thought that Creationism was true or probably true, while 31 percent thought it was false or probably false. More typically, the *Newsweek* poll taken March 28–29, 2007 reported that only 13 percent of people believe that God played no part in the evolutionary process, 30 percent believe God guided the process, and 48 percent believe that "God created humans pretty much in the present form at one time within the last 10,000 years or so." The question may legitimately be raised as to how important it is to *believe* in evolution? Is it important for the butcher, the baker, the plumber, the lawyer, the judge, the policeman, the banker, the car salesman, the store clerk? Probably not. If I don't want the plumber to fall on his knees and pray when I have water rushing across the kitchen floor, I also don't want him discussing the adaptive superiority of one pipe wrench over another! Evolution may also not be important for the engineer who builds bridges, or the architect who designs sky-scrapers, the philosopher or the professor of comparative literature. How does physics look without evolution? Pretty good, I would think. In fact, one can be a physiologist or a cellular biologist or any other biologist without *believing* in evolution, although the tension of maintaining the posture of rejecting the prevailing paradigm, expressed in the memorable words of Dobzhansky (1973), "Nothing in biology makes sense except in the light of evolu-tion," must be considerable. What is necessary is not to *believe* in evolution but to *under-stand* it. Citizenship in modern society requires that all people have some degree of understanding of science. We all benefit from the works of science, technology, and medi-cine, and we all need to have some degree of understanding of them, and we need to be able to distinguish the difference between good science, bad science, and false science.

There is no excuse for ignorance of science. There is a reciprocal burden on scientists, and that is the burden of understanding religion. There is no excuse in the United States for ignorance of the Bible. Huxley recognized well over a century ago that a British citizen could not be educated, could not possibly understand the canon of Western literature, art, or music and be ignorant of the Bible (Dyson, 2006). The same remains true today. We certainly have a broader burden today. We also most urgently need to understand Islam. One cannot hope to understand Creationists and to evaluate their arguments without some knowledge of the Bible. Darwin read his Bible on board the HMS *Beagle* on his epochal voyage around the world. Evolutionary biologist E. O. Wilson (1994) read the Bible twice before entering college and losing his religious faith. Nobody quoted Scripture more fre-quently in his voluminous writings than evolutionist Stephen Jay Gould. Gould (1999) the agnostic is famous for his view that science and religion are both necessary for the fullness of human life. Reading the Bible is not harmful to the health of a scientist, and may be help-ful in numerous ways. For example, one may respond to a claim of "The Biblical account of Creation" armed with the knowledge that there is no single account of Creation. The Bible abounds with accounts of Creation. Genesis 1 and Genesis 2 contain separate and by no means identical accounts. One might also note Creation accounts in Psalm 33, Psalm 104, Job chapters 38–41, Proverbs 8, Isaiah 40, John 1, Colossians, and elsewhere. There simply is no unitary account of Creation in the Bible, although the role of God as Creator is empha-sized throughout. The scientist may find passages throughout the Bible that encourage the belief that using the human intellect to understand the world is sanctioned. Psalm 33:4 tells us "The works of the Lord are trustworthy." Complementing this is Romans 1:20, which proclaims "We know the Creator through the works of Creation." To those who believe Genesis 1 describes a world created in six 24-hour days, 2 Peter 3:8 tells us "A thousand years is as a day to the Lord, and a day is as a thousand years." This verse is foreshadowed by Psalm 90:4: "For a thousand years in your sight are like a day that has just gone by, or like a watch in the night." The message seems clear enough that we should not look to the Bible for a rigorous chronology. I would conclude from these verses that God is not deceitful but trustworthy. God did not create the world with an *appearance* of great antiquity – it appears to be old, 4.6 billion years old in fact – because it *is* old. I also personally conclude that dinosaurs were just as much part of Creation as every living thing today, and that like all the works of the Lord, dinosaurs praised and exalted the Lord above all forever (Daniel 3:57). Indeed, dinosaurs were jewels of Creation, and surely God delighted in them, because they lasted on Earth for 160 million years, a vastly longer span than our own span of 1 or 2 million years (Dodson, 1997).

Atheism in the Public Square

Atheism has an ancient pedigree but throughout history has been a minority view both in the Classical World and in the West (McGrath, 2004). The Enlightenment saw the rise of atheism in Western Europe, but it took Charles Darwin's theory of evolution to make it possible to be an intellectually fulfilled atheist" according to Dawkins (1986). However that may be, the United States continues to be by any measure one of the most religious countries on Earth. Survey results on the frequency of atheism in the U.S. vary, although 5 percent of the population may be a reasonable estimate. A massive American Religious Identification Survey by the City University of New York taken in February – April 2001 recognized 14.1 percent of the American population as agnostics, atheists, humanists, secularists, or having no religious affiliation; 76.5 percent are Christian, 1 percent Jewish and 0.5 percent Muslim. In contrast to the population as a whole, certain subcultures are strongly supportive of atheism, for example Academia (Larson and Witham, 1997) and Journalism (Noyes, 2004). Whereas atheism has typically kept a low profile, today's new atheism has an evangelical fervor, expressed in a spate of virulently anti-religious books with lurid titles, including *The End of Faith: Religion, Terror and the Future of Reason* (Harris, 2004); *Letters to a Christian Nation* (Harris, 2006); *A Devil's Chaplain. Reflections on Hope, Lies, Science, and Love* (Dawkins, 2003); *The God Delusion* (Dawkins, 2006); *Breaking the Spell: Religion as a Natural Phenomenon* (Dennett (2006); and *god* [sic!] *is Not Great: How Religion Poisons Everything* (Hitchens, 2007). Dawkins is especially quotable:

> It is fashionable to wax apocalyptic about the threat to humanity posed by the AIDS virus, "mad cow" disease, and many others, but I think a case can be made that *faith* is one of the world's great evils, comparable to the smallpox virus but harder to eradicate. (Dawkins, 1997)

And "To describe religions as mind viruses is sometimes interpreted as contemptuous or even hostile. It is both" (Dawkins, 2003. One factor in the current outspokenness of atheists is the aftermath of the Al Qaeda terrorist attack on New York of September 11, 2001, followed by militant Islamic terrorism around the globe, and the ghastly intersectarian strife in Iraq among sects today that includes indiscriminant bombing of women and children. Another factor, at least in the United States, is in reaction to the attempted introduction of anti-evolutionary Intelligent Design instruction into public schools. Atheists have seized on these and other developments to label religion as divisive, destructive, and the fundamental cause of strife in the world. The implication would seem to be that had humans not developed religion, the lion would lie down with the lamb, and all peoples on earth would dwell together in Utopian harmony. Will they next revive Rousseau's *Noble Savage*? The naïveté of such a view seems truly astonishing; one might guess that only an academic could believe such a fantasy! All would be well in Northern Ireland, for example, if the labels Catholic and Protestant suddenly disappeared? Not likely!

Dawkins the evolutionary biologist is a brilliant expositor of evolutionary process, particularly illustrative of the power of natural selection, and his books are highly recommended, especially *The Selfish Gene* (1976); *The Blind Watchmaker* (1986); *River Out of Eden* (1995); and *Climbing Mount Improbable* (1996). This being said, one might note that his original ideas are controversial. Gould (1997) termed Dawkins a "hyperselectionist" and a "Darwinian fundamentalist," the latter charge leveled independently by Haught (2003) and McGrath and McGrath (2007). Gould believed Dawkins' interpretation of Darwin to be simplistic and too reliant on adaptation by natural selection as the sole factor in evolution. Especially controversial are Dawkins' ideas about memes, which he defined in 1976 as a "unit of cultural transmission," by which ideas jump from brain to brain. It is held to be analogous to genes. The concept of memes has not enjoyed a happy scientific reception (e.g., Conway-Morris, 2003; Orr, 2004; McGrath, 2005), as the cultural transmission of ideas from person to person is remarkably imprecise. The existence of memes is notably hard to establish, as McGrath (2005, p. 128) mischievously notes: "Dawkins talking about memes is like believers talking about God – an invisible, unverifiable postulate, which helps explain some things about experience, but ultimately lies beyond empirical investigation." Religion is held to be a powerful meme or a "mind-virus" infecting the minds of the faithful (Dawkins, 2003, 2006; Dennett, 1995, 2006). Remarkably, atheism and evolution are not regarded as memes. Right-thinking persons such as Dawkins and Dennett seem immune to memes, while the rest of us are not. "Are there memes for believing in memes?" asks McGrath.

If there is one thing Dawkins has succeeded in doing, especially in *The Blind Watchmaker*, is undermining the argument for the existence of God from design, especially as articulated by British theologian William Paley (1743–1805). Paley in 1802 wrote a very important work of natural theology entitled "*Natural Theology; Or, Evidences of the Existence and Attributes of the Deity. Collected from the Appearances of Nature.*" In a capsule, Paley argued that the complexity of the elements of nature pointed to a Creator. Darwin, while he was a student at Cambridge, was much impressed with Paley's *Evidences*. He wrote in his autobiography:

> The logic of … his *Natural Theology* gave me as much delight as did Euclid. The careful study of these works, without attempting to learn any part by rote, was the only part of the Academical Course which, as I then felt and as I still believe, was of the least use to me in the education of my mind. I did not at that time trouble myself about Paley's premises; and taking these on trust I was charmed and convinced by the long line of argumentation." (Darwin, 1887, p. 59)

Cast in a pre-Darwinian framework with a Biblical time framework of 6,000 to 10,000 years, Paley's demonstration of the Creator was comprehensible. The developing science of geology in the first half of the nineteenth century delivered to young Darwin a scientific appreciation of the antiquity of the Earth. Charles Lyell (1797–1875) was prepared to think of the age of the Earth measured in hundreds of million of years (Ruse, 1979), although precise numbers did not become available until the latter half of the twentieth century. Within the modern Darwinian paradigm, Dawkins easily demolished Paley's argument, which is nothing if not a straw man. This was not a stunning intellectual feat. McGrath (2004) pointed out that British theologian John Henry Newman rejected Paley's argument on theological grounds in 1852, prior to the publication of *On the Origin of the Species*. Dawkins seems to believe that by slaying Paley he has slain the last remaining argument for the existence of God. He has not.

Dawkins in recent years has appeared obsessed with the concept of God. Having devoted a book to the topic of God, which is unusual, to say the least, for an evolutionary biologist, one would wish that he were prepared to engage religious thought in a serious way. His attitude brings to mind the saying of G.K. Chesterton: "Christianity was not tried and found wanting. It was found difficult and left untried." Dawkins demonstrates not the slightest insight into the mind of a religious believer. The world of religion he describes is not familiar to any normal practitioner. He deals only with vulgar caricatures and excesses (Eagleton, 2006). For him any religious believer is a benighted, muddled-headed dolt trapped in the pokey Middle Ages. There is no room in his worldview for any positive contribution of Christianity to the human condition, from the preservation of Antiquity in the monasteries, to the development of hospitals ("*hôtel dieu*") in the Middle Ages, to the development of modern science, to the freeing of slaves, to the American civil rights movement (he describes the Rev. Martin Luther King, one of the most effective preachers in American history, as a political figure, not a religious one). His world is one of black and white, with nothing in between, and religion is at all times in all places an unmitigated human evil. He dismisses two millennia of rational examination of the Christian faith as not worth knowing.

The single theological question of interest to Dawkins is whether or not God exists. Philosophers have debated this question for millennia to no avail. We can freely concede that no "proof" exists either for or against the existence of God. If there were such proof, then either all believers are stupid or all atheists are stupid. This conclusion can be safely dismissed. As the late Harvard University paleontologist Stephen Jay Gould (1992) put it bluntly, "Either half my colleagues are enormously stupid, or the science of Darwinism is fully compatible with conventional religious beliefs – and equally compatible with atheism." But how can belief persist in the absence of proof? The answer is because in some sense faith is more basic than understanding; indeed, faith is prerequisite for understanding. In the words of St Anselm, "I believe in order to understand" (*credo ut intelligam*). A person without belief of any kind is like a computer without an operating system. Such a person would be an emotional cripple, completely incapable of function, literally insane. A scientist must have certain beliefs about the nature of reality. The scientist must believe that nature is orderly; that the human senses provide reliable information about reality; that our intellects are capable of understanding that reality; that we are able to communicate that understanding to others; and that others have the same understanding as we do. Beliefs are not static, and are tested and modified by encounter with reality, something we call experience. This is true no less of religious beliefs than of scientific beliefs. There is little if anything of importance that can be proven. How do I prove that I am sane? How do I prove I am awake and not asleep, dreaming that I am sitting at my computer and tapping these words? How do I prove that what you see as a red rose is the same color as what I see as a red rose? How do I prove that my wife loves me?

Science is not about proving things either. Science does not deliver absolute truth. "Scientific knowledge is a body of statements of varying degrees of certainty, some of them most unsure, some nearly sure, but none absolutely certain" (Feynman, 1989). Scientific theories are provisional explanations that account for observational data in the best possible way, but which are replaced as new data or new understandings require. Thus the determinate cosmos of Newtonian classical physics gave way to the relativistic cosmos of Einstein, and the quantum cosmos that followed. We cannot say that our present understandings of physics, cosmology, or evolution are complete and final. Who knows how our understanding will have changed a hundred years from now? A prize of $1,000 was offered a few years ago to anyone who could offer "scientific proof-positive" that the Earth is in motion; the prize went uncollected (Gingerich, 1983). We need not doubt that the Earth is in motion, and all predictions that we make on the basis of the assumption of that motion are consistent with the assumption, but likewise all observations we make can be interpreted otherwise. Mathematics at first blush appears to deliver "truth," but in reality it cannot be proven that $1 + 1 = 2$ without first assuming the value of 1. Gödel published two profoundly important incompleteness theorems in 1931 that show that "any such system that allows you to define the natural numbers is necessarily incomplete: it contains statements that are neither provably true nor provably false" (Hofstader, 1979). Provability is a weaker notion than truth. Rationality cannot yield ultimate truth. We are left staring through the glass darkly, as St. Paul (1 Corinthians 13:2) so presciently said.

Concluding Thoughts

We are left with contrasting worldviews, the worldview of the atheist and the worldview of the theist. To the atheist, matter and motion are a given. The universe we inhabit came into being some 13.8 billion years ago in a blinding flash of light. The Earth formed out of debris orbiting the Sun 4.6 billion years ago. Life appeared on Earth spontaneously out of the prebiotic chemical soup. The process of physical, chemical, and biological evolution played out. And here we are, children of star dust, an unintended accident of the uncaring cosmos. We were dead for 13.8 billion years, we are alive for our allotted span of years, then we will be dead again for untold billions of years. For the theist, God said "Let there be light" and there was light, and motion, and matter. We may agree on every scientific detail, but we cannot accept that humans are unintended by God. However vast the cosmos, we recognize that we humans play a very special role in it. With the Psalmist we exult: "What are we humans that you are mindful of us, the sons and daughter of men that you care for us? You made us a little lower than the angels and crowned us with glory and honor" (Psalm 8:4–5). Far from being hostile and uncaring, we recognize the astonishing fertility of the universe (Haught, 2003). As Dyson (1979) remarked: "The more I examine the universe and the details of its architecture, the more evidence I find that the universe in some sense must have known we were coming." We feel a profound sense of gratitude for our lives on such a hospitable planet, for the gifts we have each received, undeserving as we are – for the time and place of our births, for our intelligence, for our health, for our families and friends. We give thanks to our Creator and pray that we may use these gifts for the betterment of others. Is this worldview really such a threat to the well-being of humanity, Mr Dawkins?

Bibliography

Ayala, F. J. (2007) *Darwin's Gift to Science and Religion*. Washington, D.C: John Henry Press.

Behe, M. (1996) *Darwin's Black Box – the Biochemical Challenge to Evolution*. New York: The Free Press.

Behe, M. (2007) *The Edge of Evolution – The Search for the Limits of Darwinism*. New York: Free Press.

Brooke, J. H. (1991) *Science and Religion: Some Historical Perspectives*. Cambridge: Cambridge University Press.

Collins, F. S. (2006) *The Language of God: a scientist presents evidence for belie* (New York: Free Press.

Conway-Morris, S. (2003) *Life's Solution : Inevitable Humans in a Lonely Universe*. Cambridge University Press.

Cosans, C. (2005) *Was Darwin a Creationist? Perspectives in Biology and Medicine* 48, 362–71.

Darwin, Francis (ed.) (1887) *The Life and Letters of Charles Darwin*, including an autobiographical chapter. London: John Murray.

Dawkins, R. (1976) *The Selfish Gene*. Oxford University Press.

Dawkins, R. (1986) *The Blind Watchmaker*. New York: Norton.

Dawkins, R. (1995) *River Out of Eden – a Darwinian View of Life*. New York: Basic Books.

Dawkins, R. (1996) *Climbing Mount Improbable*. New York: Norton.

Dawkins, R. (1997) Is science a religion? *The Humanist* (Jan./Feb.).

Dawkins, R. (2003) *A Devil's Chaplain. Reflections on Hope, Lies, Science, and Love*. Boston: Houghton Mifflin.

Dawkins, R. (2006) *The God Delusion*. New York: Houghton Mifflin.

Dembski, W. (1998) *The Design Inference: Eliminating Chance through Small Probabilities*. Cambridge: Cambridge University Press.

Dennett, D. C. (1995) *Darwin's Dangerous Idea – Evolution and the Meanings of Life*. New York: Simon & Schuster.

Dennett, D. C. (2006) *Breaking the Spell: Religion as a Natural Phenomenon*. New York: Viking.

Dobzhansky, T. (1973) Nothing in biology makes sense except in the light of evolution. *American Biology Teacher* 35, 125–29.

Dodson, P. (1997) God and the dinosaurs. *American Paleontologist* 5 (2), 6–8.

Dodson, P. (1999) Faith of a paleontologist. In P. H. Kelley, J. R. Bryan, and T. A. Hansen (eds.) The evolution-creation controversy II: Perspectives on science, religion, and geological education. *Paleontological Society Papers* 5, 183–95.

Dodson, P. (2005) Fight the Good Fight – What paleontologists need to know about religion. *Journal Vertebrate Paleontolology* 25 (3) supplement 51A.

Dodson, P. (2006) How Intelligent is Intelligent Design? *American Paleontolo*gist 14 (1), 23–6.

Domning, D.P. (2006) *Original Selfishness: Original Sin and Evil in the Light of Evolution*; with foreword and commentary by Monika K. Hellwig. Burlington, VT: Ashgate.

Dyson, F. (1979) *Disturbing the Universe*. New York: Harper and Row.

Dyson, F. (1995) The scientist as rebel. *New York Review of Books* 42(9), May 25.

Dyson, F. (2006) Religion from the outside. *New York Review of Books* 53(11), June 22.

Eagleton, T. (2006) Lunging, flailing, mispunching. *London Review of Books* 28 (20), Oct. 19.

Feynman, R. P. (1989) *What Do You Care What Other People Think? Further Adventures of a Curious Character*. New York: Norton.

Gingerich, O. (1983) Let there be light: modern cosmogony and Biblical creation. In: R. M. Frye, (ed.) *Is God a Creationist? The Religious Case Against Creationism*, pp. 56–67. New York: Scribner.

Godfrey, S. J. and Smith, C. R. (2005) *Paradigms on Pilgrimage – Creationism, Paleontology, and Biblical Interpretation*. Toronto: Clements.

Gould, S. J. (1987) *Times Arrow Times Cycle – Myth and Metaphor in the Discovery of Geological Time*. Boston, MA: Harvard University Press.

Gould, S. J. (1992) Impeaching a Self-Appointed Judge. *Scientific American* 267(1), 118 (July 21).

Gould, S. J. (1997) Darwinian fundamentalism. *New York Review of Books* 44 (10, June 12).

Gould, S. J. (1999) *Rocks of Ages – Science and Religion in the Fullness of Life, Library of Contemporary Thought*. New York: Ballantine.

Grant, E. (1996. *The Foundations of Modern Science in the Middle Ages: Their Religious, Institutional, and Intellectual Contexts*. Cambridge: Cambridge University Press.

Grigg, R. (1996) Naming the animals: all in a day's work for Adam. *Creation* 18, 46–9.

Harris, S. (2004) *The End of Faith: Religion, Terror and the Future of Reason*. New York: Norton.

Harris, S. (2006) *Letters to a Christian Nation*. New York: Knopf.

Haught, J. F. (1995) *Science and Religion – from Conflict to Conversation*. Mahwah NJ: Paulist Press.

Haught, J. F. (1998) Darwin's gift to theology. In R. J. Russell, W. R. Stoeger, and F. J. Ayala, (eds.) *Evolutionary Biology and Molecular Biology: Scientific Perspective on Divine Action,* pp. 393–418. Notre Dame, IN: University of Notre Dame Press.

Haught, J. F. (2000) *God After Darwin*. Boulder, CO: Westview.

Haught, J. F. (2003) *Deeper than Darwin: The Prospect for Religion in the Age of Evolution*. Boulder, CO: Westview.

Haught, J. F. (2006) *Is Nature Enough? Meaning and Truth in the Age of Science*. Cambridge: Cambridge University Press.

Hitchens, C. (2007) *god is Not Great: How Religion Poisons Everything*. New York: Twelve.

Hodgson, P. E. (2005) Galileo the theologian, *Logos* 8, 28–51.

Hofstadter, D. (1979) *Gödel, Escher, Bach: An Eternal Golden Braid*. New York: Basic Books.

Hyers, C. (1984) *The Meaning of Genesis: Genesis and Modern Science*. Atlanta, GA: John Knox Press.

Jaki, S. (1978) *The Road of Science and the Ways to God*. Chicago: University of Chicago Press.

John Paul II (1996) *Message to the Pontifical Academy of Science on Evolution*.

Johnson, P. E. (1993) *Darwin on Trial*. Downers Grove, IL: InterVarsity Press.

Johnson, P. E. (1997) *Defeating Darwinism by Opening Minds*. Downers Grove, IL: InterVarsity Press.

Johnson, P. E. (2002) *The Wedge of Truth*. Downers Grove, IL: InterVarsity Press.

Larson, E. J. and Witham, L. (1997) Scientists are still keeping the faith, *Nature* 386, 435–6.

Lindberg, D. C. and Numbers, R. L. (1986) *God and Nature: Historical Essays on the Encounter of Christianity and Science*. Berkeley: University of California Press.

McGrath, A. (2004) *The Twilight of Atheism: The Rise and Fall of Disbelief in the Modern World*. New York: Doubleday.

McGrath, A. (2005) *Dawkins' God: Genes, Memes, and the Meaning of Life*. London: Blackwell.

McGrath, A. and McGrath, J. C. (2007) *The Dawkins Delusion? Atheist Fundamentalism and the Denial of the Divine*. Downers Grove, IL: InterVarsity press.

Miller, K. R. (1999) *Finding Darwin's God – a Scientist's Search for Common Ground Between God and Evolution*. New York: Cliff Street Books.

Newberg, A., D'Aquili, E. G., and Rause, V. (2001) *Why God Wont Go Away*. New York: Ballantine Books.

Noyes, R. (2004) The liberal media – every poll shows journalists are more liberal than the American public – and the public knows it, *Report*, Media Research Center, June 30, 2004.

Orr, H. A. (2004) A passion for evolution. *New York Review of Books* 51 (3, Feb. 26).

Orr, H. A. (2007) A mission to convert. *New York Review of Books* 54 (1, Jan. 11).

Polkinghorne, J. (1994) *Faith of a Physicist*. Princeton, NJ: Princeton University Press.

Rorty, R. (1995) Untruth and consequences, *The New Republic*, July 31, 32–6.

Roughgarden, J. (2006) *Evolution and Christian Faith – Reflections of an Evolutionary Biologis*. (Washington, DC: Island Press.

Rudwick, M. J. S. (2005) *Bursting the Limits of Time – the Reconstruction of Geohistory in a Time of Revolution*. Chicago: University of Chicago Press.

Ruse, M. (1979) *The Darwinian Revolution – Science Red in Tooth and Claw*. Chicago: University of Chicago Press.

Ruse, M. (2000) *Can a Darwinian be a Christian? The Relationship between Science and Religion*. Cambridge, MA: Harvard University Press.

Ruse, M. (2005) *The Evolution – Creation Struggle*. Cambridge, MA: Harvard University Press.

Provine, W. B. (1988) Scientists, face it! Science and religion are incompatible. *The Scientist*, Sept. 5, 10.

Sagan, C. (1996) *The Demon-Haunted World: Science as a Candle in the Dark*. New York: Ballantine.

Scott, E. C. (2004) *Evolution vs. Creationism: An Introduction*. Berkeley: University of California Press.

Slack, G. (2007) *The Battle Over the Meaning of Everything: Evolution, Intelligent Design, and a School Board in Dover, PA*. New York: Jossey-Bass.

Wilson, D. S. (2002) *Darwin's Cathedral: Evolution, Religion, and the Nature of Society*. Chicago: University of Chicago Press.

Wilson, E. O. (1978) *On Human Nature*. Cambridge, MA: Harvard University Press.

Wilson, E. O. *Naturalist*. Washington, DC: Island Press.

Wilson, E. O. (1998) *Consilience*. New York: Knopf.

Part 7

Christian Faith and Biological Explanation

Evolutionary Creation: Common Descent and Christian Views of Origins

STEPHEN MATHESON

Evolutionary theory seeks to explain fundamental aspects of the living world by proposing that living things are related by common ancestry. Common descent is an extraordinarily successful biological theory, providing explanation for many and varied phenomena in biology, ranging from biogeography (the distribution of organisms on Earth) to patterns of organization in genomes. Here I outline the theory and its success, and then discuss points at which common descent and Christian belief comes into conflict. I argue that the basic explanation of common descent is in no necessary conflict with Christian belief. Instead, the challenge faced by Christians considering common descent involves some aspects of Christian historical narratives that are difficult to place in the context of evolutionary history.

Introductory Comments

I write as a scientist, and particularly as a developmental biologist, not as a philosopher or theologian, and so my claims and comments will emphasize scientific knowledge and theory. Nevertheless my analysis, like any other, relies on key assumptions and definitions, and is influenced by commitments to science and to Christianity (at the least). So I offer these preliminary observations and definitions.

While definitions of science can vary widely, and no single definition can claim to be authoritative, I identify *explanation* as *a fundamental goal of natural science*.[1] Biological science seeks more than knowledge; it seeks explanation. And so a biological theory is judged not merely by whether it might be true, but by whether it has "explanatory power." In other words, an excellent theory provides understanding of multiple systems and phenomena, by assembling an explanation that accounts for whole assemblies of observations, including new observations that arise after the explanation has been formulated. A full discussion of this principle is beyond the scope of this chapter, but would require careful consideration of what is meant by "explanation." It is important, at least, to note that the evaluation of scientific theories is based on a system of values held by a community (the scientific community), and I take the notion of explanatory power to include many of those values.

Explanation can operate at various levels of analysis, and multiple explanations can simultaneously succeed or even excel. Consider this illustration of what John Haught calls "explanatory pluralism."[2] The kettle is boiling, and someone asks for an explanation. One might offer an explanation that describes molecular movement and the transition from liquid to gas. But one might also offer this explanation: "because the stove was turned on." Or one might explain by saying, "because I want to have tea." All of the explanations are correct, and all have some explanatory power, depending on what the questioner actually wanted to know. And so we can judge one explanation to be successful, or even excellent, without necessarily implying that other explanations are not also successful or excellent. In other words, different explanations for the same data are not necessarily in conflict with each other.

Conflict and controversy are themes of this chapter, specifically conflict between evolutionary theory and Christian belief. Conflict and controversy among Christians who are challenging science is commonplace today, at least in the United States and in other English-speaking societies. But the existence of controversy or debate does not necessarily imply the existence of substantive disagreement, or contradiction, between Christian belief and scientific explanation. Consider, for example, that significant numbers of people throughout the world claim to believe that the Holocaust never occurred, and vigorous disagreement and debate surely arise as a result of such assertions. It seems to me that it would be a mistake to conclude that there is any real controversy regarding the historical reality of the Holocaust, or to even consider the "debate" to be real in any scholarly sense. Millions of American Christians claim to reject evolutionary theory, and many hold it to be scientifically weak or invalid. Does this mean that the theory is scientifically controversial, or that the theory is inherently in conflict with Christian belief? I will argue that neither is the case. First, I examine common descent and its explanatory success, and then I turn to sources of potential conflict with Christian belief.

Evolutionary Theory and Its Explanatory Success

Evolutionary theory includes at least two broad scientific themes. The first, common descent, asserts that organisms alive today, including human beings, are related through ancient common ancestors. The second, natural selection, asserts that a major force leading to change in organisms through time is the differential survival and reproductive success of organisms in populations which contain significant variation. In this article, I focus on common descent; natural selection is a major concern of the Intelligent Design movement, which I critique in chapter 20.

Common descent is a scientific theory of extraordinary explanatory power. The strength of the theory, which enjoys effectively universal acceptance in the scientific community, is derived from this explanatory power, which is apparent when considering the relationship between the explanation and the evidence at hand. But descriptions of this relationship frequently mask the vast explanatory utility of the theory. Instead, in discussions of evolutionary theory and in debates over its validity, it is commonplace for the evidence that is explained by common descent to be described as "evidence for evolution." (The approach is adopted by both critics and defenders of the theory.) So for example, transitional forms in the fossil record are described as evidence in favor of common descent, implying that common descent is a proposition and the fossils are evidence that bolster the proposition. Certainly this reasoning strategy is valid, and even useful and appropriate in many scientific contexts. It fails, however, to describe adequately the role of common descent as an explanation for biological facts today.

To amplify this distinction, consider the investigation of a crime. Suppose that a bicycle has been stolen. Several people are considered suspects, and the investigators have collected evidence from the scene. During the early stages of the investigation, the investigators might propose a suspect, then consider whether there is evidence that implicates that suspect, perhaps by asking whether a particular footprint found at the crime scene matches the suspect's footprint. Some evidence may implicate more than one suspect, and evidence may vary in its clarity or quality. Indeed, the investigation may only establish that some of the suspects are more likely to be guilty than others, and in that case the investigation may end without an arrest, even if one particular suspect is considered the most likely perpetrator.

But the investigators' case will be bolstered significantly if they can propose a theory involving the actions of one suspect that accounts for *all* of the evidence. In other words, the case becomes *compelling* when it is more than a list of evidence against a suspect, and is instead a comprehensive explanation. Such an explanation would comprise a narrative of the events surrounding the crime, all of which involve the suspect, and all of which are connected to the various pieces of evidence that were collected.

In this era of biological science, with whole genome sequences appearing monthly and dramatic new fossil intermediates reported regularly in the scientific literature, it is no longer adequate to employ the phrase "evidence for evolution." Common descent provides a comprehensive explanation for mountains of biological data, and while there may be coexisting explanations, there is no *competing* explanation. We will now briefly consider some highlights of the evidence that is explained by common descent.

The Fossil Record

The worldwide occurrence of the fossilized remains of extinct organisms is, by itself, an observation in need of explanation, and common descent provides an excellent explanation. More importantly, however, particular features of the fossil record present a body of evidence for which common descent is the only compelling explanation. We will consider two major features that are particularly striking in this regard. First, the fossil record reveals a pattern of appearance of species through time. Second, the fossil record reveals examples of ancient species that are transitional forms, namely species that clearly represent intermediates between other species that are thought to be related by common ancestry.

The pattern of the appearance of species through geologic time is a remarkable feature of the fossil record. Scientists have known for more than two centuries that fossils in the oldest rocks are more primitive in structure than those in younger rocks, and an apparent succession of organisms through geologic time was noted long before Darwin first assembled the evidence for common descent. Mammals, for example, appear at a particular time in geologic history, preceded by certain types of tetrapods (four-legged vertebrate animals), which are preceded by certain types of fish; far older rocks contain more primitive species, and never contain a single mammal. Flowering plants appear at a particular point in the past (about 250 million years ago), and are found in younger rocks, but are never preserved in rocks older than 250 million years or so, despite the fact that plants and animals had lived on the planet for hundreds of millions of years before that. Patterns of succession like these are unmistakable and underappreciated as a body of evidence that makes sense only in light of common descent.

Common ancestry implies that species that are somewhat closely related, such as any two mammalian species, can nevertheless differ significantly in form. This leads to the prediction that the fossil record should contain examples of intermediate forms. For example, decades ago, whales and cows, though quite different anatomically and physiologically, were predicted to have a fairly recent common ancestor (another mammal of some type). Furthermore, animals that displayed a combination of terrestrial and aquatic characteristics, intermediate forms between whales and cow-like animals, were expected to have lived before whales arose. Darwin postulated a "swimming bear," but with no evidence for such intermediate forms, his idea was ridiculed. Indeed, until the last twenty years or so, such intermediate forms had not been found, and critics of evolutionary theory claimed that the lack of transitional fossils indicated that the theory was deficient. But several dramatic discoveries in recent years have uncovered a remarkable series of transitional forms, including a genus named *Ambulocetus*, which means "walking whale".[3] And there are plenty of additional well-studied evolutionary transitions: the transition from fish to terrestrial tetrapods has been superbly documented from fossils described as late as Spring 2006, and exciting new fossils unearthed in China reveal extraordinary intermediates related to dinosaurs and modern birds.[4] All of these extinct animals lived during eras that predate the modern forms we know today. Transitional species are fascinating, abundant in the fossil record, and compellingly explained by common descent.

Biogeography

Examination of the geographical distribution of organisms and fossils, or biogeography, reveals a set of patterns that are best explained by common descent. Islands, in particular, frequently display unique collections of species, and contain fossils of organisms related to those species. The Hawaiian Islands are home to thousands of species of fruit fly, but no native ants. The Galapagos Islands harbor dozens of species of finch, but no woodpeckers, even though one species of Galapagos finch can bore holes in wood. Native mammals in Australia are almost exclusively marsupials; the only placental mammals that are native to that continent are bats and rodents.[5] By combining the theory of common descent with knowledge of geological change (i.e., plate tectonics, or the movement of land masses over geologic time), scientists have provided compelling explanations for these and hundreds of related phenomena.

Comparative Anatomy and Comparative Embryology

Tetrapods form a subset of terrestrial vertebrates, and the group includes many of the most familiar animals on earth: whales, bats, birds, lizards, frogs, and humans are all tetrapods. Tetrapods are strikingly diverse in form and in size, but all have four limbs in two pairs. Comparative studies of these limbs, analyzing their structure and the developmental processes that create them, show that all tetrapod limbs display the same basic structure, and all are assembled through the same basic embryological mechanisms.[6] This means that the flipper of a whale is homologous to the leg of a horse, such that each is a modified version of a skeletal structure found in all tetrapods, including those long extinct. The wings of a bat appear to be oddly unique until one observes the skeleton (perhaps by observing the bats wings when lit from behind) and notes that the wings are basic mammalian forelimbs, with long "fingers" joined by webs of thin skin.

The tetrapod limb is the classic example of evolutionary homology, in which a biological structure is identified and understood by virtue of shared common ancestry, and the study of homology and the developmental pathways that create it forms the basis of the rapidly growing field of evolutionary developmental biology, or evo-devo.[7]

In my view, it is when considering the findings of comparative anatomy and developmental biology that the distinction between the "evidence for evolution" approach and the explanatory success approach becomes most important in an evaluation of evolutionary theory. By themselves, the facts of tetrapod anatomy or "evo-devo"[8] do not establish common descent beyond doubt. Instead, they constitute a vast body of knowledge that is best explained by the inheritance of anatomical structure and developmental mechanisms from common ancestors.

Biochemistry and Molecular Genetics

Evidence from the fossil record, biogeography, and comparative anatomy was used by Darwin in building his case for evolutionary theory in the 1850s. He knew nothing of modern biochemistry, and even less of genetics. (Gregor Mendel, considered the founder of the science of genetics, was a contemporary of Darwin's, but Mendel's work was not widely known during his lifetime, and Darwin never knew of it.) Our modern knowledge of biochemistry, and especially of DNA and molecular genetics, provides stunning confirmation of common descent, by amassing a huge collection of data that makes sense only in the light of common ancestry.

At the level of cellular function, there is striking conservation of the most basic biochemical activities in all life forms. For example, the fundamental pathways that permit cells to extract energy from chemical fuels are completely universal, employed in organisms at every level of size and complexity. Genetic information is stored by DNA in all living things, and the code is almost completely universal. Bacteria, trees, rats, and people all use the same chemical and the same information code to store and use genetic information.

Comparison of DNA sequences from various types of organisms has been yielding important clues to biological ancestry for almost three decades, but the pace of discovery has accelerated exponentially in the last five years or so, as large-scale sequencing of entire genomes has become commonplace. The first discoveries in the field of molecular evolution occurred in the 1970s and early 1980s, when comparison of gene sequences across species revealed a pattern of change that strikingly confirmed predictions of specific common ancestry as inferred from studies of the fossil record and of homologous structures. Nevertheless, these early results were focused on a small number of genes, and only on the genes themselves. (Most genomes, especially those of animals and plants, contain vast amounts of "non-coding" DNA – DNA that does not directly encode genetic information.) More modern analyses, comparing entire genomes, have uncovered fascinating genetic elements that unmistakably point to common ancestry. Here we will consider just two examples of these kinds of data.

Genomes contain thousands of genes, interspersed with large sections of DNA that do not contain genes. In most genomes, scientists have identified sequences that appear to be genes that have been inactivated, or rendered nonfunctional, by mutation. These inactivated genes, called pseudogenes, are found in the same genomic locations as fully functional genes in other species. For example, the human genome contains numerous pseudogenes that are easily identifiable as the remnants of genes for various olfactory receptors that are known to be absent in human olfactory systems. The same genes, in the same locations, are fully intact in rodents and other species known to use these particular receptors. The presence of these "fossil genes," and their precise location in the genomes of closely related species, is explained fully and simply by common ancestry.[9]

Mammalian genomes contain enormous numbers of genetic elements that represent the insertions of viruses or mobile genetic elements called retroelements. (Certain viruses, especially retroviruses such as HIV, specialize in inserting their own genome into the genome of a host organism.) About 8 percent of the human genome is composed of retroviruses, and almost half of the human genome is composed of either intact viral insertions or other retroelements. Examination of numerous insertions has revealed that the same element can be found *in the same genomic location* in the genomes of closely related species. Indeed, scientists have used these retroelements as lineage tracing tools, to test hypotheses regarding common ancestry of very closely related species.[10] As predicted, elements that were present in more ancient common ancestors display more changes (mutations) than those present in more recent common ancestors. In other words, a retroelement insertion in the genome of a rat and a whale, in the same location, will display more sequence differences than would an insertion in two different species of whale. Inheritance of these elements through common ancestry, with steady accumulation of mutations in the elements over time, provides the explanation for these striking facts of genomic biology.

In my view, the voluminous findings of comparative genomics, merely sampled here, would represent a compelling case for common ancestry *in the absence of any other evidence*. Only in light of inheritance via common ancestors do these findings make sense. But of course, the evidence explained by common descent *does* include data from fields as diverse as paleontology and molecular genomics, and the explanation of common descent explains all of the evidence together. To conclude and reiterate: it is not sufficient to claim that this evidence supports common descent, as one proposal among others. Common descent explains all of the evidence, and no other explanation even approaches its success.

Points of Conflict with Christian belief

So, common descent is an excellent and successful scientific explanation, providing a convincing account of the history of organisms alive today. How is this explanation in conflict with Christian belief? I suggest that there are exactly two points of conflict, which I will summarize as two objections to the theory that are raised by Christians.

(1)   The first objection is that the explanation for the development and current form of organisms is a natural explanation, that includes no supernatural elements. So, it is claimed, there is "no room for God." Or perhaps it is claimed that there is no place for God's creative activity. One corollary might go something like this: "It doesn't seem like God's way."

(2)   A second objection is that the history of life as outlined by common descent seems different from the Biblical history of life. The Christian view of history is framed, basically, as proceeding from creation, through fall, ending with redemption. Briefly, God created the world in a state that was free of sin, but sin and death entered this world through the disobedience of humans (the Fall).[11] Subsequent events are building toward the redemption of the world through God's own actions. This view of history does not easily fit into the view of evolutionary history, and there are two problems. One problem is somewhat broad: the Christian narrative usually assumes that death did not occur before the Fall. The second problem is more specific: the Christian narrative asserts that sin in all humans is inherited from particular human ancestors, namely Adam and Eve. Each problem arises due to a Christian historical claim that seems difficult to place into evolutionary history.

So, I assert that the points of potential conflict between Christian belief and common ancestry can be summarized thus: (1) common descent as an explanation is somehow a problem for Christians; and (2) the long history of life that precedes the appearance of humans is somehow a problem for Christians.

Are These Conflicts Real or Necessary?

Both of the broad types of objection mentioned above are raised by Christians (most especially, English-speaking Christians) while confronting common descent. Whether the challenge is raised by a Christian Young Earth creationist organization or by Christians involved in the Intelligent Design movement, I maintain that the challenge is motivated by one or both of those basic objections. So it might seem that there is real conflict between Christian belief and common descent. Certainly many Christians point to conflict, and controversy is real and intense. But is the conflict real?

Problems with the explanation

In my view, there is no necessary conflict of any kind between the scientific explanation of common ancestry and Christian belief. In other words, I believe the first objection above is mistaken and misguided.

It is certainly true that the explanation of common ancestry is natural, as opposed to supernatural, in that it never relies on supernatural phenomena to provide explanation. But this fact alone does not make the explanation problematic for Christians. On the contrary, the claim that a natural explanation for *any* phenomenon "leaves no room for God" is a significant error in Christian thought.

In fact, in Psalm 104, various biological processes, including animal birth, death, and predation, are plainly asserted to be God's own work.[12] Similarly, Psalm 139 refers to human prenatal development, claiming every detail to be God's personal handiwork.[13] We now understand the processes of mammalian development fairly well, but Christians do not object to scientific theories concerning human embryology, nor do they point to any conflict between the explanations of developmental biology and Christian belief. I believe it is notable that Christians simply do not express concern when presented with an explanatory description of the first events in the formation of a human body, in which a sperm and an oocyte fused, followed by cell division and implantation of a tiny shapeless embryo into a uterus. I am certain that essentially all Christians, after learning these fascinating truths of developmental biology, remain convinced that their life and development are works of God. Why? Because natural explanations do not – and usually cannot – rule out God's influence, at least because of the fact that different explanations, answering different questions, can coexist.

Perhaps, however, the objection is more subtle: "this doesn't seem like God's way." In other words, some Christians claim that there is an inconsistency between the evolutionary mechanism and the "ways" of God. The objection typically focuses on the necessity of death in the evolution of organisms, and in particular it highlights the existence of death long before the Fall. (The objection also raises a potential conflict with Christian historical narrative that will be discussed below.)

But again, Psalm 104 claims these very processes (death, and even predation by carnivorous animals)[14] as God's direct responsibility. The workings of the natural world, whether they are biological processes such as birth, death, and development, or physical processes involved in the formation of mountains and climate, are the works of God. It seems to me that any objection to the mechanisms of the biological explanation of common descent must either point to some aspect of evolutionary theory that is clearly different from the mechanisms described in Biblical passages like Psalm 104, or must explain how it is that these mechanisms became "God's way" when they weren't before. As it stands now, I find the objections wholly unconvincing, and I conclude that common descent, as a scientific explanation, is not a problem for Christian belief.

Problems with the historical account

In my view, the second objection, that Christian beliefs about the past are contradicted by assertions of evolutionary theory, is more serious and is worthy of continued thought and research by Christian scientists and theologians.

The broad area of conflict, as I have defined it, is the existence of animal and human death for eons, indeed throughout the existence of complex life, presumably eons before the historical event of the Fall. This is a serious conflict, but only if the Fall is understood to be the *beginning* of animal and human death. This is clearly a common view throughout Christian history. But it is not completely clear that the Biblical account intends to claim the complete absence of death before the Fall. For example, plants were given to Adam and Eve as food, and would have suffered death before the Fall occurred according to any reading of the Biblical account. The Garden of Eden contained a Tree of Life, which apparently conferred immortality to those who ate from it, and this tree existed before the Fall occurred. And although Adam and Eve were warned that they would "surely die" upon disobedience, they lived for hundreds of years after the Fall.[15] These observations suggest that "death" in the early Biblical narrative may be better understood as different from basic biological death, and Christians have long considered this possibility. It seems to me that death before the Fall, while worthy of careful thought by Christians, is not a serious problem for believers who accept evolutionary theory.

A more specific and serious problem arises, however, when considering the Christian belief in original sin, wherein all human beings are born with a sinful nature, inherited by way of common ancestry with exactly two original disobedient parents, Adam and Eve, who were the first human beings to exist. It is clear that if Christianity claims that Adam and Eve were individual human beings, then either (1) the Christian historical narrative is contradicted by evolutionary theory, which holds that humans, like any other species, arose as a population of hundreds or thousands, or (2) humans other than Adam and Eve were alive at the time of the Fall, and were unaffected by it (since they did not descend from Adam and Eve). These alternatives are both significantly problematic for the standard Christian narrative of early human history. This dilemma, and others like it, can be solved by asserting that Adam and Eve were not actual human beings. For example, Adam and Eve could be viewed as representative humans, whose actions then somehow influenced others. But this interpretation represents a significant departure from traditional Christian understanding of human origins.[16]

It seems to me that the question of original sin in the context of evolutionary history is one area of potential conflict between Christian belief and scientific explanation, and the issue calls for serious effort on the part of Christian scholars. I do not consider the dilemma to be unsolvable, and there are very good resources available to those considering the question.

Unfortunately, the question of original sin and common ancestry is not the main focus of the widespread debates about evolution among English-speaking Christians. (More accurately, and unfortunately in my view, these debates tend to pit English-speaking Christians against scientists.) Instead, most Christians who are concerned about evolution are attacking the explanation. I believe this strategy to be a significant mistake.

The Evolutionary Creation View

My comments have sought mostly to address what I see as mistaken claims of serious conflict between Christian belief and common descent and have not emphasized a cogent alternative outlook. I will end by assembling an outline of my view, as a Christian, of evolutionary theory. With others, I refer to this position as an "evolutionary creation" position. The phrase is meant to contrast with "theistic evolution," which is the currently popular descriptor for this viewpoint, but which I find unsatisfactory for largely semantic reasons.[17]

The evolutionary creation view takes common descent and natural selection to be valid explanations for biological data, and acknowledges that common descent is a theory with formidable explanatory power. As such, the view considers common descent the same way it considers theories of embryology, judging both as excellent explanations of biological phenomena. The evolutionary creation view asserts, however, that these explanations do not rule out, or even address, the reality of God's creative activity. God's creative work is taken to be real and ongoing, and the possibility that aspects of this work can be understood is not feared, but expected and embraced. Obtaining a better understanding of the Fall in the context of ancient common ancestry is a challenge that presents abundant opportunities for fruitful work by Christian scholars.

Notes

1   See Del Ratzsch, *Science and Its Limits: The Natural Sciences in Christian Perspective* (2nd edn., Downers Grove, IL: InterVarsity Press, 2000), for more on the nature and definitions of science and of explanation.

2 Haught, Distinguished Research Professor of Theology at Georgetown University, has used this illustration repeatedly; see, for example, the transcript of the Dover trial, *Kitzmiller vs. Dover Area School District*, in which Haught testified. (This trial concerned the teaching of "intelligent design" in a public school district.) The transcript is freely available online at sites like this one: http://www.paamd.uscourts.gov/kitzmiller/kitzmiller_342.pdf.

3 For excellent overviews of these and other evolutionary transitions, see Carl Zimmer, *At the Water's Edge* (New York: Simon & Schuster, 1999), Stephen Jay Gould, "Hooking Leviathan by its past," in *Dinosaur in a Haystack* (New York: Harmony Books, 1995) or Keith B. Miller, "Common Descent, Transitional Forms, and the Fossil Record," in *Perspectives on an Evolving Creation* (Grand Rapids, MI: Eerdmans, 2003).

4 See the April 6, 2006 issue of *Nature* (vol. 440, no. 7085) for articles describing a newly discovered transitional form intermediate between fish and tetrapods, and the Jan. 23, 2003 issue (vol. 421, no. 6921) for reports on a particularly exciting feathered dinosaur.

5 In each of these examples, evidence from biology and geology indicates that a population was established at some point in the past, then diverged into multiple species through continued evolution. The peculiar collections of populations (e.g., multitudes of fruit fly species and the absence of ants, in Hawaii) are explained by geographic isolation, in the form of islands, in these examples. Specifically, birds and flies would be expected to reach remote islands with more frequency than non-flying species, and this colonization of remote islands is rare in any case. Common descent from peculiar and specific founder populations provides an excellent explanation for the presence of these strange and interesting communities of organisms.

6 See Zimmer, *At the Water's Edge*, for an overview.

7 See Sean B. Carroll, *Endless Forms Most Beautiful* (New York: W. W. Norton, 2005) for an introduction to evo-devo; also see the April 25, 2000 issue of *Proceedings of the National Academy of Sciences USA* (vol. 97, no. 9), which was completely devoted to the subject. Most articles in this journal are freely available online at www.pnas.org.

8 Evo-devo is short for evolutionary developmental biology, a subfield of biology which examines the roles of embryonic development in the evolution of body form.

9 See Sean B. Carroll, *The Making of the Fittest* (New York: W.W. Norton, 2006); olfactory receptor pseudogenes are described by Yoshito Niimura and Masatoshi Nei, Evolution of olfactory receptor genes in the human genome. *Proceedings of the National Academy of Sciences* 100 (2003), 12235–40).

10 See, for example, Salem, A. H., Ray, D. A., Xing, J., Callinan, P. A., Myers, J. S., Hedges, D. J., et al., Alu elements and hominid phylogenetics. *Proceedings of the National Academy of Sciences USA* 100 (2003), 12787–91.

11 These events are described in the first three chapters of Genesis, the first book of the Bible.

12 Consider these excerpts from Psalm 104, New International Version (NIV):"How many are your works, O LORD! In wisdom you made them all; the earth is full of your creatures" (24); and

These all look to you to give them their food at the proper time. When you give it to them, they gather it up; when you open your hand, they are satisfied with good things. When you hide your face, they are terrified; when you take away their breath, they die and return to the dust. When you send your Spirit, they are created, and you renew the face of the earth. (Psalm 104:27–30)

13 From Psalm 139:13–16, NIV:

For you created my inmost being; you knit me together in my mother's womb. I praise you because I am fearfully and wonderfully made; your works are wonderful, I know that full well. My frame was not hidden from you when I was made in the secret place. When I was woven together in the depths of the earth, your eyes saw my unformed body. All the days ordained for me were written in your book before one of them came to be.

14 Psalm 104:21, NIV: "The lions roar for their prey and seek their food from God."

15 These observations come from the second and third chapters of Genesis.

16 For an excellent and extensive discussion of these issues, see Davis A. Young, "The Antiquity and the Unity of the Human Race Revisited," *Christian Scholar's Review* XXIV, no. 4 (1995), 380–96c. This article is also available online at: http://www.asa3.org/ASA/resources/CSRYoung.html

17 The phrase "theistic evolution" emphasizes evolution, and modifies it with theism, whereas the phrase "evolutionary creation" emphasizes God's creation, and modifies it with evolution.

20

A Scientific and Religious
Critique of Intelligent Design

STEPHEN MATHESON

The Intelligent Design movement challenges naturalism in science, most prominently by asserting that facets of the natural world exhibit properties that could not have arisen through purely natural mechanisms, and then concluding that these phenomena exhibit intelligent design. I critique these ideas, and find significant confusion regarding the role of naturalism in science. Moreover, although I find questions regarding the origins of biological complexity to have scientific merit, I conclude that the movement's proposals fail to mount a significant challenge to evolutionary theory.

Defining the Intelligent Design Movement

Over the past 1 to fifteen years,[1] the Intelligent Design (ID) movement has emerged as a significant force in debates concerning evolutionary biology and Christian faith, most prominently in the United States. Hailed by proponents as a full-scale scientific revolution, and dismissed by opponents as nothing more than creationism with sophisticated terms, the ID movement is neither highly organized nor officially defined. Perhaps for this reason, ID is often misrepresented and misunderstood. It is important, therefore, to carefully identify ID and its distinctive ideas and activities.

As I see it, the ID movement has two major facets.[2] First, it is a social and political struggle against naturalism, and specifically against naturalism in the teaching and practice of science. Second, it is a scientific and philosophical effort to define and identify "design" in the natural world. These two aspects of ID are quite different, but are very much intertwined in the works of many of the prominent thinkers in the movement. In my view, by keeping these two overall goals separate, it is possible to identify scientific and religious ideas and assumptions that are characteristic of ID, and thereby to analyze and critique these ideas.

Darwin and Design

Debates surrounding Darwinian theory and design are not new; in fact, the concept of design has been associated with Charles Darwin and his theory from its inception. Darwin conceived his ideas as alternatives to divine (i.e., miraculous) design and his theory was an answer to a seemingly unanswerable question posed by eighteenth-century adherents of natural theology: how can the design and complexity that is evident in nature have arisen if not through the work of a Creator God?[3]

Natural theology, in which reasoning based on facts of nature is employed to argue for the existence of a Designer God, is an ancient tradition in Christianity. Natural theology was prominent in Christian thought in the nineteenth century, and the classic work on the subject, William Paley's *Natural Theology*, was widely read and embraced by many (perhaps most) scientists of the time. Darwin, in particular, admired Paley's work, which included the famous illustration of the discovery of a watch lying in a heath. The watch is clearly designed, and its existence can only be explained through reference to a designer; likewise, aspects of nature appear to be clearly designed, and their existence can only be explained through reference to a Designer God. Darwin's theory, in effect, provided a natural explanation for apparent design, an explanation that did not directly involve a divine designer, and Darwin noted this fact explicitly. By the end of his life, Darwin had largely ruled out purposeful design as an explanatory aid, and he died an agnostic.[4]

Thus, from the very beginning, evolutionary theory was tied to naturalism, purposelessness, and the denial of any role for a divine creator or designer. Darwin's ideas were soon seen to be more than mere refutations of natural theology; divine purpose itself was seen as unnecessary and trivial by many Darwinists. And while many Christians rejected the theory outright, some Christian thinkers of the time noted that Darwin's scientific ideas could (and should) be separated from the naturalistic assumptions and conclusions of Darwin and many of his supporters. Charles Hodge was the most prominent Christian scholar to respond to Darwin in his time.

Darwinism and Naturalism

Charles Hodge was one of the most influential American theologians of the nineteenth century. A Presbyterian, he taught at Princeton Theological Seminary from 1822 until his death in 1878. In 1874, he published his famous analysis of Darwin's theory and its philosophical underpinnings, called "What is Darwinism?" Noting that the theory had "agitated the whole world," and that Darwin had plainly rejected purposeful design in nature, Hodge sought to separate scientific theories of evolution from the rejection of teleology embraced by Darwin and others. Darwinism, according to Hodge, was constituted by three main elements: evolution, natural selection, and the denial of design. Hodge claimed that the rejection of purposeful design was the only distinctive element of Darwin's theory, and he emphasized that any theory of evolution through natural selection that does not deny design is *not* Darwinism. And although he discussed scientific criticisms of the theory, he recognized the ideas as validly scientific, and insisted that the concepts of evolution and natural selection could coexist with divine purpose and guidance. Hodge's answer, then, to the question he posed, was: "It is atheism."[5]

More than a hundred years later, in the early years of the ID movement, Phillip Johnson revisited the question.[6] But for Johnson, it seems that evolution and natural selection can't be separated from purposelessness. He insists, instead, that common descent and Darwinian theories of variation and natural selection are accepted by the scientific community in spite of little or no evidential support, and that this acceptance is due solely to the influence of "scientific naturalism," which is the same atheism that Hodge identified. So Johnson, too, concludes that Darwinism is atheism, but he seems to believe that the scientific explanations of common descent and natural selection are almost worthless without a commitment to the denial of design (in other words, a commitment to naturalism). And so, the ID movement, in which Johnson is a recognized leader, seeks to destroy Darwinism, by objecting to naturalism but also by attacking the evidence for common descent and natural selection.[7]

Why do so many in the ID movement reject common descent and natural selection? Most claim to find the evidence unconvincing, although their analyses are typically inaccurate and incomplete. It seems to me that the fundamental objection raised by ID is an objection to the pervasive naturalism expressed by many, if not most, defenders of evolutionary theory (Darwin included). Johnson, for example, argues ineffectively against common descent and natural selection, concluding that neither is of explanatory value, and then claims that the only reason that science accepts the theories is because of a commitment to naturalism.[8] Moreover, it is common for both opponents and proponents of evolutionary theory to assume that the mechanisms underlying genetic variation, which are thought to be "random," are inherently naturalistic, meaning that they cannot be related to any supernatural activity, which would entail purpose or direction.

Thus, while seeking to oppose philosophical naturalism in education and elsewhere, ID finds itself opposed to evolutionary theory, in so far as evolutionary theory is seen to be based on wholly naturalistic assumptions. I consider the ideas and arguments of ID as they relate to the issues at hand to be distinctly religious, although ID claims not be religious in nature.[9]

Identifying Design in Nature

The definition and identification of "design" in the natural world is a major goal of the ID movement. Although rigorous definition of the term is challenging and beyond the scope of this article,[10] the concept of design (and its detection) is intuitively straightforward. Consider the international Search for Extraterrestrial Intelligence, or SETI. This comprehensive research program includes large, ongoing, around-the-clock scans of the heavens, listening and watching for signals from possible civilizations elsewhere in the universe. What does SETI hope to find in these scans? No one knows, of course, what an extraterrestrial message should look like, but the basic assumption is that a message of this sort should bear signs of artificiality, of designedness, of nonrandomness. SETI searches, therefore, for signals known not to arise randomly, often looking in channels (such as radio frequencies) that do not typically carry natural information.[11] In a way, then, SETI is a search for intelligent design. Similarly, any search for human activity in nature, whether by archaeologists at an excavation site or by treasure hunters scanning the ocean floor for shipwrecks, involves a deliberate search for evidence of design against what is viewed as a backdrop of "natural" randomness.

It is important to note that all of these examples constitute legitimate scientific endeavors. Thus, the identification of intelligent design is not unscientific, as some critics of ID have claimed; indeed, the detection of intelligent design (created by humans or aliens) is the very basis of many scientific activities. But while attempts to identify design are not themselves unscientific, the ID movement engenders significant criticism from the scientific community precisely because it takes evidence *for* design as evidence *against* common descent and natural selection, and the movement is rightly criticized as unscientific when some of its most prominent thinkers attack the explanatory power of common descent and the evidence for the widespread involvement of natural selection in evolutionary change.

The ID movement advances two main proposals as supportive of its argument for the presence of intelligent design in nature. First, ID thinkers claim to have defined and identified "specified complexity" in nature, especially in biological information as encoded by DNA. Second, ID theorists claim to have identified "irreducible complexity" in biological structures, especially in molecular machines that make up living cells.

Specified complexity

The concept of *specified complexity*[12] has been championed by William Dembski, a leading ID theorist whose books are some of the best-known works of the ID movement. Dembski maintains that biological systems contain structures which exhibit specified complexity, and he concludes that these systems and structures cannot come about through purely natural means. The argument combines the concepts of probability and "specification," which refers to a type of pattern that "warrants a design inference." So for example, a page of letters from the English alphabet (like this page) exhibits a certain amount of complexity, but the *pattern* of letters (i.e., the spelling out one page of this article) is a case of *specified* complexity. If this page were covered with an apparently random collection of letters of the alphabet, it might still be complex, but it would lack specified complexity. Dembski argues that the appearance of such complexity is extremely improbable in the absence of deliberate design, and concludes that this "complexity-specification criterion" is therefore a means for the detection of design. He further argues that biological systems are rife with specified complexity, and that this is evidence that such systems have been deliberately designed.

Irreducible complexity

The concept of *irreducible complexity* was developed in the context of ID by biochemist Michael Behe. Behe defines an irreducibly complex system as one "which is composed of several interacting parts that contribute to the basic function, and where the removal of any one of the parts causes the system to effectively cease functioning."[13] He offers a mechanical mousetrap as a simple example: the mousetrap is composed of several parts which, when assembled and acting together, yield a particular function but which, individually and separate from the assembled system, are worthless. Behe contends that an irreducibly complex system cannot come together through a standard Darwinian process, in which natural selection leads to improvement of some existing structure or function, because any incomplete version of that system is non-functional by definition. And the non-functional system, like an incomplete mousetrap, is worthless at best, and would not be maintained by natural selection within cells or organisms. To make this point clear, Behe focuses on some particular examples from biochemistry and cell biology, and the best-known of these examples is the bacterial flagellum.

The flagellum is a *molecular machine* used by some bacteria for movement, and its complexity and elegance has long fascinated scientists. The flagellum acts in a way analogous to a propeller, turned by an analogously conceived electrically powered rotary motor. According to Behe, the machine is composed of at least three essential parts (the propeller, a rotor, and a motor) and therefore the flagellum is irreducibly complex (in the sense that it cannot function thus without all of the parts in question). Because the individual parts seem to have no function in isolation, Behe concludes that they would not have arisen gradually via natural selection. After all, a propeller without a rotor or motor has no value to the organism (to produce a result) – in fact, it would seem to represent a significant waste of resources – and so such a structure would not be favored by natural selection. Behe's claim, then, is that the only way flagella can arise in evolution is all at once, and this means that the origin of flagella is extremely improbable. This reasoning rules out standard Darwinian evolution, with its gradual change through variation and natural selection, and leaves only deliberate design. Similar conclusions follow when ID thinkers consider any of the myriad *molecular machines* that make up even the simplest known cells.

Critique of ID'S Religious and Philosophical Aspects

Overlap with discredited creationist views

As I have noted above, ID thinkers maintain that their movement is not a religious one, and they have explicitly distinguished their ideas from those of Christian creationism.[14] I agree that the core ideas of ID with respect to the existence of design in nature are not explicitly Christian or creationist in nature, and I further agree that references to the movement as "intelligent design creationism" constitute inappropriate maneuvers intended to discredit ID and its proposals. In my view, however, ID theorists fail to acknowledge *why* the movement is so frequently associated with creationism. For example, some of the most prominent ID proponents came to ID from creationist movements, and testimony in the Dover trial showed a clear historical relationship between creationist and ID projects involving the preparation of textbooks for public schools.[15] But more importantly, some ID advocates attack evolutionary theory employing rhetorical tactics long associated with creationism. Examples of these excesses include: (1) the association of evolutionary theory with social evils of various kinds; (2) selective quotation of scientists or other experts such that their words are misrepresented in various ways; and (3) highly selective citation of scientific data, resulting in significantly skewed impressions of the scientific literature. It seems to me that ID theorists could earn additional credibility by addressing the significant overlap between some ID claims and various discredited aspects of creationism, and then by renouncing such tactics.

Views on naturalism and explanation

As I discussed in chapter 19, I reject the notion that natural explanations for biological phenomena rule out (or even address) the existence of supernatural influences. A major theme in ID thought, it seems to me, is that natural explanations exclude, by their nature, divine agency. According to Phillip Johnson, for example, Darwinism describes how creation must have occurred "if we assume that God had nothing to do with it." In general, ID writing reveals a tendency to emphasize the distinction between "naturalistic mechanisms" and supernatural design, and the resulting separation between "natural" explanations and perceptions of God's work is unworkable for me as a Christian biologist. As I will discuss below, the concept of design, even supernatural design, is not inherently problematic in my view; rather, I reject the implication that appreciating design, or acknowledging God's creative activity conceived in any other way, is diminished by natural explanations of the processes through which the design could have arisen.

As noted earlier, ID is a movement that aims to challenge naturalism, and ID work in this area is at its best when identifying the inappropriate claims of philosophical naturalism, especially in science. For example, the National Association of Biology Teachers declared in 1995 that evolution is "an unsupervised, impersonal, unpredictable and natural process." The statement is a clear assertion of philosophical materialism, and it was subsequently changed after Christian scholars noted its inappropriate implications.[16] The ID movement is right to resist such claims, especially in the realm of public education. Unfortunately, ID proponents often fail (or refuse) to distinguish between philosophical naturalism and what is called "methodological naturalism."

The practice of science is characterized by methodological naturalism, an operational stance in which scientific explanations are sought and constructed as if naturalism is true, meaning that scientific explanations are currently sought and constructed without reference to supernatural influences. As Del Ratzsch and others have noted, the commitment of science to methodological naturalism can be reasonably challenged, and a complete rejection of all nonnatural explanations can, at least in principle, limit the explanatory effectiveness of science (when and if such explanations are true).[10] And so ID proponents, it seems to me, are right to call attention to the potential limitations of the effective prohibition on supernatural explanation in science. But it is a significant error, in my view, to equate the practice of methodological naturalism with a commitment to philosophical naturalism, especially when natural explanations cannot rule out supernatural action or intention.[17]

Finally, with regard to religious implications of ID, it seems to me that much of the appeal of ID arguments rests on the assumption that the scientific understanding of "chance" or of "random events" is inherently naturalistic. This confusion is common in non-technical discussions of evolution and design: aggressive proponents of philosophical naturalism, as well as creationists and many ID supporters, are prone to conflating "random" with "purposeless" or "undirected" (recall the NABT statement above). But this is a significant misconception. The basic scientific concept of chance implies only that scientists in such cases cannot "completely predict the final state of a system based on their knowledge of earlier states."[18] In other words, chance events cannot be predicted. Whether such events could have been directed or decreed by God is simply not addressed by the scientific conception of random or chance events.

Critique of ID's Scientific Proposals

Is specified complexity an argument for design?

The technical aspects of Dembski's formulation of the concept of specified complexity are well beyond my areas of expertise. My critique, therefore, will not address the existence or detectability of *specified complexity*. In fact, I find the idea useful and intriguing, as I will explain below. A scientific critique of Dembski's ideas, however, should address his claim that selection, acting on variation, cannot yield structures that exhibit specified complexity. I find this specific claim to be unconvincing. First, recent work has demonstrated how such complexity can arise through random mutation and selection in simulations using digital organisms.[19] Second, Francisco Ayala has asserted that arguments such as Dembski's, which calculate immense improbabilities associated with the random emergence of complexity, are irrelevant due to the involvement of natural selection, which is not only nonrandom, but also directed in the sense that traits can be selected by virtue of "functional utility."[20] And lastly, it seems to me that Dembski and other ID proponents consistently underestimate the demonstrated power of selection and variation in the emergence of biological change. For example, observed rates of evolutionary change are more than adequate to account for biological evolution over tens and hundreds of millions of years; in fact, such evolutionary rates are significantly faster than the rate required to drive evolutionary change over vast amounts of time.[21]

Behe's concept of *irreducible complexity* is an example of specified complexity, and so the criticisms in the previous paragraph apply similarly to that idea. But Behe's proposal is specifically grounded in cell biology and biochemistry, and so it can be further evaluated in the context of specific scientific data.

Is the bacterial flagellum irreducibly complex?

Recall that Behe asserts that the bacterial flagellum is irreducibly complex because its parts are each essential for its function. A careful look at current scientific knowledge regarding flagella reveals several observations that significantly weaken Behe's case. First, there are, in fact, many different flagellar designs, using a large array of protein components, and exhibiting striking variation in form and function. Recent genome-sequencing studies suggest that nature displays thousands, perhaps millions of different types of flagella. Given the evidence for common ancestry among these systems (Behe does not dispute common descent), it seems that flagellar systems have changed dramatically, millions of times, in evolution, without evident interference from irreducible complexity. So, elaborate design has not impeded significant change. Second, and most importantly, subsets of the flagellar components have known functions. The best known is the type III secretion system, a bacterial system that performs a distinct task using a portion of the parts of the flagellum. This fact, omitted completely from Behe's original analysis of the flagellum, removes most of the impact from the assertion of irreducible complexity, since now it can be seen how a significant function can remain in a small portion of the system's parts. The contention, after all, is that natural selection can only act on an intact system. In the case of the type III secretion system, it is clear that the flagellum's parts can be put to use in subsets, and the objection that the parts would not have been maintained by natural selection collapses. Similar findings have uncovered interesting functions for other subsets of flagellar components, suggesting that natural selection has indeed acted to preserve and modify those components, even when they were not or are not functioning in a flagellum.[22]

Did the flagellum arise through standard evolutionary mechanisms?

Although Behe does not deny common ancestry, even for the bacterial flagellum, his challenge to evolutionary biology is clear. He insists that the flagellum could not have arisen through selection acting on variation, and he maintains that science has never produced an explanation of how Darwinian mechanisms produced it. While it is true that a complete and detailed account of the evolution of the flagellum has not been published, it is also true that rapid progress in the discovery and understanding of flagellar genes has led to extensive evidence of common descent among flagella and flagellar proteins. Many flagellar proteins appear to share common ancestry with non-flagellar proteins, implying that the flagellar proteins are modified versions of proteins that serve non-flagellar functions. And interesting "intermediate forms" of flagella are common in bacteria, as would be expected in a set of systems that have descended with modification from other systems. These types of observations have led to the formulation of evidence-based hypotheses for how previous structures were modified to form flagellar systems,[23] and these hypotheses reveal, in my view, significant weaknesses in Behe's challenge to evolutionary theory. Irreducible complexity is surely interesting, but it seems not to present an insurmountable hurdle to standard evolutionary explanations, and further analysis of Behe's questions seem only to strengthen the explanatory power of selection acting on variation.

A further conceptual weakness in ID thought

As a scientist, I identify an overall weakness in ID proposals which significantly reduces their explanatory power. Essentially all of the scientific conclusions reached by ID proponents are by nature negative, focused almost exclusively on what is asserted *not* to be possible. (To ID's credit, this makes the proposals falsifiable, as long as the proposals are sufficiently specific and are not altered in the face of contradictory evidence.) The weakness arises in the formulation of the arguments: they are very often based on what science does not currently know or cannot currently see. It seems to me that the irreducible complexity argument reduces to an argument from ignorance: we cannot understand how intermediate structures could have been altered to yield flagella (or wings or eyes), and so we conclude that this did not occur. Clearly, there is another possibility: that we do not (yet) know enough to understand how the intermediate structures did indeed precede the current systems, and how selection acting on variation could have driven the change.

I assert that this kind of argument from ignorance is wholly unsatisfactory. Consider two illustrations of how such thinking can mislead. Suppose one comes upon a simple stone arch bridge, such as have been built by humans for centuries.[24] The bridge is composed of chunks of stone, cut so that they fit together to form the arch, which stands without further support and without the need for the stones to be attached to one another. The structure exhibits the key aspects of irreducible complexity: it cannot be built piece-by-piece, and it will immediately collapse if any part is removed. One might wonder how such a structure could ever be built. The solution is straightforward: the arch was supported by a scaffold of some kind until it was complete, and then the scaffold was removed. The irreducible complexity of the current structure, then, does not entail the impossibility of functional precursors, since the precursors may well have had components or features that have since been removed and can no longer be seen.

Consider a second illustration, a case study from the history of evolutionary biology. The problem of non-functional precursors was noted by Darwin himself, and was emphasized by one of Darwin's contemporary critics, St. George Jackson Mivart. Darwin worried about the plausibility of evolutionary explanations for the vertebrate eye, and Mivart asked a now-famous question: "what use is half a wing?" Mivart's challenge, it seems to me, is the same as Behe's: how can an incomplete version of a functional system be maintained by natural selection? And the conclusion of Behe and other ID thinkers, it seems to me, is based almost completely on the same reasoning of Mivart; namely, that because we cannot understand, or do not know, how the precursors could have been functional, then natural selection could not have sculpted the resulting final structure. But Mivart's challenge is being answered.

Recent findings have provided a scientific answer to the rhetorical question that he posed. The question was "what use is half a wing?" The answer: it is useful for enhancing traction while running uphill. Such functions are documented in existing organisms, and provide explanation for the development and functional utility of feathered limbs and "proto-wings" in ancient species (dinosaurs) thought to be ancestors of modern birds.[25]

ID theorists are usually correct when they assert that science does not know the particular developmental trajectory that explains how a certain biological system could have evolved. But they are unwise, in my view, to conclude that this rules out the possibility of assembling such an explanation, and I predict that the current explosive growth of genomic information will lead to a host of new explanations for precisely the events that ID theorists identify as effectively impossible.

Valuable contributions of ID

As discussed above, ID is equated with creationism by many of its critics, and there is clear affinity between the two movements. But I maintain that such a casual dismissal of ID misses a very important distinction between its ideas and those of Christian creationists: the core ideas of ID, with respect to the detection of design in nature, have stimulated a robust scientific response, both in the form of articles in the scientific literature and, significantly in my view, in the form of specific experiments and research projects intended to test ID-related proposals.[26] By contrast, while creationism is widely popular among Christian non-scientists, its challenges to evolutionary science are ill-conceived and scientifically insignificant, and creationist ideas and claims are not regularly engaged in the scientific literature. Opponents of ID correctly note that the central questions posed by the ID movement are not new, and indeed problems concerning complexity and design have been debated for centuries. But the abundance of current scientific work on issues of self-organization, complexity, and variation (to name a few areas of recent research)[27] makes it clear that ID proponents have identified questions of interest to science in general, and of interest to evolutionary biologists in particular. If ID thinkers can translate their questions into a serious research agenda, the movement may yet achieve recognition as something bigger than a sophisticated creationist challenge to evolutionary theory.

Conclusions

In summary, I find the ID movement's focus on design in nature to be intriguing, and generally worthy of scientific attention, even though I find the proposals unconvincing as challenges to natural selection acting on variation. Unfortunately, ID ideas are currently being used in an unsuccessful attempt to undermine evolutionary biology. This effort, considered in the context of the creationist leanings (and tactics) of some of ID's proponents, has led to the dismissal of the movement as a new form of creationism, which has diminished the movement's credibility significantly. Moreover, ID thinkers incorrectly conflate natural explanation and naturalism, and ignore the important distinction that scientists typically make between methodological naturalism and philosophical naturalism. Misled by these errors, and because the movement seeks to oppose naturalism and lessen its influence, ID finds itself in conflict with evolutionary science, hoping to deprive naturalism of a significant asset.[28]

As I argued in the previous chapter, there is no serious conflict between evolutionary science and Christian belief. Christians, in my view, should not embrace ID as an alternative to evolutionary theory, since it has failed to advance any competing explanation. Instead, it seems to me that Christians who seek to oppose the appropriation of science by naturalism would do better to reclaim science as an exploration of God's world, and welcome the natural explanations that result. As far as they take us.

Notes

1 Although the modern ID movement was born in the late 1980s, the first clear articulations of its ideas are found in Phillip Johnson's *Darwin on Trial* (Downers Grove, IL: InterVarsity Press, 1991) and Michael Bee's *Darwin's Black Box* (New York: Free Press, 1996).

2 Thanks to Ted Davis for particularly helpful clarifications of the nature of the ID movement. See, for example, "Intelligent Design on trial," in *Religion in the News* 8, no. 3, 2006. This article is available on Prof. Davis' website: http://home.messiah.edu/~tdavis

3 For an excellent discussion of Darwin and the evolution of his attitudes toward design, see Michael Ruse, *Darwin and Design* (Cambridge, MA: Harvard University Press, 2003), especially chapter 6, "A subject too profound."

4 See Ruse, *Darwin and Design*, for details on the history of natural theology.

5 Charles Hodge, *What Is Darwinism? And Other Writings on Science and Religion*, ed. Mark A. Noll and David N. Livingstone (Grand Rapids, MI: Baker Books, 1994). The article is also available online at Project Gutenberg: http://www.gutenberg.org/etext/19192.

6 Phillip E. Johnson, "What is Darwinism?" in *Objections Sustained* (Downers Grove, IL: InterVarsity Press, 1998). The article is also available online: http://www.arn.org/docs/johnson/wid.htm.

7 There is significant confusion regarding the stance of the ID movement toward evolutionary biology. Some prominent ID proponents, such as Michael Behe, accept common descent, and most acknowledge at least a limited role for natural selection in observed changes in populations over time. Others, however, such as Phillip Johnson and Jonathan Wells, reject most of evolutionary science, including common descent. More significantly, the popular perception of ID, which the movement's leaders do not actively discourage, is that ID represents a distinct alternative to common descent and natural selection as well as to the naturalism that Hodge identified with Darwinism.

8 See Johnson, *Darwin on Trial*. For critical reviews of Johnson's failed attack on evolutionary theory, see Stephen Jay Gould's review of *Darwin on Trial* in *Scientific American* (July 1992, vol. 267, no. 1, available online at http://www.stephenjaygould.org/ctrl/gould_darwin-on-trial.html), or Ken Miller's *Finding Darwin's God* (New York: HarperCollins, 1999), chapter 4, "God the Magician."

9 The Discovery Institute is the predominant think tank of the ID movement, and its website is a good source of basic information on the movement: http://www.discovery.org/csc/

10 See the extensive work of Del Ratzsch on this subject. *Science and Its Limits: The Natural Sciences in Christian Perspective*, 2nd Edition (Downers Grove, IL: InterVarsity Press, 2000) contains an excellent introduction to the issues, while *Nature, Design, and Science* (Albany, NY: SUNY Press, 2001) is a deeper and more complete analysis.

11 Some ID proponents claim that SETI is a search for "specified complexity"; see, for example, William A. Dembski, "The logical underpinnings of intelligent design," in W. A. Dembski and M. Ruse, eds., *Debating Design* (Cambridge: Cambridge University Press, 2004). This is disputed by SETI researchers themselves, who note that the signals being sought are actually very simple and are identified as potentially extraterrestrial by their probable source and not by their content. See Seth Shostak, "SETI and intelligent design," Space.com, Dec. 1, 2005; available online at http://www.space.com/searchforlife/seti_intelligentdesign_051201.html.

12 Specified complexity is also known as complex specified information. For a basic introduction, see Dembski, "The logical underpinnings of intelligent design," or "Science and design," *First Things*, October 1998 issue, pp. 21–7; available online at www.firstthings.com. The full-length account is found in Dembski's *The Design Inference* (Cambridge: Cambridge University Press, 1998).

13 See Behe's "Molecular machines: experimental support for the design inference," *Cosmic Pursuit*, March 1998 (available online at design.org/csc) or "Irreducible complexity" in Dembski and Ruse, *Debating Design* for an introduction to irreducible complexity. The complete account in found in his *Darwin's Black Box* (New York: Free Press, 1996).

14 "Creationism" is a term that is often used imprecisely; it is here understood to refer to the assertion of supernatural creation by God accompanied by the denial of most aspects of evolutionary theory. For the ID movement's claims to be distinct from creationism, see Stephen C. Meyer, "Intelligent Design is Not Creationism," in *The Daily Telegraph* (London), Feb. 9, 2006. Available online at discovery.org/csc.

15 See Davis, "Intelligent Design on trial," and work by philosopher Barbara Forrest on the reworking of creationist textbooks. An article by Forrest, and links to her testimony at the Dover trial, can be found at www.ncseweb.org.

16 See Eugenie C. Scott, "NABT statement on evolution evolves," NCSE website, May 21, 1998. Available online at www.ncseweb.org.

17 See John F. Haught, "Darwin, design, and divine providence," in Dembski and Ruse, *Debating Design*.

18 See Loren Haarsma, "Does science exclude God?" in *Perspectives on an Evolving Creation* (Downers Grove, IL: Eerdmans, 2003) and Miller's *Finding Darwin's God*, ch. 8, "The road back home."

19 See R. E. Lenski, C. Ofria, R. T. Pennock, and C. Adami, "The evolutionary origin of complex features" (*Nature* 423:139–44, 2003); J. T. Bridgham, S. M. Carroll, and J. W. Thornton, "Evolution of hormone-receptor complexity by molecular exploitation" (*Science* 312, 97–101, 2006; C. Adami, "Reducible complexity" (*Science* 312, 61–3, 2006); and R. M. Hazen, P. L. Griffin, J. M. Carothers, and J. W. Szostak, "Functional information and the emergence of biocomplexity" (*Proceedings of the National Academy of Sciences USA* 104, 8574–81, 2007).

20 F. J. Ayala, "Darwin's greatest discovery: Design without designer" (104, 2007, 8567–73).

21 The classic study by D .N. Reznick, F. H. Shaw, F. H. Rodd, and R. G. Shaw, "Evaluation of the rate of evolution in natural populations of guppies (*Poecilia reticulata*)," (*Science* 275, 1934–7, 1997) found that observed rates of change (after selection) can exceed rates estimated from the fossil record, by several orders of magnitude. See also H. E. Hoekstra, J. M. Hoekstra, D. Berrigan, S. N. Vignieri, A. Hoang, C. E. Hill, et al. "Strength and tempo of directional selection in the wild" (*Proceedings of the National Academy of Sciences USA* 98, 9157–60, 2001).

22 Pallen and Matzke, "From *The Origin of Species* to the origin of bacterial flagella" (*Nature Reviews Microbiology* 4, 2006, 784–90).

23 See Behe, *Darwin's Black Box*, or "Irreducible complexity," in Dembski and Ruse, *Debating Design*.

24 At least one such bridge survives from the 2nd century AD, built by the Romans. See Ruse, "Turning back the clock," in *Darwin and Design* for a similar use of this illustration.

25 See K. P. Dial, R. J. Randall, and T. R. Dial, "What use is half a wing in the ecology and evolution of birds?" *BioScience* 56, 437–45, 2006; and K. P. Dial, "Wing-assisted incline running and the evolution of flight," *Science* 299, 402–4, 2003. Articles available online at the laboratory's website: http://dbs.umt.edu/research%5Flabs/flightlab.

26 F. J. Ayala, "Darwin's greatest discovery"; Pallen and Matzke, "From *The Origin of Species* to the origin of bacterial flagella."

27 For very recent examples, see Hazen et al. "Functional information," Ayala "Darwin's greatest discovery," and other articles in the May 15, 2007 supplemental issue of *Proceedings of the National Academy of Sciences USA*, vol. 104, Suppl. 1.

28 The success of evolutionary theory is taken by some to be of profound help to naturalism. Hence the famous claim by atheist Richard Dawkins: "… although atheism might have been *logically* tenable before Darwin, Darwin made it possible to be an intellectually fulfilled atheist." Richard Dawkins, *The Blind Watchmaker* (New York: W.W. Norton, 1986); see also Alvin Plantinga, "When faith and reason clash: Evolution and the Bible," *Christian Scholar's Review* XXI (1991), 8–33 (available online at www.asa3.org).

21

Biology, the Incarnation, and Christian Materialism

STEPHEN MATHESON

Christianity has a long history of embracing dualism, wherein human persons are believed to consist of both bodies and immaterial souls. But modern neuroscience is poised to provide biological explanations, through analysis of brain function and dysfunction, for nearly every aspect of human nature that has been traditionally attributed to the immaterial soul. If such entities exist, they seem not to provide useful explanatory resources in the understanding of properties such as moral agency. I sketch an overview of relevant biological theories, then discuss an alternative to dualism which provides a useful framework for the understanding of embodied human nature.

Introducing the Problem

All three of the chapters I present in this volume have a common theme: scientific explanation, particularly biological explanation, in the context of Christian faith. The previous two chapters have explored some interactions between Christian faith and evolutionary theory. Here, I turn to interactions between Christian faith and modern neurobiology, focusing on the concept of the soul as it relates to scientific explanation. Partly because the relevant fields of inquiry are less well-developed, and partly because the questions I raise here are heavily philosophical in nature, this chapter will range into terrain more speculative and philosophical than the first two. My primary purpose is not to address theological or philosophical debates surrounding dualism, though I will mention these discussions. Instead, my intent is to maintain a specific focus on the value of dualism in the arena of biological scientific explanation.

The phrase "Christian materialism" will seem like an oxymoron to many readers, since materialism is often understood to refer to a philosophical view which asserts that matter is all that exists. The latter type of materialism, variously referred to as *nothing-but material-ism*[1] and *reductive materialism,*[2] is clearly not compatible with Christianity or any other type of theism. Here, however, and from this point forward, I use the term solely to refer to materialism about the human person. Materialism about the human person does not deny supernaturalism in general; it denies *dualism* with respect to the human person. This means that materialism denies that human persons are composed of, or include, immaterial essences; in other words, materialism denies the existence of immaterial *souls*.

Here, I will explore the concept of the soul as an explanation for various phenomena. My question, then, is this: does dualism provide significant biological (mostly neurobiological) explanatory resources? I conclude that it does not; in other words, I argue that immaterial souls offer little in the way of biological explanatory value. I close by arguing that Christians who reject dualism will find abundant resources for the construction of a robust Christian materialism, which embraces the embodied view of life that has always undergirded Christian faith.

The Soul and Christian Dualism

The dualistic concept of an immaterial soul is both ancient and pervasive in Christian and Western thought.[3] In one of the Biblical accounts of the creation of humankind, the first human is first formed from the dust of the ground, but does not become a "living being" until he is exposed to God's breath: "And the Lord God formed a man from the dust of the ground and breathed into his nostrils the breath of life, and man became a living being."[4] In the other creation account, humans are said to be created in God's image; God is elsewhere asserted to be a spirit, and a reasonable conclusion is that humans share in God's image in so far as they are composed at least in part by an immaterial spirit, or soul.[5] A well-known and pivotal Bible passage urges people to love God "with all your heart and with all your soul and with all your strength."[6] And at various points throughout the Bible, writers seem to refer to human beings in disembodied states.[7] While a careful review of dualistic thought in the Bible is beyond the scope of this chapter, it is clear that Christians have always been inclined toward dualism, and that the Bible provides ample justification for this belief.

Dualism and Scientific Explanation

Dualism, despite its widespread acceptance by Christians, is the subject of robust debate among Christian scholars, some of whom have identified both philosophical and theological problems presented by Christian dualism. The specifics of these problems lie beyond the scope of this article, but most of the philosophical and theological problems presented by dualism arise when considering the relationship(s) between the soul and the body.

Christian scholars have identified another category of problem with dualism, and it is this issue on which I will concentrate here. For centuries, the soul has been identified as the source of most of the most important aspects of uniquely human existence: free will, reason, moral agency, love, spirituality, among others. And the problem is simply this: modern neuroscience is proposing scientific explanations that account for, or strongly influence, all of these properties of human beings. To the extent that the immaterial soul is understood to be an explanation, or *the* explanation, for these formerly mysterious aspects of personhood, it is clearly threatened by newly proposed alternative scientific explanations. More precisely: the existence of immaterial souls is no longer the sole explanation, and clearly no longer a *necessary* explanation, for the most unique and special aspects of human nature. So what are these central human attributes, and how has science begun to explain them biologically?

Central human attributes and their emerging biological explanations

Moral agency

The ability of human beings to make moral choices has long been linked to the image of God and the activity of the soul,[8] and moral agency is a fundamental human trait acknowledged universally (i.e., the concept is not peculiarly Christian). But the capacity to make moral judgments can be compromised by damage to particular areas of the brain, and this is best illustrated by a case study that is commonly marked as a signal event in the founding of modern neuroscience.

When Phineas Gage was 25 years old (in 1848), he worked as a supervisor for a company that was building railroads in the New England region of the United States. Gage was one of the company's finest employees, and was responsible for the preparation of holes filled with explosive powder for the blasting of rock. Gage's job was to compact the blasting powder in the hole, using a large iron bar, pounding on sand that had been added on top of the blasting powder. The compacted powder exploded more forcefully; the sand enabled Gage to pound on the powder without touching it. The bar was more than 1 meter long, and 3 cm in diameter, tapering to a point about 0.5 cm across. (The taper enabled Gage to grip the bar while pounding on the sand.) One day, when Gage was momentarily distracted, he began to pound on the powder in a hole to which no sand had been added. The resulting explosion shot the bar out of the hole with the velocity of a bullet fired from a gun. The bar pierced Gage's cheek, entered the base of his skull behind his eye, then exited through the top of his skull, having passed through the most frontal regions of his brain. It shot into the air, and landed more than 30 meters away. Amazingly, Gage was not killed, and appeared to lose consciousness only momentarily. He was able to walk and speak within minutes, and made an almost complete recovery within two months.[9]

Gage's survival and recovery were extraordinary, but his case is famous for a different reason. Gage's recovery seemed complete: he could walk and speak, and his basic cognitive faculties seem to have been intact. But his personality was completely altered. Before the accident, Gage was considered to exhibit exemplary character; after the accident, he became so obnoxious and profane that his friends could barely recognize him as the same person. "Gage was no longer Gage," his friends noted, and his employer would not hire him again. He was physically quite able to do his job, but his character had changed dramatically, and he was unable to remain employed for the rest of his life.

Detailed studies of Gage's skull, combined with new findings from more modern cases involving similar damage to the brain, have led to the development of increasingly sophisticated theories regarding the interactions of emotion and rationality in moral reasoning. These fascinating advances, focused on one particular type of moral function, represent a fraction of the progress achieved by scientific examination of moral reasoning and neurobiology over the past few decades.[10] Consider, for example, Tourette's syndrome, in which sufferers exhibit regular and involuntary actions called tics. The tics can be merely odd movements, such as elaborate twitches, but often take the form of verbal outbursts that can be rude or profane. The syndrome is somewhat common, and is thought to result from dysfunction in particular brain systems. Moral agency, it seems, is mediated by brain systems that can be understood through the tools of neuroscience, and the scientific explanations that are being assembled do not require reference to the immaterial.

Capacity for love

Few things seem more uniquely human than the ability to love and the giving of unconditional love is a foundational Christian commandment. And yet this capacity can be altered profoundly by brain damage, as evidenced by the rare but fascinating Capgras delusion.[11] In this syndrome, the affected individual can recognize loved ones, but will insist that they are impostors. Although the affected person will acknowledge, for example, that the woman in his home looks exactly like his mother, he is convinced that she is not his mother, but is a different person who looks just like her. The hypothesized explanation for the delusion is that damage to the brain has uncoupled visual processing from emotional processing, such that the affected person experiences no sense of love or connection when looking at his loved ones. The affected person's profound sense of disconnection results in the delusion that the other person is not who they appear to be. If an immaterial soul causes us to love others, it appears that this ability can be severely impaired by damage to certain areas of the brain, and this significantly diminishes the explanatory value of the immaterial soul.

Religious experience

What about religious experiences? Do we need to postulate immaterial souls to explain feelings associated with worship and spirituality, or a sense of the divine? Scientific explanations of religion and religious behavior have become quite popular recently, focusing mostly on theoretical accounts of how religion could have arisen through standard evolutionary mechanisms.[12] But the strongest evidence that religious experience is biologically explainable comes from studies of a particular form of epilepsy, in which the seizures hyperactivate the temporal lobes of the brain. Such seizures can induce feelings of religious awe or ecstasy, and sufferers sometimes exhibit long-lasting spiritual fixations.[13] That such religious experiences can be triggered by hyperactivity in particular regions of the brain suggests that the experiences have a biological explanation, that they are anchored to the human body. Reference to an immaterial soul may not be necessary to provide explanation for human religious experience.

Sense of self

Humans typically experience their cognitive life in a unified way; indeed, this aspect of consciousness is a major focus of work on the ancient mind – body problem, and the accompanying sense of self, of unified ownership of one's experience, is a common argument for the existence (and explanatory efficacy) of immaterial souls.[14] V. S. Ramachandran has referred to the self as "the last remaining great mystery in science," and identifies five defining characteristics of the self: (1) continuity (through time); (2) unity or coherence of self; (3) a sense of ownership and embodiment, or a sense of being attached to one's body; (4) a sense of agency; and (5) a sense of self-awareness by which one can reflect on oneself.[15] These attributes of human experience are indeed mysterious, and yet every one of them is known to be affected by certain types of brain dysfunction.

For example, continuity of the self through time can be completely abolished through destruction of neural systems responsible for the production of long-term memory, and this type of brain disease has produced some of the best-known case studies in neuroscience and psychology. These patients live in a moving window of time, acquiring no memory as they go, with no anchor to the past. So profound is this disruption of the self that neurologist Oliver Sacks, writing about one such patient he calls Jimmie G., wondered whether Jimmie had a soul.[16]

The sense of being anchored to one's body would seem to be a very basic function of an immaterial soul, especially a soul thought to live inside a body. But even this mysterious aspect of the self can be disrupted by brain damage.[17] Consider the bizarre and fascinating delusion called Cotard's syndrome, in which the patient claims that he or she is dead. The proposed explanation for the delusion is similar to that for the Capgras delusion: emotional centers in the brain have been disconnected from the senses, so that the person feels completely disconnected from his or her body, and is apparently forced to conclude that he or she is dead. The syndrome is rare, but psychiatry is quite familiar with less extreme manifestations of this type of disconnectedness, in the form of depersonalization disorders that can accompany depression and other maladies. In these disorders, the patient will report feeling utterly disconnected, certain that the world is unreal. The causes of these syndromes are not well understood, but specific and testable hypotheses have been proposed, and it seems clear that biological explanations will emerge.

And what of split-brain patients and sufferers from multiple personality disorder? In both cases, there seem to be multiple selves within a single body. In split-brain patients, the two hemispheres of the brain have been mostly disconnected from one another, due to severing of the *corpus callosum*, the brain structure that normally allows the two hemispheres to communicate. Extensive research on split-brain patients has led to increasing understanding of the significantly different roles of the two hemispheres in the construction of human consciousness.[18] For example, the left hemisphere specializes in hypothesis formation, so much so that it is variously referred to as the "interpreter" or the "general." Remarkably, Ramachandran reports that in one split-brain patient, the left hemisphere claimed to believe in God, while the right hemisphere identified itself as an atheist. While even in these strange cases only one self is experienced at any given time, the fact that brain dysfunction can cause a single human body to harbor multiple selves or personalities suggests that the self, even when fractured or multiplied within a single body, arises through the activity of neural systems.

Free will

Free will, or the capacity to choose, represents an area of significant conflict between dualists and non-dualists, and a topic of widespread and ongoing debate. One might reasonably attribute free will (i.e., non-deterministic decision-making) to an entity outside of naturalistic cause and effect: an immaterial soul. But studies of human brain activity during simple decision-making raise interesting questions about the source of the human will to act. Most provocative are the experiments of Libet and coworkers, who measured the timing of activation of various brain regions in people performing simple motor tasks (i.e., moving a finger).[19] They found specific brain activity that preceded, by at least half a second, the conscious decision to move the finger. (More precisely, the activity preceded the "reported time of conscious intention to act.") This pattern of brain activity, observed repeatedly in experiments since the original study, is called the readiness potential, and the implication is almost unbelievable: the brain seems to decide to act before the self is conscious of the decision. The will to move, however it works, does not seem to be well explained through the actions of an immaterial soul, unless the soul is proposed to act without the conscious awareness of the self.

Souls, persons, and explanation

It is important to reiterate the purpose of the preceding section. It is my view that neuroscience has significantly eroded the explanatory value of immaterial souls. As Malcolm Jeeves and Warren Brown put it, neuroscience "strongly questions a separate, non-material agency for the soul by which certain domains of human experience can remain unaffected by changes in brain function."[20] This view in no way establishes that the existence of immaterial souls is impossible or even unlikely. It does mean that a Christian might hesitate to accept the existence of immaterial souls based only on the asserted explanatory value of the concept. Why else might a Christian adopt a dualistic stance on the nature of persons? I see two remaining arguments: (1) an argument based on Biblical assertion of the existence of immaterial souls; and (2) an argument based on Christian understandings of human nature, which assert that humans are something more than biological machines.

I find the first argument unpersuasive. Although I and others see Christian dualism as reasonable and defensible, I find the Biblical case for the existence of immaterial souls to be indecisive. Although an exhaustive account of the theological and Biblical arguments[21] is beyond the scope of this chapter, I join others who see Biblical redemptive history as pervasively embodied, emphasizing the physical and bodily aspects of human (and divine) existence, as I will explain below.

The second argument, on the other hand, represents a significant challenge for Christian scholars seeking to place human nature in a natural context while avoiding the pitfalls of dualism. But thanks to some excellent work by Christian philosophers and neuroscientists, a framework has emerged of an understanding of human nature that is wholistic (i.e., non-dualist) but not reductionist. The perspective is called non-reductive physicalism, and I turn now to some thoughts on the advantages of this view for Christian reflection on biology and personhood.

Non-Reductive Physicalism

Non-reductive physicalism is a non-dualist perspective on human nature, in that it assumes there is no need to invoke immaterial entities to account for the attributes of humanness that are traditionally associated with souls. It is a non-reductive perspective in that it assumes that human behavior cannot be completely explained by understanding biological phenomena; in other words, it denies determinism with respect to higher-level human capacities, asserting instead that such capacities (such as thinking) are causally efficacious. Importantly, non-reductive physicalism does not deny the existence of souls; it denies the *non-material nature* of souls. As Warren Brown puts it: "Humans *are* bodies – they do not have bodies; they *are* souls – they do not have souls." Christians who adopt this view can acknowledge the centrality of the image of God and the concept of human souls, without embracing dualism, and I find this approach quite fruitful.

How, though, can a human being be both a soul and a body? In other words, how does a Christian assert that a human being is purely physical, without asserting that a human being is *nothing but* physical? Kevin Corcoran has described a useful perspective on human nature that resolves this dilemma.[22] His view is the Constitution View (CV) of human persons. CV maintains that a human person is *constituted* by his or her body, but is not *identical* to it. The concept is best explained with the illustration of a statue. Consider a statue of some sort of metal, such as the Statue of Liberty in New York harbor. The statue is not identical with the metal plates from which it is made, because the metal plates can still exist without the statue continuing to exist. (If the statue were pounded flat with an enormous hammer, the metal plates would survive, but the statue would be destroyed.) The statue is made of exactly the same stuff as the metal plates, and no additional metaphysical entity need be asserted in order to completely account for the statue's properties. But the statue and the metal plates are different kinds of things; they are not identical, even though they are spatially coincident.

I maintain that non-reductive physicalism, especially as expressed as the Constitution View of persons, provides an excellent framework within which to explore the biological properties of human nature, and this view is the "Christian materialism" that I outlined at the beginning of this article. This framework does not hinder the pursuit of scientific explanation, and does not encourage the introduction of unnecessary metaphysical entities into biological accounts of human attributes. Just as importantly, non-reductive physicalism integrates well with fundamental assertions of Christian faith that bear on the very nature of redemptive history, by affirming the central importance of human bodies in Christianity.

Incarnation, resurrection and ascension: All about bodies

Bodies have always been important in Christianity. Jesus Christ though the son of God was born a human being, with human flesh and completely human nature. This event, called the Incarnation, is so pivotal in Christian narrative history that special declarations of Christian faith, called creeds, were established during early Christian history for the purpose of affirming its truth and centrality.[23] The Nicene Creed, for example, written in the fourth century AD, states that Jesus "became incarnate by the Holy Spirit and the Virgin Mary, and was made human." The humanity of Jesus is the basis of his identification with human weakness and his ability to conquer human death through his own death.[24] In the Incarnation, God became flesh, human flesh, and lived among humans.[25]

A further central Christian belief is the hope of resurrection from the dead, meaning the resurrection of the *body*. As the Nicene Creed states, "We look forward to the resurrection of the dead, and to life in the world to come. Amen." The Apostles' Creed is more direct, professing belief in "the resurrection of the body, and the life everlasting." Jesus' resurrection is the founding event, the so-called firstfruit of many resurrections to come.[26] And Jesus' resurrection was clearly a resurrection of the body: at one point, he ate food in order to demonstrate his existence as a physical body, and not as a ghost.[27]

The completion of work of Jesus on earth occurred when he ascended from earth "into heaven." The significance of the ascension is several folds in Christianity, but its key aspect is this: Jesus went into heaven *with a body*. This remarkable event has a remarkable implication, namely that God's nature now includes human flesh, in the person of Jesus Christ. As one historic Christian document, the Heidelberg Catechism, puts it, "we have our own flesh in heaven." The stuff of biology, cells and DNA and flesh and bones, is in heaven, somehow, in the form of Jesus' ascended body. Bodies are important in Christianity. Bodies are forever in Christianity. Non-reductive physicals is, in my view, a robust affirmation of the embodied nature of humans, including Jesus Christ, an affirmation that embraces biological scientific explanation without denying any aspect of the image of God in humans or of the foundational nature of Jesus himself.

Summary

In chapters 19–21, it has been my intention to focus mainly on the interactions between scientific explanations and Christian faith. Many scientific explanations do touch on issues of interest to Christians, and conflicts are inevitable. On closer inspection, however, I find that most of the conflicts and controversies are centered on misunderstandings or questionable assumptions. When the conflicts are real, they tend to be conflicts between Christianity and naturalism, not between Christianity and science.

In summary, I have attempted to highlight some basic principles for the effective consideration, by Christians, of biological explanations. First, it is my contention that careful attention to the various types of explanation can eliminate numerous errors, such as those I discuss in chapter 19 on evolutionary creation. Second, I maintain that a unified view of God's creative activity, which does not artificially distinguish between natural and supernatural aspects of God's actions, enables Christians to consider biology as the exploration of God's created world, as I discuss in chapter 20 on intelligent design. And finally, I believe that a strong affirmation of the embodied nature of Christianity, and of Christ himself, can provide an excellent framework for the understanding of biological human nature by Christians.

Notes

1   See Kevin J. Corcoran, *Rethinking Human Nature: A Christian Materialist Alternative to the Soul* (Grand Rapids, MI: Baker Academic, 2006).
2   See Warren S. Brown, "Evolution, Cognitive Neuroscience, and the Soul," in *Perspectives on an Evolving Creation* (Grand Rapids, MI: Eerdmans, 2003).
3   Kevin Corcoran notes that "a dualist view of human nature has been the majority view of Christians throughout the history of the church" (n. 1, p. 20). Malcolm Jeeves examines these topics in "Neuroscience, evolutionary psychology, and the image of God" (*Perspectives on Science and Christian Faith* 57, 2005, 170–86), available online at www.asa3.org.) And readers of the immensely and internationally popular Harry Potter stories have explored a wholly dualistic world, in which the only fate worse than death is to have one's soul removed from one's body by an evil creature called a dementor.
4   Genesis 2:7. (All Bible passages are taken from the New International Version, hereafter referred to as NIV.)
5   Genesis 1:26–7; John 4:24 (NIV).
6   Deuteronomy 6:5; see also Mark 12:29–31 and Luke 10:25–8 (NIV).
7   For example, I Samuel 28 (NIV) describes a scene in which a sorceress (the witch of Endor) summons a dead person from the grave. See Corcoran, *Rethinking Human Nature*, ch. 6 for more examples and a discussion of their significance.

8 See Jeeves, "Neuroscience."

9 An excellent account of the accident and its aftermath can be found in Antonio R. Damasio, *Descartes' Error* (New York: HarperCollins, 1994).

10 See Jeeves, "Neuroscience." For fascinating accounts of persons suffering from Tourette's syndrome, see Oliver Sacks, "Witty Ticcy Ray" and "The possessed," in *The Man Who Mistook His Wife for a Hat* (New York: Touchstone, 1985), or "A surgeon's life," in *An Anthropologist on Mars* (London: Vintage Books, 1995).

11 See Brown, "Evolution," and V. S. Ramachandran, *A Brief Tour of Human Consciousness* (New York: Pi Press, 2004). This book contains Ramachandran's 2003 Reith Lectures, which can be found online at http://www.bbc.co.uk/radio4/reith.

12 See, for example, Daniel Dennett's *Breaking the Spell: Religion as a Natural Phenomenon* (New York: Penguin Books, 2006).

13 V. S. Ramachandran, *Phantoms in the Brain* (New York: William Morrow 1998).

14 See, for example, Joel B. Green, "Body and soul, mind and brain: Critical issues," in J. B. Green and S. L. Palmer (eds.), *In Search of the Soul* (Downers Grove, IL: InterVarsity Press, 2005), or Ramachandran, *A Brief Tour*.

15 Ramachandran, *A Brief Tour*, pp. 96–7.

16 Oliver Sacks, "The lost mariner," in *The Man Who Mistook His Wife for a Hat*. For more examples of this kind of amnesia and its effects on persons, see Brown, "Evolution," p. 517, and descriptions of Clive Wearing, whose story is told in his wife's recent memoir: Deborah Wearing, *Forever Today* (New York: Doubleday, 2005).

17 Ramachandran, *A Brief Tour*, pp. 91–3. See also Sacks, "The Disembodied Lady," in *The Man Who Mistook His Wife for a Hat*.

18 Ramachandran, *A Brief Tour*, pp. 104 and 154–5; Ramachandran, "The Sound of One Hand Clapping," *Phantoms in the Brain*; Michael S. Gazzaniga, "Cerebral specialization and interhemispheric communication: Does the corpus callosum enable the human condition?" (*Brain* 123, 2000, 1293–1326; available online at http://brain.oxfordjournals.org).

19 Ramachandran, *A Brief Tour*, pp. 86–7; B. Libet, C. A. Gleason, E. W. Wright, and D. K. Pearl, "Time of conscious intention to act in relation to onset of cerebral activity (readiness-potential): The unconscious initiation of a freely voluntary act" (*Brain* 106, 623–42, 2000; available online at http://brain.oxfordjournals.org).

20 Warren S. Brown and Malcolm A. Jeeves, "Portraits of Human Nature: Reconciling Neuroscience and Christian Anthropology" (*Science and Christian Belief* 11, 1999, 139–50; available online at www.asa3.org).

21 Green, "Body and Soul"; Joel B. Green, "'Bodies – that is, human lives': A re-examination of human nature in the Bible," in W. S. Brown, N. Murphy, and H. N. Malony (eds.), *Whatever Happened to the Soul?* (Minneapolis: Augsburg Fortress Press, 1998).

22 Kevin Corcoran, "The constitution view of persons," and various responses, in Green and Palmer, *In Search of the Soul*.

23 These creeds, and historical documents called confessions, are available online at http://www.crcna.org/pages/beliefs.cfm.

24 Hebrews 2:14–18 (NIV).

25 John 1:14 (NIV).

26 I Corinthians 15:20–3 (NIV).

27 Luke 24:36–43 (NIV).

Part 8

Religion, Naturalism, and Science

22

Science and Religion: Why Does the Debate Continue?

ALVIN PLANTINGA

In this chapter I try to make a contribution to an answer to the question, why does the debate continue between science and religion? Specifically, I address two related topics: (1) the association of science with secularism, the so-called "scientific world-view"; (2) the alleged conflict between scientific theories of evolution and essential teachings of Christianity and other religions, for example, that humans are created in God's image.

First, *is* there a debate? Well yes, I suppose there is. Many Christians have the vague impression that science is somehow unfriendly to religious belief; for other Christians it's less a vague impression than a settled conviction. Similarly, many scientists and science enthusiasts argue that there is opposition between serious religious belief and science; indeed, some claim that religious belief constitutes a clear and present danger to science. Still others see religious belief as steadily dwindling in the face of scientific advance. Our question is: Why does this debate continue?

I shall try to answer that question; more modestly, I will try to make a contribution to an answer. This debate displays several different loci or topics.

1) There is the association of science with *secularism* or the so-called "scientific world-view."[1]
2) There is alleged conflict between scientific theories of evolution and essential aspects of Christianity and other theistic religions – for example, that human beings are created in the image of God.
3) There is alleged conflict between science and the claim, common to theistic religions, that God *acts especially* in the world. Miracles would be one example of special divine action, but there are others as well: for example, Calvin's "Internal Witness of the Holy Spirit" and Aquinas' "Internal Instigation of the Holy Spirit."
4) There is conflict between religious claims and many explanations in evolutionary psychology of such human phenomena as love, altruism, morality, and religion itself.

5) There is conflict between certain classical Christian doctrines – the resurrection of Jesus, for example – and certain varieties of scientific or historical Biblical criticism.
6) Finally, there is alleged conflict between the *epistemic attitudes* of science and religion. The scientific attitude, so it is said, involves forming belief on the basis of empirical investigation, holding belief tentatively, constantly testing belief and looking for a better alternative; the religious attitude involves believing on faith.

Clearly I cannot address all six of these topics of debate here; I will confine myself to the first two.

1 Science and Secularism

Science is often thought to endorse, promote, enforce, imply, or require *secularism*; but what exactly, or even approximately, *is* secularism? Suppose we start with the adjective and sneak up gradually on the noun. According to my dictionary the term *secular* means "of or relating to the worldly or the temporal as distinguished from the spiritual or eternal: not sacred." Here *eternal* wouldn't refer to propositions, properties, numbers and other abstract objects, which could also be thought of as eternal; perhaps we could replace "eternal," here, with "supernatural." On this account, raking your lawn could be secular; praying or worshipping would not. How about secular*ism*? This would be an attitude or a position of some sort: perhaps the position, with respect to some particular area of life, that secular approaches are all that is necessary or desirable in that area of life; no reference to the spiritual or supernatural is needed for proper prosecution of the activities or projects in that area. One might thus embrace secularism with respect to raking the lawn or getting your car repaired: no reference to the supernatural or spiritual is necessary. This is secularism *with respect to x*, for some department or aspect of life *x*; but then what is secularism *tout court*? For present purposes, that would be the idea that a secular approach to *all* of life is satisfactory or required; there is no department or aspect of life where there needs to be, or ought to be, a reference to the supernatural or spiritual. Secularism, so construed, has been an increasing feature of much of Western life, in particular of Western academic and intellectual life, for the last couple of centuries.

There are two basic and vastly different versions of secularism present in contemporary Western academia. One is limned and examined (and rejected) by Bas van Fraassen in his absorbing book *The Empirical Stance* (2002), initially given as lectures in the very series we are celebrating. This variety is intimately connected with science, and can be briefly if imprecisely described as the thought that scientific inquiry, or more accurately what van Fraassen calls "objectifying inquiry," is enough. Perhaps a bit more accurately, but still requiring nuance and qualification, it is the position that the broadly scientific picture of the world is enough. Enough for what? Enough for understanding, and enough for practice. Enough as a guide to life, and enough for rightly fixing opinion. This scientific worldview encompasses all we need to know and indeed all we *can* know about our world and about ourselves; if there is anything beyond or in addition to what science (present or future) reveals, it is something with which we neither have nor can have contact.

This variety of secularism is our main focus; but it is important to see that there is another and wholly different species of the same genus. And just as the first, scientific, variety is outlined in van Fraassen's book, so the second, nonscientific variety is sketched in a review of van Fraassen's book by Richard Rorty.[2] As Rorty points out, there is a kind of secularism that pays little attention to science, or at any rate sees its value as merely utilitarian. Rorty may or may not be right about the nature of the practical goals endorsed by this version of secularism; I'll comment instead on its intellectual or perhaps ideological side. Here what is fundamental is a turning away from science and objectifying inquiry, rejecting that whole endeavor as a failed project. And instead of seeing human beings as trying to achieve the truth about our world, it would instead see us, at some deep level, as *constructing* or, better, *constituting* the truth about the world. This way of thinking goes back, of course, to Kant and perhaps indeed to the ancient world, to the Protagorean claim that "man is the measure of all things." Here the fundamental idea is that we human beings, in some deep and important way, are ourselves responsible for the structure and nature of the world – either individually or communally. At this point, naturally, I would like to talk about Kant, but I don't have the space.

Another version of fundamentally the same idea is the claim that there really is no such thing as Truth (with a capital T, as they like to put it); what there are instead are various substitutes. Sticking with Rorty, for example, there is truth (now with a small 't') as "what our peers will let us get away with saying" (Rorty 1979a). This kind of secularism, like scientific secularism, embraces the idea that we have no need to resort to the spiritual or supernatural; we human beings are autonomous, and must make our own way, must fashion our own salvation. We are responsible for ourselves, and indeed (as Rorty says), can redefine, and remake ourselves. This lust for human autonomy can assume truly heroic proportions, as (if Rorty's account is accurate) with Heidegger's standing appalled at the thought that he was not his own creation (Rorty 1989, p. 109), and his remarkable idea that he was *guilty* by virtue of existing in a universe he had not himself created. (Talk about moral scruples and a tender conscience!) The contrast between these two forms of secularism is enormously fascinating. From a Christian perspective the one vastly overestimates us, tending to see us, we ourselves, as the real creators of the world, or at least the real source of its structure; the other vastly underestimates us, tending to see us as just another animal with a peculiar way of making a living.

But our present concern is with scientific secularism. Let's look a bit further. According to van Fraassen, the development of modern science involves what he calls, perhaps following Rudolf Bultmann, "objectifying inquiry." Objectifying inquiry, he says, is neither necessary nor sufficient for science; nevertheless, he says, it is a prominent and profoundly important feature of most scientific investigation. There are several aspects to this kind of inquiry, but a number of them can be subsumed under the striking phrase "getting ourselves out of the picture".[3] There is getting ourselves *individually* out of the picture: my own likes and dislikes, my own hopes and fears and loves are not to enter into what I do or say as a scientist, although of course they may serve as motivation for engaging in science in the first place and for pursuing one scientific inquiry as opposed to another. The surgeon who dispassionately cuts into another human being displays this kind of objectivity; to achieve it, surgeons ordinarily refuse to operate on family members. Similarly, my own private and idiosyncratic moral judgments are not to enter, either into my reports of the data, or into my theories. Objectivity in this sense is a matter of ignoring or bracketing what pertains to one or some individual(s) as opposed to others.

But science, notoriously, is also said to refrain from moral judgments more generally – not just those that do not enjoy universal assent. And the same goes for likes and dislikes. So there is a stronger sense of objectivity also operative here: stepping away from, bracketing, at least some aspects or characteristics of human subjectivity more generally, hoping in this way to achieve objectivity in the sense of faithfulness to the object of inquiry. There is our nearly inevitable propensity for making moral judgments; objectivity requires that, in doing science, we see this as something "from our side" as it were, not to be found in the things themselves (at least for the purposes of science. Similarly for *teleology*: human subjects display a nearly ineluctable tendency to think in terms of teleology, perhaps because of our inveterate practical bent. Another part of objectifying inquiry, therefore, another part of "taking ourselves out of the picture" is to think of the world, at least as scientific object, as involving no purposes, no teleology. This thought goes all the way back to Francis Bacon:

> Although the most general principles in nature ought to be held merely positive, as they are discovered, and cannot with truth be referred to a cause; nevertheless the human understanding being unable to rest still seeks something prior in the order of nature. And then it is that in struggling towards that which is further off it falls back upon that which is more nigh at hand; namely, on final causes: which have relation clearly to the nature of man rather than to the nature of the universe; and from this source have strangely defiled philosophy.[4]

Still further: human beings display a powerful inclination to *personify* the world: to see it as populated by living spirits who, like us, love and hate, think, believe, and reason;[5] for the animist the whole world is alive, permeated by living spirits. And a very special case of this – a limiting case, as we might think – is our human tendency to think of the world itself as created and governed by just one transcendent spirit; theism can thus be thought of as a limiting case of animism. Now part of taking ourselves out of the picture is rejecting, at least for scientific purposes, this tendency to personify the world. And if we do think of theism as a limiting case of animism, then this taking ourselves out of the picture can be seen as the source of *methodological naturalism* (MN).[6]

MN is widely proposed as a constraint on proper science, and indeed it seems to characterize most if not all of contemporary science. MN is not to be confused with *philosophical* or *ontological* naturalism, according to which there is no such person as God or any other supernatural beings. The partisan of MN doesn't necessarily subscribe to ontological naturalism. MN is a proposed condition on proper science, not a statement about the nature of the universe. (Of course if philosophical naturalism were true and if we thought of science as an effort to find the truth about our world, then MN would presumably be the sensible way to proceed in science.) The rough and basic idea of MN is that science should be done *as if*, in some sense, ontological naturalism were true; as Hugo Grotius put it, we should proceed as if God is not given. According to MN, therefore, a proper scientific theory cannot refer to God or other supernatural agents such as angels or devils or Satan and his cohorts. Further, scientific description or presentation of the data relevant to a given inquiry cannot be in terms or categories involving the supernatural. Still further, a scientific theory cannot employ what one knows or thinks one knows by way of divine revelation. There will be more to MN than this: for example, it will also involve a constraint on the appropriate body of background knowledge or belief with respect to which a scientific discipline is to be conducted: that background information, presumably, will contain no propositions obviously entailing[7] the existence of God (or other supernatural beings).

I shall try to say more about MN later; for the moment, we may note that it can nicely be seen as secularism with respect to science. The claim is that science, that striking and important human activity or form of life, has no need of the supernatural or spiritual for its proper prosecution, and indeed is best done by deleting any such references. Note the vast difference between *secularism with respect to science* and *scientific secularism*. The former is the claim that *science* can or should proceed without reference to the supernatural; it says nothing about the rest of life. The latter is a variety of secularism *tout court*; it is the claim that *all* of life can or should proceed without reference to the supernatural, because objectifying inquiry is enough for practice as well as for understanding. And now we can note one source of the continuing debate or mistrust between science and religion. Secularism *tout court*, of course, is the enemy of religion; it is the declaration that there is no department or aspect of life where there needs to be, or ought to be, a reference to the supernatural or spiritual. But the religious attitude towards life just is the attitude that the most important project in human life is getting into the right relation with the supernatural. Specified to Christianity, the religious attitude is that the final good, the *summum bonum* for human beings, is to get into the right relationship with God, which is made possible by the incarnation and atonement of the divine son of God. From that perspective, secularism is a maximally mistaken attitude; it's about as far from right as you can get. And the same will go, then, for *scientific* secularism, the variety of secularism according to which objectifying inquiry, the kind of inquiry characteristic of science, is enough for understanding and practice. According to Christian belief, objectifying inquiry, inquiry characterized by getting ourselves out of the picture, isn't anywhere nearly enough either for theoretical understanding or for knowing how to live a good life. To say it is woefully inadequate would be colossal understatement.

It is crucially important to see that science itself doesn't support or endorse scientific secularism, or the scientific world picture. Science is one thing; the claim that it is *enough* is a totally different thing. It is not part of science to make that claim. One will not find it in textbooks of science as such, whether physics, chemistry, biology, or whatever. There are scientists who make this claim; but there are nearly as many who reject it. One can be wholly enthusiastic about science without thinking objectifying inquiry is enough. Indeed, that is the sensible attitude towards science from a Christian perspective. The confusion of science with scientific secularism is egregious; it is little better than confusing, say, music history with the claim that music history is enough, stamp collecting with the claim that stamp collecting is enough. But I believe this confusion, colossal as it is, is widely perpetrated, and by people from both sides of the divide between science and religion. There are many who enthusiastically endorse science; but they go on to confuse it with scientific secularism. Perhaps this is because they see secularism with respect to science, that is, methodological naturalism, as essential to science, but then confuse it with secularism *simpliciter*. Others who emphatically reject secularism fall into the same confusion. They are suspicious, distrustful of science, because of its association with scientific secularism or the so-called scientific worldview. But the fact that science is associated with secularism – the fact that some people associate the two – is not a decent reason for suspicion of science; it is no better than being suspicious of music history just because someone thinks it's enough. This confusion, I believe, is one factor underlying the continuing mutual distrust between science and religion. So one factor here is really no more than a confusion.

2 Evolution

In Galileo's time, so they say, the main source of conflict between science and religion was astronomical; at present it is biological (in general see Drake 1980). Ever since Darwin's day, there has been friction, misunderstanding, and mutual recrimination between those who accept Darwinism in one form or another, and Christians of various kinds; and of course this conflict is a main source of the continuing debate between religion and science. Many Christian fundamentalists find incompatibility between the contemporary Darwinian evolutionary account of our origins and their version of the Christian faith. Many Darwinian fundamentalists (as the late Stephen Jay Gould called them) second that motion: they too claim there is conflict between Darwinian evolution and classical Christian or even theistic belief. Contemporaries who champion this conflict view would include, for example, Richard Dawkins (1986), (2003), Daniel Dennett (1995), and, far to the opposite side, Phillip Johnson (1993). In Darwin's own day, this opposition and strife could assume massive proportions. Now Darwin himself was a shy, retiring sort; he hated public controversy and confrontation, but given what he had to say, he was often embroiled in controversy. Fortunately for him, there was his friend Thomas H. Huxley, who defended Darwin with such fierce tenacity that he, came to be called "Darwin's bulldog." Huxley himself continued the canine allusion by referring to some of Darwin's opponents as "curs who will bark and yelp" (Huxley to Darwin, Nov. 23, 1859. This canine connection has proved resilient, or at least durable, extending all the way to the present, where we have Richard Dawkins described as "Darwin's Rottweiler," and Daniel Dennett described, unkindly, by the late Stephen Jay Gould, as "Dawkins' lapdog."

Now where, exactly, does conflict or alleged conflict arise? Evolution, of course, is manifold and various; the term covers a multitude – not necessarily a multitude of sins, but a multitude nevertheless. There is:

(1)   the *Ancient Earth Thesis*, the claim that the earth is billions of years old.

(2)   There is the claim that life has progressed from relatively simple to relatively complex forms. In the beginning there was relatively simple unicellular life, perhaps of the sort represented by bacteria and blue green algae, or perhaps still simpler unknown forms of life. (Although bacteria are simple compared to some other living beings, they are in fact enormously complex creatures.) Then more complex unicellular life, then relatively simple multicellular life such as seagoing worms, coral, and jellyfish, then fish, then amphibia, then reptiles, birds, mammals, and finally, as the culmination of the whole process, and the crown of creation, human beings: the *Progress thesis*, as we humans like to call it (jellyfish might have a different view as to where the whole process culminates).

(3)   There is the thesis of *descent with modification*: the enormous diversity of the contemporary living world has come about by way of offspring differing, ordinarily in small and subtle ways, from their parents. Connected with the thesis of descent with modification is

(4)   the *Common Ancestry thesis*: that life originated at only one place on earth, all subsequent life being related by descent to those original living creatures – the claim that, as Gould (1983) put it, there is a "tree of evolutionary descent linking all organisms by ties of genealogy." According to the Common Ancestry thesis, we are all cousins of each other – and indeed of all living things.[8] You and the summer squash in your garden, for example – are really cousins under the skin (rind).

(5)   There is the claim that a certain particular mechanism drives this process of descent with modification: the most popular candidate is natural selection culling or winnowing random genetic mutation. Since Darwin made a similar proposal ("Natural

selection has been the main but not exclusive means of modification"), call this thesis *Darwinism*. Finally,

(6)   There is the claim that life itself developed from nonliving matter without any special creative activity of God but just by virtue of processes described by the ordinary laws of physics and chemistry: call this the *Naturalistic Origins thesis*.

These six theses are of course importantly different from each other. They are also logically independent in pairs, except for the third and fifth theses: the fifth entails the third, in that you can't sensibly propose a mechanism for a process without supposing that the process has indeed occurred. Suppose we use the term "Evolution" to denote the conjunction of these six theses, making distinctions among them when needed.

So where does real or apparent conflict arise? Many Christian evangelicals or fundamentalists accept a literal interpretation of the creation account in the first two chapters of *Genesis*; they are inclined therefore to think the Earth and indeed the universe vastly younger than the billions of years of age attributed to them by current science. This seems to be a fairly straightforward conflict, and hence part of the answer to our question is that current scientific estimates of the age of the Earth and of the universe differ widely (not to say wildly) from Scripturally based beliefs on the part of some Christians and other theists (Muslims for example). The ranks of Young Earth creationists seem to be thinning; they are being succeeded by adherents of Intelligent Design, who ordinarily hold neither that the Earth is young, nor that God has directly created representatives of most lineages in more or less their present forms.

A more important source of conflict has to do with the Christian doctrine of creation, in particular the claim that God has created human beings *in his image*. This requires that God *intended* to create creatures of a certain kind – rational creatures with a moral sense and the capacity to know and love him – and then acted in such a way as to accomplish this intention. It does not require that God *directly* create human beings, or that he did not do so by way of an evolutionary process, or even that he intended to create precisely human beings, precisely our species. (Maybe all he actually intended to create were rational, moral and religious creatures; he may have been indifferent to the specific form such creatures would take.) But if he created human beings in his image, then at the least he intended that creatures of a certain sort come to be, and acted in such a way as to guarantee the existence of such creatures. This claim is consistent with the Ancient Earth thesis, the Progress thesis, the Descent with Modification thesis, and the Common Ancestry thesis. It is important to see that it is also consistent with Darwinism. It could be, for example, that God directs and orchestrates the Darwinian process; perhaps, indeed, God causes the right genetic mutation to arise at the right times. There is nothing in the scientific theory of evolution to preclude God from causing the relevant genetic mutations.

What is *not* consistent with Christian belief, however, is the claim that this process of evolution is *unguided* – that neither God nor anyone else had a hand in guiding, directing, orchestrating, or shaping it. But precisely this claim is made by a large number of contemporary scientists and philosophers who write on this topic. There is a veritable choir of extremely distinguished experts insisting that this process is unguided, and indeed insisting that it is part of contemporary evolutionary theory to assert that it is unguided. Examples would be Stephen Jay Gould (1983), Douglas Futuyma (1986), G. G. Simpson (1984) and many others; but the loudest voices in the choir (the soloists, perhaps) are Richard Dawkins and Daniel Dennett.

One of Dawkins's most influential books is entitled *The Blind Watchmaker*. Its thesis is that the enormous variety of the living world has been produced by natural selection unguided by the hand of God or any other person:

> All appearances to the contrary, the only watchmaker in nature are [*sic*] the blind forces of physics, albeit deployed in a very special way. A true watchmaker has foresight: he designs his cogs and springs, and plans their interconnections, with a future purpose in his mind's eye. Natural selection, the blind, unconscious automatic process which Darwin discovered, and which we now know is the explanation for the existence and apparently purposeful form of all life has no purpose in mind. It has no mind and no mind's eye. It does not plan for the future. It has no vision, no foresight, and no sight at all. If it can be said to play the role of watchmaker in nature, it is the *blind* watchmaker. (Dawkins 1986, p. 5)

This thought is trumpeted by the subtitle of the book: "Why the evidence of evolution reveals a universe without design." Why does Dawkins think natural selection is blind and unguided? Why does he think that *"the Evidence of Evolution Reveals a Universe without Design"*? How does the evidence of evolution reveal such a thing? What Dawkins does in his book, fundamentally, is three things. First, he nicely recounts some of the fascinating anatomical details of certain living creatures and their ways (bats, for example). Second, he tries to refute arguments for the conclusion that blind, unguided evolution could not have produced certain of the wonders of the living world – the mammalian eye, or the wing. Third, he makes suggestions as to how these and other organic systems could have developed by unguided evolution.

His refutations of these objections are not always successful; what is most striking, however, is the general form of his argument for the conclusion that the universe is without design. His detailed arguments are all for the conclusion that it is *biologically possible* that these various organs and systems should have come to be by unguided Darwinian mechanisms, where he takes it that an outcome is biologically possible if it is not *prohibitively improbable*. Of course there are problems with measuring probability here, with saying what degree of improbability is acceptable, and the like. What is truly remarkable, however, is the form of the main argument. The premiss he argues for is something like

(1)   We know of no irrefutable objections to its being biologically possible that all of life came to be by way of unguided Darwinian processes;

the conclusion is

(2)   All of life has come to be by way of unguided Darwinian processes.

It is worth meditating, if only for a moment, on the striking distance, here, between premiss and conclusion. The premiss tells us, substantially, that for all we know it is possible that unguided evolution has produced all of the wonders of the living world; the conclusion is that unguided evolution has indeed produced all of those wonders. The argument form seems to be something like *there are no irrefutable objections to the possibility of p; therefore p*. Many widely endorsed philosophical arguments are invalid; few display the truly colossal distance between premiss and conclusion flaunted by this one. I come home and announce to my wife that I have just been given a $50,000 raise; naturally she wants to know my reason for thinking so; I tell her that no irrefutable objections to its possibility have been produced. The reaction would not be pretty.

Dawkins utterly fails to show that "the facts of evolution reveal a universe without design"; at best he argues that we do not know that it is astronomically improbable that the living world is without design. Still, the fact that he and others assert his subtitle loudly and slowly, as it were, can be expected to convince many, in particular those with no particular expertise in the subject, that the biological theory of evolution is in fact incompatible with the Christian belief that the living world has been designed. Another source of the continuing debate, therefore, is the mistaken claim on the part of such writers as Dawkins that the scientific theory implies that the living world and human beings in particular have not been designed and created by God.

A second prominent authority on the subject is Daniel Dennett; his views are similar to those of Dawkins (which may be why Gould called him "Dawkins' lapdog"). Dennett's main contribution to the subject is entitled "*Darwin's Dangerous Idea*" (Dennett, 1995); what is Darwin's idea and why is it dangerous? In brief, Darwin's idea, an idea Dennett of course endorses and defends, is the thought that the living world with all of its beauty and wonder, all of its marvelous and apparent ingenious design, was not created or designed by God or anything at all like God; instead it was produced by natural selection, a blind, unconscious, mechanical, algorithmic process – a process, he says, which creates "design out of chaos without the aid of Mind" (p. 50). The whole process has happened without divine aid. It all happened just by the grace of mindless natural selection: "An impersonal, unreflective, robotic, mindless little scrap of molecular machinery is the ultimate basis of all the agency, and hence meaning, and hence consciousness, in the universe" (p. 203). The idea is that mind, intelligence, foresight, planning, design, are all latecomers in the universe, themselves created by the mindless process of natural selection. Human beings, of course, are among the products of this mindless process; they are not designed or planned for by God or anyone else.

> Here, then, is Darwin's dangerous idea: the algorithmic level *is* the level that best accounts for the speed of the antelope, the wing of the eagle, the shape of the orchid, the diversity of species, and all the other occasions for wonder in the world of nature. (Dennett 1995, p. 59)

He could have added that the same goes for the moral sense we humans display, as well as our religious sensibilities, our artistic strivings, and our interest in and ability to do science and mathematics or compose great music or poetry.

Now why is Darwin's idea dangerous? Because if we accept it, thinks Dennett, we are forced to reconsider all our childhood and childish ideas about God, morality, value, the meaning of life, and so on. Christians, naturally enough, believe that God has always existed; so mind has always existed, and was involved in the production and planning of whatever else there is. In fact many have thought it *impossible* that mind should be produced just from unthinking matter; as John Locke puts it, "… it is as impossible to conceive that ever pure incogitative Matter should produce a thinking intelligent Being, as that nothing should of itself produce Matter" (Locke 1959, IV, x, 10). Darwin's idea is that this notion is not merely not impossible; it is the sober truth of the matter. This idea, then, is inconsistent with any form of theism, and Dennett sees serious religion as steadily dwindling with the progress of science. Never one to shrink from the practical applications of what he believes, he suggests that we keep a few Baptists and other fundamentalists in something like "cultural zoos" (no doubt with sizable moats to protect the rest of us right-thinking non-fundamentalists. We should preserve a few Baptists for the sake of posterity – but not, he says, at just any cost. "Save the Baptists", says he, "but not *by all means* [Dennett's emphasis]. Not if it means tolerating the deliberate misinforming of children about the natural world" (p. 516). Save the Baptists, all right, but only if they promise not to misinform their children by teaching them "that 'Man' is not a product of evolution by natural selection" (p. 519) and other blatantly objectionably views.[9]

Darwin's idea is incompatible with theism (and most varieties of religion). Of course this doesn't automatically make it *dangerous* to theism – theists might just note the inconsistency and reject it. Many propositions are inconsistent with theism (e.g., *nothing but turtles exist*), but not a danger to it. This idea is dangerous to theism only if it is *attractive*, only if there are good reasons for adopting it and rejecting theism. Why does Dennett think we should *accept* Darwin's idea? Concede that it is audacious, with-it, revolutionary, anti-medieval, quintessentially contemporary, appropriately reverential towards science, and has that nobly stoical hair-shirt quality Bertrand Russell said he liked in his beliefs: still, why should we believe it? First, Dennett seems to think Darwin's idea is just part of current biology – that the contemporary neo-Darwinian theory of evolution just is a theory according to which the living world in all its beauty and diversity has come to be by unguided natural selection. That's Darwin's idea, and that idea, he thinks, is a solid part of contemporary biology. But what does he think is the *evidence* for this idea?

Here Dennett follows the same route as Dawkins. He proposes that it is *possible* that all the variety of the biosphere be produced by mindless natural selection: "The theory of natural selection shows how every feature of the world *can* be the product of a blind, unforesightful, nonteleological, ultimately mechanical process of differential reproduction over long periods of time" (p. 315, Dennett's emphasis). Now clearly the theory of natural selection doesn't show this at all. Dennett quotes John Locke (Dennett 1995, p. 26) as holding that it is impossible that "pure incogitative Matter should produce a thinking intelligent Being"; Locke believed it impossible in the broadly logical sense that mind should have arisen apart from the activity of mind. Supposing, as he did, that matter and mind exhaust the possibilities for concrete beings, he believed that there are no possible worlds in which there are minds at a given time, but no minds at any earlier time; minds can have been produced only by minds. Or by Mind; Locke and other theists will agree that mind is a primitive feature of the universe. God has always existed, never come into existence, and exists necessarily; at any time *t*, God is present at *t*. The scientific theory of natural selection certainly hasn't shown that Locke is wrong: it hasn't shown that it is possible, in the broadly logical sense, that mind arises from "pure incogitative Matter." It doesn't so much as address that question. But set aside such metaphysical qualms for the moment. What does the theory show, then? It gives us detailed and empirically informed stories – or perhaps a recipe for such stories about how various features of the living world[10] could have come to be by way of natural selection winnowing genetic mutation. Could have come to be in what sense of "could"? Perhaps the thing to say is that these stories are successful if they are reasonably probable – where of course there is no real way to say how probable *reasonably* probable is.

The important point to see is that Dennett just identifies Darwin's idea – the idea that the living world has been produced by a process of unguided natural selection – with the deliverances of contemporary biological science. But how can that be right? True: there is no canonical source telling us exactly and precisely what the contemporary neo-Darwinian theory of evolution comprises. But does it include, not merely the idea that the living world has been produced by a process in which natural selection is the chief mechanism, but the vastly more ambitious idea that this process has been unsupervised, unplanned, unintended by God or any other intelligent agent? That hardly seems to be an appropriate part of an empirical scientific theory. It looks instead like a metaphysical or theological add-on. Dennett himself is of course a naturalist; he just adds naturalism to the scientific theory, shakes well, and declares the result part of current science, thus confusing natural selection with *unguided* natural selection.

Here we have another important source of the continuing debate between science and religion. Dawkins and Dennett both hold that contemporary evolutionary theory – Darwinism, in particular – is incompatible with the Christian and theistic claim that God has created human beings in his own image. Both claim that Darwinism, the theory that the principal mechanism driving the process of evolution is natural selection winnowing random genetic mutation, implies that the universe – the living universe, anyway – is without design. Dennett does so simply by identifying current evolutionary theory with the result of annexing to it the proposition that evolution is unguided; Dawkins does so by arguing – ineptly, as we have seen – that Darwinism implies that proposition.

This confusion or alleged connection between Darwinism and unguided Darwinism is one of the most important, perhaps the most important, source of continuing conflict and debate between science and religion. According to theistic religion, God has created human beings in his own image. According to current evolutionary theory – Darwinism, anyway – the main mechanism driving the process of evolution is natural selection culling random genetic mutation. So far there is no conflict. God could shape, supervise, direct, this process, for example, by protecting certain populations from extinction, arranging for their having a sufficient food supply, and so on. He could be more intimately involved; he could cause the genetic mutations, and cause the right mutations to arise at the right times. But when Dennett, Dawkins and their friends go on to add that the process is unguided by God or any other intelligent agent, then, of course, conflict and inconsistency arise. Hence if you confuse Darwinism with *unguided* Darwinism, a confusion Dennett makes and Dawkins encourages, you will see science and religion as in conflict at this point (see Ruse, 2005).

There are many manifestations of this confusion. Consider the conflict raging over Intelligent Design. Here both friends and foes and allegedly neutral arbiters like Judge Jones of Dover fame claim that ID is *incompatible* with evolution. Some of its friends propose that ID be taught as an *alternative* to evolution; foes, naturally, reject that proposal. Both claim that ID is inconsistent with evolution. Now the central claim of ID is that certain organisms or organic systems cannot be explained by unguided natural selection, and that the best scientific hypothesis, with respect to those phenomena, is that they have been intelligently designed. This claim, that intelligent design in the living world can be empirically detected, is consistent with Darwinism as such; but of course if you confuse Darwinism, with *unguided* Darwinism, or evolution with *unguided* evolution, then you will see ID as incompatible with evolution. This confusion of Darwinism with unguided Darwinism is to be found even in official proclamations of such organizations as the National Association of Biology Teachers. Until 1997 that organization stated as part of its official position that "the diversity of life on earth is the outcome of evolution: an unsupervised, impersonal, unpredictable and natural process...."

This confusion between Darwinism and unguided Darwinism is a crucial cause of the continuing debate. Darwinism, the scientific theory, is compatible with theism and theistic religion; unguided Darwinism, a consequence of naturalism, is incompatible with theism, but is not entailed by the scientific theory. It is instead a metaphysical or theological add-on.

I close with two objections to my assertion that the scientific theory does not entail unguided Darwinism. One of these is of little consequence; the other is more puzzling. To start with the easy one: Darwinism and theism are compatible, so I say, because it could be that God *causes* the random genetic mutations involved. But, says the objector, if those mutations are caused by God, how could they possibly be *random*? Doesn't randomness imply that they are uncaused, or at least unplanned? Doesn't it mean that they happen just by chance?

The answer is easy enough: to say that a mutation is random, in the biological sense, is only to say that it does not arise out of the design plan of the creature to which it accrues, and is not a response to its adaptational needs. Thus Ernst Mayr, the dean of post-World War II biology: "When it is said that mutation or variation is random, the statement simply means that there is no correlation between the production of new genotypes and the adaptational needs of an organism in the given environment" (Mayr 1988, p. 99; see also Sober 1993). He adds that:

> If we say that a particular mutation is random, it does not mean that a mutation at that locus could be anything under the sun, but merely that it is unrelated to any current needs of the organism or is not in any other way predictable. (Mayr 1997, p. 69; see also Sober 1993)

But clearly a mutation could be random in this sense and also caused, indeed, caused by God. In this way God could guide and orchestrate the whole course of evolution, and do it by way of causing the right random mutations to arise at the right time, allowing natural selection to do the rest.

Some will object to this suggestion as improperly involving divine action in the world; God should not be thought of as intervening in the world he has created. That is, of course, a theological objection that doesn't really bear on the question of compatibility. But for those who find this theological objection compelling, there is another possibility worth exploring: frontloading. God could create initial conditions that he knows will issue, given the laws he sets for the world, in the right mutations arising at the right time. There is little real difference between

(1)   God's decreeing at the beginning that at *t*, such and such will happen,

on the one hand, and

(2)   At *t*, God's decreeing that such and such happen then.

Our issue, however, is the question whether Darwinism is compatible with God's creating and designing human beings, and creating them in his own image. Clearly these two are compatible.

Turning now to the second objection, Alex Pruss[11] claims that current evolutionary theory is incompatible with Christian belief, but it is a suggestion of a very different kind. According to Pruss, the modern neo-Darwinian theory asserts at least two things. It asserts, first, that there is a "full ancestral history" of each population of organisms, and indeed of each individual organism. This would be a proposition specifying the ancestors of the individual in question, going all the way back to its very first ancestor. According to most contemporary experts, life began in just one place; therefore that first ancestor would also be the first ancestor of all living things. This history would also report which mutations occurred to which ancestors, and which of those mutations (by way of natural selection) came to spread to the rest of the relevant population. (It goes without saying that we don't have access to these ancestral histories.) According to Pruss, the claim that there is such a complete ancestral history for each individual is compatible with theism, as is the claim that no special divine action is required for the mutations or for their spreading to the rest of the population by natural selection.

But evolutionary theory makes a further claim: that an *explanation* of all the current diversity of life is given by the assertion that it has come to be by way of natural selection working on random genetic mutation:

> It is the ambitious claim that evolution provides a true explanation of why such marvellously complex and adapted animals as horses, pine trees and frogs exist, with complex organs such as equine eyes and human brains, and why intelligent animals like humans exist, an explanation whose possibility competes with, and undercuts, Paley-type teleological arguments. (p. 9)

It is *this* claim, the claim

(E)   Darwinism provides a true explanation of the variety of life, including the existence of human beings,

says Pruss, that is incompatible with the theistic claim that God has created human beings in his own image.

Where, exactly, is the incompatibility? The first thing to note is that explanations come in a wide variety, and the term "explanation" is a bit of a weasel word. A paradigm case of explanation: my car won't start; I take it in to the garage; the mechanic checks the electrical system, finds no problem, and finally concludes that the problem is a defective fuel pump; he replaces the fuel pump, whereupon the car starts properly. The explanation of its failing to start is that it had a defective fuel pump; that is, the answer to the question *Why did that car fail to start?* is *It had a defective fuel pump.* Note that (depending on just how we understand "defective") it is very unlikely that a car with a defective fuel pump will start.

The explanation E says that what Darwinism offers is of a different kind: it is *statistical*. This means, says Pruss, that the explanation works by showing how the *explanans* is not unlikely: "… it is claimed that some set of mutations and environmental interactions that would lead to the occurrence of a species containing the 'notable' features … is not unlikely" (p. 4). Pruss proposes that this statistical variety of explanation is the sort current scientific evolutionary theory claims to give for the variety of terrestrial life. According to the scientific theory of evolution, therefore, the correct answer to the question, Why is there such a thing as human beings or the human brain, or the equine eye? is "It is not unlikely that these things have come to be by way of natural selection working on random genetic mutation, starting originally from some very simple unicellular form of life."

Pruss goes on to say, however, that no theist could accept E – that is, no theist could accept the claim that the presence and activity of these processes is the *explanation* of the existence of human-like creatures (intelligent animals made in the image of God. That is because the theist accepts another proposition that *undercuts* the explanation proposed in E. This proposition, of course, is that God intended all along to create human beings, or at any rate creatures in his image. Pruss's claim is that if you accept *that* proposition, then you cannot also accept E; you cannot also accept the evolutionary story *as an explanation*.

By way of analogy: suppose Sam contracts lung cancer; one explanation is that he was a smoker for forty years. But now suppose we learn that an ill-disposed physician injected Sam with a serum that invariably causes lung cancer. Then, we might think, Sam's long-term smoking is no longer an explanation, at least for us; it has been undercut, as an explanation, by our knowledge of that rogue physician's malicious activity. When we knew that Sam was a heavy smoker but didn't know about the rogue physician, then the fact that he was a smoker was a probabilistic explanation of his getting lung cancer; once we learn about that malevolent physician, the fact of his smoking is no longer a probabilistic explanation, or indeed an explanation of any kind at all.

According to Pruss, therefore, you can't both be a theist and sensibly think natural selection is the explanation of the existence of human or humanlike creatures. Is he right? The question divides itself. First, is he right in claiming that it is part of current science, part of the scientific theory of evolution, to claim that natural selection is indeed the true explanation of the existence of humanlike creatures? As I said earlier, there is no canonical axiomatization of the scientific theory of evolution emblazoned on the walls of the National Academy of Sciences or the American Association for the Advancement of Science. Where do you go to find out precisely what this theory says? How can we tell whether this claim of explanation is or isn't part of the scientific theory as such, as opposed to an add-on by those who don't accept theism? That is a hard question, and the answer is far from obvious.

Second, is E, the claim that natural selection is a (statistical) explanation of there being humanlike creatures, really incompatible with theism? Not obviously. Let's concede for purposes of argument that a theist can't sensibly accept E; is that sufficient for the proposition that theism is incompatible with E? Maybe not. As Pruss sees it, a proposition's being an explanation sometimes depends on what else you know: if you know that God intended that there be humanlike creatures, then natural selection won't be, for you, a statistical explanation of their existence; if you don't know that, however, it could be. That Sam is a smoker is a statistical explanation of his coming down with cancer – but it is not an explanation for you if you know about that nefarious physician.

This means that a proposition of the sort in question is an explanation *relative to* some body of background information; P can be an explanation relative to my background information without being an explanation relative to yours. We live in North Dakota; the overnight temperature drops below $-40°F$ ($-36°C$); my car won't start. The proposition that most cars will not start at that temperature may be a probabilistic explanation of that event for me, but not for you; that is because you have more detailed knowledge of the cause of this car's failing to start on this occasion (you know I always buy cheap oil that congeals at $-40°F$ and that my car is equipped with an inhibitor that prevents its starting when the oil is congealed. But then, strictly speaking, the claim that natural selection is a probabilistic explanation of the variety of life doesn't make sense, just as it stands; it's like saying "Chicago is to the west of." To get a proper assertion, we need to specify which background information it is with respect to which this proposition is an explanation.

Of course the scientific theory in question does not explicitly say. But it seems sensible to suppose, first, that any scientific inquiry proceeds relative to some array of background information. It seems sensible to suggest, second, that the relevant background information will not include propositions obviously implying the existence of God or other supernatural agents; this would be a consequence of the assumption of methodological naturalism, which, at present anyway, constrains most if not all scientific projects. That means, however, that E is not really incompatible with theism. For E is as it stands incomplete; it's the claim that *the coming to be of humanlike creatures by way of natural selection* is not massively improbable with respect to an implicitly but not explicitly specified array of background information. That array, however, whatever precisely it is, is constrained by methodological naturalism and therefore contains no propositions implying the existence of supernatural beings. That (1) is a probabilistic explanation of the variety of life relative to *that* array is surely not inconsistent with theism.

I am therefore inclined to think Pruss has not given us a good reason for thinking theism incompatible with evolutionary theory.

Acknowledgment

The editor and publishers wish to thank Yale University Press for permission to include, in both Chinese and English-language editions, "Science and Religion: Why Does the Debate Continue?" from *The Religion and Science Debate, Why Does It Continue?*, ed. Harold W. Attridge (New Haven, CT: Yale University Press, 2009).

Notes

1 What Peter Unger calls "the scientific worldview." In his mind, as in mine, there is no intrinsic connection between science and the scientifical worldview.

2 Review of van Fraassen, *The Empirical Stance*, in *Notre Dame Philosophical Reviews* (July 7, 2002).

3 A phrase van Fraassen gets from the historian Catherine Wilson.

4 Quoted in Leon Kass (1985), p. 250.

5 A tendency that, for what it is worth, has been confirmed by studies in evolutionary psychology: see, for example, Justin Barrett (2000), and (2004); Pascal Boyer (1994); and Todd Tremlin (2006).

6 Obviously we don't take ourselves *completely* out of the picture, in doing science: we continue to endorse *modus ponens* as opposed to affirming the consequent; we rely on logic, mathematics, perception, measurement, the idea that there has been a past, etc., all of which are characteristically human ways of proceeding. Other, more subtle ways in which our human proclivities enter into scientific inquiry are pointed out in detail in Del Ratzsch (2009). And of course there can be controversy as to whether a given part of the human cognitive constitution *should* be bracketed in science: if theism is true, for example, it is far from obvious that methodological naturalism gives us the best shot at reaching the truth. See Plantinga (1996).

7 "Obviously": if, as many theists have thought, God is a necessary being, the proposition that there is such a person as God is necessarily true and thus entailed by every proposition.

8 Why not suppose that life has originated in more than one place, so that we needn't all be cousins? This suggestion is occasionally made, but the usual idea is that life originated just once – if only because of the astounding difficulty in seeing how it could have originated (by merely natural processes) at all.

9 But what if they *do* insist on teaching these heresies to their children? (Baptists will be Baptists, after all.) Will we be obliged to remove Baptist children from their parents' noxious influence? Will we have to put barbed wire around those zoos, maybe check to see if perhaps there is room for them in northern Siberia? Dennett and Richard Rorty come from opposite ends of the philosophical spectrum, but Dennett's views here nicely match Rorty's declaration that in the new liberal society, those who believe there is a "chief end of man," as in the Westminster Shorter Catechism, will have to be regarded as "insane" (and perhaps deprived of the vote and institutionalized pending recovery from the seizure?)

10   Of course many claim that there are features of the world such that at the moment there are not any plausible stories of that sort – see, for example, Michael Behe's *Darwin's Black Box*. So perhaps the idea is that the theory of natural selection gives us reason to think such stories will be forthcoming, or would be forthcoming given sufficient time and resources.

11   Alexander Pruss, "Divine creation and evolution," unpublished paper.

References

Barrett, Justin (2000) Exploring the Natural Foundations of Religion, *Trends in Cognitive Science* 4.

Barrett, Justin (2004) *Why Would Anyone Believe in God?* Walnut Creek, CA: AltaMira.

Behe, Michael (1996) *Darwin's Black Box.* New York: Free Press.

Boyer, Pascal (1994) *The Naturalness of Religious Ideas: A Cognitive Theory of Religion.* Berkeley: University of California Press.

Dawkins, Richard (1986) *The Blind Watchmaker: Why the Evidence of Evolution Reveals a Universe without Design.* London: W. W. Norton.

Dawkins, Richard (2003) *A Devil's Chaplain: Reflections on Hope, Lies, Science, and Love.* Boston, MA: Houghton Mifflin.

Drake, Stillman (1980) *Galileo.* New York: Hill and Wang.

Dennett, Daniel (1995) *Darwin's Dangerous Idea.* New York: Simon & Schuster.

Draper, J. W. (1881) *History of the Conflict between Religion and Science.* New York: D. Appleton.

Futuyma, Douglas (1986) *Evolutionary Biology*, 2nd edn. Sunderland, MA: Sinauer Associates.

Gould, Stephen Jay (1983) Evolution as fact and theory. In *Hen's Teeth and Horse's Toes.* New York: W. W. Norton.

Johnson, Phillip (1993) *Darwin on Trial*, 2nd edn. Downers Grove, IL: InterVarsity Press.

Kass, Leon (1985) *Toward a More Natural Science: Biology and Human Affairs*, (New York: Free Press.

Locke, John (1959) *An Essay Concerning Human Understanding*, ed. A. C. Fraser, 2 vols. Mineola, NY: Dover Publications.

Mayr, Ernst (1997) *This is Biology: The Science of the Living World.* Cambridge, MA: Harvard University Press.

Mayr, Enst (1988) *Towards a New Philosophy of Biology: Observations of an Evolutionist.* Cambridge, MA: Harvard University Press.

Plantinga, Alvin (1996) Science: Augustinian or Duhemian? *Faith and Philosophy*, 13 (3), 368–94.

Ratzsch, Del (2009) Humanness in their hearts: Where science and religion fuse. In Jeffrey Schloss and Michael Murray, *The Believing Primate.* Oxford: Oxford University Press.

Rorty, Richard (1979) *Philosophy and the Mirror of Nature.* Princeton, NJ: Princeton University Press.

Rorty, Richard (1989) *Irony, Contingency and Solidarity.* Cambridge: Cambridge University Press.

Ruse, Michael (2005) *The Evolution Creation Struggle.* Cambridge, MA: Harvard University Press.

Simpson, George G. (1984) *Tempo and Mode in Evolution.* (Columbia Classics in Evolution Series). New York: Columbia University Press.

Sober, Elliott (1993) *Philosophy of Biology.* Boulder, CO, and San Francisco: Westview.

Tremlin, Todd (2006) *Minds and Gods: The Cognitive Foundations of Religion.* Oxford: Oxford University Press.

Van Fraassen, Bas (2002) *The Empirical Stance.* New Haven, CT: Yale University Press.

23

Divine Action in the World

ALVIN PLANTINGA

One of the most important spiritual/intellectual questions of the twenty-first century concerns the relation between religion and science. Many people believe that there is conflict between them; more exactly, they believe current science conflicts specifically with Christian belief, and more generally with theistic belief as also found in Judaism and Islam. There is alleged to be conflict in at least six areas.

1) There is the association of science with secularism or the so-called 'scientific world-view.'
2) There is alleged conflict between scientific theories of evolution and essential aspects of Christianity and other theistic religions – for example, that human beings are created in the image of God.
3) There is alleged conflict between science and the claim, common to theistic religions that God acts specially in the world; miracles would be one example of special divine action, but there are others as well: divine providence, and the way in which God acts in the hearts of believers.
4) There is conflict between religious claims and many explanations in evolutionary psychology of such human phenomena as love, altruism, morality, and religion itself.
5) There is conflict between certain classical Christian doctrines – the resurrection of Jesus, for example-and certain varieties of scientific or historical Biblical criticism.
6) Finally, there is alleged conflict between the epistemic attitudes of science and religion. The scientific attitude, so it is said, involves forming belief on the basis of empirical investigation, holding belief tentatively, constantly testing belief and looking for a better alternative; the religious attitude involves believing on faith.

What follows is a synopsis (prepared by Professor John Cottingham) of a lecture in which I address (3); this lecture was given at Fudan University on December 20, 2006.

In my second chapter I take up the alleged conflict between science and the claim, common to theistic religions, that God acts specially in the world, and I want to begin by quoting a statement of the classical Christian idea of Providence, as found in the Heidelberg Catechism:

> Providence is the almighty and ever-present power of God by which he upholds, as with his hand, heaven and earth and all creatures, and so rules them that leaf and blade, rain and drought, fruitful and lean years, food and drink, health and sickness, prosperity and poverty – all things, in fact, come to us not by chance but from his fatherly hand.[1]

Such a conception implies a *regularity* and *dependability* in the divinely created world. But traditional Christian belief also includes the idea of God's *special action* in the world – for example in the miracles described in the Old Testament (such as the parting of the Red Sea) and many of the events reported in the Gospels, such as Jesus' walking on water, his changing of water into wine, his miraculous healings, and his rising from the dead). Such miracles, moreover, are not just supposed to have occurred in Biblical times: according to classical Christian belief, God also now responds to prayers, for example by healings, and by working through the Holy Spirit in the hearts and minds of his children. In short, God constantly causes events in the world.

A belief in divine causal action in the world is thus standard Christian orthodoxy. But does it clash with any of the tenets of modern science? Many theologians seem to think that there is indeed a "science/religion problem,." Thus Robert Bultmann speaks of the historical method as including "the presupposition that history is a unity in the sense of a closed continuum of effects in which individual events are connected by the succession of cause and effect." And he goes on to assert that this continuum "cannot be rent by the interference of supernatural, transcendent powers."[2] In another passage, he goes so far as to say that: "It is impossible to use electric light and the wireless and to avail ourselves of modern medical and surgical discoveries, and at the same time to believe in the New Testament world of spirits and miracles."[3] This general line is supported by John Macquarrie:

> The way of understanding miracles that appeals to breaks in the natural order and to supernatural intervention belongs to the mythological outlook and cannot commend itself in a post-mythological climate of thought … The traditional conception of miracle is irreconcilable with our modern understanding of both science and history. Science proceeds on the assumption that whatever events occur in the world can be accounted for in terms of other events that also belong within the world; and if on some occasions we are unable to give a complete account of some happening … the scientific conviction is that further research will bring to light further factors in the situation, but factors that will turn out to be just as immanent and this-worldly as those already known.[4]

In like manner, Langdon Gilkey observes that

> contemporary theology does not expect, nor does it speak of, wondrous divine events on the surface of natural and historical life. The causal nexus in space and time which the Enlightenment science and philosophy introduced into the Western mind … is also assumed by modern theologians and scholars; since they participate in the modern world of science both intellectually and existentially, they can scarcely do anything else. Now this assumption of a causal order among phenomenal events, and therefore of the authority of the scientific interpretation of observable events, makes a great difference to the validity one assigns to biblical narratives and so to the way one understands their meaning. Suddenly a vast panoply of divine deeds and

events recorded in scripture are no longer regarded a having actually happened … Whatever the Hebrews believed, we believe that the biblical people lived in the same causal continuum of space and time in which we live, and so one in which no divine wonders transpired and no divine voices were heard.[5]

These various assertions of a "religion/science problem" do not, however, succeed in making it clear what exactly the problem is supposed to be. According to the classical Christian and theistic picture of the world, God is a person, one who has knowledge, loves and hates, and aims or ends; he acts on the basis of his knowledge to achieve his ends. Second, God is all-powerful, all-knowing, and wholly good. God has these properties essentially, and indeed necessarily: he has them in every possible world in which he exists, and he exists in every possible world. (Thus God is a necessarily existent concrete being, and the only necessarily existent concrete being.) Third, God has created the world. Fourth, as noted above in the quotation from the *Heidelberg Catechism*, God conserves, sustains, or maintains in being this world he has created. None of these claims of standard theistic belief appear in themselves to create a science/religion problem.

But there is a fifth claim, one that we are invited to see as problematic, namely that at least sometimes God acts in a way going beyond creation and conservation (for example in the case of miracles, but also in God's providential guiding of history, and his working in the hearts of people, and so on). Thus a divinely caused miracle would be a case of God's "interfering," as Bultmann puts it – a violation of the "hands-off theology" he advocates. Yet why should such "interference" be somehow contrary to science? According to Philip Clayton, science has created a "challenge to theology by its remarkable ability to explain and predict natural phenomena," and "any theological system that ignores the picture of the world painted by scientific results is certain to be regarded with suspicion." He goes on:

> In a purely deterministic universe there would be no room for God to work in the world except through the sort of miraculous intervention that Hume – and many of his readers – found to be so insupportable. Thus many, both inside and outside of theology, have abandoned any doctrine of divine action as incompatible with the natural sciences.[6]

Many scientists seem to share this view, for example H. Allen Orr, who in connection with miracles writes that "no sensible scientist can tolerate such exceptionalism with respect to the laws of nature."[7]

So one might summarize the supposed problem as follows: science promulgates natural laws; if God did miracles or acted specially in the world, he would have to contravene these laws and miraculously intervene; and that's contrary to science.

The Old Scientific Picture

Bultmann and those who follow him in thinking miracles are contrary to science are apparently thinking in terms of classical science (viz. Newtonian mechanics, and the later physics of electricity and magnetism represented by Maxwell's equations). According to the Newtonian world picture, God has created the world, which is like an enormous machine proceeding according to fixed laws – the laws of classical physics. Yet this not sufficient for anti-interventionism or hands-off theology; Newton himself (presumably) accepted the

Newtonian world picture, but he did not accept hands-off theology. Newton's laws describe how the world works *provided that the world is a closed (isolated) system*, subject to no out-side causal influence. The great conservation laws deduced from Newton's laws are stated for *closed* or *isolated* systems. Thus, the principle of conservation of linear momentum states that "where no resultant external force acts on a system, the total momentum of the system remains constant in magnitude and direction"; and the principle of conservation of energy states that "the internal energy of an isolated system remains constant."[8]

So these principles apply to closed or isolated systems. There is nothing here to prevent God from changing the velocity or direction of a particle, or from creating, *ex nihilo*, a full-grown horse. Energy is conserved in a closed system; but it is not part of Newtonian mechanics of classical science generally to declare that the material universe is indeed a closed system. (How could such a claim possibly be verified experimentally?)

To get to hands-off theology, we need more than classical science as such. We would need, in addition, *determinism*, which is commonly defined as the thesis that the natural laws plus the state of the universe at any given time entail the state of the universe at any other time. Thus, Pierre Laplace states that

> we ought to regard the present state of the universe as the effect of its previous state, and as the cause of the one which is to follow. Given for one instant a mind which could comprehend all the forces by which nature is animated and the respective situation of the beings that compose it – a mind sufficiently vast to subject these data to analysis – it would embrace in the same formula the movements of the greatest bodies of the universe and those of the lightest atom; for it, nothing would be uncertain and the future, as the past, would be present to its eyes.[9]

The idea, then, is that the material universe is a system of particles such that whatever happens at any time, together with the laws, determines whatever happens at any other time; that is, the state of the universe at any time t together with the laws entails the state of the universe at any other time t^*. This deterministic picture is supposed to preclude special divine action (and also human freedom).

Several points about this should be noted. First, we need to ask: what are the laws like? If the laws are Humean descriptive generalizations (exceptionless regularities), determinism so conceived *does not* preclude either divine action or human action or even libertarian human freedom. On this Humean picture of natural laws, compatibilism would be perfectly correct: determinism is compatible with libertarian freedom. The same goes for David Lewis' conception of laws as supervening on particular matters of fact (being exceptionless regularities that display the best combination of strength and simplicity). Determinism is incompatible with human freedom only if the laws of nature are outside human control.

Second, Laplace is clearly thinking of the laws as the laws of classical science.

The Laplacian picture is accurate only if the universe is closed: only if God doesn't act specially in the world. If he did, that great Laplacian mind would not be able to make those calculations. In other words, the Laplacian picture consists of the Newtonian picture *plus* the principle of closure – that the universe is a closed system. This is the picture guiding the thought of people like Bultmann, Macquarrie, and Gilkey. An interesting point here is that in the name of being scientific and up to date they urge on us a picture of the world that is scientifically out of date by many decades. But in any case, classical science doesn't assert or include closure (or determinism). The laws describe how things go when the universe is causally closed, subject to no outside causal influence.

In this context, it is worth referring to J. L. Mackie's contrast between "the order of nature"and "a possible divine or supernatural intervention." According to Mackie,

> the laws of nature describe the ways in which the world – including, of course, human beings – works when left to itself, when not interfered with. A miracle occurs when the world is not left to itself, when something distinct from the natural order as a whole intrudes into it.[10]

If we accept this, the natural laws would take the form:

*(NL)*When the universe is causally closed (God is not acting specially in the world), then *P*.

This seems a good description of the laws of nature and fits with the Newtonian picture. So thought of, the natural laws offer no threat to divine special action, including miracles. The Laplacian picture results only if we add that the universe is in fact a causally closed system and God never acts specially in it.

At this point someone might object: why can't we just as well say that the law is *P* itself, rather than *NL*? We could indeed say this; but then classical science as such doesn't imply that *P* is an exceptionless generalization; *P* holds just when nature is causally closed, and it is no part of classical science to assert that nature is causally closed. So again, there is no conflict with divine special action, including miracles.

In short, there is in classical science no objection to special divine action (or indeed to human free action, dualistically conceived). To get such an objection, we must add that the (material) universe is causally closed. But that is a metaphysical or theological add-on, not part of classical science. Classical science is perfectly consistent with special divine action including miracles (walking on water, rising from the dead, creating *ex nihilo* a full-grown horse). There is no religion/science conflict here; only a religion/metaphysics conflict.

So why do the theologians we have mentioned reject miracles and so on? The answer seems to be that they (mistakenly) think that miracles are contrary to science. A possible further objection they may have is that miracles would involve God's intervening in the world, which would involve his establishing regularities with one hand but undermining them with the other. But this is a theological objection, not one drawn from science. Nothing in classical science conflicts with miracles or special divine action.

The New Scientific Picture

The old Laplacian (and Newtonian) scientific picture has now been superseded by quantum mechanics. In particular, the laws of quantum mechanics are probabilistic rather than deterministic. Given a quantum mechanical system, for example a system of particles, these laws do not say which configuration will in fact result from the initial conditions, but instead they assign probabilities to the possible outcomes. Miracles (walking on water, rising from the dead, etc.) are clearly not incompatible with these laws. (They are no doubt very improbable; but we already knew that.) Further, on Copenhagen interpretations, for example the collapse theories of Ghirardi, Rimini, and Weber, God could be the cause of the collapses, and of the way in which they occur. (One might perhaps think of this as a halfway house between occasionalism and secondary causation.) And on hidden-variable interpretations, the laws describe how things go when God isn't acting specially. A further point to note is that if higher-level laws supervene on (are determined by) lower-level laws, nothing compatible with lower-level laws will be incompatible with higher-level laws.

Despite this, very many philosophers, theologians, and scientists who are wholly aware of the quantum mechanics revolution still apparently find a problem with miracles and special divine action generally. A typical example may be found in the Divine Action Project,[11] a 15-year series of conferences and publications that began in 1988. So far these conferences have resulted in five or six books of essays involving some fifty or more authors from various fields of science together with philosophers and theologians, including many of the most prominent writers in the field: John Polkinghorne, Arthur Peacocke, Nancey Murphy, Philip Clayton, and many others. This is certainly a serious and most impressive attempt to come to grips with the topic of divine action in the world. Nearly all of these authors believe that a satisfactory account of God's action in the world would have to be non-interventionistic. According to Wesley Wildman in his account of the Divine Action Project:

> The DAP project tried to be sensitive to issues of theological consistency. For example, the idea of God sustaining nature and its law-like regularities with one hand while miraculously intervening, abrogating or ignoring those regularities with the other hand struck most members as dangerously close to outright contradiction. Most participants certainly felt that God would not create an orderly world in which it was impossible for the creator to act without violating the created structures of order.

According to Philip Clayton, the real problem here, apparently, is that it is very difficult to come up with an idea of divine action in the world in which such action would not constitute "breaking natural law" or "breaking physical law." Arthur Peacocke comments as follows on a certain proposal for divine action, a proposal according to which God's special actions would be undetectable:

> God would have to be conceived of as actually manipulating micro-events (at the atomic, molecular, and according to some, quantum levels) in these initiating fluctuations on the natural world in order to produce the results at the macroscopic level which God wills. But such a conception of God's action … would then be no different in principle from that of God intervening in the order of nature, with all the problems that that evokes for a rationally coherent belief in God as the creator of that order.

But what, exactly, is the problem with intervention? More poignantly, what is intervention? We can say what it is on the old picture. As we saw, on the old picture the form of a natural law is

(NL) When the universe is causally closed (when God is not acting specially in the world), then P.

Let us now consider the result of deleting the antecedents from the laws, and call the conjunction of the Ps "L." There is an intervention when an event E occurs such that there is an earlier state of the universe S such that $S \& L$ entails $-E$. But nothing like this is available on the New Picture of science. So what would an intervention be? Four possible answers suggest themselves.

1) The first suggestion is that an intervention occurs when God does something A that causes a state of affairs that would not have occurred if God had not done A. But on this

account, any act of conservation would be an intervention; and presumably no one is worried about conservation.

2) Alternatively, an intervention might be defined as what occurs when God performs an act *A*, which is neither conservation nor creation, that causes a state of affairs that would not have occurred if he had not performed *A*. But this appears to make intervention come down simply to God's acting specially in the world. Yet the original objection to special divine action was that it involves intervention. And in answer to the question "What is intervention?" we are now told: "Special divine action." So apparently the problem with special divine action turns out to be special divine action.

3) A third possibility is that one might define intervention as happening when God performs an act that is very improbable, given the previous states of the world. But in that case it is unclear what the problem is supposed to be. Why shouldn't God perform very improbable acts?

4) Finally, one might define intervention in terms of the various low-level generalizations, not entailed by quantum mechanics, on which we normally rely: bread nourishes, people don't walk on water or rise from the dead, and so on. God would then be said to intervene when he causes an event contrary to one of those generalizations. But again, it is not clear what the problem with such interventions is supposed to be. Are we to suppose that the lower-level regularities are like the laws of the Medes and the Persians, so that once God has established one of them, not even he can act contrary to it? In any event, this kind of objection is philosophical or theological not scientific. There is nothing in science, under either the old or the new picture, that conflicts with, or even calls in to question, special divine action, including miracles.

Notes

1 *Heidelberg Catechism,* Question 27.
2 Rudolf Bultmann, *Existence and Faith: Shorter Writings of Rudolf Bultmann,* trans. S. M. Ogden (New York: Meridian Books, 1960), pp. 291–2.
3 Rudolf Bultmann, "New Testament and mythology," in *Kerygma and Myth: A Theological Debate,* ed. H. W. Bartsch, trans. R. H. Fuller (London: SPCK, 1957), p. 5.
4 John Macquarrie, *Principles of Christian Theology* (New York: Scribner, 1966), pp. 226–7.
5 Langdon Gilkey, "Cosmology, ontology and the travail of biblical language," *Journal of Religion* (July 1961), 185.
6 Clayton, Philip D. *God and Contemporary Science* (Edinburgh: Edinburgh University Press, 1997), p. 209.
7 *New York Review of Books,* May 13, 2004.
8 Sears and Zemanski, *University Physics* (Reading, MA: Addison-Wesley, 1964), pp. 186, 415.
9 Pierre Simon Laplace, *A Philosophical Essay on Probabilities,* trans. F. W. Truscott (Mineola, NY: Dover Publications, 1995), p. 4.
10 Mackie, J. L. *The Miracle of Theism* (Oxford: Clarendon, 1982), pp. 19–20.
11 So-called by Wesley Wildman, *Theology and Science* 2, 31 ff.

24

The Evolutionary Argument Against Naturalism

ALVIN PLANTINGA

As it stands, naturalism is presumably not a religion. But if we examine it, we find that it performs one of the central functions of a religion: it provides its followers with a worldview. And as such, it might be called an "honorary religion." And as such, we are led to ask, is there a conflict between naturalism understood in this way and science? And if the answer is "yes," there is a science/religion conflict, but not between science and religion, but between science and naturalism.

Naturalism is the view that there is no such person as God or anything like God. So taken, it is stronger than atheism; it is possible to be an atheist without rising to the heights (or sinking to the depths) of naturalism. A follower of Hegel could be an atheist, but, because of his belief in the Absolute, fail to qualify for naturalism; similarly for someone who believed in the Stoic's Nous, or Plato's Idea of the Good or Aristotle's Prime Mover. This definition of naturalism is a bit vague: exactly how *much* must an entity resemble God to be such that endorsing it disqualifies one from naturalism? Perhaps the definition will be serviceable nonetheless; clear examples of naturalists would be Bertrand Russell ("A Free Man's Worship"), Daniel Dennett (*Darwin's Dangerous Idea*), Richard Dawkins (*The Blind Watchmaker*), the late Stephen Jay Gould, David Armstrong, and the many others that are sometimes said[1] to endorse "the scientific worldview."

Naturalism is presumably not, as it stands, a religion. Nevertheless it performs one of the most important functions of a religion: it provides its adherents with a worldview. It tells us what the world is fundamentally like, what is most deep and important in the world, what our place in the world is, how we are related to other creatures, what (if anything) we can expect after death, and so on. A religion typically does that and more; it also involves worship and ritual. These latter are ordinarily (but not always) absent from naturalism; naturalism, we could therefore say, performs the *cognitive* or *doxastic* function of a religion. For present purposes, therefore, we can promote it to the status of an honorary religion, or at any rate a quasi-religion. And now we must ask the following question: is there a conflict between naturalism, so understood, and science? If so, then indeed there is a science/religion conflict – not, however, between science and Christian (or Judaic, or Islamic) belief, but between science and naturalism.

Why should we think there might be such a conflict? Here the place to look is at the relation between naturalism and current evolutionary theory. But why should we think there might be conflict there, in particular since so many apparently believe that evolution is a main supporting pillar in the temple of naturalism?[2] Note, first, that most of us assume that our cognitive faculties, our belief-producing processes, are for the most part reliable. True, they may not be reliable at the upper limits of our powers, as in some of the more speculative areas of physics; and the proper function of our faculties can be skewed by envy, hate, lust, mother love, greed, and so on. But over a broad range of their operation, we think the purpose of our cognitive faculties is to furnish us with true beliefs, and that when they function properly, they do exactly that.

But isn't there a problem, here, for the naturalist? At any rate for the naturalist who thinks that we and our cognitive capacities have arrived upon the scene after some billions of years of evolution (by way of natural selection and other blind processes working on some such source of genetic variation as random genetic mutation)? The problem begins in the recognition, from this point of view, that the ultimate purpose or function of our cognitive faculties, if they have one, is not to produce true beliefs, but to promote reproductive fitness.[3] What our minds are *for* (if anything) is not the production of true beliefs, but the production of adaptive behavior. That our species has survived and evolved at most guarantees that our behavior is adaptive; it does not guarantee or even suggest that our belief-producing processes are reliable, or that our beliefs are for the most part true. That is because our behavior could be adaptive, but our beliefs mainly false. Darwin himself apparently worried about this question: "With me," says Darwin,

> the horrid doubt always arises whether the convictions of man's mind, which has been developed from the mind of the lower animals, are of any value or at all trustworthy. Would any one trust in the convictions of a monkey's mind, if there are any convictions in such a mind?[4]

Perhaps we could put Darwin's doubt as follows. Let R be the proposition that our cognitive faculties are reliable, N the proposition that naturalism is true and E the proposition that we and our cognitive faculties have come to be by way of the processes to which contemporary evolutionary theory points us: what is the conditional probability of R on $N\&E$? i.e., what is $P(R/N\&E)$? Darwin fears it may be low.

There is much to be said for Darwin's doubt. Natural selection rewards adaptive behavior and penalizes maladaptive behavior, but it cares not a whit what you believe. How, exactly, does this bear on the reliability of our cognitive faculties? In order to avoid irrelevant distractions or species chauvinism, suppose we think, first, not about ourselves and our ancestors, but about a hypothetical population of creatures a lot like ourselves on a planet similar to Earth. Suppose these creatures have cognitive faculties; they hold beliefs, change beliefs, make inferences, and so on; and suppose these creatures have arisen by way of the selection processes endorsed by contemporary evolutionary thought. And suppose naturalism is true in their possible world. What is the probability that their faculties are reliable? What is $P(R/N\&E)$, specified, not to us, but to them?

We can assume that their behavior is for the most part adaptive; but what about their beliefs; is it likely that they are for the most part true? In order to evaluate $P(R/N\&E)$, for those creatures, we must look into the relation between their beliefs and their behavior.

Their behavior, we suppose, is adaptive; but what does that tell us about the truth of their beliefs or the reliability of their cognitive faculties? We'll consider the probability of R on $N\&E$ and each of two possibilities (C and $-C$), possibilities that are mutually exclusive and jointly exhaustive. Given $P(R/N\&E\&C)$ and $P(R/N\&E\&-C)$, we can determine $P(R/N\&E)$. (Of course we won't be able to assign specific real numbers, but only vague estimates such as "high," or "low," or "in the neighborhood of .5.")

What are these two possibilities C and $-C$? First, what sort of thing will a belief *be*, from the perspective of naturalism? Here I will assimilate materialism (about human beings) to naturalism: human beings are material objects and neither are nor contain immaterial souls or selves. (All or nearly all naturalists are materialists, so there will be little if any loss of generality.) And from this point of view, that is, naturalism so construed as to include materialism, a belief would apparently have to be something like a long-term event or structure in the nervous system – perhaps a structured group of neurons connected and related in a certain way. This neural structure will have *neurophysiological* properties (NP properties): properties specifying the number of neurons involved, the way in which those neurons are connected with each other and with other structures (muscles, sense organs, other neuronal events, etc.), the average rate and intensity of neuronal firing in various parts of this event, and the ways in which the rate of fire changes over time and in response to input from other areas. It is easy to see how *these* properties of a neuronal event should have causal influence on the behavior of the organism. Beliefs, presumably, will be neurally connected with muscles; we can see how electrical impulses coming from the belief could negotiate the usual neuronal channels and ultimately cause muscular contraction.

So a belief will be a neuronal structure or event with an array of NP properties. But if this belief is really a *belief*, then it will also have *another* sort of property: it will have *content*; it will be the belief that p, for some proposition p – perhaps the proposition *naturalism is all the rage these days*. And now the question is this: does a belief – a neural structure – cause behavior, enter into the causal chain leading to behavior, *by virtue of its content*? C is the possibility that the content of a belief *does* enter the causal chain leading to behavior; $-C$ is the possibility that it does not.

Lets begin with $-C$ (which we could call *semantic epiphenomenalism*): what is $P(R/N\&E\&-C)$? Well, it is of course the *content* of a belief that determines its truth or falsehood; a belief is true just if the proposition that constitutes its content is true. But given $-C$, the content of a belief would be *invisible* to evolution. Since natural selection is interested only in adaptive behavior, not true belief, it would be unable to modify belief-producing processes in the direction of greater reliability by penalizing false belief and rewarding true belief. Accordingly, the fact that these creatures have survived and evolved, that their cognitive equipment was good enough to enable their ancestors to survive and reproduce – that fact would tell us nothing at all about the *truth* of their beliefs or the reliability of their cognitive faculties. It would tell something about the *neurophysiological* properties of a given belief; it would tell us that, by virtue of these properties, that belief has played a role in the production of adaptive behavior. But it would tell us nothing about the truth of the *content* of that belief: its content might be true, but might with equal probability be false. Now reliability requires a fairly high proportion of true beliefs – for definiteness, say three out of four. On this scenario (i. e., $N\&E\&-C$), the probability that three-quarters of these creatures' beliefs are true is low. Alternatively, we might think this probability is inscrutable – such that we simply cannot tell, except within very wide limits, what it is. This too seems a sensible conclusion. $P(R/N\&E\&-C)$, therefore, is either low or inscrutable.

Turn to *C*, the other possibility, the possibility that the content of a belief *does* enter the causal chain leading to behaviour. As I will argue below, it is difficult to see, on the materialist scenario, how a belief *could* have causal influence on behavior or action by virtue of its content. Nonetheless, suppose *C* is true. This is the common-sense position: belief serves as a (partial) cause and thus explanation of behavior – and this explicitly holds for the *content* of belief. I want a beer and believe there is one in the fridge; the content of that belief, we ordinarily think, partly explains the movements of that large lumpy object that is my body as it heaves itself out of the armchair, moves over to the fridge, opens it, and extracts the beer. What is P(*R*/*N*&*E*&*C*)? Not as high as one might think.

Could we argue that beliefs are connected with behavior in such a way that false belief would produce maladaptive behavior, behavior that would tend to reduce the probability of the believer's surviving and reproducing? No. First, false belief by no means guarantees maladaptive action. For example, religious belief is nearly universal across the world; even among naturalists, it is widely thought to be adaptive; yet naturalists think these beliefs are mostly false. Clearly enough false belief can produce adaptive behavior. Perhaps a primitive tribe thinks that everything is really alive, or is a witch; and perhaps all or nearly all of their beliefs are of the form *this witch is F* or *that witch is G*: for example, *this witch is good to eat*, or *that witch is likely to eat me if I give it a chance*. If they ascribe the right properties to the right "witches," their beliefs could be adaptive while nonetheless (assuming that in fact there aren't any witches) false.

Our question is really about the proportion of true beliefs among adaptive beliefs – that is, beliefs involved in the causation of adaptive behavior. What proportion of adaptive beliefs are true? For every true adaptive belief it seems we can easily think of a false belief that leads to the same adaptive behavior. The fact that my behavior (or that of my ancestors) has been adaptive, therefore, is at best a third-rate reason for thinking my beliefs mostly true and my cognitive faculties reliable – and that is true even given the common-sense view of the relation of belief to behavior. So we can't sensibly argue from the fact that our behavior (or that of our ancestors) has been adaptive, to the conclusion that our beliefs are mostly true and our cognitive faculties reliable. It is therefore hard to see that P(*R*/*N*&*E*&*C*) is very high. To concede as much as possible to the opposition, however, let's say that this probability is either inscrutable or in the neighborhood of 9.

Now the calculus of probabilities (the theorem on total probability) tells us that

$$P(R/N \ \& \ E) = [P(R/N \ \& \ E \ \& \ C) \times P(C/N \ \& \ E)] + [P(R/N \ \& \ E \ \& -C) \times P(-C/N \ \& \ E)],$$

i.e., the probability of *R* on *N*&*E* is the weighted average of the probabilities of *R* on *N*&*E*&*C* and *N*&*E*&–*C* – weighted by the probabilities of *C* and –*C* on *N*&*E*.

We have already noted that the left-hand term of the first of the two products on the right side of the equality is either moderately high or inscrutable; the second is either low or inscrutable. What remains is to evaluate the weights, the right-hand terms of the two products. So what is the probability of –*C*, given *N*&*E*, what is the probability of semantic epiphenomenalism on *N*&*E*? Robert Cummins suggests that semantic epiphenomenalism is in fact the received view as to the relation between belief and behavior.[5] That is because it is extremely hard to envisage a way, given materialism, in which the content of a belief *could* get causally involved in behavior. According to materialism, a belief is a neural structure of some kind – a structure that somehow possesses content. But how can its content get involved in the causal chain leading to behavior? Had a given such structure had a *different* content, one thinks, its causal contribution to behavior would be the same. Suppose my belief *naturalism is all the rage these days* – the neuronal structure that does in fact display that content – had had the same neurophysiological properties but some entirely different content: perhaps *nobody believes naturalism nowadays*. Would that have made any difference to its role in the causation of behavior? It is hard to see how: there would have been the same electrical impulses traveling down the same neural pathways, issuing in the same muscular contractions. It is therefore exceedingly hard to see how semantic epiphenomenalism can be avoided, given N&E. (There have been some valiant efforts but things don't look hopeful.) So it looks as if P ($-C/N\&E$) will have to be estimated as relatively high; let's say (for definiteness) .7, in which case P($C/N\&E$) will be.3. Of course we could easily be wrong; we don't really have a solid way of telling; so perhaps the conservative position here is that this probability too is inscrutable: one simply cannot tell what it is. Given current knowledge, therefore, P ($-C/N\&E$) is either high or inscrutable. And if P ($-C/N\&E$) is inscrutable, then the same goes, naturally enough, for P($C/N\&E$). What does that mean for the sum of these two products, i.e., P($R/N\&E$)?

We have several possibilities. Suppose we think first about the matter from the point of view of someone who doesn't find any of the probabilities involved inscrutable. Then P($C/N\&E$) will be in the neighborhood of .3, P ($-C/N\&E$) in the neighborhood of .7, and P($R/N\&E\&-C$) perhaps in the neighborhood of .2. This leaves P($R/N\&E\&C$), the probability that R is true given ordinary naturalism together with the common-sense view as to the relation between belief and behavior. Given that this probability is not inscrutable, let's say that it is in the neighborhood of .9. Under these estimates, P($R/N\&E$) will be in the neighborhood of .41.[6] Suppose, on the other hand, we think the probabilities involved are inscrutable: then we will have to say the same for P($R/N\&E$). P($R/N\&E$), therefore, is either low – less than .5, at any rate – or inscrutable.

In either case, however, doesn't the naturalist – at any rate one who sees that P($R/N\&E$) is low or inscrutable – have a defeater for R, and for the proposition that his own cognitive faculties are reliable? I think so. Note some analogies with clear cases. I hear about a certain substance *XXX*, a substance the ingestion of which is widely reputed to destroy the reliability of one's belief-forming faculties; nevertheless I find it difficult to estimate the probability that ingestion of *XXX* really does destroy cognitive reliability, and regard that probability as either high or inscrutable. Now suppose I come to think you have ingested *XXX*. Then I have a defeater for anything I believe just on your say-so; I won't (or shouldn't) believe anything you tell me unless I have independent evidence for it. And if I come to think that I myself have also ingested *X* – at an unduly high-spirited party, perhaps – then I will have a defeater for R in my own case. Suppose, in the modern equivalent to Descartes' evil demon case, I come to think I am a brain in a vat, and that the probability of my cognitive faculties being reliable, given that I am a brain in a vat, is low or inscrutable: then again I have a defeater for R with respect to me.

Perhaps it seems harder to see that one has a defeater for R in the case where the relevant probability is inscrutable than in the case where it is low. Suppose you buy a thermometer; then you learn that the owner of the factory where it was manufactured is an Audited who aims to do what he can to disrupt contemporary technology, and to that end makes at least some instruments that are unreliable. You can't say what the probability is of this thermometer's being reliable, given that it was made in that factory; that probability is inscrutable for you. But would you trust the thermometer? It is outside your window, and reads 30°F; if you have no other source of information about the temperature outside, would you believe it is 30°F?

Another analogy: you embark on a voyage of space exploration and land on a planet revolving about a distant sun, a planet that apparently has a favorable atmosphere. You crack the hatch, step out, and immediately find what appears to be an instrument that looks a lot like a terrestrial radio; you twiddle the dials, and after a couple of squawks it begins to emit strings of sounds that, oddly enough, form English sentences. These sentences express propositions only about topics of which you have no knowledge: what the weather is like in Beijing at the moment, whether Caesar had eggs on toast on the morning he crossed the Rubicon, and whether the first human being to cross the Bering Strait was left-handed. Impressed, indeed awed, by your find, you initially form the opinion that this instrument speaks the truth, that the propositions expressed (in English) by those sentences are true. But then you recall that you have no idea at all as to who or what constructed the instrument, what it is for, whether it has a purpose at all. You see that the probability of its being reliable, given what you know about it, is inscrutable. Then you have a defeater for your initial belief that the thing does in fact speak the truth. In the same way, then, the fact that P(R/N&E) is low or inscrutable gives you a defeater for R.

But here an objection rears its ugly head. In trying to assess P(R/N&E), I suggested that semantic epiphenomenalism was probable, given materialism, because a neural structure would have caused the same behavior if it had had *different* content but the *same* NP properties. But, says the objector, it *couldn't* have had the same NP properties but different content; having a given content *just is* having a certain set of NP properties. This is a sensible objection. Given materialism, there is a way of looking at the relation between content (as well as other mental properties) and NP properties according to which the objector is clearly right. We must therefore look a bit more deeply into that relation. Here there are fundamentally two positions: *reductionism* or *reductive materialism* on the one hand, and *nonreductive materialism* on the other. Consider the property of having as content the proposition *naturalism is all the rage these days*, and call this property *C*. According to *reductive* materialism, *C just is* a certain combination of *NP* properties.[7] It might be a disjunction of such properties; more likely a complex Boolean construction on *NP* properties, perhaps something like

$$[P1 \,\& \, P7 \,\& \, P28...) \vee (P3 \,\& \, P17 \,\& ...) \vee (P8 \,\& \, P83 \,\& \, P107...) \vee ...$$

(where the *Pi* are *NP* properties).

Now take any belief *B* you like: what is the probability that *B* is true, given N&E and reductive materialism? What we know is that *B* has a certain content; that having that content just is having a certain combination of NP properties; and (we may assume) that having that combination of NP properties is adaptive (in the circumstances in which the organism finds itself). What, then, is the probability that the content of *B* is *true*? Well, it doesn't *matter* whether it is true; if it is true, the NP properties constituting that content will be adaptive, but if it is false, those properties will be equally adaptive, since in each case they make the same causal contribution to behavior. That combination of NP properties is the property of having a certain content; it is the property of being associated with a certain proposition *p* in such a way that *p* is the content of the belief. Having that combination of NP properties is adaptive; hence having that belief is adaptive; but that combination of NP properties will be equally adaptive whether *p* is true or false. In this case (reductionism) content does enter into the causal chain leading to behavior, because NP properties do, and having a certain content just is displaying a certain set of NP properties. But those properties will be adaptive, whether or not the content the having of which they constitute, is true. Content enters in, all right, but not, we might say, *as* content. Better, content enters the causal chain leading to behavior, but not in such a way that its truth or falsehood bears on the adaptive character of the belief.

But, someone might object, given that the belief is adaptive, isn't there a greater probability of its being true than of its being false? Why so? Because, the objector continues, the belief's being adaptive means that having this belief, in these or similar circumstances, helped the creature's ancestors to survive and reproduce; having this belief contributed to reproductive fitness. And wouldn't the best explanation for this contribution be that the belief accurately represented their circumstances, in other words *was true*? So, probably, the belief was adaptive for the creature's ancestors because it was true. So, probably, the belief is adaptive for this creature in *its* circumstances because it is true.[8]

This objection, beguiling as it sounds, is mistaken. The proper explanation of this belief's being adaptive is that having the NP properties that constitute the content of the belief causes adaptive behavior, not that the belief is true. And of course having those NP properties can cause adaptive behavior whether or not the content they constitute is true. At a certain level of complexity of NP properties, the neural structure that displays those properties also acquires a certain content C. That is because having that particular complex of NP properties just is what it is to have C. Having those NP properties, presumably, is adaptive; but whether the content arising in this way is true or false makes no difference to that adaptivity. What explains the adaptivity is just that having these NP properties, this content, causes adaptive behavior.[9]

So consider again a belief B with its content C; what, then, given that having that belief is adaptive, is the probability that C is true, is a true proposition? Well, since truth of content doesn't make a difference to the adaptivity of the belief, the belief could be true, but could equally likely be false. We'd have to estimate the probability that it is true as about .5. But then if the creature has 1,000 independent beliefs, the probability that, say, three-quarters of them are true (and this would be a minimal requirement for reliability) will be very low — less than 10^{-58}.[10] So on naturalism and reductionism, the probability of R appears to be very low.

That's how things go given reductive materialism; according to *non-reductive materialism*, the other possibility, a mental property is not an NP property or any Boolean construction on NP properties, but a new sort of property that gets instantiated when a neural structure attains a certain degree of complexity – when, that is, it displays a certain sufficiently complex set of NP properties. (We might call it an "emergent" property.) Again, take any particular belief B: what is the probability, on N&E & non-reductive materialism, that B is true? What we know is that B has a content, that this content arises when the structure has a certain complex set of NP properties, and that having that set of NP properties is adaptive. But once again, it doesn't matter for adaptivity whether the content associated with those NP properties is true or false; so once again, the probability that the content is true will have to be estimated as about .5; hence the probability that these creatures have reliable faculties is low. Either way, therefore, that probability is low, so that P(R/N&E) is also low – or, as we could add, if we like, inscrutable.

Now for the argument that one cannot rationally accept N&E. P(R/N&E), for those hypothetical creatures, is low or inscrutable. But those creatures aren't relevantly different from us; so of course the same goes for us: P(R/N&E) specified to us is also low or inscrutable. We have seen furthermore that one who accepts N&E (and sees that P(R/N&E) is either low or inscrutable) has a defeater for *R*. But one who has a defeater for *R*, has a defeater for any belief she takes to be a product of her cognitive faculties – which is of course *all* of her beliefs. She therefore has a defeater for *N&E* itself; so one who *accepts N&E* has a *defeater* for *N&E*, a reason to doubt or reject or be agnostic with respect to it. If she has no independent evidence then the rational course would be to reject belief in *N&E*. If she has no independent evidence, *N&E* is self-defeating and hence irrational.

But of course defeaters can in turn be themselves defeated; so couldn't she get a defeater for this defeater – a defeater-defeater? Maybe by doing some science, for example, determining by scientific means that her faculties really are reliable? Couldn't she go to the MIT cognitive-reliability laboratory for a check-up? Clearly that won't help. Obviously that course would *presuppose* that her faculties are reliable; she would be relying on the accuracy of her faculties in believing that there is such a thing as MIT, that she has in fact consulted its scientists, that they have given her a clean bill of cognitive health, and so on. Thomas Reid (*Essays on the Intellectual Powers of Man*)[11] put it like this:

> If a man's honesty were called into question, it would be ridiculous to refer to the man's own word, whether he be honest or not. The same absurdity there is in attempting to prove, by any kind of reasoning, probable or demonstrative, that our reason is not fallacious, since the very point in question is, whether reasoning may be trusted.

Is there any sensible way at all in which she can argue for *R*? It is hard to see how. Any argument she might produce will have premises; these premises, she claims, give her good reason to believe *R*. But of course she has the very same defeater for each of those premises that she has for *R*; and she has the same defeater for the belief that if the premises of that argument are true, then so is the conclusion. So it looks as if this defeater cannot be defeated. Naturalistic evolution gives its adherents a reason for doubting that our beliefs are mostly true; perhaps they are mostly mistaken. But then it won't help to *argue* that they cannot be mostly mistaken; for the very reason for mistrusting our cognitive faculties *generally*, will be a reason for mistrusting the faculties that produce belief in the goodness of the argument.

This defeater, therefore, cannot be defeated. Hence the devotee of *N&E* has an undefeated defeater for *N&E*. *N&E*, therefore, cannot rationally be accepted – at any rate by someone who is apprised of this argument and sees the connections between *N&E* and *R*.

But if *N&E* can't rationally be accepted, there is indeed a conflict between naturalism and evolution: one cannot rationally accept them both. But evolution is an extremely important scientific doctrine, one of the chief pillars of contemporary science. Hence there is a conflict between naturalism and science. The conclusion seems to be that there is a religion/science conflict, all right, but it isn't between Christian belief and science: it is between naturalism and science.[12]

Notes

1   Erroneously, in my opinion. There is no inner connection between science and naturalism; indeed, as I will argue, naturalism clashes with science.

2   Thus Richard Dawkins: "Although atheism might have been logically tenable before Darwin, Darwin made it possible to be an intellectually fulfilled atheist." *The Blind Watchmaker* (New York: Norton, 1986), pp. 6–7.

3   As evolutionary psychologist Donald Sloan Wilson puts it, "the well-adapted mind is ultimately an organ of survival and reproduction." *Darwin's Cathedral* (Chicago: University of Chicago Press, 2002), p. 228.

4   Letter to William Graham Down, July 3, 1881. In *The Life and Letters of Charles Darwin: Including an Autobiographical Chapter*, ed. Francis Darwin (London: John Murray, 1887), vol. 1, pp. 315–16. Evan Fales has suggested that Darwin is thinking, here, not of belief generally, but of religious and philosophical convictions and theoretical beliefs. If he is right, Darwin's doubt would not extend to everyday beliefs to the effect, e.g., that bread is nourishing but mud is not, but to religious and philosophical beliefs – such as naturalism.

5   *Meaning and Mental Representation* (Cambridge, MA: MIT Press, 1989), p. 130.

6   Of course these figures are the merest approximations; others might make the estimates somewhat differently; but they can be significantly altered without significantly altering the final result. For example, perhaps you think the $P(R/N\&C)$ is higher, perhaps even 1; then (retaining the other assignments) $P(R/N)$ will be in the neighborhood of .44. Or perhaps you reject the thought that $P(-C/N)$ is more probable than $P(C/N)$, thinking them about equal. Then (again, retaining the other assignments) $P(R/N)$ will be in the neighborhood of .55.

7   Or (to accommodate the thought that meaning "ain't in the head") a combination of NP properties with environmental properties. I will assume but not mention this qualification in what follows.

8   Here I am indebted to Tom Crisp.

9   In this connection, consider dream beliefs. Take a given dream belief with its content C: Having the NP properties that constitute the property of having C is presumably adaptive; but it makes no difference whether or not that content is true.

10   As calculated by Paul Zwier. This is the probability that the whole battery of cognitive faculties is reliable; the probability that a given faculty is reliable will be larger, but still small; if its output is, say, 100 beliefs, the probability that three-quarters of them are true will be no more than .000001.

11   Thomas Reid, *Essays on the Intellectual Powers of Man*, ed. Derek R. Brookes (Philadelphia: Penn Press, 2002).

12   For wise counsel and good advice, I am grateful to Thad Botham, E. J. Coffman, Robin Collins, Tom Crisp, Chris Green, Jeff Green, Dan McKaughan, Brian Pitts, Luke Potter, and Del Ratzsch.

Part 9

Science and Theology as Faithful Human Activities

25

Two For the Ages:
Origen and Newton

GARY PATTERSON

The history of Christianity is replete with examples of highly original thinkers, both with regard to science or natural philosophy and with regard to theology. Two of the most original minds were Origen, a Patristic theologian, philosopher, and Bible scholar from Alexandria, and Isaac Newton, the inventor of the calculus, classical mechanics, modern optics, and modern critical study of the Bible. The present paper reviews and compares the lives and thoughts of these two men. They were both characterized by exceptionally large minds. Origen blended this with an expansive heart and a wise judgment. Newton formed the nucleus of both a public scientific world and a more private world of alchemy and theology. He was a major influence on latitudinarian Anglican thought in the early eighteenth century. They both were committed to the search for the Truth and adopted a highly multidisciplinary approach.

Introduction

The history of Christianity is a story of people from many times and many places. It started in Palestine twenty centuries ago with a man named Jesus. Jesus was a Jew from the city of Nazareth in the region of Galilee. Although he died a martyr's death, his disciples continued to preach his message, and Christianity spread over the known world. One of the places where the Christian Church became established in the second century AD was Alexandria in Egypt. It was the intellectual capital of the Roman world. Although there are many names associated with the church in Alexandria, one name stands out in the late second and early third century: Origen.

Another place that welcomed Christianity was seventeenth-century England. Although the religious and political history of this time was tumultuous, the Anglican establishment at Oxford and Cambridge reigned in their academic world. Standard religious histories of this time and place seldom make any mention of Isaac Newton, but recent scholarly work on original manuscripts from the Yahuda collection in Jerusalem have enlightened us with regard to the religious work of this great natural philosopher and mathematician. A good reference source for this material is *The Religion of Isaac Newton* by Frank E. Manuel (1974).

Tertullian, the great Roman contemporary of Origen, questioned "What indeed has Athens to do with Jerusalem?"; the present chapter will examine the interesting relationship between Origen of Alexandria and Newton of Cambridge. While they were separated by many years in time and came from two very different societies, they shared many traits and beliefs that united them. Above all they shared a passion for Truth that has rarely been equaled, either then or now.

Origen

Origen was born in AD 185 in Alexandria into a wealthy Christian family. This was significant in that time and culture, because then, as now, conversion was a crime in Egypt! Origen had a devout father, Leonides, who raised him to love Jesus, the Bible, other Christians, and Truth. When his father was arrested during the persecution of Septimus Severus in 202, Origen wrote him a touching encouragement in the face of his martyrdom. He would have joined his father in death, but his mother hid his clothes! The theme of martyrdom colored Origen's whole life and one of his most famous writings was the *Exhortation to Martyrdom*, written to his friend Ambrose in 235.

Origen found himself the head of his household, with a family to support. He was well educated and earned his living as a teacher of literature, a *grammateus*. In spite of the danger, many pagans came to Origen and asked him to instruct them in the ways of Christianity. Within a year he was asked by Bishop Demetrius to head the catechetical school in Alexandria. He was a very persuasive catechist and the local authorities were outraged that so many of his pupils converted to Christianity. One of his most solemn duties was to prepare them for the almost certain martyrdom that accompanied their conversion.

Origen caught the attention of a wealthy widow who served as his patron. She enabled him to study with the foremost teacher in Alexandria, Ammonius Saccus. Saccus was also the teacher of the great neo-Platonic philosopher, Plotinus. Origen established his own *Didascalion* in Alexandria in which he taught from 212–31. This school produced a very large number of books, many of which are extant. Most of them are commentaries on the Bible. The method of instruction at the *Didascalion* was very interesting. The students were encouraged to read the best books they could find; perhaps from the great Jewish philosopher Philo or the great Greek philosopher Plato. The students would then gather and discuss the books in light of all they knew. The strong belief in the unity of knowledge and the faith to follow the arguments carefully were inculcated by Origen. His ability to work in a group and his openness to the arguments of others were soon noticed by other Bishops. Origen was invited to come to places such as Cappodocia, Arabia, or Jerusalem to help settle disputes. While he was away, his school was ably managed by Ambrose.

Since Origen was frequently in Caesarea or Jerusalem teaching the Bible, the local bishop recommended that he be ordained. This act was condemned by Demetrius of Alexandria, and Origen spent the rest of his life at a new school established at Caesarea. During the reign of Decius in 247 Origen was arrested and tortured for his faith. He died around 253.

Since Origen believed that the Truth was found in many places, he learned the ancient languages of faith, including Hebrew. He read the rabbinic writings and consulted with Jewish scholars on the meaning of the text. He knew and read the early Christian writings, in addition to the current text of the New Testament, such as the Shepherd of Hermas and the works of Clement of Alexandria. His mind was open to the best that was known in his time, but he did not just read. He actively synthesized his faith with all that was known and produced a masterpiece: *On First Principles*.

Origen and Neoplatonic theology

The theological program of Origen is well-expressed in a letter he wrote to Gregory Thaumaturgus:

> I should like to see you use all the resources of your mind on Christianity and make that your ultimate object. I hope that to that end you will take from Greek philosophy everything capable of serving as an introduction to Christianity and from geometry and astronomy all ideas useful in expounding the Holy Scriptures; so that what philosophers say of geometry, music, grammar, rhetoric and astronomy – that they assist philosophy – we too may be able to say of philosophy itself in relation to Christianity.

Rather than denouncing Greek thought, as did Tertullian, he embraced it, in so far as it assisted true theology.

The basic worldview of Origen was elaborate, but it was based on an essential unity: the One of Greek philosophy was identified as God the Father. Everything proceeded from the Father. In particular, the Word proceeded from the Father. This theme is sounded strongly in the Gospel of John, and Origen tried to synthesize his understanding of both sources. The identification of Jesus as the Word had profound implications for Origen. It meant that Jesus was the Creator. The history of Christian theology has had many twists and Origen was not a favorite of some medieval theologians, but he was greatly inspired by the relationship between the Father and the Son and Orthodox thought still reveres his memory.

One phrase that helps to explain neo-Platonic thought is the "great chain of being." Everything is related to everything else. This monistic thread in Origen is constantly in view. One of the entities that proceeds from the Word is the rational mind or soul. In this system, all humans are directly related to God through the Soul, through the Word. The simplicity and purity of this vision allowed Origen to see the value in every single human being. The simplicity and purity of his life gave considerable force to his words during his lifetime. Arguments about words have sometimes obfuscated the issues involved, but Origen lived above some of those problems.

With such a grand and sweeping vision, what can be made of the actual world in which we live? The reality of evil in the world was all too apparent to Origen. He had experienced it personally. One of the most important properties of the One was immutability. The Word retained that same perfect character. But, as time and distance away from the One increased, mutability appeared. The Fall is accepted as a fact, but no explanation for it is given. Nevertheless, after the Fall, the rational natures "cooled" and they became human "souls." The body was given to humankind in order to make the "journey" back to God. This picture has not persisted in Christian theology as neo-Platonism has not retained its appeal, but in the time of Origen, it provided a grand metanarrative that organized certain aspects of reality.

Neoplatonic theology became complicated with regard to Jesus. He had a body, but it was believed that he was the Word, and hence not mutable. Origen believed in the principle of dynamic tension: Jesus was both the Word and a man. He was sent to help humankind in their journey back to God. He was presented as the mediator between God and man.

Because he had a body, the basic stance towards matter was positive; the body was given as a gift to humankind. This is in contrast to many ancient theologies that had a very negative view of matter.

There were also two active principles that were held in tension: Freedom and Providence. Historical attempts to resolve the tension in favor of one or the other have not produced satisfactory solutions. Origen felt no need to resolve the tension since human life was inherently complicated.

Origen created a theology of hope since he believed that in the end there would be a restoration. Humans would receive resurrection bodies in which the rational soul would find its stasis. There is considerable current discussion about the nature of a final state that emphasizes the ultimate importance of resurrection to a new body, rather than reconstitution of an old one. While the conceptual world of current theologies is quite different in many respects, there are some issues that seem to transcend time.

The story of human existence is envisioned as a great drama, where every person has a part to play. The metaphor for human life is the journey. The constant factor in human life is change and only hope in God makes the journey understandable. Origen also had a very communal view of the Christian life; God has given us many things to help us on our way. The great English classic *Pilgrim's Progress* would have been enjoyed immensely by Origen. God has given us Jesus and one another to help us along. Origen also had a very thick ontology of beings that could be encountered on our journey. Since he believed in the great chain of being, he had no problem with multiplying beings. Current thinking along this line includes the haunting novel *All Hallows Eve* by Charles Williams.

Origen believed that the Christian life should be both contemplated by the rational soul and actively lived in community. He was a good personal model of this way of life. He observed all he could in the natural world, and reasoned about the natural order. He was especially clear in his belief that the created order is contingent on God. He read everything he could find that might contain a measure of Truth needed by humankind. But, he related everything he did find to the book that he had learned to love as a child.

Newton

Isaac Newton was born in 1643 in the manor house of Woolsthorpe. His father died before he was born, and when he was three his stepfather, Barnabas Smith, an Anglican clergyman, sent him away. Isaac Newton developed very specific views about clergy and their influence on the Christian Church. He could have easily rejected Christianity as well, but he chose to revere the Bible, and to seek to dwell in peace with his fellow Cantabs. He was raised by his maternal grandmother and the Ayscough family helped him to make his way to Cambridge. Barnabas Smith died in 1653 and Newton's mother Hannah returned to live at Woolsthorpe with her three new children. She also brought Smith's extensive library. Isaac soon moved to Grantham to attend grammar school and lived with a local apothecary. His lifelong love of chemistry may have been sparked by this environment.

Isaac Newton eventually enrolled in 1661 at Trinity College, Cambridge as a subsizar, a poor student. He was a servant to some of the wealthier students. However, he worked very hard and mastered the curriculum of his time. It consisted of Aristotelian logic, ethics, and rhetoric, as well as Latin and Greek. But Newton was not content to merely look towards the past. He began to read many current books on a wide range of subjects, especially natural

Figure 25.1   Isaac Newton 1643–1727. From Frank Edward Manuel, *A Portrait of Isaac Newton* (Cambridge, MA: Belknap Press, 1968). Picture courtesy of Wellcome Library, London.

philosophy. In addition to his academic studies, he gave serious consideration to the state of his soul. He formulated a series of "Quaestiones" that helped to organize his insatiable curiosity. Newton fell in love with Descartes' geometry, and soon was able to progress well beyond it. He graduated in 1665 with a BA degree. Isaac Newton's time at Cambridge was interrupted by the plague, but his sojourn back at Woolsthorpe did not interrupt his rapid mathematical development. The basis of the calculus was developed and several important papers were published. He also progressed beyond both Descartes and Galileo in his understanding of mechanics. He read and interacted with Boyle and Hooke on colors and produced a better optics. This time spent back home with his mother was especially fruitful and helped to launch Newton on the rest of his life.

Newton returned to Cambridge and was elected a Fellow of Trinity College in 1667. He progressed to the MA degree in 1668 and became a major Fellow, with enough of a stipend to provide his living. Isaac Newton tutored students, as was required of the Fellows, but mostly he read everything he could get his hands on. He was interested in mathematics, natural philosophy, chemistry, and theology. He was never content to just read about things; he followed up his reading with attempts to verify his conclusions, using whatever means were available. Often this meant trying things out on himself. He carried out some truly gruesome experiments on his own eyeballs. He was also exposed to many chemicals, including heavy metals. He is mostly celebrated today for his mathematics and natural philosophy, but he spent far more time on chemistry and theology!

Isaac Newton began to share his mathematical developments with Isaac Barrow, the Lucasian Professor of Mathematics at Trinity. His celebrated paper on *Analysis* led to his appointment as Lucasian Professor, in Barrow's stead, in 1669. Barrow went on to serve as Master of Trinity and had a close relationship to Newton all his life. Newton also benefited greatly from Barrows' extensive library. Newton was now free to pursue his interests wherever they might take him. Although he did give lectures, they mostly served to organize his growing understanding of natural philosophy, and few students either attended or could have understood them. Unlike Origen, Newton worked mostly by himself on his deepest subjects. He may have stood on the shoulders of other giants, but he kept his own best work private.

Isaac Newton was now well-known both in Cambridge and in London at the Royal Society. He made major contributions to natural philosophy and to practical matters such as his invention of a reflecting telescope. He published major works on optics and his magisterial *Principia*. With all this activity, it might be wondered how Newton could have done anything else. In actual fact, he was an obsessively busy man. Although modern chemistry books rarely mention Newton, he formulated a conceptual scheme and a research program that inspired research in this field for more than 100 years. But, even more effort was put into theology. One of Newton's other Cambridge friends was Henry More, the celebrated Cambridge Platonist. More was a consummate Bible scholar and he and Newton often discussed prophecy and other religious topics.

Newton's later years were dominated by public service and the Royal Society. He was made the Master of the Mint and served the Crown well. He was knighted for his contributions to both science and the nation. He served as the President of the Royal Society. He died a wealthy and celebrated man in 1727.

The religion of Isaac Newton

Newton did not confine his religious thoughts to his private writing. A good statement of his stance is contained in the General Scholium to his *Philosophiae Naturalis Principia Mathematica*:

> This Being governs all Things, not as a Soul of the World, but as Lord of the Universe; and upon Account of his Dominion, he is stiled Lord God, supreme over all. For the Word God is a relative Term, and has Reference to Servants, and Deity is the Dominion of God not (such as a Soul has) over a Body of his own, which is the Notion of those, who make God the Soul of the World; but(such as a Governor has) over Servants. The supreme God is an eternal, infinite, absolutely perfect Being: But a Being, how perfect soever without Dominion is not Lord God. For we say, my God, your God, the God of Israel, the God of Gods, and Lord of Lords. But, we do not say, my Eternal, your Eternal, the Eternal of Israel, the Eternal of Gods: We do not say, my Perfect, (your Perfect, the Perfect of Israel:) For these Terms have no relation to Servants. The Term God very frequently signifies Lord; but every Lord is not God. The Dominion of a spiritual Being constitutes him God. True Dominion, true God: Supreme Dominion, supreme God: Imaginary Dominion, imaginary God. And from his having true Dominion it follows, that the true God is living, intelligent, and powerful; from his other Perfections it follows that he is supreme or most perfect.

This would be considered a strange introduction for a modern physics text, but in Newton's world nothing made sense apart from the Lord God. But, it is not neo-Platonic. The God of Newton was viewed in very different terms than the impassive One of Greek thought. Another good insight can be gained from Newton's commentary on II Kings 17:

To celebrate God for his eternity, immensity, omnisciency, and omnipotence is indeed very pious and duty of every creature to do it according to capacity, but yet this part of God's glory as it almost transcends the comprehension of man so it springs not from the freedom of God's will but the necessity of his nature … the wisest of beings required of us to be celebrated not so much for his essence as for his actions, the creating, preserving, and governing of all things according to his good will and pleasure. The wisdom, power, goodness, and justice which he always exerts in his actions are his glory which he stands so much upon, and is so jealous of … even to the least tittle. (Yahuda MS 21)

The God of Newton was revealed by his actions in the physical world and by his written revelation in the Bible. He chose to accept both of these spheres as valid places to probe the work of God and to think deeply about what was found. Since Isaac Newton was quite successful in revealing many aspects of the physical world, he viewed himself as ordained by God to be a revealer of spiritual truths as well. Newton viewed himself as a priest-scientist, just as Origen viewed himself as a searcher for all truth.

Newton and the Bible

Isaac Newton believed that the Bible was given by God to humans and that it should be searched thoroughly, just as the physical world was open to investigation. The analogy of the Two Books of Nature and Scripture was very common in the seventeenth century, but as with many other things, Newton gave it his own form. He believed that

Truth is ever to be found in simplicity, and not in the multiplicity and confusion of things. As the world, which to the naked eye exhibits the greatest variety of objects, appears very simple in its internall constitution when surveyed by a philosophic understanding, and so much the simpler by how much better it is understood, so it is in these prophetic visions. It is the perfection of God's works that they are all done with the greatest simplicity. He is the God of order and not of confusion. (Yahuda MS 1.1)

Since he believed that there was an underlying simplicity in both nature and scripture, he applied himself to finding the key to the Bible.

In order to carry out this search, he learned the languages needed to read the text in its original form. He had friends at Cambridge who could help in this project, such as Henry More. Since he was searching for pure truth, he attempted to establish a pure text. He examined all the known versions of the texts of the Old and New Testaments and tried to make judgments about the best text. This project continues today, but Isaac Newton stands in the line of critical scholars of the Bible.

The text he found was still very heterogeneous; there were many different genres from many different periods. Newton read all he could find on the interpretation and nature of the Bible by the best scholars of former times, such as Spinoza and Abraham Ibn Ezra, and of his own time, such as Lightfoot and Pocock. He formed his own opinions based on considerable evidence. Since he worked so hard on this project, and since he was "Newton," he had a high opinion of his opinions, but he was wise enough to share these opinions mostly in private. He concluded that the form of narrative writing used in the Bible was largely conformed to the community for which it was written, and that modern notions of "objective" history were not followed. Even so, the Bible was considered a much more reliable source of historical evidence than any other ancient document. The recognition of the human element in the text of the Bible is very modern in its insight, and it produced a greater appreciation of the text in Newton.

Isaac Newton was especially interested in the prophetic books such as Daniel and the Revelation of John. Since they are written in symbolic language, the greatest revealer of the secrets of nature was eager to serve this world as well. He studied a very large number of commentaries on these books, and made his own judgments about the meaning of the symbols. He expected the truth to be simple and coherent, and he tried to produce an interpretation that satisfied his criteria. He constructed a correspondence between the Biblical texts and known events in world history. He was generally careful to look towards the past when making these connections. However, occasionally he could not resist the temptation to look forward to the Millennium. He believed strongly in the resurrection of Christians and other godly souls, and genuinely looked forward to his part in this blessed time. His ontology of the blessed future was rich with beings, so even though the underlying principle was simple the outworking was diverse. Newton shares much with Origen in this area.

Isaac Newton had a circle of friends who were Anglican clergy, such as Samuel Clarke and Richard Bentley, and they talked about many things together. The Boyle lectures were established to promote the irenic cooperation of science and theology, and while Newton did not give one himself, he played a role behind the scenes. However, he understood the nature of science and the character of theology far too well to be happy with the so-called *physica sacra* that attempted to use the explicit arguments of current science to "prove" explicit propositions abstracted from the Bible. Newton did believe strongly in the personal pursuit of truth, and he wrote an extended treatise called the *Irenicum* that promoted the free exploration of both nature and the Bible. Attempts to "claim" Newton by various religious groups are a misunderstanding of who he was and what he was doing. He remained a member in good standing of the Anglican Church, but his private thoughts were unconstrained by official orthodoxy. He rejected polemical efforts and even rejected his friend William Whiston for admission to the Royal Society when he openly promoted Unitarianism. He would not have been pleased with French efforts to divinize him in the nineteenth century.

Newton and Christian Church history

Isaac Newton was an avid student of history. He read everything he could find on the history of Christianity. He did not like what he found! He expected the religion established by God the Father and his son, the Lord Jesus Christ, to be simple and coherent. He wrote his own take on the development of the Christian Church.

Since Jesus was the Son of God, he expected him to preach the simple message of belief in the Creator God who was the Lord of the Universe. Since the text of the New Testament does not sound quite that simple, he proposed that it had been corrupted along the way. He identified several sources of early corruption in metaphysical religions such as Gnosticism. But he was just as critical of those who sought to create confusion:

> We are commanded by the Apostle (I Tim. 1.13) *to hold fast the form of sound words*. Contending for a language which was not handed down from the Prophets and Apostles is a breach of the command and they that break it are also guilty of the disturbances and schisms occasioned

thereby. It is not enough to say that an article of faith may be deduced from scripture. It must be exprest in the very form of sound words in which it was delivered by the Apostles. Otherwise there can be no lasting fixity nor peace of the Church catholick. For men are apt to vary, dispute, and run into partings about deductions. All the old Heresies lay in deductions; the true faith was in the text. (Yahuda MS. 15.1)

Newton sought a simple common ground for all Christians, with liberty to follow their faith wherever else it led them.

While Isaac Newton was truly unique, he was a man of his time and place. He often engaged in the anti-papal rhetoric that was so common in the seventeenth century. He was especially upset at the use of civil power to enforce discipline in the church:

By violence a Church may increase her numbers but ever allays and debases her self with impure mixtures, force prevailing with none but Hypocrites. Every Persecutor is a Wolf (Matth. 10.16,17) and every Christian that preaches it is one of the fals Prophets called Wolfs in sheeps cloathing (Math. 7). (Yahuda MS. 39)

Newton had the faith that an honest search for the Truth would not be disappointed, and the patience to realize that the future might reveal things not known to him.

The seventeenth century was also a time of religious enthusiasm, and many "prophets" made many claims of inspiration. Newton did believe in prophecy, but he did not believe that ecstatic utterances were valid in his time. Newton did believe in miracles, but he also did not believe they were being done in Cambridge. He was a firm believer in the admonition: "Let all things be done decently and in order" (1 Corinthians 14:40).

Conclusions

A full understanding of the history of Christianity requires very many perspectives, but a view of two of the most singular actual people that were pleased to identify themselves as Christians provides an interesting insight. Both Origen and Newton devoted themselves to the pursuit of Truth, and both looked in the Bible as one source for this search. They believed in the value of a multidisciplinary approach that incorporated insights and methods from other people. They believed that after the hard work of analysis had been done, it was useful to synthesize the results into a coherent story. The validity of the stories told by Origen and Newton may be questioned in the twentieth century, but the energy and devotion that they both displayed still inspires us today.

References

Origen

There are many good sources for the life and thought of Origen. The basic biographical and historical reference is the Church history of Eusebius: *Eusebius:The Church History,* tr. Paul L Meier (Grand Rapids, MI: Kregel, 1999).

Another classic biography is by Jean Danielou, the great Patristic scholar: Jean Danielou, *Origen,* tr. Walter Mitchell (London: Sheed and Ward, 1955).

A good edition of *Peri Archon* is: Origen, *On First Principles,* ed. G.W. Butterworth, Introduction by Henri de Lubac (New York: Harper Torchbooks, 1966).

Three good compilations with extended introductions are: Joseph W. Trigg (ed.) *Origen* (London: Routledge, 1998); Hans Urs von Balthasar (ed.), *Origen: Spirit and Fire: A Thematic Anthology of His Writings* (Washington, DC: Catholic University Press, 1984); Rowan A. Greer (ed.), *Origen: An Exhortation to Martyrdom, Prayer, and Selected Works* (Mahwah, NJ: Paulist Press, 1979).

Newton

There are many good sources for the life of Isaac Newton, but this chapter is based primarily on the magisterial work: Richard S. Westfall, *Never at Rest: A Biography of Isaac Newton* (Cambridge: Cambridge University Press, 1980). The Freemantle Lectures for 1973: Frank E. Manuel, *The Religion of Isaac Newton* (Oxford: Clarendon Press, 1974). And the unique biography of Newton by Manuel: Frank E. Manuel, *A Portrait of Isaac Newton* (Cambridge, MA: Belknap Press, 1968).

26

The Holy Trinity of Nineteenth-Century British Science: Faraday, Maxwell, and Rayleigh

GARY PATTERSON

The great age of British physics was the nineteenth century. Three of the most notable, both as scientists and Christians, were Michael Faraday, James Clerk Maxwel, and Lord Rayleigh. Faraday was born into a very poor family but rose to become famous but not wealthy. He remained a religious Sandemanian throughout his life. Maxwell was born into a landed Scottish family and rose through the ranks of Cambridge University. He collaborated with Faraday to produce a lasting theory of electricity and magnetism. He was born into a Presbyterian world but attended Anglican worship in Cambridge and Baptist services in London. Rayleigh was a hereditary peer, but he transcended his station in life every bit as much as Faraday. He was part of the very devout English Anglican aristocracy. He was a brilliant physicist who enriched both his field and his friends.

Introduction

The nineteenth century was the great age of British science. Major advances in natural history and philosophy occurred throughout this period. It was also an especially fruitful period in the interaction of science with religion. It was the age of the Bridgewater treatises written by outstanding scientists such as William Whewell and William Prout. Among the many scientists who were personally very devout but were not ordained clergy, three names stand out as exemplars of both science and Christian faith: Michael Faraday, James Clerk Maxwell, and John William Strutt, Lord Rayleigh. The present essay will survey briefly some aspects of each of their lives that are remarkable, both then and now.

Michael Faraday (1791–1867)

Biographical studies of Michael Faraday are enriched by two special portraits: *Faraday as a Discoverer* was written in the year after his death by John Tyndall, his coworker and successor at the Royal Institution; *Michael Faraday: Sandemanian and Scientist* is a recent (1991) biography by Geoffrey Cantor that is especially sensitive to the personal and religious aspects of his character. While a large number of books and original papers have been consulted in the course of writing this chapter, a special debt is owed to the sources named above.

Michael Faraday was born on September 22, 1791, in London to a poor family. He had little formal education and was apprenticed at 14 to a bookbinder. His advantage was that he was able to read the books that he was binding, and he had the initiative to attend the many lectures available in London, especially those at the Royal Institution. He made a fine set of notes from four of Sir Humphry Davy's lectures and presented them to him. Faraday was hired as a laboratory assistant to Davy in 1813, and made rapid progress. He was even taken along on a grand tour of Europe as Davy's amanuensis. He experienced both the peaks of scientific stimulation from the finest scientists on the Continent, and the sting of European class distinctions at the hands of Lady Davy. In spite of all Faraday did to advance the career of Humphry Davy, his master resented Faraday's scientific success and even opposed his election as a Fellow of the Royal Society in 1824. Five years later Davy died.

Faraday was appointed Director of the Laboratory at the Royal Institution in 1825 and instituted traditions and practices that continued for many years. His Friday Evening Discourses were open to the public and were one of the hottest tickets in London. John Tyndall absorbed the best of Michael Faraday's public lecture style and continued the tradition in high style. Each lecture included actual demonstrations of physical phenomena and the discourse was clear enough to be understood by any educated person. For his many discoveries in chemistry he was appointed the Fullerian Professor of Chemistry at the Royal Institution in 1833.

Faraday is even better known today for his research in electricity and magnetism. The facilities of the Royal Institution and the many instruments designed by Faraday made his laboratory the premier scientific center for this research. The discoveries of Faraday provided the inductive grist for Maxwell's theoretical mill. His approach to the physical world was based on his belief that God had created a world that was capable of being understood, and it was the duty of mankind to search out and present the wonderful ways of the Creator. His hard work and high standards were communicated to the world of English science at the Royal Institution, the Royal Society and the British Association for the Advancement of Science. Faraday was lionized in all these communities, but he refused merely ceremonial honors, such as knighthoods. He shunned politics and avoided high society.

Victorian British scientists were expected to contribute their expertise to the nation as a whole and Faraday gave his time graciously to such causes as Trinity House, the Admiralty, and various Royal Commissions. One of his most celebrated public services was to debunk spiritualism in a series of experiments that demonstrated the technique used to confuse the gullible. Prince Albert expressed his personal gratitude for Faraday's public exposé at the Royal Institution in 1854.

While Faraday gave more to science than we can adequately recognize here, his personal world was not centered there. His father, James, was a member of a small Christian sect known as the Sandemanians. They believed that the Bible was the infallible guide for life and godliness and that the established Church of England had forsaken the way of Truth. This close-knit group looked out for one another and provided employment for those in need; thereby he acquired the job as a smithy in London. Michael Faraday was raised in this community and it provided both a sturdy worldview and a practical source

Figure 26.1 Michael Faraday, 1791–1867. From Geoffrey N. Cantor, David Gooding, and Frank A. J. L. James, *Michael Faraday* (Humanity Books, 1996). Picture courtesy the Wellcome Library, London.

of encouragement and fellowship. He met and married Sarah Barnard, and soon made a life commitment to the group. He even received a fine portrait from one of his Sandemanian brothers, John Z. Bell.

Faraday interacted with most of the leading scientists in Europe concerned with electricity and magnetism. Hermann von Helmholtz described his "perfect simplicity, modesty and the undimmed purity of his character." Faraday always sought to establish empirically solid facts and was never satisfied with inconsistent or preliminary results because he wanted to know the actual world created by God. He carried on a long and fruitful correspondence with James Clerk Maxwell, both on scientific and on spiritual subjects. He tried to bring the egalitarian character and loving fellowship of his Sandemanian church to the worldwide community of scientists. He was a loyal citizen of England, but there was no hint of the nationalistic spirit so common in nineteenth-century Europe. He was given major awards by both France and Prussia, based solely on the quality of his science.

Unlike the world of politics, commerce, and high society, Faraday viewed pure science as a place of peace and order, just as God had created it. He preferred to commune with physical reality in all its purity and perfection. As a result, he was able to discover the secrets of nature that required patience and ingenuity. Although he did attend meetings of public bodies such as the Royal Society and the British Association, he preferred the calm of the laboratory. He was offered the Presidency of the Royal Society, but quietly demurred.

Although Faraday was world famous, his position in the Sandemanians was independent of all worldly position. He served as an elder and visited the sick and needy. He regularly took his turn as a preacher and rightly divided the Word of Truth. He took attendance at Sabbath meetings seriously and often rushed back to London when he was away during the week. He also donated a significant portion of his income to the church. This religious community provided the solid ground needed to live the kind of life that made Faraday the great scientist that he was. It also allowed him to die happy and content with this testimony:

> I am, I hope, very thankful that in the withdrawal of the powers and things of this life, the good hope is left with me, which makes the contemplation of death a comfort – not a fear. Such peace is alone the gift of God; and as it is he who gives it, why should we be afraid? His unspeakable gift in his beloved son [Jesus] is the ground of no doubtful hope.[1]

James Clerk Maxwell (1831–79)

The biographical corpus on James Clerk Maxwell is large and diverse. The present chapter has benefited greatly from the first and still the best personal biography by his friend Lewis Campbell and his fellow Cambridge scientist William Garnett, *The Life of James Clerk Maxwell* (London: Macmillan 1882). It includes many letters both to and from Maxwell, and a good collection of his poetry. It is sensitive to the full range of Maxwell's life, not just his scientific achievements.

James Clerk Maxwell was born on June 13, 1831, in Edinburgh, Scotland. He retained a lifelong connection to Edinburgh, and it helped to form his personal world. He moved to the family estate, Glenlair, in the parish of Parton, in the Stewartry of Kirkcudbright, when he was two years old, and it provided the solid rock on which his life was built. He had free rein of the house and grounds and never tired of exploring. His insatiable curiosity and his love of nature were exhibited his whole life. He also developed another love that colored his personality and his behavior; he loved the Bible and could recite Psalm 119 from memory when he was only eight years old. His command of the text of the Bible allowed him to interact at the deepest levels with the leading religious figures of the nineteenth century. His mother guided his early education and taught him to "look up through Nature to Nature's God." They were especially close, but she died when he was eight. The character of James Clerk Maxwell is well displayed in his words on her death: "Oh, I'm so glad. Now she'll have no more pain." Maxwell himself later experienced that pain and died of the same cancer at the same age. He was always close to his aunt, Jane Cay, and they carried on a very active correspondence.

The idyllic childhood was followed by formal grammar school at the Edinburgh Academy. It was at the center of Edinburgh society; Lord Cockburn was one of the directors and the Rector, Archdeacon John Williams, MA, was an Oxford first-classman. James was treated by the other boys as a country bumpkin, but he proved the value of the phrase, "if you can't beat'em, join'em," and eventually established his place. He lived in Edinburgh with his widowed Aunt Isabella Wedderburn. This congenial home made the many years spent in Edinburgh a happy time, and he benefited from the companionship of his cousin Jemima. His father spent the winters in Edinburgh, and James returned to Glenlair for the summers. While James passed his time in school, at home he read voraciously in the extensive library. James Clerk Maxwell was one of the most widely read men of the nineteenth century, and knew the wealth of English and Scottish poetry and hymnody. On Sundays he went to both the Scottish Presbyterian St Andrews Church and to St John's Episcopal. He exhibited a

Figure 26.2   James Clerk Maxwell. From *Nature*, October 27th, 1881. Photo courtesy of the Wellcome Library, London.

broadness of heart and spirit that served him well throughout his life; he even frequently attended a Baptist church when he was a Professor at King's College in London. He welcomed all Christians into his fellowship, and was consulted by people from the church pew to the cathedral.

James Clerk Maxwell was also taken to meetings of the Edinburgh Royal Society by his father starting when he was 12. He made rapid progress in visualizing the concepts of geometry and constructed models of the Platonic solids. He entered into much deeper questions of geometry and his first paper on the construction of generalized ovals was read before the Society when he was 15 by Professor James D. Forbes of Edinburgh University. This led to a lifelong friendship between the great Scottish natural philosopher and his world-famous pupil. Forbes is also famous for his book on glaciers, and the study of viscoelastic solids became a lifelong object of study by Maxwell. While still in grammar school, James Clerk Maxwell also carried out experiments in optics, magnetics, and astronomy. All the phenomena of nature interested him and he was never content just to read about things. He loved to try them out for himself. He also made two lifelong friends at Edinburgh Academy, Lewis Campbell, who wrote his biography, and P. G. Tait, the famous physicist. He shared both a scientific and a religious correspondence with them as well.

Maxwell entered the University of Edinburgh at 16 and took a wide range of courses for three years. The spirit of natural philosophy, mathematics, and moral philosophy was well represented at Edinburgh in these years and Maxwell absorbed all he could and added much besides. He took many courses with the great Scottish philosopher William Hamilton and was never at a loss philosophically with anyone after that. He took many courses in both physics and chemistry, both practical and theoretical, and he was already fully conversant with the latest work by the time he entered Cambridge. No aspect of natural philosophy was beyond his grasp, and by the end of his life he had revolutionized virtually every aspect of our understanding of the material world.

Cambridge was the center of mathematical studies and theological discussions; Maxwell thoroughly entered into both aspects. He reached the highest levels in mathematics and was equal first for the Smith's Prize. He listened to great natural philosophers like Stokes and Whewell. One of his greatest distinctions was election to the Select Essay Club, also known as the "Apostles." This group of 12 included the great English theologians and text scholars Lightfoot, Westcott, and Hort. They all commended Maxwell for his theological acuity and for his willingness to discuss any significant question. These were tumultuous times for the Anglican Church and strong personalities were urging very different courses of action. Maxwell was solid like a rock, but flexible like natural rubber, a good reflection on his natural philosophy of elastic bodies! The depth of his religious thought is reflected in the following poem from this period, written in 1853.

A Student's Evening Hymn

Now no more the slanting rays
With the mountain summits dally,
Now no more in crimson blaze
Evening's fleecy cloudlets rally,
Soon shall Night from off the valley
Sweep that bright yet earthly haze,
And the stars most musically
Move in endless rounds of praise.

While the world is growing dim,
And the Sun is slow descending
Past the far horizon's rim,
Earth's low sky to heaven extending,
Let my feeble earth-notes, blending
With the songs of cherubim,
Through the same expanse ascending,
Thus renew my evening hymn.

Thou that fill'st our waiting eyes
With the food of contemplation
Setting in thy darkened skies
Signs of infinite creation,
Grant to nightly meditation
What the toilsome day denies –
Teach me in this earthly station
Heavenly Truth to realize.

Give me wisdom so to use
These brief hours of thoughtful leisure,
That I may no instant lose

In mere meditative pleasure,
But with strictest justice measure
All the ends of life pursues,
Lies to crush and truths to treasure,
Wrong to shun and Right to choose.

Then, when unexpected Sleep,
O'er my long-closed eyelids stealing,
Opens up that lower deep
Where Existence has no feeling,
May sweet Calm, my languor healing,
Lend me strength at dawn to reap
All that Shadows, world-concealing,
For the bold inquirer keep.

Through the creatures Thou hast made
Show the brightness of Thy glory,
Be eternal Truth displayed
In their substance transitory,
Till green Earth and Ocean hoary,
Massy rock and tender blade
Tell the same unending story –
"We are Truth in Form arrayed."

When to study I retire,
And from books of ancient sages
Glean fresh sparks of buried fire
Lurking in their ample pages –
While the task my mind engages
Let old words new truths inspire –
Truths that to all after-ages
Prompt the Thoughts that never tire.

Yet if, led by shadows fair,
I have uttered words of folly,
Let the kind absorbing air
Stifle every sound unholy,
So when Saints with Angels lowly
Join in heaven's unceasing prayer
Mine as certainly, though slowly,
May ascend and mingle there.

Teach me so thy works to read
That my faith,-new strength, accruing,-
May from world to world proceed,
Wisdom's fruitful search pursuing;
Till, thy truth my mind imbuing,
I proclaim the Eternal Creed,
Oft the glorious theme renewing
God our Lord is God indeed.

Give me love aright to trace
Thine to everything created,
Preaching to a ransomed race

> By thy mercy renovated,
> Till with all thy fullness sated
> I behold thee face to face
> And with Ardour unabated
> Sing the glories of thy grace.[3]

James Clerk Maxwell was truly the poet laureate of the scientific world.

His success in his undergraduate studies continued and he obtained a position as a Fellow of Trinity College, Cambridge. He tutored students, as expected, but his major occupation was in searching out the truth with regard to color, electricity, and hydrodynamics. During these years he wrote a remarkable note that characterized his mode of life and work:

> He that would enjoy life and act with freedom must have the work of the day continually before his eyes. Not yesterday's work, lest he fall into despair, nor tomorrow's, lest he become a visionary,-not that which ends with the day, which is a worldly work, nor yet that only which remains to eternity, for by it he cannot shape his actions.
>
> Happy is the man who can recognize in the work of today a connected portion of the work of life, and an embodiment of the work of Eternity. The foundations of his confidence are unchangeable, for he has been made a partaker of Infinity. He strenuously works out his daily enterprises, because the present is given him for a possession.
>
> Thus ought Man to be an impersonation of the divine process of nature, and to show forth the union of the infinite with the finite, not slighting his temporal existence, remembering that in it only is individual action possible, nor yet shutting out from his view that which is eternal, knowing that Time is a mystery which man cannot endure to contemplate until eternal Truth enlighten it.[4]

As his father's health began to fail, James Clerk Maxwell felt the pull of Scotland. He helped his father settle in Edinburgh and was appointed Professor of Natural Philosophy at Marischal College in Aberdeen. While Maxwell carried out many important scientific investigations while at Aberdeen, the most important event in his life during this period was his marriage to Katherine Mary Dewar, the daughter of the Principal of Marischal College. They were deeply devoted to one another and carried on an active correspondence when temporarily apart. A typical example of one of these notes:

> I have been reading again with you Eph. vi. Hereer is more about family relations. There are things which have meanings so deep that if we follow on to know them we shall be led into great mysteries of divinity. If we despise these relations of marriage, of parents and children, of master and servant, everything will go wrong, and there will be confusion as bad as in Lear's case. But if we reverence them, we shall even see beyond their first aspect a spiritual meaning, for God speaks to us more plainly in these bonds of our life than in anything that we can understand. So we find a great deal of Divine Truth is spoken of in the Bible with reference to these three relations and others.[5]

The machinations of Scottish politics led to the unification of the two colleges in Aberdeen and the suppression of his Professorship, but Maxwell was appointed to a better post at King's College, London. He had established an ongoing relationship with Michael Faraday while in Edinburgh and now this collaboration flourished. The result was the classic paper on

"A Dynamical Theory of the Electromagnetic Field"[6] and the book *Treatise on Electricity and Magnetism*. Since he was now resident in London, he became a regular at the Royal Society and the Royal Institution. He carried out seminal measurements of the viscosity of gases, and he continued his work on the three-color theory of vision. He combined his interests in light and his theory of the electromagnetic field to discover that light is an electromagnetic wave. He spent his summers at Glenlair and eventually decided to reside there and resigned his Professorship at King's College. But, rather than hindering his scientific work, he was more prolific than ever at his country estate. He built many instruments and made many theoretical advances. He also finished his book on the theory of heat. He continued to interact strongly with his friends at Cambridge, to preside at meetings of the British Association, and to carry on an extensive correspondence with scientific and religious colleagues.

When a new Chair of Experimental Physics in the University of Cambridge was established in 1871, many leading physicists such as G. G. Stokes and J. W. Strutt (Lord Rayleigh) urged him to take the post. Maxwell accepted the job and supervised the construction of the Cavendish Laboratories for Experimental Physics. This facility made Cambridge the world leader in studies of electricity and magnetism and his successor, Lord Rayleigh, continued the brilliant tradition. For one man to give to England both the fundamental theory that guided research for 50 years and the laboratory in which it was pursued was remarkable. Even more remarkable was the eulogy of Professor Reverend Westcott:

> It was impossible to think of him whom they had so lately lost, to whom the first charge of the Cavendish Laboratory had been committed, Prof. Clerk Maxwell, and to recollect his genius and spirit, his subtle and profound thought, his tender and humble reverence, without being sure that the close connection between Physics and Theology which was consecrated by the past was still a living reality among them. That was an omen for the future. He felt, as probably all present felt, that he owed a deep debt of gratitude to him, both for his researches, and for the pregnant words in which he gathered up their lessons.[7]

Since Maxwell was once again resident in Cambridge, he participated in stimulating theological discussions with some of his old friends (now major figures in the English church) and some new ones. He was also frequently consulted by prelates such as the Archbishop of Canterbury. He was urged to become a member of the Victoria Institute, which was established to promote the irenic interaction of theology and science. Maxwell understood the nature of science far too well to recommend that theologians latch onto any particular theory, since it would soon be superseded by a better one. His polite reply to the secretary of the Victoria Institute is still worth remembering.

> Sir – I do not think it is my duty to become a candidate for admission into the Victoria Institute. Among the objects of the Society are some of which I think very highly. I think men of science as well as other men need to learn from Christ, and I think Christians whose minds are scientific are bound to study science that their view of the glory of God may be as extensive as their being is capable of. But I think that the results which each man arrives at in his attempts to harmonize his science with his Christianity ought not to be regarded as having any significance except to the man himself, and to him only for a time, and should not receive the stamp of a society. For it is of the nature of science, especially of those branches of science which are spreading into unknown regions to be continually [*changing*].[8]

James Clerk Maxwell died young (1879), but he gave more to science and theology than almost any other man.

John William Strutt (1842–1919)

The story of the life and work of Lord Rayleigh is extensively and lovingly told by his son, Robert John Strutt, 4th Baron Rayleigh. This biography remains the best source for both the scientific and personal aspects of his life.

John William Strutt was born on November 12, 1842. His father, John James Strutt, was a country squire and was extremely religious. John William was raised listening to the Bible at meals and to prayer. He was born prematurely and had many episodes of illness during his childhood. He continued to grow stronger and to make great progress in mathematics at his grammar school run by the Rev. G. T. Warner.

He entered Trinity College, Cambridge, in 1861 and had the benefit of Lightfoot as his tutor. As the son of a peer, he was frequently invited to dine with other members of high society, including HRH, the Prince of Wales. But, it was the Gentlemen of Science that he enjoyed the most; he attended his first British Association meeting at Bath in 1864. He met Sir John Herschel at a party and had a long conversation on spectrum analysis. His first real exposure to formal natural philosophy was from G. G. Stokes on optics. He was a lover of light for ever after. His course of study was crowned by achieving Senior Wrangler in mathematics.

Because of his position he traveled extensively over the next few years both in Europe and America. He was a keen observer and understood many political issues. He did become a Fellow of Trinity College, but he did not habitually reside there. He corresponded with P. G. Tait and with William Thomson. He also purchased experimental apparatus and began studies of optics, electricity, and magnetism. This led to extensive correspondence with James Clerk Maxwell on a wide range of subjects. One of Rayleigh's earliest triumphs was to use Maxwell's electrodynamic theory to explain the blue color of the sky in terms of light scattering by the gas particles. They also discussed the kinetic theory of gases. When the time came to appoint the new Professor of Experimental Physics at Cambridge, Rayleigh played a leading part in convincing Maxwell to accept it. Had Maxwell refused, it was widely believed that Rayleigh himself would have been approached, even though he was only 29 at the time. In the event, he eventually did sit in Maxwell's seat.

John William Strutt traveled well in the highest circles, and was a frequent guest of many lords and ladies, including the prime minister William Gladstone and Lord Salisbury. This was a very pious crowd and Rayleigh's vast knowledge of the Bible and history helped him to contribute to the conversation. He also met many of the most eligible girls, and married Evelyn Balfour, sister of his good friend Arthur Balfour (later the prime minister). Upon his marriage he forfeited his Fellowship at Trinity and retired to a cottage on the family estate. While on his extended honeymoon, he attended the British Association meeting at Edinburgh, and met many of the Scottish natural philosophers such as William Thomson (Lord Kelvin) and P. G. Tait. While on a visit to another noble family, the Beresford Hopes, he became very ill with rheumatic fever and was never physically vigorous again. However, his mental capacity was not diminished. Rather than spend a cold English winter on the estate, he took an extended trip to Egypt along with his wife and sister-in-law Eleanor Balfour. During the long voyage up the Nile, Rayleigh worked out many of the details for his famous book on the theory of sound. Upon returning to London they spent an extended visit in Arthur and Eleanor Balfour's new house, which became their London dwelling when needed.

Figure 26.3   John William Strutt, (1842–1919). From Robert John Strutt, *The Life of John William Strutt, Third Baron Rayleigh: An Augmented Edition with Annotations by the Author* (Madison: University of Wisconsin Press, 1968).

Upon his father's death in 1873, John William Strutt became the 3rd Baron Rayleigh and moved into the large house at Terling. An experimental laboratory was added to the house where many of Rayleigh's most famous investigations were carried out. He was a frequent visitor to London for meetings of the Royal Society, where he was elected a Fellow in 1873. He made the Royal Society one of his strongest communities of interest, and the benefit was mutual. He also interacted strongly with John Tyndall at the Royal Institution. Because of his brilliant scientific intuition, his complete mathematical sophistication and his open approach to other scientists, Rayleigh was able to live at the center of late nineteenth-century science.

Upon Maxwell's death, the Chair in Experimental Physics was offered to Rayleigh and he took up his post in 1879. He continued the progress in experimental physics both by raising money for new equipment and by contributing himself. He is best known for his extremely precise measurements of the fundamental constants of electricity and magnetism. One of Rayleigh's lasting achievements at the Cavendish Laboratory was to pass it on to J. J. Thomson, who carried British physics to even higher heights. They both received the Nobel Prize in the twentieth century.

One of the responsibilities of someone in Rayleigh's position was to present plenary lectures at meetings like the British Association for the Advancement of Science. He used these occasions to encourage an efficient and irenic practice of science, as exemplified in the following remarks:

> The different habits of mind of the two schools of physicists sometimes lead them to the adoption of antagonistic views on doubtful and difficult questions. The tendency of the purely experimental school is to rely almost exclusively upon direct evidence, even when it is obviously imperfect, and to disregard arguments which they stigmatize as

theoretical. The tendency of the mathematicians is to over-rate the solidity of his theoretical structures, and to forget the narrowness of the experimental foundation upon
which many of them rest.[9]

Rayleigh believed firmly in the unity of truth and the need for all the tools available to reach
a good understanding of nature. He included the following remarks in his Presidential
Address at the British Association meeting in Montreal in 1884:

> Many excellent people are afraid of science as tending towards materialism. That such appre-
> hension should exist is not surprising, for unfortunately there are writers, speaking in the
> name of science, who have set themselves to foster it. It is true that among scientific men, as
> in other classes, crude views are to be met with as to the deeper things of Nature; but that the
> life – long beliefs of Newton, of Faraday, and of Maxwell, are inconsistent with the scientific
> habit of mind, is surely a proposition which I need not pause to refute. It would be easy,
> owever, to lay too much stress upon the opinions of even such distinguished workers as these.
> Men, who devote their lives to investigation, cultivate a love of truth for its own sake, and
> endeavour instinctively to clear up, and not, as is too often the object in business and politics,
> to obscure a difficult question. So far the opinion of a scientific worker may have a special
> value; but I do not think that he has a claim, superior to that of other educated men, to
> assume the attitude of a prophet. In his heart he knows that underneath the theories that he
> constructs there lie contradictions which he cannot reconcile. The higher mysteries of being,
> if penetrable at all by human intellect, require other weapons than those of calculation and
> experiment.[10]

Upon his return from a triumphant American tour after Montreal, Lord Rayleigh retired
to Terling and his science and family life. He built a laboratory that allowed him to carry out
many optical experiments; he made major contributions to spectroscopy and the theory of
gratings. He was a true natural philosopher and for him there was no demarcation between
physics and chemistry. He carried out high – precision measurements of gas densities and
eventually this led to the discovery of the inert gas argon (from the Greek word for idle), for
which he received the Nobel Prize.

One of the most important aspects of the community of science is the official publications that are refereed before acceptance. Rayleigh became the Secretary of the Royal Society
in 1885 and served valiantly in producing the *Proceedings*. His exceptionally broad mind
comprehended the full range of science and he sought to advance it wherever he could. His
scientific world transcended national boundaries and he championed excellence wherever
he found it; he promoted the work of J. Willard Gibbs many years before the rest of the
English scientific community realized the brilliance of his work.

One area of common interest among all three of the scientists considered here was human
color-blindness. This subject was brought to a practical level by Rayleigh and instituted in
commercial practice, where issues of safety were paramount. All three were also asked to
serve on national committees where scientific expertise was helpful in naval affairs, or other
government activities.

The Scottish aristocracy was a devout group and Rayleigh was welcome in this society. He
and his family often visited the country houses and castles in the Highlands. The evangelical
practices of his friends were noted by his son. Rayleigh was quite regular in his church
attendance and was welcomed wherever he went.

Figure 26.4   Lord Kelvin and Lord Rayleigh. Fom Robert John Strutt, *The Life of John William Strutt, Third Baron Rayleigh: An Augmented Edition with Annotations by the Author* (Madison: University of Wisconsin Press, 1968).

Lord Rayleigh was also on intimate terms with Tory party leader Lord Salisbury and many of the most important politicians in England. He treated them with the same gracious manner he displayed to others. He was welcomed in the highest aristocratic company, again because he could discuss matters in an irenic and informed manner. He often mediated disputes because he could impartially advise each side. He was admired by both Kelvin and Tait, and by T. H. Huxley! He cared for Truth more than for any particular party.

Although Rayleigh's scientific papers are models of precision and arcane erudition, he also was able to explain scientific subjects to the general public. He served as the Professor of Natural Philosophy and hence Saturday lecturer at the Royal Institution from 1887–1905 and was a great success, in the tradition of Faraday and Tyndall. He also gave Friday evening lectures which were often attended by the Prince of Wales.

There was a close friendship between Lord Rayleigh and Lord Kelvin, but they were very different in their approaches to science. Rayleigh was eager to consider the truth that might be contained in new work, while Kelvin tended more to look for the errors. Kelvin often found himself on the wrong side of a scientific development because he allowed small ambiguities to spoil the bigger picture. They carried on an extensive correspondence in addition to their many personal meetings both in public and at Terling. They both shared a deep love of science and an even deeper love of Jesus. Although his son could not absolutely prove that Rayleigh nominated William Thomson to be a peer, his close relationship to Lord Salisbury, and his deep affection for his friend, coupled with Lord Kelvin's great service to England and Scotland, make this conjecture reasonable.

The daily life at Terling was quiet, devout, and organized. Each day began with family prayers. Rayleigh took great delight in his children and grandchildren. Meals were scheduled and were considered ceremonial events. Sundays were observed as a Sabbath and church services were often attended both morning and evening. Because Terling was an easy drive from London, weekend parties were attended by many nobles and other society friends. "When appealed to for his opinion, he always gave it modestly, and without cocksureness."[11] Rayleigh set a tone for late – nineteenth – century English society that may never be seen again. A civil search for Truth was carried out with grace. He made everyone better!

Notes

1   Quoted in Cantor and Faraday from a letter of Faraday to August de la Rive, p. 81.
2   Campbell and Garnett, *The Life of James Clerk Maxwell*.
3   Written at Cambridge, April 25, 1853 and printed in Campbell and Garnett, p. 386.
4   Written in 1854 and printed in Campbell and Garnett, p. 144.
5   Written to K. M Dewar, May 13, 1858 and printed in Campbell and Garnett, p. 225.
6   Maxwell, *A Treatise*.
7   As quoted in Campbell and Garnett.
8   As quoted in Campbell and Garnett, p. 312.
9   As quoted in Strutt, *Life*, p. 132.
10   As quoted in Strutt, p. 142.
11   Strutt, p. 261, a gracious opinion of his son.

References

Campbell, Lewis and William Garnett, *The Life of James Clerk Maxwell* (London: Macmillan, 1884).
Cantor, Geoffrey and Michael Faraday, *Sandemanian and Scientist* (London: Macmillan, 1991).
Maxwell, J.C., *A Treatise on Electricity and Magnetism* (Oxford: Clarendon, 1873).
Strutt, Robert John, *Life of John William Strutt: Third Baron Rayleigh* (London: University of Wisconsin Press, 1968).
Tyndall, John , *Faraday as a Discoverer* (London, 1868).

27

A Professor in Dialogue with His Faith

GARY PATTERSON

My forthcoming book *An Evangelical Stance* is the product of more than forty years of interaction and reflection. Two themes from the book are presented here: (1) An Evangelical Natural Philosophy and (2) An Evangelical Anthropology. While belief in God as Creator is central to an Evangelical stance, it is important to recognize that the world that was actually created is more complex and more interesting than we can imagine. The appropriate stance to take with regard to the current discourse in science is to be knowledgeable about the past and present, engaged in the present, and open to the future. This approach is explored over a wide range of current scientific topics. While humankind is created in God's image, it is important to recognize that we are "fearfully and wonderfully made." The major advances in understanding of the physiology, psychology, and sociology of humankind are examined in light of an Evangelical view.

One of the fruits of more than forty years of study and discussion of the relationship of science and Christianity is my forthcoming book: *An Evangelical Stance*. The present talk will explore two of the themes from this book: (1) An Evangelical Natural Philosophy, (2) An Evangelical Anthropology. The presentation will be brief, but an attempt will be made to explore the flavor of the complete work.

An Evangelical Natural Philosophy

We live in a universe of great complexity and heterogeneity. As Christians we choose to relate all of natural reality to our Creator. But, what does that mean when applied to the physical world? An Evangelical stance towards the created world is that we must look at what God has actually done in order to understand its true nature. The following essay will survey the broad aspects of what is known from such observations and will reflect on the meaning of what is seen for our lives as Christians.

While there have been periods in history when space and time were considered absolute quantities independent of anything, including God, an Evangelical stance is that both space and time were created by God to regulate the physical world. A more modern approach to space-time is instantiated in the theory of general relativity (Ohanian and Ruffini, 1994) and its application to the history of the universe. A thoroughly Evangelical example (Page, 2005) of this field is provided by Professor Don Page of the University of Alberta, a former student and postdoctoral Fellow with Stephen Hawking (Hawking and Penrose, 1996). There is often a human tendency to hold on to outmoded ways of describing physical reality. This tendency is also encouraged by religious leaders who stake a claim to an archaic form of science. We should be ready to follow the Truth wherever it may be found, but not in a hurry to embrace every "new" thing. While the details of natural philosophy constantly change, and the attempts to create a coherent ontology are only provisional, an Evangelical stance is that the human activity known today as science is valuable and contributes to our physical and spiritual wellbeing.

The current ontology of the universe is almost completely foreign to most clergy and their parishioners. It is even dimly perceived by most professional scientists, including this one. The latest announcement is that at least 90 percent of the universe contains "dark" matter and energy (Nicolson, 2007). If we are ignorant of most of physical reality, it behooves us to be especially humble when making pronouncements about what "can" and "cannot" happen! I predict that we will continue to discover that physical reality is more complex and more interesting than we ever imagined. A challenge for both scientists and theologians is to remain truly open to the present so that all of the known facts and ideas of human history can be employed to produce the best current picture.

The currently accepted scenario for the early history of the universe, the "Big Bang," has no competing views which command wide devotion (Hogan, 1998). Before a very short time, known as the Planck time, the universe was very small. Very soon a dramatic event took place known as the "inflation" (Guth, 1997). After this period, matter as we know it became more common. As the universe expanded, the light that filled the system also kept expanding and today we can see the current state of this process as the microwave background radiation that fills the universe (Smoot, 2007). The "Big Bang" theory is based on observations in the present that allow us to infer events in the past. This approach is the basis for the human activity known as natural history. No such reconstruction can be granted the status of certainty, but in the early twenty-first century, no wise Christian will denigrate the "Big Bang" theory if they wish to have any credibility in the public square. Observation of the spectrum of visible light from the stars has allowed astronomers to infer the motion and location of distant galaxies and to estimate an age for the universe, 13.7 billion years (Snoke, 1998). Christians assert that God is the Creator of this universe (Hebrews 11:3); wise Christians look at the actual universe to find out what God has actually created. A clear and inspiring vision of a Christian cosmology is presented in the book, *God's Universe* (Gingerich, 2007).

The conceptual framework for the description of the universe includes several conservation principles and the laws of thermodynamics. The assertion that energy is conserved (a form of the First Law of Thermodynamics) has proven to be highly fruitful in the history of physics; new forms of energy have been identified, including mass-energy. The Second Law of Thermodynamics introduces a physical quantity known as the entropy. In a closed system, either the state is already one of equilibrium, in which case entropy is conserved and maximized, or it is not, in which case the entropy increases until equilibrium is reached.

The thermodynamic state function known as the entropy is an explicit and monotonically increasing function of the total energy and volume of a macroscopic equilibrium system. There are no known violations of the Second Law, but there are constant denigrations of this principle in certain theological circles. Wise Christians follow the advice of Augustine and refuse to utter nonsense in public on subjects about which they know little or nothing. Equating a foundational physical quantity with a moral category, such as sin, betrays a profound misunderstanding of both science and theology. An extensive discussion of this subject is contained in the web document "In Praise of Entropy". As the universe expanded and cooled, low-energy states of matter became more likely. Another important phenomenon also became more evident: local fluctuations led to local inhomogeneities. This process continues to this day and we can be viewed in cosmic context as a local fluctuation. For those for whom this is the only relevant context, humankind is a meaningless anomaly in a highly nonequilibrium local state of the universe. But, there are a very large number of other contexts that matter to most Evangelicals.

Another important paradigm in modern physics is quantum mechanics. Matter behaves in nonintuitive ways when it is very small and very light. It is no longer useful to talk about point particles, because every bit of matter has a "size" that depends on its mass and relative velocity, and its location and momentum are related in the famous "uncertainty principle." A statement about the variance in measurements of position and momentum has often been co-opted as a theological or philosophical statement about the inherent nature of physical reality. Since ambiguity is often welcomed by theologians, the "uncertainty principle" of quantum mechanics has often been invoked as the "secret" to understanding psychological concepts such as consciousness or theological concepts such as "free will." A clear statement of the physics of quantum mechanics and its relevance to theology has been given by John Polkinghorne (Polkinghorne, 2007). He understands both physics and faith at the deepest levels and I can recommend any of his many books. An Evangelical stance is that, while every field of human thought can be mined for inspiration and analogy, it is wise to avoid conflating precise scientific concepts with vague theological constructs: it is both bad science and bad theology.

The state of ordinary matter more than a billion years after the "Big Bang" was mostly a mixture of hydrogen and helium. If it had stayed this way, life as we know it would never have appeared. The complex world we see today was not a necessary outcome of the mixture of H and He. For those for whom the present can only be viewed as a completely determined result of the past, an atheistic "miracle" had to happen. While miracles can be bravely denied and elegantly dismissed by the cold hand of philosophy, there is no good reason why we are here, from a strictly physical perspective. However, astronomical observations do record what actually happened. As first generation stars collapsed under their own gravity, after the initial nuclear reactions had reached equilibrium, new nuclear reactions occurred at the higher pressures and temperatures of the supernova, and chemistry as we know it was born (Arnett, 1996). I choose to give thanks to God for these explosions and to study the nuclei more complex than hydrogen and helium. One of the more miserable efforts of some Christians in the twenty-first century is an attack on nuclear chemistry. While the principles of this discipline are very firmly established (Friedlander, 1981), some Christians seem to think they can just shout that no one knows how radioactivity works and that we should reject the decay rates for such nuclei measured in the laboratory. The net effect of this effort is to completely marginalize such Christians in the public square. It also tarnishes local congregations since thinking Christians are placed in tension between legitimate science and obscurantist ideologues. More discussion of this topic is contained in the book, *Science and Christianity: Four Views* (Carlson, 2000).

While many of the details of the formation of our own solar system are still vague, the timescale appears to have reached a stable estimate of 4.5 billion years. We continue to learn new things about our solar system every year. Its history is indeed more complex and it abounds with features that stagger the imagination. The earliest years were very chaotic, and violent collisions dominated the local dynamics. Eventually, a chunk of matter we now call Earth and a highly related chunk of matter we now call the Moon reached a stable orbital arrangement. But, why are they so different today? Nuclear reactions continue to happen regularly in the interior of the Earth, as well as complex chemical reactions. The atmosphere of the Earth has changed substantially over its history. And the surface of the Earth continues to change due to physical, chemical, and biological processes. The present Earth shows the marks of its history and allows reasonable conjectures to be formulated about its history. While the Psalms are not a science textbook, a good stance for Christians is contained in Psalm 148: "Praise the Lord from the earth, ye dragons and all deeps: Fire and hail; snow and vapors; stormy wind fulfilling his word." The great age of Earth science is right now! The Earth has an intricately woven history that fascinates the mind. The attempt of some Christians to reduce all of Earth science to a focus on the "Genesis flood" does a great disservice to the faith. Evangelical Christians were in the forefront of Earth Science and chemistry at the beginning of the nineteenth century. It is time to free present Christians to pursue the study of God's good Earth!

One of the wonders of natural history is the rapid appearance of life on the Earth. The present remnants of stromatolite colonies are dated at more than three billion years old. Christians believe that all life owes its existence to God. Wise Christians look at the present evidence of current and former living creatures to find out what God has actually done. A beautiful summary of the appropriate stance for an Evangelical Christian towards the biological world has been published by Francis Collins in his book *The Language of God* (Collins, 2006). Following the DNA that we can observe today has led to a unified picture of the biological world. A deeper appreciation of biology only increases our admiration for our Creator. The richness and diversity of the biological world is a never-ending source of joy for the Christian naturalist. Many of the most famous nineteenth-century naturalists were devout Christians. One of my favorite naturalists wrote Psalm 147. It is time to praise God for the richness of life on Earth and to truly appreciate the details of what He has done.

God created matter Good. But what does this mean in our current context? Rain still falls on the just and the unjust. We live in a highly nonequilibrium system. The miracle is not that there are fluctuations in such a system; the surprise is that life can be sustained at all. What conceptual paradigm is appropriate for our understanding of the natural world? John Polkinghorne (1997) likes to generalize the properties of our world as faithful and flexible. If our world was not faithful, no life would be possible, since reproduction would not be effective. If our world was not flexible, no life would be possible, since it could not adapt to a changing environment. Ungrateful atheists may rail against the world we actually inhabit, but a rigid or a chaotic world would never achieve life at all. Surprisingly, many Christians join the chorus of complaint about our physical world. An Evangelical stance is that we should be grateful for the life we currently enjoy and hopeful about the life we will share with Jesus in eternity.

The physical world can be described in terms of two basic concepts: structure and dynamics. For reasons that are not completely clear to me, many Christians are attracted to notions of "perfect" structure. Greek Christians were tempted to view God as spherical, since the sphere was the perfect shape. Our actual world is characterized by a very complex structure. Does this mean it is bad!? Greek philosophers were impressed with the virtue of *stasis*. Change was bad! We live in a world of constant change. Does this mean our world is bad!? While there may be many things of value in Greek philosophy, the natural philosophy of this era leaves much to be desired. The sad fact is that many Christians feel bound by the errors of Aristotle, since it has been sold as Christian orthodoxy. An Evangelical stance is that Christians should not feel bound by any system of natural philosophy, but they should be aware of the current state of discussion. We should be thankful for the gift of life and busy in the active management of the good Earth. We are stewards of God's creation and we should remember our Creator in all that we do. While we should love God first, we show our devotion by our faithful care over the Earth and its inhabitants.

The current understanding of physical reality has always inspired an appreciation of the Creator: "The heavens declare the Glory of God and the firmament showeth his handywork" (Psalm 19:1). What kind of God is revealed by our current science? Theologians such as Nancey Murphy, Alister McGrath, and Alan Padgett have all reflected on this question. While the power of God has been a consistent theme throughout history, the present science features his subtlety. While Greek theology emphasized God's simplicity, modern science emphasizes the complexity of the Creator. Some theologies emphasize the discontinuous nature of creation *ex nihilo*, while current science features the continuity and patience of God. We should not think that one perspective alone does justice to God; multiple views are necessary to create even a dim view of his majesty! No attempt to produce a tight little system should keep us from appreciating the grandeur of God.

An even deeper issue is raised by Nancey Murphy and George Ellis (Murphy, 1996). This world is a place of suffering. Why would God create such a place? They embrace the reality to infer that God is actively involved in the suffering of the universe. Henri Blocher suggests that God chose to create a world where evil could be defeated in the death and resurrection of Jesus (Blocher, 1994). This kenotic view of the Incarnation and Resurrection is mirrored in the physical universe as well. It may be a great mystery, but it is an Evangelical stance that we should try to understand the world God actually created rather than complain about the world we would have made. The God revealed in the Bible is the same God that created the universe. Better science has helped us envision a more satisfying picture of the God and Father of our Lord Jesus Christ.

An Evangelical Anthropology

> What is man, that thou are mindful of him?
> And the son of man, that thou visitest him?
> For thou hast made him a little lower than the angels,
> And hast crowned him with glory and honour.
> Thou madest him have dominion over the works of thy hands;
> Thou hast put all things under his feet.
>
> (Psalm 8:4–6)

An Evangelical anthropology starts with God and our relationship to Him. We have been created by Him in order to have fellowship with Him. We have been made "in His image" and are expected to administer the Earth in His stead. The simple faith expressed in these verses should never be forgotten in the swamps of scholarship that will follow in this chapter. It is my belief that our faith is strengthened by looking at what God has actually done, rather than founding our doctrinal thoughts on figurative Psalms alone. The nature of humankind is an area of scholarship that is currently in flux in both science and theology. Especially in such a time it is important to identify an appropriate stance.

The history of humankind on the Earth has now achieved some kind of scholarly consensus. This does not make it true, as any scholarship is contingent, but it behooves wise Christians to know what is believed by the scholarly community. Skeletal remains of humanoid creatures have now been recovered from a wide range of locations on Earth. The oldest remains are dated in the million-year range. Does this mean that *Homo sapiens* have been around for a million years? The current view is that a wide variety of creatures have populated the Earth and that our own species appeared around 200,000 years ago. There are other humanoid species such as Neanderthals that also existed at that time. There are no known Neanderthals living today. However, the heterogeneity of the current human population is quite large. Is it the bones that define humans? Christians should embrace historical realities, but should never forget the words of Psalm 35:10: "All my bones shall say, Lord, who is like unto thee?" One Christian scientist who is intimately acquainted with bones is Peter Dodson, Professor of Gross Anatomy at the University of Pennsylvania (Dodson, 1999).

Conditions on the surface of the Earth are constantly changing. The mean temperature of the Earth has undergone drastic changes during the 200,000 years of human existence. Few cultural artifacts have been recovered that are much older than 20,000 years, the end of the last Ice Age. One type of evidence of human activity that has been preserved is paintings in caves. Signs of an affective mental life are one of the defining features of our species. Other animals do not appear to paint pictures. Another important locus for human activity is burial sites. All animals die, but humans take the time to remember and sometimes preserve the dead. The importance of art and religion in the consideration of humanity cannot be overemphasized. Both are clear signs of our place as made in the image of God. The free creativity of art reveals the spirit of humanity at its best, and unfortunately, its worst. But, Christians should embrace the expression of our humanity in art, since it was given to them by God. Death is one of the surest facts of existence. It could be ignored as inevitable, but Christians choose to remember the death of Jesus and to commemorate the deaths of all His saints. I do not think it is an accident that death is a part of human existence; it is part of God's plan for His people: "Precious in the sight of the Lord is the death of his saints" (Ps. 116:15).

We live in an age of cowardice; taking responsibility for ourselves is definitely out of vogue. We are all either "victims" or "mentally ill abusers." Sorting out the psyche in our time is big business, but the level of confusion is horrendous. On one side of the scholarly debate are the biological "determinists" who think that we are our genes and that everything we do is programmed in advance. Even a casual perusal of the Bible reveals that this is not acceptable to children of God. However, the insights of evolutionary psychology cannot be dismissed entirely; every person is influenced by biological factors that affect our psychology and our behavior. Ignoring the realities of human biology is not an acceptable stance for an Evangelical Christian. We should seek to know the best of current biology, but not be eager to rush to judgment. We can confidently assert that before this book goes to print, the current view of human biology will change. But, the message of the Bible is that these factors do not "determine" who we are or what we do. Another form of determinism focuses on social factors in our personal history. We are then programmed by our parents and our society to do the awful things that are reported with increasing frequency in our news media. Fobbing off our sins as normal aspects of human society will not work in a Biblical world. We are subjected to malignant forces in society and there is tremendous pressure to commit some form of idolatry. But, we are not forced to sin; we choose to do it (Rom. 7). An Evangelical stance is that there are demonic forces in our world and we are subjected to malevolent influences, but the power of the Holy Spirit is also available to Christians, just as to Jesus. From my perspective, any form of Christian determinism is unacceptable.

The other side of the divide is occupied by the "Americans." "I am the captain of my soul; I am the master of my fate." Untrammeled free will is promoted as the answer to every ill. The goal of many people in our time is self-realization. There is a great desire to be "true to ourselves." Biological and social factors are ignored in the rush to become "all that we can be." Spiritual factors are ignored as well. Health and wealth are freely available to anyone who truly believes (and sends in a big enough donation). Even the largest association of Evangelicals openly welcomes the spiritual hucksters. Is there a simple path in the jungle? An Evangelical stance is that we should take into account all we know about physics, chemistry, biology, psychology, and sociology, but it must be integrated into the framework provided by the Bible. We should resist the temptation to worship any human perspective that dehumanizes us or tries to rob us of the place given to us by God Himself. We are God's representatives on the Earth, and we must tend the Garden with integrity. We must take responsibility for our own actions. It is not possible for humans to avoid mistakes, but we can admit them and seek to correct the damage.

Humans are highly complex and must be described on many levels. From a strictly physical perspective, humans are highly nonequilibrium open systems. Energy is constantly radiating from each one of us as infrared light. Gaseous matter is constantly being exchanged with our environment. Upon occasion, large inputs of liquid or solid matter are ingested or excreted. The systems biology and chemistry description of humans is now very detailed, and should not be forgotten in the subsequent discussion, but the main function of these processes is to provide energy for higher-level activities.

Conscious thought requires large amounts of energy to sustain. But where do our thoughts come from? Some thoughts are highly correlated with external inputs. Some thoughts seem to arise from purely internal factors. But, humans are characterized by thoughts! Our genetic legacy influences the nature of our thoughts, and the biological level of description should never be forgotten; but humans are still characterized as much by their history as they are by their genes. We are not genetically determined, nor are we culturally determined, but we are influenced by both of these factors. Many animals are born with a fully developed behavioral program. Humans learn most of what they need to survive after they are born. If the conditions are right, they continue to learn throughout their life and their total person is a function of their genes and their history. The search to find one's "true self" is a serious misunderstanding. We are constantly in the process of becoming and, like the rainbow, we never reach the end. Our humanity must be understood as a *process* involving the whole person.

The whole question of the human mind and "consciousness" is a subject of current controversy. Physical reductionists wish to explain thought entirely in terms of the physics or chemistry of life; the focus is on mechanisms like quantum indeterminacy or messenger molecules. While these stories are fascinating, and will continue to change daily for a long time, my own stance is that the lowest-level processes that are required for human thought are not the most interesting aspect of the problem. Many other microscopic mechanisms could be used to produce thinking machines, and are currently being used in sophisticated new robots. Biological reductionists wish to explain thought entirely in terms of neural activity: our thoughts are merely the functioning of our neurons. This reminds me of the days when the brain was viewed as an air conditioner for the body; it gave off large amounts of heat! Yes, neural activity is involved in all thought, but it is not the most interesting part of the problem. Neural activity could be simulated with sophisticated chips, and is currently being studied entirely in the virtual world, as well as in the biological world. Neurons are organized in remarkable ways in the brain. Each neuron is capable of making connections to thousands of other neurons. This enormous change in perspective requires new concepts and new paradigms to grasp the significance of the actual functioning human brain. Even so, the reductionists insist that human thought is "nothing but" the functioning of neurons. My own stance is that, while neurons are the structures used in human thought, they are not the most interesting part of the problem. Neurons are organized into higher-level regions in the brain and are connected to sensors outside the brain. This area of research is very active at present and is sure to remain so for the foreseeable future. Perhaps some day we will have a very sophisticated understanding of the functioning of the biological human brain. Perhaps we will even be able to build a device that can carry out many of the functions of the human brain. Computer programs can already compose music and paint pictures. However, I do not know of a computer system that contemplates its own "death" and commemorates outstanding former computers. I believe that God has "given" us a sophisticated brain so that we can engage in activities that are worthy of beings created in His image. Christians should embrace all the knowledge gained about our brain, but never forget the purpose for which we have a mind.

In all the frenzy about the brain, the subject of the mind often is either forgotten, or is marginalized as an epiphenomenon (Churchland, 2000). There is a large and very active community of philosophers of mind who try to think about consciousness at levels higher than the neural, or even the "regional" level (Chalmers, 1996). No dominant paradigm commanding wide devotion has emerged, even though the "emergentist" perspective has fans in the Evangelical Christian community (including me) (Brown, 1998). The history and philosophy of science can be a real help on this problem, since there is often a tendency to forget how other complex problems were solved. At the highest level, examples of human thought can be studied on their own, as phenomenological subjects. These data provide strong "controls" on more speculative work. Denial of the relevance of actual human thought to the problem of consciousness has hindered much progress. As the concepts needed to explain the lower-level processes becomes more advanced, new paradigms that encompass broader and broader areas of brain activity will be developed. There may be a phase where complementary but paradoxical concepts must be held in tension until a more unified theory emerges. In the meantime, an excellent book on this subject, *Minding God* by Greg Peterson, is highly recommended (Peterson, 2003).

Religious thinkers throughout history have chosen to denote a particular aspect of humans as a "soul." This function of humans allows us to communicate with one another on subjects deeper than food, drink, and sport. In addition to physiological appetites such as hunger and thirst, humans "feel" anger, love, and awe. While there is certainly a chemical and biological cognate to these emotions, it is an Evangelical stance that emotions are just as "real" as molecules. Attempts to reduce humanity to nothing more than an epiphenomenon are pitiful, both in detail and as an effective philosophical stance. Detailed experiments with simpler animals have shown that specific molecules are true causal agents of particular behavior. The extension of this biological truth to all of human behavior is a serious error known as sociobiology. It is an Evangelical stance that mindless ideology is just as destructive in the practice of science as it is in religion.

Classical thought postulated a separable "soul" that did not require a body. An Evangelical stance rejects the preexistence of "Platonic souls" in favor of the biblical notion of a whole person that starts at conception and grows forever. Descartes also proposed a separable "soul" that did the thinking and imposed its will on the body. Modern cognitive psychology views the mind as a dynamic process that involves the whole person. In a highly dualistic age, the soul was viewed as immaterial and pure and was contrasted to the material (and degraded) body. An Evangelical stance is that the human body is good and has been given to humankind by God. It should be remembered that Jesus had a human body. Nancey Murphy has been a leader in the conceptualization of the soul as instantiated in our body (Murphy, 2006). The details of the "eternal" or "resurrected" state are not understood, but for the present we require bodies. Christians should embrace the "emotions" that have been provided by our Creator, but not either worship them or denigrate them.

In addition to our affective natures, religious humans have a strong intuition that there is a human capacity for interacting with the divine: this function is called the spirit. Christians believe the spirit is a direct gift from God, but the nature of this gift is envisioned as an inherently unpredictable force that goes where it wills. Attempts to localize a causal nexus in the body have been unsuccessful, just as in the case of the Cartesian soul, but there is substantial debate over whether the spirit should be envisioned as a human mental function, just like the soul, or whether it is qualitatively different. Active scholarly effort is being carried out in this area, but practicing Christians have known experientially for millennia that God communicates through the Holy Spirit with the spirits of His people (Rom. 8:16). While scholars study and debate this question, we can confidently practice the daily life of the spirit in fellowship with the Holy Spirit.

One of the other requirements for our humanity is other humans, both for better and for worse. A modern understanding of original sin includes the notion that we learn how to sin from our parents and other significant others. We also model our life on other humans (both current and historical). The importance of the social world of humans cannot be overemphasized. Christians believe that the family is ordained of God for the benefit of humankind; both mothers and fathers serve as examples of the love of God. It is in families that children learn those daily patterns of thought and behavior that are the basis of civil society. An Evangelical stance strongly supports the family as an essential element of humanity.

Christianity offers a social world that is called the "Kingdom of God." Socially constructed modes of living are instantiated in actual humans. If we live in accordance with the principles of the "ecclesia", we are changed physically and mentally into the image of Jesus in addition to being created in the image of God. Unless the local church operates as a "family" structure, it fails to accomplish one of its primary functions; the growth and development of the saints.

Individuals and families are embedded in human cultures. Christians assert that God was involved in the history of human culture and that He gave revelations to us through prophets and teachers, especially in the person of Jesus of Nazareth. Cross-cultural studies by anthropologists have revealed incredible diversity in the cultural paradigms of present and historical societies. Some cultures value dissimulation above all else while others glory in violence. Nevertheless, it is an Evangelical stance that the message of Jesus can be communicated to all humans in a meaningful manner. One of the great challenges of the modern Church is to make it so.

The human race is highly heterogeneous in both physical and cultural terms. One of the greatest insights of religious thought is the essential unity of humankind. This stance permeates the Bible and is strongly reinforced in Christian theology. Biological studies of the geography of the human genome have emphasized the continuity of the variability of our heredity. One of the great evils of some human cultures is the focus on differences as the basis of inhuman treatment of others. An Evangelical stance emphasizes the unity of humanity as the basis for the love of all other humans, as demanded by Jesus of Nazareth.

References

Arnett, David, *Supernovae and Nucleosynthesis* (Princeton, NJ: Princeton University Press, 1996).

Blocher, Henri, *Evil and the Cross* (Downers Grove, IL: InterVarsity Press, 1994).

Brown, Warren S., Nancey Murphy, and H. Newton Malony (eds.),*Whatever Happened to the Soul? Scientific and Theological Portraits of Human Nature* (Minneapolis: Fortress Press, 1998).

Carlson, R. F. (ed.), *Science and Christianity: Four Views* (Downers Grove, IL: InterVarsity Press, 2000).

Chalmers, David J., *The Conscious Mind: In Search of a Fundamental Theory* (New York: Oxford University Press, 1996).

Churchland, Paul M., *The Engine of Reason, the Seat of the Soul* (Cambridge, MA: MIT Press, 2000).

Collins, Francis S., *The Language of God* (New York: Free Press, 2006).

Dodson, Peter, Faith of a paleontologist, *The Paleontological Society Papers* 5 (1999), 183–95.

Friedlander, Gerhardt, Joseph W. Kennedy, Edward S. Macias, and Julian Malcolm Miller, *Nuclear and Radiochemistry* (New York: John Wiley and Sons, 1981).

Gingerich, Owen, *God's Universe* (Cambridge, MA: The Belknap Press, 2006).

Green, Joel B. and Stuart L. Palmer (eds.), *In Search of the Soul: Four Views of the Mind-Body Problem* (Downers Grove, IL: InterVarsity Press, 2005).

Guth, Alan H., *The Inflationary Universe* (New York: Basic Books, 1997).

Hawking, Stephen and Roger Penrose, *The Nature of Space and Time* (Princeton, NJ: Princeton University Press, 1996).

Hogan, Craig I., *The Little Book of the Big Bang* (Kirkwood, MO: Copernicus, 1998).

McGrath, Alister, *Science and Religion: An Introduction* (Oxford: Blackwell, 1999).

Murphy, Nancey and George F. R. Ellis, *On the Moral Nature of the Universe* (Minneapolis: Fortress Press, 1996).

Murphy, Nancey, *Theology in the Age of Scientific Reasoning* (Ithaca, NY: Cornell University Press, 1990).

Murphy, Nancey, *Bodies and Souls, or Spirited Bodies* (Cambridge, Cambridge University Press, 2006).

Nicolson, Iain, *Dark Side of the Universe* (Baltimore: Johns Hopkins University Press, 2007.)

Ohanian, Hans C. and Remo Ruffini, *Gravitation and Spacetime* (New York: W.W. Norton, 1994).

Page, Don N., Hawking radiation and black hole thermodynamics, *New Journal of Physics* 7 (2005), 203.

Patterson, Gary, In praise of entropy, http://thytestimonies.com/articles.htm

Patterson, Gary, *An Evangelical Stance* (forthcoming).

Peterson, Gregory R., *Minding God: Theology and the Cognitive Sciences* (Minneapolis: Fortress Press, 2003).

Polkinghorne, John, *Quantum Physics and Theology: An Unexpected Kinship* (New Haven, CT: Yale University Press, 2007).

Polkinghorne, John, *Quarks, Chaos and Christianity* (New York: Crossroad, 1997).

Smoot, George and Keay Davidson, *Wrinkles in Time* (New York: Harper Perennial, 2007).

Snoke, David, *A Biblical Case for an Old Earth* (Hatfield, PA: IBRI, 1998).

Part 10
Cosmology and Theology

28

Our Place in the Vast Universe

DON N. PAGE[1]

Scientists have measured that what we can see of space is about a billion billion billion billion billion billion billion billion billion billion (10^{81}) times the volume of an average human. Inflationary theory suggests that the entirety of space is vastly larger. Quantum theory suggests that there are very many different copies of space of the same basic kind as ours (same laws of physics). String theory further suggests that there may be many different kinds of space. This whole collection of googolplexes of galaxies within each of googolplexes of different spaces within each of googols of kinds of space makes up an enormously vast universe or multiverse. Human beings seem to be an incredibly small part of this universe in terms of physical size. Yet in other ways, we may still be a very significant part of our vast universe.[2]

The monotheism of Judaism, Christianity, and Islam asserts that the universe was created by God. For example, the first verse in the Bible, Genesis 1:1, says, "In the beginning God created the heavens and the Earth" [1]. In the New Testament, the third verse of the Gospel of John, John 1:3, says, "All things were made through Him [Jesus Christ as the Son of God], and without Him nothing was made that was made."

Astronomers, cosmologists, physicists, and other scientists who study the universe continue to discover that the universe is larger than previously thought. Human beings seem to be an incredibly small part of the universe in terms of physical size. Yet in other ways, we still believe that we are a very significant part.

Ancient people knew that the universe was much larger than humans. For example, Psalm 8 in the Bible, composed perhaps around 3,000 years ago, refers to this qualitative knowledge: "When I consider Your heavens, the work of Your fingers, the moon and the stars, which You have ordained, what is man that You are mindful of him, and the son of man that You visit him?"

The Greeks were perhaps the first to try to measure how much larger than humans the Earth and other astronomical objects are. Around 2,200 years ago, Eratosthenes measured the size of the Earth to within a few percent of the correct value. About the same time,

Aristarchus of Samos made observations of the size of the shadow of the Earth on the Moon during an eclipse to deduce the distance to the Moon. He had correct geometric reasoning but made poor measurements, getting the distance from the Earth to the Moon as 20 times the radius of the Earth, whereas the actual average distance is about 60 times.

Aristarchus also measured the angle between the Sun and the Moon when the Moon was half-illuminated (quarter moon), as well as other angles, to estimate the distance from the Earth to the Sun to be nearly 400 times the radius of the Earth. This estimate was actually too small by a factor of about 60 because of errors in measuring the angles, some of which were too small or too near a right angle to be measured accurately at that time. However, if one combined these measurements with the viewpoint of some of the ancient Greeks who contended that the radius of the universe was the distance from the Earth to the Sun, one could have deduced that the universe was over a billion times larger than an average human.

Aristarchus thought that the stars were actually much further away than the Sun, which led him to believe the universe was considerably larger than the distance from the Earth to the Sun. Although none of Aristarchus' writings on this matter have survived, Archimedes wrote that Aristarchus believed the Sun and stars were at rest and that it was the Earth that revolved around the Sun. (This reference makes Aristarchus the first person to propose the heliocentric theory, that the Sun is at the center of the solar system.)

In order to avoid observable changes in angles between the directions to the stars as the Earth moved around the Sun (stellar parallax), Aristarchus had to assume that the distances to the stars were much larger than the distance from the Sun to the Earth. But most people accepted neither this heliocentric view nor the belief that the stars were much farther away than the Sun, until Copernicus proposed similar ideas again in the sixteenth century.

Part of the objection to Aristarchus' heliocentric view may have been an assumption that as the home of humans, the Earth ought to be the center of the universe. However, a larger reason for assuming that the Earth was at the center seems to have been the argument of Aristotle (who lived about 100 years before Aristarchus), that as something heavy, the Earth would have settled at the center of the universe. Furthermore, it might have seemed incredible that the stars were so far away that their changes in direction would be unnoticeable from the Earth if it really did revolve around the Sun.

Aristotle did not conceive of the Earth as the source of the gravity around it, as Newton did 2,000 years later, but rather assumed that what we now call gravity would pull things toward the center of the whole (what we would now call the universe) [2]. Aristotle argued that this pull toward the center is why the Earth settled there, the effect rather than the cause of things falling. Although this Aristotelian concept of gravity has proved to be wrong regarding the actual gravitational field surrounding the Earth, something resembling it would occur even in Einstein's theory of gravity, general relativity, if there were a sufficiently large negative cosmological constant. This occurs in the hypothetical anti-de Sitter spacetime that is a favorite toy model of many gravitational theorists today, though not as an accurate model of our universe.

By the Middle Ages, whatever exalted view of the central position of the Earth some of the ancients may have had was generally replaced by the view of the central position of the Earth as mundane, located at what Galileo called the "dump heap of the filth and dregs of the universe" [2]. Copernicans' praise of the Sun's central location in the solar system is now misinterpreted as a degradation of the Earth to a demoted position away from the center. However, at the time, the praise of the Sun's new central position was an attempt to restore the lofty status of the Sun after it had fallen from a more exalted position.

After Aristarchus tried (and inevitably failed) to find the true size of the solar system, it took a long time before an accurate size was discovered. The size of the Earth could be accurately measured to a certain degree by the ancient Greeks because people could traverse a sufficient fraction of the circumference around it to measure the difference in the upward direction (say relative to the direction of the rays of the Sun at high noon). Then the relative size of the Moon could be measured by comparing it with the shape of the shadow of the Earth on the Moon during a lunar eclipse. From the size of the Moon in the sky (its angular diameter of about half a degree), one could deduce the distance to the Moon. However, since the Sun and planets are considerably further away than the Moon, their relative distances could not be measured until centuries later.

The first precise measurements of the size of the solar system were made during the transits of Venus of 1761 and 1769, when Venus passed directly in front of the Sun and could be seen as a small black disk covering a tiny part of the Sun. The time it takes for Venus to cross the observed disk of the Sun depends on how far from the center it crossed, and this depends slightly on the viewing position on the Earth. (The rotation of the Earth also affects the transit time.) Therefore, by taking precise timing measurements of the transit durations from different locations on Earth, one could deduce the distance to Venus and to the Sun in terms of the known distances between the locations on the Earth. (The ratios of the distances to Venus and to the Sun at various times, though not their actual values, could be deduced centuries earlier from the angles between the directions to the Sun and to Venus at various times.)

Many countries cooperated in sending expeditions to distant parts of the Earth to take these measurements of the 1761 and 1769 transits of Venus. Wars and bad weather hampered many attempts, such as the one made by the unfortunate Guillaume Le Gentil of France [3]. In 1761 he could not land at Pondicherry, a French colony in India, because the British had seized it, and he could not make his measurements from his ship that was tossing about at sea. He stayed eight years to make measurements of the 1769 transit (the last transit before 1874) and this time was able to set up his equipment on Pondicherry, which was restored to France by then. But after a month of clear weather, the sky turned cloudy on the morning of the transit, and he again saw nothing. He nearly went insane but gained enough strength to return to France, which took another two years. After being away for nearly 12 years in his fruitless mission to help measure the size of the solar system, Le Gentil finally got back home to find that his "widowed" wife had remarried and his possessions had gone to his heirs.

Once the size of the solar system had been determined, the next prodigious step was to measure the distances to the stars. For a sufficiently nearby star, this could be determined by measuring the change in the direction from the Earth to the star as the Earth revolved around the Sun. The first successful measurement of stellar parallax was done by Friedrich Bessel in 1838, for the star 61 Cygni, a little more than 10 light years away (about 700,000 times as far away from Earth as the Sun). Since then, the stellar parallaxes of over 100,000 other stars have been measured, notable by Hipparcos (High Precision Parallax Collecting Satellite).

To measure the distances to stars and galaxies that are farther away, one must use other methods, such as the apparent brightness of stars or galaxies for which there is independent evidence of how bright they would be at a given distance (their intrinsic brightness or absolute luminosity). One obtains what is sometimes called a whole "ladder" of cosmic distance scales, with a sequence of "rungs" or classes of objects used to determine ever-greater distances. That is, the distances to nearby objects of one class are measured by one method (e.g., by stellar parallax), and the same class of objects (say with apparently the same absolute luminosity) is used to calibrate the next class of objects at greater distances, which is in turn used to calibrate another class of objects at still greater distances.

There are also some methods, such as measuring the angles, times of variability, and velocities of multiple images of objects focused by gravitational lensing, that allow one to get direct measures of some distances without using other rungs of the ladder. (The velocities of distant stars and galaxies can be determined by measuring how much the wavelengths of the light they emit is shifted, a "redshift" toward longer or redder wavelengths for objects moving away from us. Gravitational lensing is the bending of light by a mass, say of a galaxy, that is close to the line of sight from a more distant object, the source of the light. In some cases the light can be bent to reach us in two or more routes from the more distant source.)

Planets are grouped in solar systems. Stars like the Sun are grouped in galaxies containing about 100 billion stars, with our galaxy being called the Milky Way, or simply the Galaxy. Galaxies themselves are generally arranged in groups of less than 50 galaxies, clusters of 50–1,000 galaxies, and superclusters of many thousands of galaxies.

It has been found that very distant galaxies are at distances nearly proportional to their velocities away from us, the proportionality constant being roughly the time since the galaxies would have been on top of each other at the beginning of the universe. Therefore, measuring both the distances and the velocities of distant galaxies can tell us the age of the universe. For most of my academic career this age had an uncertainty factor of nearly 2, but in recent years it has been determined much more precisely to be roughly 13.7 billion years, likely between 13.56 and 13.86 billion years [4].

Since we cannot see beyond the distance light has traveled since the beginning of the universe, we cannot see further than about 14 billion light years away. (Actually, what we see as nearly 14 billion light years away has been moving away from us since the light we now see left it; one may estimate that today it might be about 50 billion light years away, but of course we cannot see that distance yet.)

This size of the observable universe, say 13.7 billion light years, is nearly a million billion (10^{15}) times the average distance between the Earth and the Sun (499 light seconds), and almost 100 million billion billion (10^{26}) times the height of a human. If one includes the recession of the most distant observed galaxies up to their unobserved present distance of about 50 billion light years, one can say that the universe we have observed now has a volume more than a billion billion billion billion billion billion billion billion billion (10^{81}) times the volume of an average human.

However, this is not the end regarding our thoughts on the size of the universe. The furthest distances we can see within the universe are limited by the age of the universe, since light can travel only 13.7 billion light years if the age of the universe is only 13.7 billion years. But what we see at that distance shows no sign of being near an edge or being an end to space; consequently, it appears likely that the universe extends far beyond what we can see. (There is also no sign that the universe is curled up into a finite volume, as the surface of the Earth is curled up into a finite area in one lower dimension.)

How much further the universe might extend of course we cannot directly observe, but we can ask how far it might extend. Basically, no one has thought of any convincing limit that would prevent the entire universe from being infinite. (It often seems as if the universe would be easier to understand if it was finite, but that is not persuasive enough to imply that the universe must be finite.) Even if the universe is finite, it might be enormously larger than what we can see of it.

Indeed, in the past few decades, a theory called *inflation* [5, 6, 7] has been developed to explain several of the mysteries of the universe, and it generally predicts that the universe is much, much larger than what we can see. One of these mysteries is the large-scale homogeneity of the universe, the fact that at the largest distance we can see, averaging over many superclusters of galaxies, the universe appears to be statistically the same everywhere. (There do not seem to be significant structures much larger than superclusters, or larger than about 1 percent of the furthest distance we can see.) The universe is also highly isotropic, with the superclusters of galaxies statistically nearly the same in all directions. A third mystery is the fact that the universe has expanded to become very large, and yet gravity is still important.

Inflation gives partial explanations of these mysteries by postulating that the early universe expanded exponentially to become enormously larger than it originally was. This expansion would smooth out whatever lumps there might have been (within some limits) and hence make the present universe highly homogeneous and isotropic at the largest distances. It would also tend to lead to a balance between expansion and gravity, so that the universe would not have already recollapsed as it otherwise might have, and it would not have thinned out so much that gravity would have become unimportant.

Of course, we may note that within superclusters of galaxies, the universe is far from homogeneous and isotropic, and gravitational collapse has occurred to form planets, stars, and black holes. Although inflation was not originally designed to explain the departures from the overall approximate homogeneity and isotropy that it successfully explained, it was a bonus that with a simple starting point, inflation could partially explain the observed inhomogeneities and anisotropies of our universe, which of course are essential for our existence. The idea is that although inflation apparently smoothed out the early universe to a very high degree, it could not make it completely smooth, because of what are called quantum fluctuations.

Quantum fluctuations result in the Heisenberg uncertainty principle, which contends that one cannot have precise values for both the location and the momentum (mass-energy times velocity) of any object. Normally for objects of everyday experience that are much larger than atoms, these quantum fluctuations are too small to be noticed, though some of the fuzziness and tiny ring-like appearance of floaters in the eye is due to the diffraction of light, which might be viewed as one form of quantum fluctuations. So one might expect that quantum fluctuations would be negligible for astronomically larger objects, such as planets, stars, galaxies, clusters, and superclusters of galaxies.

On the other hand, the universe is expanding, so in the past it was much smaller. The entire universe we can now see was apparently once smaller than the width of a hair. And if inflation is right, it was even astronomically smaller than that. For such a tiny universe, smaller than the size of a present-day atom, quantum fluctuations can be significant.

One can calculate that quantum fluctuations in the early universe would lead to variations in the density of ordinary matter that formed later, and these density variations would then clump because of their gravitational attraction to form the planets, stars, galaxies, clusters, and superclusters we see today. Therefore, it appears that inflation, acting on the inevitable quantum fluctuations, can lead to the structured universe we see today. Indeed, our very existence depends upon this structure that apparently can be explained by inflation that amplifies initially tiny quantum fluctuations.

Although we are not absolutely certain that inflation really occurred, it does offer quite a lot of partial explanations for what we observe. Therefore, it is interesting to see what other predictions inflation makes.

One of inflation's most important predictions is that the universe is most likely to be enormously larger than what we can see, which is limited by the present age of the universe. This is not just saying that the universe is likely to be billions of times larger than what we can see. Rather, suppose that we wrote a sequence of billions to tell how much larger the universe is. (Above we gave a sequence of nine billions multiplied together, 10^{81}, or one with 81 zeros after it, to denote the number of humans who could fit into the volume of the part of the universe today that we have seen.) Not enough ink would exist in the world to write down the number of billions multiplied together to give the size of the universe. The size of the universe might be even enormously greater than a googol, 10^{100}, 1 followed by 100 zeros, and perhaps even greater than a googolplex, $10^{10^{100}}$, 1 followed by a googol of zeros, which would require a googol of digits to write down as an ordinary integer.

As a googol is itself far larger than the number of elementary particles in the part of the universe we can now see, a googolplex could not be written down in the ordinary way (as a sequence of digits), even if one could write each digit with only a single elementary particle from all those within sight. And inflation tends to predict that the whole universe is even larger than a googolplex.

To put it another way, with only 10 digits we could in principle assign a different telephone number for every human now on earth. But with each particle from the whole observable part of the universe taken to be a digit, we could not count the size of the total universe, according to many inflationary theories. Thus inflation suggests that the entire universe is enormously larger than what we can see of it, so much larger that it boggles the imagination.

Furthermore, one of the most prominent modern ways to understand quantum theory and its fluctuations (the Everett "many worlds" theory [8]) implies that there may be an exorbitant number of universes, perhaps as many as the staggeringly large number of particles within the entirety of our universe if inflation is correct. So we think that not only is our universe very, very large, but also there are very, very many of them.

Many experts believe that string/M theory, which is the leading contender to be the physics Theory of Everything, predicts that there are many different kinds of universes [9]. The law of physics in each of them would be different. There might be one relatively simple overarching set of laws for the collection of all universes, but in each kind of universe, the apparent laws would differ, being merely "bylaws" for that kind of universe.

In many kinds of universes the "constants of physics" that lead to the structures of molecules we know would be different, so that these molecules would be replaced by different ones. In many other kinds of universes, there would be no molecules at all. In many others it is believed that even spacetime would not exist, though what would exist in its place is still rather murky in the minds of the theorists trying to understand string/M theory.

Some estimates are that it would require perhaps 500 digits just to list the different "laws of physics" of the distinctly qualitatively different kinds of universes within string/M theory [10]. And remember, each of these different kinds of universes can have googolplexes of particular universes (Everett worlds), and many of these particular universes can be so large as to have googolplexes of particles, planets, stars, galaxies, clusters, and superclusters of galaxies within them.

Suppose it took 500 digits to say which kind of universe one is in, a googol of digits to say which of the Everett "many worlds" or universes of that kind one is in, and another googol of digits to say where within one of those inflated enormous universes one is. Then it would take 500 + 2 googols to specify where we are. This would make us an incredibly tiny part of the entire collection of universes, which is sometimes called the multiverse.

One might seek an analogy of our place in the multiverse in terms of human experience within all the humans on the Earth. Then one could take the 500 or so digits that specifies which kind of universe to be analogous to a specification of the genome of a person. However, listing the genetic code of a human, in the form of listing the sequence of about 3 billion DNA base pairs, requires specifying about 2 billion digits, many more digits than the 500 digits that some think would be needed to specify the kind of universe in string/M theory. Thus in this regard string/M theory would apparently be much simpler than human genetics, though at present it is perhaps even less well understood.

The googol of digits that specifies which of the Everett many-worlds describes our universe could be taken to be analogous to a specification of which person one is out of all those with the same genes. For people living on the Earth at the same time, in most cases one would not need further specification beyond their genes, although identical twins or other multiplets that originated from a single fertilized egg would.

However, if one considered the possible memories and synaptic connections in the brain of a human with specified genes but with arbitrary experiences, one would need even more digits to specify those than just to specify the genes. For example, there are about 100 billion neurons in the human brain, and each is linked to as many as ten thousand others, giving perhaps a million billion (10^{15}) connections. If this were the total possible number of connections, and we had to say which ones were actually connected, we would need a million billion binary digits to specify this or roughly 30 percent as many decimal digits. In this manner, there may be hundreds of thousands of times more information in "nurture" (the conscious and unconscious memories recorded in synaptic connections that one gains from experiences) than in "nature" (one's genes). In a similar manner, a googol of information about which Everett many-world one exists in would be far more than the 500 digits of information which reveals which kind of universe one is in.

On the other hand, each of these 500 digits would likely have a far larger effect on the nature of the universe than each of the googol of digits specifying the particular universe, just as the information in each gene for a human may exude more of an effect than the information stored in a single unit of memory. Thus the nature vs. nurture debate does not end merely with the observation that there is generally far more information in nurture than in nature.

Finally, there is a second googol of information that specifies where one exists within a particular Everett "many world". This may be taken to be analogous to which lifetime experience a particular human of particular genes is experiencing. If one takes a person who is conscious for two-thirds of a 70-year lifetime, roughly 1.5 billion seconds, and says that he or she has one experience each tenth of a second, then this person would have about 15 billion experiences within his or her lifetime. This would require just 11 digits to specify which lifetime experience a particular person is presently experiencing. These 11 digits are enormously less than the googol of digits it might take to specify where we are within our particular universe of a particular kind that has undergone inflation. But then, unlike the universe, we have not exponentially inflated.

The vast size of the entire multiverse makes it seem likely that almost all possible human experiences would occur somewhere. Indeed, if inflation is true, it seems likely that there are very many copies of us, spread throughout our vast universe, that have exactly the same genes and memories.

This existence of an enormous number of humans or other intelligent life forms would be true even if the probability per planet for intelligent life and consciousness were very small. In particular, we would likely exist in all of our details even if the probability per planet were so small that it is unlikely that there would be any other intelligent life and consciousness on any of the other million billion billion (10^{24}) or so planets that may exist within the part of our universe that we can see.

One implication is that we would have no real evidence to suggest that the probability per planet is large enough for us to have contact with other intelligent life. We cannot rule out the possibility of contact either, but the fact that the probabilities per planet could be so much smaller than one in a million billion billion suggests to me that it may well be just wishful thinking to suppose that we can ever be in contact with extraterrestrial intelligence.

Does this picture of a vast universe or multiverse make us insignificant, since we make up such a tiny part of it? I believe not. The mere size of something does not determine its importance. Perhaps because of our past human history, when human physical strength (often correlated with size) was important for obtaining food, we have a tendency to admire physical size and strength in humans, for example, referring to someone as a giant in his or her field. But now, if we stop to think about it, we realize that this is mainly just a metaphorical expression, and importance really has very little to do with physical size.

For example, the author of Psalm 8, after implicitly recognizing that a human is far smaller than the heavens responded with a praise of human glory: "For You have made him a little lower than the angels, and You have crowned him with glory and honor."

Even on a purely physical or mechanical level, it seems very likely that we are the most complex beings within our solar system, and perhaps even within the entire part of the universe that we can see.

Another issue arises with the view that the entire multiverse contains not just the observed humans on Earth, but also presumably huge multitudes of other humans and other intelligent and conscious beings, widely distributed across space in our universe and across different universes and maybe even across different types of universes. We might fear that in this view we would lose significance because of our loss of uniqueness.

It is indeed human nature to appreciate being considered unique. I remember feeling flattered when John Wheeler once wrote about me, "No one else has his combination of talents." However, I quickly realized that he could have written the same about any person on Earth (at least if the comparison were to other people on this same Earth). One might fear that this distinction that each of us has in comparison with the hundred billion or so humans that have lived on earth would be lost if we extended our comparison to the vast reaches of space, where we are likely not to be so unique.

But on further reflection, I do not understand why being unique is so important. Even without considering his or her unique combination of talents, each person on Earth is important just for being human, despite the fact that there have been nearly 100 billion other humans living on earth. So why can't each person be important for being who he/she is, even if there are googolplexes of copies spread over the entire universe?

The urge to achieve importance through uniqueness has led humans to seek roles that are obviously unique within a society, such as being the ruler. But if we can realize that each of us is important, whether or not he/she is unique in any particular way, then we can be happy with our lives and fulfill our roles to show love to others who are also equally important.

Note

1   Internet address: don@phys.ualberta.ca.

References

[1]   This and all other Scripture taken from the New King James Version. Copyright © 1982 by Thomas Nelson, Inc. Used by permission. All rights reserved.

[2]   Dennis Richard Danielson (ed.) *The Book of the Cosmos: Imagining the Universe from Heraclitus to Hawking* (Cambridge, MA: Perseus Publishing, 2000).

[3]   Helen Sawyer Hogg, "Le Gentil and the transits of Venus, 1761 and 1769," *Journal of the Royal Astronomical Society of Canada* 45(1951), 37–44, 89–92, 127–34 and 173–8.

[4]   D. N. Spergel et al. (WMAP Collaboration), "Wilkinson Microwave Anisotropy Probe (WMAP) three year results: Implications for cosmology," *Astrophysical Journal Supplement Series* 170, 377 (2007), astro-ph/0603449, online at: <http://arxiv.org/abs/astro-ph/0603449>.

[5]   Andrei D. Linde, *Particle Physics and Inflationary Cosmology* (Chur, Switzerland: Harwood, 1990).

[6]   Alan Guth, *The Inflationary Universe: The Quest for a New Theory of Cosmic Origins* (Reading, MA: Addison-Wesley, 1997).

[7]   Alex Vilenkin, *Many Worlds in One: The Search for Other Universes* (New York: Hill & Wang, 2006).

[8]   Bryce DeWitt and R. Neill Graham (eds.), *The Many-Worlds Interpretation of Quantum Mechanics* (Princeton, NJ: Princeton University Press, 1973).

[9]   Leonard Susskind, *The Cosmic Landscape: String Theory and the Illusion of Intelligent Design* (New York: Little, Brown, 2006).

[10]   Michael R. Douglas and Shamit Kachru, "Flux compactification," *Reviews of Modern Physics* 79, 733–796 (2007), hep-th/0610102 <http://arxiv.org/abs/hep-th/0610102>.

29

Does God So Love the Multiverse?

DON N. PAGE

Monotheistic religions such as Judaism and Christianity affirm that God loves all humans and created them in His image. However, we have learned from Darwin that we were not created separately from other life on earth. Some Christians opposed Darwinian evolution because it undercut certain design arguments for the existence of God. Today there is the growing idea that the fine-tuned constants of physics might be explained by a multiverse with very many different sets of constants of physics. Some Christians oppose the multiverse for similarly undercutting other design arguments for the existence of God. However, undercutting one argument does not disprove its conclusion. Here I argue that multiverse ideas, though not automatically a solution to the problems of physics, deserve serious consideration and are not in conflict with Christian theology as I see it.

1 God's Love for All Humans

A central point of Judaism and Christianity is that God loves everyone. For Christians, one of the most famous verses in the Bible is in the Gospel of John, John 3:16: "For God so loved the world that He gave His only begotten Son, that whoever believes in Him should not perish but have everlasting life" [1]. However, this idea starts way back in the Old Testament (the first part of the Bible, the part accepted by both Jews and Christians).

In Genesis, the first book of the Old Testament, God began a revelation through the family of Abraham, Isaac, and Jacob (who became the Israelites, Hebrews, and/or Jews). In God's original call to Abraham in Genesis 12:1–3, He said, "I will make you a great nation; I will bless you and make your name great; … and in you all the families of the earth shall be blessed." As a personal example of this, my family is not Jewish, and yet academically I have been marvelously blessed by the remarkable contributions of a vast number of brilliant Jewish scientists, and spiritually I have been immeasurably blessed by the teachings, life, death, and resurrection of the Jewish rabbi Yeshua, known in English as Jesus, whom we Christians believe to be the Christ or Messiah, the anointed Son of God and Savior.

Later in the Old Testament, in the book of Ruth, God's love was extended beyond the Israelites to Ruth, a woman of the foreign country of Moab who married an Israelite who had settled there during a famine in Israel. After both Ruth and her mother-in-law Naomi were widowed, Ruth moved with Naomi to Israel and became an ancestor to Israel's greatest king, David, as well as an ancestor of Jesus.

Jonah is another book in the Old Testament stressing the extension of God's love beyond the Israelites. This famous short story tells of the prophet Jonah who was sent by God to preach against the evils of Nineveh, a great city of ancient Assyria, on the eastern bank of the Tigris River at the location of the present city of Mosul, Iraq. As an Israelite enemy of Nineveh, Jonah wanted Nineveh to remain unrepentant and be destroyed by God. Therefore, initially he refused to go warn that evil city but rather fled in the opposite direction. As Jonah later admitted to God, "Therefore I fled previously to Tarshish; for I know that You are a gracious and merciful God, slow to anger and abundant in lovingkindness, One who relents from doing harm." However, through a remarkable event God got Jonah to obey Him, and the Ninevites repented and were spared, still to the bitter anger of Jonah. The book closes with God's emphasizing His love for the foreign city: "And should I not pity Nineveh, that great city, in which are more than one hundred and twenty thousand persons who cannot discern between their right hand and their left – and much livestock?"

In the New Testament, God sent His Son Jesus Christ to live, die on the cross for our sins, and defeat death by His resurrection, to bring forgiveness and salvation to all of us who cannot meet God's standards as set down by the laws God had given to the Israelites in the Old Testament. As the Apostle Paul expressed it in Romans 3:23–4: "For all have sinned and fall short of the glory of God, being justified freely by His grace through the redemption that is in Christ Jesus." This Gospel message of salvation by faith was offered to all people, not just the Jews. The last recorded words of Jesus Christ, in the Gospel of Matthew 28:18–20, are these:

> All authority has been given to Me in heaven and on earth. Go therefore and make disciples of all the nations, baptizing them in the name of the Father and of the Son and of the Holy Spirit, teaching them to observe all things that I have commanded you; and lo, I am with you always, even to the end of the age.

The first book of the history of Christianity, after the Gospel stories of the life, death, and resurrection of Jesus, is the Acts of the Apostles. It particularly records how the Apostles Peter and Paul began the work of extending the Gospel message beyond the Israelites to all nations.

> God not only loves all people, but He also said that He created all people in His own image. As it is written in the first book of the Bible, in Genesis 1:27, "So God created man in His own image; in the image of God He created him; male and female He created them."

The question arises as to how unique does that make us? The Bible certainly emphasizes that the image of God extends to all humans. But are we created entirely separately from the rest of creation?

Some have taken the image of God for humans to imply that God created us individually and separately from other living beings. However, Darwin's theory of evolution suggests that we are related to the rest of life. It also suggests that we humans were not separately created by an individual act, independent of the creation of the remainder of the Earth's biosphere.

2 Parallels Between Evolution and Multiverse Ideas

When Darwin proposed evolution, many conservative Christians accepted it. One famous example was Benjamin B. Warfield (1851–1921), the conservative Christian theologian and principal of Princeton Seminary from 1887 to 1921. Warfield wrote the chapter on "The Deity of Christ" in *The Fundamentals*, from which the term *Fundamentalism* arose. Thus one of the most famous original fundamentalists accepted Darwinian evolution, writing [2], "I am free to say, for myself, that I do not think that there is any general statement in the Bible or any part of the account of creation, either as given in Genesis 1 and 2 or elsewhere alluded to, that need be opposed to evolution."

However, many Christians later came to oppose evolution, perhaps most famously some other fundamentalists. Although there were many reasons for this, which I cannot get into here, one possible reason is that evolution did remove one particular design argument for the existence of God, that all of the marvelously many different species of living things on earth had been separately designed and created by God. Nevertheless, evolution did not disprove the existence of God or of some overall design. Indeed, there are many leading theologians and scientists today that accept both evolution and creation by God, such as Francis Collins, the head of the Human Genome Project [3].

It seems to me that there may be a parallel development occurring today. Before Darwin, some Christians took the marvels of humanity as evidence of separate and individual design. Now, some Christians take the marvels of the fine-tuning of the constants of physics as evidence of theism and often of separate and individual design of these constants by God [4, 5, 6, 7, 8, 9, 10, 11, 12, 3]. Here I wish to argue that this could be equally mistaken.

I have found that my views are rather similar to those of a minority of theists, notably John Leslie [13, 14], Stephen Barr [15], Robin Collins [16, 17, 18], Gerald Cleaver [19, 20], Klaas Kraay [21], and others that Kraay cites, who break tradition and argue that a multiverse could reveal an even more grand design of the universe, since the physical process that generates the multiverse would have to have suitable basic laws and initial conditions to produce any life at all (no matter what the constants of physics are, since often they seem to be fine-tuned for several different reasons [13, 14]). The laws and initial conditions would apparently have to be even more special to produce not just life, but life like ours observing the order we actually do see around us. Leslie, Barr, Collins, Cleaver, Kraay, and others claim that since God is infinitely creative, it makes sense to say that He might create a physical reality much larger than the single visible part of the universe or multiverse that we can observe directly.

3 Fine-Tuning in Our Universe

Now it does seem to be true that we could not be here if many of the constants of physics were significantly different, so that in our part of the universe, the constants of physics do in fact seem to be fine-tuned for our kind of life. This is generally agreed upon both by those who attempt to use this fine-tuning to support theism, as in the references above, and by many scientists who are usually neutral or opposed to such an attempt [22, 23, 24, 25, 26, 27, 28, 29, 30, 31, 32, 33, 34, 35]. Of course no one knows what other forms of life might be possible if the constants of physics were significantly different, but the general consensus seems to be that it would be very difficult to imagine the possibility of any complex life at all existing if certain combinations of the constants of physics were greatly different.

For example, one of the most remarkable fine-tunings is the value of the cosmological constant or energy density of the "dark energy" responsible for the current acceleration of distant galaxies away from each other. (Even though a positive cosmological constant corresponds to positive energy density which normally would gravitate or tend to pull things together, it is also accompanied by tension or negative pressure that antigravitates by an amount that is larger by a factor of three, the number of dimensions of space. Thus the net observed effect of the positive cosmological constant or dark energy is antigravity, the gravitational repulsion of otherwise empty space that causes distant galaxies now to be accelerating apart.)

Measurements show that the cosmological constant is more than 120 orders of magnitude smaller than unity in certain natural units (called Planck units, obtained by setting to unity the speed of light, Planck's quantum constant of action, and Newton's gravitational constant). With the other constants kept fixed, it would be difficult to have a universe with gravitationally formed structures lasting long enough for life if the cosmological constant were even just a few orders of magnitude (powers of 10) larger than its observed value. But even if one tuned the other constants to allow the possibility of such structures when the cosmological constant has a value many orders of magnitude larger than its observed value, one still seems to need it to be many orders smaller than unity. So one does not see how to avoid at least some significant amount of fine-tuning of this parameter. (Basically, if the cosmological constant were of the order of unity in the natural Planck units, the spacetime of the universe would always have large quantum mechanical fluctuations, and no one knows any plausible way to have persisting complex structures that one could call life in such a case.)

Another constant that is many orders of magnitude away from unity, in this case about 36 orders of magnitude larger than unity, is the ratio of the electrostatic repulsion to the gravitational attraction between two protons (the nuclei at the centers of hydrogen atoms). With other constants kept fixed, it seems that one could not have the types of stars that appear to be necessary for life if this constant differed by much more than even one order of magnitude (factor of 10) from its actual value. Again one could try to imagine a universe hospitable to some other form of life when this constant is significantly different by also tuning other constants to an appropriate range, but again it seems that complex life of any form relying mainly on the electromagnetic and gravitational forces would be impossible if this constant were close to unity. (Then it seems that one could not have stars, planets, and living organisms with large numbers of atoms, since the number of atoms in such structures generally scales as a positive power of this constant and would approach some small number near unity if this constant were itself near unity [34, 35].)

Martin Rees [28] discusses in much more detail these two constants and four others in our universe that are crucial for its properties. Life as we know it would apparently be impossible if any one of them was greatly different (with the others held fixed). So although it might not be necessary for all of them to have their observed values, there are some combinations of them that apparently could not be very much different and yet give a universe with life, at least life at all similar to present life on earth.

4 Explanations for Fine-Tuning

So there is a general consensus that there is at least some fine-tuning of the constants of physics in our part of the universe, though not that all of the constants had to have values close to what we observe. But what is the explanation for this phenomenon? There are three general types of explanations that are often put forward.

Some suggest that the fine-tuning was done by a separate act of God to allow life. Others say that it is presumably an accidental fluke. And yet others propose that it arises from a huge multiverse of very many different possible constants of physics. It is also noted in several of the references that I have given, such as [13, 36], that the three explanations are not mutually exclusive, so that virtually any combination of them is logically possible. However, it is the multiverse explanation that is now rapidly growing in favor, though not without a lot of opposition from both theists and nontheists.

One must quickly point out that each of these three explanations really stands for a class of explanations, so that one should actually compare specific proposals taken from these classes rather than the classes themselves. Theists of different theological convictions might propose different ideas of how God would choose the constants. Those saying that the fine-tuning is a fluke might say that the constants are determined by any number of different mathematical structures that just happened to give biophilic values, or they might propose that there is truly some random process determining the constants in some way not derivable from any simple mathematical structure. And of course there are a huge number of possible multiverse theories.

Some multiverse theories seem to me to be too general to be plausible, such as the idea of David Lewis [37] that all logical possibilities actually exist, or the original idea of Max Tegmark [38] that all mathematical structures have physical reality. These would seem to leave it unexplained why what we see has the order that it does, whereas a random possibility from all logical possibilities or from all mathematical structures would surely be far more chaotic [13, 14, 15, 36] (though I now admit that my objection to Tegmark's original Level IV multiverse as logically inconsistent was wrong, since I misinterpreted each mathematical structure to be a description of reality rather than being simply a part of reality). However, there might be other multiverse theories that are more explanatory of the order that we do observe, perhaps arising naturally out of elegant but specific laws of nature. For example, Tegmark's more recent ideas [39] that physical reality might be restricted to the mathematical structures of computable functions seems to me more hopeful, though I would disagree with his view that physical reality is just mathematical structure or syntax and instead believe that it includes at least the semantics of consciousness.

One natural way to get a multiverse is to have a universe so large that highly varied conditions occur somewhere. Another is from Everett many-worlds [40], that all the quantum possibilities are actually realized. However, those possibilities do not necessarily give varying constants of physics.

One scenario that seems more hopeful is to get multiverses from inflation [41, 42, 43], which is a very rapid exponential expansion of the early universe that may make the universe enormously larger than what we can observe of it. If the inflationary scenario can include phase transitions, and if the constants of physics can differ across phase transitions, inflation tends to produce all such possibilities.

Recently it has been realized that string/M theory apparently leads to a huge multiverse of 10^{500} or so different vacua or sets of constants [44]. This would apparently be enough for the constants we see to occur somewhere (maybe once per 10^{200} vacua or so). Then perhaps 10^{300} or so vacua would fit what we see.

If only one universe in 10^M could fit our observations, but if 10^N different universes exist in the multiverse, then it might not be surprising that what we observe exists if $N > M$. E.g., in the previous paragraph, I was saying that perhaps N is around 500 and M is around 200, so then indeed $N > M$. However, the actual numbers are known very poorly [44]. We really don't yet know whether $N > M$ in string/M theory, but that seems plausible. Then what we see could be explained without its having to be individually selected.

One might still ask whether the multiverse explanation always works, assuming that it has enough universes (e.g., $N > M$). Is it sufficient to explain what we see by a multiverse theory in which there are enough different conditions that ours necessarily occurs somewhere?

I would say no, but rather that there is the further requirement that the conditions we observe should not be too rare out of all the conditions that are observed over the entire multiverse. A theory making our observations too rare should not be considered a good theory.

Good theories should be both intrinsically plausible and fit observations. Intrinsic plausibility is quantified by what is called the *a priori* probability of the theory, the probability that one might assign to it from purely theoretical background knowledge, without considering any observations. The fit to observations is quantified by the conditional probability of the observation given the theory, what is called the likelihood. Then the probability of the theory after taking into consideration the observation, what is called the *a posteriori* probability of the theory, is given by Bayes' theorem as being proportional to the product of the *a priori* probability and the likelihood [45].

I take the *a priori* probabilities of theories (intrinsic plausibilities before considering the observations) to be subjective but to be generally assigned higher values for simpler theories, by the principle that is called Occam's razor. One problem with this is that David Deutsch [46, 47] notes that simplicity depends on one's background knowledge that itself depends on the laws of physics.

The likelihood of a theory is itself neither the *a priori* nor the *a posteriori* probability of the theory, but rather the conditional probability, not of the theory, but of the observation given the theory. A theory that uniquely gives one's observation would have unit likelihood but might have very low *a priori* probability.

For example, consider an extreme solipsistic theory that only one's actual momentary observation exists, not anyone else's or even any of one's own in either the past or the future, and perhaps not even that an external world exists at all. This theory would predict that observation with certainty if it were correct. (If the theory were true, certainly the observation would be that single one predicted by the theory.) Therefore, for that observation the likelihood is unity. However, such an extreme solipsistic theory, giving all the details of one's observation or conscious perception without an external world giving other observations, would surely be highly complex and so would be viewed as extremely implausible, much more implausible than an alternate theory in which the observation resulted from the existence of an external world that also gives other observations. Therefore, this extreme solipsistic theory would be assigned very low *a priori* probability.

At the other extreme, consider the simple theory that predicts all possible observations equally (arguably a consequence of something like the modal realism of David Lewis [37]). Since this theory is so simple, it might be assigned a high *a priori* probability, but then because of the enormous number of observations it predicts with equal probability, it would give very low likelihood.

5 Applying Bayes' Theorem

Let us consider a simple example with three possible theories and use Bayes' theorem to calculate the resulting *a posteriori* probabilities. Suppose that we have theory T_1 with *a priori* probability .000 0001 that would give probability 1 for what we see (unit likelihood; the observation would be certain if this theory were true), theory T_2 with *a priori* probability .001 that would give probability .01 for what we see (1 per cent likelihood), and theory T_3 with *a priori* probability .998 999 9 that would give probability .000 000 1 for what we see (.00001 percent likelihood). Assume for simplicity that these three theories exhaust all possible theories.

Then the product of the a priori probability and of the likelihood for the first theory, T_1, is .000 000 1, for T_2 is .000 01, and for T_3 is nearly .000 000 1. The *a posteriori* probabilities of these three theories, by Bayes' theorem, is proportional to these products, so all we need to do is to normalize the products by dividing each of them by their sum, which is nearly .000 010 2. After dividing by this, we then get that to two-digit accuracy, the approximate *a posteriori* probability of T_1 is .01, of T_2 is .98, and of T_3 is .01. That is, after the observation, we would think that theories T_1 and T_3 each have only about 1 percent probability of being correct, whereas in the end theory T_2 is seen to be 98 percent probable.

In this case, neither T_1 with its unit likelihood, nor T_3 with its nearly unit *a priori* probability, gains the highest *a posteriori* probability, which instead goes to the compromise theory T_2, which had both its *a priori* probability (.001) and its likelihood (.01) rather low. Of course, there is no guarantee that a compromise theory will gain the greatest *a posteriori* probability, since the result depends on the particular *a priori* probabilities and likelihoods of the theories being tested. However, if the theories were ranked in order from most specifically predictive, say giving unit likelihood or unit probability for the specific observation, to the simplest theory with the highest *a priori* probability, it would seem unusual for either of the two extreme theories to end up with the greatest *a posteriori* probability. In this way I would be surprised if the theory for the universe or multiverse with the greatest *a posteriori* probability turned out to be either the most specifically predictive theory (giving precisely one's own observation with certainty, and no probability of any other possible observation one might have had instead) or the simplest (say predicting all possible observations with equal likelihood).

Suppose that as a theist one wants to assign *a priori* probabilities to different theories of what kind of universe or multiverse God might want to create. One might guess that God might want to create the simplest or most elegant universe or multiverse that has beings like us that He considers to be in His image or that can have fellowship with Him or that have some other moral good in it. Then the theist might try to guess whether it would be simpler for God to create just one universe with a single set of constants of physics, or whether it would be simpler for Him to create a multiverse with a variety of sets of constants.

If there were a simple principle for choosing the particular constants that we observe (e.g., simple laws of physics that give these uniquely), then one might suppose that God would prefer just using those laws and creating a unique set of constants. However, we do not see any reason why the constants we observe should be uniquely preferred over other possibilities. Of course, this could easily just be a failure of our imagination and knowledge, so we might continue looking. Even non-theistic scientists like David Gross might prefer a single-universe theory with a single set of constants of physics and persist in looking for simple laws of physics that would give this unique result, following Winston Churchill in saying, "Never, never, never, never, never give up" [48].

On the other hand, not finding a simple principle from which one can deduce uniquely the constants of physics we observe, and having some potential theories like string/M theory that strongly suggest a multiverse instead, might lead many, both theists and non-theists, to look for a multiverse theory instead. From a theistic perspective, it might seem simpler (or better in other regards) for God to choose a variety of the sets of constants of physics, a multiverse rather than a single universe.

The situation is reminiscent of that facing Johannes Kepler, who attempted to explain both the number of planets and their orbits. He was remarkably successful in describing the shape of the orbits, but his attempted explanation that the number was 6 failed, as was directly shown by the discovery of more planets. Now we know that different solar systems can have different numbers of planets, so there would not have been a way for Kepler successfully to explain a unique value. We are faced with a similar situation with the constants of physics, in that at present we do not know whether they are like the orbital shapes, which can be explained by simple principles (e.g., Newton's law of universal gravitation) or whether they are like the number of planets, which can have different values for different systems. I do not see that it ultimately makes a significant difference theologically which way the answer turns out, but as seekers of the truth we would like to find what is actually the case, or in theistic terms, what God actually did. Given our present knowledge, to me it currently seems simpler to hypothesize that God created a multiverse, and I would argue that that is a theologically acceptable option for Christians and other theists to consider.

6 Toy Multiverse Model from Arithmetic

For those of you who are mathematically inclined, the following example from arithmetic might be a helpful analogue, illustrating how observations within just one universe can give evidence of whether or not other universes also exist.

Suppose that we imagine possible universes to be analogous to positive integers, and one's observed universe to be analogous to a particular integer. For example, suppose that there were a simple prescription for translating the constants of physics into a single integer (e.g., some binary string encoding the values of the constants). Then we might seek the simplest explanation for the integer corresponding to the observed universe or to the observed constants of physics in that universe.

If the integer itself were simple, such as 2^{2222}, which is very large (19,729 decimal digits) but quite simple to state, one might suppose that the simplest explanation would be an explanation that postulates just the existence of one universe and hence just that one simple integer. On the other hand, if the integer were a very complex member of a simple set of integers, then it might be simpler to postulate that the entire set exists.

For example, any large positive integer, no matter how complex, is a member of the set of all positive integers, which is a very simple set. If the observed universe corresponded to such a very complex integer (not given by a simple algorithm such as the example 2^{2222} above), one might suppose that it would be simpler to suppose that the much simpler set of all possible positive integers existed. (Note that although this set is infinite, it does not encompass negative integers, rational numbers, algebraic numbers, real numbers, complex numbers, quaternions, or any number of other mathematical structures, so that even an infinite multiverse need not encompass all logical possibilities.)

However, one might worry that if the set of possibilities is infinite (even the highly limited infinity of the positive integers), then the probability of getting the particular observed integer would be zero, so the hypothesis or theory that the multiverse corresponded to the simple set of all possible positive integers would be assigned zero likelihood. (One way to avoid this would be to put a simple normalizable weight upon all the positive integers, so that the total weight is finite, allowing one to get non-zero probabilities for all finite positive integers, but for now let us try something else.)

To allow equal weights for all positive integers corresponding to universes in a multiverse, one might hypothesize that the multiverse corresponds to some finite set of positive integers. As an example of a large but finite simple set, consider the following set of what I call *pili-increasers*: *positive integers n for which $\Pi(n)/li(n)$ is both greater than one and greater than that of any smaller n.* Here $\Pi(n)$ is the number of primes not greater than n, and $li(n)$ is the Cauchy principal value of the integral of the reciprocal of the natural logarithm of x from 0 to n, which by the prime number theorem gives a good asymptotic estimate for $\Pi(n)$ but which oscillates around $\Pi(n)$ an infinite number of times as n increases [49].

This set of pili-increasers is a fairly simple set to define, and yet it apparently has more members than particles in the observable universe (the part of our universe we can see from light emitted after most of the electrons and ions combined in the early universe to make it transparent, which contains roughly 10^{90} particles). Each member of this set of pili-increasers likely has more than a thousand binary digits, so almost all individual members of this set are almost certainly much more complex than the entire set. (Imagine trying to memorize one of these thousand-binary-digit numbers, in comparison with trying to memorize my short definition of the set.)

The smallest member of this set of pili-increasers has been estimated to be about 1.398×10^{316} [50]. Smaller candidate pili-increasers, for example near 10^{190}, have not yet been rigorously ruled out, although such smaller numbers appear unlikely actually to be pili-increasers. (Ref. [50] only gives rigorous upper bounds on the smallest pili-increaser, the smallest $x \geq 2$ for which $\Pi(x) > li(x)$.)

Less is known about the largest pili-increaser, which I call the *pili-maximizer*, the positive integer n that maximizes the ratio of $\Pi(n)$ to $li(n)$. However, from Figure 2b of [50], it appears that it might be about 10^{311} larger than the most likely candidate for the smallest pili-increaser (i.e., larger by roughly one part in 140,000 of the smallest pili-increaser that is likely to be near 1.4×10^{316}), and give a maximum value of $\Pi(n)/li(n)$ approximately $1 + 10 - 154$. The number of pili-increasers would be expected to be about twice the value of $\Pi(n) - li(n)$ at the pili-maximizer, which from Figure 2b of [50] appears to be nearly 10^{154}. Thus one might expect somewhat more than 10^{154} pili-maximizers, but spread over a range of roughly 10^{311} from the smallest to the largest, so that if one picked a number at random within that range, the probability might be of the order of 10^{-157}, or one part in more than 13 trillions multiplied together, of picking a pili-increaser.

In fact, no one knows the precise value of any of the individual members of this set of pili-increasers. I am hereby offering to pay US$1 for each of the binary digits (probably 1,051, if the estimates above are indeed applicable for all the members and are not just upper bounds for the smallest member) of the first member of this set that is found explicitly as a binary integer and is proved to be a member of the set. I am also offering a more attainable prize of US$1 for each binary digit proved to be correct for the logarithm to base 2 of the pili-maximizer (up to as many binary digits of this logarithm as are needed to give the integer precisely, perhaps 1,061; I won't pay any more for the arbitrarily large number of additional digits that can be found trivially if and when the exact pili-maximizer integer is found).

Although there is thus apparently an enormous number of members of this simple finite set, they are also apparently extremely rare among all integers in the same range. If one chose a random integer between the smallest and the largest member of this set, the chance that it would be in the set would apparently be smaller than the chance of choosing one particular particle out of all those in the observable universe. Therefore, if in some hypothetical universe some observer found the constants of the physics translated into one member of that extremely sparse set, it would certainly be strong evidence of fine-tuning, strong evidence against a multiverse corresponding to all possible positive integers and even against a finite multiverse corresponding to all positive integers within one part in 140,000 of the smallest pili-increaser.

If one then further found that this integer were a special member of the set of pili-increasers, say the smallest or the largest, that would be such extreme fine-tuning that it would be strong evidence for the hypothesis of a single value or a single universe (or at least for just a small number of integer values or universes).

On the other hand, if the evidence were strong that this number were not a special member of the set (though there is no algorithm for proving this), then that particular integer would apparently be much more complex than the simple set of all pili-increasers. In this case, I would say that the observer would be justified to postulate the existence of a multiverse giving the entire simple set, and not just the particular complex though fine-tuned example directly observed.

Although one might accuse this observer of being extravagant in postulating this enormous set of perhaps roughly 10,154 multiverses, in reality the entire set would be much simpler than the individual member observed (at least if the individual member were in fact a random member of the set, as almost all members are, though there is no algorithm for proving that any particular member is). This is one sense in which an observation in one single universe can be more simply explained by postulating a large set of universes in a multiverse, though without needing to postulate that all possible universes exist.

This simple toy example from arithmetic illustrates the fact that in principle even from one single observation result (the one integer) in a single universe, one can gain strong evidence (though even here not a rigorous proof) for the much greater simplicity of either a single-universe or a multiverse hypothesis, depending on what is observed. Of course, in practice, even in this toy example it would be very difficult to calculate whether the integer were in the simple set of pili-increasers and then whether it were a special member such as the smallest or the largest. However, one might develop a suspicion that it might be a member if one found that the integer were a prime (as all pili-increasers are) in the relatively narrow range between the smallest member and the largest member, for which one can imagine fairly good approximate estimates being made in the foreseeable future. Then if one found that it were within a narrow uncertainty of the estimate for one of the endpoints of the range, one might suspect that it is at the endpoint and interpret that as evidence for the single-universe hypothesis, whereas if one found that it were not near an endpoint, one might take that as evidence for the multiverse hypothesis that the entire simple set existed.

Thus one can gain theoretical evidence for (or against) a multiverse even from observations restricted to one single universe, and in principle one might even gain evidence of how large the multiverse is. One's limited observations within a single universe are just a small sample of the whole, but if it is a sufficiently rich sample, it can give much information about the rest that is not directly observed.

7 The Growth of Our Knowledge of the Universe

Our whole growth of knowledge of the universe has been an expansion of its scope. As one grows as an infant, one rapidly grows beyond the view that one's present observation is all that is real, as one develops memories about the past and anticipations of the future. One then goes beyond solipsism and gains an understanding that other persons or observers exist as well. In the early stage of human development, there was the focus on one's family, which was then gradually extended to one's tribe, one's nation, one's race, and, one might hope, to all humans. But then when one further considers what other conscious observations may be going on, one might well believe that consciousness extends to other creatures, such as other animals.

Of course, one's direct observation never extends beyond one's own immediate conscious perception, so one can never prove that there are past or future perceptions as well (and I know philosophers who do not believe the future exists). Similarly, one can never directly experience even the present conscious perceptions of another, which engenders the problem of other minds in philosophy. Nevertheless, most of us believe that we have fairly good indirect evidence for the existence of other conscious experiences, at least for other humans on Earth with whom we can communicate, though it is logically possible that neither they nor any external world actually exists. (For me, I believe that it is much simpler to explain the details of my present observation or conscious perception or experience by assuming that an external world and other conscious experiences also exist, than by assuming that just my own momentary conscious perception exists.)

We may now extend the reasoning to suppose that if the universe is large enough, it will also include conscious extraterrestrials, even though we do not have even indirect evidence for them that is so nearly direct as our (inevitably still indirect) evidence for other conscious beings on earth. We can further theorize that if the universe is so large that there never will be any contact between its distant parts and our part, there still might be other conscious beings not in causal contact with us, so that we never could communicate with them to get, even in principle, the indirect evidence of the same qualitative nature that we have for other humans here on Earth with us.

A next step might be to postulate conscious beings and experiences in other universes totally disconnected from ours, so that even if one could imagine traveling faster than the speed of light, there would simply be no way to get there from here; the two parts would be in totally disconnected spacetimes. A similar situation would occur for putative conscious experiences in other branches of an Everett many-worlds wave function or quantum state. From accepting the existence of such disconnected observers, it hardly seems an excessive additional step to imagine observers in universes or parts of the multiverse with different constants of physics. One might even imagine observers in entirely different universes, not related to ours in the way an entire multiverse might be related by having one single over-arching set of natural laws.

So in this sense, the idea of a multiverse seems to be rather a natural extension of our usual ideas of accepting a reality beyond one's immediate conscious perception, which is all the experience for which one has direct access. All the rest of one's knowledge is purely theoretical, though one's brain (assuming that one's brain exists and not just the logical minimum of one's immediate conscious awareness as a single disembodied entity with absolutely nothing else) is apparently constructed to bring this knowledge into one's awareness without one's having to be consciously aware of the details of why one seems to be aware of the existence of other conscious beings.

Despite the naturalness of the progression of ideas that leads to multiverse theories, there are various objections to it. However, none of the objections seems to me to be convincing, as there are highly plausible rebuttals to the objections.

8 Objections to Multiverse Ideas

A scientific objection to a multiverse theory might be that the multiverse (beyond our observed part, which is within one single universe) is not observable or testable. But if one had precise theories for single universes and for multiverses that gave the distributions of different conditions, one could make statistical tests of our observations (likely or unlikely in each distribution). Unfortunately, no such realistic theory exists yet for either a single universe or a multiverse, so I would agree that at present we simply do not have any good theories for either to test.

Another objection is that a multiverse is not a clear consequence of any existing theory. Although it is beginning to appear to be a consequence of string/M theory, that is not yet certain, which is why there can be theorists like David Gross who are still holding out hope that string/M theory might turn out to be a single-universe theory after all, possibly enabling theorists (if they could perform the relevant calculations) to fulfill their wildest dreams of being able to calculate the constants of physics uniquely from some simple principles. One first needs to make string/M theory into a precise theory and calculate its consequences, whether single universe or multiverse. And if that theory gives predictions that do not give a good statistical fit to observations, one needs to find a better theory that does.

A philosophical objection to a multiverse theory is that it is extravagant to assume unfathomable numbers of unobservable universes. This is a variant upon the psychological gut reaction that surely a multiverse would be more complex than a single universe, and hence should be assigned a lower *a priori* probability. But this is not necessarily so, as I have explained above. The whole can be simpler than its parts, as the set of all integers is quite simple, certainly simpler than nearly all the (arbitrarily large) individual integers that form its parts. The mathematical example above of the simple set of pili-increasers also shows how even a very large finite set can be much simpler than almost all of its individual members.

As a further rebuttal of the accusation of extravagance, a theist can say that since God can do anything that is logically possible and that fits with His nature and purposes, then there is apparently no difficulty for Him to create as many universes as He pleases. He might prefer elegance in the principles by which He creates a vast multiverse over paucity of universes, that is, economy of principles rather than economy of materials.

Another philosophical objection to multiverses is that they can be used to explain anything, and thereby explain nothing. I would strongly agree with this criticism of multiverse theories that are too vague or diffuse, which do not sufficiently restrict the measure on the set of observations to favor ordered ones such as what we observe. There is a genuine need for a multiverse theory not to spread out the probability measure for observations so thinly that it makes our observation too improbable. So this objection would be a valid objection to vast classes of possible multiverse theories, but I do not see that it is an objection in principle against a good multiverse theory. Certainly not just any multiverse theory is acceptable, and even if simple single-universe theories do not work for explaining our observations, it will no doubt be quite a challenge to find a good multiverse theory that does succeed.

Most of the objections I have raised and attempted to answer so far would apply both to theistic and non-theistic scientists. However, if one is a theist, one might imagine that there are additional objections to multiverse theories, just as some theists had additional objections to Darwin's theory of evolution beyond the scientific objections that were also raised when that theory had much less support.

For example, a theist might feel that a multiverse theory would undercut the fine-tuning argument for the existence of God. I shall not deny that it would undercut the argument at the level of the constants of physics (though I think there would still be such a design argument from the general apparently elegant structure of the full laws of nature once they are known). However, the loss of one argument does not mean that its conclusion is necessarily false.

I personally think it might be a theological mistake to look for fine-tuning as a sign of the existence of God. I am reminded of the exchange between Jesus and the religious authorities recorded in the Gospel of Matthew 12:38–41:

> Then some of the scribes and Pharisees answered, saying, "Teacher, we want to see a sign from You." But He answered and said to them, "An evil and adulterous generation seeks after a sign, and no sign will be given to it except the sign of the prophet Jonah. For as Jonah was three days and three nights in the belly of the great fish, so will the Son of Man be three days and three nights in the heart of the earth. The men of Nineveh will rise up in the judgment with this generation and condemn it, because they repented at the preaching of Jonah; and indeed a greater than Jonah is here."

In other words, I regard the death and resurrection of Jesus as the sign given to us that He is indeed the Son of God and Savior He claimed to be, rather than needing signs from fine-tuning.

Another theistic objection might be that with a multiverse explanation of the constants of physics, there is nothing left for God to design. But God could well have designed the entire multiverse, choosing elegant laws of nature by which to create the entire thing. In any case, whatever the design is, whether a logically rigid requirement, a simple free choice God made, or a complex free choice God made, theists would ascribe to God the task of creating the entire universe or multiverse according to this design.

A third more specifically Christian objection might be that if the multiverse (or even just our single part of the universe) is large enough for other civilizations to have sinned and needed Christ to come redeem them by something similar to His death on the Cross here on earth for our sins, then His death may not sound so unique as the Bible says in Romans 6:10: "For the death that He died, He died to sin once for all; but the life that He lives, He lives to God." But the Bible was written for us humans here on Earth, so it seems unreasonable to require it to describe what God may or may not do with other creatures He may have created elsewhere. We could just interpret the Bible to mean that Christ's death here on earth is unique for our human civilization.

9 Conclusions

In conclusion, multiverses are serious ideas of present science, though certainly not yet proven. They can potentially explain fine-tuned constants of physics but are not an automatic panacea for solving all problems; only certain multiverse theories, of which we have none yet in complete form, would be successful in explaining our observations. Though multiverses should not be accepted uncritically as scientific explanations, I would argue that theists have no more reason to oppose them then they had to oppose Darwinian evolution when it was first proposed. God might indeed so love the multiverse.

Note

This chapter will also be published in Chinese in Melville Y. Stewart and Fu Youde (eds.), 《科学与宗教：当前对话》(*Science and Religion: Current Dialogue*) by Peking University Press, Beijing).

Acknowledgments

I am indebted to discussions with Andreas Albrecht, Denis Alexander, Stephen Barr, John Barrow, Nick Bostrom, Raphael Bousso, Andrew Briggs, Peter Bussey, Bernard Carr, Sean Carroll, Brandon Carter, Kelly James Clark, Gerald Cleaver, Francis Collins, Robin Collins, Gary Colwell, William Lane Craig, Paul Davies, Richard Dawkins, William Dembski, David Deutsch, Michael Douglas, George Ellis, Debra Fisher, Charles Don Geilker, Gary Gibbons, J. Richard Gott, Thomas Greenlee, Alan Guth, James Hartle, Stephen Hawking, Rodney Holder, Richard Hudson, Chris Isham, Renata Kallosh, Denis Lamoureux, John Leslie, Andrei Linde, Robert Mann, Don Marolf, Greg Martin, Alister McGrath, Gerard Nienhuis, Cathy Page, Gary Patterson, Alvin Plantinga, Chris Polachic, John Polkinghorne, Martin Rees, Hugh Ross, Peter Sarnak, Henry F. Schaefer III, Paul Shellard, James Sinclair, Lee Smolin, Mark Srednicki, Mel Stewart, Jonathan Strand, Leonard Susskind, Richard Swinburne, Max Tegmark, Donald Turner, Neil Turok, Bill Unruh, Alex Vilenkin, Steven Weinberg, Robert White, and others whose names I don't recall right now, on various aspects of this general issue, though the opinions expressed are my own. My scientific research on the multiverse is supported in part by the Natural Sciences and Research Council of Canada.

References

[1]   This and all other Scripture taken from the New King James Version © 1982 by Thomas Nelson, Inc. Used by permission. All rights reserved.

[2]   Mark Noll and David Livingstone (eds.) *B. B. Warfield: Evolution, Science and Scripture* (Grand Rapids, MI: Baker Books, 2000).

[3]   Francis S. Collins, *The Language of God: A Scientist Presents Evidence for Belief* (New York: Free Press, 2006).

[4]   Hugh Ross, *Genesis One: A Scientific Perspective* (Pasadena, CA: Reasons to Believe, 1983).

[5]   Hugh Ross, *Design and the Anthropic Principle* (Pasadena, CA: Reasons to Believe, 1983).

[6]   Hugh Ross, *The Fingerprint of God* (Orange, CA: Promise, 1989).

[7]   Richard Swinburne, "Argument from the fine-tuning of the universe," in John Leslie (ed.), *Physical Cosmology and Philosophy* (New York: Macmillan, 1990), pp. 154–73; and in John Leslie (ed.), *Modern Cosmology and Philosophy* (Amherst, NY: Prometheus, 1998), pp. 160–79.

[8]   Richard Swinburne, *The Existence of God* (Oxford: Clarendon Press, 1991).

[9]   Hugh Ross, *The Creator and the Cosmos*, 3rd edn. (Colorado Springs: NavPress, 2001).

[10] Neil A. Manson (ed.), *God and Design: The Teleological Argument and Modern Science* (London: Routledge, 2003).

[11] Rodney D. Holder, *God, the Multiverse, and Everything: Modern Cosmology and the Argument from Design* (Burlington, VT: Ashgate, Burlington, Vermont, USA, 2004).

[12] Robert B. Mann, "Inconstant multiverse," *Perspectives on Science & Christian Faith* 57, 302–310 (2005).

[13] John Leslie, *Universes* (London and New York: Routledge, 1989).

[14] John Leslie, *Infinite Minds* (Oxford: Clarendon Press, 2001).

[15] Stephen Barr, *Modern Physics and Ancient Faith* (Notre Dame, IN: University of Notre Dame Press, 2003).

[16] Robin Collins, "Design and the many-worlds hypothesis," in William Lane Craig (ed.), *Philosophy of Religion: A Reader and Guide* (New Brunswick, NJ: Rutgers University Press, 2002), pp. 130–148.

[17] Robin Collins, "Design and the designer: new concepts, new challenges," in Charles S. Harper, Jr. (ed.), *Spiritual Information: 100 Perspectives on Science and Religion* (West Conshohocken, PA: Templeton Foundation Press, 2005), pp. 161–7.

[18] Robin Collins, "The multiverse hypothesis: a theistic perspective," in Bernard Carr (ed.), *Universe or Multiverse?* (Cambridge: Cambridge University Press, 2007), pp. 459–80.

[19] Gerald Cleaver, "String/*M*-theory cosmology: God's blueprint for the universe," presented at ASA 2003, National Faculty Leadership Conference 2004, and International Institute for Christian Studies, 2005.

[20] Gerald Cleaver, "Before the Big Bang: String theory, God, & the origin of the universe," presented at Metanexus 2006, <www.metanexus.net/conferences/pdf/conference2006/Cleaver.pdf>.

[21] I thank Jonathan Strand (private communication) for drawing my attention to Klaas Kraay, "Theism and the multiverse" and "Theism and modal collapse" at <http://www.ryerson.ca/_kraay/>, which for more purely philosophical reasons support the view that God created a multiverse and cite many other theists who have also proposed multiverses, often as a solution for the problem of evil, as I discuss in my companion paper at <http://arxiv.org/abs/0801.0247>.

[22] Brandon Carter, "Large number coincidences and the anthropic principle in cosmology," in M. S. Longair (ed.), *Confrontation of Cosmological Theory with Observational Data* (Dordrecht: Riedel, 1974), pp. 291–8; reprinted in John Leslie (ed.), *Physica Cosmology and Philosophy* (New York: Macmillan, 1990), pp. 125–33.

[23] Bernard J. Carr and Martin J. Rees, "The anthropic principle and the structure of the physical world," *Nature* 278 (1979), 605–12.

[24] Paul Davies, *The Accidental Universe*, (Cambridge: Cambridge University Press, 1982).

[25] Brandon Carter, "The anthropic principle and its implications for biological evolution," *Philosophical Transactions of the Royal Society of London* A310 (1983), 347–63.

[26] John D. Barrow and Frank J. Tipler, *The Anthropic Cosmological Principle*, (Oxford: Clarendon Press, 1986).

[27] Paul Davies, *The Mind of God* (New York: Simon & Schuster, 1992).

[28] Martin Rees, *Just Six Numbers* (New York: Basic Books, 2000).

[29] John D. Barrow, *The Constants of Nature* (New York: Pantheon Books, 2002).

[30] Nick Bostrom, *Anthropic Bias: Observation Selection Effects in Science and Philosophy* (New York and London: Routledge, 2002).

[31] Leonard Susskind, *The Cosmic Landscape: String Theory and the Illusion of Intelligent Design* (New York: Little, Brown, 2006).

[32] Paul Davies, *Cosmic Jackpot: Why Our Universe Is Just Right for Life* (Boston: Houghton Mifflin, 2007).

[33] Bernard Carr (ed.), *Universe or Multiverse?* (Cambridge: Cambridge University Press, 2007).

[34] Brandon Carter, "Objective and subjective time in anthropic reasoning," arXiv:0708.2367 <http://arxiv.org/abs/0708.2367>.

[35] Brandon Carter, "The significance of numerical coincidences in nature," arXiv:0710.3543; <http://arxiv.org/abs/0710.3543v1>.23

[36] Don N. Page, "Predictions and tests of multiverse theories," in Bernard Carr (ed.), *Universe or Multiverse?* (Cambridge: Cambridge University Press, 2007), pp. 411–429, hep-th/0610101; <http://arxiv.org/abs/hep-th/0610101>.

[37] David K. Lewis, *On the Plurality of Worlds* (Oxford: Blackwell, 1986).

[38] Max Tegmark, "Is 'The Theory of Everything' merely the ultimate ensemble theory?" *Annals of Physics* 270, 1–51 (1998), gr-qc/9704009; <http://arxiv.org/abs/gr-qc/9704009>.

[39] Max Tegmark, "The mathematical universe," to be published in *Foundations of Physics*, arXiv:0704.0646; <http://arxiv.org/abs/0704.0646>.

[40] Bryce DeWitt and R. Neill Graham (eds.), *The Many-Worlds Interpretation of Quantum Mechanics* (Princeton, NJ: Princeton University Press, 1973).

[41] Andrei D. Linde, *Particle Physics and Inflationary Cosmology* (Chur,Switzerland: Harwood, 1990).

[42] Alan Guth, *The Inflationary Universe: The Quest for a New Theory of Cosmic Origins* (Reading, MA: Addison-Wesley, 1997).

[43] Alex Vilenkin, *Many Worlds in One: The Search for Other Universes* (New York: Hill & Wang, 2006).

[44] Michael R. Douglas and Shamit Kachru, "Flux compactification," *Reviews of Modern Physics* 79 (2007), 733–796, hep-th/0610102;<http://arxiv.org/abs/hep-th/0610102>.

[45] Richard Swinburne (ed.), *Bayes's Theorem: Proceedings of the British Academy* 113 (Oxford: Oxford University Press, 2002).

[46] David Deutsch, *The Fabric of Reality* (Harmondsworth, UK: Penguin Books, 1998).

[47] David Deutsch, private communication (Jan. 22, 2007).

[48] Peter Woit, *Not Even Wrong: The Failure of String Theory and the Search for Unity in Physical Law* (New York: Basic Books, 2006).

[49] John E. Littlewood, "Sur la Distribution des Nombres Premiers," *Comptes Rendus de l'Acad'emie des Sciences* 158, Paris (1914) 1869–72.

[50] Carter Bays and Richard H. Hudson, "A new bound for the smallest x with $(x) > li(x)$," *Mathematics of Computation* 69 (2000), 1285–96.

30

Scientific and Philosophical Challenges to Theism

DON N. PAGE

Modern science developed within a culture of Judeo-Christian theism, and science and theism have generally supported each other. However, there are certainly areas in both science and religion that puzzle me. Here I outline some puzzles that have arisen for me concerning everlasting life, human free will, divine free will, the simplicity and probability of God, the problem of evil, and the converse problem of elegance.

1 Introduction

Modern science developed within a culture of Judeo-Christian theism for several reasons [1]. For example, the idea of a lawgiver for nature (i.e., God) encouraged belief in laws of nature. Also, the need to study the laws of nature was encouraged by the Biblical command in the first book of the Bible, Genesis 1:28: "Be fruitful and multiply; fill the Earth and subdue it; have dominion over the fish of the sea, over the birds of the air, and over every living thing that moves on the Earth" [2].

But once the idea of laws of nature was derived from the idea of a lawgiver, one could often forget the lawgiver and just study the laws, rather as citizens in a nation can obey its laws without thinking about who made those laws. There is then a tendency to conclude that there is no lawgiver at all. Since both science and religion are human activities, and since humans often have conflicts, it is not surprising that there are science – religion conflicts. Since science and religion tend to claim jurisdiction over territories that have historically overlapped, it is no wonder that conflict should on occasion have arisen between them, as the aftermath of the Galileo affair would illustrate [3].

At other times there are genuine human uncertainties and differences of opinion. For example, theists have differed over whether the evidence for biological evolution is convincing, though now it seems that most theologians accept it. Somewhat similarly, today there is disagreement among both theists and scientists about whether the multiverse ideas are correct [4].

Generally I see science and religion as supporting each other, but there are certainly areas in both that puzzle me. Let me discuss some that to me have seemed to be the biggest challenges to theism, and give some thoughts I have had on them. These thoughts are certainly tentative, so I would certainly appreciate any help others can provide on these mysteries.

2 The Afterlife Awareness Problem

One rather arcane challenge that has occurred to me is the application of the Carter – Leslie – Nielsen – Gott doomsday argument [5, 6, 7, 8, 9, 10] to the afterlife. The original doomsday argument is that the observation that we are among the first hundred billion or so humans reduces the prior probability that we find ourselves in a species whose total lifetime number of individuals is much higher. If humans were to continue at present or growing populations for more than a few hundred additional years, it would be unlikely for us to have found ourselves in the very small fraction alive by now. On the other hand, if the human race were to end sooner, we would not be so unusual.

The doomsday argument implies that unless the *a priori* probability is very high for far more humans in the future than in the past, then our observations of how many humans there have been in the past makes the *a posteriori* probability low for far more humans in the future. Although this argument has been widely debated and disputed (too widely for me to give a comprehensive list of references), it has never been refuted, and I believe that it is basically valid.

I realized several years ago that similar consequences would seem to apply to hypotheses about an afterlife, experiences after physical death. If one were not absolutely certain of an afterlife that would last enormously longer than the predeath life, then the observation that we are experiencing (presumably) pre-death life rather than the afterlife would significantly reduce the *a posteriori* epistemic probability for a very long afterlife. Otherwise, our present experiences would seem to be highly unusual if there were in fact far more afterlife experiences than pre-death experiences.

After puzzling over this for several years (and having long series of email discussions with a small number of people, most particularly Richard Swinburne, who were kind enough to consider my thoughts on it without necessarily agreeing with the presuppositions), I stumbled upon an analogous possibility in physics, the formation of brains by vacuum fluctuations, which gives a similar problem if the universe lasts too long [11, 12, 13]. These brains are rather similar to those which had been earlier proposed to arise from thermal fluctuations and which had been named Boltzmann brains [14], following a somewhat analogous suggestion by Boltzmann [15] that he actually attributed to his assistant Dr. Schuetz (leading Andreas Albrecht, the originator of the phrase *Boltzmann brain*, to quip that they might actually be better named Schuetz's Schmartz). Therefore, I generally followed the usage of this catchy name for my related idea of brains as vacuum fluctuations, though so far as I know I was to first to raise the problem with vacuum fluctuations themselves.

The problem with these generalized Boltzmann brains is that if the universe lasts too long (e.g., infinitely long), then per comoving volume (i.e., in a region that expands with the universe and would contain a fixed number of atoms if they are not created or destroyed), there would only be a fixed number of ordinary observers (conscious beings like us who presumably evolved by natural selection), since they can surely last only a finite time, say when there are still stars burning, but on the other hand there would be a much larger (e.g., infinite) number of Boltzmann brains. Then almost all observations per comoving volume would be made by Boltzmann brains. So if this scenario were correct, we would most likely be Boltzmann brains.

But Boltzmann brains are very unlikely to observe the order that we actually see, so our ordered observations (with rather coherent detailed memories, etc.) are strong evidence against our being Boltzmann brains and therefore also against there being far more Boltzmann brains than ordinary observers. In this way we have observational evidence against a universe that lasts too long, at least under the assumption that Boltzmann brains can form from vacuum fluctuations at similar rates at any time arbitrarily far into the future, and under the assumption that we count the ratio of Boltzmann brains to ordinary observers in a fixed comoving volume before our universe possibly tunnels into something different.

There are many conceivable solutions to the Boltzmann brain problem [16, 17, 18, 19, 20, 21, 22, 23, 24, 25, 26, 27, 28, 29, 30, 31, 32, 33, 34, 35, 36, 37, 38, 39, 40, 41], some of which abandon the assumptions of the previous paragraph, though none that is universally accepted. For the analogous problem with the afterlife, which I might call the afterlife awareness (AA) problem instead of the Boltzmann brain (BB) problem, what seems to me possibly most relevant is the solution I suggested [11, 12, 13] that instead of persisting indefinitely into the future, our universe could be decaying quantum mechanically at a rate comparable to its exponential expansion rate, decaying at least fast enough to make the expectation value of the four-volume of the comoving region (the three-volume multiplied by the persistence probability and integrated over the time) finite and not so large that Boltzmann brains would dominate over ordinary observers (OOs). This proposed solution has its own problem of the fine tuning of the decay rate (which is not one of the fine tunings that might be explained by the observational selection of the anthropic principle), since the decay rate has to be great enough and yet not so great to make it highly improbable that the universe has lasted as long as it already has.

However, whether or not my suggested solution to the Boltzmann brain problem in our physical universe is correct, it occurred to me that something similar might conceivably be a solution to the analogous afterlife awareness problem. But before explaining this, I need to reformulate the problem in terms of the measures of conscious experiences.

All of the problems discussed here, the doomsday (DD) argument, the Boltzmann brain (BB) problem, and the afterlife awareness (AA) problem, arise from comparing the probability of an experience to be one of those (which does not fit our observations) to that of being an ordinary observer (OO) (which apparently would fit our observations). (I am tempted to think of other related problems, such as that of CCs or conscious clouds [42], but I haven't yet thought of analogous problems for all of the letters of the alphabet after D to O, though it did occur to me that EEs could be eternal experiences, conscious experiences that are each eternal, unlike our experiences that are each momentary.)

One might well postulate that each conscious perception or experience (all that one is momentarily conscious aware of) has a measure associated with it, giving the probability of that experience's being selected at random if a random selection were made [43, 44, 45, 46]. (One does not need to suppose that there actually is any such random selection in order to be able to calculate likelihoods as if such a selection occurred.) Then any set of conscious perceptions would have a corresponding measure obtained by summing the measures for the individual perceptions. (It could be the case that conscious perceptions form a continuum rather than a discrete set, in which case one would only have positive measures for continuous sets of perceptions, rather than for individual perceptions, analogous to the way that there is positive volume only for continuous sets of spatial points and not for the individual points. But for simplicity here I shall consider just the alternative logical possibility that the perceptions are discrete rather than continuous.)

In a classical physics picture of a single conscious being having a unique temporal sequence of perceptions, one might make an approximation that the measure for a particular sequential set of perceptions is proportional to the time taken to have that set. So if during 16 waking hours (960 minutes) in a day one is conscious of eating for 96 minutes, say, one might take the measure for experiences of eating during that day to be 0.1 or one-tenth of the measure for all the conscious experiences of the waking hours. (I don't mean to be denying that one is having conscious perceptions while asleep during dreams, but I am avoiding the question of how to compare their measure with perceptions while awake.)

In a quantum physics picture, there are also what are usually interpreted as the quantum probabilities of various alternative possibilities. So, for example, if there is a quantum probability of 0.2 that one is fasting during those 16 waking hours and 0.8 that one spends 96 minutes eating, then the relative measure of the experiences of eating would be only 0.8 times 0.1, or 0.08. Or, if one would be eating caviar for 96 minutes in a day if one won a lottery for which the quantum probability of winning is one in a million (and if one would not be eating caviar at all otherwise), the relative measure of the experience of eating caviar, out of all the experiences in that day with all results of the lottery, would be 10–7.

I have formulated a framework for connecting consciousness to physics [43, 44, 46] in which each conscious perception has a measure given by the expectation value of a corresponding quantum operator. However, for the present discussion, it is not important whether or not this framework is correct, but just that conscious perceptions do have objective measures that give frequency-type probabilities of the perceptions' being selected if they were selected at random. (Since I believe that the random selection is purely hypothetical, these probabilities, while being perfectly objective for each possible theory giving them, are also hypothetical, what I might call objective hypothetical probabilities, to be distinguished from the subjective epistemic probabilities that one might assign to various theories that are not known to be correct or incorrect.)

Now suppose that one has various theories Ti that each tell what fraction fi of the measure of all conscious perceptions or experiences are pre-death rather than afterlife. (For simplicity I shall just focus on these two possible types and also assume that the content of each experience clearly identifies which type it is, leaving out such experiences as those here in the present life in which one might feel that one has gone to heaven or hell.) Then in each Ti, the probability that a randomly selected conscious experience would be a pre-death experience would be fi. Given the information that one is observing a pre-death experience (and no other information), this fi would then be the likelihood of the theory Ti. (If one includes other information from the particular conscious perception being experienced, that would further restrict the fraction and give a lower likelihood.)

For a theory Ti predicting no afterlife, all experiences would be pre-death, so $fi = 1$. For a theory predicting an afterlife with far greater measure of experiences, $fi \ll 1$. In the limit of an infinite measure of experience for afterlife awarenesses but still only a finite measure for pre-death experiences, $fi = 0$.

Now suppose that various theories of these different types are all assigned non-zero *a priori* probabilities, so that one is originally not epistemically certain of any of them (though one might have strong preferences). Then by Bayes' theorem, the final epistemic *a posteriori* probabilities to be assigned to the theories would be proportional to their *a priori* probabilities multiplied by their likelihoods f_i. This then has the effect of reducing the *a posteriori* probabilities more for the theories in which the fraction of the measure of pre-death experiences is smaller. For a theory in which f_i is very tiny (a very large relative measure of afterlife awarenesses), the *a posteriori* probability would be less than ½ unless the total *a priori* probability of all the theories with higher f_i is smaller than f_i. In particular, if the total *a priori* epistemic probability of all the theories with $f_i = 1$ (theories with no afterlife; all experiences pre-death experiences) is positive, larger than zero, then in the limit that any theory gives $f_i = 0$ (i.e., by having an infinite measure of afterlife awarenesses and only a finite measure of pre-death experiences), it would have zero *a posteriori* epistemic probability.

Thus it seems that unless one started absolutely certain of an infinite afterlife, after considering the evidence that one is having a pre-death experience instead, one should then assign zero epistemic probability to the idea of an infinite afterlife.

Given that I had previously had faith in an infinite afterlife, though not quite 100 percent faith, this conclusion certainly seemed contrary to how I had interpreted the afterlife. It has bothered me ever since I first thought of it.

One possible solution, suggested to me by the originator of the doomsday argument, Brandon Carter [47], is that the afterlife is not an infinite set of afterlife awarenesses (AAs) but a single eternal experience (EE), or a single one for each person. This finite number of eternal experiences could then have a large but finite measure, leaving f_i and the resulting *a posteriori* probability non-zero (assuming one was not absolutely certain that this theory is wrong and so assign it zero *a priori* probability). Perhaps this would be a more sophisticated way of looking at eternal life, not as an infinite set of experiences but as one single eternal experience, or as one single eternal experience for each person.

Another suggested solution was given me by the person who has expounded the doomsday argument the most thoroughly, John Leslie [48], following arguments by Andrei Linde that Leslie previously disputed [10]. Linde's argument applied to an infinite afterlife would be that although any pre-death experience would be infinitely early if there is an infinite afterlife, it would not be *specially* early, since all experiences at finite time, even in the afterlife, would also be infinitely early. Maybe Leslie's change of mind in now accepting this argument is correct, but to me the pre-death experiences would still seem to have zero probability in comparison with an infinite measure of afterlife awarenesses, so it does not solve the problem in my own mind.

Another point made by Leslie [48] is that it is just subjective epistemic probabilities that are being discussed, not true objective probabilities that are "out there" in reality. That is, it presumably is the case that either an afterlife of infinite measure definitely exists or definitely does not exist, so the objective probability is either 1 or 0. As Leslie notes, "God's infinitely powerful and benevolent!" Therefore, one might remain confident that the probability of an infinite afterlife is really 1, even though applying a Bayesian analysis to an uncertain epistemic *a priori* probability (not quite unity for an infinite afterlife) might give zero *a posteriori* epistemic probability for it. Nevertheless, it does bother me that a line of Bayesian reasoning that apparently works in finite cases seems to give zero *a posteriori* epistemic probability for a theistic doctrine that I formerly was much more certain about.

However, another possible way to solve the afterlife awareness problem and avoid the infinite measure of those experiences that would give $f_i = 0$ for the presumably finite measure of pre-death experiences (or at least finite measure of pre-death experiences per person), would be to have the measures of each of the infinitely many AAs not constant but decaying sufficiently rapidly in some ordering of them. That is, if one orders the afterlife in decreasing order of their individual measure, one could have the measure per AA decreasing fast enough that the sum converges to a finite total measure that is not too much greater than the corresponding sum of the measures of all the pre-death experiences.

For example, one might postulate that in some theory T, there is a countably infinite set of AAs, and the nth AA has the measure $A(1 - x)x - n$ for some x between 0 and 1, so that the sum over n is the finite total measure A of the AAs. Then if the sum of the measures of the pre-death experiences in this theory is B, the fraction of the measure that is pre-death is $f = B/(A + B)$. This is the likelihood of this theory under the observation of a pre-death experience.

Assume for simplicity that this is the only theory under consideration in which there is an afterlife, and that its *a priori* probability is assigned to be p. Then all the other (non-afterlife) theories have total *a priori* probability $1 - p$ and have unit likelihood under the observation of a pre-death experience (since all of their experiences are pre-death). The product of the *a priori* probability and the likelihood for this afterlife theory T is then pf, and the sum of the products of the *a priori* probabilities and the (unit) likelihoods for all the non-afterlife theories is $1 - p$. Normalizing by the sum of these products, which is $pf + 1 - p$, Bayes' theorem gives the *a posteriori* probability of this afterlife theory T as $pf/(pf + 1 - p) = pB/(A + B - pA)$, which is not too small so long as pf is not too small in comparison with $1 - p$, the total *a priori* probability of all the (non-afterlife) theories. In particular, the afterlife theory T has an *a posteriori* probability greater than $\frac{1}{2}$ if its *a priori* probability is $p > 1/(1 + f) = (A + B)/(A + 2B)$, or if $A/B < (2p - 1)/(1 - p)$.

If one is nearly certain a priori of this afterlife theory T, so p is near unity, then the afterlife can have much more measure A than the pre-death measure B and yet still give an *a posteriori* probability greater than $\frac{1}{2}$. For example, if one were initially 99 percent certain of the afterlife, $p = 0.99$, then its *a posteriori* probability would be greater than $\frac{1}{2}$ for all A up to $98B$, a total afterlife measure up to 98 times that of the pre-death measure. However, if one initially had only 60 percent confidence in the afterlife, then its *a posteriori* probability would be greater than $\frac{1}{2}$ only for all A up to $B/2$, a total afterlife measure only up to half that of the pre-death measure.

If such an afterlife theory were true, one could have an infinite number of afterlife experiences and yet their total measure would not necessarily swamp that of the predeath experiences to such an extent that it would have low *a posteriori* probability in view of our observation of having a pre-death experience. Of course, the total measure would not be infinitely greater than the pre-death experiences, and the probability for finding oneself experiencing an AA far along the sequence of ever decreasing measure would be very small.

In this proposed possible solution of the AA problem, earthly pre-death experiences would not be an infinitesimal fraction of the total, though they could still be a rather small fraction of the total. Furthermore, the quality of the afterlife experiences could presumably be arbitrarily more intense than those of our present pre-death experiences. Although the New Testament and the Koran stress the superiority of heaven, I do not see that they say it is infinitely more important than life, justice, and righteousness here on this Earth. Therefore, it is not obvious that this solution to the AA problem is incorrect, though it is certainly speculative and highly tentative, since to the best of my knowledge both the AA problem and its possible solutions have not been discussed in the traditional theological literature.

3 Human Free Will

Another potential problem, or at least controversial issue within theistic beliefs, is the question of human free will, which has often been invoked to explain human responsibility and the existence of evil caused by humans. Is there any room for human free will in a universe with definite laws of nature and a definite quantum state? That is, if the initial conditions and the dynamical laws of evolution are determined, how could humans act otherwise than what would be predicted by these initial conditions and dynamical laws? (Here I am taking free will in the libertarian or incompatibilist sense of being incompatible with determinism or complete determination ultimately by causes or entities other than the being to whom the free will is ascribed.)

One logically possible answer is that human free will could help choose the laws and the quantum state of the universe. But since that would involve determining the quantum state of the very early universe, far before humans existed, that would seem rather implausible. If one assumed that causality acts only forward in time, and if time indeed goes forward from the early universe to the existence of humans, this logical possibility would seem to be physically impossible. However, we do not fully understand the nature of causation, so it is not completely obvious that causality backward in time really is physically impossible. Indeed, the ordinary concept of causality in physics says that the state of a closed system is completely determined by the laws of evolution and the state at any time, so from the state at one time, the state at all times, both before and after, would be determined, and therefore there is no obvious restriction just to causality forward in time. Nevertheless, even though I do accept timeless views of the universe in which there is no fundamental asymmetry in time and no time asymmetry in causality, I do personally find it rather implausible that human free will choices can help determine the quantum state of the universe from the very beginning.

However, I find an even stronger argument against human free will to be the realization that if God creates everything logically contingent other than Himself, then free will by any created being seems to me to be logically impossible. That is, I see the concept of free will of created beings to be a logical contradiction to the concept that they are created ex nihilo by God (or even just to the concept that one can trace back all causation to God). For if God entirely creates or ultimately causes everything contingent other than Himself, as I believe, He creates or causes all such entities not just as one time but at all times, including all actions of the beings He creates. If God creates or causes everything other than Himself that does not exist necessarily, then it seems to me that nothing other than necessary entities (e.g., logical tautologies) can lie outside the purview of this creation or causation, including any actions or choices by created beings. If God totally creates us or causes our entire existence that would seem to imply that He creates or causes everything that we do, so that all we are and do would be completely created or caused, and hence determined by God, with our having no true (libertarian) free will.

Now I will admit that if we had some independent existence and were not entirely created or caused by God, then logically we could have free will. God might adopt us, or at least our independent free will choices, within a universe that He otherwise creates. (I do not even see a contradiction between this logical possibility and God's always knowing what free will choices we would make, since the only contradiction I see is with His creating or ultimately causing all that we are and do and the claim that what we do is free from His determination.) However, this adoption picture, that our free will choices have some existence independent of God and were adopted by God within His universe, seems to leave God's not creating or causing everything contingent other than Himself and hence seems less simple than the traditional monotheistic view that God creates everything contingent other than Himself.

4 Divine Free Will and Information Content

So far I have implicitly assumed that God Himself truly has libertarian free will and can do whatever is not logically inconsistent (though I am arguing that it seems logically inconsistent for Him to create beings with libertarian free will, and, if so, that is truly impossible for Him). Sometimes it is assumed that if the laws of nature are fixed and if the initial conditions or quantum state are also fixed, then even God would not be free to make things otherwise. For example, when the Hartle – Hawking "no-boundary" proposal for the quantum state of the cosmos [49, 50] was first proposed, I was defending it at a small gathering of quantum cosmologists [51], and the late Bryce DeWitt, often considered the father of quantum cosmology, objected, "You don't want to give God any freedom at all!" But before I could think of an answer, Karel Kuchař responded, "But that's His choice." In other words, even if we correctly deduced the quantum state of the universe, it would have been God's choice to create the universe in that state. That is, God's determining the universe to be in a particular deterministic state would not contradict His free will in making this determination, though it would seemingly preclude the independent free will of any creatures created by God in this state.

However, there is a strand of traditional monotheistic thought, going back at least to Anselm [52], that God Himself is a necessary being. If that is interpreted to mean that God is an entirely necessary being, then even God has no free will. Furthermore, if the necessity of God includes all of His activity, such as His activity in creating the universe or multiverse, then the created universe or multiverse is also necessary and not contingent. Assuming that God indeed creates everything otherwise contingent other than Himself (e.g., leaving out the apparent logical possibility of other partially independent beings with independent free will, perhaps themselves contingent rather than necessary, that God might adopt within His creation without directly creating their free will choices), then the entirety of existence, what philosophers call *the World*, would be necessary [53].

However, it is not clear to me that God must be a completely necessary being. Anselm's ontological argument just seems to imply the necessary existence of the greatest necessary being, but if only tautologies such as mathematical theorems have necessary existence, then Anselm's proof would only imply that the greatest tautology necessarily exists, and not what one would traditionally interpret to be God. Therefore, it seems to me that, so far as we know, God and the universe might be at least somewhat contingent, not necessarily the way they actually are.

We might consider these various conceptual possibilities in terms of the information content of God. (I say "conceptual possibilities" to denote concepts that we are not sure are impossible, since if in fact God is a necessary being, then it is necessarily impossible for Him not to exist, and on the other hand, if in fact God is not a necessary being, then it is necessarily impossible for Him to have necessary existence. So one or the other of these "possibilities" presumably must be the case, and the other necessarily impossible rather than really being a "possibility," is such that we don't know for certain which is necessary and so may epistemically regard both as "conceptual possibilities." I suppose an atheist might also raise the conceptual possibilities not only that God might contingently not exist but also that God might necessarily not exist. I recall hearing this question being asked, perhaps without realizing the full philosophical content, by Lucy Hawking when she was quite young: "Is God impossible?")

If God were entirely necessary, He would have no information content, since the information content of an entity is the minimum that needs to be specified in order from that information to deduce fully the properties of the entity. On the other hand, if God were contingent but simple, He would have small but non-zero information content. And yet a third conceptual possibility is that God is contingent and irreducibly complex, having large information content.

5   The Complexity and Probability of God

This third conceptual possibility is what Richard Dawkins assumes in his popular book, *The God Delusion* [54]. For much of the book, Dawkins sounds like an Old Testament prophet railing against idolatry, except that he believes the worship of any God or gods is idolatrous. But the philosophical heart of his argument is chapter 4, where he argues against the existence of God by saying that God would have to be extremely complex. Since his arguments are not very tightly stated, I formulated the heart of Dawkins' argument as a syllogism and then, with the help of an email exchange with several colleagues, especially William Lane Craig, I revised it to the following form:

(1)   A more complex world is less probable than a simpler world.
(2)   A world with God is more complex than a world without God.
(3)   Therefore a world with God is less probable than a world without God.

After circulating this form, I did get the obviously hurried reply from Dawkins: "Your three steps seem to me to be valid [sic]. Richard Dawkins" (Feb. 1 2007).

Now that I have summarized Dawkins' basic argument in a brief form that he seems to agree with, *modulo* typos, one can ask whether Dawkins is right. The conclusion of the syllogism seems to follow from the two premises (or at least I have intended this to be the case), so it is a question of whether the premises are correct.

One might question whether complexity is improbable, an unproved assumption. There is also the fact that complexity depends on background knowledge and may be only subjective. For example, David Deutsch [55] has emphasized to me that

> complexity cannot possibly have a meaning independent of the laws of physics. ... If God is the author of the laws of physics (or of an overarching system under which many sets of laws of physics are instantiated – it doesn't matter) then it is exclusively God's decision how complex anything is, including himself. There neither the idea that the world is 'more complex' if it includes God, nor the idea that God might be the 'simplest' omnipotent being makes sense.

This argument makes sense to me, but it did have the effect of shaking my fundamentalist physicist faith in the simplicity of the laws of nature. However, more recently Deutsch has pointed out [56] that these considerations do not mean that the concept of the simplicity of the laws of physics is circular: "I don't think it's circular, because the fact that simplicity is determined by the laws of physics does not mean that all possible laws are 'simple' in their own terms." So I suppose one might still ask whether in a universe apparently governed by simple laws of physics, God appears to be simple. However, since as Deutsch notes, God could have made Himself appear to have arbitrary complexity, it is a bit dubious to say that His probability is determined by His complexity.

Nevertheless, since we scientists (and indeed most others) prefer hypotheses that are ultimately simple, we might for the sake of argument grant the first premise I have ascribed to Dawkins and ask whether the second premise is correct. Again Deutsch's comments should lead us to be cautious in drawing such conclusions. However, even if we take the naïve view that one can define the complexity of God (say with respect to the laws of physics in our universe), then it is still not obvious that God is complex, or that He would add complexity to the world. Perhaps God is indeed simple [57].

If God were necessary, then He would have no complexity at all. Even if God were contingent, He might be simple. For example, perhaps God is the best possible being (assuming sufficient background knowledge that this apparently simple definition uniquely specifies some possible entity, though it is certainly unclear that our background knowledge within this universe is sufficient for this). Even if it is not necessary for such a God to exist, He might be simple (if simplicity can indeed be defined).

Even if one concedes that the philosophical idea of God might be simple, there is the question of whether God is simple in traditional monotheism. At first sight, the God of the Bible and of the Koran seems complex. But analogously, Earth's biosphere seems complex. However, the full set of biospheres arising by evolution in a huge universe or multiverse with simple laws of physics might be simple. Similarly, the limited aspects we experience of God might be complex, but the entirety of God might be simple.

6 The Problem of Evil and Elegance

Perhaps the most severe problem of traditional theism is the problem of evil. If God is the best possible being and created everything, why does evil exist? If instead of being totally created and determined by God, we were adopted and bring in evil by our own free will choices this might explain human evil, but one would still have the problem of natural evil: disease, earthquakes, storms, floods, and other evils not caused by humans. So whereas human free will is often invoked to solve the problem of evil, it does not seem to give a full solution, and therefore I do not regard the problem of evil as sufficient for me to give up my simple hypothesis that God created and determined everything contingent other than Himself.

Perhaps because I independently stumbled upon it myself, though many years later, I regard the best tentative solution for the problem of evil to be the multiverse theodicy [58, 59, 60, 61, 62, 63, 64, 65, 66, 67, 68, 69, 70, 71, 72] that God created all universes that are better to exist than not to exist. So rather than God's just creating one or more universes that have no evil, one might imagine that God thought it better to create all universes that are better to exist than not to exist. In other words, instead of minimizing evil by avoiding creating any universes with evil, God might be seeking to maximize the net good over evil. Therefore, instead of leaving our universe uncreated because it has evil in it as well as good,

God might have seen that it has more good than evil and decided that it would be better to exist than not to exist.

I would think that it is certainly common to make analogous judgments about the existence of persons rather than of universes. For example, I have certainly done evil and hurt other people. Yet I still feel that it is better for me to exist than not to exist. I believe that it is the same for you and hope that you feel similarly, that it is indeed better for you to exist than not to exist. If an entity has good that is accompanied by a lesser amount of evil, then it indeed seems better for that entity to exist, rather than that all evil be eliminated.

For me, particularly as one who has worked with and lived with the wheelchair-bound Stephen Hawking, one of the most horrific scenes in the movie *The Pianist* was when the Nazis entered a Jewish apartment in Warsaw and ordered the people sitting around the table to stand. An elderly man in a wheelchair could not comply, so the Nazis then heaved him out the third floor window to his death on the street below. In realizing that the inhuman Nazis were not actually non-human but exhibited some of the same sinful tendencies that I see in myself, it occurred to me that perhaps in their twisted minds they were trying to eliminate what they saw as evil, disabilities and weaknesses. Without endorsing the Nazis' ideas of what is good and evil, which were also quite distorted, I would indeed be sympathetic to efforts to reduce disabilities and weaknesses in a person, with his or her consent, while also working to enhance the good that the person has. However, the Nazis' procedure of cruelly eliminating entire persons and communities that they saw as having evils or weaknesses (or often just differences from themselves) was barbaric and totally unjustified. Perhaps analogously, we should not expect God to eliminate (or avoid creating) entire universes that have both good and evil in them.

Now although I do believe that the many-universes solution to the problem of evil is the best one I have heard of, I also think that so far it has not completely solved the problem. With this solution, one might expect that if our universe is a typical one with more good than evil, it would not have enormously more good than evil. That is certainly consistent with my general impression as a human of the moral goodness and evil on the Earth. However, if one applies the same idea to the elegance of the laws of physics as another good that God might be seeking to promote, one might expect that the laws of physics of our universe would have more elegance than ugliness, but not enormously more. On the other hand, my impression as a scientist is that the laws of physics are enormously more elegant than ugly, so it seems doubtful that God created all universes with just more elegance than ugliness in the natural laws.

In other words, for me the problem of evil (which might be explained by having God create all universes better to exist than not) has been replaced by the problem of elegance (why on the level of the beauty of the laws of nature our universe seems enormously more elegant than ugly). Another expression of the problem is the question of why God seems to have so much higher standards of mathematical elegance (not allowing our universe much mathematical ugliness) than of moral good and evil (apparently permitting a much higher ratio of moral evil to good).

7 Conclusions

Challenges to theism go back to one of the oldest books of the Bible, the Book of Job, whose lead character wrestled with the problem of evil that was basically left unexplained to him.

As finite beings, like Job we should not expect to understand everything, though it is good to seek as much understanding as possible. We can wrestle with the problems, but in the end we have to live life with the limited knowledge that we do have.

In summary, theism and science generally support each other, though there are occasionally conflicts. Everlasting life has raised a puzzle for me. Human and/or divine free will are also puzzling. Whether God is seen as probable or improbable depends on one's assumptions. The problem of evil may be reformulated as the problem of elegance.

Let me close with an aphorism that I coined to summarize my thoughts as a scientist and as a Christian:

> Science reveals the intelligence of the universe; the Bible reveals the Intelligence behind the universe.

Acknowledgments

I am indebted to discussions with Andreas Albrecht, Denis Alexander, Stephen Barr, John Barrow, Nick Bostrom, Raphael Bousso, Andrew Briggs, Peter Bussey, Bernard Carr, Sean Carroll, Brandon Carter, Kelly James Clark, Gerald Cleaver, Francis Collins, Robin Collins, Gary Colwell, William Lane Craig, Paul Davies, Richard Dawkins, William Dembski, David Deutsch, the late Bryce DeWitt, Michael Douglas, George Ellis, Debra Fisher, Charles Don Geilker, Gary Gibbons, J. Richard Gott, Thomas Greenlee, Alan Guth, James Hartle, Stephen Hawking, Rodney Holder, Chris Isham, Werner Israel, Renata Kallosh, Klaas Kraay, Karel Kucha˘r, Denis Lamoureux, John Leslie, Andrei Linde, Robert Mann, Don Marolf, Alister Mc-Grath, Ernan McMullin, Gerard Nienhuis, Andrew Page, Cathy Page, John Page, Gary Patterson, Alvin Plantinga, Chris Polachic, John Polkinghorne, Martin Rees, Hugh Ross, Henry F. Schaefer III, Paul Shellard, James Sinclair, Lee Smolin, Mark Srednicki, Mel Stewart, Jonathan Strand, Leonard Susskind, Richard Swinburne, Max Tegmark, Donald Turner, Neil Turok, Bill Unruh, Alex Vilenkin, Steven Weinberg, Robert White, and others whom I don't recall right now, on various aspects of these general issues, though the opinions expressed herein are my own. I particularly thank Klaas Kraay for providing me with many references on multiverse theodicies. My scientific research on the multiverse is supported in part by the Natural Sciences and Research Council of Canada.

References

[1]   Reijer Hooykaas, *Religion and the Rise of Modern Science* (Vancouver, Canada: Regent College Publishing, 2000).

[2]   This and all other Scripture taken from the New King James Version. © 1982 by Thomas Nelson, Inc. Used by permission. All rights reserved.

[3]   Ernan McMullin (ed.), *The Church and Galileo* (Notre Dame, IN: University of Notre Dame Press, 2005); Ernan McMullin (private communication).

[4]   Don N. Page, Does God So Love the Multiverse? chapter 29, this volume. Also at: arxiv:0801.0246;<http://arxiv.org/abs/0801.0246>.

[5]   Brandon Carter, "The anthropic principle and its implications for biological evolution," *Philosophical Transactions of the Royal Society of London* A310 (1983), 347–63.

[6]   John Leslie, *Universes* (London and New York: Routledge, 1989), p. 214.

[7]   Holger B. Nielsen, "Random dynamics and relations between the number of fermion genera-
      tions and the fine-structure constants," *Acta Physica Polonica* B20 (1989), 427–68.

[8]   John Leslie, "Time and the anthropic principle," *Mind* 101 (1992), 521–40.

[9]   J. Richard Gott III, "Implications of the Copernican principle for our future- prospects," *Nature*
      363 (27 May 1993), 315–19.

[10] John Leslie, *The End of the World: The Science and Ethics of Human Extinction* (London and
      New York: Routledge, 1996).

[11] Don N. Page, "Is our universe likely to decay within 20 billion years?" hepth/0610079;<http://
      arxiv.org/abs/hep-th/0610079>.

[12] Don N. Page, "Return of the Boltzmann Brains," hep-th/0611158; <http://arxiv.org/abs/
      hep-th/0611158>.

[13] Don N. Page, "Is our universe decaying at an astronomical rate?" hep-th/0612137; <http://
      arxiv.org/abs/hep-th/0612137>.

[14] Andreas Albrecht and Lorenzo Sorbo, "Can the Universe Afford Inflation?" *Physical Review*
      D70 , 063528 (2004), hep-th/0405270; <http://arxiv.org/abs/hep-th/0405270>.

[15] Ludwig Boltzmann, "On certain questions of the theory of gases," *Nature* 51 (1985), 413–15;
      for a pdf file online, see <http://cosmicvariance.com/2007/05/04/a-glimpse-into-boltzmanns-
      actualbrain/>.

[16] Raphael Bousso and Ben Freivogel, "A paradox in the global description of the multiverse,"
      Journal of High Energy Physics 0706 , 018 (2007), hep-th/0610132; <http://arxiv.org/abs/hep-
      th/0610132>.

[17] Don N. Page, "Susskind's challenge to the Hartle – Hawking no-boundary proposal and pos-
      sible resolutions," *Journal of Cosmology and Astroparticle Physics* 0701, 004 (2007), hep-
      th/0610199 <http://arxiv.org/abs/hepth/ 0610199>.

[18] Raphael Bousso, "Precision cosmology and the landscape," presented at Amazing Light: Visions
      for Discovery: An International Symposium in Honor of the 90th Birthday Years of Charles H.
      Townes, Berkeley, California, 6–8 Oct. 2005, hep-th/0610211;<http://arxiv.org/abs/hep-
      th/0610211>.

[19] Andrei Linde, "Sinks in the landscape, Boltzmann Brains, and the cosmological constant prob-
      lem," *Journal of Cosmology and Astroparticle Physics* 0701, 022 (2007), hep-th/0611043; <http://
      arxiv.org/abs/hep-th/0611043>.

[20] Alexander Vilenkin, "Freak observers and the measure of the multiverse," *Journal of High
      Energy Physics* 0701, 092 (2007), hep-th/0611271; <http://arxiv.org/abs/hep-th/0611271>.

[21] Lee Smolin, "The status of cosmological natural selection," hep-th/0612185; <http://arxiv.org/
      abs/hep-th/0612185>.

[22] Don N. Page, "Boundary conditions and predictions of quantum cosmology," invited talk at
      11th Marcel Grossmann Meeting on Recent Developments in Theoretical and Experimental
      General Relativity, Gravitation, and Relativistic Field Theories, Berlin, Germany, 23–29 Jul
      2006, hep-th/0612194; <http://arxiv.org/abs/hep-th/0612194>.

[23] Vitaly Vanchurin, "Geodesic measures of the landscape," *Physical Review* D75, 023524 (2007),
      hep-th/0612215; <http://arxiv.org/abs/hepth/0612215>.

[24] Tom Banks, "Entropy and initial conditions in cosmology," hep-th/0701146; <http://arxiv.org/
      abs/hep-th/0701146>.

[25] Steven Carlip, "Transient observers and variable constants, or repelling the invasion of the
      Boltzmann's Brains," *Journal of Cosmology and Astroparticle Physics* 0706, 001(2007), hep-th/
      0703115; <http://arxiv.org/abs/hepth/0703115>.

[26] Max Tegmark, "The mathematical universe," to be published in *Foundations of Physics*,
      arxiv:0704.0646 <http://arxiv.org/abs/0704.0646>.

[27] James B. Hartle and Mark Srednicki, "AreWe Typical?" *Physical Review* D75, 123523 (2007),
      arxiv:0704.2630; <http://arxiv.org/abs/0704.2630>.

[28] Steven B. Giddings and Donald Marolf, "A global picture of quantum de Sitter space," *Physical
      Review* D76, 064023 (2007), arxiv:0705.1178; <http://arxiv.org/abs/0705.1178>.

[29] Steven B. Giddings, "Black holes, information, and locality," arxiv:0705.2197; <http://arxiv.org/abs/0705.2197>.

[30] Artyom V. Yurov, Artyom V. Astashenok, and Pedro F. Gonzalez-Diaz, "Astronomical bounds on future big freeze singularity," arxiv:0705.4108; <http://arxiv.org/abs/0705.4108>.

[31] Brett McInnes, "Good babies vs. bad babies; or, inheriting the arrow of time," arxiv:0705.4141; <http://arxiv.org/abs/0705.4141>.

[32] Don N. Page, "No-Bang quantum state of the cosmos," arxiv:0707.2081; <http://arxiv.org/abs/0707.2081>.

[33] Don N. Page, "Typicality defended," arxiv:0707.4169; <http://arxiv.org/abs/0707.4169>.

[34] Andreas Albrecht and Alberto Iglesias, "The clock ambiguity and the emergence of physical laws," arxiv:0708.2743; <http://arxiv.org/abs/0708.2743>.

[35] Miao Li and Yi Wang, "Typicality, freak observers and the anthropic principle of existence," arxiv:0708.4077; <http://arxiv.org/abs/0708.4077>.

[36] Raphael Bousso, "TASI lectures on the cosmological constant," arxiv:0708.4231;<http://arxiv.org/abs/0708.4077>.

[37] Brett McInnes, "The arrow of time in the landscape," arxiv:0711.1656; <http://arxiv.org/abs/0711.1656>.

[38] Anthony Aguirre, "Eternal inflation, past and future," arxiv:0712.0571; <http://arxiv.org/abs/0712.0571>.

[39] John D. Barrow and Douglas J. Shaw, "Some late-time asymptotics of general scalar-tensor cosmologies," arxiv:0712.2190; <http://arxiv.org/abs/0712.2190>.

[40] Don N. Page, "Observational selection effects in quantum cosmology," arxiv:0712.2240;<http://arxiv.org/abs/0712.2240>.

[41] Raphael Bousso, Ben Freivogel, and I-Sheng Yang, "Boltzmann babies in the proper time measure," arxiv:0712.3324; <http://arxiv.org/abs/0712.3324>.

[42] Fred Hoyle, *The Black Cloud* (Cutchogue, NY: Buccaneer Books, 1992).

[43] Don N. Page, "Sensible quantum mechanics: are only perceptions probabilistic?", quant-ph/9506010; <http://arxiv.org/abs/quant-ph/9506010>.

[44] Don N. Page, "Sensible quantum mechanics: are probabilities only in the mind?" *International Journal of Modern Physics* D5, 583–596 (1996), grqc/9507024; <http://arxiv.org/abs/gr-qc/9507024>.

[45] Nick Bostrom, *Anthropic Bias: Observation Selection Effects in Science and Philosophy* (New York and London: Routledge, 2002).

[46] Don N. Page, "Mindless sensationalism: a quantum framework for consciousness," in Quentin Smith and Aleksandar Jokic (eds.), *Consciousness: New Philosophical Perspectives* (Oxford: Clarendon Press, 2003), pp. 468–506, quantph/0108039; <http://arxiv.org/abs/quant-ph/0108039>.

[47] Brandon Carter (private communication).

[48] John Leslie (private communication).

[49] Stephen W. Hawking, "The boundary conditions of the universe," in H. A. Brück, G. V. Coyne, and M. S. Longair (eds.), *Astrophysical Cosmology: Proceedings of the Study Week on Cosmology and Fundamental Physics*, Sept. 28–Oct. 2, 1981 (Vatican City: Pontificiae Academiae Scientiarum Scripta Varia, 1982).

[50] Stephen W. Hawking and James B. Hartle, "Wave function of the universe," *Physical Review* D28, 2960–2975 (1983).

[51] Don N. Page, "Hawking's timely story," *Nature* 332, 742–3 (1988).

[52] Anselm of Canterbury, "Proslogion," in Sidney N. Deane, *St. Anselm: Basic Writings*, trans. Sidney D. Deane (Chicago: Open Court, 1962).

[53] Jonathan Strand (private communication) drew my attention to Klaas Kraay, "Theism and modal collapse" at <http://www.ryerson.ca/_kraay/>, which comes to similar conclusions from slightly different assumptions.

[54] Richard Dawkins, *The God Delusion* (Boston: Houghton Mifflin, 2006).

[55] David Deutsch (private communication, Jan. 22, 2007).

[56]   David Deutsch (private communication, Sept. 29, 2007).

[57]   Richard Swinburne, *The Existence of God* (Oxford: Clarendon Press, 1991).

[58]   R. Adams, "Must God create the best?" *Philosophical Review* 81 (1972), 317–32.

[59]   J. D. McHarry, "A theodicy," *Analysis* 38 (1978), 132–4.

[60]   R. K. Perkins, "McHarry's theodicy: A reply," *Analysis* 40 (1980), 168–71.

[61]   P. Forrest, "The problem of evil: Two neglected defences," *Sophia* 20 (1981), 49–54.

[62]   Keith Ward, *Rational Theology and the Creativity of God* (New York: Pilgrim Press, 1982).

[63]   Melville Y. Stewart, "*O felix culpa*, redemption, and the greater-good defense," *Sophia* 25 (1986), 18–31.

[64]   M. J. Coughlan, "Must God create only the best possible world?" *Sophia* 26 (1987), 15–19.

[65]   John Leslie, *Universes* (London and New York: Routledge, 1989).

[66]   Melville Y. Stewart, *The Greater Good Defence: An Essay on the Rationality of Faith* (London and New York: Macmillan and St. Martin's Press, 1993).

[67]   P. Forrest, *God Without the Supernatural: A Defense of Scientific Theism* (Ithaca, NY: Cornell University Press, 1996).

[68]   John Leslie, *Infinite Minds* (Oxford: Clarendon Press, 2001).

[69]   Donald Turner, "The many-universes solution to the problem of evil," in Richard M. Gale and Alexander R. Pruss (eds.), *The Existence of God* (Aldershot, UK: Ashgate, 2003), pp. 143–59.

[70]   P. Draper, "Cosmic fine-tuning and terrestrial suffering: Parallel problems for naturalism and theism," *American Philosophical Quarterly* 41, 311–321.

[71]   H. Hudson, *The Metaphysics of Hyperspace* (Oxford: Oxford University Press, 2006).

[72]   Klaas Kraay, "Theism and the multiverse," <http://www.ryerson.ca/_kraay/>.

Part 11

Science Under Stress in the Twentieth Century: Lessons from the Case of Early Nuclear Physics

Part II

31

The Copenhagen Spirit of Science and Birth of the Nuclear Atom

RICHARD PETERSON

Nurtured in the shadows of Søren Kierkegaard and Harald Høffding, the deeply philosophical Niels Bohr led fellow workers toward a sub-nuclear, atomic, and molecular foundation for modern science that is based on complementarity – yet still anchored solidly in the real world. Starting with the experimental mentorship of Rutherford, we trace the Copenhagen impact on quantum mechanics, neutron physics, and fission, and Bohr's engaging approach for doing science while inspiring experimental and theoretical teamwork on an international scale. The chapter concludes with the aftermath of Lise Meitner and Otto Frisch deliberations on the mechanism of nuclear fission in the woods near the little Swedish town of Kungälv.

1 Background

As an experimental physicist who is perhaps most at home in the optics laboratory (enjoying holographic and interferometric measurements in acoustics, surface metrology, plasma physics, and fluids), I step with both fear and some anticipation into this more philosophical arena that surely draws on the interplay of the process of science and worldview foundational values of those who practice it. More than most of the speakers in this series I have also worked closely for many years with those who passionately teach physics at all levels (high school through graduate school), and consequently I will sometimes encourage us to ponder how these foundational issues might impact how we can best interact with our students. For 30 years I have taught undergraduate students about the history of nuclear physics and nuclear weapons in the twentieth century, and it is that experience which especially motivates these chapters. These historically based courses have been replete with issues involving the foundational values of the scientists and their worldviews, the quest for sound and personally affirming ethical decisions, and an observation of the scientific establishment sometimes uneasily plodding forward – even in difficult times for international consensus. Liberal arts students (e.g., business, arts, and humanities, social science, along with science and engineering students) often find this intimate and rather human view of science and technology most revealing.

I assume my readers have very diverse backgrounds in science, history, religion, and philosophy, and I will *not* assume a familiarity with nuclear or atomic physics. Because I am not a philosopher or historian of science (nor a nuclear physicist), my comments will necessarily be quite "down to earth," yet my underlying goal is to still take you at least momentarily into one period of science history where some human frailties, triumphs, and insecurities have been laid bare. We will consider what underlying human values have served to guide and motivate science and its world leaders in such situations.

I trust the examples of this venture into one brief period of scientific history may serve to bring us closer to how the process of science functions in actuality, and it may take us momentarily away from abstractions to existence in the twentieth century – at least in the lives of a few scientists. And ultimately I want all of us to try to put ourselves in the shoes of those who faced these tough and turbulent times and consider how our own worldviews would fare in providing personalized responses to the situations, pressing questions and dilemmas that have been encountered in the previous century.

2 A Motivating Mentorship during a Paradigm Shift – Rutherford and Bohr (1911–16)

Following the discovery of natural radioactivity by Henri Becquerel and the isolation and concentration of radioactive materials by Marie and Pierre Curie, it largely fell to British Ernest Rutherford to work with colleagues in England and Canada to further study the alpha and beta radiations coming from elements as they are transmuted into other forms of matter. In chapter 2 of Richard Rhodes', *Making of the Atomic Bomb* (*MAB*) [1] we are introduced in some detail to the clever experiments of this brilliant, but practical experimenter who clearly sets the pace within early experimental nuclear physics. After foundational nuclear transmutation work with Frederick Soddy at McGill University, Rutherford responded to the opportunity to return to England at Manchester University, and it was at Manchester where he led a most famous experiment. Using a collimated beam of positive alpha particles, he worked with Ernest Marsden and Hans Geiger to collide this beam with a very thin gold foil, and upon careful and patient observation of scattered particles from the foil, they concluded that a few of them had been scattered through large angles after encountering a massive but tiny nucleus of positive charge. Yet the stability of any so-called nuclear atom model thus suggested appeared inconsistent with classical physics, as any "orbiting" charged electrons about the nucleus would quickly radiate their energy.

Science can find the most confidence and relative stability within a time of revolutionary change as it strives to network individuals of differing perspectives and abilities while working toward a consensus within this introspective and critical community. As Hungarian philosopher of science and chemist Michael Polanyi is quoted by Rhodes (*MAB*, ch. 2),

> This network is the seat of scientific opinion, of an opinion which is not held by any single human brain, but which, split into thousands of different fragments, is held by a multitude of individuals, each of whom endorses the other's opinion at second hand, by relying on the consensual chains which link him to all the others through a sequence of overlapping neighborhoods.

And Richard Rhodes goes on to summarize: "Science, Polanyi was hinting, worked like a giant brain of individual intelligences linked together. That was the source of its inexorable power."

Thus it seems most fortunate that shortly after Marsden's result showing alpha particles scattering and reflecting off gold atoms, the very young and theoretically inclined Danish physicist Niels Bohr makes the transition from Copenhagen to Cambridge and then to Rutherford's now renowned experimental fiefdom at the University of Manchester.

Anyone who seeks to "light fires" [2] within the context of undergraduate or graduate level teaching, can hardly help but ask why this Manchester environment so effectively nurtured the leap of faith that birthed the "Bohr atom" – a very revolutionary construct, while the model still daringly and creatively built on the earlier quantum ideas of Planck and Einstein [MAB, Ch. 3]. This nuclear Bohr atom becomes a crucial early "stepping-stone" toward the maturing of a much more sophisticated "full-blown" quantum mechanics in the late 1920s and the blossoming of nuclear physics in the 1930s.

So why did Rutherford's Manchester environment work so well in bringing out the first manifestation of genius in the young Bohr? On the surface the down-to-earth and practical minded New Zealand "farm boy" Rutherford could not have seemed more different than the cultured Bohr, who was raised in an intellectual and philosophical home where Søren Kierkegaard's ideas would often have been discussed with their close family friend and philosophy professor, Harald Høffding – and in the shadows of Bohr's father, Christian, a very highly respected Copenhagen professor of physiology. And as is pointed out in Chapter 7 of Abraham Pais' "Niels Bohr's Times" (NBT), it is not that Rutherford immediately gave this intensely philosophical young theoretician the most inspiring task, but rather his patience and wise leadership in enthusiastically supporting Bohr's request to largely stay away from the lab and work on theory – first on alpha-ray penetration of matter and eventually (five years after the initial work of Marsden and Geiger) his three published papers of 1913 on a revolutionary model of atomic matter. Surely the time was right for this early work of Bohr. Yet it also seems it was the classic scientific spirit of Rutherford - his endless enthusiasm and optimism, willingness to work extremely hard with his young colleagues, and "no nonsense" common sense that most impressed, inspired, and motivated the young Dane. And the spirit of this mentorship appears to "stick" with Bohr, as Pais remarks (NBT, p. 129) in quoting Rutherford's collaborator Andrade,

> Nor would those who later worked in Bohr's institute fail to recognize his own style in what another collaborator has written about Rutherford: "Although there was no doubt as to who was boss, everybody said what he liked without constraint.... He was always full of fire and infectious enthusiasm when describing work into which he had put his heart and always generous in his acknowledgement of the work of others."

It is well to note that seldom is revolutionary science done without such an enterprising and highly motivated spirit. The sources of such motivation are legion – but are often grounded in a passionate, deep curiosity about nature, sometimes a quest for human recognition and practical impact (or tenure!), and for many scientists the drive may involve a religious foundation that especially celebrates the study and analysis of all aspects of the universe. It is unfortunately not uncommon for those who teach the sciences and mentor future scientists to almost ignore such underlying motivations, while concentrating only on the difficult and important concepts that drive their particular discipline.

3 Complementarity Rises from a Maturing Quantum Mechanics (1926–8)

Much has been written (including in this volume) regarding the development of a maturing quantum mechanics in the late 1920s. Especially to be noted are the elegant mathematical formalism of Werner Heisenberg, the wave mechanics of Erwin Schrödinger (and Max Born's statistical interpretation of the wave function), and Bohr's growing emphasis on the philosophical basis of complementarity – especially in relating the foundations of this dizzying new science to classical physics. I would like here to only summarize some physics and philosophical implications of this rather broad idea and briefly consider some personal reflections of a close colleague of Bohr.

The heart of physical science complementarity in the late 1920s resulted from the wave particle behavior of particles (like electrons) or photons (comprising a beam of light), as Heisenberg's formation of the uncertainty principle quantified the ultimate limitations on specifying the position or momentum within particle/wave phenomena. And Bohr went so far as to clearly define any "phenomenon" itself as inseparable from the experiment being used in the observation process. Thus we find a sharp observation of the momentum of an electron to exclude an arbitrarily precise measurement of its position, and we say that these two physical properties are inherently complementary to each other. Similarly, detail of the exact quantum state of a hydrogen atom is lost as it is studied by an apparatus that would locate its electron – yet the original eigenstate may again be restored as the atom becomes sufficiently isolated for a time.

While a fiercely intense and perseverant thinker who often depended on brilliant young colleagues for a "sounding board," Bohr seemed to find complementarity a naturally useful perspective while intellectually working toward the best description possible for phenomena, situation, or even an ethical dilemma. For example he is often said to have suggested the complementarity between *Klarheit* (clarity) and *Wahrheit* (truth) in dealing with all aspects of life. Indeed in his chapter in the *Niels Bohr Centenary Volume* [3] entitled, "Niels Bohr, the Quantum, and the World," Victor Weisskopf suggests that this is why Bohr was such a notoriously confusing lecturer, as the many cross-connections of ideas covered would continuously bubble up during his all-too-thoughtful and personally reflective presentations. Even in his pondering of the ethics of work on the atomic bomb (see chapter 32), Bohr insisted and convinced others that they should consider the complementary perspectives of a tragically destructive and cruel weapon versus the need to actually use it to convince nations that it must make war impossible and bring lasting peace and international controls.

Pais reminds us in his chapter, "We are suspended in Language" (*NBT*, chapter 19) that Bohr considered the goal of scientific writing to express as best possible "what we can say about nature." Bohr continually struggled with draft after draft of papers and was observed to spend more time on words than equations in many cases. Following many conversations with Bohr, Pais strongly suggests that most of Bohr's philosophical positions were driven by his struggles in physics and not by formal training in philosophy. On the other hand Bohr wrote of his admiration for the writing and presentation of Kierkegaard – at the same time stating he could not accept some of it. Part of this may have followed from Kierkegaard being a very avowed, yet rather circuitous proponent of a costly Christian faith, while after a youth of confirming faith Bohr himself was a non-believer. One can't help but observe however that Bohr's frustration with the limits of language were closely shared by the nineteenth-century Danish hero Kierkegaard and would have been an assumed background in the philosophical household of the young Bohr. Rhodes in his Bohr *Tvi* chapter of *MAB*, makes the case for a considerable (even if unconscious) philosophical impact on the young Bohr as he seemed to struggle with issues of multiple identities and doubt. Whether a direct or indirect cultural influence, Rhodes sees the likely impact of following the Danish philosophical lineage through Poul Martin Møller (author of Bohr's favorite novel, *The Adventures of a Danish Student*) to Kierkegaard (Møller's student) to family friend Høffding (Kierkegaard's early and strong proponent in Denmark) to Bohr himself. It is also clear that paradox remains a central theme in writings of Kierkegaard, and this could surely have led indirectly through this Danish cultural lineage to Bohr's beloved complementarity. In Frederick Sontag's *Kierkegaard Handbook* [4] we read in the chapter on "Paradox/Passion" – what might be seem to be an intellectual cornerstone for Bohr,

> Almost anyone who knows anything about Søren Kierkegaard knows that he loved to stress the inevitability of paradox… In the first place, we will be poorer if we eliminate all paradox, since paradox is the pathos of the intellectual life. Ordinary people may live simple lives, but great thinkers are exposed to paradoxes …

In *The Privilege of Being a Physicist* [5], an early and close younger colleague of Bohr, MIT's late professor Victor Weisskopf, suggests additional cases where a complementary relationship surely exists in our lives. In a chapter entitled, "Art and Science," he first conveys the fundamental, yet complementary, differences between science and art – and then also science and religion.

> This difference has very much in common with Niels Bohr's complementarity …. The scientific approach to a phenomenon is complementary to the artistic approach. The artistic experience evanesces when the phenomena are scientifically explored, just as the quantum state is temporarily destroyed when the position of a particle is observed. We cannot at the same time experience the artistic content of a Beethoven sonata and also worry about the neurophysiological processes in our brains. But we can shift from one to another …. Both aspects are necessary to get at the full reality of the phenomenon …
>
> A similar complementarity characterizes science and religion or myth. Religious approaches to human experiences are contradictory to the scientific one only in a superficial way … Jean Hamburger expresses the complementary situation succinctly in his book, *La Raison et la Passion*. "We must accept the idea that man can acquire all kinds of truths. But let us not mix them up; we would risk that the mixture would dissolve them all."
>
> The decay of previously existing sources for meaning, sense, and purpose – such as myth and religion – has left a great void in our minds, a void that craves to be filled. Every human being craves meaning and sense to his existence. The answers to these cravings must, by necessity, be holistic.

As Weisskopf well knew, an analogous quest for a holistic approach to the atom (both classical and quantum) was the driving force for Bohr in developing his complementarity emphasis. And in many classic religious writings the quest for wholeness brings one clearly into the world of complementarity and apparent paradox. For example, in the well-known prayer of St Francis, its conclusion reminds us, "for it is in giving that we receive, it is in pardoning that we are pardoned, and it is in dying that we are born to eternal life."

4 Basic to Applied Physics: A Conversation
in the Kungälv Woods (1938)

Bohr deeply influenced the basic early physics of the nucleus, even in the midst of the evolution of quantum mechanics (QM) in the 1920s – including an application of QM to the process of alpha decay, the formation of a liquid drop nuclear model by George Gamow (at Copenhagen), and working with Pauli and others on what is happening with beta decay. But nuclear physics really blossomed in the 1930s, particularly as stimulated by James Chadwick's 1932 discovery of the neutron – and the nearly simultaneous "invention" of experimental hardware like mass spectrometers and cyclotrons that made measurements and perturbations of the atom's nucleus rather commonplace at centers for nuclear physics and chemistry (see "Machines" in *MAB*). The neutron becomes such a powerful tool, since it is not repelled by the positive nucleus electrically and is found to make the triggering of nuclear transmutations much easier. Following the Nobel prize-winning work of Enrico Fermi's group in Rome (in the increasingly fascist Italy of 1934–6), it became apparent that a neutron striking and attaching to a nucleus will often initiate beta decay, a process in which one of the atom's neutrons may effectively be converted into a proton and an electron – with that electron becoming a beta particle, flying out of the nucleus with a velocity and kinetic energy. Thus it became almost "child's play" to produce and study a plethora of nuclear reactions and new artificially produced radioactive materials (*MAB*, ch. 8). Enrico, his Jewish wife Laura, and their children used the occasion of the Nobel award for an escape from Italy and made their way to New York. At about the same time, a widely respected nuclear physicist (Lise Meitner) and a nuclear chemist (Otto Hahn) teamed up as leaders at the Kaiser Wilhelm Institute for Chemistry at Dahlem, Germany – near Berlin – to take on the difficult task of trying to understand the process occurring when the most massive naturally occurring element (uranium) is struck by neutrons.

With the help of friends and on account of her Jewish roots, Meitner narrowly escaped Germany. She found a position in neutral Sweden with the assistance of Niels Bohr. But, by all accounts, she did not find welcome, comfort, or respect in the laboratory space of K. Manne Siegbahn, a Nobel laureate in X-ray spectroscopy – and she felt in exile, if not prison. Still, at Christmas time in 1938, Lise left Stockholm and traveled west across Sweden to share the holidays with her relatives near the small town of Kungälv that lies a few miles north of the western harbor of Göteborg. Her nephew Otto Frisch of the Bohr Institute also came from Copenhagen to join the family in Kungälv. Lise carried a fresh letter from Otto Hahn that would change history and open up the atomic age – but Hahn, a nuclear chemist, could not provide any plausible explanation for his strange, but well confirmed results. His letter reported to his primary physics advisor and friend that his German team had decisively found traces of the element barium after uranium had been irradiated with neutrons.

So Meitner and Frisch eventually sought the solitude of the Kungälv woods. They skied and walked in the snow across a stream and sought a log for a long talk in the Swedish forest. Eventually they reasoned what was normally believed impossible - was possible. Namely that energetically a large nucleus could indeed split into two fairly large chunks (like barium and krypton) – rather like a splitting liquid drop on a hot frying pan – if it were to accept an extra neutron that would initiate the split or fission. It became clear why uranium was the most massive naturally occurring element, since forces analogous to surface tension on a drop were not sufficient to hold large nuclei together. Meitner apparently had the necessary nuclear data in her head to rapidly calculate the energy that would be released in such a fission and how much mass would be converted into energy in the fission of just one nucleus. Frisch anxiously reported their speculation to Bohr upon return to Copenhagen on January 3, 1939 (*MAB*, p. 261), recalling "I had hardly begun to tell him, when he struck his forehead with his hand and exclaimed, 'Oh what idiots we have all been! Oh but this is wonderful! This is as it must be!'" As soon as possible the aunt and nephew composed a paper of the basic physics behind nuclear fission for *Nature*, while Hahn and Strassmann published their nuclear chemistry findings even faster in *Naturwissenschaften* on January 6, 1939. Niels Bohr left as planned immediately for a trip to the United States for conferences and work at Princeton's Center for Advanced Studies, and in spite of his caution, the word of the new discovery spread throughout the world. A few physicists departed from subsequent conferences quickly to return home so they could also check and observe the splitting of large nuclei.

And so it was that within a few weeks of this discovery and the Kungälv conversation, a blackboard in Robert Oppenheimer's office at Berkeley had a sketch of a crude bomb that could result if each fission were to yield the needed extra neutrons to keep the process building. And the always practical Enrico Fermi, now at Columbia University in New York, looked out his window over Manhattan Island. He cupped his hands is a softball size globe and said, "A little bomb like that, and it would all disappear" (*MAB*, p. 275). Thus the beautiful basic nuclear physics about which Bohr exclaimed, "this is wonderful!" would soon be drawn upon and applied by both sides in an explosive worldwide conflagration, and scientists over the globe would be under intense pressure to play a unique contributing role.

References

[1]   Richard Rhodes, *Making of the Atomic Bomb* (New York: Simon & Schuster, 1986). Abbreviated *MAB* here, this 880-page book plays the role of a primary reference for many sections of these presentations. This Pulitzer Prize-winning history on science, history, and human events during this period was written shortly after quite a bit of World War II material was declassified in the 1980s. Rhodes also wrote a major documentary book on the H-bomb and cold war era that followed World War II, *Dark Sun - The Making of the Hydrogen Bomb* (New York: Simon & Schuster, 1995). It was a 1996 Pulitzer Prize finalist.

[2]   Abraham Pais, "Niels Bohr's times," in *Physics, Philosophy, and Polity*, (Oxford: Clarendon Press, 1991). Abbreviated *NBT* in these writings. Pais followed his legendary biography of Einstein, *Subtle is the Lord*, with this warm and authoritative biography of Bohr. A review in the *American Journal of Physics* notes, "Pais has seemingly done the impossible; he has broached the irreconcilable combination of myth and humanity, and in the process he has contributed massively to the Bohr legend."

[3]   A. P. French and P. J. Kennedy, *Niels Bohr – A Centenary Volume* (Cambridge, MA: Harvard University Press, 1985). This beautifully edited volume included intimate and spirited sections by many who knew Bohr well and presents them largely in a chronological order. For these writings the entries by Weisskopf, Stuewer, Bethe, and Ruth Moore have been particularly helpful.

[4]   Michael Frayn, *Copenhagen* (London: Methuen, 2000; edition with extended postscript by Frayn). *Copenhagen* premiered in May 1998 at the Royal National Theatre, London, and in April 2000 at the Royale Theater, New York. Both productions were directed by Michael Blakemore.

[5]   Victor F. Weisskopf, *The Privilege of Being a Physicist* (New York: W. H. Freeman, 1989). Here a close colleague of Bohr and renowned professor of nuclear and high energy physics at MIT steps forward to discuss the ties between physics and several aspects of broader world culture. His insights on the complementarity between science and both art and religion are written with personal insight and conviction.

32

When Scientists Go to War

RICHARD PETERSON

Beset by the ethical imperatives and dilemmas of racism, fanatical dictatorships, weapons for mass civilian destruction, human egotism, and pride, the physicists still persevere to build a "gadget" that can shake the Earth and usher in a new perspective of warfare on a new and frightening scale. We will consider the pacifism of Einstein, the Quaker heritage of Robert R. Wilson, and the Christian Mennonite background of Arthur H. Compton as these internationally renowned physicists are confronted with the pressures of national survival and moral outrage. Can we say real "science" is being done when wartime censorship of work becomes the norm, and open publication among peers stops? Is there a legitimate case for scientific work on weapons designed for massive destruction of hundreds of thousands of civilians? This chapter will conclude with my own reflections on the responses of Los Alamos scientists in the aftermath of the first atomic bomb test.

1 Science and Scientists in Conflict – the Case of Bohr and Heisenberg

The word of nuclear fission spread quickly over the globe in the very troubled months of 1939. Not only would nearby nations soon be divided into warring camps, but consensus science itself would be seen to suffer and stall as nationalism and censorship quickly formed barriers between close friends and colleagues. Later 1939 saw the quick movement of German forces throughout Western Europe – first Austria and Czechoslovakia with little resistance, and then with the attack on Poland in September 1939 World War II is underway, with France and England pulled formally into the war on Septtember 3 (*MAB*, ch. 10 [1]).

A deeper understanding of nuclear fission in this period can still be seen as centering about Niels Bohr. An authoritatively detailed 25-page paper on fission was produced in Spring of 1939 during the extended visit of Bohr to Princeton and an intensive time of work with John Wheeler. This included the eventually confirmed hypothesis that the fission of uranium observed with slow neutrons was actually that of its rare isotope U-235 (with

92 protons and 143 neutrons) and not the naturally more plentiful U-238. This fission model was built upon the Bohr, Frisch, and Meitner extension of George Gamow's original liquid-drop model of the nucleus, combined with Bohr's long successful emphasis on a composite, compound nuclear interaction with incident particles – such as neutrons. In late 1939 Bohr also summarized and quantified the necessary conditions for the release of nuclear energy, as described in Roger Stuewer's chapter "Niels Bohr and Nuclear Physics" of the Bohr centenary volume [2].

That fall and winter Bohr also gave several lectures on nuclear fission. One, which he delivered in December before the Society for Dissemination of Natural Science in Copenhagen, was particularly memorable to those who heard it, because in it Bohr outlined the entire problem of how to liberate nuclear energy on a practical scale, including the ominous possibility of its use in a weapon of enormous destructive power.

Meanwhile at this time Columbia University in New York was blessed by the presence of some of the best nuclear experimentalists in the world – including Enrico Fermi, Herbert Anderson, and the always visionary Hungarian Leo Szilard. In addition Otto Frisch and others working in England had done approximate calculations of the amount of U-235 that might be needed to sustain a rapid, explosive chain reaction, and they came to the conclusion (eventually strongly conveyed in confidence to U.S. wartime science and technology leaders) that it really was technically feasible to design and build a bomb if U-235 could somehow be separated in multi-kilogram quantities from the more common U-238 isotope (*MAB*, ch. 11, 12). But it was known to be extremely difficult to separate isotopes with only slightly different masses.

Within months of the German sweep through Europe they were found to be occupying the area of Bohr's Institute in Copenhagen. Bohr and fellow workers tried to go on with their physics and some humanitarian efforts during the early months of this occupation, and it is to this discomforting scene that Bohr had a visit by his younger friend and quantum mechanics colleague Werner Heisenberg. Heisenberg's short visit to the Bohr home gave rise to the controversial and still debated conversation between these two famous physicists now found on opposing sides during the war – with Heisenberg becoming the leading German physicist during World War II.

First it should be recognized that Heisenberg has never been accused of being an enthusiastic Nazi; however some feel he did not sufficiently battle the wartime science/technology power structure of Germany, and without question he did in fact become the leader of a significant (but rather unsuccessful) German effort to make wartime progress toward fission energy release for military use. Niels Bohr of course was the half-Jewish dominant leader of the worldwide development of quantum and nuclear physics of the twentieth century, and he had worked actively to help many Jews escape from German areas of Europe and from Denmark into Sweden. So, as might be expected, this was to be an uncomfortable conversation that seemed to bring to a focus several ethical issues regarding the proper stance of scientists in such a difficult time.

What should be the highest goals of scientists in such a time? Heisenberg later claimed he came to Copenhagen to probe Bohr on the ethics of atomic bomb work, including a push toward a united front of physicists on each side to quietly agree to slow or stop fission bomb work. But clearly Bohr heard things quite differently or at least with very different intent – and the conversation did not go at all well. Bohr apparently learned with a fright that Heisenberg was indeed the head of an ambitious German bomb project and seemed to primarily hear Heisenberg telling him of considerable German progress under his leadership, and at the same time a petitioning to discourage Allied efforts. Others however note that Heisenberg at this time did not commonly address ethical issues with visits to other European laboratory leaders and spoke of the benefit of a presupposed future German dominance in Europe as opposed to that of the Soviets. And as shown in the release of a post-World War II unsent letter (written to Heisenberg by Bohr) by the Bohr family in 2002 [3], Bohr recalls clearly that Heisenberg came to the conversation with an assumption that the Germans would "win."

The complex and blurry history of this conversation was the backdrop for the play *Copenhagen* completed by British playwright Robert Frayn in 1998 [4]. The play had very successful runs in both London and New York during the 1998–2001 period and surely pushed the audience to awareness of some twentieth-century physics and to also consider the optimal course of action at such a time. Frayn builds on the complementarity of differing possible interpretations of the conversation, and different scenes of the play depict the ethical and historical implications of these "uncertain" options – as they might be juxtaposed in this analogy to parameters subject to Heisenberg's uncertainty principle.

It would appear that two well-known German Nobel prize recipients Werner Heisenberg (quantum theory) and Otto Hahn (nuclear chemistry discovery of fission) took it as their professional responsibilities to support the German frontline troops and their leaders with nuclear science. Some have argued that scientists in time of war belong to their country and have a professional duty to do so if they do not find fundamental ethical issues making it impossible. The argument is sometimes considered similar to that of a lawyer who takes on the responsibility to defend the accused [5]. Such an argument might stipulate that if one takes on the job of scientific and technological support, regardless of guilt or innocence of overall national efforts, your professional obligation is clear if troops can be assisted or kept alive by your actions. However if an individual sees foundational ethical difficulties in performing the scientific support duty, they should surely not sign up for the job – just as a lawyer may choose to not take on a case that would be inconsistent with his or her conscience. Eventually both Hahn and Heisenberg took criticism that they should have been willing to step forward in moral outrage for a known mass murderer. For example, Lise Meitner (see chapter 31), after the war wrote personally to her scientific colleague Hahn and accused Heisenberg and fellow-workers of all trying to take passive positions that indirectly contributed to the murder of millions of Jews. And I suspect that Bohr in the famous Copenhagen conversation may have hoped Heisenberg would come forward with at least a nuanced anti-Nazi stance and perhaps have secretly conveyed information that could help the Allied cause.

In terms of tough ethical decisions during this time, one can hardly help but also consider the stance and sustaining strength of German Christian pastor and theologian Dietrich Bonhoeffer as he consciously made the costly decision to return to Germany from New York at the onset of the war. While generally a strong supporter of pacifism, he still felt the evils of Nazi leadership (especially murdering millions of Jews) required him to speak out and act to "throw a spike" into the Nazi regime. With other collaborating members of his family, he was killed by hanging during Hitler's last days for participating in multiple plots on Hitler's life. Bonhoeffer believed that one's costly faith in God leaves really little choice but to respond when presented with a clear religious calling – even at the risk of death. And regardless of personal views of the justice of a particular war, it would be traditional belief of Christ's followers that one must be willing to sacrifice, work, and identify with those who suffer at the hands of a ruthless power structure. Many Christian theologians would argue that such an identity with the powerless should be more visible and effective than any political or nationalistic struggles.

2   Professional/Personal Ethics in a Time Of War – Meitner, Einstein, Compton, and Wilson

Without judgmental conclusions as to "right or wrong" (or being able to more than briefly summarize the scientific history), I would like to consider some motivational factors and positions taken by a few visible participants who either limited or enhanced their roles in the resultant race to build an atomic bomb in World War II. In considering brief summaries of such examples and case studies it is possible to obtain some sense of the complexity of the situation and the diversity of human responses.

Lise Meitner

With her contributions to nuclear physics and nuclear chemistry (with Otto Hahn) for decades, and then stepping up to lead in the explanation of the underlying physics of fission (see chapter 31), it is clear that Lise Meitner stands as a leading nuclear scientist of the twentieth century. Still the months and years prior to her frightening exodus into Holland from Berlin in summer 1938 (initially with the clothes on her back, no money, outdated passport, no equipment, no books) were fraught by tensions with fellow leaders of the Kaiser Wilhelm Institute (KWI) of Chemistry regarding her increasingly unwelcome position within the rising Nazi power structure. Hailing from Austria, she was Jewish in background but had split off from formal ties with the Jewish community while in Vienna in 1908 [6], and she was baptized at the Evangelical (Protestant) Congregation. In *Lise Meitner, A Life In Physics*, Ruth Sime suggests the conversion may have been impacted by the life and stature of Max Planck, whose steady integrity and values were always a mentoring force for Meitner. Moreover, Sime indicates that the ethical tenants of her faith were significant for all of Meitner's life. In later years Meitner emphasized that she deeply regretted not leaving Germany earlier, in identification with the many Jewish colleagues who chose or were forced to immigrate. Still she was momentarily protected from 1933 to 1938 by Austrian citizenship and in spite of losing her academic position she was comfortable with the laboratory support, friends, and fellow leaders at the KWI for Chemistry. Her life was wrapped up in physics and the option of leaving her laboratory and colleagues was simply too painful, until Austria was annexed and her entire wellbeing was in danger.

Besides her close colleagues in fission work, Hahn and Fritz Strassmann, other sources of support prior to and during her exodus came from many directions, including very prominent physicists James Franck, Max von Laue, Max Born, and Max Planck (with both Born and Franck publicly resigning in 1933 and taking their leaves of Germany in strong protest of the crackdown onJews in academia). It can be said that all of these individuals faced the issue of professional pressure for funding and prestige within their organizations in Berlin or Göttingen (of KWI branches and the university), in stark tension with the almost daily ethical dilemmas manifested by blatant anti-Semitism. Frontline service in World War II allowed some individuals to speak out more openly without as much professional risk, while compromise with the Third Reich sometimes seemed advisable for management leaders to continue financial support and perhaps to lend some protection to valued Jewish colleagues. Other non-Jews like Fritz Strassmann were willing to pay the professional pen-alty for taking a strong, idealistic position of Jewish support. He also risked his life and his family by befriending and hiding Jewish friends in their apartment for months, and he was honored in 1986 at Yad Vashem, the holocaust memorial in Israel.

Lise Meitner was eventually invited to participate in the work on the atomic bomb, and this would have provided much welcome release from her lonely and uncomfortable situation in Stockholm, reestablishing interactions with close colleagues – including Bohr, Frisch, and many others. Deeper values prevailed. Sime notes that Meitner's response "arose from a deep revulsion, 'I will have nothing to do with a bomb!'" Sime goes on to observe: [6]

> Meitner wanted no part of deaths anywhere; she could not commit herself and her physics – the two were not distinct – to a weapon of war. She had seen the casualties firsthand in 1915–1916; she had heard the screams. She could not do it. Her decision was instantaneous and absolute; there was not discussion. She would not work on the bomb.

Upon her death in 1967, Lise Meitner asked to be buried in a country cemetery in Hampshire. Only family members attended and no speeches or sermons were delivered. Her nephew and fellow-worker, Otto Frisch, selected the gravestone and inscription [6]: *Lise Meitner: A physicist who never lost her humanity*. While I do not know any scientists who would want their lives to be in conflict with their humanitarian values, I know few who have followed through as resolutely as Lise Meitner.

Albert Einstein

To initiate financial support for atomic bomb work in the US, an aging Albert Einstein's fame and reputation for genius were called upon to increase the chances of getting the attention of President Roosevelt. Biographers of Einstein note that his public pacifist stance diminished in the 1930s through World War II, and his hatred and distrust of Nazi German leaders was clear. He had left Germany for the Center of Advanced Studies at Princeton in 1933, and at the time of the exodus predicted correctly that he would never be on German soil again. He signed a letter to President Roosevelt that (1) drew attention to the possibility of a fission explosive chain reaction, (2) noted the likely beginning of work on such a device in Germany, and (3) suggested starting an effort in the US. Like many scientific workers on the developing Manhattan Project (code name for the US project to obtain materials, design, and test the atomic bomb) he was motivated almost purely by fear of German atomic bomb developments and believed that resistance to the evils of this threat required the option of a violent response. After it became clear post-World War II that German efforts had been slow and unsuccessful, he observed that if he had known of this lack of German success, he never would have signed the letter.

The combination of Einstein's avowed pacifism of the past, his socially rebellious person-ality, and perhaps his strong identity with the Jewish Zionist movement, apparently made him an unwelcome weapons worker in the eyes of security and clearance people in the US. National Defense Research Council (NDRC) head Vannevar Bush expressed his misgivings about laying the bomb project details before Einstein (*MAB*, p. 635), "… I wish very much I could place the whole thing before him … but this is utterly impossible in view of the attitude of people here in Washington who have studied into his whole history."

Arthur Compton

Arthur Holly Compton, professor of physics at the University of Chicago, was one Nobel Prize winner leader of the Manhattan Project who took his religion very seriously. He was a Christian who made no secret of it, and his faith clearly impacted everything about his life. Richard Rhodes (*MAB*, p. 363) quotes a student of Fermi's at Chicago, Leona Woods, who worked around Compton, "Arthur Compton and God are daily companions." Moreover, Compton had Mennonite roots, a denomination known for pacifism and non-violence, with his mother dedicated to Mennonite missionary causes, and in 1939 American Mother of the Year.

As one of America's most respected scientists, Compton needed to decide if his pacifist roots should stand in the way of becoming a Manhattan project major leader. Rhodes (*MAB*, p. 364) quotes Compton's remembrance of his decision:

> In 1940, my forty-eighth year, I began to feel strongly my responsibility as a citizen for taking my proper part in the war that was then about to engulf my country, as it had already engulfed so much of the world. I talked, among others, with my minister in Chicago. He wondered why I was not supporting his appeal to the young people of our church to take a stand as pacifists. I replied in this manner: "As long as I am convinced, as I am, that there are values worth more to me than my own life, I cannot in sincerity argue that it is wrong to run the risk of death or to inflict death if necessary in the defense of those values."

When Vannevar Bush and the NDRC called upon Arthur Compton to lead the Columbia University and University of Chicago efforts to design and build a slow neutron chain reaction, he was ready. He became the highly respected managerial leader of the likes of Enrico Fermi, Leo Szilard, and Glenn Seaborg as they learned to run a nuclear reactor and then scale it up to produce the plutonium needed for the most complex version of the initial atomic bombs. He would be the one to call Washington to report the achievement of the world's first controlled fission chain reaction under Fermi's firm hand, as Compton reported, "The Italian navigator has just landed in the new world." Leo Szilard, the source of the first physics patent for such a chain reaction in earlier years, and surely one of Compton's most challenging Chicago "employees," then went on to comment that he thought, "… this day will go down as a black day in the history of mankind. (*NAB*, p. 442)

This author knew one nuclear chemist at Los Alamos in 1970 who had been a student of Compton's in Chicago prior to that intensive effort. This man regularly attended the Sunday school class that Arthur taught each week in church, even in the midst of stress. He recalled vividly that Compton's approach to his awesome responsibilities was marked by both confidence and considerable somberness. It was a weight that needed to be borne; yet it was as if his Mennonite mother were still looking over his shoulder.

Robert R. Wilson

The nationwide Manhattan project went on in secrecy during the height of World War II under the hard-driving management of the US Army's General Leslie Groves (*MAB*, chs. 14–18). Groves let everyone know that he was boss, but still managed usually to work effectively with several physicists who took leadership and management positions – like Arthur Compton in Chicago. Others included Ernest Lawrence (electromagnetic isotope separation),

Fermi and Eugene Wigner (reactor physics and plutonium production), and most influential of all, Robert Oppenheimer (bomb physics and design at Los Alamos, NM). It was Los Alamos director and Berkeley physics professor Oppenheimer who chose the very young accelerator physicist Robert R. Wilson (in his late twenties) to be the youngest group leader (cyclotron group R-1) at the remote Los Alamos laboratory established to actually design and make the first atomic bombs.

Wilson, like Compton, was raised in a Christian pacifist tradition (in his case Quaker), and indicated he was a pacifist up to the time of World War II [7]. In the following quote recorded by Mary Palevsky at Cornell, he talks about his feelings regarding work at Los Alamos:

> So it was quite a change for me to find in fact that I would be working on this horrible project. On the other hand I certainly understood what that entailed and it would probably be used – if we were successful.... And I kept hoping that we would find something [that would show an atomic bomb was not possible]. And we could have. For example if all the neutrons had been delayed there would have been no bomb. And so, I thought that would be a successful ending.

But like others, Wilson felt the driving force for his own involvement with the project to be the real possibility of long world domination by the Third Reich. As a young instructor at Princeton (after extensive experimental work with Lawrence's cyclotron group at Berkeley) he was chosen by Oppenheimer to help bring the Princeton cyclotron up the hill to the Los Alamos lab. At the lab he ran the cyclotron, helped determine the needed critical mass of plutonium, and was a leader in nuclear measurements when the complex plutonium implosion bomb was to be tested in south-central New Mexico (Trinity Test).

After VE (Victory in Europe) day, a determined Robert Wilson went ahead (over Oppenheimer's objections) and organized a laboratory evening meeting at which people could talk about their motivations for the Los Alamos efforts in light of the German surrender. The posters advertising the meeting featured the eye-catching title, "The Impact of the Gadget on Civilization." Oppenheimer came to the meeting and instead presented the Bohr complimentarity model of the bomb – a weapon so horrible that it could bring an era of peace, as nations would realize war was not an option. Wilson notes in fact that he found the argument quite convincing in light of the anticipated organization sessions of the UN to occur in 1945, and that Oppenheimer felt that knowledge of the possibilities of nuclear weapons would be an important backdrop to forming a realistic United Nations. So the work went on.

As reported in the classic documentary video, *The Day After Trinity* [8], Wilson was one of the last people up in the bomb tower during the thunder-and-lightning storm within hours of the Trinity Test shot. The tricky "Fat Man" plutonium implosion bomb worked as planned to the great elation and relief of almost all present. They knew their work and all the money spent in the midst of war had accomplished its immediate goal, and it would likely make possible a shortening of the war. In "Surely You're Joking Mr. Feynman," future Nobel laureate Richard Feynman recorded the Trinity Test celebration, but "one man, I remember, Bob Wilson, was just sitting there moping." When asked why, Wilson replied, "It's a terrible thing that we have done." Yet the fact is that even 40 years later shortly before his death, Bob Wilson was not sure that given the World War II circumstances their "terrible" work was still not a necessary task that was important to do.

3 An Existential Experience: The Epiphany of the First Atomic Bomb Test

Almost everyone present at Trinity (both those in the 10,000-yard front shelters and those on Campania Hill 20 miles away) reflect that it was an epiphany experience that changed their lives. Palevsky [7] asked Wilson how he was impacted by the event.

> It certainly was an epiphany. … From then on I certainly took myself more seriously. Up to that point I thought of myself as a physicist and what I could do in physics. Now I was concerned with what we could do what a group of people, and what I in particular could do, about passing the word along and trying to have an effect to get people to take it [the bomb] seriously.

Columbia's Nobelist I. I. Rabi is quoted (*MAB*, p. 675):

> We turned to one another and offered congratulations, for the first few minutes. Then there was a chill, which was not the morning cold; it was a chill that came to one when one thought, as for instance when I thought of my wooden house in Cambridge, and my laboratory in New York, and of the millions of people living around there, and this power of nature which we had first understood it to be – well, there it was.

And Oppenheimer himself:

> … and then it was extremely solemn. We knew the world would not be the same. A few people laughed, a few people cried. Most people were silent. I remembered the line from the Hindu scripture, the Bhagavad-Gita: Vishnu is trying to persuade the Prince that he should so his duty and to impress him he takes on his multi-armed form and says, "Now I am become Death, the destroyer of worlds." I suppose we all thought that, one way or another.

References

[1] Richard Rhodes, *Making of the Atomic Bomb* (New York: Simon & Schuster, 1986). Abbreviated *MAB* here, this 880-page book plays the role of a primary reference for many sections of these presentations. This Pulitzer Prize-winning history on science, history, and human events during this period was written shortly after quite a bit of World War II material was declassified in the 1980s. Rhodes also wrote a major documentary book on the H-bomb and cold war era that followed World War II, *Dark Sun – The Making of the Hydrogen Bomb* (New York: Simon & Schuster, 1995). It was a 1996 Pulitzer Prize finalist.

[2] A. P. French and P. J. Kennedy, *Niels Bohr – A Centenary Volume* (Cambridge, MA: Harvard University Press, 1985). This beautifully edited volume included intimate and spirited sections by many who knew Bohr well and presents them largely in a chronological order. For these writings the entries by Weisskopf, Stuewer, Bethe, and Ruth Moore have been particularly helpful.

[3] See www.nba.nbi.dk for a variety of archive documents related to Niels Bohr.

[4] Michael Frayn, *Copenhagen* (London: Methuen, 2000; edition with extended postscript by Frayn). Copenhagen premiered in May 1998 at the Royal National Theatre, London, and in April 2000 at the Royale Theater, New York. Both productions were directed by Michael Blakemore.

[5] Charles Hatfield, *The Scientist and the Ethical Decision* (Downers Grove, IL: InterVarsity Press, 1973); a book of essays from 14 Christian scholars regarding ethical considerations to be faced in physical, life, and social sciences.

[6]   Ruth Lewin Sime, *Lise Meitner, A Life In Physics* (Berkeley: University of California Press, 1996). No book better conveys the human dimension of ethical dilemmas faced by scientists working in Germany (e.g., Meitner, Hahn, Planck, Frank, and Von Laue) at the time of the Nazi crackdown on Jewish scientists. Meitner's own reflections about the foundational values of many of her closest colleagues are especially insightful.

[7]   Mary Palevsky, *Atomic Fragments, A Daughter's Questions* (Berkeley: University of California Press, 2000). Palevsky does interviews with many of the bomb physicists during their last years. Many of her interviews are direct quotes from folks like Hans Bethe, Edward Teller, Philip Morrison, Robert Wilson, Joseph Rotblat, and Herbert York. They are motivated to share deeply by her honest questions that follow from her late father's defense work.

[8]   Jon Else, documentary video, *The Day After Trinity – J. Robert Oppenheimer & the Atomic Bomb* (1980), currently distributed by Image Entertainment. This Oscar-nominated film intensely studies the progress of the twentieth century in nuclear physics and focuses on the actions, ideas, and tragedy of Robert Oppenheimer's life.

33

Scientific Responsibility: A Quest for Good Science and Good Applications

RICHARD PETERSON

Prior to and after Hiroshima and Nagasaki, nuclear scientists and engineers have debated their proper and most influential role in trying to guide in the use of their work. Some scientists like Leo Szilard, Niels Bohr, Edward Teller, Robert Oppenheimer, Joseph Rotblat, and Andrei Sakharov have played strong roles in speaking out in politics and public affairs. Atomic bomb leader Robert Oppenheimer stated after World War II that "physicists have known sin" in the war years, and we will consider the implications of such a statement and what might properly comprise "sin" within the process of science. H-bomb development (by the United States, Soviet Union, England, France, and China) in the decades that followed the war presented technical, strategic, and ethical problems that are still with us today. The chapter will conclude with examples of exemplary human motivations for active participation and teaching within the global scientific community.

1 The Historical Cases of Hiroshima and Nagasaki

The so-called "Met Lab" of the Manhattan Project was managed by Arthur Compton in the war years, and Leo Szilard and Eugene Rabinowitch led efforts of a few staff there to gather the attention of President Roosevelt as to how the "gadget" would be used [1] (*MAB*, chapter 18). As needed supplies of fissile materials (Pu-239 and U-235) were finally available and as the implosion design of the Pu-239 gadget was be tested at the Trinity site, it was a crucial time if scientists were to exert any control over the results of their labors. Rhodes (*MAB*, p. 635) notes:

> With the successful operation of the production reactors and separation plants at Hanford, the work of the Met Lab had slowed; Compton's people, Szilard particularly, found time to think about the future. Szilard says he began to examine "the wisdom of testing bombs and using bombs." Rabinowitch remembers, "many hours were spent walking up and down the Midway … with Leo Szilard and arguing about these questions and about what can be done. I remember sleepless nights."

Szilard wrote a memo to President Roosevelt (FDR) that argued against both bomb testing or dropping the bomb on population centers, and he again used his old friend Einstein to obtain the attention of the Roosevelt's. On May 8, 1945 he was able to arrange an appointment with Mrs Roosevelt to present his concerns. He told Compton of these activities and was surprised in this case by being cheered on by his boss. Szilard apparently made his argument on both humanitarian and US strategic grounds, and in many ways he represented the arguments presented earlier by Bohr. He felt it was critical for the US to prepare for the years ahead and for a world in which international control of nuclear energy technology was imperative. In World War II the US had tremendous long- term fighting power due to abundant resources and an unparalleled industrial base, while in the future nuclear fighting capabilities might be determined more solely by technical expertise and access to uranium. Unfortunately a few days before his appointment the entire nation was in grief over the sudden death of FDR, and Szilard was back to "ground zero" in his efforts. He would not give up, and eventually personally presented his memorandum and concern to the President's advisor and Secretary of State, Jimmy Byrnes. Byrnes was not impressed, and Szilard's political and military naiveté for these turbulent times in the US became more evident.

The decisions as to how and where to use the bomb were to be made by a committee at the highest level (including the Secretary of War, top-level military leaders, plus several Nobel level scientists (including Oppenheimer, Compton, Fermi, Lawrence and others). A subcommittee of this group plus other scientific advisors comprised the "Target Committee" that would advise on expected physical impacts on targets and assorted bombing strategies. As described in the Wilson section of chapter 32, in these times Oppenheimer was prone to argue for the Bohr perspective of bomb complementarity – thus this awesome weapon of mass destruction should be visibly big and bad enough to make conventional war nearly impossible in the future and stimulate international reform so as to lead to a lasting peace. Within such a model the use of the bomb in Japan seemed to follow as a necessary evil to bring sufficient visibility and awareness to enable world peace in the future – and the shadow of the cold war of the next half-century appears to loom large in the minds of strategic thinkers. In this context Nobel Peace Prize winner Joseph Rotblat recalled the dinner conversation in Los Alamos in which General Groves said that the "real purpose of the atomic bomb was to subdue the Russians."[2] Palevsky notes that Groves repeated this personal conviction in his testimony during the security trial of Oppenheimer in 1954. In the same interview Rotblat talks about how his respect for Oppenheimer continued to fall because of his acquiescence to the attacks on Japanese cities and civilians – as opposed to a possible demonstration of the weapon to international observers. In such deliberations Oppenheimer and other scientists at this point seemed to often try to play the role of an amoral advisor who could authoritatively guide at the highest level on technical matters, but would not push from any particular moral or humanitarian position. It is interesting that the record shows it was Secretary of War Stimson who took a very strong stand to remove the religious and cultural center of Kyoto as a primary target.

As we all know, the eventual decision at that time was to use the two types of bombs (the U-235 gun device first; and complex Pu-239 spherical implosion device second) without warning on cities that had not been previously attacked by fire bombing and would therefore show bomb impacts graphically. Many believe the effectiveness of these attacks in bringing a quick Japanese surrender (and thus likely saving many thousands of lives on both sides) more than justified their use. But the immediate reaction to the bomb usage was mixed among the scientists. In the classic and powerful documentary film, *The Day After*

Trinity [3], Robert Wilson emotionally tells how he became physically ill upon hearing of these attacks, in spite of a spirit of celebration that predominated in Los Alamos. In the same documentary, Frank Oppenheimer (Robert's physicist brother) recalls considerable relief that the bombs were not "duds," but in the next breath especially laments the use of the second bomb on Nagasaki – as perhaps unnecessary in bringing surrender. Palevsky [2] recalls her physicist father's continuing grief, even shortly before his death, in which he asks her, "Did you know that Nagasaki was the center of Christianity in Japan." And after learning more, she goes on to recall:

> Nagasaki is the Japanese city with which Westerners have had the longest contact, a trading center whose port was opened in the sixteenth century; the center of Christianity in Japan. Jesuit priests brought the word of the Christian God, the God of Love, the three person'd God, the God of the Golden Rule. The blast of the atomic bomb destroyed nearly two square miles in the heart of the city – 70,000 injured 70,000 dead. Where does it fit in the sacred teachings about the meaning of suffering? What does it mean to have caused such great suffering?

Leo Szilard's laments the first use of his chain reaction in war, as described by Rhodes (*MAB*, Epilogue, p. 750):

> Upon hearing of the Nagasaki bombing he immediately asked the chaplain of the University of Chicago to include a special prayer for the dead and a collection for the survivors of the two Japanese cities in any service commemorating the end of the war. He drafted a second petition to the President calling the atomic bombing "a flagrant violation of our own moral standards" and asking that they be stopped. The Japanese surrender mooted the issue and the petition was never sent.

If the Trinity Test was an "epiphany" experience to people like Robert Wilson, the actual use of the weapon to end the war promptly, and in the words of Nobel laureate I. I. Rabi "to treat human beings like matter," was for many a life-changing call to responsible action. For some such action was to actively work toward international controls, while for others it was a call to return to basic science that could sustain their lives within the many pains of the end of the war.

2 "Physicists Have Known Sin?" – Reflections on the Manhattan Project

In the aftermath of World War II and given some time for reflection, the leader of Los Alamos intimated, "In some sort of crude sense, which no vulgarity, no humor, no overstatement can quite extinguish, the physicists have known sin; and this is a knowledge which they cannot lose." This controversial statement was one of many from within the physics community as several of its members were able to pull away from Los Alamos, think about the completed project from within their research and teaching occupations, and try to make their own personal decision as to whether they would continue to contribute to weapons work. I would like us to consider what Oppenheimer may have meant by his "sin" statement and compare it to responses from many of his colleagues.

In *The Day After Trinity* documentary [2] on the post-World War II period, Frank Oppenheimer speaks for himself and his brother's deep concern shortly after Hiroshima about the irresistible nature of this project as they experienced it. The temptation to take this (fission) pulsed power of nature and harness it toward usage within an atomic bomb was very hard to put down once it was underway. Yes, Quaker-heritage Robert Wilson states that he wishes he had walked away after VE day, but for hundreds of other physicists and engineers such a notion was not even a question. Their creativity was flowing, human ego and nationalistic pride were at stake, the materials had been accumulated, the money had been spent, and a Pacific war needed to be ended – and indeed the United Nations was being formed, now with knowledge of the "gadget." So in many ways the entrapping "sin" that their leader glimpsed in himself and his "team" was seemingly driven by technological pride, the lack of real reflection about the expected application (after the Nazis were done), and the simultaneously needed drive toward international controls that would help prevent a nuclear arms race that could destroy the world. Palevsky [3] quotes Freeman Dyson, p. 226 – also orally in [2],

> I have felt it myself, the glitter of nuclear weapons. It is irresistible if you come to them as a scientist. To feel it there in your hands – to release this energy that fuels the stars, to let it do your bidding ... It is something that gives people an illusion of illimitable power and it is, in some ways, responsible for all our troubles, I would say – this, what you might call technical arrogance that overcomes people when they see what they can do with their minds.

Morrison [4], p. 316, quotes from Oppenheimer's well-known speech given to his friends and colleagues at Los Alamos shortly after the war.

> ... If atomic bombs are to be added as new weapons to the arsenals of a warring world, or to the arsenals of nations preparing for war, then the time will come when mankind will curse the names of Los Alamos and Hiroshima. ... The nations of this world must unite, or they will perish. This war, that has ravaged so much of the earth, has written these words. The atomic bomb has spelled them out for all men to understand. Other men have spoken them, in other times, of other wars, of other weapons. They have not prevailed. There are some, misled by a false sense of human history, who hold that they will not prevail today. It is not for us to believe that. By our work we are committed, committed to a world united, before this common peril, in law, and in humanity.

Oppenheimer at this point has not lost the Bohr complementarity view of the bomb. This is not a vision of a mere balance of powers or deterrence, but one can see an extraordinary (some would doubtlessly say impractical) hope for the global expectations of the world. It seems to imply that all the major powers of the world would yield much of their sovereignty to make major wars impossible in light of this threat that has totally changed the nature of ultimate warfare.

Nobel laureate I. I. Rabi helped lead the MIT radar project that may have played the most crucial role in actually turning the tide of the war on both fronts, and he also advised Oppenheimer at Los Alamos. On the occasion of the fortieth anniversary of the Los Alamos lab, he gave a memorable speech entitled, "How Well We Meant." Palevsky [2] quotes his remarks,

> "The world seemed about to be engulfed by a fanatic, barbarian culture. And it did look then, as it turned out to be, that only through science and its products could western civilization be saved ... Well, we saved it; I say this proudly, and I think truly." He went on to say that this great

new power put the US in a position "to start on a new road to a new world" in the post-war era. Then the question changed. It was no longer about how to save civilization but how to destroy another culture - how to destroy other human beings. "We have lost sight of the basic tenets of all religions – that a human being is a wonderful thing. We talk as if humans were matter."

Robert Wilson himself never did any weapons work after Hiroshima, and he first went into academia at Cornell University and later became the acclaimed director of the Fermi Lab (the US high-energy physics accelerator complex in Illinois). He thought it not his calling to help build more efficient fission bombs or to lend his experimental skills to the H-bomb work of the 1950s. Yet it is interesting in his interviews with Mary Palevsky [2] that he very much hesitates to criticize those like his colleague Hans Bethe who made the other choice. Wilson emphasizes that while he maintained a bit of an activist role in the Federation of American Scientists, he never again would be able to really impact national policy on weapons and international control like Bethe – or Oppenheimer, before his security trial. It is a little like pastor Bonhoeffer's tough decision to go back to Germany before the war and painfully participate in the debates regarding racist policy and contribute in the power struggle to remove the Nazi leaders – even to the point of martyrdom for what he saw as a righteous cause. There is often a real price in pulling out of the picture and taking a more separatist position on a difficult ethical issue.

3 The Human Dimensions of "Good Science" – Some Research and Teaching Perspectives

Science support in the years that followed the Manhattan project were good ones in the United States. Money flowed freely as science and engineering were viewed as good for a country as we entered the "cold war" period in which several countries built both fission and fusion bombs. However there were often "strings attached" as governmental leaders were well aware that our science and technological "edge" was crucial in our global position. Yet support was also present for basic science, as the case was made that the best applications (even in national defense) often were stimulated by fundamental, curiosity-driven basic science. Nuclear physics matured and was broadened in perspective, especially in the area of high-energy physics made possible by gigantic, expensive accelerators.

In June of 1996, the *American Journal of Physics* (vol. 64, no. 6, p. 682) published a response by Robert Wilson to my question regarding his testimony before Congress. In 1969 he was called before the US Senate in support of funding for the Fermi national accelerator. Senator John Pastore asked whether this expensive nuclear physics machine would really help defend our country in the midst of the cold war, and Wilson said the new accelerator had "nothing at all" to do such a defense. Rather,

"It has only to do with the respect with which we regard one another, the dignity of men, our love of culture. It has to do with: Are we good painters, good sculptors, great poets? I mean all the things we really venerate in our country and are patriotic about. It has nothing to do directly with defending our country except to make it worth defending."

While this powerful extemporaneous statement does little to define science, I believe it has much to say about the human dimension of science and why we do it. It surely is not a statement about the many applications of science that may either help or hurt our daily lives, but rather that the process of science is humanly driven by our passionate desire to know about the smallest and largest parts of the universe - and ascertain our place in it. In her correspondence with Hans Bethe, Mary Palevsky [2], p. 239, passes on her conviction that "science is a marriage, the relationship between human intellect and the intelligibility of a dynamic nature – nature that is both mysterious and knowable and in who's knowing we learn something about ourselves." Thus the best of science is (in the phrase of Einstein's) driven by a "holy curiosity" which he says we must not lose. Bethe responded to Palevsky's marriage metaphor of science by saying, "yes, you have got the essence of science. It is the desire to understand nature, not the things that science creates." He added the question, "How can we make that clear to people?"

To those of us who teach about science, Bethe's final question is a very, very big one – and it has no simple answer since we are all so different. I am sure of one thing; it is really hard to help people understand or support the scientific quest when we are elitist. Some of the recent century's best scientists have been at their best when conveying their craft to very young people and children. Einstein's "holy curiosity" is most apparent in the very young and it is no accident that much of the best physics has been done by the giants like Newton, Einstein, and Bohr before they were 35.

I would like to tell a story of one of my physics conference experiences at which an award was to be given by the American Institute of Physics (AIP) for the best physics book written for children during the last year. Following a presentation to Elaine Scott for her wonderful children's book on remarkable findings from the Hubble telescope [5] we fidgeted in our chairs when she asked if she could make a few remarks. But to many physicists at that meeting, the story she told continues to be a very memorable moment from that week.

> When I first told (my daughter) about the award and the venue in which it would be presented, she was quiet for a moment. "Physics teachers, huh," she said. Then added, "Gosh Mom, I hope they don't ask you any hard questions." I'll briefly tell you how an English major came to write a book about astronomy in general and the Hubble Space Telescope in particular.
>
> It begins with questions and an incident from my early childhood that has remained with me and may have contributed to the career path I have taken. I was about five or six years old, and I went to a Vacation Bible School at a new church where I was a stranger. The young teacher … began to tell a story about Joseph, his brothers, and a gaudy coat his father had given him. As she spoke, she reached into a basket by her side, and one by one, she pulled out figures and bits of scenery … placing them on a vertical board by her side, and they stayed there as if by magic. When she finished her story, she looked at her class and asked brightly, "Are there any questions?" Dead silence ensued. Well, I had a question, and I raised my hand. "Yes," she said, obviously delighted to call on someone. "How did you do that?" I asked. Perplexed, she looked at me. "Do what?" "Get those people to stick up there," I said.
>
> For some reason this question seemed to bother her. … She frowned and said, "That's not a good question." The class laughed, and I was humiliated. I remember that moment from over 50 years ago to this very day. I knew the Bible story well, but I didn't know how a flannel board worked. A teachable moment was lost, and I was an adult before I conquered the fear of asking a question and having it deemed stupid. I grew up and became an author of non-fiction books for young people, and in each of my titles I've been trying to answer that question for myself, as well as my readers. *How does it work?*

So I would emphasize that as we do and teach science we must first be alert to our own "holy curiosity" and be sensitive to its manifestation in the lives of those we teach and mentor. Our science must always be humble and be especially open and honest about all those things that are still very uncertain. My own reading and study about the driving forces and people within the Manhattan project still affirms that our science is at its best when following the guidance of a Jewish prophet who gave a simple admonition regarding how we can best live our lives,

"to do justice, to love kindness and to walk humbly with your God" (Micah 6:8).

Surely this foundational ethical principle also can guide us to "good science" and to the right applications – and both motivate and enable us to share it with others.

References

[1]   Richard Rhodes, *Making of the Atomic Bomb* (New York: Simon & Schuster, 1986). Abbreviated *MAB* here, this 880-page book plays the role of a primary reference for many sections of these presentations. This Pulitzer Prize-winning history on science, history, and human events during this period was written shortly after quite a bit of World War II material was declassified in the 1980s. Rhodes also wrote a major documentary book on the H-bomb and cold war era that followed World War II, *Dark Sun - The Making of the Hydrogen Bomb* (New York: Simon & Schuster, 1995). It was a 1996 Pulitzer Prize finalist.

[2]   Mary Palevsky, *Atomic Fragments, A Daughters Questions* (Berkeley: University of California Press, 2000). Palevsky does interviews with many of the bomb physicists during their last years. Many of her interviews are direct quotes from folks like Hans Bethe, Edward Teller, Philip Morrison, Robert Wilson, Joseph Rotblat, and Herbert York. They are motivated to share deeply by her honest questions that follow from her late father's defense work.

[3]   Jon Else, documentary video, *The Day After Trinity – J. Robert Oppenheimer & the Atomic Bomb* (1980), currently distributed by Image Entertainment. This Oscar-nominated film intensely studies the progress of the twentieth century in nuclear physics and focuses on the actions, ideas, and tragedy of Robert Oppenheimer's life.

[4]   Philip Morrison, *Nothing is too Wonderful to be True* (Woodbury, NY: AIP Press, 1995). This is a collection of essays and reflections from MIT's late Philip Morrison. As a student of Oppenheimer's, his insights into the motivations and personality of Oppenheimer and the Los Alamos years are relevant to thes lectures. Morrison was one major atomic scientist of the Los Alamos period who devoted much of his later energy and skills to physics and science education for the public. Another would be Frank Oppenheimer who played a major role in the founding of San Francisco's *Exploratorium,* a world-class, highly interactive science museum for "children" of all ages.

[5]   Elaine Scott, *Close Encounters – Exploring the Universe with the Hubble Space Telescope* (New York: Hyperion Books for Children, 1998)

Part 12

The Science of Religion

34

The Evolution of Religion: Adaptationist Accounts

MICHAEL J. MURRAY

Anthropologists, psychologists, and evolutionary theorists have developed a number of scientific accounts of the origin and persistence of religion. Some of these accounts explain religious belief and behavior in terms of native cognitive faculties or the social utility of religion, while others explain religion in evolutionary terms. Evolutionary explanations divide between those that explain religion as an adaptation, and those that explain it as a byproduct or spandrel. In this chapter I describe the three most widely defended adaptationist evolutionary models and consider the liabilities of each, both with respect to their internal coherence and as purported explanations for the human phenomenon of religion. Those accounts are punishment theories, commitment signaling theories, and group selection theories.

I Introduction

Human beings share many characteristics in common. We are vertebrates. We are mammals. We are bipedal. We are omnivorous. We have unusually large brains. We give birth to live offspring. We are conscious. We experience emotion; and we signal our emotions with facial expression. We live in groups. We construct tools. We have and use language. These are some among our many similarities. Some of these are strictly biological. Others are cultural. And some are a mixture of the two. The biological universals are easy to pick out of the list. However, it is much harder to distinguish purely cultural universals from those that are a mixture of the two. In many cases cultural similarities count as similarities only in very broad terms. For example, while it is true that we are all "language users," we don't all speak English, or French, or Chinese. We are all "tool users" and yet we don't all use chopsticks. Part of the reason we speak the particular language that we do, or use the particular tools that we do, is that there is something about the way the human cognitive architecture is put together that makes us naturally disposed – hard-wired, you might say – for these cultural activities. We are wired to acquire and use languages and tools naturally; though which languages and tools we use will be decided by local culture and custom.

Tool and language use are, of course, cultural universals of a fairly coarse-grained sort. Are there cultural universals with a more specific character? There are. There is one cultural practice in particular that is quite specific, and is found everywhere human beings are or have ever been. That cultural universal is religion. Human beings are inescapably and incurably religious. Any time we stumble upon human culture, past or present, East or West, it is inevitable that there will be churches, temples, mosques, synagogues, shamans, seers, mediums, and the like. Indeed across the globe, religion not only persists, but continues to proliferate – sometimes even in spite of deliberate efforts to prevent it. In China alone, where places of religious worship were shuttered during the Cultural Revolution, it is estimated that there are between 65 and 100 million among the ranks of Christians alone – and that number is increasing as rapidly as it is anywhere in the world.

What accounts for the unstoppable infectiousness of religion through times and cultures? What explains the fact that humans, as far as we can tell, are "wired" for religious belief and practice? That is the question we will be discussing in the next three chapters.

Whenever we encounter human traits that are universal in this way, they will admit of one or the other of two types of explanation. The first type of explanation is horizontal transmission. While it is not true that all human beings use the Internet, it certainly appears that we are moving in that direction. If the day of universal Internet use were ever to arrive, the explanation for this universal phenomenon would simply be this: one person told another person, who in turn told another person, and so on, until the whole world got the message. If that were to happen, the universal trait of "Internet use" would have arisen because one person spread a good idea to another. Such traits would be and are *purely* cultural in nature, since they spread by word of mouth or by imitation. The second type of explanation appeals to natural biological disposition. Human beings, for example, have a universal and natural aversion to human waste, dead bodies, and rotting flesh. This phenomenon, known in psychology as "contagion avoidance," leads us to engage in some very useful behavior. It is a good thing for us to have an aversion towards waste products since contact with waste is often a mode of transmission of harmful pathogens (bacteria and viruses) and thus of disease. And while this aversion is found across times and cultures, it was not something that was learned by each culture from another one. Instead, the disposition to feel disgust at sources of contagion is hard-wired into us, being passed down "vertically" from our parents through our genes.

Notice that some widespread traits have both a vertical and a horizontal dimension. My love for sugar and fat is vertical, and it disposes me to eat French fries when I can. But my love for *McDonald's* French fries, while motivated by this vertically transmitted trait is, technically speaking, horizontal. I only like *those particular fries* because someone once told me that they were good and that I should eat them. And so I did. If my love for McDonald's French fries becomes a human universal (and that seems to be a real possibility given the spread of the McDonald's empire), this fact would be explained both vertically and horizontally. The love for things of that *sort* (fatty things) would be conferred on us vertically, and the love of that very kind of fatty thing (McDonald's fries) is conferred on us horizontally.

Widespread traits that spread through horizontal transmission are strictly cultural traits. Widespread traits that spread vertically are biological traits. And those that have a dual character (like our love for McDonald's French fries) are explained partially by culture and partially by biology.

Is religion, a human universal, transmitted vertically, horizontally, or through a combination of both modes? The answer is undoubtedly: both. Even cultures that are and have been isolated from other human populations develop religion. Having religion does not seem to require horizontal transmission. Furthermore, like love for McDonald's French fries, religious belief and practice springs from a common core of human dispositions which gets specified and diversified in light of cultural factors that shape them. This common core of dispositions is, it is reasonable to think, something that is transmitted to us vertically. There is some sense, that is, in which we are hard-wired for religious belief and practice.

Describing religion as springing from a common core of universal human dispositions might initially sound odd since it seems to imply that religions share a common core that is explained by these dispositions. But is this right? That is, is there some common core to religious expressions – religious beliefs and practices – that makes them *religious* as opposed to moral or political or merely cultural? We might think that the answer is obviously: yes. Religion is a distinct and identifiable phenomenon that is the object of study in, for example, the field of religious studies. So to find the common core, we must simply ask scholars in the field what religion *is* – what is it that is the object of their study?

If some of you are chuckling to yourselves right now it is probably because you know that the project of defining religion is, as Paul Griffiths once wrote, like the project of writing diet books: it never stops, and none of it does much good. Defining religion is a notoriously difficult and contentious matter. Though it is worth pointing out that it is not much more difficult than defining core concepts that lie at the very heart of other disciplines. Ask a dozen biologists what "life" consists in, or ask a dozen philosophers what philosophy is, and you will likely get 12 different answers. In light of that, perhaps trying to come up with a definition of religion will be a diversion not worth our time.

While it is true that setting off in search of a set of necessary and sufficient conditions for a belief system or set of practices to count as religious would be a wasted journey on our part, it is still true that we need to know what phenomenon it is we are trying to explain. So for our purposes we will use the following characterization, adapted from psychologist Scott Atran (2002):

Religion is a community's costly commitments to a world of strange and unusual supernatural agents which serve to master people's existential anxieties, such as death and deception.

While these commitments take on very different forms in different communities, they are found across times and cultures.

All universal traits that are passed along vertically have an ultimate biological explanation. Furthermore, all such traits are connected, directly or indirectly, with evolutionary adaptation. Some of these traits, contagion avoidance for example, exist and are universal because they are adaptive. But not every universal trait is adaptive. Some traits, like our love for fat, *were once adaptive but no longer are*. Changes in our environment can make some adaptive traits turn on us and cause us harm. Still other traits have no adaptive value either in the present or in the past. These traits are instead by-products that result from other traits that we have. Human beings have belly buttons. These are inevitable by-products that result from our having been connected to the placenta in our mother's womb during development. Is the belly button adaptive? Does having it (now or in our ancestral past) increase our chances of surviving to reproductive age? No. But it is a consequence of another trait that is adaptive. These by-products are called *spandrels*. Spandrels are not adaptations. And indeed, spandrels can even be maladaptive. Nonetheless, spandrels will persist in a population as long as they are by-products of adaptive traits that carry greater fitness benefits than the spandrel does fitness costs.

What does all of this have to do with religion? If I am right that religion is a human universal, and I am right that all human universals are transmitted vertically, and I am right that all vertically transmitted traits have a biological basis, then religion too has a biological basis. Many biologists, psychologists, and anthropologists have drawn the same conclusion. And yet, it is a conclusion they find deeply troubling. The trouble is not that religion can be explained scientifically. Rather, the problem is that religion, while universal, seems to be profoundly *maladaptive*. Religion encourages people to do such things as: become celibate for a lifetime (Catholic priests and Hindu sadhus); build huge structures with no obvious benefit (pyramids); sacrifice one's crops or cattle to unseen gods; kill one's healthy offspring, chopping off fingers and toes to give to dead relatives; burn one's house for a family member killed in a tragedy; knock out one's own teeth; give up the opportunity to work on special "holy" days, or eating important sources of nutrition (pigs for Jews, cows for Hindus); stopping to utter strange words and perform weird gestures several times a day. And so on and so on. What could explain the universality of a trait that seems to carry so many liabilities?

Boiled down to a single slogan, the Darwinian theory of evolution contends that characteristics evolve because they help the organisms that have them survive and reproduce. Once one grasps the theory, it can easily become a parlor game to hypothesize about how many of the characteristics we see in organisms might be accounted for in Darwinian terms. Zebras run quickly because such a capacity allows them to avoid predators, Great White sharks can detect aquatic electrical discharges because such a capacity helps them find prey, and so on. Yet even Darwin recognized that some characteristics of organisms seem to defy the evolutionary picture. The peacock's tail seems to render it gratuitously vulnerable to predators. How could such a characteristic persist? In addition to puzzling morphological traits like peacock coloration, a number of organismic behaviors can be identified which likewise seem to detract from fitness by harming the reproductive success or fitness of the organisms that exhibit them. Honeybees naturally sacrifice their lives by stinging intruders which strike the nest for example. Darwin himself recognized the anomalous nature of such characteristics and he proposed a variety of supplementary explanations for them aimed at showing their consistency with his overarching theory.

Scientists have continued to catalog cases of widespread while apparently maladaptive characteristics and behaviors and have likewise continued to look for explanations for them that are consistent with a broadly Darwinian picture of the biological world. In the last quarter of the twentieth century, Darwinians from many disciplines focused special attention on animal behaviors, like intruder-stinging bees, which seemed to detract from the fitness of the organism exhibiting it. Such behaviors are not especially uncommon, and they are usually accompanied by a corresponding fitness benefit for others associated with the organism. As a result, such behaviors bear a surface resemblance to actions that among humans we would describe as altruistic, in other words behaviors in which the altruist sacrifices his or her own interests to secure the well-being of others. A variety of explanations for such altruistic behaviors has been cataloged, though there is still widespread disagreement over which of the explanations are in fact in play. Attempts at providing such explanations now fall broadly under the name "evolutionary psychology."

Over the last decade a number of evolutionary psychologists have turned their attention from altruistic behavior to another form of behavior common among human beings which initially seems at least as intractable from an evolutionary perspective as altruistic behaviors once did, namely, religious behavior. Religious behavior seems to be a Darwinian anomaly since it seems to carry such high fitness costs. In this sense, religious behavior appears eminently maladaptive. Scott Atran describes what we might call the evolutionary "problem of religion" as follows:

> religion is materially expensive and unrelentingly counterfactual and even counterintuitive. Religious practice is costly in terms of material sacrifice (at least one's prayer time), emotional expenditure (inciting fears and hopes), and cognitive effort (maintaining both factual and counterintuitive networks of beliefs). (Atran, 2002, p. 6)

This new wave of evolutionary psychologists has thus turned their attention toward explaining the evolutionary problem of religion.

Attempts to explain religious belief and practice in human beings is thus in one sense of a piece with attempts to explain other apparently maladaptive beliefs and practices (the *belief*, for example, that one should love one's neighbor as oneself, and the *practice* of actually doing so). In another sense, such evolutionary explanations fit a general pattern in that area of psychology concerned with explaining how evolutionary history might be relevant to explaining why we have the sensory and cognitive processing mechanisms that we have. Such explanations range from attempts to explain our ordinary ability to sense light in the visible spectrum to our extraordinary abilities to produce works of art.[1]

II One Preliminary

Evolutionary explanations or religion aim to answer the question of why religion is pervasive and persistent despite its apparent maladaptiveness. However, as we will see, the different answers that are given often seem quite orthogonal to one another. The reason for this is that there are, in fact, many facets to the question, and no single answer, even if correct, will tell us all we want to know. For example, we might come up with one type of explanation when considering the *origins* of religious belief, and a quite different type of explanation if we were to consider the *persistence* of religious belief. We can see this by considering a parallel. Scientists who are interested in abiogenesis are looking to explain why there is life in a universe that was initially lifeless. Such explanations sometimes focus on how life originated, that is, on accounts that describe, for example, the probability of the natural occurrence of phosopholids, their tendency to form micelles and bilipid layers, the tendency of these structures to form cytoplasmic spheres, and so on. This provides a story about the *origin* of cellular life. But someone interested in the question of why there is life in the universe might be equally interested in providing an account of the *persistence* of cellular life. That sort of explanation would look strikingly different of course. Here one might instead talk about the ability of cellular life to survive and reproduce in environments in which it is found, and its ability to successfully recruit scarce resources in an environment which is perhaps competitive and so on.

Robert Hinde has demarcated a variety of questions which one might be trying to answer when it comes to evolutionary explanations of religion. In particular he highlights the following:

(1) *The causal question*: What proximate causal factors caused the behavior in the organism?
(2) *The developmental question:* How did the proximate causal factors yielding the behavior develop in the organism?
(3) *The functional question:* What is the immediate benefit of the behavior to the organism? And on what did natural selection act in order to maintain the behavior?
(4) *The evolutionary question*: What are the evolutionary stages of the development of the behavior?[2]

Distinguishing these questions is important since, as we will see, some theorists offering intriguing explanations for how religious beliefs or practices arise, but are then unable to provide any plausible account of why such strange or maladaptive features did, or even could, persist. A complete explanation of religion should address both issues.

III Adaptationist Theories

For as long as academics have studied the phenomenon of religion they have marveled at its power both to unify and to divide. Religion is among the most powerful motivating forces in human culture, serving to foster strong cooperation among members of the same religious community as well as gross and even lethal hostility to those outside the group. All adaptationist scientific explanations of religion argue that the adaptive character of religion arises because of its capacity to sustain cooperation among groups of individuals in the face of forces that threaten their unity. It is uncontroversial that living in cooperative groups brings significant adaptive benefits to the individuals in the group as well as to the group as a whole. Social organization permits groups of organisms to interact with their local environment in ways that allow them to extract greater benefits from it, and to do so with greater efficiency. Cooperating groups can work together to harvest more resources from their environments, groups of hunters can bring down more and larger game, and groups of farmers can divide their labor in order to make efficient agriculture production possible. Large cooperating groups can ward off predators and other threats. Furthermore, groups permit members to develop technical and intellectual specializations that allow specific individuals to develop specialized adaptive talents, while leaving other needs to be handled by other members of the group. The result is that groups can have doctors, soldiers, scientists, and so on, each bringing specialized and valuable assets to the group that would not be possible without the contributions of others.

However, while the potential benefits of group life are substantial, these benefits are hard to get and sustain in the face of threats of defection. For example, you and I both benefit if I agree to protect your property in return for you growing my food. But if I can get away with having you grow my food without having to spend my time protecting you, so much the better for me. Or take another example: the whole group benefits if we work together to run the herd over the cliff so that we can eat their carcasses. But if I can enjoy the fruits of the hunt without expending any energy or putting myself at risk, I reap the rewards without paying the cost. The prospect of defection without loss of reward provides powerful

Table 34.1   The Prisoners' Dilemma

	Confess	Stay Silent
Confess	−6	−10
	−6	0
Stay Silent	0	−1
	−10	−1

incentives for members of the group to free-ride on the efforts of others. This prospect constitutes the central problem of group life, and it is a problem that must be solved if groups of organisms are going to enjoy the adaptive power of their numbers.

Scholars from many disciplines have sought to map this problem of group cooperation in order to consider various strategies that might be used to solve it. One simple model is provided by game-theoretic consideration of the Prisoner's Dilemma. Mark and Jim take guns into a local grocery store and rob the owner at gunpoint. They are later arrested by the police and placed in separate rooms where they are questioned. Unfortunately, the police have no solid evidence that either Mark or Jim is guilty. As a result, the only way they will be convicted of the crimes is if they confess. The police thus decide to make each of them the following offer: if you confess to the crime and your accomplice does not, we will set you free and give him the maximum sentence of 10 years. If you both confess you will both go to jail, but we will make sure that the prison sentences are not too harsh. If neither of you confesses, we will only be able to convict you on the charge of having unregistered guns (but beware of the powerful incentives that your partner has to confess!). Mark and Jim cannot communicate with one another. What is it rational for them to do?

We can plot their choices graphically to see their dilemma (see table 34.1). Mark considers his options by thinking about what it would be best for him to do if Jim confesses, and what it would be good for him to do if Jim does not confess. If Jim confesses, it is better for Mark to confess as well. At least that way he will get 6 years in jail rather than 10. If Jim does not confess, Mark should still confess since, in that case, he will serve no time in jail (though, unfortunately, Jim will serve the maximum sentence – too bad Jim!). As a result, no matter what Jim does, Mark should confess. As a result, he is going to confess. In one sense, this dilemma is no dilemma at all. When rational agents are faced with a decision in which one decision is best no matter how the others involved behave, that decision is called a "dominant" one. So, in this case, as we have seen, the dominant strategy is to confess.

Notice that while confessing is dominant for both Mark and Jim, there is one sense in which they do better collectively if they do the exact opposite: that is, if they both refuse to confess, they will collectively serve only 6 years in jail. If only one confesses they collectively spend 11 years in jail, and if they both confess they get the worst outcome: 16 collective years in jail. These outcomes are only compounded if Mark and Jim are confronted with this dilemma repeatedly.

The situation in the Prisoner's Dilemma reflects, on a small scale, the problem of group cooperation on the large scale. If all members of the group cooperate, contributing their resources to serve the common good, the group as a whole reaps the maximal benefit. However, each member of the group has incentives to cheat others, reaping the benefits for themselves, without having to contribute any of their own resources. In a situation like this, in which cheating is the dominant strategy, the fragile economy of cooperation threatens to erode rapidly, splintering the former cooperators into cheating opportunitists, ultimately losing any of the benefits the cooperation formerly earned them. Cooperating groups thus face a deep and vexing problem: how to insure continued cooperation in the face of these temptations?

The first strategy that naturally comes to mind is: punish cheaters. Punishment is the system that nations implement to deter those who want to free-ride on their fellow citizens. For example, you might be tempted to reap the benefits of the protection afforded by the state, while trying not to pay the taxes that you rightly owe. You let others pay the price while you enjoy the benefit. The state responds by implementing laws and punishments that remove these incentives. If you are caught, the punishments for tax evasion are certain and severe. This leads to a revision of the decision matrix with the result, when done properly, that incentive no longer exists.

IV Punishment Theories

However, punishment is a far less than ideal way to sustain cooperation. There are four central problems with punishment.

(1)   It is costly. In order to sustain a system of punishment, members of the group will have to contribute some of their resources to detecting, detaining, and punishing those who fail to cooperate. As we know, this is expensive: police forces, courts, judges, and prisons and so on all incur high costs that make lower the ultimate payoff for the cooperators. In cases where the payoff for cooperation is not extremely high, the cost of punishing might outstrip its benefits.

(2)   The mechanisms of punishment typically involve other members of the group doing the policing, judging, and incarcerating. Unfortunately, situations like that are highly liable to corruption. If, for a small price, I can pay the police, the judge, or the jailer to lower my fee or prison sentence, the deterrent power of punishment is correspondingly lower. And when that happens, punishment loses its effectiveness.

(3)   Any system of punishment is only as good as its detectives. If there is a system of punishment, cheaters will find increasingly sophisticated ways of avoiding detection. This leads to an escalation of costs as punishers are forced to find new ways to catch more sophisticated cheaters.

(4)   Finally, any system of punishment is susceptible to the problem of second-order cheating. The same incentives that lead me to consider cheating in the first place are now in place when it comes to the system of punishment. If I can find a way to keep from making my contribution to the system of punishment, I can enjoy its benefits, without paying any of the costs. As a result, we now face an unstable situation at the higher level.

An ideal system of punishment would involve minimal or no cost, no possibility of corruption, and no chance of failure of detection. Notice that a system like this would avoid the last problem above as well: if a system of punishment is cost-free, there is no way to second-order cheat, since members of the group are not required to make a contribution to punishing in the first place. But how could we implement such an ideal system of punishment? The answer: religion. It is interesting to notice that religious systems commonly have all of these features. Disinterested gods, spirits, forces, or ancestors take a deep and abiding interest in the moral behavior of members of human groups. These supernatural beings do not need to be paid for their work (though they may need to be satisfied by various forms of sacrifice), they infallibly discover our failings, and they are not liable to corruption or bribery by cheaters. According to "Supernatural Punishment" theories of religion, religion exists and spreads because groups which postulate supernatural entities of this sort do better at fostering low-cost, stable cooperation than groups that do not. (Johnson 2005, Johnson and Kruger 2004, Johnson and Bering 2005).

Initially this theory of the origin and persistence of religion might seem highly implausible. Perhaps we can instill and experience fear of supernatural punishment for a while. But once an individual cheats and "gets away with it," surely the cheater (and perhaps others) will realize that the gods can be fooled after all (or perhaps that the gods don't exist). For this reason, we might conclude, religion could not in the end foster cooperation. Defenders of this theory point out, however, this problem can be skirted in cases where religious systems come prepackaged with a handful of additional features. For example, religious systems that teach that punishments for cheating will largely or exclusively be dealt out in the afterlife will never be falsified in this way. Further, religious systems that evolve elaborate systems of punishment which are administered by other human beings who pose as divine agents will be able to avoid this problem. If I know that the Taliban regularly shows up at the doorstep of those who violate Islamic law, I will have reason to fear that God will punish me through these indirect means. Finally, if human beings had a natural tendency to attribute cosmic significance to events that involve great fortune and misfortune, we might naturally tend to assume that when good things happen to me, the gods or the ancestors are responsible for my fortunes, and when bad things happen to me, that these are due to supernatural cursing.

In fact, one or more of these features are in fact found in human populations and the religious systems they embrace. It is common for religions to invoke instruments like purgatory, hell, karma, and so on as instances of supernatural punishment in the afterlife (Rappaport 1999). In addition, it is common for religious organizations to administer this-worldy forms of justice on those who violate the social and religious norms. Finally, recent research in cognitive psychology shows a widespread human tendency to ascribe cosmic significance to our successes and failures (Barrett 2004, Boyer 2001). As a result, religious systems use a variety of amendments and natural human tendencies to sustain belief in the face of what might appear to be undermining evidence.

While all of this makes a good just-so story, there is powerful empirical evidence to support this theory as well. First, there is strong evidence that human beings have a natural tendency to act in accordance with social norms when they are subjected to cues that indicate that they are under the watchful eye of neutral observers. To show this, a collection box was placed in a university lounge in which students were supposed to voluntarily place the money for their purchases. The study took place under two conditions. In one condition the collection box was an ordinary wooden box with a lock and slot in the top for depositing the money. In the second condition, an identical box was used, with images of two large human shaped eyes on the front. Even though the "watchful eyes" were not real, the presence of the eyes led far more students to pay (and to pay the full price!) for the items they removed from the store (Bateson, Nettles, and Roberts 2006). Similarly, Haley and Fessler (2006) have shown that students have a much higher rate of cooperative behavior when performing a competitive task on a computer screen which has stylized human eyes as part of the desktop artwork.

This research shows a general tendency on the part of human beings to cooperate when they are primed with cues that indicate that their behavior is being observed. But does belief in supernatural observers add any additional force to these cooperation fostering tendencies? There is good evidence that they do.

Jesse Bering (2004) has shown that, even from an early age, children tend to follow rules more consistently when they are primed to believe that a supernatural agent is watching them. In one experiment, subjects were brought into a room and shown a box under two conditions. In one condition, the child is told that there is an invisible princess in the room named Alice, who is watching the whole experiment very carefully. In the control condition, children are not told any story about Alice. The children were then told that inside the box was a very special prize, and that they could have the prize if only they could guess what it was. However, they must guess what the prize is without looking in the box. After giving the child the instructions, the experimenter tells the child that he needs to step out of the room for the moment. Children who had received the Alice prime cheated significantly less than those who did not, and even among cheaters, it took much longer for primed subjects to cheat than subjects who were not primed.

Similar results were found for adult subjects. College-aged subjects were engaged in a competitive game on a computer. The game required students to select the correct answers to a series of questions. In one condition, the subjects were told that the game was designed by a graduate student at the university, in another they were told that the experiment was designed by a graduate student at the university who had died, and in a third they were told that the experiment was designed by a graduate student who had died and was believed by some to haunt the laboratory. All subjects were then told that the computer program had a small glitch which would sometimes cause the correct answer to appear on the screen *before* they were prompted to give the answer. They were further told that, to keep the game honest, they should simply hit the space bar on the keyboard when the glitch happened to clear the answer. Not to do so would, they were told, be cheating. Interestingly, subjects who received the ghost prime hit the space bar, clearing the correct answer, in about *half* the time of those who did not receive the prime. The results indicate that those prompted to think that their behavior might be observed by invisible agents are more likely to engage in rule following, cooperative behavior (Bering 2004).

Norenzayan and Sharif had pairs of students play the Dictator Game. In this game, one student is given a sum of money which he can share with his partner. The game is played only one time, and the giver can choose to give the receiver all of the money, only some of it, or none of it. The giver then keeps the rest. Prior to playing the game students are required to read scrambled sentences. In one condition, the scrambled sentences contained one or more of the following words: spirit, divine, God, sacred, and prophet. In the other condition the sentences contained no words with religious connotations. Givers were provided with $10 to distribute. The results showed the student primed with the religious words before the start of the game gave, on average, $2 more to the receiver than those without the prime ($4.56 *versus* $2.56). This is at least some indication that distinctively religious concepts dispose us towards greater cooperative behavior (*Psychological Science*, Sept. 2007).

Perhaps this feature of religion explains its unreasonable success in fostering group cooperation over long spans of time, especially in contrast to purely secular groups (Sosis and Bressler 2003). Supernatural punishment views are still in their infancy and a great deal more work needs to be done to assess their merits. While there is some powerful empirical and game-theoretic evidence favoring such a view, the view faces a few crucial difficulties. We don't have time to deal with all of them here. However, the most serious objection to this view is that, for all appearances, its success depends on human agents believing claims for which they have a great deal of counter-evidence. Without direct evidence of afterlife punishments – or indeed any punishments except for those we see meted out by other human agents – cheaters would still have good evidence that cheating pays. In fact, cheating *would* still pay on this view. If cheating is not in fact punished in ways that outweigh the value of cheating, it would be adaptive for individual organisms to recognize this, and to take advantage of those who have been hypnotized by religion. As a result, Supernatural Punishment theories seem to have a serious instability at their core.

Perhaps defenders of this view will argue that religion only acts as an adaptation when all of the additional requirements are met (when we tend to think that fortune and misfortune are rewards and punishments, and so on). In cases where they are not, the fragile balance is fractured. But if religion requires that all of these factors be present and balanced in this way, the pervasiveness of religion is itself a mystery. How likely is it that this constellation of characteristics would arise repeatedly across times and cultures? There is as yet no good answer to this question.

V Commitment Signaling

As human beings began to interact in larger social groups, the cognitive demands placed on them increased accordingly. (Humphrey 1976; Byrne and Whiten 1988; Humphrey 1992; Dunbar 1998 b.; Dunbar 2005). The more people I interact with, the more I must be able to police relationships, predict behaviors of others, and maintain positive social dispositions. Since individuals have both one-on-one relationships as well as relationships with various groups of individuals (kin, hunting groups, trade partners, etc.) the social cognitive demands increase more quickly than the raw numbers of individuals do.

As social demands of this sort increase, so do techniques that serve to reduce the cognitive and computational demands required to manage and negotiate them. As a result, individuals in group benefit from the creation norms which structure relationships and behavior in ordered routinized ways (Boehm 1999). If there are strict rules for dividing the harvest or the kill or the war spoils, social relationships can be managed with minimal cognitive demand. Furthermore, we can and do manage many of our social alliances through perceptual and emotional signals that further reduce the cognitive demands of social life. The Buddhist monk, with shaved head and brown robe, is easily recognizable to those who are part of the social group to which he belongs, as is the gang member and the leather-clad Nazi skinhead.

Religious groups can serve similar purposes. Those who attend my temple, church, synagogue, prayer group and so on identify themselves as part of the group to which I belong and display solidarity with me that leads me to trust them. Of course, as with supernatural punishment theories, members of the group can still successfully cheat other members, ultimately leading to the dominance of imposters and the collapse of the signals that allowed groups to recognize cooperating partners.

The same problem was illustrated earlier in the Prisoner's Dilemma. Mark and Jim each confront a situation in which defection is dominant. Yet it is also true that Mark and Jim together do better if they cooperate. If the Prisoner's Dilemma is to be a useful model of society however it must take account of the fact that our social interactions are not exclusively (or even largely) restricted to single encounters. Instead we repeatedly interact with many of the same individuals over and over again. If this were not the case, the prudent strategy might be for me to cheat those I encounter. Since I don't have to fear being punished in future encounters, I can take the money and run. Of course, in real life, I have reason to fear future reprisals. As a result, I prosper in the long run if I can find other individuals that will reliably cooperate with me over the long run. One way to secure this sort of cooperation is by agreeing to subject myself to some enforcement mechanism, as we saw above. Even better would be some network of signaling that would allow me to reliably distinguish between likely cooperators and likely cheaters. If agents develop a sign that allows them to them to signal their cooperative intentions for others, members of the cooperating group will ultimately jointly benefit.

Without filling in any of the details here it is easy to see that establishing alliances on the basis of a seemingly reliable signal is ultimately unstable. Eventually, cheaters will find some way to mimic the signal so that they can enjoy the benefits of cooperation while not paying the cost. So how can we develop reliable signals that exclude fake signals? There are two ways to solve the problem of fake signalers. The first is to establish signals that are costly enough that cheaters would be unlikely to pay the price of displaying them. "Costly Signaling" theorists argue that religious signals can play such a role. Religions often require members of the group to pay a price for admission to or continued participation in the group that is very high – high enough, on this view, to deter potential cheaters from paying it (Irons 1996c; Irons 2001; Sosis 2003; Sosis and Alcorta 2003; Sosis 2004; Bulbulia 2004a.). If one is willing to spend hours memorizing countless theological claims, make enormous sacrifices to god or the ancestors, allow others to inflict pain and suffering in the context of religious ritual, all for the sake of showing commitment to the group, members of the group can develop a reliable way of showing their willingness to cooperate with others in the group.

As an alternative, if members of the group can develop ways of reliably signaling commitment that cannot easily be faked or mimicked by others, worries about cheaters can also be avoided. "Hard to fake" signals might include internalizing detailed theological knowledge, showing avid displays of emotion in worship, prayer, or ritual, expressing sincere commitment to the importance of the religious activities or organizations. All of these represent modes of signaling that are difficult to express with apparent sincerity.

The most reliable hard-to-fake signals are likely to have direct connections to our emotions. Emotions are directly connected to motivation. If a person is not genuinely motivated to seek the good of the group, they will be unlikely to be able to express the commitment-signaling emotion. On the other hand, those with such a commitment will signal commitment emotions reflexively. Shedding tears when members of the group experience misfortune and evincing joy at others' successes displays genuine concern for and commitment to others. Furthermore, emotional displays represent powerful signals since they are routinely scrutinized by others.

Are there reliable hard-to-fake signals that humans display and scrutinize that are capable of discriminating between cooperators and cheaters? Brown, Palameta, and Moore (*Evolutionary Psychology* 2003) conducted experiments on groups of college students which sought to find subtle signals that humans use to signal and detect likely cooperation. They began by surveying subjects to determine the degree to which they are inclined to altruistic or helping behavior. Subjects were then asked to read a famous Western children's story (*Little Red Riding Hood*) into a video camera. The videos were then shown to other subjects who were asked to rank the story-readers on a number of different measures, one of which was: how likely they would be to help others in need. The study showed that subjects showed a strongly statistically significant correlation between measured altruism and perceived altruism. What signals were story-readers sending that allowed others to peer into their souls? Further scrutiny of the films showed that perceived altruism correlated directly with concern furrows on the brow, head nods, and symmetrical smiles. On the other hand, perceived altruism correlated inversely with length of smile. It is well-known that felt or genuine smiles are hard to fake, and perceivers were using genuineness of smile as an indicator of the genuineness of the reader (Ramachandran and Blakeslee 1998).

Brown et al. shows us that human beings are capable of managing hard-to-fake signals in ways that can potentially help solve the key problem of group living: cheaters or free riders. Costly signaling and hard-to-fake signaling both represent ways in which individuals signal a solidarity with or commitment to a group so that others can reliably trust the signaler not to cheat. Thus both types of signaling are members of a broader genus we can now call "commitment-signaling" (following Joseph Bulbulia[in press]).

There are a number of ways that religion could be tied to commitment signaling. First, religious belief and ritual all by themselves might count as commitment signals in so far as religious knowledge is hard to acquire and maintain, and religious ritual is often quite costly to perform. The problem with this explanation of religion, however, is that there is nothing here that explains why *religion itself* is so effective at achieving group solidarity that it is culturally recurrent. What we would expect to find is *some cultural practice or other* that involves knowledge that is hard to acquire and practices that are costly to perform. But since many cultural activities satisfy this description, there is nothing about it that explains the pervasiveness of religion.

Bulbulia argues for a more complex connection between signaling and religion. On his view, religion has played a dual role in solving the free-rider problem. First, religion solves the problem of cooperation as described in the Prisoner's Dilemma by changing the expected outcomes. If supernatural beings care about our cooperative behavior, and have the power to reward cooperators and punish free-riders, the perceived utilities of our options change. If the punishments and rewards are sufficiently weighty, it will be easy to change the matrix so that cooperation is strongly dominant for both players. (This is the same claim defended, – as we saw above – by Bering and Johnson.) But committed religious individuals will need one other element before they can gain from this adjustment: a reliable way of finding others who have the same cooperative intent. Here commitment signaling comes to the rescue. If affective states associated with the religious commitment are hard-to-fake or costly, these will be good indicators that those displaying the signal have commitments that are genuine.

There are two problems with commitment signaling. The first concerns signals that display commitment because of their cost. Let's break down the sorts of benefits that can be secured and lost by cooperation and defection into the *secular benefits* and the (perceived) *religious benefits*. If you and I are cooperating members of a religious kibbutz in Israel, we will each devote equal resources to our enterprise and we will yield a much higher return for our labor than we would toiling individually. But we also perceive a religious benefit: reward in the afterlife for cooperation, and punishment for defection.

A free-rider would have perfect incentive to fake commitment in this case since, if she could fake the religious commitment, she would receive the secular benefit. Costly signals are supposed to fix this. How? If the price of the signal is so high that only the religious believer perceives an all-things-considered benefit in the cooperative arrangement, the free-rider won't see any benefit in trying to exploit this group. The admission price (the costly signal) cancels out the secular benefit. That all works fine if religion is true – since the religious believers will come out better in the end by cooperating, though not in virtue of the secular benefits, those being outweighed by the costly signal. But if the only benefits are the secular benefits, costly signaling makes for trouble. If the price of admission (the costly signal) wipes out all the secular benefit, then it is the religious believer that has been fooled.

So perhaps costly signals cannot perform the function they are supposed to perform. But recall that commitment signals come in one of two forms: costly and hard-to-fake. Might hard-to-fake signals avoid costly signaling liabilities? It seems that the answer is yes. If we develop an involuntary signal which shows cooperative intent, then those who display the signal can much more easily find reliable cooperative partners. Since religious rituals often involve a number of hard-to-fake signals, perhaps religion plays this cultural role.

However, while costly signaling can avoid this pitfall, it is still not entirely satisfactory as a scientific account of the origin and persistence of religion, for two reasons. First, hard-to-fake signaling does not explain why religion is pan-cultural and second, it does not explain why religions have the broad similarities they have with respect to belief and ritual structure. Let's consider these in turn.

(1)   Any scientific account of religion which aims to explain the phenomenon in terms of its functional benefits will be forced to explain why religion is uniquely successful in playing this role. This would *not* be the case if religion were not as pervasive as it is. Police forces play an important functional role in some cultures, namely, providing citizens with disincentives for breaking fundamental cultural norms. But not every culture has a police force; other cultures find other ways to present members of the group with disincentives. If religion plays the role of sending signals of cooperative intent, then it plays an important functional role. But there is no reason to think that other hard-to-fake signals would not be just as effective. Indeed there are many ways in which human beings could form voluntary associations which rally around hard-to-fake emotional commitments and signals: the Houston Rockets fan club, the Nazi Party, the Chinese Communist Party (CCP), the Harley-Davidson motorcycle association, the numismatists society. Why would religion be more successful if its only utility derives from generating hard-to-fake signals of cooperative intent? There are easier ways to find cooperators.

(2)   Commitment signaling does not explain why religion has the similarities it does across times and cultures. As we saw earlier, religions almost always include belief in the existence of invisible, supernatural agents who support and enforce norms of human behavior. These agents demand our attention not only because of their norm-supporting character, but because they are also involved in orchestrating the good or ill fortune that we experience both in this life and the next. Such agents also require that we engage in activities with distinct ritual structure (McCauley and Lawson 2002) and belief (Whitehouse 2004). Nothing in commitment signaling theory gives us any clue as to why these features exist and are as pervasive as they are.

VI Group Selection

Perhaps we have been going about this the wrong way. To this point we have been looking at religious behaviors in which organisms sacrifice their own interests for the sake of others and which thus give the appearance of being maladaptive. We have looked at explanations of such behavior which aim to show that while these behaviors seem to carry a net fitness cost to the one making the sacrifice, there is a hidden benefit which makes the behavior ultimately fitness-enhancing for the individual. One way or another, the trait in question does (or is a by-product of a trait that does) increase the frequency of the individual's genes in succeeding generations.

While this style of explanation allows us to successfully explain many pervasive yet seemingly maladaptive traits, there are still some where an explanation eludes us. For a controversial example of this we can consider the Lancet Fluke. This small organism has a very elaborate life-cycle. The cycle begins with eggs in the feces of cows and sheep which are eaten and hatch in the digestive system of snails. The resulting larvae are then excreted through the snail's slime, which is in turn ingested by ants (who eat the slime as a source of moisture). After developing in the ant, one of the mature flukes migrates to the nervous system of the ant where it causes the ant to crawl to the top of a blade of grass and latch onto it with its mandible until it is eaten by a cow or sheep, where the life cycle will begin all over again. The lancet fluke raises a problem because the one fluke that migrates to the ant's nervous system does not survive or pass on its genes to succeeding generations. It receives no benefit for this action, an action which in turn greatly benefits the other members of its group. What explains this?

According to David Sloan Wilson (2002) the explanation is found in the fact that the activities of this ant benefit the group of which it is a member. Our earlier explanations of religion all assume that the only sort of traits natural selection can favor are those that favor the individual. What this example shows us is that selection can also select for traits that benefit *the group as a whole*, even at one individual's expense. If the genetic complement for the lancet fluke disposes at least some members of the group towards behaviors which are disastrous for some, but which significantly enhance the reproductive success of the whole group, such a group will thrive. On the other hand, if the lancet fluke evolved so that it exhibited only traits which were ultimately beneficial for the organism that had them, lancet flukes would not exist. Without the one that gives its life for the others, the others would have no descendents.

On Wilson's view, groups of organisms can be adaptive units in just the same way that individual organisms are. In fact, Wilson argues, in the same way that groups of cells, working together to constitute an organism, can be favored or disfavored by natural selection, so can collections of organisms, working together to form a group. And just as it is adaptive for some cells to sacrifice themselves to preserve the life of the organism as a whole, it will (or can) sometimes be adaptive for members of groups to sacrifice themselves to preserve the life of the group (Wilson 2002; Wilson and Wilson 2008).

Wilson argues, in keeping with a longstanding anthropological tradition, that: "In most human social groups, cultural transmission is guided by a set of norms that identifies what counts as acceptable behavior" and that "function largely … to make human groups function as adaptive units." (Wilson 2002) However, we can expect that those norms will sometimes call for some members of the group to make sacrifices for the benefit of others. For

Wilson, religion plays the role of creating and establishing norms that lead religious groups to act in ways that enhance the overall fitness of their group.

In his book *Darwin's Cathedral* (2002), Wilson illustrates the group fitness benefits of religion with a few key examples. Prominent among these is the case of the Balinese water temples. The Balinese landscape is punctuated by high volcanic peaks that make agriculture difficult. Not only must farmers carve out small level plots of ground from the face of the peaks, they must also find effective ways of channeling the water in order to produce effective irrigation. The task of overseeing irrigation falls to disciples of Dewi Danu, goddess of the waters that are thought to flow out of the volcano itself. Below the large temple that stands at the Crater Lake at the volcanic peak are a series of temples which control the flow of water at every branch in the elaborate irrigation system. Decades of study have shown conclusively that the complicated irrigation system operated by the priests and priestesses has given rise to the most effective agricultural output possible for these farmers. The elaborate system of temples and channels is operated by the priests in accordance with an elaborate set of religious rules and rituals that ultimately control the fate of thousands of farmers spread over hundreds of square kilometers. The divine sanction of the priests and their activities give them, among other things, the power to regulate and distribute a precious resource that allows the group as a whole to survive (Wilson 2002).

Religion often functions in such a way that it requires members of the religious community to make sacrifices that benefit not the one making the sacrifice, but the community as a whole. This makes no sense from the standpoint of individual selection. But once we turn our focus to the survival and reproduction of groups, the phenomenon makes perfectly good sense. If it is good for a group to have all or a subset of its members altruistically serve the individual well-being of other members of the group, and it is possible for the group to pass along this behavioral pattern, then this sort of altruism will have the same selective advantages that the group does.

Group selectionist theories of religion offer a very different account of the origin and persistence of religion as a cultural phenomenon. Unlike punishment and signaling theories, group selection theories need not come up with special explanations for how altruists can avoid being exploited into extinction. On group selection theories it may, in fact, be the fate of altruists to make their contribution to group fitness without even getting any individual fitness benefit ever. In addition, they explain how altruistic behavior which has no individual benefit for the one performing it can arise and evolve, something which, from the individualistic perspective would appear to be genuinely impossible.

However, group selection theory still remains the minority position in this field for some very good reasons. First, while most biologists agree that group selection is, in principle, a possible force in evolutionary development, many argue that it in fact played no role (or perhaps played a role that is exceedingly small in comparison with individual selection) (Dicks 2000; Atran 2002, p. 214)

Second, and perhaps more important in this context, group selection accounts of religion are, what Scott Atran calls "mindblind" (Atran 2002, p. 197). For Wilson and other defenders of group selection, what is passed on from one generation to the next – and what selection acts on – is not really *religion*, but rather behaviors performed by religious people following religious norms. In other words, it is not the religion that is adaptive, it is the behavioral practices. Once we see this, it is also easy to see that group selection theories explain only the origin and persistence of the adaptive behaviors. What it does not explain is why these adaptive behaviors are always explained against the background of religious belief. If any old set of beliefs and desires that gave rise to adaptive behaviors could be adaptive, then we would expect that religious belief would be just one among many sorts of cultural constructs that human beings use to motivate altruistic behavior. Perhaps some groups would simply hit upon a compelling yet thoroughly naturalistic commitment to moral sympathy. Perhaps others would hit upon a cultural system of behavior control in which mortal fear of a political ruler generates the group adaptive behavior. But, as far as we can tell, these alternatives hardly ever arise in human culture. Why is it that these adaptive practices are most commonly accompanied by beliefs in supernatural agents who establish and police those behavioral norms? Group selection theory tells us nothing that could explain this.

Finally, group selection theories of religion, at this stage of development, simply assume that benefits of altruism lead to greater group fitness than would be realized without the presence of the altruists. The argument proceeds by looking at the contribution that altruists make to the fitness of the group, and arguing that if those benefits were absent, the group would be correspondingly less well off. But these arguments as they stand are just invalid. What is needed to make them valid is a testable model which predicts what degree of fitness would be had by a group made up entirely of egoists. Imagine that I am part of an army. Most members of the army are committed to battle against armies of other countries that we are trying to conquer. However, a few members of our group are routinely chosen to provide medical assistance to those who are wounded in battle. These medical personnel are defenseless and thus frequently killed during conflict. But while they are alive they provide sufficient care to injured warriors so that most of them ultimately recover. It thus appears that the altruistic contribution of the medical personnel ultimately enhances overall group fitness. However, this argument only works if the fortunes of the army would not be better served by having everyone standing on the frontline wielding their swords or firing their guns. It sure is nice and helpful when some members stay back and help the injured recover. But it just may be the case that the group as a whole will win more battles if everyone gets to the frontline and fights as hard as they can. The same is true when it comes to group selection arguments for religion. It is easy to point out the many benefits that arise when some members of the religious community sacrifice their well-being for others. What this (alone) does not tell us, is whether or not (and why and how) the fitness of the group is higher in this condition than it would be were no one behaving altruistically.

V Conclusion

Adaptationist theories of the origin and persistence of religion bring take an old theory and dress it in new garb. For centuries functionalist anthropologists and sociologists argued that religion plays a powerful role in securing successful group cooperation and integration. And in fact, looked at in a charitable light, religion does seem to bring these benefits. With Darwinism, we have a way to quantify those benefits, and then look for the specific ways in which religion might enhance them. Yet while religion is often connected with securing the sorts of benefits adaptationists cite, it is not clear that there is anything about religion in particular that accounts for those benefits. As we have seen, other beliefs and desires would, as far as one can tell, be equally suited to the task of securing the adaptive ends. And if that is so, the pervasiveness of religion remains a troublesome mystery on these views. In the next chapter we will look at non-adaptationist theories to see if and how they fare better.

Notes

1   For the latter there are both adaptationist explanations, such as those proposed by Geoffrey Miller in *The Mating Mind* (2000) as well as non-adaptationist explanations such as one finds in, for example, E. O. Wilson in *Consilience* (1998).
2   Hinde (2005), pp. 38–9.

References

Barrett, J. (2004) *Why Would Anyone Believe in God?* Walnut Creek, CA: AltaMira Press.

Bateson, M., Nettle, D. & Roberts, G. (2006) Cues of being watched enhance cooperation in real-world setting. *Biology Letters*.

Bering, J. M. (2005) The evolutionary history of an illusion: Religious causal beliefs in children and adults. In B. Ellis and D. F. Bjorklund (eds.) *Origins of the social mind: Evolutionary psychology and child development.* New York, Guilford Press.

Boehm C. (1999) *Hierarchy in the Forest: The Evolution of Egalitarian Behavior.* Cambridge, MA: Harvard University Press.

Boyer, P. (2001) *Religion Explained.* New York: Basic Books.

Brown, M, Palameta, B, and Moore, C. (2003) Are there nonverbal cues to commitment? An exploratory study using the zero-acquaintance video presentation paradigm. *Evolutionary Psychology* 1, 42–69.

Bulbulia, J. (2004) Religious costs as adaptations that signal altruistic intention. *Evolution and Cognition* 10 (1), 19–38.

Dicks L. (2000) All for one! *New Scientist* 167 (2246), 30.

Dunbar, R. I. (1998) The Social Brain Hypothesis. *Evolutionary Anthropology* 6, 178–90.

Griffiths, P. (2002). The origins of religious thought (faith seeking explanation). *First Things,* 119.

Haley, K. J. & Fessler, D. M. T. (2005) Nobody's watching? Subtle cues affect generosity in an anonymous economic game. *Evolution and Human Behavior* 26 (3), 245–56.

Hinde, R. (2005). Modes theory. In H. Whitehouse and R. McCauley (eds.) *Mind and Religion: Psychological and Cognitive Foundations of Religiosity.* Walnut Creek, CA: AltaMira Press.

Humphrey, N. K. (1976) The social function of intellect. In P. Bateson and R. Hinde (eds.) *Growing Points in Ethology.* Cambridge: Cambridge University Press, pp. 303–17.

Humphrey, N. K. (1992) *A history of the mind: Evolution and the birth of consciousness.* New York: Simon & Schuster.

Irons, W. (1996) Morality as an Evolved Adaptation. In J. P. Hurd (ed.) *Investigating the Biological Foundations of Morality,* Lewiston: Edwin Mellon Press, pp. 1–34.

Irons, W. (2001) "Religion as a hard-to-fake sign of commitment." In Randy Nesse (ed.) *Evolution and the Capacity for Commitment,* pp. 292–309. New York: Russell Sage Foundation.

Johnson, D. (2005) God's punishment and public goods: a test of the supernatural punishment hypothesis in 186 world cultures. *Human Nature* 16(4), 410–46.

Johnson, D. and Bering, J. (2009) Hand of God, Mind of Man: Punishment and cognition in the evolution of cooperation. In Jeffrey Schloss and Michael Murray (eds.) *The Spiritual Primate: Scientific, Philosophical, and Theological Reflections on the Origin of Religion.* Oxford: Oxford University Press.

Johnson, D. and Krüger, O. (2004) The Good of Wrath: Supernatural Punishment and the Evolution of Cooperation. *Political Theology* 5.2.

McCauley, R. N. and E. T. Lawson (2002). *Bringing Ritual to Mind.* New York: Cambridge University Press.

Miller, Geoffrey (2000) *The Mating Mind: How Sexual Choice Shaped the Evolution of Human Nature.* New York: Doubleday.

Rappaport, R. A. (1999) *Ritual and Religion in the Mmaking of Humanity*. Cambridge Studies in Social and Cultural Anthropology 110. Cambridge and New York: Cambridge University Press.

Ramachandran, V. S. and Blakeslee, S. (1998) *Phantoms in the Brain: Probing the Mysteries of the Human Mind*, New York: Quill William Morrow.

Sharif, A. and Norenzayan, A. (2007) God is watching you: Supernatural agent concepts increase prosocial behavior in an anonymous economic game. *Psychological Science* 18, 803–9.

Sosis, R. and Alcorta, C. (2003) Signalling, solidarity, and the sacred: The evolution of religious behavior, *Evolutionary Anthropology* 12, 264–74.

Sosis, R. (2003) Why aren't we all Hutterites? Costly signaling theory and religious behavior. *Human Nature* 14(2), 19–127.

Sosis, R. (2004) The adaptive value of religious ritual: Rituals promote group cohesion by requiring members to engage in behavior that is too costly to fake. *American Scientists*, 92(2): 166–74.

Sosis, R. and Bressler, E. R. (2003) Cooperation and commune longevity: A test of the costly signaling theory of religion. *Cross-Cultural Religion* 37(2), 211–39.

Whitehouse, H. (2004) *Modes of Religiosity: A Cognitive Theory of Religious Transmission*. New York: AltaMira Press.

Wilson, D. S. and Wilson, E. O. (2008) Rethinking the Foundations of Sociobiology, *Quarterly Review of Biology* 82(4), 327–48.

Wilson, D. S. (2002) *Darwin's Cathedral*. Chicago: University of Chicago Press.

Wilson, E. O. (1998) *Consilience*. New York: Knopf.

35

The Evolution of Religion: Non-Adaptationist Accounts

MICHAEL J. MURRAY

Not all evolutionary explanations of religion see religious belief and practice as adaptations. Indeed, the most popular evolutionary explanation of religion take to be either a non-adaptive or even a maladaptive consequence of other traits which are adaptations. Traits of this sort of commonly referred to as "spandrels." In this chapter I describe the two most widely held spandrel theories of religion, cognitive theories and meme theories, and go on to assess their adequacy as scientific accounts of religion.

In chapter 34 we looked at a variety of accounts that attempt to explain the origin and persistence of religion as an adaptation. Traits count as adaptations when the fitness of the organism (or the group in the case of group selection) is increased because of the role that they play for the organism in their environment. Fitness as we saw, is a technical notion in biology. Specifically, a trait enhances an organism's fitness when it tends to increase the frequency of that organism's genetic code in subsequent generations. As a result, fitness is a relative notion: since fitness requires an *increasing frequency in subsequent generations* a trait is not adaptive merely because it helps the organism survive and reproduce; rather, the trait must help the organism that has it survive and reproduce *in greater numbers* than those who lack the trait.

Because of this fitness-enhancing traits will, over time, begin to proliferate. Since, by definition, fitness-enhancing traits increase the frequency of the genes that give rise to them in subsequent generations, the trait will become more widespread as time goes by (all other things being equal). This tempts many people to assume that when we see a trait that is widespread, or at least a trait that is increasing in frequency, that this trait must serve some adaptive purpose, now or in our ancestral past. This, however, is a mistake – a very common mistake among scholars and non-scholars alike.

First, some traits will become widespread simply because they have no fitness benefit and little in the way of fitness cost. Near-sightedness might provide a good contemporary example. In the past, near-sightedness would likely have been a fatal genetic flaw. If I cannot see my prey in the distance (or even worse, the predators stalking me), it is not likely that

I would survive very long. However, once inexpensive glasses become available to us, the gene that causes nearsightedness (a gene that happens to be dominant) will spread in the population because of its dominance and its fitness neutrality. Since it is dominant, it will increase in frequency since selection has no power to stop its advance. These traits piggy-back on the genetic code of the organism, without being associated with any adaptive mechanism. For our purposes we can call these traits "piggybackers."

Second, some are non-adaptive by-products of a distinct trait that is adaptive. Traits of this sort are called *spandrels*. The English word originally referred to the spaces that are formed as an inevitable architectural by-product when interior archways meet in a building. In medieval European cathedrals these spaces were often decorated with elaborate carvings and paintings, and thus became artistic focal points of the building. However, the *real reason* for their existence was not their artistic function. They were merely by-products that were used for good purposes later. In the same way that human architectural design can spawn non-functional by-products, so can biological architectural design. A commonly discussed (though recently controversial) example of a spandrel is female orgasm. While female orgasm is possible in a number of female primates, it is typically manifested only after lengthy stimulation. However, since sex among primates ends quickly, orgasm is rare in any primates other than humans. The capacity is there, but it is not a target of selection since it is never or rarely manifested. The capacity is rather a by-product of human genital embryological development.[1]

Note that while piggybackers are fitness neutral, spandrels might not be. There might be some cases in which adaptive traits give rise to by-products which are, taken in isola-tion, harmful. However, as long as the benefits of the beneficial trait outweigh the costs of the maladaptive by-product, both traits will continue to increase in frequency in the population.

While few evolutionary theorists would argue that widespread cultural traits, like reli-gion, are piggybackers, many would argue that they are spandrels. Indeed, the spandrelist account of the origin of widespread cultural traits is the dominant view. Human cogni-tive capacities in the areas of music (the ability to discover principles governing harmon-ics, for example), art (the capacity for aesthetic appreciation or the ability to discover principles of perspective drawing), abstract mathematics (in topology, for example), and so on are not, on this view adaptive (directly or indirectly), but are rather spandrels which result from other capacities which are themselves adaptive. So, the capacity for manipulating mathematical ideas at the level of, say, arithmetic and geometry might be adaptive, but the ability to solve problems in calculus arises naturally out of this adaptive, and thus evolutionarily more fundamental, phenotype. Since such traits are blind to selection, and explainable as evolutionary free-riders, adapationist explanations are not warranted.[2]

As in other areas, evolutionary accounts of religion are most often cast in these non-adaptationist terms. Some of these accounts argue that religion is a fitness-neutral by-product of other fitness-enhancing capacities, while others argue that religion is a maladaptive by-product. If we could keep the fitness-enhancing trait while dispensing with the by-product, we would be better off – and those defending this theory argue that this is exactly what we should do.

In this chapter we will consider the two most widely defended non-adaptationist theories of religion: cognitive theories and memetic theories.

I Cognitive Theories of Religion

On what is now called "the standard model," religions across times and cultures revolve around concepts that share a number of central features in common:

1) They are counterintuitive in ways that make them optimally suited for recall and transmission.
2) They spring from cognitive mechanisms that generate beliefs about agents and agency.
3) They are "inference rich" and thus allow us to generate narratives about them that enhance their memorability, make them attractive as objects of ritual, and increase our affective reaction toward them.
4) They typically represent the religious entities as minded agents who, because of their counterintuitive character, stand to benefit us in our attempt to maintain stable relationships in large interacting groups (Barrett 2004, Boyer 2001).

Religions are, by nature, communal and thus religious ideas are ideas shared by a community. In order for religious ideas to become communal they must have characteristics which make them memorable and readily transmissible. As it happens, human minds are structured in such a way that ideas of certain sorts are more naturally memorable and transmissible than others. In particular, human minds find it very easy to remember and talk about ideas that are strange. But not any old strangeness will do. Rather, only strangeness that involves specifiable sorts of deviations from our innate ontological categories seems to do the trick.

Human beings are naturally inclined to sort objects they encounter into ready-made or innate ontological categories such as animal, plant, inanimate natural object, artifact, and so on. This "folk ontology" allows us to classify objects in our environment in ways that allow us to make quick calculations about the objects we happen upon, and such computational simplicity confers fitness advantages. Empirical data demonstrates quite conclusively that when we encounter ideas of particulars which violate these general ontological categories in minimal ways, the ideas are highly memorable and transmissible (Boyer (2001, ch. 2); Barrett (2004, chs. 2–4)) We can thus predict that successfully shared religious ideas will be strange in what cognitive theorists describe as "Minimally Counterintuitive" (or "MCI") ways. Harvey Whitehouse explains the role of such beliefs as follows:

> MCI concepts will, all else being equal, be easy to recall in all human societies … on this view we should expect concepts of ghosts and witches to be globally recurrent, whereas concepts of statues made of cheese or that can see into the future will be either localized or entirely absent from human cultures (Whitehouse 2004, p. 31)[3]

The latter concepts will not be fit objects of religious attention and devotion because they fail to satisfy the MCI test; such concepts instead violate our innate ontologies in large scale ways that make them hard to remember and transmit. As a result, we can expect the entities which are central to religious belief will be strange, but not merely strange. As Barrett puts it,

> A tree that hears prayers is a religious concept and *minimally counterintuitive*. But a tree that hears prayers you will make next week is not a religious concept and is more than minimally

counterintuitive – not only has expectations on trees been violated but also our intuitive assumptions about communication. A person who can foretell the future is a religious concept (and minimally counterintuitive), but a person who vanishes whenever you look at him, knows how many insects are in the Amazon basin at any given moment, and sustains itself on crude oil, is not a religious concept. It is massively counterintuitive.[4]

The minimally counterintuitive nature of religious ideas might explain why those ideas routinely display certain general features, but it still leaves us to wonder about their origins. According to (2), religious ideas are spawned from an online cognitive tool aimed at agency-detection. Humans are, thankfully, equipped with specialized cognitive mechanisms that hypothesize the existence of *agents* when we detect special sorts of stimuli in our environments. When, for example, we see "unnatural" configurations in nature (crop circles or traces in the grass), or unnatural types of motion (rustling bushes), or unnatural sounds (things going bump in the night) we naturally hypothesize the existence of unseen agents as their source. This Hyperactive Agency Detection Device, or HADD, enhances fitness since it leads us to be especially wary in circumstances where, for example, predators might be on the prowl. Of course, such cognitive mechanisms are less adaptive when they are less sensitive, more adaptive when more sensitive. As a result such a mechanism will tend towards greater sensitivity and thus tend to produce a fairly high number of false positives (those beliefs about ghosts in the attic are, inevitably, always wrong). Concepts of supernatural beings thus arise at least in part as a way of explaining natural phenomena that trigger our HADD. Justin Barrett explains the role of HADD in religious cognition as follows:

> Our minds have numerous pattern detectors that organize visual information into meaningful units. HADD remains on the lookout for patterns known to be caused by agents. If this patterned information matches patterns … known to be caused by agents, HADD detects agency and alerts other mental tools …. More interesting is when a pattern is detected that appears to be purposeful or goal directed and, secondarily, does not appear to be caused by ordinary mechanical or biological causes. Such patterns may prompt HADD to attribute the traces to agency yet to be identified: unknown persons, animals, or space aliens, ghosts, or gods. (Barrett 2004, p.37)

Once we generate counterintuitive ideas via HADD, other cognitive tools can enhance their significance in the ways described in (3) and (4). Let's begin with (4). As our primate ancestors began to live in larger interacting groups, it became highly valuable to be able to predict the behaviors of others in the group. Since these behaviors are motivated by beliefs and desires of the agents, having access to those beliefs and desires not only allowed for prediction of their behaviors, but also for the cultivation of strategies for outsmarting others to gain resources – strategies such as deception. If I understand how your actions are motivated, I can seek to hijack those motivations in ways that get you to act for my advantage. Such selective pressures are cited as the explanation for the human tendency to attribute mindedness to other human (or human-like) entities, and to explain behaviors by appeal to hypothesized beliefs and desires. When we conjoin this tendency to anthropomorphize with (1) and (2) we are led to predict that human beings will be liable to take HADD-triggering events as occasions to form beliefs about *minded agents* which are the causes of these events. Since many of these natural events (floods, thunder, etc.) could only be caused by very powerful and unseen agents, it is natural for us to form beliefs in the existence of *powerful, invisible, and minded agents*, that is, something very like the objects of religious experience and devotion. And since, returning to (1), *invisible agents* are counterintuitive, they are memorable and easily transmissible.

In addition to the above characteristics, these powerful, invisible, and minded agents become even more memorable and liable to transmission in light of their "inference richness" (as noted in characteristic (3) above). Ideas are "inference rich" when they lead or invite us to draw conclusions or construct narratives concerning the sorts of activities that might be undertaken by the hypothesized entity. Since we can easily generate narratives concerning these powerful, invisible agents, such "proto-religious" ideas have the potential to become highly emotionally gripping (see Atran 2002, p. 81, Boyer 2001b, p. 50; and Boyer 2001b, p. 59, Barrett 2004, p. 15). For example, the standard model claims that we are highly liable to take these beliefs in minded invisible agents and infer that, since they are not confined by ordinary spatial boundaries, they must have *wide-ranging knowledge* of what is happening, even at distant places (and perhaps distant times). Indeed, the tendency to regard supernatural agents as having super-knowing and super-perceiving powers is one towards which we are developmentally biased (Barrett 2004). Cross-cultural empirical studies demonstrate quite clearly that the human tendency to regard all minded agents as infallible shifts radically at age 4 in such a way that children no longer regard humans as infallible though the overwhelming majority still regard gods as such (Richert and Barrett 2005). Such supernatural agents are thus likely to possess information about what I am doing and what others are doing. Hypothesizing supernatural agents with super-knowing powers thereby undermines our beliefs that we can ever get away with violating social, cultural, or moral norms wholly undetected. Supernatural agents are thus naturally connected with morality because they deter me from trying to get away with norm-violating behavior, and because I can have some confidence that the behavior of others is similarly monitored. Recognition of these formidable powers of supernatural agents thus helps those in large interacting groups to follow the dictates of the social contract and refrain from trying to cheat others.[5]

Such so-called "strategic information" makes these invisible agents quite important and thus worth exploiting, pleasing and/or placating. This in turn further invites us to construct *religious rituals* in which such exploiting, pleasing, or placating can go on.[6]

The confluence of the workings of these cognitive mechanisms, it is argued, make us highly liable both to form religious ideas and to sustain them in and through religious rituals and practices.

Notice that there is nothing in the account of the *origins* of religious ideas that involves appeal to the adaptiveness of the ideas themselves. Perhaps these religious beliefs are mere spandrels. Yet one might argue that once such beliefs and practices emerge they can be co-opted for adaptive work. And indeed some argue that the primary reason that religion *persists* is that it confers such additional advantages.[7] For example, as we have seen, belief in such agents might tend to generate or supplement our motivation for altruistic or moral behavior. This in turn might be beneficial either because it encourages alliances that lead to reciprocal altruism, or because it enhances the fitness of my kin or group. If adaptive cognitive mechanisms work in concert to make religious beliefs likely, and especially if these religious beliefs can be co-opted to do additional fitness enhancing work, there are strong selective pressures favoring the formation and maintenance of religious beliefs and practices amongst human beings.

However, as noted earlier, the most prominent advocates of the standard model are quite adamant that religion confers no fitness benefits at all.[8] These non-adaptationists argue that religion is to be explained as a mere by-product brought about by a chance confluence of cognitive circumstances. We happen to find counterintuitive ideas memorable, we happen to attribute mindedness to agents, we happen to engage in HADD, and we happen to have a moral code, the force of which can be bolstered by hypothesized strategic agents. The result is religion.

II Assessing Cognitive Accounts

On these cognitive accounts, religious commitment coalesces around concepts of minimally counterintuitive minded agents that are inference rich and which spawn both affective reactions and religious ritual. But there are a host of such ideas that do not, and seemingly cannot, become the object of religious devotion despite having these same characteristics: the tooth fairy, Mickey Mouse, Batman, Sponge Bob, and the like. So the problem is: Why are there Muslims but not Batmanians? The question is posed by Pyysiainen as follows:

> ...symbolism, as explained by Atran, Sperber and Boyer, cannot be distinguished from mere fiction, such as Mickey Mouse cartoons, without some additional criteria ... Boyer's earlier work does not contain anything that would allow us to differentiate between religious and nonreligious counterintuitiveness or between religion and superstition or fiction, although he clearly thinks that these are different categories.[9]

The problem is that the list of "religious" properties is insufficient to distinguish *religious ideas* from *merely strange and MCI ideas that are taken to be fanciful*. So what is it that accounts for our commitment to the *reality* of one set of ideas and not the other?

While current theorists have offered no response to this challenge, there are at least two potentially complementary responses worth considering. The first goes as follows: Evolutionary psychologists argue that counterintuitive religious beliefs often *arise* in part from the operation of a hyperactive agency detection device (HADD) which is in general adaptive despite generating a large number of false positives (a relatively harmless fault). In this way, religious ideas have a different origin than that of mere creatures of fiction. This might help solve the Sponge Bob objection since beliefs formed by way of inferences from our agency-detection device have two important features. First, they commit the believer to the *reality* of the hypothesized purposeful agent, and second the commitment is accompanied by heightened emotional arousal. A commitment to *reality* of agents hypothesized by HADD is expected since it explains the adaptive value of HADD in the first place. When I hear a certain sort of rustling in the brush or see "traces in the grass" or hear things going bump in the night, it is adaptive for me to respond in a way that allows me to avoid a potential threat (from a predator for example). But I will hardly be motivated to engage in the right sorts of avoidance behavior unless I am genuinely committed to the *existence* of the hypothesized agent. Thus, one would expect that beliefs in counterintuitive entities triggered by the HADD will carry existential commitment, while beliefs concerning counterintuitive entities encountered first in dreams or works of fiction will not. Such commitment is adaptive in the former case, but not in the latter. Of course it is part and parcel of the existential commitment to a perceived threat that the belief arouses powerful emotions, such as fear, as well. Believing that the rustling in the bushes signals a real predator leads to a fear that at least in part motivates me to flee. But it is also true that the emotional arousal itself strengthens my commitment to the reality of the hypothesized agent.[10]

Second, for reasons that are still not quite clear, human beings exhibit a demonstrable natural tendency to hypothesize the existence of supernatural beings with a cluster of super-powers. Above I referred to empirical research which showed a developmental tendency to favor belief in the existence of supernatural beings with super-knowing and super-perceiving faculties. But it is equally true that human beings cross-culturally are developmentally biased towards accepting belief in the existence of supernatural beings that are super-powerful, immortal (Gimenez, Guererro, and Harris [in press]), and creators. (Keleman 2004). If HADD leads us to hypothesize the existence of supernatural minded agents, and this is coupled with a developmental bias towards belief in beings with super-powers, these two factors taken together make it likely that beings of this sort will become likely objects of religious devotion while Mickey Mouse and Sponge Bob will not.

Yet, even this response will not satisfy all of the relevant worries. Since we are committed, cognitively and emotionally, to the reality of religious entities, and since we are liable to remember and transmit ideas of emotionally arousing MCI agents generated by HADD, and since we are biased towards belief in super-powered, supernatural beings we possess powerful starting ingredients for religious cognition. But it is also true that agents hypothesized by the activation of HADD are still highly liable to empirical defeat. If I hear a noise in the closet but find nothing there when I look, I surrender the belief in the hypothesized agent. If I think I hear something moving in the bushes, and then the noise stops, I soon give up the belief that there is something there. False positives are common with HADD, and once we detect their falsity, belief in the hypothesized agents are quickly abandoned. So an important question remains: shouldn't we expect that religious belief would be equally liable to defeat when the religious hypothesis is not confirmed by independent evidence, or when we come to discover natural explanations for the events that originally led us to hypothesize supernatural agency? Many "primitive cultures" invoke agentive explanations for natural phenomena until natural explanations are shown to suffice. Why do those religious beliefs persist even when natural explanations for the "traces in the grass" are subsequently discovered?

Let's assume that defenders of this model can answer the question of how such false positives are able to survive. There is still the further question of why concepts spawned in this way would amount to anything other than mere objects of predatory fear. These unseen agents would be regarded as nothing more than super-powerful, bizarre, and scary. Why then would these things become the focus of *religious devotion*? We can imagine one arguing as follows:

Supernatural concepts don't emerge from HADD ready made for religious devotion. Rather, these unseen agents, hypothesized to be minded, are on occasion taken to be not merely unseen but invisible. In virtue of that, they are counterintuitive. And such invisible, MCI agents then are understood to have strategic information. This makes the concepts inference rich, allowing them to rally emotional commitment, and further makes them fit objects of ritual devotion. This in turn spawns routine activities in which we take ourselves to engage in commerce with these special agents. Combine this with our tendency to believe in supernatural super-beings and we have a recipe for religious belief and practice. It is only then the confluence of *all* of these factors occurs that religion emerges.

The main problem with this version of the story is that it seems to render the view incapable of explaining what it set out to explain: the *pervasiveness* of religion across times and cultures. If the emergence of religion requires this apparently highly contingent confluence of cognitive circumstances, we may have an explanation of why religion sometimes emerges – here and there. But given the highly contingent nature of the processes described here, it does not seem likely that religion is something we would expect to find everywhere and always. Why would concepts spawned by HADD become layered with all of the additional properties that attend religious concepts?[11] If that were to happen in some cases, we could chalk it up to a chance. But could we expect this to be common? One could, of course, hypothesize that human cognitive capacities and the environment in which they are placed are calibrated in a way that makes this special outcome likely. But this sort of special pleading raises an important question: why are human cognitive capacities and the human cognitive environment structured in a way that makes religious belief so widespread? Is this special fact about human and their environment evidence of a form of cosmic, cognitive design?

III Memetic Accounts

I have spent most of my time in this chapter on non-adaptationist cognitive accounts of religion because they are the most widely endorsed. There are, however, other non-adaptationist accounts of religion that are somewhat less developed. We will look at one of these in the final portion of this chapter.

When we think about evolution, it is most natural for us to think about organisms and their genes. But organisms and genes are not the only things that are capable of evolutionary development. In fact evolution can occur any time we have (a) replicating entities, (b) which can copy themselves with a high degree of fidelity, while still allowing for occasional variation, and (c) a mechanism that provides selective pressure on variants which meet a standard more or less well. These three elements: *replicators, fidelity/variation*, and *selection*, are present in organisms which reproduce and pass on their traits through genetic coding and which are in turn selected for or against by environmental conditions (natural selection). But these three elements can be present in other conditions as well. Computer viruses provide an apt example. We all know that the most effective computer viruses are those that can spread themselves from computer to computer while varying their code slightly so that they can avoid detection by virus-protection software. As long as the variations keep the virus one step ahead of the protection software, it will continue to evolve and thrive. Likewise, human political arrangements can evolve. As democracy spreads around the globe, emerging democratic countries will copy central political elements from other countries: free elections of government officials, a constitution guaranteeing protection of individual rights, a system of checks and balances for state leaders, and so on. Of course, elements of these political arrangements can and do change, and some are likely to be more effective at governing group behavior and securing political success than others. Those that do will be followed by others, while those that do not will perish. The same is going to be true about short fictional stories, urban legends, recipes, business plans, and many, many other aspects of human culture.

Noting this allows us to see that it is not only organisms that evolve – units of culture can evolve as well since they satisfy the three conditions. Units of culture replicate (from one mind to another, and from one group to another), they can vary (as with political arrangements and folk tales) and they can be selected for or against (though as we will see, there are some distinctive problems with each of these three elements when it comes to cultural units). As a result, units of culture will be susceptible to the same sort of explanation and analysis. Advocates for this evolutionary picture of the development of culture label these cultural units *memes*. So-called "meme theorists" insist on a few important distinctions. First, the replicators in this case are not human beings, nor are they the human minds which carry and transmit the memes. Rather what evolves is the meme itself. In genetic evolution, we measure fitness in terms of the increasing or decreasing frequency of genes in succeeding generations. In memetic evolution, we measure fitness in terms of increasing or decreasing frequency of a meme and the cultural expression it codes for. Thus it is the meme itself which is evolvable.

All of this still leaves the notion of a meme quite vague. What actually are these units of culture? Initially it seems that memes are nothing more than potentially spreadable forms of behavior. But meme theorists are keen to emphasize that memes are units around which culture develop and, as such, are *conceptually* mediated. As a result, many forms of spreadable behavior (yawning, laughing, coughing) would not count as memes. But what does "conceptual mediation" amount to? Early meme theorists held that any unit of "cultural information" would count as a meme. On this account stories, songs, technological techniques (like the English language or the Chinese language), theoretical frameworks (like deconstructionism or pragmatism), pornography, technological innovations (wheels, plastic) all would count as memes. However, early critics of meme theory argued that units of cultural information were not capable of evolutionary development because they lack one of the essential ingredients: replication with fidelity. There is a common game played among children in which one child whispers a message to another, who in turn whispers it to another, and so on until all the children have heard "the message." Inevitably, there are "copying errors" that are made, errors which mount very quickly. It could be that "copying errors" are not fatal after all. Perhaps all they do is provide the source of small variation that is also necessary for evolution to occur. The problem is that when the changes are radical and/or very high in frequency, there is not enough stable, heritable content to allow adaptive changes to be selected for. What the children's message-passing game shows us is that when it comes to cultural units, change is radical and frequent indeed. In games like this sentences that begin as "Dickens was a charming young man" are soon transformed into "Chicken was harming the land." (In case you cannot see why fidelity matters to evolvability consider this: An organism comes to have an adaptive trait. This trait makes the organism able to produce lots of offspring. And so it does. Do the offspring retain the adaptive trait? Only if the trait can be faithfully reproduced in the offspring, otherwise not.)

Because of this problem, more recent meme theorists argue that memes are not merely units of cultural information but rather units of information which (a) code for a behavior, and that (b) is learned by imitation. How does this help? Let's consider each of these conditions, starting with the second. Learning by imitation helps because memes learned in this way are learned not by verbal communication but behavioral imitation. This is a good thing since behaviors are more coarse-grained instruments that are not as susceptible to information loss. Consider an example. I am trying to teach you how to make a paper airplane. There are two ways I can do it. First, I can give you oral instructions. They might go something like this:

Take the paper and hold it the long way. Fold it in half until the opposite corners touch. Now take the upper left corner and fold in back until it makes a 45-degree crease. Press the crease. Flip the paper over and repeat the last step for the corner of the paper that was opposite the last corner that you folded back. Next ... Now I want you to turn to your neighbor and give him or her the instructions.

We can't do it. It is too complicated. But if I *show* you how to make the paper airplane, passing the information along to others is easy. Part of the reason is that *showing* allows for a lot more sloppiness – it doesn't matter if I fold it exactly in half, or whether or not the corners meet exactly, or whether or not the angle is 45 degrees.

This condition in turn mandates the first condition. If learning memes is something that happens through imitation, then memes will be restricted to units of culture that script for behaviors. We learn them through behaviors, and we pass them along through behaviors. This might mean that the mental contents associated with the meme will not be stable from individual to individual. But the cultural unit can be passed on because of the stability of the behavior.

This covers two of the characteristics that must be satisfied for something to be evolvable. We can see how memes can replicate and how they can admit of variation. But what does the work of *selection*? What brings it about that memes are selected for or against? There are, in fact, multiple factors. In some cases the selecting factor is clearly real, but very hard to identify. Advertising jingles make good examples. For some reason, McDonald's "I'm lovin' it" jingle is hard for people to purge from their minds. They walk down the sidewalk humming it, and those that pass them start humming it too. Why? There is something about the way our brains are configured that make certain sounds attractive to us. And we tend to mimic them.

Other memes replicate not because they take advantage of some neurological quirk, but because they take direct advantage of our cognitive architecture, appealing to our tendency to embrace what is good or pleasurable, and what is right or true. In the first category we might include the memes of fast food, pornography, horror films, gossip, or ecstatic religious experience. These cultural activities proliferate not because we think that participating in them is good, but because we regard them as good or pleasurable in some way. It is for that reason that these "desire satisfying" cultural activities spread to others. Similarly, units of information that we regard as true not only stick with us, but compel us to pass them on. Here gossip would be another good example, as might myths about the Loch Ness monster, the Abominable Snowman, or Bigfoot.

Although no one has yet developed a full blown memetic theory of religion, a number of people have asserted that religion is a meme. The suggestion has been made a number of times by Oxford biologist Richard Dawkins, for example, who writes that humans minds are susceptible to all sorts of memes, especially religious ones:

A beautiful child close to me, six and the apple of her father's eye, believes ... in Father Christmas, and when she grows up her ambition is to be a tooth fairy. She and her schoolfriends believe the solemn word of respected adults that tooth fairies and Father Christmas really exist. This little girl is of an age to believe whatever you tell her. If you tell her about witches changing princes into frogs she will believe you. If you tell her that bad children roast forever in hell she will have nightmares. I have just discovered that without her father's consent this sweet, trusting, gullible six-year-old is being sent, for weekly instruction, to a Roman Catholic nun. What chance has she? A human child is shaped by evolution to soak up the culture of her people. Most obviously, she learns the essentials of their language in a matter of months. A large dictionary of words to speak, an encyclopedia of information to speak about, complicated syntactic and semantic rules to order the speaking, are all transferred from older brains into hers well before she reaches half her adult size. When you are pre-programmed to absorb useful information at a high rate, it is hard to shut out pernicious or damaging information at the same time. With so many mindbytes to be downloaded, so many mental condoms to be replicated, it is no wonder that child brains are gullible, open to almost any suggestion, vulnerable to subversion, easy prey to Moonies, Scientologists and [Roman Catholic] nuns. (Dawkins 1991)

For Dawkins, we can explain the costly behavior and bizarre belief associated with religion not because religious beliefs are true, but rather because they hijack the cognitive and affective weaknesses, loopholes, and security measures our minds usually deploy. In fact, for Dawkins, it is only because religion can exploit these weaknesses that it can spread as successfully as it does. For Dawkins then, religion is like a virus that is passed along from one host mind to the other. And like viruses, according to Dawkins, religious memes are harmful to their hosts.

Is meme theory a useful tool for explaining the widespread and persistent nature of religion? Perhaps. That is, perhaps part of the reason religion is such a pervasive religious phenomenon is that it is a successful cultural replicator that is selected for by various memetic selective forces. But as a scientific theory of religion, meme theory has some severe weaknesses. I will highlight just two here.

The first weakness is that meme theory is, at best, an *epidemiology* of religion. That is, meme theory can point out that religious claims, like other memes, are good at infecting minds and spreading from mind to mind. Meme theory might also be able to explain why religions spread in the way that they do. They might first show us why religion tends to spread *by contact*, that is, why Buddhist parents tend to have Buddhist children, and Christian parents Christian children. They might even be able to locate the mechanisms that explain why religious memes are successful replicators. Eating McDonald's fast food is a successful meme because the food has ingredients that exploit desires developed in our ancestral past – passionate desires for fats. Perhaps meme theorists can identify something analogous when it comes to religion. Religion exploits ancestral fears of the dangers associated with things we cannot control (perhaps we could call this the Freudian memetic theory), or perhaps, as Dawkins suggests, religion just exploits the powerful tendency that children have to internalize whatever is told to them by their parents at a very young age.

But even if meme theory can give us all this, and it is by no mean clear that it can, it still does not explain any of the most important aspects of religion. Before we see that, let me say briefly why it is not even clear that it can deliver the modest sorts of explanatory benefits I mention above. Take Dawkins' theory. How likely is it that the explanation of the persistence of religion is that children have a powerful tendency to internalize, believe, and act in accord with what their parents tell them from a very young age? Just think about that for a moment. Did you eat your vegetables? Do all of your homework? Avoid video games? Shun sex? My guess is that if there was ever a falsified scientific theory it is one that claims that children tend to internalize and obey principles promoted by their parents from an early age, even when those principles involve a high cost.

However, as I said, it does not seem that meme theory can take us much farther. What meme theory does not tell us *at all* is why religion exists and persists as a pan-cultural human phenomenon. Why is religion found across times and cultures? Meme theory really cannot answer this question at all. It can tell us why it spreads among cultures within which it arose. But why is it so pervasive? This fact indicates that it is, or is associated with, a good solution to a common ancestral problem. But meme theory gives us no hints about what that problem and solution might be (and if it did, we wouldn't need meme theory to account for religion in any case). Further, meme theory does absolutely nothing to explain the recurrent features of religious belief and practice in the way that, say, the cognitive theories outlined above do. Why is it that religions promote the existence of strategic access agents which support moral norms, are interested in human behavior, afford various forms of temporal and eternal reward, and so on. Meme theory tells us nothing about how to explain these commonalities. It is, to repeat, at best nothing more than an *epidemiology* of religion.

We should note one other thing about meme theory before we conclude. Dawkins tries to explain the persistence of religious memes by arguing that cognitive memes that are "resistant to" or "immune to" evidence are not only hard to eradicate but, because of their evidence-free status, cognitively harmful. Dawkins claims that we should regard such individuals as ill "patients" in need of a cure. He characterizes the disease as follows:

> The patient typically finds himself impelled by some deep, inner conviction that something is true, or right, or virtuous: a conviction that doesn't seem to owe anything to evidence or reason, but which, nevertheless, he feels as totally compelling and convincing. We doctors refer to such a belief as "faith." Patients typically make a positive virtue of faith's being strong and unshakable, in spite of not being based upon evidence. Indeed, they may feel that the less evidence there is, the more virtuous the belief. A related symptom, which a faith-sufferer may also present, is the conviction that "mystery, " per se, is a good thing. It is not a virtue to solve mysteries. Rather we should enjoy them, even revel in their insolubility. (Dawkins 1991)

We might say, then, that memes that commend themselves to us as true will come in one of two varieties. First there are those that commend themselves to us because they seem to be "confirmed by the evidence." Second there are those that, like religion, present themselves as immune to evidence. Dawkins claims that memes of this second source are especially resilient. Once they enter a population they are hard to eradicate and thus quickly stabilize in a population (a population of minds).

But Dawkins is wrong to think that the most dangerous and virulent of memes are those that are "immune to evidence." Generally speaking, human minds rebel at the idea of believing things in the absence of evidence. Philosophy professors know this especially well. Any of us who have taught epistemology know that students' strongest sympathies are with the view that justified belief positively requires evidence. In light of this, the most resilient types of meme would *not* be those that present themselves as *immune to evidence*; they would rather be those that trick us into thinking that ordinary beliefs/experiences count in favor of them even if they do not (or perhaps that they belong in the category of the obvious or of common sense – beliefs that seem just "self-evident"). Memes like that would be very hard to eradicate because we take ourselves to be in possession of unmistakable evidence of their truth already.

But notice that if some memes can gain success from making it appear to us that they are well-supported by the evidence, a serious skeptical problem looms on the horizon, namely: if there can be memes like this, how can we ever distinguish them from beliefs that are supported by genuine evidence, or from genuine common sense? Dawkins' viral meme now emerges a competitor to Descartes' evil demon. Memetic selection thus provides us with the ingredients for a potent argument for general skepticism. Let's call memes that seem to be fully supported by ordinary evidence but that are not *false-confidence-inducing memes* (FCIM) and distinguish those from genuinely *well-supported beliefs* (WSB).

(1)   If ideas evolve by memetic selection, false-confidence-inducing memes (FCIM) are going to be indistinguishable from ideas that are well-supported by the evidence (WSB).
(2)   If I am unable to distinguish FCIM from WSB, I can never be confident that any idea I have is an FCIM rather than a WSB.
(3)   Thus, for all I know, all ideas are FCIM.
(4)   Thus, I cannot regard any belief as truly well supported by the evidence.

Of course, if this is right, then, for all we know, empirical science and its deliverances is an FCIM meme, and one that will be much harder to detect and weed out than Dawkins takes religion to be.

IV   Conclusions

In this chapter we have fixed our attention entirely on non-adaptationist explanations of religion. According to these views, religion emerges either because it piggybacks on other traits that are adaptive, or is a mere spandrel. Meme theory does not seem to offer much in the way of a satisfying scientific account of religion. On the other hand, cognitive accounts of religion seem to have a great deal of explanatory power and empirical evidence in their favor. We have seen however, that neither view can be judged ultimately successful.

Notes

1   The example springs from widely discussed research performed by Frances Burton on macaques, see Burton (1970).
2   For an engaging discussion of different ways of approaching adaptationist explanation of human cognitive capacities see Atran (2005).
3   See also Boyer (2001,ch. 2), Pyysiainen (2002, p. 113), Barrett (2004, ch. 2).
4   Presentation at the conference "Nature and Belief" Calvin College, November 2005.
5   See especially Johnson and Krüger 2004.
6   I give little attention to the topic of ritual here though the literature presents important arguments concerning the role of ritual in the evolutionary advancement of religious practice. Most important here are the works by McCauley and Lawson (2002) and Whitehouse (2004).
7   See for example Robert Hinde (2005:52 ff), and Pyysiainen (2004, pp. 45–52), Bering 2005, Johnson and Bering 2009, Sosis 2003.
8   Both Atran and Boyer insist on this point strenuously. See Atran (2002, p. 12) and Boyer (2001, ch. 1). However, Atran wavers on this point, sometimes arguing that adaptive advantages play no role in the origin of religion, though they may play a role in its persistence. See, most notably: Atran (2005, p. 54).
9   Pyysiainen (2004, p. 45). The objection is also raised by Hinde (2005, pp. 39–40).
10   In the interests of full disclosure it appears that Boyer rejects an account of this sort (2001, pp. 144–8) while Barrett (2004, ch. 3) seems to defend it.

11 One might hold that the pervasiveness is explained by common origin. Perhaps this confluence occurred once early in our hominid ancestry and all subsequent manifestations of religion are cultural descendants of this manifestation. This claim would depend on a history of religions that none would accept as far as we know. And it is further disowned by prominent defenders of the view such as, for example, Atran who says:

If we reject the unlikely possibility that these thematic occurrences stem from historical contact and diffusion or are spontaneous instantiations of a Platonistic set of innate religious forms ..., then how else could such apparent recurrences independently take place across cultures without specific and strong universal cognitive constraints? (2002, p. 88)

References

Atran, S. (2005) Adaptationism for Human Cognition: Strong, Spurious or Weak? *Mind & Language* 20 (1), 39–67.

Barrett, J. (2004) *Why Would Anyone Believe in God?* Walnut Creek, CA: AltaMira Press.

Bering, J. M. (2005) The evolutionary history of an illusion: Religious causal beliefs in children and adults. In B. Ellis and D. F. Bjorklund (ed.) *Origins of the Social Mind: Evolutionary Psychology and Child Development*. New York: Guilford Press.

Boyer, P. (2001) *Religion Explained*. New York: Basic Books.

Burton, F. D. (1970) Sexual climax in female Macaca mulatta. *Proceedings of the 3rd International Congress of Primatology*, Zurich, 3, 180–91.

Dawkins, R. (1999) Viruses of the mind at http://www.cscs.umich.edu/~crshalizi/Dawkins/viruses-of-the-mind.html

Giménez-Dasi, M., Guerrero, S., and Harris, P. L. (2005) Intimations of immortality and omniscience in early childhood. *European Journal of Developmental Psychology* 2, 285–97.

Johnson, D. and Bering, J. (2009) Hand of God, Mind of Man: Punishment and cognition in the evolution of cooperation. In Jeffrey Schloss and Michael Murray (eds.) *The Believing Primate: Scientific, Philosophical, and Theological Reflections on the Origin of Religion*. Oxford: Oxford University Press.

Johnson, D. and Krüger, O. (2004) The good of wrath: Supernatural punishment and the evolution of cooperation. *Political Theology* 5.2, 159–76.

Hinde, R. (2005) Modes theory. In H. Whitehouse and R. McCauley (eds.) *Mind and Religion: Psychological and Cognitive Foundations of Religiosity*. Walnut Creek, CA: AltaMira Press.

Kelemen, D. (2004) Why are rocks pointy? Children's preferences for teleological explanations of the natural world. *Developmental Psychology* 35, 1440–53.

McCauley, R. N. and E. T. Lawson (2002) *Bringing Ritual to Mind*. New York: Cambridge University Press.

Pyysiainen, I. (2002). Religion and the counterintuitive. In I. Pyysiainen and V. Anttonen (eds.) *Current Approaches in the Cognitive Science of Religion*, London: Continuum.

Pyysiainen, I. (2004) *Magic, Miracles, and Religion: A Scientist's Perspective*. Walnut Creek, CA: AltaMira Press.

Richert, R. A., and Barrett, J. L. (2005) Do you see what I see? Young children's assumptions about God's perceptual abilities, *International Journal for the Psychology of Religion* 15, 283–95.

Sosis, R. (2003) Why aren't we all Hutterites? Costly signaling theory and religious behavior. *Human Nature* 14(2), 19–127.

Whitehouse, H. (2004) *Modes of Religiosity: A Cognitive Theory of Religious Transmission*. New York: AltaMira Press.

36

Evolutionary Accounts of Religion: Explaining or Explaining Away

MICHAEL J. MURRAY

Popular and professional commentators on scientific accounts of religion often argue that such accounts raise serious troubles for the justification of religious belief. Once we show that religious belief arises as a result of the operations of a cognitive tool selected for during our evolutionary history, the argument runs, we have good reason for thinking those beliefs false or unjustified. In any case, scientific accounts of religion show us that religious belief cannot be taken with the seriousness religious believers claim. In this paper I look at detailed arguments for this conclusion and show why they are, in the end, wanting.

As we have seen in the last two chapters a handful of cognitive and evolutionary models of religious belief have begun to emerge in the scholarly literature. Attempts to offer "scientific explanations of religious belief" are nothing new, of course, stretching back at least as far as David Hume, and perhaps as far back as Cicero (who explained religious belief as arising from bombardment of our brains by atoms emanating from the gods themselves).[1] What is also not new is a common belief that scientific explanations of religious belief serve in some way to undermine the justification for those beliefs. Sometimes, defenders of these scientific explanations are quite clear about these purported implications – and here Freud comes to mind as perhaps the most famous example, illustrated by the title (and the contents) of his discussion of religion in *Future of an Illusion*. However, most contemporary defenders of cognitive and evolutionary models of religious belief have been more cautious – or at least subtle – than Freud. Michael Persinger, Professor of Behavioral Neuroscience at Laurentian University, argues that this work shows us that "God is an artifact of the brain" (Chu et al. 2004). Arch-atheist Richard Dawkins concludes that "The irrationality of religion is a by-product of the built in irrationality mechanism in the brain" (Dawkins 2008). Dean Hamer (2005), author of *The God Gene*, argues as follows:

> If belief in God is produced by a genetically inherited trait, if the human species is "hardwired" to believe in a spirit world, this could suggest that God doesn't exist as something "out there," beyond and independent of us, but rather as the product of an inherited perception, the manifestation of an evolutionary adaptation that exists exclusively within the human brain. If true, this would

imply that there is no actual spiritual reality, no God or gods, no soul, or afterlife. Consequently, humankind can no longer be viewed as a product of God but rather God must be viewed as a product of human cognition.

Even less subtle is Jesse Bering: "We've got God by the throat and I'm not going to stop until one of us is dead." For Bering, the deliverances of the psychology of religion are "not going to remain in the privileged chapels of scientists and other scholars. It is going to dry up even the most verdant suburban landscapes, and leave spiritual leaders with their tongues out, dying for a drop of faith" (quoted in Reischel 2006).

What makes these scientists think that scientific accounts of the origin of religion make religious belief disreputable? I could suggest that we now turn to the arguments these critics offer on behalf of this conclusion. Unfortunately, they don't offer any. They take it to be fairly obvious that these accounts have such consequences. But this is not obvious at all. To see why, just consider the fact that developmental psychologists have tried to explain why human beings believe such things as: that one and one equal two; that animals give birth to offspring of the same species; and that certain unnatural events are caused by agents. No one thinks those beliefs are disreputable simply because they immediately spring to mind as a result of the workings of our innate cognitive machinery.

So why are some tempted to think that religious beliefs formed by the working of various psychological mechanisms honed by natural selection are epistemically unjustified? In what follows we will consider a variety of reasons that might tempt one towards this conclusion.

The first reason might be something like this: "Scientific accounts of religion show us that religious beliefs are just a product of brain activity. But beliefs produced by mere brain activity shouldn't be taken seriously. Thus, religious belief should be rejected." Is this a good reason for rejecting religious belief? After all, these scientific accounts of religion merely aim to explain the origins of religious beliefs and, as we all learned in our introductory philosophy course, an account of a belief's *origin* tells us nothing about its *truth*. To think otherwise is to commit the notorious "genetic fallacy" (a fallacy which, in spite of our context, has nothing to do with genetics). Each philosopher has his favorite way of illustrating this fallacy. Mine comes from the story of Friedrich Kekulé, the somewhat eccentric nineteenth-century German chemist. Kekulé is famous for being the first to present chemicals in terms of structural formulas, and more famous for his discovery of the ring structure of the benzene molecule. His great discovery occurred not as a result of hard labor in the lab, but from an episode he described as follows:

> I turned my chair to the fire [after having worked on the problem for some time] and dozed. Again the atoms were gamboling before my eyes. This time the smaller groups kept modestly to the background. My mental eye, rendered more acute by repeated vision of this kind, could not distinguish larger structures, of manifold conformation; long rows, sometimes more closely fitted together; all twining and twisting in snakelike motion. But look! What was that? One of the snakes had seized hold of its own tail, and the form whirled mockingly before my eyes. As if by a flash of lighting I awoke ... Let us learn to dream, gentlemen. (Weisberg 1993)

Now this is admittedly a silly reason to believe that benzene has a ring structure. It was nonetheless *his reason*. But his coming to it on silly grounds doesn't undermine the *truth* of the belief. Likewise, nothing we say or discover about the origins of our religious beliefs is going to make any difference to our assessment of the truth of those beliefs.

However, even though genetic accounts of belief cannot undermine a belief's truth, they can (sometimes) undermine their justification. If Freud is right and religious belief arises primarily through the workings of some sort of wish-fulfillment mechanism, this would not show religious belief to be *false*. But it would give us good reason for thinking that religious beliefs – at least when they are generated that way – are *unjustified*. This invites us to ask the parallel question in this case: would scientific accounts of the origin of belief undermine the justification of religious belief in the same way?

To answer this question we first need to consider the question of whether or not the mechanisms at work in generating religious belief are, like believing via wish-fulfillment, known to be unreliable (say because they commonly generate other beliefs, the truth of which we can directly confirm or disconfirm). Below we will look at a pair of arguments that aim to show that these religious belief-forming mechanisms are indeed unreliable. If they are, then these accounts spell real trouble for religious belief. But for now, let's assume that all we know is this: the workings of these cognitive mechanisms generate religious beliefs in us, and we have no independent reason to trust or distrust these mechanisms? Are religious beliefs justified in such a case?

Philosophers have actually had a good bit to say about this question. On one very common view in epistemology, our beliefs can be divided into two fundamental categories: basic and non-basic. *Non-basic beliefs* are beliefs that require independent propositional evidence for their justification. In order to justifiably believe that the defendant is guilty, for example, I need *reasons*, *evidence*, or *arguments*. However not every belief can be non-basic. If they were, the chain of justifying reasons for any belief would have be infinitely long; and since we don't have any infinite number of beliefs, all of our beliefs would thus be rendered unjustified. Thus, in addition to basic beliefs, many philosophers suppose that there must be (and are) *basic beliefs*. Basic beliefs are those beliefs that spontaneously arise in us, sometimes on the occasion of having particular sorts of sensory experiences, and which do not require independent reasons, evidence, or argument to be reasonably held. A number of our beliefs fall into that category, including most of our beliefs based on sense experience or memory, beliefs in induction, beliefs in other minds, and so on; we hold all of these beliefs without any propositional evidence which supports their truth. As a general rule, epistemologists have held that we do, and are entitled to, hold such basic beliefs and to regard them as innocent until proven guilty. That is, unless we are in possession of other beliefs, basic or non-basic, that we hold more strongly and which undermine the truth of a basic belief we hold, then we are entitled to accept those beliefs.

If that is right, then we ought to regard religious beliefs generated by native cognitive structures as true in just the same way that we regard our sensory beliefs as true. Of course the commitment is provisional. Once sufficient evidence is amassed for the falsity of such beliefs, they should be rejected. But it is worth noting that the standard for sufficient evidence can be quite high. If someone presents me with what seems to be a sound philosophical argument that there is no external world, I am going to be inclined to reject it – not because I have strong evidence against the conclusion, but rather because our initial degree of commitment to this basic belief is so high, defeating it would take evidence of an overwhelming sort. However in this instance we are asking only how we should regard religious beliefs generated by these cognitive mechanisms in cases where we do not have any reason to regard those mechanisms as unreliable. Since such beliefs are basic we should thus regard them as true and justified unless we have sufficient reason to conclude otherwise.

One might hold, however, that this lets religious belief off too easily. Up to this point we have assumed that we have no good reason to question the reliability of the cognitive mechanisms that give rise to religious belief. But perhaps that is not right. In fact, critics might contend, there are two good reasons that readily suggest themselves for doubting the reliability of these mechanisms. First, on the standard model, HADD is directly implicated in the formation of religious belief. But part of what we know about HADD is that it is Hyperactive or Hyper-sensitive. What does that mean? Simply put, it means the mechanism is prone to lots of false positives. It oftentimes tells us that there are agents lurking about (in the bushes, in the attic, in the closet, under the bed) when there are none. And that is a problem. If HADD is prone to generate false positive in this way it is, while perhaps adaptive, generally *unreliable* as a guide to truth. But any tool that is unreliable in this way is one we ought not to believe (unless there is independent evidence supporting the conclusion that an agent, on a particular occasion, is present).

Here is a second worry. It takes no special expertise to notice that religions around the globe differ in ways that are logically incompatible. Some religions assert that ultimate reality is personal; some deny this. Some assert that we survive our deaths as individuals; some deny this. Some assert that we live through a number of bodily incarnations; others reject this. Some assert that there are many gods; some insist that there is exactly one. And so on and so on. However, if religious beliefs are rooted in or spring from the workings of a set of cognitive tools, this diversity shows us that these cognitive tools are simply not reliable. There is no way to coherently regard a cognitive tool as trustworthy when it churns out beliefs that are contradictory across so many dimensions. Or so it seems.

Does the hyper-sensitivity of HADD or the contradictory character of religious belief show that cognitive tools that generate religious belief ought not to be trusted? Let's consider these in turn. In order for the first reason to have traction, two conditions must be met. First, it must be the case that HADD does indeed play a crucial role in the formation of religious belief, and second, it must be the case that HADD is largely unreliable. Are these conditions met? With respect to the first, advocates of the cognitive model are not in agreement. One leading figure, Pascal Boyer, argues that HADD plays a minimal and dispensable role in the formation of religious belief (Boyer 2001) while Justin Barrett (2004) and Stewart Guthrie (1993) argue that it is central and necessary. If Boyer is right, then even if HADD is largely unreliable, religious belief is not thereby implicated.

What about the second condition? Is HADD generally unreliable? It is certainly reliable when we infer that an agent is present from hearing a tune whistled in the hall. It is reliable when hear a basketball being bounced and infer that an athlete is coming down the hall. However, it is unreliable when we infer the presence of a prowler or a ghost upon hearing the creaking floorboards in the kitchen. Is HADD in religious cognition more like the former cases or the latter? Posing the question makes it clear that HADD, like other cognitive modalities, is more reliable in some context that in others. So what about in this case?

The difficulties in answering this question become obvious as soon as it is posed. Unless we can show that HADD is unreliable in the case of religious cognition, we have no reason to doubt its reliability. But if we have independent reason to conclude that it is unreliable in the religious domain, we already have independent reason to think that religious beliefs are false. As a result, reflecting on HADD alone will not give us much in the way of positive reason to deny the justification of beliefs that arise from it. For that we need independent evidence.

This brings us to the next reason. Perhaps we can get positive evidence for the unreliability of HADD in particular cases, and religious cognitive processes in particular – by showing that the cognitive processes generate contradictory outputs. However, the argument here is not as straightforward as it seems. Consider an analogy. Across times and cultures humans beings have a hard-wired disposition to have aversive feelings towards dead bodies, animal waste, and rotting food. While this disposition towards "contagion avoidance" is widespread, the reasons that people give for the aversion varies widely from culture to culture. Some cultures claim that dead bodies should be avoided because they are a source of disease, while others claim that they harbor potentially dangerous spirits. Do these contradictory beliefs attending contagion avoidance show contagion avoidance to be an unreliable tool? No. They show that contagion avoidance is a non-specialized mechanism that leads us to believe certain general truths (dead bodies are dangerous) but which also allows us to fill in details about the nature of the dangers that are not dictated by the cognitive tool itself (that it is dangerous *because* it is a potential source of pathogens).

For all we know at this point, the same thing is true when it comes to the mechanisms at work in religious cognition. Perhaps those cognitive tools that dispose us towards the religious are a non-specialized mechanism that inclines us towards belief in transcendent reality, but which allows the details to be filled in by social and cultural conceptual resources. So, for example, when HADD triggers beliefs in unseen agents, I might take those agents to be ghosts, trolls, or the ancestors. Which options are live for me will depend on the conceptual resources available to me from my cultural surroundings. Thus, if there are supernatural agents, the mechanisms identified by the cognitive theory are reliable as far as they go. If we succeed in reliably describing those entities at a more specific level, that will be explained not by the operations of the non-specific cognitive mechanisms, but by the workings of mechanisms operating at a social and cultural level.

To this point we have considered worries about the justification of belief that spring from doubts about the reliability of the belief-forming processes involved. But this is not the only sort of concern one might reasonably have. In addition to worries about reliability, one might have concerns about the *underlying causal pathways* that lead to religious belief. Philosophers who are concerned about questions of the justification of belief fall into two basic categories: internalists and externalists. Internalists argue that whether or not a belief is justified depends entirely on facts "inside the head" (for example, facts about the extent to which the belief is properly supported by sensory states or other beliefs one has). Externalists argue that justification depends on whether or not the belief has the right relation to facts in the external world. For some, the right relation consists only in reliability (does the belief-forming mechanism typically succeed in "getting things right"?) while for others the right relation will require that there be certain causal connections between the external world and the belief formed. I point this out only to make it clear that even if these psychological accounts do show that there is no direct causal connection between religious beliefs and their target, only some epistemological theories would take that to be relevant to the justification of those beliefs. Exernalists will think that the unreliability of beliefs formed in this way – unreliability revealed by the mutually incompatible outputs – shows us that religious beliefs must be unjustified. Internalists, on the other hand, will be content to hold that beliefs formed in this way might still be justified since nothing about the beliefs "in the head" of the religious believer conflict or fail to cohere in ways that would undermine those beliefs.[2] As a result, these accounts of the origins of religious belief will raise concerns about justification primarily for externalists.

So should externalists conclude, if evolutionary accounts of religious belief are right, that those beliefs are unjustified? The externalist's worry, in short, is this. In cases where the target of the belief is not causally involved in the origin of the belief, the process that generates the belief would do so whether or not the belief is true. If a hallucinogenic drug causes me to have a belief that there are chickens running around the room then, if I take the drug, and the drug causes those beliefs, the chicken belief is unjustified – even if there are chickens running around the room! In such a case, the deviant causal origin of the belief undermines its justification.

Perhaps critics who think that the justification of religious belief is undermined by scientific accounts of the origin of those beliefs think that religious beliefs are analogous to drug-induced chicken belief. That is, on these accounts, religious beliefs are formed through the working of purely natural processes: purely natural stimuli activate purely natural cognitive processes to produce purely natural religious belief. On such a story, religious beliefs have no connection to the target of those beliefs (supernatural reality), in the same way that drug-induced chicken beliefs lack connections to chicken reality. As a result, the justification of religious belief is undermined in exactly the same way that chicken belief is undermined when it is induced by hallucinogenic drugs. In both cases, that is, the causal pathways that lead to the belief are deviant and the beliefs so generated are thus unjustified.

That line of reasoning just elucidated is right if and only if the following claim is true:

(P) Whether or not there is a God (or other supernatural reality), human minds, honed by such-and-such evolutionary mechanisms, would exist and would hold religious beliefs.

Is (P) true? Clearly theists (and other religious believers) will have quite different views on this question from atheists (and other religious disbelievers). Theists think that without God there would be no universe, no fine-tuning of the universe for life, no habitable worlds, no life, no minds, and no religion. Are theists right about that? We need not answer that question here. All we need to see is that *scientific accounts of the origin of religion* don't settle the question of whether theists or atheists are right when it comes to the truth of (P). Since these accounts only undermine religious belief if (P) is true, and those accounts can't themselves speak to the truth or falsity of (P), those accounts cannot, all on their own, undermine the justification of religious belief.

There is one final reason that is sometimes hinted at by those who think that scientific accounts of religion undermine religious belief. It goes something like this. Like other human phenotypes, human cognitive tools are shaped directly or indirectly by natural selection. Those tools that are directly subject to fitness pressures – that is, cognitive tools that are adaptations – can reasonably be assumed to be reliable. After all, if those cognitive tools were unreliable – say by systematically misrepresenting reality – the organisms that possessed those tools would get things wrong and ultimately be selected against. Human beings who, for example, fail to see their local environment as it really is will stumble over the log while fleeing the pursuing grizzly bear and end up a lunch! However, cognitive tools that are either spandrels or fitness neutral will not be subject to the winnowing power of natural selection in the same way. Their reliability will not have any fitness consequences, and thus there will be no way for the forces of natural selection to "keep them honest." However, most (but not all) scientists agree that religious belief and practice are cognitive spandrels. And for that reason, we should not be inclined to regard religious beliefs as reliable.

This line of argument, while initially tempting, is mistaken on many levels. First, there are a number of cognitive tools (or collections of them working in concert) which are (almost certainly) spandrels and which we nonetheless regard as eminently reliable. In fact, the claims of just about every academic discipline within the modern university result from operations of mental tools that are cognitive spandrels. Our ability to compute differential equations is not an adaptation. But that alone gives us no reason to question the reliability of mathematics.

Second, this argument mistakenly assumes that natural selection can in fact winnow reliable from unreliable belief-forming mechanisms. Unfortunately, there is no reason to think this. The only way that natural selection can winnow these belief-forming mechanisms is by winnowing the behaviors that they produce. Behaviors, in our case, arise from the interplay of beliefs *and desires*. Because of this, false beliefs can be as adaptive as true beliefs *as long as they are paired with affective systems that, together with the false beliefs, give rise to adaptive behaviors like feeding, fleeing, fighting, and reproducing.* Since false beliefs can be as adaptive as true ones, there is no reason to think that natural selection will select for reliable belief forming mechanisms and against unreliable ones.

Finally, even if it were plausible to hold that selective pressures acting on cognitive processors could insure (or raise the odds of) reliability, there is no reason to think that evolutionary pressures would lead us to false beliefs concerning religious reality. To see why, imagine that theism is true, and that God created the world in such a way that biological complexity and diversity evolved in much the way evolutionary scientists believe it did. The theist might then look on these evolutionary accounts as providing us a description of the way in which God configured evolutionary history to make belief in supernatural reality easy or natural for us. If this were true, then our coming to have belief in a supernatural reality – a reality that created us and configured our minds to make religious belief easy and natural – is something that leads us to true beliefs, and leads us in this way *because the beliefs are true*. God set up nature in such a way that natural selection in the end does succeed in selecting for reliable religious cognition. For all we know, that's the way things really are.

Notes

1   "As infinite kinds of almost identical images arise continually from the innumerable atoms and flow out to us from the gods, so we should take the keenest pleasure in turning and bending our mind and reason to grasp these images, in order to understand the nature of these blessed and eternal beings." (Cicero 1986, pp. 87, 90)
2   Of course, were the religious believer to come to believe or know that the religious beliefs of others spring from a similar mechanism and nonetheless generate conflicting outputs, that additional belief might render one's religious beliefs unjustified.

References

Barrett, J. (2004) *Why Would Anyone Believe in God?* Walnut Creek, CA: AltaMira Press.
Boyer, P. (2001) *Religion Explained*. New York: Basic Books.
Chu J. K., Liston, B., Sieger, M., and Williams, D. (2004) Is God in our genes? *Time*, October 25.
Cicero (1986) *On the Nature of the Gods,* trans. Horace C. P. McGregor. New York: Viking Penguin.
Dawkins, R. (2008) *The God Delusion*. New York: Mariner Books.
Guthrie, S. (1993) *Faces in the Clouds*. Oxford and New York: Oxford University Press.
Hamer, D. (2005) *The God Gene: How Faith is Hardwired into our Genes*. New York: Anchor.
Reischel, J. (2006) The God fossil, *Broward-Palm Beach New Times,* March 9.
Weisberg, R. (1993) *Creativity, Beyond the Myth of Genius*. New York: W. H. Freeman.

Part 13

Belief in God

How Real People Believe: Reason and Belief in God

KELLY JAMES CLARK

Reformed epistemology rejects the widely held Enlightenment evidentialist assumption that one must have evidence for belief in God to be rational, where evidence is understood as a propositional argument (a theistic proof) for the existence of God. Reformed epistemology holds that belief in God does not require the support of evidence in order for it to be rational. The evidentialist's universal demand for evidence cannot be met in most cases with the cognitive equipment that we have. There is a limit to the things that human beings can prove. We have been outfitted with cognitive faculties that produce beliefs that we can reason from. There are at least three reasons to believe that it is proper or rational for a person to accept belief in God without the need for an argument. First, because most of our cognitive faculties produce beliefs immediately, without evidence or argument, there are good inductive grounds for thinking that a god-faculty produces beliefs immediately. Second, belief in God is more like belief in a person than belief in a scientific hypothesis. If belief in God is more like belief in other persons than belief in atoms, then the trust that is appropriate to persons will be appropriate to God. Finally, contemporary cognitive science seems to have confirmed that we have cognitive faculties that produce belief in spiritual beings.

Introduction

Suppose a stranger, let's call him David, sends you a note that declares that your wife is cheating on you. No pictures are included, no dates or times, no names – just the assertion of your wife's unfaithfulness. You have had already 15 good, and as far as you know, faithful years with your wife. Her behavior hasn't changed dramatically in the past few years. Except for David's allegation, you have no reason to believe there has been a breach in the relationship. What should you do? Confront her with what you take to be the truth, straight from David's letter? Hire a detective to follow her for a week and hope against hope the letter is a hoax? Or do you simply remain secure in the trust that you have built up all those years?

Suppose, even worse, that your son Clifford comes home after taking his first philosophy course in college. He persuades you of the truth of the so-called "problem of other minds." How do you know that other minds and, therefore, other people exist? How do you know that people are not simply cleverly constructed robots with excellent make-up jobs? How do you know that behind the person's façade lies a person – someone with thoughts, desires and feelings? You can't experience another person's feelings; you can't see another person's thoughts (even if you cut off the top of their head and peered into their brain); and even Bill Clinton can't really feel another person's pain. Yet thoughts, desires, and feelings are all essential to being a person. So you can't tell from the outside or just by looking, so to speak, if someone is a person. I can know that *I* am a person because I experience my own thoughts, feelings, and desires. But I can't prove, because I don't have any access to your inner experience, that you, or anyone else, is a person.

Since you can't prove that anyone else is a person, you rightly infer that you can't prove if your wife is a person. Lacking such a proof, how do you treat her? Do you hire a philosophical detective to search the philosophical literature for a proof that people-like things really are people? Do you avoid cuddling in the meantime, given your aversion to snuggling with machines? Or do you simply trust your deep-seated conviction that, in spite of the lack of evidence, your wife is a person and deserves to be treated as such?

Two final "supposes." Suppose that you come to believe that there is a God because your parents taught you from the cradle up that God exists. Or suppose that you are on a retreat or on the top of a mountain and have a sense of being loved by God or that God created the universe. You begin to believe in God, not because you are persuaded by some argument – you are simply taken with belief in God. You just find yourself believing, what you had heretofore denied, that God exists. Now you have come across the writings of David Hume and W. K. Clifford who insist that you base all of your beliefs on evidence. Hume raises a further point: your belief in an all-loving, omnipotent God is inconsistent with the evil that there is in the world. Given the fact of evil, God cannot exist. To meet this demand for evidence, do you become a temporary agnostic and begin perusing the texts of Aquinas, Augustine, and Paley for a good proof of God's existence? Do you give up belief in God because you see Hume's point and can't see how God and evil could be reconciled? Or do you remain steady in your trust in God in spite of the lack of evidence and even in the face of counter-evidence?

My Suppose-This and Suppose-That Stories are intended to raise the problem of the relationship of our important beliefs to evidence (and counter-evidence). Since the Enlightenment, there has been a demand to expose all of our beliefs to the searching criticism of reason. If a belief is unsupported by the evidence, it is irrational to believe it.

But perhaps – contrary to the mighty Hume and Clifford – belief in God, like belief in other persons, does not require the support of evidence in order for it to be rational. The claim that belief in God is rational without the support of evidence[1] is startling for many an atheist and even for some theists. Most atheist intellectuals feel comfort in their disbelief in God because they judge that there is little or no evidence for God's existence. Many theistic thinkers, however, insist that belief in God requires evidence and that such a demand should and can be met. So the claim that a person does not need evidence in order to rationally believe in God runs against the grain for atheist thinkers and has raised the ire of many theists. In spite of this vitriolic response, the claim that rational belief in God does not require evidence is eminently defensible. In order to defend it, let us first critically examine the enlightenment demand for evidence.

The Demand for Evidence

W. K. Clifford, in "The Ethics of Belief," claims that it is wrong, always and everywhere, for anyone to believe anything on insufficient evidence. Let's examine the deficiencies of his claim that everything must be believed only on the basis of sufficient evidence (relevance: If everything must be based on sufficient evidence, so must belief in God).

Clifford, an accomplished nineteenth-century mathematician and physicist, was rather hostile to religious belief. Clifford's fetching parable involves a shipowner who knowingly sends an unseaworthy ship to sea:

> He knew that she was old, and not over-well built at the first; that she had seen many seas and climes, and often needed repairs. Doubts had been suggested to him that possibly she was not seaworthy: These doubts preyed upon his mind and made him unhappy; he thought that perhaps he ought to have her thoroughly overhauled and refitted, even though this should put him to great expense. Before the ship sailed, however, he succeeded in overcoming these melancholy reflections. He said to himself that she had gone safely through so many voyages and weathered so many storms that it was idle to suppose she would not come safely home from this trip also. He would put his trust in Providence, which could hardly fail to protect all these unhappy families that were leaving their fatherland to seek for better times elsewhere. He would dismiss from his mind all ungenerous suspicions about the honesty of builders and contractors. In such ways he acquired a sincere and comfortable conviction that his vessel was thoroughly safe and seaworthy; he watched her departure with a light heart, and benevolent wishes for the success of the exiles in their strange new home that was to be; and he got his insurance money when she went down in midocean and told no tales. (Clifford 1886, 338)

The crucial point for Clifford is not the belief itself, but how the belief was acquired. The shipowner acquired his belief that the ship was seaworthy not by carefully attending to the evidence (for the evidence was to the contrary) but rather by suppressing both the evidence and his doubts. The sincerity of his belief was irrelevant to the rightness or wrongness of his believing, because the evidence prohibited a right to believe in the ship's seaworthiness. He ought to have acquired the belief by patient inquiry, not by selfishly acceding to his passions. His intentional stifling of evidence and doubts makes him fully responsible for the deaths of his passengers.

From this parable Clifford draws the general lesson: all rational beliefs require the support of evidence. He concludes: "It is wrong, always and everywhere for anyone to believe anything on insufficient evidence" (Clifford 1886, 346).

The implications of Clifford's claim for religious belief were thought to be clear then and have been spelled out countless times since.[2] If every belief must be based on sufficient evidence, then it is irrational or unreasonable to believe in God without sufficient evidence or argument. Furthermore, he also endorsed the idea that there is not sufficient evidence or argument to support belief in God. In the absence of the evidence, Clifford's estimation of the rationality of religious belief is manifest: one must withhold belief in God.

Clifford's examples powerfully demonstrate that in cases like the seaworthiness of ships, rational belief requires evidence. No one would disagree: some beliefs require evidence for their rational acceptability. But *all* beliefs in *every* circumstance? That's an exceedingly strong claim to make and, it turns out, one that cannot be based on evidence.

The first reason to suppose that not all of our beliefs can be based on evidence is the so-called regress argument. Consider your belief *A*. If *A* is rational, according to Clifford's universal demand for evidence, it must be based on some evidence, say belief *B*. But if *B* is rational, it must likewise be based on some evidence, say, belief *C*. And if *C* is rational, it must be based on *D*, and *D* on *E*, *E* on *F* ... You get the point. If every belief must be based on evidence, then one would have to hold an infinite regress of beliefs. But in this busy day and age, most of us simply don't have the time to hold an infinite number of beliefs! So, if we rationally believe anything, there must be some beliefs which we can reasonably take as evidence but which need not be based on evidence themselves. That is, there must be some beliefs that we can simply start with.[3]

Consider what someone like Clifford might allow us to take for evidence, to start with: beliefs that we acquire through sensory experience and beliefs that are self-evident like logic and mathematics. Next rainy day, make a list of all of your experiential beliefs: The sky is blue, grass is green, most trees are taller than most grasshoppers, and slugs leave a slimy trail.... Now add to this list all of your logical and mathematical beliefs: $2 + 2 = 4$, every proposition is either true or false, all of the even numbers that I know of are the sum of two prime numbers, in Euclidean geometry the interior angles of triangles equal 180°. From these propositions, try to deduce the conclusion that it is wrong, always and everywhere, for anyone to believe anything on insufficient evidence. None of the propositions that are allowed as evidence have anything at all to do with the conclusion. So Clifford's universal demand for evidence cannot satisfy its own standard! Therefore, by Clifford's own criterion, it must be irrational (see Plantinga and Wolterstorff 1983, pp. 16–93).

But the universal demand for evidence is more than irrational.[4] It is simply false and it is easy to see why. If there were a universal demand for evidence, most of our beliefs beyond those of our immediate, present experience would be ruled out as unjustified or irrational. Let us see why in the next section.

Belief Begins with Trust

We, finite beings that we are, simply cannot meet such a universal demand for evidence. Consider all of the beliefs that you currently hold. How many of those have met Clifford's strict demand for evidence? Clifford intends for all of us, like a scientist in a laboratory, to test all of our beliefs all of the time. Could many of your beliefs survive Clifford's test? Again, make a complete list of your experiential and logical/mathematical beliefs. If you were allowed to take those as evidence, few of your non-experiential, non-logical beliefs would survive.

Think of how many of your beliefs, even scientific ones, you have acquired *just because_ someone told you*. Not having been to Paraguay, I only have testimonial evidence that Paraguay is a country in South America. For all I know, all of the mapmakers have conspired to delude us about the existence of Paraguay (and even South America!). And, since I have been to relatively few countries around the world, I must believe in the existence of most countries (and that other people inhabit them and speak in that language) without support of evidence.[5] Even if I were to fly somewhere and then land and look around and see Paraguay signposts, I'd still have to trust that not everyone was deceiving me! I believe that $e = mc^2$ and that matter is made up of tiny little particles not because of experiments in a chemistry or physics lab (for all of my experiments failed) but because my science teachers told me so. Most of the beliefs that I have acquired – including my scientific ones – are based on my trust in my teachers and not on careful consideration of what Clifford would consider adequate evidence.

And in this busy day and age, I don't really have the time to live up to Clifford's demand for evidence! If we had the leisure to test all of our beliefs, perhaps we could meet the demand. But since we cannot meet that demand, we cannot be obligated to do so.

Even if we had the time, however, we could not meet this universal demand for evidence. The demand for evidence simply cannot be met in a large number of cases with the cognitive equipment that we have.

No one, as mentioned above, has ever been able to prove the existence of other *persons*.[6] Since I don't have experiential access to the inner life of another person – their thoughts, feelings, or desires – I could not base my belief in other persons on the only sort of evidence that is relevant to establishing personhood. If my only evidence is *my* own experience, my belief in *other* persons could not be based on experiential evidence. Nor do I see any hope of constructing any other sort of non-experiential argument for belief in other persons.

No one has ever been able to prove that we were not created five minutes ago with our memories intact. Nor has anyone proven that there is an external world – a world outside of my own sensations or mind. Again, if my evidence is my own experience, how can I prove that there is something outside of or prior to my own experience? And no one has been able to prove the reality of the past or that, in the future, the Sun will rise (I cannot have experience of the past or future and my present experience is poor evidence indeed for the past and future). Note that all of science assumes these very unprovable things: the existence of the external world, other persons, the past and that the future will be like the past. Without a world and the collective wisdom of other inquirers and without the principle of induction (that the future will be like the past), science is simply impossible. This list could go on and on. There is a limit to the things that human beings can prove. A great deal of what we believe, including modern science, is based on faith or trust, not on evidence or arguments.

I use the term "faith" here but that it is misleading. I don't mean to oppose faith to knowledge in these instances. For surely we do know that other persons exists, the Earth is more than five minutes old and that the Sun will rise tomorrow (although, maybe not in perpetually cloudy Grand Rapids where I reside!) and that Paul converted to Christianity (and lots of other truths about the past), and so on and so forth. In these cases, we know lots of things but we cannot prove them. We have to trust or rely on the cognitive faculties which produce these beliefs. We rely on our memory to produce memory beliefs (I remember having coffee with my breakfast this morning). We rely on an inductive faculty to produce beliefs about the veracity of natural laws (if I let go of this book, it will fall to the ground). We rely on our cognitive faculties when we believe that there are other persons, there is a past, there is a world independent of our mind, or what other people tell us. We can't help but trust our cognitive faculties.

The recently rediscovered eighteenth-century Scottish philosopher, Thomas Reid, developed a very powerful conception of human knowledge that rejects this universal demand for evidence and affirms the veracity of trusting our cognitive faculties. Let us now turn to consideration of Reid's views.

Reid on Human Cognitive Faculties

Thomas Reid is famous for defending common sense, the opinions of "the vulgar."[7] We don't proclaim that the Reidian defense of the vulgar in this section is precisely Reid's defense of the vulgar. Rather, this is a defense of the vulgar in the spirit of Reid (see Wolterstorff 1984; Plantinga and Wolterstorff 1983, pp. 135–86.) More specifically, it is a Reidian defense of a common sense view of rationality that both endorses common sense and, unlike a lot of philosophy, has a great deal of plausibility: it defends a view of rationality that fits with the cognitive equipment that human beings have.

This Reidian conception of rationality avoids the skepticism inherent in conceptions of knowledge that restrict knowledge to experience, logic and mathematics. In a nutshell the skeptical problem is that our experiential input (present moment, finite, fleeting) is insufficient to support our belief/knowledge output: the world (past, present, future, enduring, other persons, etc.). We have minimal experiential input and massive informational output. Even if we were to use logic and mathematics to order our experience, the world presented to us in our finite experience thusly ordered would pale in comparison to the rich and vast world that we believe in. Our own experience is a paucity of information incapable of supporting our knowledge of the world. Think of the world: it extends into the distant past and will proceed into the unforeseen future; its physical dimensions are both inconceivably vast and tiny; it includes people some of whom who lived long ago and far away and it includes me (and I am conscious and self-conscious, and I persist through time, and I recall finishing first in a High School relay thanks only to three much faster teammates). Now think of your own experiences: could they, when supplemented with the rules of logic and mathematics, produce the world (or, more precisely, justified beliefs about the world)? Even if we were to add the experiences of others to our repository of information, we would be incapable of deriving the world with our joint experience and logic. Fortunately, we are equipped with cognitive faculties that produce substantial beliefs about the world where experience and logic are doomed to fail.

Reid's project was, in part, a critique of this sort of skepticism which he believed began with René Descartes and culminated in the work of the skeptic David Hume. Their beliefs about what constituted knowledge led people to skepticism about the world:

> Descartes, Malebranche, and Locke, have all employed their genius and skill to prove the existence of a material world and with very bad success. Poor untaught mortals believe undoubtedly that there is a sun, moon, stars, an earth, which we inhabit; country, friends, and relations, which we enjoy land, houses, and moveables, which we possess. But philosophers, pitying the credulity of the vulgar, resolve to have no faith but what is founded on reason[ing]. (Reid 1983, p. 5)

In the final sentence Reid notes the Cartesian reliance upon reasoning as the sole, reliable cognitive faculty; reasoning produces belief by urging assent to a proposition upon reflecting on other propositions. But reasoning is nearly impotent in the production of beliefs: one must reason from something to something else. And the things one is permitted to reason from, according to the tradition Reid was critiquing, simply do not provide adequate informational resources for reasoning to the material world. In Reid's estimation precious little was or could be proved by these philosophers, and what ought to be rejected are not our ordinary beliefs, but the philosophers' sole reliance upon reasoning.

Reid believed these philosophers to be spellbound by a deceptive theory. But Reid is determined not to let a philosophical theory take precedence over the facts:

> That we have clear and distinct conceptions of extension, figure, and motion, and other attributes of body, which are neither sensations, nor like any sensation, is a fact of which we may be as certain as that we have sensations. And that all mankind have a fixed belief of an external material world – a belief which is neither got by reasoning nor education, and a belief which we cannot shake off, even when we seem to have strong arguments against it and not a

shadow of argument for it – is likewise a fact, for which we have all the evidence that the nature of the thing admits. *These facts are phenomena of human nature, from which we may justly argue against any hypothesis, however generally received. But to argue from a hypothesis against facts, is contrary to the rules of true philosophy"* (Reid 1983, p. 61; emphasis mine).

According to Reid, any philosophical theory which entails the rejection of our strong beliefs in the external, material world should itself be rejected. The dismissal of our common-sense beliefs is evidence enough against an abstract, arid, and speculative philosophy. True philosophy affirms our deepest commitments and works from them.

In Reid's own earthy style, we have been led astray:

> A traveler of good judgment may mistake his way, and be unawares led into a wrong track; and, while the road is fair before him, he may go on without suspicion and be followed by others; but, when it ends in a coal-pit it requires no great judgment to know that he had gone wrong, nor perhaps to find out what misled him. (Reid 1983, p. 11)

The reliance upon reasoning from very finite experience has led us astray. If we have fallen into a coal-pit, it is time to find a new path. Although Reid wholeheartedly endorses reasoning as a legitimate belief-producing faculty, he rejects the idea that it is *the* legitimate belief-producing faculty. We have many cognitive faculties, not just reasoning, that produce beliefs. He calls all of these faculties, taken together, "Common Sense."

One of our common-sense faculties is our disposition in certain circumstances, to believe what we sense and remember:

> There is a smell, is the immediate testimony of sense; there was a smell, is the immediate testimony of memory. If you ask me, why I believe that the smell exists, I can give no other reason, nor shall ever be able to give any other, than that I smell it. If you ask why I believe that it existed yesterday, I can give no other reason but that I remember it. Sensation and memory, therefore, are simple, original, and perfectly distinct operations of the mind, and both of them are original principles of belief. (Reid 1983, p. 15)

The belief-producing faculties of sense and memory are as much a part of the human constitution as reasoning and there is no reason to exalt reasoning over sense and memory. They are all "equally grounded on our constitution: none of them depends upon, or can be resolved into another. To reason against any of these kinds of evidence, is absurd; nay to reason for them is absurd" (Reid 1983, pp. 18–19).

Another of our common-sense faculties is belief in a mind or self that unifies me and my experiences and which persists through time. Hume rightly recognizes that no one has offered a proof that we have minds; although we have a strong tendency to believe that we do (it might not always be quite so strong in the case of some people!). We have sensations but they are discrete and apparently disconnected; an enduring mind or self would unify those experiences making them uniquely mine. But we cannot infer an enduring self from discrete experiences. So, if our belief in our self must be based on an argument from experiences, the belief in a mind or self is folly. Reid rejects this, accepting the belief in the self that our cognitive constitution forces upon us:

> What shall we say, then? Either those inferences which we draw from our sensations-namely, the existence of a mind, and of powers or faculties belonging to it – are prejudices of philosophy or

education, mere fictions of the mind, which a wise man should throw off as he does the belief of fairies; or they are judgments of nature – judgments not got by comparing ideas, and perceiving agreements and disagreements, but *immediately* inspired by our constitution. (Reid 1983, p. 23; my emphasis)

Reid believes that we are under some necessity in our cognitive constitution to believe that we have minds and that to reject this belief is "not to act the philosopher, but the fool or the madman" (p. 23). Just because I don't see, hear, touch, taste or smell my self, it doesn't follow that I don't have one or that my belief in my self is not rational.

Our make-up also gives us belief in the past which is assumed in every historical belief. For example, most of us believe that Caesar crossed the Rubicon, and that Chinese invented gunpowder and that I won that relay in High School. These beliefs, of course, assume that there's a past of which no one can any longer have sensations or experiences. And my beliefs concerning Caesar and the inventor of gunpowder are certainly not based on any sensations of Caesar or any ancient Chinese inventor. Suppose you were to take a history examination and you turned in a blank document assuring the professor that either the past had not been proven to exist or that no one had any experiential contact with the past, therefore no one had any reason to believe in any past events or even the past at all!

Memory beliefs are also produced directly and immediately by a cognitive faculty that triggers a belief in us when prompted. For example, what did you have for breakfast this morning? Perhaps this prompting triggered your memory faculty which produced a memory belief such as – "I had oatmeal (or cereal or toast)." Now you have no sensations of oatmeal – you don't see, hear, taste, or smell it. And you don't infer your belief that you had oatmeal for breakfast from any of your current sensations. You just immediately formed the belief upon my prompting.

Even in the domain of science, the redoubtable domain of experiential and experimental confirmation and refutation, one must simply accept without proof the regularity of nature that the future will be like the past. Science makes generalizations about the behavior of everything everywhere based on a finite set of extremely limited experiences. We can have no experiences or sensations of those parts of the universe that exceed our senses (we cannot see everything in the universe); in addition, the future likewise exceeds our puny experiential grasp. How can we make rational judgments about things we do not or cannot see? The law of universal gravitation, for example, states that every object in the universe is attracted to every other object in the universe in direct proportion to their masses but in disproportion to their distance:

$$F_g = \frac{Gm_1 m_2}{r^2}$$

Where, in the above formula, F_g is the gravitational force, m_1 and m_2 are the masses of two objects, r is the distance between the two objects and G is the universal gravitational constant. This is true of every two objects, everywhere in the universe, past, present, and future. But we can see the behavior of only the tiniest proportion of objects in the universe. We can pile finite experiences on top of finite experiences ad nauseum, but we will never be able to generalize to every object everywhere without assuming the uniformity of nature. The practice of science would be impossible without our natural cognitive ability to generalize from a finite set of data to everything, past, present, and future.

So, Reid recognizes, we have a tendency or disposition to believe, in the appropriate circumstances, that there is an external world, that we have a mind or self, that there are other persons; and we tend to believe inductively supported statements, what we remember, what we sense, and so on. What is significant about these cognitive faculties is that, with the exception of the reasoning faculty, they produce their effects immediately, without the evidential support of other beliefs. For example, belief in an enduring mind and belief in sensate knowledge, Reid says, are "immediately inspired by our constitution" (1983, p. 23). And, as with senses and memory, these cognitive faculties do not need to be justified by reasoning.

Reid also recognizes – a psychological point of some philosophical significance – that the vast majority of our beliefs are produced in us by our cognitive faculties, by our innate tendencies or dispositions to believe in an immediate, noninferential manner. That is, we don't reason to such beliefs; if anything, we simply trust them and use them to comprehend the world and live our lives. We really have no options here: these are our cognitive faculties – this is our intellectual equipment – it's all we have to work with.

Of course, not all of our beliefs are immediate. Some beliefs are acquired and maintained because of other beliefs we hold. Typically, specific scientific theories; say, the belief that there are electrons or that $e = mc^2$ – are acquired upon performing certain experiments in a laboratory or examining the observational evidence. Nonetheless, even the physicist must simply assume the uniformity of nature. After hearing testimony at a trial one might form the non-basic, inferential belief that the defendant is guilty. Suppose that after weighing the evidence one comes to believe that giving up French fries will reduce one's cholesterol count. Upon reading the medical reports one may conclude that secondary smoke is dangerous to one's health or that one ought to reduce one's exposure to the sun because of the declining ozone layer. Upon considering the mathematical formulas relating to the orbits of the planets one may acquire the belief in the universal law of gravitation. All of the beliefs that one reasons to, are beliefs produced by reasoning.

But the vast majority of beliefs we hold are not ones that we reason to. The vast majority of our beliefs are produced immediately, non-reflectively by our various cognitive faculties. We see or hear something and, if our attention is called to something, we immediately form a belief (and we find that in many of these beliefs we are assuming that there is a world outside of our minds). Someone speaks to us and we respond to them as a person (without inferring that they are a person). Our very reasoning assumes the unproven validity of logic and our scientific reasoning assuming the unproven uniformity of nature. And, if we are honest, a huge proportion of what we believe is acquired simply because someone told us (in person, or in a newspaper, or in a magazine, or by a teacher, etc.).

Consider our acceptance of what others tell us. Reid calls this "the credulity" disposition; others call it the principle of testimony. Whatever it is called, it is a profound and extensive source of human beliefs. From believing the response to one's question, "Do you have the time?" to accepting what your teachers told you in your classes or what you read in your textbooks, the reliance upon others for our beliefs is virtually limitless. Even in science – the paradigm of weighing evidence and affirming only what can be proved – a great deal of human belief is based on what others tell us. I said previously that one – a physicist one – might affirm $e = mc^2$ only after carefully weighing the evidence. But most of us non-physicists can barely understand the evidence. And even if we could, when I did the experiment in physics class my data proved that $e = mc^3$ not

$e = mc^2$!^{8} I accept the belief simply because someone told me that $e = mc^2$. It might be unfitting for a physicist to accept a scientific hypothesis without carefully considering and weighing the evidence; the physicist must carefully attend to the evidence and to the counter-evidence and not assent to a scientific hypothesis without the support of the evidence. We would not look kindly upon a scientist who committed herself to a scientific hypothesis because it just occurred to her on a whim or because it just seemed to be true. Yet even the best and most fastidious scientist must accept a great deal of what other scientists tell her. The physicist, incapable of proving every theory, must accept some theories' experimental results and observations on the authority of her peers. And I, *qua* non-physicist, believe in electrons, that the Sun is made mostly of hydrogen, that black holes exist, and so on, only because people have told me. And I believe there's a country called Uzbekistan and that is has a population of 28 million, that the best coffee is Jamaica Blue Mountain (and from Jamaica), and that Julia Child wrote a very famous French cookbook because others have told me. Even if I were to try to confirm these matters, I'd have to rely on what others told me (mapmakers, census counters, historians, importers, sales people, museum guides, etc.).

Reid notes that the credulity disposition is "unlimited in children" – children accept without question whatever anyone tells them. But as they grow and mature, children begin to question what others tell them. And they begin to ask questions of what others tell them in part because what they've been told sometimes conflicts with other things they've been told. In short, beliefs produced by the credulity disposition are not infallible. When such beliefs come in conflict, one must call upon one's other cognitive faculties to resolve the conflict.

One might look at Reid's discussion of our human cognitive faculties as both descriptive and prescriptive. In the first instance, Reid seems content simply to describe the cognitive faculties that we have. In the second instance, he seems content to permit us, rationally speaking, to rely on or trust our cognitive faculties. One might look at matters this way: Reid has developed an epistemology (a theory of knowledge) for creatures. Creatures are finite, limited, dependent, and, typically, fallible. We are not epistemological gods – we don't have infallible and indubitable access to basic aspects of the world and we aren't infallible reasoners from those basic aspects. Yet our cognitive equipment seems to work fairly well in helping us cope with reality. We have to rely on what we've been equipped with. We can do no other.

Reid and Rationality

What sort of general lessons might we learn from Reid about what it means for creatures like us to be rational?

Reid recognizes our many cognitive faculties that produce beliefs immediately that are without the support of evidence or argument. This leads him to part company with the grand tradition of modern philosophy which demands that most beliefs be supported by evidence or argument to be rational or justified. The paradigm instance of this principle is the Cartesian method of doubt in Descartes' famous *Meditations on First Philosophy*. Descartes determined to reject any belief that can possibly be doubted and accept only what is indubitable or what can be established by absolutely certain evidence. "Doubt first, believe second," was his motto; and rational belief is permitted only when it could be established on

the basis of solid evidence and sound reasoning. Reid views this guilty-until-proven innocent principle as the guiding philosophy of modem epistemology at least since the time of
Descartes. But it is precisely this sort of philosophy which leads to skepticism given our
human cognitive faculties and limitations. So Reid rejects this tradition that treats human
beliefs as guilty until proven innocent.

In its stead, Reid suggests an innocent-until-proven-guilty principle of rationality. Belief
begins with trust, not with doubt. We ought to trust, he contends, the deliverances of our
cognitive faculties, unless reason provides us with substantial grounds for questioning that
belief. With respect to our plethora of cognitive faculties, Reid states:

> I have found her in all other matters an agreeable companion, a faithful counselor, a friend to
> common sense, and to the happiness of mankind. This justly entitles her to my correspondence
> and confidence, till I find infallible proofs of her infidelity. (1983, p. 12; emphasis mine)

Under the presumption of innocence, a belief ought to be accepted as rational until it is
shown to be specious.

Contemporary philosopher Nicholas Wolterstorff affirms Reid's intuitions and develops
them into a criterion of rationality. Wolterstorff contends that

> A person is rationally justified in believing a certain proposition which he does believe unless
> he has adequate reason to cease from believing it. Our beliefs are rational unless we have reason
> for refraining; they are not nonrational unless we have reason for believing. They are innocent
> until proved guilty, not guilty until proved innocent. (Wolterstorff 1984, p. 163)

On this conception of rationality, beliefs produced by our cognitive faculties are rational
unless or until one has good reason to cease believing them. That is, we can trust a belief
produced by our cognitive faculty until that belief is undermined or defeated by stronger or
better corroborated beliefs.

One of the reasons that Reid thinks that our cognitive faculties typically produce rational
beliefs is his belief that our cognitive equipment has been given to us by our Creator. If we
are endowed by God with cognitive faculties, then we have sufficient reason for trusting
them. Because of the divine power and goodness, there is no good reason to prefer reasoning to common sense:

> Common Sense and Reason[ing] have both one author; that Almighty Author in all whose
> other works we observe a consistency, uniformity, and beauty which charm and delight under-
> standing: there must, therefore, be some order and consistency in the human faculties, as well
> as in other parts of his workmanship. (Reid 1983, p. 53)

Reid also believes that reasoning is empty unless Common Sense supplies it with materials for thought. We need something to reason *from*. If we, in a Cartesian and Humean vein,
admit only what can be established by reasoning, we will admit nothing. They permit so
little into the bases upon which one can reason, one could not reasonably believe in anything outside of one's own present experience. Without the principles of common sense, we
will believe nothing:

> All reasoning must be from first principles; and for first principles no other reason can be given
> but this, that, by the constitution of our nature, we are under a necessity of assenting to them.

Such principles are parts of our constitution, no less than the power of thinking: reason can neither make nor destroy them; nor can it do anything without them: it is like a telescope, which may help a man see farther, who hath not eyes; but, without eyes, a telescope shows nothing at all. A mathematician cannot prove the truth of his axioms, nor can he prove anything, unless he takes them for granted. We cannot prove the existence of our minds, nor even of our thoughts and sensations. A historian, or a witness, can prove nothing, unless it is taken for granted that the memory and senses may be trusted. A natural philosopher can prove nothing, unless it is taken for granted that the course of nature is steady and uniform. (Reid 1983, pp. 57–8)

Without the beliefs produced by our manifold cognitive faculties, reasoning would not lead us to embrace much of anything. Fortunately, we have been equipped with a plethora of cognitive faculties to supply us with materials for reasoning about the world. But most of the beliefs supplied by our cognitive faculties are ones that we must simply accept or trust, not ones that we can or should reason to. So we can and must trust the beliefs delivered to us by our cognitive faculty unless or until such beliefs are undermined or defeated.[9]

Why should we be interested in being rational? The goal of rationality is to get more amply in touch with the truth. Most of us would like to orient our lives around the truth. If there is a God, let it be known and let us live our lives accordingly. But if there be no God, then let that be known and let us get on with our lives. Seeking to be rational is seeking the truth. Rationality, in short, aims at the truth.

But while being rational aims at the truth, it does not always hit that target. Surely it was rational in 200 BC to believe that the Earth was flat and that the Earth was at the center of the universe. After all, we don't see the Earth's curvature and we don't feel the Earth rotating at roughly 1,000 miles per hour or hurtling through space in orbit around the sun at 67,000 miles per hour. Using our commonsensical cognitive faculties produced rational but false beliefs about the place of the Earth in the cosmos. Our perceptions misled us about the nature of physical reality. It was only as evidence mounted against geocentrism that such a commonsensical view was abandoned. And heliocentrism became the rational view for most people due to the accumulation of evidence.

So we need to amend our understanding of rationality. If we want to discover the truth, we need to be sensitive to the accumulation of evidence and counter-evidence. Indeed, gaining evidence is one of the best guides to truth. However, for reasons stated above, gaining evidence cannot be a rational requirement for the discovery of truth. We still have to start somewhere and so we have to trust our cognitive faculties; rational belief still begins with trust.

But being willing to revise our beliefs in the face of counter evidence and the accumulation of favorable evidence will surely and powerfully assist our quest for the truth. So let us propose the Rational Stance:

The Rational Stance: *trust* the deliverances of reason, *seek* supporting evidence, and *open* yourself to contrary evidence

The Rational Stance captures the Reidian insight that belief begins with trust but also captures the truth-aimed goal of rationality in the seeking of supporting evidence and openness to counter evidence.

Let us take these Reidian insights and apply them to belief in God.

The God Faculty

We have been outfitted with cognitive faculties that produce beliefs that we can reason from. The kinds of beliefs that we do and must reason to is a small subset of the kinds of beliefs that we do and must accept without the aid of a proof. That's the long and short of the human believing condition. We, in most cases, must rely on our intellectual equipment to produce beliefs, without evidence or argument, in the appropriate circumstances. Do we have a cognitive faculty or capacity (or set of faculties or capacities); let us call it the "god faculty," that produces belief in God?

Theologian John Calvin believed that God had provided us with an innate sense of the divine. He writes:

> "There is within the human mind, and indeed by natural instinct, an awareness of divinity." This we take to be beyond controversy. To prevent anyone from taking refuge in the pretense of ignorance, God himself has implanted in all men a certain understanding of his divine majesty. Ever renewing its memory, he repeatedly sheds fresh drops.... Indeed, the perversity of the impious, who though they struggle furiously are unable to extricate themselves from the fear of God, is abundant testimony that this conviction, namely that there is some God, is naturally inborn in all, and is fixed deep within, as it were in the very marrow. From this we conclude that it is not a doctrine that must first be learned in school, but one of which each of us is master from his mother's womb and which nature itself permits no one to forget. (Calvin 1960, bk. 1, ch. 3, pp. 43–4)

Calvin contends that people are accountable to God for their unbelief not because they have failed to submit to a convincing theistic proof, but because they have suppressed the truth that God has implanted within their minds.

If there is a God who cares for human beings, it is natural to suppose that if God created us with cognitive faculties which by and large reliably produce beliefs without the need for evidence, he would likewise provide us with a cognitive faculty which produces belief in him without the need for evidence. So there is some theological or philosophical reason for supposing there might be a god-faculty.

Reformed epistemologists – theistic philosophers who on this matter follow the theologian John Calvin, whose ideas can be traced back through Aquinas, Anselm, and Augustine to St Paul) find contemporary expression in the work of analytic philosophers such as Alvin Plantinga, Nicholas Wolterstorff, and William Alston.[10] Reformed epistemologists hold that one may properly believe in and even know that God exists without the support of proof or inferential evidence (like an argument for the existence of God). Alvin Plantinga, the most famous of the Reformed epistemologists, considers the god faculty as analogous to our other cognitive faculties:

> The *sensus divinitatis* is a disposition or set of dispositions to form theistic beliefs in various circumstances, in response to the sorts of conditions or stimuli that trigger the working of this sense of divinity. There are many circumstances, and circumstances of many kinds (glories of nature, grave danger, awareness of divine disapproval, etc) that call forth or occasion theistic belief. Here the *sensus divinitatis* resembles other belief-producing faculties or mechanisms. If we wish to think in terms of the over-worked functional example, we can think of the *sensus divinitatis* too, as an input-output device: it takes the circumstances mentioned above as input and issues as output theistic beliefs, beliefs about God. (Plantinga (200), pp. 173–5)

It should be noted that Plantinga contends that, unlike Calvin's general sense of the divine, the *sensus divinatis* produces belief in God – an omnipotent, omniscient, perfectly good Creator of the universe.

But appeals to a theologian, theistic philosopher, or to God himself are not likely to persuade many people that belief in God is rational because of an implanted god-faculty. Are there any non-theological reasons for supposing (a) that we have a god-faculty, and (b) that beliefs produced by the god-faculty are "innocent until proven guilty"?

There now seems to be good empirical reason, established by cognitive science, to believe what some philosophers and theologians affirmed only on theological grounds: that we have an innate god-faculty, although "religious faculty" or *sensus divinitatis* may be more precise and relevant terms. Cognitive science is a relatively new discipline that unites psychology, neuroscience, computer science, and philosophy in the study of the operations of the mind/brain. It is concerned with how the mind processes information – how it is acquired, stored, retrieved, ordered, and used. The scientific study of the thinking mind has considered, among many other things, perception, attention, memory, pattern recognition, concept formation, consciousness, reasoning, problem-solving, language-processing and forgetting. Interestingly, the results of cognitive science about the operations of the mind suggest empirical confirmation for Thomas Reid's speculations: that, in a large number of cases, we have an inbuilt cognitive mechanism, faculties, or modules that process information and produce immediate, non-reflective beliefs. And the Reidian faculties – perception, external world, inductive principle, memory, other persons, and so on – parallel those affirmed by cognitive science. The mind seems to work roughly as Reid conceived.

With respect to belief in God, it appears that we do, indeed, have a natural, instinctive religious sense.[11] It is likely impossible to offer a definition of religion that captures every type of religious belief (and only religious belief) including, for example, theistic religious such as Judaism (one god), Hinduism (many gods) or Christianity (one god in three persons), on the one hand, and non-theistic religions such as Buddhism and Taoism on the other; religions involving an eternal judgment (Islam, for example) and those that don't (say state Confucianism); religions that hold to human immortality (Greek religions) and those that deny it (various forms of Buddhism and Christianity); religions that posit a supernatural source of morality and those that are humanistic, and so on. The best we can say is that there is family resemblance among the various religious beliefs and practices even if they do not share any features in common (the way features of a family – build, color and shape of eyes, gait, temperament, etc. – overlap but are not possessed by each and every member of that family). I take it that near-cousins to the term "religion" are "spirituality", "the supernatural" "ritual," and "worldview".

Anthropologists have increasingly come to recognize that spirituality/religious beliefs/rituals universally occur across cultures and times. Darwin himself, while rejecting the universality of belief in God, concedes the universality of religious beliefs:

> The belief in God has often been advanced as not only the greatest but the most complete of all the distinctions between man and the lower animals. It is however impossible to maintain that this belief is innate or instinctive in man. On the other hand a belief in all-pervading spiritual agencies seems to be universal, and apparently follows from a considerable advance in man's reason, and from a still greater advance in his faculties of imagination, curiosity and wonder. (Darwin 1871, pp. 609–19)

Every culture seems to have a firm belief in spiritual beings and an afterlife. E. O. Wilson writes: "Religious belief is one of the universals of human behavior, taking recognizable form in every society from hunter gatherer bands to socialist republics" (Wilson 1976, p. 176). And just as universal human traits such as language and emotion are explained by a mind-brain disposed to language and emotion, it is now widely accepted that universally occurring spiritual beliefs indicate that humans are naturally disposed to spiritual beliefs; humans are "hard-wired" for belief in spiritual beings. While these innate dispositions find culturally particular expression (just as with language), there is a hard core of dualistic belief/practice – dividing the world into the spiritual and the material – that is common to every culture.

Robert McCauley contends, on the basis of the recurrence of religious beliefs and rituals that the acquisition of religious beliefs is due to "the possession and operation of ... naturally occurring cognitive inclinations" (McCauley 2000, p. 62). Just as the acquisition of a natural language is natural, so, too, the acquisition of religious beliefs is natural. Religious beliefs are natural in the sense of (a) being "self-evident, intuitive, or held or done without reflection" and (b) being developed with very little cultural input.

Contemporary cognitive scientists of religion include Pascal Boyer, Scott Atran, and Justin Barrett. According to Barrett, Senior Director of Oxford University's Centre for Anthropology and Mind, "Belief in God or gods is not some artificial intrusion into the natural state of human affairs. Rather, belief in gods generally and God particularly arises through the natural, ordinary operation of human minds in natural ordinary environments" (Barrett 2004, p. 124). Atran is research director in anthropology at the National Center for Scientific Research in Paris. He is also visiting professor of psychology, anthropology and public policy at the University of Michigan and presidential scholar in sociology at the John Jay College of Criminal Justice, New York City. Atran writes: "Supernatural agency is the most culturally recurrent, cognitively relevant, and evolutionarily compelling concept in religion. The concept of the supernatural is culturally derived from an innate cognitive schema ..." (Atran 2002, p. 57).[12] Boyer, Henry Luce Professor of Individual and Collective Memory at Washington University in St Louis, contends that religious beliefs are natural, arguing that "the explanation for religious beliefs and behaviors is to be found in the way that all human minds work. I really mean all human minds, not just the minds of religious people" (Boyer 2001, p. 2).

More sensational claims have been made about the god-faculty. In 2004 *Time* magazine's cover article trumpeted the discovery of the "God gene." In the accompanying article, we read:

> Far from being an evolutionary luxury then, the need for God may be a crucial trait stamped deeper and deeper into our genome with every passing generation. Humans who developed a spiritual sense thrived and bequeathed that trait to their offspring.

Matthew Alper, in *The "God" Part of the Brain* claims: "If there is any behavior that has been universally exhibited among every human culture, that behavior must represent an inherent characteristic of our species, a genetically inherited instinct" (Hamer 2005, p. 49). Belief in God and its accompanying practices is just such a trait. Dean Hamer, in *The God Gene: How Faith Is Hardwired Into Our Genes*, claims to have isolated the "God gene" (VMAT2). The so-called God gene is loosely associated with brain receptors that, he alleges, are pronounced in the feelings of spirituality not with belief in God per se. He claims to have isolated the "God gene" in those who report self-transcendent experiences; such experiences are a curious combination of self-forgetfulness, interconnectedness (with others and the cosmos) and mysticism. However, the sensational title is belied by the evidence; at best, his book suggests a spiritual sense or faculty of the brain.

Let's assume that cognitive science affirms that we do have a natural god-faculty which produces religious beliefs immediately, non-inferentially, or non-reflectively. What should our initial judgment be of the beliefs thusly produced?

Reason and Belief in God

There are at least four reasons to believe that it is proper or rational for a person to accept belief in God without the need for an argument.

First, and most importantly, we have argued that belief begins with the trust in our cognitive faculties unless or until they are proven unreliable; inductively we should extend this privilege to our god-faculty (unless or until it proves unreliable or our belief in God is defeated by other beliefs). If we are permitted to trust our cognitive faculties and the god-faculty is one of those faculties, then we are permitted to trust the god-faculty and accept the beliefs produced by it. So if one's belief in God is produced by the god-faculty in the appropriate circumstances then one is rational in accepting that belief unless or until one has adequate reason to cease holding that belief.

Second, although philosophers are fond of touting arguments in favor of their positions, it surely is not a requirement of reason that ordinary folks understand and hold philosophical arguments before they believe in, say, the external world or other persons. This would be especially problematic given that there are no good arguments for other persons and the external world! And even in areas where philosophers have decent arguments, there are very few people who have access to or the ability to assess most philosophical arguments. It is hard to imagine, therefore, that the demand for evidence would be a requirement of reason. Even Hegel, no paragon of lucidity, could see that rational belief in God did not hang on grasping a theistic argument:

> The (now somewhat antiquated) metaphysical proofs of God's existence, for example, have been treated, as if knowledge of them and a conviction of their truth were the only and essential means of producing a belief and conviction that there is a God. Such a doctrine would find its parallel, if we said that eating was impossible before we acquired a knowledge of the chemical, botanical, and zoological characters of our food; and we must delay digestion till we bad finished the study of anatomy and physiology. (Hegel 1974, pp. 20–1)

The demand for evidence is an imperialistic attempt to make philosophers out of people who have no need to become philosophers. It is curious that very few philosophers (like most ordinary folk) have come to belief in God on the basis of theistic arguments. I commissioned and published a collection of spiritual autobiographies from prominent Christian philosophers just to see if philosophers were any different from my grandmother on this count. They weren't.

Third, if there is a God it seems that God has given us an awareness of himself that is not dependent on theistic arguments. It is hard to imagine that God would make rational belief as difficult as those that demand evidence contend. I encourage anyone who thinks that evidence is required for rational belief in God to study very carefully the theistic arguments, their refutations and counter-refutations, and their increasing subtlety yet decreasing charm. Adequate assessment of these arguments would require a lengthy and torturous tour through the history of philosophy and may require the honing of one's logical and metaphysical skills beyond the capacity of most of us. Why would God put that sort of barrier between us and himself? If you are a religious believer, think back to the origin of this belief (not your subsequent attempts to understand that belief through reasoning). Have you believed since childhood, because you were brought up in a believing family? Did you come to belief on a retreat, in the mountains, or while gazing at a starry sky? Were you destitute and sought God as your only hope? Did you feel moved to pray or attend church and gradually find yourself embracing what people who pray and worship believe? Were you made aware of God's providential action in the world by a series of apparently chance events through which you came to see the benevolent hand of God? Did you feel increasingly guilty, as if you were responsible to someone greater than human persons, and find in God the open arms of forgiveness? Were you moved by the worldviews powerfully portrayed in the fiction of, say, C. S. Lewis or G. K. Chesterton? Were you impressed by the joyful and centered lives of Christian friends? Were you moved to despair by the absurdity of life without God through reading Sartre and Kierkegaard and took a leap of faith into the abyss of the divine? Did you make a pact with God that if he existed and saved you from some peril you would reorient your life around him? I suspect you did not come to belief in God through the study of the great proofs of Anselm and Aquinas and find your intellect moved to belief in God? Again, if there is a God who wishes us to be in relation to him, why put an obscure and complicated proof in the way of knowing him?[13]

Fourth, belief in God is more like belief in a person than belief in a scientific theory. Consider the examples that started this essay. Somehow the scientific approach – doubt first, consider all of the available evidence, and believe later – seems woefully inadequate or inappropriate to personal relations. What seems manifestly reasonable for physicists in their laboratory is desperately deficient in human relations. Human relations demand trust, commitment, and faith. If belief in God is more like belief in other persons than belief in atoms, then the trust that is appropriate to persons will be appropriate to God. We cannot and should not arbitrarily insist that the scientific method (supposing there is one) is appropriate to every kind of human practice. The fastidious scientist, who cannot leave the demand for evidence in her laboratory, will find herself cut off from relationships that she could otherwise reasonably maintain – with friends, family and, perhaps even, God.

Conclusion

This approach to belief in God has been rather descriptive. We need to pay a lot more attention to how actual people actually acquire beliefs. The psychology of believing may tell us a lot about our cognitive equipment. The lessons learned from observing people and their beliefs support the position that I have defended: rational people may rationally believe in God without evidence or argument. But, recalling the rational stance, we should seek supporting evidence for God's existence and open ourselves to evidence contrary to God's existence. In my next chapter, I will consider in more depth the philosophy, psychology, and theology of belief in God.

Notes

1   By "evidence" I mean propositional arguments or proofs of the sort one might find in a theistic argument. There might be non-propositional evidence for the existence of God, say religious experience, but that is not how I will take the term "evidence" in this chapter. Historically, I believe evidentialists have restricted evidence to propositional arguments.

2   See for example the discussions of Michael Scriven and Antony Flew in Plantinga and Wolterstorff, *Faith and Rationality* (1983), pp. 24–39.

3   Another alternative is coherentism. The coherentist claims that all of our beliefs are justified by other beliefs but avoids the regress argument by contending that our beliefs form an interconnecting web of beliefs. So our beliefs are justified by being part of a coherent or logically consistent set or web of beliefs. The problem with construing knowledge along coherentist lines is that we can have a consistent set of beliefs with little or no connection to reality.

4   William James's (1956) ingenious strategy at this point is to show that the Cliffordian himself has unwittingly made a passional decision. James recognizes that there are two possible ways to approach truth and avoid error. First, James's preferred way considers "the chase for truth as paramount, and the avoidance of error as secondary" (James 1956 p. 18). Secondly, Clifford's way regards the avoidance of error as paramount and the attainment of truth as secondary. James's disapproval of Clifford is evident:

Clifford's exhortation … is like a general informing his soldiers that it is better to keep out of battle forever than to risk a single wound. Not so are victories either over enemies or over nature gained. Our errors are surely not such awfully solemn things. In a world where we are so certain to incur them in spite of all our caution, a certain lightness of heart seems healthier than this excessive nervousness on their behalf. (James, *The Will to Believe,* p. 19).

5   Recall that by evidence, I mean "propositional argument" of the sort accepted or acceptable by an Enlightenment evidentialist: from premises that are self-evident, evident to the senses or incorrigible. Of course, there is testimonial evidence in these sorts of cases but this is not acceptable to the Enlightenment evidentialist unless it can be demonstrated from propositions that are self-evident, evident to the senses or incorrigible. Testimonial evidence is (a) neither self-evident, evident to the senses, nor incorrigible and (b) cannot be demonstrated from such propositions. Furthermore, we generally simply accept testimony, we don't seek independent proof.

6   Again, to be a person is to have an inner life – a minded life – that is not accessible to other persons.

7   By "the vulgar," he means common, uneducated, ordinary folks, not the educated, cynical, and perhaps skeptical elite.

8   I actually did not perform any experiments in physics class designed to prove Einstein's famous theorem. But my point is illustrative – few, if any, of our own attempts to replicate the evidence work, so few if any of our scientific beliefs are based on good evidence.

9   Michael Bergmann, following Plantinga, develops this more formally and fully. His main contention is that, roughly speaking, "*S*'s belief *B* is justified iff i) *S* does not take *B* to be defeated and ii) the cognitive faculties producing *B* are a) functioning properly, b) truth-aimed and c) reliable in the environments for which they were 'designed'" (Bergmann, 2006, p. 135).

10 See Plantinga (2000), Wolterstorff (1976), Plantinga and Wolterstorff (1983) and Alston (1991). For a more popular introduction to Reformed epistemology, see Clark (1990).

11 Is it a single module of the mind-brain or is it a complex involving various parts of the mind-brain? Is it a part of the brain dedicated to belief in God or is belief in God a by-product of cognitive faculties that serve other purposes?

12 Atran contends that this faculty is our ordinary agency-detection faculty, aimed at detecting a wide variety of ordinary agents (people, animals, etc.) which is extended to divine agency detection.

13 There may nonetheless be evidence of God's existence. Belief in God may quickly and immediately affirmed upon appreciating the beauty and wonder of creation. But even in this case one need to be aware of an explicit, formal, propositional argument.

Bibliography

Alper, Matthew (2006) *The God Part of the Brain*. New York: Sourcebooks.

Alston, William (1991) *Perceiving God*. Ithaca, NY: Cornell University Press.

Atran, Scott (2002) *In Gods We Trust*. New York: Oxford University Press.

Barrett, Justin (2004) *Why Would Anyone Believe in God?* Lanham, MD: AltaMira Press.

Bergmann, Michael (2006) *Justification Without Awareness*. New York: Oxford University Press.

Boyer, Pascal (2001) *Religion Explained: Evolutionary Origins of Religious Thought*. New York: Basic Books.

Calvin, John (1960) *Institutes of the Christian Religion*, trans. Ford Lewis Battles. Philadelphia: Westminster Press.

Clark, K. J. (1990) *Return to Reason*. Grand Rapids, MI: Eerdmans.

Clifford, W. K. (1886) The ethics of belief. In *Lectures and Essays*, pp. 339–63. London: Macmillan.

Darwin, Charles (1871) *Descent of Man*. New York: D. Appleton.

Hamer, Dean (2005) *The God Gene: How Faith Is Hardwired into Our Genes*. New York: Anchor.

Hegel, G. W. F. (1974) *Hegel: The Essential Writings*, ed. Frederick G. Weiss. New York, Harper.

James, William (1956) *The Will to Believe*. New York: Dover.

McCauley, Robert (2000) The naturalness of religion and the unnaturalness of science. In F. Keil and R. Wilson (eds.) *Explanation and Cognition*, pp. 61–85 Cambridge, MA: MIT Press.

Plantinga, Alvin (2000) *Warranted Christian Belief*. New York: Oxford University Press.

Plantinga, Alvin and Wolterstorff, Nicholas (1983) *Faith and Rationality*. Notre Dame, IN: University of Notre Dame Press.

Reid, Thomas (1983) *Inquiry and Essays*, ed. Ronald Beanblossom and Keith Lehrer. Indianapolis: Hackett.

Wilson, E. O. (1976) *On Human Nature*. New York: Bantam Books.

Wolterstorff, Nicholas (1984) Thomas Reid on rationality. In Hendrik Hart, Johan van der Hoven, and Nicholas Wolterstortf (eds.)*Rationality in the Calvinian Tradition*, pp. 43–69. Lanham, MD: University Press of America.

38

Reformed Epistemology and the Cognitive Science of Religion

KELLY JAMES CLARK

Reformed epistemology and cognitive science have remarkably converged on belief in God. Reformed epistemology holds that belief in God is basic – that is, belief in God is a natural, non-inferential belief that is immediately produced by a cognitive faculty or capacity. "Cognitive science also holds that belief in gods is non-reflectively and instinctively produced," that is, non-inferentially and automatically produced by a cognitive faculty or system. Reformed epistemology finds its inspiration in the theologian John Calvin and finds contemporary expression in the work of prominent analytic philosophers. Cognitive science, on the other hand, is the relatively recent work of empirical psychologists who find inspiration in empirical psychology and in the work of Darwin. Both groups contend that we have natural cognitive faculties or faculties which produce belief in God immediately without the support of an inference. In this chapter, I will show some remarkable points of convergence, and a few points of divergence, between Reformed epistemology and the cognitive science of religion.

Introduction

Reformed epistemology and cognitive science have remarkably converged on belief in God. Reformed epistemology holds that belief in God is basic – that is, belief in God is a natural, non-inferential belief that is immediately produced by a cognitive faculty or capacity. Cognitive science also holds that belief in gods is nonreflectively and instinctively produced – that is, non-inferentially and automatically produced by a cognitive faculty or system.[1] But there are *prima facie* differences. Reformed epistemologists hold that the god-faculty was implanted in each person by God while the cognitive scientist typically holds that the god-faculty developed in each person through evolutionary processes. Reformed epistemology finds its inspiration in the theologian John Calvin (although the idea goes back through Aquinas, Anselm and Augustine to St. Paul) and finds contemporary expression in the work of prominent analytic philosophers such as Alvin Plantinga, Nicholas Wolterstorff, and William Alston.[2] According to Calvin, "There is within the human mind, and indeed by natural instinct, an awareness of divinity. ... God himself has implanted in all men a certain understanding of his divine majesty" (Calvin 1960, I. iii. 1). Cognitive science, on the other hand, is the relatively recent work of empirical psychologists who find inspiration in empirical psychology and in the work of Darwin; contemporary cognitive scientists of religion include Pascal Boyer, Scott Atran, and Justin Barrett. Both groups contend that we have natural cognitive faculties or faculties which produce belief in God immediately without the support of an inference. According to Barrett, "Belief in God or gods is not some artificial intrusion into the natural state of human affairs. Rather, belief in gods generally and God particularly arises through the natural, ordinary operation of human minds in natural ordinary environments" (Barrett 2004, p. 124).

In this chapter, I will show some remarkable points of convergence, and a few points of divergence, between Reformed epistemology and the cognitive science of religion. I will do so through the work, primarily, of Plantinga. I will first set up Reformed epistemology by showing it as a response to Enlightenment evidentialism. Next I will present the basic arguments in favor of Reformed epistemology. Before turning to Reformed epistemology, let us first consider explanations of religious belief afforded by various cognitive scientists.

The Cognitive Science of Religion

There are various accounts of the cognitive faculties that produce religious belief. I will focus here on cognitive science's accounts of belief in God. Cognitive science of religion rejects the popular anthropological assumption of radical incommensurability among cultural groups. Rather studies seem to show that our common biological heritage and relatively similar environments produce relatively similar minds and, often, beliefs. Rejecting the empiricist assumption of the mind as a blank slate, cognitive science holds that our minds come equipped with cognitive faculties that actively process our perceptions and shape our conceptions of the world (see Boyer 1994, Pt. II). These common cognitive faculties are relatively specialized and discrete subsystems that structure, inform, enhance, and limit our worldview. Some of these cognitive faculties structure, inform, enhance and limit religious beliefs. Belief in gods, to take one characteristic form of religious belief, arises from the stimulation of universal cognitive faculties. Hence, religious belief is a natural product of our common cognitive faculties. Humans have a natural tendency to believe in gods.

A general picture has emerged of how our common cognitive faculties produce belief in God. Our cognitive faculties are believed to have been generated evolutionarily in response to rather specific environmental pressures. Religious beliefs, it is claimed, have arisen in part because human beings are equipped with a cognitive unit – an agency-detecting device – that generates beliefs about agency, sometimes with only the slightest stimulation. When appropriately stimulated, humans are equipped with cognitive faculties that immediately, that is non-reflectively or non-inferentially, produce beliefs in the existence of agents. Without such immediate beliefs/responses to certain motions (rustling bushes) or sounds (things going bump in the night) we might end up food for a predator or victim of an enemy. Because this "hypersensitive agency detection device" (HADD) is sensitive and is triggered sometimes with the slightest provocation, it has obvious adaptive advantages; if it were less sensitive, less hyperactive, it would prove less adaptive.[3] In addition to beliefs in animals and enemies, beliefs about gods are also explained by HADD. If ordinary agents seem unsuited to account for one's experiences, one might find oneself immediately believing in extraordinary, supernatural agents (including ghosts, angels, or gods); these might better account for, say, apparently miraculous events or weather patterns than ordinary agents. HADD works not only when stimulated by sounds or motions; it is also triggered in the face of apparent but odd design, design with "traces" of agency (such as crop circles). Human beings, it seems, are naturally predisposed to seek agentive explanations of unusual phenomena that appear to be like things that we know humans have designed. Barrett explains:

> Our minds have numerous pattern detectors that organize visual information into meaningful units. HADD remains on the lookout for patterns known to be caused by agents. If this patterned information matches patterns … known to be caused by agents, HADD detects agency and alerts other mental tools. … More interesting is when a pattern is detected that appears to be purposeful or goal directed and, secondarily, does not appear to be caused by ordinary mechanical or biological causes. Such patterns may prompt HADD to attribute the traces to agency yet to be identified: unknown persons, animals, or space aliens, ghosts, or gods (Barrett 2004, 36–7)

We are equipped with pattern detectors (in some cases, pattern creators) which are fine-tuned to detect agency (see Atran 2002, pp. 59–61). Upon the detection of agency, another cognitive faculty, Theory of Mind begins operating and attributes beliefs, desires, purposes, and so on to the postulated agent.[4]

Cognitive science also has explanations of the sustainability and transmissibility of religious belief (see Boyer 1994, chs. 2–3; and Barrett 2004, pp. 21–30). Religious beliefs are sustainable and transmissible because they are, typically, minimally counterintuitive. They are *minimally* counterintuitive: if they were maximally counterintuitive they would not fit within our cognitive expectations and so would be rejected as fanciful or bizarre. They are minimally *counterintuitive*: by virtue of being counterintuitive, they capture our attention, account for phenomena that are otherwise inexplicable, and are easy to remember and to faithfully transmit (see Atran 2002, ch. 4). In addition, successful religious beliefs "have good *inferential potential*": they can unite, in a single explanation, a wide variety of diverse and otherwise inexplicable phenomena and can find themselves embedded in deep and informative narrative contexts. Once again, successful religious beliefs are successful in so far as they prove memorable and readily transmissible, which traits are maximized by increased explanatory power and the affective dimensions of story (See Atran 2002, pp. 88–9; Boyer 2001, pp. 50–9; and Barrett 2004, p. 15). And, finally, religious beliefs are reinforced and transmitted through ritual practices (see Lawson and McCauley 1990, and McCauley and Lawson 2002).

The cognitive science of religion is often allied with evolutionary explanations of the origins of our cognitive faculties. Most evolutionary accounts agree that belief in God is a spandrel. A *spandrel*, to use a term coined by Gould and Lewontin, is a trait that is a byproduct, not a direct consequence of natural selection. That is, natural selection selects for a an adaptive trait, a trait that increases one's chances of spreading one's seed, but such traits are sometimes accompanied by another trait that is non-adaptive; on its own, the spandrel would not have been selected (see Gould and Lewontin 1979; Atran 2002, pp. 43–5). For example, the redness (or blueness) of blood or the precise number of fingers and toes on a human hand or foot may be spandrels. Spandrels are more ornamental epiphenomena, non-adaptive leftovers, than adaptive traits. Some spandrelists contend that religious beliefs are spandrels with no adaptive advantage. So, for example, Atran claims: "Religions are not adaptations and they have no evolutionary functions as such." He goes on to claim that religion did not originate primarily to cope with death, keep moral and social order, recover the security of father or mother, provide causal explanations, or provoke intellectual surprise (Atran 2002, pp. 12–13).

But some spandrels, including cultural traits, may in the long run prove adaptive. David Sloan Wilson, for example, contends that religious belief is adaptive because religious systems encourage pro-social behavior such as cooperation and lack of stealing and so will tend to out survive groups that lack these traits.[5] Indeed, the pervasiveness and intractability of religious beliefs may be explained by postulating survival advantages to groups that maintain religious beliefs. For example, God as a perfectly just, super-knower may serve to prevent defections from the social contract. It may be rational (i.e., rational in the sense of maximizing one's interests) to defect occasionally from the social contract if one can get away with it. If one's community includes merely finite knowers, the opportunities for defection will be great given the relative ease with which one can avoid detection. However, if one's community includes an all-knowing, perfectly just God, one can never escape detection and, ultimately, punishment. So if one's community includes belief in god, it is never rational to defect. That is, it is always rational, indeed always one's overall best interest, to abide by the rules. As Scott Atran writes:

> Because human representations of agency and intention include representations of false belief and deception, human society is forever under the threat of moral defection. Simple consent among individuals seldom, if ever, sustains cooperation among large numbers of people over long periods of time ... Supernatural agents thus *also* function as moral Big Brothers who keep constant vigil to dissuade would be cheaters and free riders. (Atran 2002, p. 112)

But a super-knowing god is not sufficient to prevent defections. Since punishments/rewards for bad/good behavior are meted out imperfectly in this life, in order to rationally preclude defections, there must be a next life in which punishments/rewards are meted out perfectly. Interestingly, cognitive science has shown a natural human tendency to regard supernatural agents as having super-knowing and super-perceiving powers. Furthermore, cognitive science has shown that human beings have a natural impulse to believe in an afterlife (Bering 2002 and 2006; Bering and Bjorklund 2004). The survival advantages of a community that has the full explanatory resources for reward of good behavior and the punishment of bad behavior are obvious.

Studies in the cognitive science of religion suggest that people are naturally religious, that is, they have natural cognitive faculties which produce, perhaps indirectly, belief in gods. As we turn to Reformed epistemology's understanding of our natural knowledge of God, we will need to limit our discussion to just two of the claims of cognitive science of religion (which are most suggestive of Reformed epistemology). We will consider both the proposed HADD and pattern-detecting faculties.

The Internal Witness: The *Sensus Divinitatis*

In this section, I will focus on the ideas, primarily, of John Calvin on knowledge of God. Calvin holds that there are two primary sources of knowledge of God, one internal and one external. Internal knowledge of God is either innate or immediately produced by a divinely instilled cognitive faculty. Here we will also consider the arguments of contemporary Reformed epistemologists that belief in God is properly basic. External knowledge of God is produced through an inference, perhaps inchoate, from the order both of the human body and of the cosmos. As we proceed we will consider similarities and differences between the views of Reformed epistemology and the cognitive science of religion.

John Calvin believed that God has provided all humans with a natural, instinctual sense of the divine. He writes:

> There is within the human mind, and indeed by natural instinct, an awareness of divinity. This we take to be beyond controversy.... God himself has implanted in all men certain understanding of his divine majesty. Ever renewing its memory, he repeatedly sheds fresh drops. ... Indeed, the perversity of the impious, which though they struggle furiously are unable to extricate themselves from the fear of God, is abundant testimony that this conviction, namely that there is some God, is naturally inborn in all, and is fixed deep within, as it were in the very marrow.... From this we conclude that it is not a doctrine that must first be learned in school, but one of which each of us is master from his mother's womb and which nature itself permits no one to forget ... (Calvin 1960, I.iii.1–3).

This natural, internal sense of the divine, the *sensus divinitatis*, is inscribed or written on the hearts of all people; there is "no nation so barbarous, no people so savage" that is not imbued with the conviction that there is a god (Calvin 1960, I.iii.1). Even those who deny God's existence will, in various circumstances, "feel an inkling of what they desire not to believe" (I.iii.2). This natural knowledge of God is that "primal and simple knowledge to which the very order of nature would have led us if Adam had remained upright" (I.ii.1). It is quite limited, according to Calvin, revealing God only as Creator, not God as Creator and Redeemer. Because we are sinners, in a post-Adamic, fallen state, we "lack the natural ability to mount up unto the pure and clear knowledge of God" (I.v.15). This "slight taste of his divinity" (II.ii.18) amounts to little more than the conviction that there is a God, that humans acquire the true belief that there is a majestic creator. This knowledge includes all of the properties necessary for being creator – super powers and intellect – but little of what is necessary for human redemption. In commenting on St Paul's claim in Romans that "the invisible things of God from the creation of the world are clearly seen, being understood by the things that are made" (Romans 1:20), Calvin remarks:

> He [Paul] does not mention all the particulars which may be thought to belong to God; but he states, that we can arrive at the knowledge of his eternal power and divinity; for he who is the framer of all things, must necessarily be without beginning and from himself. When we arrive at this point, the divinity becomes known to us, which cannot exist except accompanied with all the attributes of a God, since they are all included under that idea .... We conceive that there is a Deity; and then we conclude that he ought to be worshiped: but our reason here fails, because it cannot ascertain who or what sort of being God is.[6]

While everyone has some knowledge of God and the benefits of allegiance to God, most lack "pure and clear knowledge of God" (Calvin 1960, 1.v.15). So, while one may have primal and natural knowledge of a superpowerful, eternal, intelligent and morally providential creator, one cannot thereby gain knowledge of God as redeemer. For that, the unredeemed must seek information in Scripture. We shall return to this after a discussion of Reformed epistemology, a contemporary defense of Calvin's natural and primal, non-inferential knowledge of God.

Reformed Epistemology

Reformed epistemology's claim that belief in God is a basic, non-inferential belief developed first and foremost as a response to Enlightenment evidentialism, the claim that belief in God is justified only if it is supported by an argument for God's existence. If a belief cannot survive the scrutiny of reason, where reason is understood primarily in the sense of *inference* or *argument*, it should be rejected as irrational.[7] Some, such as W. K. Clifford, claim that belief in God is irrational because of the lack of evidence for God's existence; belief in God cannot survive the scrutiny of reason.

According to Reformed epistemologists, Enlightenment thinkers assume classical foundationalism, a culturally dominant but defective understanding of reason. Classical foundationalism attempts to elucidate the structure of rational believings (beliefs and their proper relationships to one another). It divides our beliefs into two parts: those that are inferred from other beliefs (non-basic beliefs) and those that are not inferred (or inferable) from other beliefs (basic beliefs). Of course, not all basic and non-basic beliefs are rational, so classical foundationalism offers criteria for determining which of our beliefs are properly or justifiably basic or non-basic. Properly basic beliefs include beliefs that are self-evident, evident to the senses or incorrigible. Self-evident beliefs include, for example, logical and mathematical truths such as *2 + 2 = 4*, *every statement is either true or false*, and *when equals are added to equals you get equals*. Beliefs that are evident to the senses include *grass is green*, *honey tastes sweet*, and *sandpaper feels rough*. Since we can be mistaken about perceptual beliefs, some certainty-mongering classical foundationalists rejected perceptual beliefs as properly basic in favour of incorrigible beliefs, beliefs about which we cannot be wrong. I might be wrong, for example, in believing that the grass is green, but I can hardly be wrong in believing that the grass appears to me to be green. And I can scarcely be wrong in asserting that the honey seems sweet. Incorrigible beliefs are first-person psychological states (typically of how things appear or seem to me) about which one cannot be mistaken such as *the grass appears green* and *honey seems sweet* (both first-person indexed).

When classical foundationalism has been applied to belief in God, belief in God has been found wanting. Since God's existence is neither self-evident, evident to the senses, nor incorrigible, according to classical foundationalism, it requires the support of evidence in order to be rational. If the evidence is lacking, belief in God is irrational.

Classical foundationalism, however, is irretrievably flawed. First, classical foundationalism is self-referentially inconsistent. Classical foundationalism itself is neither self-evident, evident to the senses, nor incorrigible. In addition, it cannot be inferred from beliefs that are self-evident, evident to the senses, or incorrigible. If classical foundationalism were true, it would be irrational to accept it! The second sort of defect of classical foundationalism is that it entails skepticism about the world. We cannot infer anything about the existence of the external world, the past, the future, other persons and so on given the basis of the slim body of evidence that classical foundationalism permits. Indeed, classical foundationalism is a crippled epistemology. It imagines the human knower as a homunculous spectator trapped inside his own mind, seeing if his own, private sensations can unlock the door to the external world. So classical foundationalism must be rejected as the proper structure of rational belief.

Can belief in God be rational for a person? Is there a conception of rationality that is not obviously defective (as is classical foundationalism) yet permits rational belief in God? The

Reformed epistemologist holds that one is perfectly within one's epistemic rights, that is, perfectly rational, in believing in God even without the support of, for example, a sound theistic argument. How can this be so?

Reformed epistemology recognizes that we have been outfitted with many cognitive faculties that produce beliefs that we can reason from. The kinds of beliefs that we do and must reason to is small relative to the kinds of beliefs that we do and must accept without the aid of a proof. That's the long and short of the human believing condition. We, in most cases, must rely on our (God-given) intellectual equipment to produce beliefs, without evidence or argument, in the appropriate circumstances. Is it reasonable to believe that God has created us with a cognitive faculty which produces belief in God without evidence or argument? The primary reason to believe that it is proper or rational for a person to accept belief in God without the need for an argument is a parity argument: It is rationally permissible, in general, to accept the deliverances of our cognitive faculties, so it is rationally permissible to accept the deliverance of our god-faculty. We simply must trust that our cognitive faculties generally produce true beliefs or we will know nothing at all. The Humean lesson learned from the failure of classical foundationalism is that excluding the deliverances of our cognitive faculties inevitably results in skepticism. We must, if we are to know much of anything at all beyond our immediate sensations, accept the deliverances of our cognitive faculties. Furthermore, it is impossible to offer non-circular justifications of the general reliability of our cognitive faculties. To show that our cognitive faculties are reliable, we would have to use our cognitive faculties (see Alston 1991, pp. 146–9). All we can do is accede to our cognitive faculties and the beliefs that they prompt within us. Because this is all we can do, this is all we should do (employing an "ought implies can" principle). That is, we are perfectly within our rights in accepting the deliverances of our cognitive faculties. If we have a god-faculty, then we are within our rights in maintaining the belief(s) that it produces.

One caveat: our faculties can deliver contradictory or competing beliefs and so some beliefs may serve to defeat the justification of other beliefs. The justification of which I've been speaking is *prima facie* justification which may not be *ultima facia*, all-things-considered justification in the face of belief-competitors. But, in general, we are *prima facie* justified in accepting the deliverances of our cognitive faculties and so by induction are *prima facie* justified in accepting the deliverance of our god-faculty.

Reformed Epistemology and Cognitive Science

Let us compare the views of Plantinga and Calvin on the inner sense of the divine. Plantinga contends that our god-faculty is dispositional and that belief in God is grounded in human experience. Plantinga argues that belief in God is produced in response to a variety of widely realized circumstances such as moments of guilt, gratitude, or a sense of God's handiwork in nature (while beholding the articulate beauty of a flower or the purple mountains majesty); in these or any other circumstances, people find themselves believing in God. While Plantinga holds that belief in God, thusly produced, is based on experience, and so is not groundless, it is not, however, based on beliefs, and so is not the conclusion of an argument (Plantinga and Wolterstorff 1983, pp. 78–82). While Calvin holds that the sense of the divine is likewise not the conclusion of an argument, he seems to hold that the *sensus divinitatis* is not a faculty of the soul that is triggered in various circumstances; indeed, Calvin seems to hold that the knowledge itself of God's existence and basic attributes is innate: "A certain understanding of the divine majesty" has been "implanted in all men" (Calvin 1960, I.iii.1); and, the conviction that there is some God "is naturally inborn in us all, and is fixed deep within, as it were in the very marrow" (I.iii.3). That is the god-faculty may not so much be dispositional as innate; it is "engraved on men's minds" (I.iii.3).

On this matter, Plantinga's dispositional understanding of the *sensus divinitatis* seems more in line with the deliverances of the cognitive science of religion than Calvin's innatist understanding of the *sensus divinitatis*. Cognitive science, of the HADD persuasion, sees the god-faculty as more dispositional than an innate belief and as being triggered by a variety of circumstances. However, HADD is not a perfect match with Plantinga's account because Plantinga's understanding of the widely realized grounding circumstances has little in common with HADD's attribution of belief in God to, basically, those circumstances under which the immediate response is flight or fight. Plantinga's grounding conditions are more pastoral, tranquil, and thoughtful (but non-inferential). HADD's grounding conditions are ignorance and terror. On this matter, Calvin may be closer to the cognitive science of religion; he quotes Statius favorably: "Fear first made gods in the world" (Calvin 1960, I.iv.4).

While Calvin surely did not have HADD in mind when he affirmed Statius's sentiment, he did believe that humans are compelled to believe in God under conditions of fear. Furthermore, Plantinga does not treat belief in God as an evolutionary spandrel as suggested by those who offer evolutionary accounts of HADD (or other accounts of the god-faculty). According to Plantinga, belief in God is the direct and intended product of the god-faculty, not an epiphenomenal by-product of an agency-detecting device. And, finally, Calvin and Plantinga both seem to believe that the god-faculty produces belief in God (an omnipotent, omniscient, non-material, creator of the world). If HADD is correct, and here I emphasize its hyperactivity, polytheism (and a world of ghosts, fairies, and goblins) is the direct by-product of our god-faculty not monotheism. And here we might expect to find some empirical confirmation of the theory: for we might find in the recesses of history a universal polytheism with monotheism as a later theological development. Interestingly, this is precisely what we find in the Hebrew narratives, the ultimate source of Calvinistic theology (Clark 2005).

Plantinga might need to revise his view that the *sensus divinitatis* is present in humans but not in quite the shape that he originally specified; that is the *sensus divinitatis* is HADD. Why, after all, could God not have produced in us, through the processes of evolution, a god-faculty that makes humans universally aware of God under widely realized circumstances (just different ones from those that he asserted)? There are analogues here to, say, the Freudian critiques of religious belief. Freud contended that we wish God into existence and "God" hears our prayers: God can tame nature, help us accept our fate, and reward us for our sufferings. By revealing our desire for the divine, masking deeply insecure self-interest, Freud thinks he has explained God away. But a Plantingian might think that Freud is right in his explanation of belief in God but not in his explaining it away; that is, a Plantingian might think that Freud's account is an accurate description of the divinely implanted, truth-aimed *sensus divinitatis* and so is a proper ground of belief. Why, after all, could God not have produced in humans a Freudian god-faculty that makes humans universally aware of God under widely realized circumstances? After all, the *sensus divinitatis*, assuming there is one, must have some determinate shape or form. Why not the Freudian or HADD shape and form? As Plantinga writes of Freud – Marx critiques of belief in God: "To show that there are natural processes that produce religious belief does nothing ... to discredit it; perhaps God designed us in such a way that it is by virtue of those processes that we come to have knowledge of him" (Plantinga 2000, p. 145). Surely God can use ignoble vessels, even spandrels, to transport belief in God.

Why think that the cognitive science of religion has or ever will have access to all of our cognitive faculties? Perhaps in addition to HADD, humans also have a god-faculty precisely as described by Plantinga and/or Calvin. I am sure that no cognitive scientist believes that they have exhaustively mapped the human mind; I wonder if it is a commitment of cognitive science that an exhaustive map is possible. I am not making an argument from ignorance here; I am not arguing as follows: no one knows if we have a god-faculty as Plantinga has described, therefore, there is a god-faculty as Plantinga has described. I only mean to preclude the hasty generalization of those who believe that cognitive science explains religion away; those who argue: we have found an ignoble god-faculty, therefore belief in God is intellectually subpar. This arguments works, if at all, only under the assumption that the ignoble god-faculty is the only god-faculty; and this has simply not been established. At this primitive stage of the cognitive science of religion, it is still possible that a god-faculty as described by Plantinga or Calvin might be discovered. And even if not, little of consequence follows (except that either Plantinga was mistaken about some details or the human mind has depths inaccessible by cognitive science).

The atheist cognitive scientist might respond that the god-faculty cannot produce justified religious beliefs because it is not reliable. After all, HADD produces beliefs in a multiplicity of gods, angels, fairies, demons, and the like. Even supposing the truth of monotheism, the reliability of the god-faculty is surely less than half (supposing we take as the denominator the number of kinds of entities produced by HADD and as the numerator the single class of Yahwistic monotheism, that is 1). Plantinga might have two responses to this.

1) Plantinga might think that part of the function of HADD is to make humans aware of the divine dimension of reality rather than clearly defined Judeo-Christian conceptions of God; on this view, God might be willing to concede a host of religious "false positives" – say, elves or mountain deities – to secure, by and large, belief in a supreme heavenly being. So, while HADD may be unreliable in securing belief in Yahweh and Yahweh alone, HADD is reliable in producing belief in a divinity.[8] Calvin himself claimed little specific knowledge of divinity through the *sensus divinitatis*; one's slight taste of divinity, recall, is impure and unclear. Indeed, such impurities and unclarities might include elves and fairies.

2) With respect to belief in God, we cannot know if HADD is unreliable unless we already know that there is no God. Of course, if one does not believe in God, one will not believe HADD to be unreliable but one's beliefs on this matter scarcely constitute evidence that there is no God.

Calvin claims that all humans have the *sensus divinitatis* – a sense of the divine – not the *sensus dei* (sense of God). This vaguer notion of divinity – that there are supernatural powers, that there is a creator, that these powers have more force – is consonant with the various forms of spiritual beliefs that we find throughout human history. That is, Calvin does not claim that people have precise knowledge of Yahweh, the God of Abraham, Isaac, and Jacob. Rather, they have an inchoate sense of divinity – of various forms of nonnatural powers and moral forces – and so have a sense of duty or obligation to divinity. While Calvin claims that the sense of the divine produces true beliefs about God (that is, beliefs consonant with the truths revealed in Scripture), he also contends that scripture serves as "spectacles gathering up the otherwise confused knowledge of God in our minds" (Calvin 1960, I.vi.1). He attributes this confusion not to a poor source of knowledge but to our own "dullness': to various forms of human misappropriation of genuine knowledge. So Scripture serves to correct us (it corrects our eyesight) more than to correct the natural revelation. Indeed, Calvin cites as empirical support for his view just the sort of evidence evolutionary psychologists of religion cite in support of their view: the universality of religious belief, including idolatry, shows that it is a "common conception" found in "the minds of all" (I.iii.1) Again, Calvin's account is fully consonant with the plethora of religious beliefs found in the world. Plantinga, on the other hand, claims that the *sensus divinitatis* produces a more theologically precise belief in God – belief in an omnipotent, omniscient, perfectly good Creator. One might expect, then, to find universal belief in God. However, like Calvin (I.iv), he believes that the sense of the divine can be, indeed has been, overlaid by the noetic consequences of sin and so we find a wide variety of false religious beliefs among the people. Interestingly, Calvin takes idolatry and various forms of unbelief, including atheism, as evidence both in favor of his *sensus divinitatis* and of its corruptions.

Obstinacy in Belief

One area of agreement between Calvin and cognitive science is that belief in God is the natural state of belief for humans and can never be entirely gotten rid of. Belief in God is produced by our primal and instinctive dispositions to believe in various circumstances. Unbelief is unnatural in the sense that rejection of God's existence involves suppressing our natural belief dispositions. It may not be unnatural all things considered (for presumably unbelief involves other, natural cognitive faculties such as reasoning), but it is not primitive and instinctual and so must be cultivated. Yet, given the promptings of our primitive and instinctive god- and immortality-faculties, belief in God may never be entirely erased from one's set of beliefs; it will repeatedly find its way back in spite of our best efforts to resist it. Studies in cognitive science and personal reflection on the part of atheistic cognitive scientists has shown that religious beliefs come creeping back into one's consciousness despite one's best efforts to rid oneself of them. For example, the death of a loved one can provoke a native belief in the immortality of souls and very frightening experiences can lead one to pray to or blame God (see Barrett 2004, ch. 8; Bering 2002 and 2006).

The External Witness: The Order of the Cosmos

While affirming the *sensus divinitas* as productive of a primitive, undeveloped belief in God, Calvin claims that there is an additional, external source of knowledge of God; he writes:

> Lest anyone, then, be excluded from access to happiness, he not only sowed in men's minds that seed of religion of which we have spoken but revealed himself and daily discloses himself in the whole workmanship of the universe. As a consequence, men cannot open their eyes without being compelled to see him. (Calvin 1960, I.v.1)

Indeed, the title of the chapter that discusses inferential knowledge of God is "The Knowledge of God Shines Forth in the Fashioning of the Universe and the Continuing Governing of It"

(I.v.1). He contends that people can behold the glory of God through the manifestation of the divine in "the whole workmanship of the universe" (I.v.1). We can, Calvin claims, see God in both the vastness of the cosmos and the human person. Of the human person, "the loftiest proof of divine wisdom," he writes:

> In the first place, no one can look upon himself without immediately turning his thoughts to the contemplation of God, in whom he "lives and moves." For, quite clearly, the mighty gifts with which we are endowed are hardly from ourselves; indeed, our very being is nothing but subsistence in the one God. (Calvin 1960, I.i.1)

In addition, he writes: "… the human body shows itself to be a composition so ingenious that its Artificer is rightly judged a wonder-worker" (I.V.1,2). And of the universe he speaks of the "innumerable evidences both in heaven and on earth that declares his wonderful wisdom" (I.v.2).

Proofs? Calvin's talk of "proof" suggests a crucial role for inference of the kind adduced in the theistic arguments. Yet while, say, medicine and the natural sciences afford us learned and complex examples, the "proofs" force themselves on the notice of the most illiterate peasant, who "cannot open their eyes without being compelled to witness them" (Calvin 1960, I.v.2). Such "proofs" involve an inference but the inferential nature of such proofs is surely slight and easy. Indeed, Calvin believes that knowledge of God is so manifest and evident that detailed arguments are unnecessary; the "elegant structure" of the cosmos, he writes, is a "kind of mirror, in which we may behold God" (I.v.1). The mirror image suggests that such beholding is a kind of perception. As a consequence, people cannot open their eyes "without being compelled to see him" (I.v.1). Because God has made himself so readily available to us in his creation, arguments are redundant:

> We see that no long or toilsome proof is needed to elicit evidences that serve to illuminate and affirm the divine majesty; since the few we have sampled at random, withersoever you turn, it is clear that they are very manifest and obvious that they can easily be observed with the eyes and pointed out with finger. (Calvin 1960, I.v.9)

While detailed arguments are unnecessary, Calvin does seem to affirm an inferential step from nature and humanity to the divine nature.

The kind of evidence that Calvin believes so perspicuously displays the divine nature is the order or pattern found in nature. Although the cosmos contains an endless variety, it is "well-ordered." The human body itself bears "proofs of ingenious contrivance." Perhaps Calvin views these as not explicitly but implicitly inferential. Belief in God may be based on other beliefs but not explicitly inferred from those beliefs.[9] Unlike beliefs immediately produced by the *sensus divinitatis*, the basing beliefs constitute evidence for the non-basic belief in God. The order of nature betokens or is a sign of the divine orderer.

> Even the common folk and the most untutored, who have been taught only by the aid of the eyes, cannot be unaware of the excellence of divine art, for it reveals itself in this innumerable and yet distinct and well-ordered variety of the heavenly host. … Likewise, in regard to the structure of the human body … the human body shows itself to be a composition so ingenious that its Artificer is rightly judged a wonder-worker" (Calvin 1960, I.V.1,2).

Calvin, no friend of scholastic theist arguments, nonetheless holds that belief in God is based on, among other things, the order and symmetry of the cosmos and the human person. One, whether peasant or physiologist or physicist, can quite simply see that order and symmetry and so become of aware of the being on whom that order and symmetry depend. While the physiologist and physicist can see the order and symmetry better and in more detail, there is enough order and symmetry that is plainly available to the untutored to foster belief in God.

Plantinga himself seems to hold something like Calvin's view although he calls beliefs produced by the order and symmetry of the universe "grounded" rather then "inferential." He writes of the various circumstances that ground our immediate beliefs such as *God disapproves of what I've done*, or *this flower was created by God*, or *this vast and intricate universe was created by God*; these propositions, in turn, self-evidently entail that God exists (Plantinga and Wolterstorff 1983, pp. 80–1). The dispute may be merely verbal here. There seems little cognitive distance between Calvin's implicitly inferential and Plantinga's grounded beliefs (which self-evidently entail their conclusion).

The External Witness and the Cognitive Science of Religion

The cognitive science of religion also supposes to have found cognitive faculties or faculties that are reminiscent of the external witness. Barrett, for example, contends that humans are equipped with "pattern detectors" that organize information or experiences into orderly, meaningful patterns (Barrett 2004, pp. 36–9; see also Kelemen 2004). While we are pattern detectors in general, HADD focuses some pattern detection on agent causes. HADD takes certain "traces" and attributes those traces to an agent, especially when those traces appear to be (a) teleological or purposeful, and (b) inexplicable by biological or mechanical means. Barrett contends that pattern detecting is seldom an originating source of belief in God but it is more a source of reinforcing belief in God.

Conclusion

The cognitive psychology of religion offers an account of why human beings believe in God. We have, they contend, natural cognitive faculties which, under certain circumstances, produce an automatic, non-inferential belief in supernatural agents. This, they allege, is the natural believing state of all human beings. That such thusly produced beliefs are not very determinate and find a variety of expressions in various cultures is more conducive to Calvin's *sensus divinitatis* than to Plantinga's de facto commitment to a *sensus dei*. On the other hand, the dispositional nature of such beliefs is more conducive to Plantinga's dispositional understanding of the *sensus divinitatis* than Calvin's more innatist conception of divine knowledge.

Let me conclude with a bit of speculation.[10] We have assumed, with the evolutionary accounts of the psychology of religious believing, that religious belief is a spandrel. That is, religious belief is an unintended by-product of faculties "designed" to produce other sorts of beliefs or behaviors. Those intended beliefs and behaviors are essential to human survival while belief spandrels are not. Belief spandrels are simply accidentally dragged along with those beliefs and behaviors that are essential to survival. Might it not be, however, that religious beliefs with their moral concomitants are not spandrels after all? That is, might it be the case that belief in the supernatural and a beyond-the-human grounding of morality and a next life are conducive to even if not necessary for human survival (and so give proto-humans with such beliefs an advantage over those without such beliefs)? If belief in the supernatural as thusly construed is conducive to human survival, then we have *prima facie* reason to think such belief-producing mechanisms are reliable, that is truth-tracking.[11] If there is a God who wishes humans to be in relationship with him and who superintends the evolutionary process, he may then guide evolutionary history so that such favorable traits naturally develop in human beings.

Notes

1   Cognitive scientists of religion differ as to whether a single cognitive device accounts for theistic beliefs (e.g., Guthrie 1993), or whether a constellation of devices converge to promote belief in God (e.g., Boyer 2001). The term *god-faculty* is used here to refer to the cognitive functional unit or units responsible for generating belief in God.

2   See Plantinga (2000), Wolterstorff (1976), Plantinga and Wolterstorff (1983) and Alston (1991). For a more popular introduction to Reformed epistemology, see Clark (1990).

3   So HADD, in addition to producing many true beliefs that elicit appropriate fight or flight responses, produces many false-positives (see Atran 2002: 69).

4   One might speculate that ToM developed as it became increasingly advantageous for primates to be able to successfully "guess" the beliefs, desires, and intentions of competitors. This tendency to speculate about the intentions of competitors would then have been generalized and applied to agentive accounts that HADD engendered. As Atran writes, "Identifying animate beings as agents, with goals and internal motivations, would allow our ancestors to anticipate goal-directed actions of predators, prey, friends, and foe and to profit from this in ways that enhanced survival and reproductive success" (Atran 2002, p. 61).

5   Some have criticized Wilson because of his reliance on group selection rather than individual selection.

6   John Calvin, *Commentaries on the Epistle of St. Paul to the Romans*, trans. John Owen, ed. Henry Beveridge (Grand Rapids, MI: Baker Books ., 1979; reprint).[date of reprint]

7   I take "Enlightenment" to refer more to an attitude or stance than to an historical epoch.

8   "Gods" might be a better term here. I assume that if our ancestors were equipped with HADD, polytheism not monotheism would be the most primitive form of theistic religion. But polytheism bears a family resemblance to monotheism and, so, need not be viewed as a defeater of Plantinga's account of belief in God.

9   Michael Sudduth explores and defends a similar distinction in Sudduth (1998).

10 It should be finally noted that evolutionary psychology is itself a very speculative enterprise. Its just-so stories are only more or less plausible.

11 Unfortunately, I don't know of any empirical way of determining if belief in God is a belief-spandrel or a belief that is directly conducive to our survival. In spite of, for example, Atran's insistence that religious beliefs have no survival value as such, it is not clear how that could be known.

Bibliography

Alston, William (1991) *Perceiving God*. Ithaca, NY: Cornell University Press.

Atran, Scott (2002) *In Gods We Trust*. New York: Oxford University Press.

Barrett, Justin (2004) *Why Would Anyone Believe in God?* Lanham, MD: AltaMira Press.

Bergmann, Michael (2006) *Justification Without Awareness*. New York: Oxford University Press.

Boyer, Pascal (1994) *The Naturalness of Religious Ideas: A Cognitive Theory of Religion.* Berkeley: University of California Press.

Boyer, Pascal (2001) *Religion Explained: Evolutionary Origins of Religious Thought.* New York: Basic Books.

Calvin, John (1960) *Institutes of the Christian Religion,* trans. Ford Lewis Battles. Philadelphia: Westminster Press.

Clark, Kelly James (1990) *Return to Reason.* Grand Rapids, MI: Eerdmans.

Clark, Kelly James (2005) The gods of Abraham, Isaiah and Confucius, *Dao: A Journal of Comparative Philosophy,* vol. V, no. 1, Winter, 109–36.

Clifford, W. K. (1886) The ethics of belief. In *Lectures and Essays,* pp. 339–63 London: Macmillan.

Darwin, Charles (1871) *Descent of Man.* New York: D. Appleton.

Gould, Stephen and Lewontin, Richard (1979) The spandrels of San Marco and the Panglossian Paradigm: A critique of the adaptationist program, *Proceedings of the Royal Society of London* B 205, 581–98.

Guthrie, Stewart (1993) *Faces in the Clouds: A New Theory of Religion.* New York: Oxford University Press.

Kelemen, Deborah (2004) Are children 'intuitive theists?' Reasoning about purpose and design in nature, *Psychological Science* 15, 295-301.

Lawson, Thomas and McCauley, Robert (1990) *Rethinking Religion: Connection, Cognition and Culture.* Cambridge: Cambridge University Press.

McCauley, Robert. (2000) The naturalness of religion and the unnaturalness of science. In F. Keil and R. Wilson (eds.) *Explanation and Cognition,* pp. 61–85 Cambridge, MA: MIT Press.

McCauley, Robert and Lawson, Thomas (2002) *Bringing Ritual to Mind: Psychological Foundations of Cultural Forms.* Cambridge: Cambridge University Press.

Plantinga, Alvin. (2000) *Warranted Christian Belief.* New York: Oxford University Press.

Plantinga, Alvin and Wolterstorff, Nicholas (1983) *Faith and Rationality.* Notre Dame, IN: University of Notre Dame Press.

Reid, Thomas (1983) *Inquiry and Essays,* ed. Ronald Beanblossom and Keith Lehrer. Indianapolis: Hackett.

Sudduth, Michael (1998) Calvin, Plantinga, and the natural knowledge of God: A response to Beversluis, *Faith and Philosophy,* vol. 15, no. 1, Jan.

Wilson, David Sloan (2002) *Darwin's Cathedral: Evolution, Religion, and the Nature of Society.* Chicago: University of Chicago Press.

Wolterstorff, Nicholas (1976) *Reason Within the Bounds of Religion.* Grand Rapids, MI: Eerdmans.

Wolterstorff, Nicholas (1984) Thomas Reid on rationality. In Hendrik Hark, Johan van der Hoven, and Nicholas Wolterstortf (eds.) *Rationality in the Calvinian Tradition,* pp. 43–69. Lanham, MD: University Press of America.

39

Explaining God Away?

KELLY JAMES CLARK

We will examine the claim that evolutionary explanations of religion undermine the rationality of belief in God. We will first discuss the findings of the cognitive psychology of religion which suggest that we have a natural, built-in god-faculty. Next we consider evolutionary explanations of the origin of the god-faculty and the alleged consequences that follow. We conclude with responses to arguments that claim to demonstrate that evolutionary psychology undermines rational belief in God.

Science shows us, or so it is claimed, that God exists in the mind alone; God is a human creation, a collective illusion or a delusion fobbed off on us by our genes. So Boyer writes:

> In a cultural context where this hugely successful [scientific] way of understanding the world has debunked one supernatural claim after another, there is a strong impulse [in religious believers] to find at least one domain where it would be possible to trump the scientist. But evolution and microbiology crushed all this. (Boyer 2001, p. 76)

Evolution and genetics, so it is claimed, explain God away; rational belief in God is crushed.

In this chapter we will examine the claim that evolutionary explanations of religion undermine the rationality of belief in God. We will first discuss the findings of the cognitive psychology of religion which suggest that we have a natural, built-in god-faculty. Next we consider evolutionary explanations of the origin of the god-faculty and the alleged consequences that follow. We conclude with responses to arguments that claim to demonstrate that evolutionary psychology undermines rational belief in God.

The Cognitive Psychology of Religion

A generally accepted picture of cognitive science's account of belief in God has emerged in the past twenty or so years. The cognitive science of religion rejects the popular anthropological assumption of radical incommensurability among cultural groups. Rather, studies seem to show that our common biological heritage and relatively similar environments produce both relatively similar minds and relatively similar beliefs. Rejecting the empiricist assumption of the mind as a blank slate, most cognitive scientists today hold that our minds come equipped with cognitive faculties that actively process our perceptions and shape our conceptions of the world (see Boyer 1994, Pt. II). These common cognitive faculties include relatively specialized and discrete "subsystems" that structure, inform, enhance and limit our worldview. Some of these systems structure, inform, enhance, and limit religious beliefs. Belief in god, to take one characteristic form of religious belief, arises from the stimulation of universal cognitive faculties; religious belief is a natural product of our common cognitive faculties. Humans have a natural tendency to believe in God.

A general picture has emerged of how our common cognitive faculties produce belief in God. Our cognitive faculties are believed to have been generated evolutionarily in response to rather specific environmental pressures. Religious beliefs, it is claimed, have arisen in part because human beings are equipped with a cognitive unit – an agency-detecting device – that generates beliefs about agency, sometimes with only the slightest stimulation. When appropriately stimulated, humans are equipped with cognitive faculties that immediately – that is, non-reflectively or non-inferentially – produce beliefs in the existence of agents. Without such immediate beliefs/responses to certain motions (rustling bushes) or sounds (things going bump in the night), we might end up as food for a predator or the victim of an enemy.

One can imagine the survival benefits if the agency-detecting device were extremely sensitive; if it were triggered with just the slightest provocation, one would more likely avoid dangerous situations involving one's predators and enemies than if one were to routinely respond sluggishly to such promptings; sluggish and sleepy responders are more likely to end up dead. So ADD is highly sensitive and hyperactive – provoking us to respond instantly to the slightest provocation; Justin Barrett has fetchingly named the disposition to form beliefs about agents in such slightly stimulated fight or flee situations the "hypersensitive agency detection device" (HADD). HADD has obvious adaptive advantages; if it were less sensitive, less hyperactive, it would prove less adaptive. So HADD, in addition to producing many true beliefs that elicit appropriate fight or flight responses, produces many false-positives. You can see remnants of HADD in the relatively safe confines of your home: consider your response when, in the midst of the night's deep sleep, you are awaked by a sound coming from your living room; you are immediately ready to anxiously spring into action and then need time to calm yourself down. HADD immediately produces agent beliefs and an immediate response.

In addition to beliefs in animals and enemies, beliefs about gods are also explained by HADD. If ordinary agents – animals and enemies – are unsuited to account for one's experiences, one might find oneself immediately believing in extraordinary, supernatural personal beings (including ghosts, angels, or gods); really big agents better account for really big events such as apparent miracles, floods, or thunder than ordinary agents; only a super-powerful, minded agent could cause such extraordinary events; we attribute super-qualities – omnipotence and omniscience, for example – to the causes of super-events.

HADD works not only when stimulated by sounds or motions; it is also triggered in the face of apparent design, design with "traces" of agency (such as crop circles). Human beings, it seems, are naturally predisposed to seek agentive explanations of unusual phenomena that appear to be like things that we know humans have designed. Barrett explains:

> Our minds have numerous pattern detectors that organize visual information into meaningful units. HADD remains on the lookout for patterns known to be caused by agents. If this

patterned information matches patterns … known to be caused by agents, HADD detects agency and alerts other mental tools. … More interesting is when a pattern is detected that appears to be purposeful or goal directed and, secondarily, does not appear to be caused by ordinary mechanical or biological causes. Such patterns may prompt HADD to attribute the traces to agency yet to be identified: unknown persons, animals, or space aliens, ghosts, or gods. (Barrett 2004, pp. 36–7)

We are equipped with pattern detectors (in some cases, pattern creators) that are fine-tuned to detect agency (see Atran 2002, pp. 59–61). Upon the detection of agency, another cognitive faculty called the Theory of Mind begins operating and attributes beliefs, desires, purposes, and so on to the postulated agent.[1]

For the sake of shorthand, let us call HADD plus ToM "the god-faculty."[2] Cognitive science also has explanations of the sustainability and transmissibility of religious belief (see Boyer 1994, chs. 2–3, and 2001; Barrett 2004, pp. 21–30). Religious beliefs are sustainable and transmissible in part because they are memorable. They are memorable, according to cognitive psychologists, because they are, typically, minimally counterintuitive. They are *minimally* counterintuitive: if they were maximally counterintuitive they would not fit within our cognitive expectations and so would be rejected as fanciful or bizarre. They are minimally *counterintuitive*: by virtue of being counterintuitive, they capture our attention, account for phenomena that are otherwise inexplicable, and are easy to remember and to faithfully transmit (see Atran 2002, ch. 4). In addition, successful religious beliefs "have good *inferential potential*": they can unite, in a single explanation, a wide variety of diverse and otherwise inexplicable phenomena and can find themselves embedded in deep and informative narrative contexts. Once again, successful religious beliefs are successful insofar as they prove memorable and readily transmissible; such traits are more memorable insofar as they include explanatory power and the affective dimensions of story (see Atran 2002, pp. 88–9; Boyer 2001b, pp. 50–9; and Barrett 2004, p. 15); these affective dimensions engage and enflame the passions necessary for religious devotion.

The cognitive psychology of religion also claims to have found a cognitive faculty or set of faculties that detect the kind of design that is often alleged to support God's existence. Barrett, for example, contends that humans are equipped with "pattern detectors" that organize information or experiences into orderly, meaningful patterns (Barrett 2004, pp. 36–9). While we are pattern detectors in general, HADD focuses some pattern detection on agent causes. HADD takes certain "traces" and attributes those traces to an agent, especially when those traces appear to be (a) teleological or purposeful, and (b) inexplicable by biological or mechanical means. Barrett contends that pattern detection is seldom an originating source of belief in God, but it is often a source of reinforcing belief in God.

Belief in God, according to these accounts, is the natural state of belief for humans and can never be entirely eliminated. Belief in God is produced by our primal and instinctive dispositions to believe in various circumstances. Unbelief is unnatural in the sense that rejection of God's existence involves suppressing our natural belief dispositions. It may not be unnatural all things considered (for unbelief may involve other natural cognitive faculties such as reasoning), but unbelief is not primitive and instinctual and so must be cultivated. Yet, given the promptings of our primitive and instinctive god faculties, belief in God may never be entirely erased from one's set of beliefs; it will repeatedly find its way back in spite of our best efforts to resist it. Studies in cognitive science and personal reflection on the part of atheistic cognitive scientists have shown that religious beliefs come creeping back into one's consciousness despite one's best efforts to rid oneself of them; "there are no atheists in foxholes" seems well substantiated.

Studies in the cognitive science of religion suggest that people are naturally religious; that is, they have natural cognitive faculties which produce belief in God.

Evolutionary Explanations of Religious Belief

So where does this god-faculty come from? Why is it that humans are naturally inclined to believe in God? Explanations of the god-faculty typically ally the cognitive science with evolutionary explanations of the origins of our cognitive faculties. Evolutionary explanations of our cognitive faculties seek to account for the development of our various mental faculties and concepts as our primitive ancestors faced the pushes and pulls of human experience. Just as the opposable thumb, under various evolutionary pressures, helped us gain reproductive success so too our brains (minds) developed under similar pressures and for similar purposes. Our brains developed the intellectual tools that fit us for survival against enemies, natural disasters, and predators. So our cognitive faculties were cobbled together in ways that enabled us to perceive middle-sized objects (not the astronomically large or microscopically small) in a three-dimensional world; to take into account past, present, and future; to anticipate the plans of our enemies; to contemplate, initiate, and complete plans of our own; to communicate, feel, and remember. These and other cognitive abilities developed for the same purpose: to help us feed, flee, fight, or reproduce.

How can we account for belief in God in evolutionary terms? As Dawkins states:

> If neuroscientists find a "god center" in the brain, Darwinian scientists like me want to know why the god center evolved. Why did those of our ancestors who had a genetic tendency to grow a god center survive better than our rivals who did not? (Dawkins, 2004b, p. 14)

What follows here is the standard account of the evolutionary origin of god beliefs, culled from the various and quite differing accounts of the evolutionary origins of religious belief.

Religious beliefs, according to this standard account, are an evolutionary problem. With respect to adaptive fitness, *many* religious practices seem positively maladaptive. They are maladaptive because they are, in evolutionary terms, costly; the don't seem very conducive to reproductive success. As Scott Atran writes:

> Religion is materially expensive and unrelentingly counterfactual and even counterintuitive. Religious practice is costly in terms of material sacrifice (at least one's prayer time), emotional expenditure (inciting fears and hopes), and cognitive effort (maintaining both factual and counterintuitive networks of beliefs). (Atran 2002, p. 43)

Severe religious practices such as celibacy and the sacrifice of virgins run counter, to say the least, to reproductive success; a religious group that consistently practiced both would be quickly removed from the gene pool. Likewise, in times of scarcity, animal sacrifice and grain offerings do not conduce to survival. Even less severe practices such as worship and prayer take time away from hunting, gathering, and reproducing. So why would anyone believe in religion? How is it that throughout human existence, belief in religious reality has been the norm? How could behaviors so costly survive the cruel but precise culling of natural selection? If evolution outfitted us with our cognitive equipment, how could we have developed a god-faculty?

The most popular and widely discussed evolutionary accounts of religion, and those assumed by Dawkins and Dennett, claim that the faculties that produce belief in God did help us to survive better than our rivals but that god beliefs themselves did not have survival value: god beliefs did not help us fight, flee, feed, or reproduce. Another example of such a belief is the belief that various astral spectra can help us determine the chemical structure of stars: that belief did not help any of our primitive ancestors survive but it was produced by perceptual and reasoning faculties which did. That is, belief in God and the beliefs concerning astral spectra are spandrels or by-products.

A spandrel, to use a term coined by Gould and Lewontin, is a trait that is a by-product, not a direct consequence of natural selection. That is, natural selection selects for an adaptive trait, a trait that increases one's chances of spreading one's seed or increasing one's descendants, but such traits are sometimes accompanied by another trait that is non-adaptive; on its own, the spandrel would not have been selected (see Gould and Lewontin 1979; Atran 2002, pp. 43–5). For example, the redness (or blueness) of blood or the precise number of fingers and toes on a human hand or foot may be spandrels. While redness of blood may have developed to render us more sexually attractive or make us able to hide beneath autumn's auburn leaves, it is more likely a by-product of hemoglobin's ability to store oxygen (hemoglobin turns red when oxygenated). Spandrels are more ornamental epiphenomena, non-adaptive leftovers, than are adaptive traits. Spandrels are evolution's by-products and, when they prove adaptive, are sometimes called "exaptations."[3]

A "belief-spandrel," to coin a term, is a belief that is a by-product of faculties designed for the production of other sorts of beliefs. Belief-spandrels include god, if the standard picture of the evolution of religious beliefs is correct, astral spectra, and, as we shall see later, modern science. None of these were produced by faculties with the specific intention of helping us fight, feed, flee or reproduce (but immediately relevant perceptual and reasoning beliefs were).

Some evolutionary psychologists contend that religious beliefs are spandrels with no adaptive advantage. So, for example, Atran claims: "Religions are not adaptations and they have no evolutionary functions as such." He goes on to claim that religion did not originate primarily to cope with death, keep moral and social order, recover the security of father or mother, provide causal explanations, or provoke intellectual surprise (2002, pp. 12–13). Religious beliefs are mere by-products of something else.

Why, then, do religious beliefs arise? They arise as spandrel or by-product beliefs of our hyperactive agency-detecting device. Scary, big, and/or portentous phenomena that cannot be explained by appeal to man or beast are attributed to agents – spiritual (i.e., non-physical) beings with super-powers and, through ToM (theory of mind), various intentions. These non-physical beings, then, are either for us or against us and we need to begin devising plans to appease or please them, entertain them or otherwise keep them at bay (and keep ourselves out of harm's way). HADD creates belief in non-physical agents and ToM embellishes that initial belief into (anthropomorphic) gods. We take a little bit of HADD, shake it together with a dash of ToM, and create gods.

Of those countless spiritual entities that are postulated as a result of the god-faculty, only a few survive to be passed on to future generations. While memorability (or memorizability) is a factor in the transmission of deities, so too, Dawkins claims, is the natural credulity of children. As Dawkins writes: "Natural selection builds child brains with a tendency to believe whatever parents and tribal elders tell them" (Dawkins 2004a, p. 12). The key here is not children's credulity but that beliefs in unseen causal agents are "inference rich" – they are generously suggestive of a variety of meaningful connections. Such beliefs attract attention and invite narrative development. These, in turn, make them the focus of attention which, once again, makes them memorable.

Let's assume, at least for the next two sections, that the god-faculty (roughly HADD plus ToM) produces religious belief as a by-product – that belief in God was not the intended product of the cognitive faculties that produced it. If the god-faculty developed as the evolutionary psychologists suggest, what follows?

Explaining God Away

The belief that cognitive science has discovered the natural processes that produce belief in God has led some to claim that belief in God is, thereby, irrational. Evolutionary explanations of the development of these processes are alleged to show that survival forces, not a supernatural being, caused various religious beliefs and practices. These forces produced agency-detecting devices which were designed to get us to fight or flee when alarmed by a suspicious sight or sound. In short, they were designed originally to get us to behave appropriately when confronted by a possible predator or enemy. If anything should be produced by way of belief, it should be a belief in an animal or human competitor. But when our hyperactive agency detector (HADD) turns fairly minimal beliefs over to theory of mind (ToM), extravagant and unintended beliefs in spiritual agencies and powers are produced. Spiritual or religious beliefs are the accidental by-product of otherwise effective behavior-producing modules. When applied outside of its domain, the god-faculty is, Dennett claims, a "fiction generating contraption" (Dennett 2006, p. 120). Dawkins concurs: "The irrationality of religion is a by-product of a particular built-in irrationality mechanism in the brain" (Dawkins 2006, p. 184).

By showing the ignoble, non-divine, natural origins of religious belief, the claim is that one has shown that belief in God is irrational. Michael Shermer, in a review of Dennett's *Breaking the Spell,* summarizes thusly:

> Humans have brains that are big enough to be both self-aware and aware that others are self-aware. This "theory of mind" leads to a "Hyperactive Agent Detection Device" (HADD) that not only alerts us to real dangers, such as poisonous snakes, but also generates false positives, such as believing that rocks and trees are imbued with intentional minds or spirits… This is animism that, in the well-known historical sequence, leads to polytheism, and, eventually, monotheism. In other words, God is a false positive generated by our HADD. (Shermer 2006)

Religion, according to this line of thought, is a trick of the brain: God is an illusion or a delusion.

Has the evolutionary psychology of religion broken the spell of the god delusion once and for all? Will Dawkins and Dennett lead us from the darkness of religion into the brightness of unbelief?

Critique

Have Dawkins, Dennett, and the evolutionary psychology of religion crowd undermined rational religious belief? How exactly might the argument go?

Since the critics of religious belief in the previous section either don't explicitly state their argument against the rationality of religious belief or do so only somewhat inchoately, we will reconstruct their arguments for them. There seem to be four sorts of arguments in the neighborhood, so we will consider and respond to them one at a time.

The natural versus supernatural explanation argument

This argument assumes a rigid dichotomy between natural and supernatural explanations, assuming that one precludes the other. It assumes that if there is a natural explanation for some phenomenon, there cannot be a supernatural explanation. E. O. Wilson issued this challenge early on: "If religion … can be systematically analyzed and explained as a product of the brain's evolution, its power as an external source of morality will be gone forever …" (Wilson 1978, p. 201)

The argument may be stated as follows:

(1)   If a belief can be explained by a natural process, it cannot also be explained by a supernatural process.
(2)   Religious belief can be explained by a natural process.
(3)   Therefore, religious belief cannot be explained by a supernatural process.

This argument assumes that God could not have used natural processes to produce belief in God.

Does identifying and believing in a natural process that produces belief in God preclude a supernatural explanation of belief in God? Can there be two non-competing, perhaps complementary, explanations of the same phenomenon?

Suppose someone offered a complete natural explanation of why the water was boiling. The complete natural explanation of the boiling water is that the mean kinetic energy of its molecules is 100°C. Have we, by providing a natural explanation, precluded an explanation in terms of agency (say a person with relevant powers and intentions)? Surely not. A personal explanation of the phenomenon might also be true. For example, it could also be true that the water is boiling because I want to make some tea. This sort of explanation, a personal and teleological explanation (in terms of goals or desired ends) is not precluded by the natural explanation.

So, too, there might be a perfectly good and complete natural explanation of the god-faculty (along the lines of evolution, HADD and ToM) but it might also be true that God providentially directs the natural process so that people are given sufficient moral and spiritual knowledge to transcend their animal natures and become, in the long run, children of God. Both the natural and the supernatural explanations may be true. By pointing out the natural explanation, then, one has not thereby precluded a supernatural explanation.[4]

Why, after all, could God not have produced in us, through the processes of evolution, a god-faculty that makes humans universally aware of God under widely realized circumstances?

There are analogies here to other natural explanations of religious belief. Consider the Freudian critiques of religious belief. Freud contended that we wish God into "existence" and "God" hears our prayers: God can tame nature, help us accept our fate, and reward us for our sufferings. By revealing our desire for the divine, masking deeply insecure self-interest, Freud thinks he has explained God away. But one might think that Freud is right in his explanation of belief in God but not in his explaining it away; that is, one might think that Freud's account is an accurate description of a divinely implanted, truth-aimed god-faculty and so is a proper ground of belief. Why, after all, could God not have produced in humans a Freudian god-faculty that makes humans universally aware of God under widely realized circumstances? After all, the god-faculty, assuming there is one, must have some determinate shape or form. Why not the Freudian or HADD shape and form? As Plantinga writes of Freud – Marx critiques of belief in God: "To show that there are natural processes that produce religious belief does nothing ... to discredit it; perhaps God designed us in such a way that it is by virtue of those processes that we come to have knowledge of him" (Plantinga 2000, p. 145). Surely God can use natural processes to transport belief in God.

One might argue that the principle of parsimony or simplicity requires us to believe only in the natural explanation; if there is a fully naturally explanation of the phenomena in question, it is explained full stop. While one *can* put a theological overlay on the natural processes that produce belief, one should not bring in the supernatural unless it is rationally required. To cite Occam's razor: do not multiply explanations beyond necessity. One should not because one need not bring in the supernatural.

While appeals to the supernatural are surely precluded by the scientist using methodological naturalism to explain the data, the question posed is not about how the scientist should proceed or what one should believe *qua* scientist. We are not offering the God hypothesis as a better or more complete scientific explanation of the data. Indeed, we believe that science should proceed by the principles of methodological naturalism and so scientific appeals to the supernatural are precluded. It should be noted that the scientist, precluded methodologically from considering such matters, should simply be silent, qua scientist, about whether or not there are or are not also non-competing supernatural explanations of the data. Such matters are simply beyond the ken of the scientist *qua* scientist. When the evolutionary psychologist ventures into theological speculation – denying or affirming God's existence – she is scientifically out of bounds. She, *qua* scientist, is no more an authority on the relevance of this data to the existence or non-existence of God than any person on the street. Just as science may find a complete natural explanation of the patterns of sun and rain so too it may find a complete natural explanation of religious belief. But whether or not God is the primary and ultimate cause of everything that exists, science must remain silent. When scientists claim to preclude the existence of God on allegedly scientific grounds, they are no longer speaking as scientists; they are betraying their philosophical prejudices, not informing us of their scientific discoveries.

The question posed is the rationality of belief in God in the face of various evolutionary challenges. Does a natural explanation of religious belief defeat one's *prima facie* justification of belief in God? I don't see how. Just as one might say in the case of a natural explanation of the weather – "So, that's how God does it," so one might say in the case of a natural explanation of religion – "So, that's how God did it." What one didn't know before, one knows now. And what one knows now is logically irrelevant to whether or not God exists.

The by-product argument

Let us call this second argument "the by-product argument." Recall that HADD and ToM developed in circumstances conducive to fighting and fleeing behavior in response to the threat of, say, lions, tigers, and bears and to early hominid enemies; given the seriousness of the threat, hyperactive vigilance is desirable and, by attributions of agency and mind, successful planning is facilitated. But the whistling wind in the grass produces not only lion, tiger, and bear beliefs but also many "unintended" beliefs such as beliefs in spirits and gods. So, HADD and ToM, under ideal conditions, should (rationally) be restricted to lion-tiger-bear-enemy beliefs but not god beliefs. The by-product argument may be stated as follows:

(1)   Beliefs that are by-products of cognitive faculties are irrational.
(2)   Religious beliefs are by-products of cognitive faculties.
(3)   Therefore, religious beliefs are irrational.

In his *Atlantic Monthly* article "Is God an Accident?" psychologist Paul Bloom seems to have this sort of argument in mind when he affirms his titular question. For instance, he explains that natural systems "go awry" and consequently give rise to religion, by "inferring goals and desires where none exist" (Bloom 2005, p. 8). Here we have no direct argument or evidence that gods or other entities do not exist. Bloom also speculates about what would happen if religious people allowed for insights from science to permeate their belief system: "Scientific views would spread through religious communities. Supernatural beliefs would gradually disappear as the theologically correct version of a religion gradually became consistent with the secular world view."

The problem with this type of argument is that it cuts too wide a swath. Beliefs that are by-products of our cognitive faculties may be true and are often widely and rationally accepted as such. Consider the following generalized argument type:

(1)   Beliefs that are by-products of cognitive faculties are irrational.
(2)   Belief in x is a by-product of cognitive faculties.
(3)   Therefore, x beliefs are irrational.

Assuming the evolutionary origins of our cognitive faculties, the whole of modern science is a belief-spandrel. It is a by-product of cognitive faculties that were developed long before, say, 1600. The relevantly specified cognitive faculties developed to help us fight, flee, feed, and reproduce.[5] These proved enormously useful for millennia. Yet they were not developed to help *homo sapiens* grasp relativity theory or the advanced mathematics that relativity theory includes. Noam Chomsky puts the problem thus: "The experiences that shaped the course of evolution offer no hint of the problems to be faced in the sciences, and the ability to solve these problems could hardly have been a factor in evolution" (Chomsky 1987, p. 158). Molecular biologist Gunther Stent has argued that the innate structures of the evolved brain are well suited to handling immediate experience but are poorly suited to those areas of most interest to scientific inquiry (Stent 1975). So we could construct a By-product argument against modern science. Let x be modern science:

(1)   Beliefs that are by-products of cognitive faculties are irrational.
(2)   Scientific beliefs are by-products of cognitive faculties.
(3)   Therefore, modern science is irrational.

Atran's claim that religious beliefs are not adaptations, have no evolutionary functions, and were not produced directly via natural selection could be made of modern scientific beliefs (and, no doubt, many other domains of human inquiry) as well. If one rejects belief in God because it is an evolutionary by-product, one should also, *mutatis mutandis*, reject belief in quarks, black matter, natural selection, and other products of modern science.

Substituting "the evolutionary psychology of religion" for *x* will produce a similar argument. Evolutionary speculations about the origins of religious belief are themselves by-product beliefs: therefore, evolutionary psychology is irrational. And those – like Dawkins and Dennett – who rely on by-product arguments, likewise condemn their own beliefs to irrationality. So we get:

(1)   Beliefs that are by-products of cognitive faculties are irrational.
(2)   The evolutionary psychology of religion is a by-product of cognitive faculties.
(3)   Therefore, the evolutionary psychology of religion is irrational.

If by-product arguments are successful, evolutionary psychology is irrational. And we could construct countless similar arguments that "prove irrational" what might seem to be quite rational.

Dawkins and Dennett should simply reject the by-product argument against rational theism.

The unreliability argument

The atheist cognitive scientist might respond that the god-faculty cannot produce justified religious beliefs because it is not reliable. Perhaps this is what Dawkins had in mind when he claimed that religious belief is produced by a built-in irrationality mechanism. After all, the hypersensitive agency detection device (HADD) working with the theory of mind sub-system (ToM) produces beliefs in a multiplicity of gods, angels, fairies, demons, and so on. And even if there is a god, most religious beliefs (in this case, beliefs in gods) simply cannot be true (because they are often contradictory).

There are, so the argument might go, too many religious false-positives to trust HADD and ToM in the religious domain. So the unreliability argument:

(1)   A belief produced by an unreliable cognitive process cannot be justified.
(2)   Religious beliefs are produced by an unreliable cognitive process.
(3)   Therefore, religious beliefs cannot be justified.

The first point that needs to be made is that HADD and ToM are not unreliable. If I were to walk into a bookstore and see you reading this book (eager to purchase it, of course), I would immediately form the belief that you were a minded person (though redundant, that is the point to be made). HADD and ToM are instantly effective in a wide variety of circumstances. I walk through the mall and person-beliefs pop up instantly and regularly. When I check out at the grocery store I attribute both agency and intention to the clerk. Common sense testifies that HADD and ToM are, quite simply, reliable.[6]

But perhaps we should think that HADD and ToM are reliable with embodied persons, but they are unreliable when it comes to gods (this takes us back to the by-product belief issue, but let us press on). HADD is after all H. Because of the god-faculty we see faces in clouds, posit elves and fairies, and liberate gods from dead bodies. Recall Dennett's claim that outside of its domain, the god-faculty is a "fiction generating contraption" (Dennett 2006, p. 120). How can we trust a cognitive faculty that seems so unreliable in this area?

But perhaps HADD and ToM are not spiritually unreliable, they are simply spiritually imprecise or coarse-grained. Perhaps the function of the god-faculty is to make humans aware of the divine/moral dimension of reality rather than of clearly defined, say, Judeo-Christian conceptions of God; the function would be then to secure, by and large, belief in a supreme transcendent and moral being. So, while the god-faculty may be unreliable in securing belief in Yahweh and Yahweh alone, the god-faculty is reliable in producing true beliefs about a divinity, that is, some kind of supernatural agency.[7]

Given the earliest stages of human spiritual development, such coarse-grained, primitive beliefs as produced by the god-faculty proved sufficient for human moral and spiritual improvement. John Calvin, reflecting on much later stages of human development, claimed little specific knowledge of divinity through the *sensus divinitatis*; this slight taste of divinity, he thought, is impure and unclear. Such unclarity and impurity will find a variety of cultural manifestations as, say, fairies and elves. Yet such imprecise and spiritual/moral awareness may be sufficiently true to begin the process of human moral and spiritual development (the unselfing necessary to move into more substantial communities). It may take further reflection and even revelation to refine these inchoate inklings of the divine.

We find a similar sort of problem and solution in the moral domain. When one looks at the plethora of "souped up" moral beliefs held throughout human history, one might think the moral faculties unreliable. Foot-binding, widow-burning, cannibalism, infanticide, and slavery are but a few of the moral practices held by long and venerable moral traditions. I suspect a complete list of diverse moral practices would parallel a complete list of religious practices. So we might construct an unreliability argument against morality:

(1)   A belief produced by an unreliable cognitive process cannot be justified.
(2)   Moral beliefs are produced by an unreliable cognitive process.
(3)   Therefore, moral beliefs cannot be justified.

Rather than think of the plethora of resultant culturally specific moral beliefs, one should think that our original moral cognitive processes produced primitive, coarse-grained moral beliefs that are imprecise yet basically true. It is plausible to believe that evolutionary forces led our distant ancestors to develop certain basic evaluative tendencies that were conducive to reproductive success. As the cognitive capacities of our ancestors developed over time, these tendencies contributed to our distant ancestors forming certain basic evaluative judgments. And, given the importance of the group to human survival, altruistic impulses are likely to develop as well along with altruistic evaluative judgments. Thus, at the earliest points in human development, an inchoate and imprecise moral system based on the satisfaction of human needs within a human family/community will arise. It will soon find very different cultural representations but the basic moral impulses, sentiments and actions are correct. With subsequent rational reflection (and perhaps revelation) further justified moral beliefs will develop.

So the religious sense may parallel the moral sense. Humanity's incipient and primitive moral and spiritual impulses, behaviors, and corresponding judgments may be truth-aimed but coarse-grained. They will subsequently find culturally specific and widely varying manifestations. In general we might expect to find rather coarse-grained cognitive faculties with a great deal left open to culture to specify. Culturally varying and divergent beliefs are likely to trace back to more fundamental behaviors/beliefs that are both adaptive and widely shared. Rational reflection (and revelation) may lead one to more, deeper, more precise, and truer moral and religious beliefs (which, of course, provides the opportunity for false beliefs as well). But, given the coarse-grained nature of our moral and spiritual faculties, widely divergent beliefs are to be expected very early on even from relatively truth-aimed but imprecise faculties.

One final, logical point. With respect to belief in God, we cannot know if the god-faculty is unreliable unless we already know that there is no God. Of course, if one doesn't believe in God, one won't believe the god-faculty to be reliable, but one's personal beliefs on this matter scarcely constitute evidence that there is no God.

Conclusion

The evolutionary psychology of religion offers a naturalistic account of the origin of the human god-faculty in terms of a by-product belief. While some have seen fit to claim that evolutionary psychology undermines the rationality of religious belief, we have shown that this claim is simply unwarranted. We have not proved that there is a god but we have argued that belief in God need not be irrational given the findings of evolutionary psychology. The various arguments from evolutionary psychology of religion that might be alleged to defeat rational theistic belief are unsuccessful. Or, one might argue, they are too successful and undermine both modern science and morality. What's good for the evolutionary goose is good for the gander.

Notes

1 One might speculate that ToM developed as it became increasingly advantageous for primates to be able to successfully "guess" the beliefs, desires and intentions of competitors. This tendency to speculate about the intentions of competitors would then have been generalized and applied to agentive accounts that HADD engendered. As Atran writes: "Identifying animate beings as agents, with goals and internal motivations, would allow our ancestors to anticipate goal-directed actions of predators, prey, friends, and foe and to profit from this in ways that enhanced survival and reproductive success" (Atran 2002: 61).

2 Let us not assume that the god-faculty is a single cognitive faculty or that it consists simply in HADD plus ToM (it may include more than HADD plus ToM).

3 A trait whose origin was not the direct result of natural selection but becomes coopted for a current use.

4 One might, thereby, have precluded a *miraculous* supernatural explanation. That is, the natural explanation would preclude God directly intervening in non-normal ways with the physical processes.

5 One might think, given that truth is irrelevant to the selection process, that true beliefs are irrelevant; that is, that survival behavior is all that is selected. Indeed, Alvin Plantinga has argued that in Plantinga (1993), pp. 216–37.

6 One could attempt to tabulate how often HADD and ToM accurately deliver beliefs about the presence of minds against how often they deliver false-positives or false-negatives. Such an exercise, if possible, would produce a measure of HADD-ToM's accuracy rate. If such a rate were low, we would have grounds to be suspicious of HADD-ToM's deliverances. Unfortunately, such accuracy testing assumes we have a way of knowing when an agent or mind has been accurately detected that is independent of HADD-ToM, a dubious assumption. As Reid argued regarding our perceptual and mnemonic faculties, we may be forced to simply assume their reliability.

7   "Gods" might be a better term here. I assume that if our ancestors were equipped with HADD, polytheism not monotheism would be the most primitive form of theistic religion. But polytheism bears a family resemblance to monotheism and, so, need not be viewed as a defeater of Plantinga's account of belief in God.

Bibliography

Alston, William (1991) *Perceiving God*. Ithaca, NY: Cornell University Press.

Atran, Scott (2002) *In Gods We Trust*. New York: Oxford University Press.

Barrett, Justin (2004) *Why Would Anyone Believe in God?* Lanham, MD: AltaMira

Bloom, Paul (2005) Is God an accident? *Atlantic Monthly* (Dec.), 1–8.

Boyer, Pascal (1994) *The Naturalness of Religious Ideas: A Cognitive Theory of Religion*. Berkeley: University of California Press.

Boyer, Pascal (2001) *Religion Explained*. New York: Basic Books.

Calvin, John (1979) *Commentaries on the Epistle of St Paul to the Romans*, trans. John Owen, ed. Henry Beveridge. Grand Rapids MI: Baker Book House.

Chomsky, Noam (1987) *Language and the Problem of Knowledge*. Cambridge, MA: MIT Press.

Clark, Kelly James (1990) *Return to Reason*. Grand Rapids, MI: Eerdmans.

Dawkins, Richard (2006) *The God Delusion*. New York: Houghton Mifflin Harcourt.

Dennett, Daniel (2006) *Breaking the Spell: Religion as a Natural Phenomenon*. New York: Viking.

Gould, Stephen and Lewontin, Richard (1979) The spandrels of San Marco and the Panglossian Paradigm: A critique of the adaptationist program. *Proceedings of the Royal Society of London* B 205, 581–98.

Guthrie, Stewart (1993) *Faces in the Clouds: A New Theory of Religion*. New York: Oxford University Press.

Murray, Michael (forthcoming) Four arguments that the cognitive psychology of religion undermines warrant of religious belief. In Murray and Schloss, (eds.), *The Believing Primate*. New York: Oxford University Press.

Plantinga, Alvin (1993) *Warrant and Proper Function*. New York: Oxford University Press.

Plantinga, Alvin (2000) *Warranted Christian Belief*. New York: Oxford University Press.

Plantinga, Alvin and Wolterstorff, Nicholas (1983) *Faith and Rationality*. Notre Dame, IN: University of Notre Dame Press.

Ruse, Michael (1986) *Taking Darwin Seriously*. New York: Basil Blackwell.

Shermer, Michael (2006) Review of Dennett's *Breaking the Spell*, *Science*, Jan. 27.

Stent, Gunther (1975) Limits to the scientific understanding of Man, *Science* 187, no. 4181, 1052–7.

Wilson, David Sloan (2002) *Darwin's Cathedral: Evolution, Religion, and the Nature of Society*. Chicago: University of Chicago Press.